A RHETORICAL HISTORY OF THE UNITED STATES

VOLUME V

Significant Moments in American Public Discourse

A Rhetorical History of the United States
Significant Moments in American Public Discourse
Volumes I–X

Under the General Supervisory Editorship of
Martin J. Medhurst
Baylor University

Editors:

Volume I: James R. Andrews, *Indiana University*

Volume II: Stephen E. Lucas, *University of Wisconsin, Madison*

Volume III: Stephen Howard Browne, *The Pennsylvania State University*

Volume IV: David Zarefsky, *Northwestern University*, and Michael Leff, *University of Memphis*

Volume V: Martha Solomon Watson and Thomas R. Burkholder, *University of Nevada, Las Vegas*

Volume VI: J. Michael Hogan, *The Pennsylvania State University*

Volume VII: Thomas W. Benson, *The Pennsylvania State University*

Volume VIII: Martin J. Medhurst, *Baylor University*

Volume IX: David Henry and Richard J. Jensen, *University of Nevada, Las Vegas*

Volume X: Robert Hariman, *Northwestern University*, and John Louis Lucaites, *Indiana University*

The Rhetoric of Nineteenth-Century Reform

Edited by
MARTHA S. WATSON
and
THOMAS R. BURKHOLDER

A RHETORICAL HISTORY OF THE UNITED STATES

Significant Moments in American Public Discourse

VOLUME V

Michigan State University Press
East Lansing

♾ The paper used in this publication meets the minimum requirements of ANSI/NISO Z39.48-1992 (R 1997) (Permanence of Paper).

Michigan State University Press
East Lansing, Michigan 48823-5245

Printed and bound in the United States of America.

14 13 12 11 10 09 08   1 2 3 4 5 6 7 8 9 10

LIBRARY OF CONGRESS CATALOGING-IN-PUBLICATION DATA

The rhetoric of nineteenth-century reform / edited by Martha S. Watson and Thomas R. Burkholder.
        p. cm.—(A rhetorical history of the United States : significant moments in American public discourse ; v. 5)
    Includes bibliographical references and index.
    ISBN 978-0-87013-836-2 (hardcover : alk. paper) 1. Social reformers—United States—History—19th century. 2. Social problems—United States—History—19th century. 3. Rhetoric—United States—History—19th century. I. Watson, Martha S. II. Burkholder, Thomas R.
    HN64.R46 2008
    303.48'4097309034—dc22   2008015733

Cover and book design by San Serif, Inc., Saline, Michigan

g green
  press
  INITIATIVE Michigan State University Press is a member of the Green Press Initiative and is committed to developing and encouraging ecologically responsible publishing practices. For more information about the Green Press Initiative and the use of recycled paper in book publishing, please visit www.greenpressinitiative.org.

Visit Michigan State University Press on the World Wide Web at:
www.msupress.msu.edu

The following individuals, departments, colleges, and universities provided subvention funds to help offset the initial publication costs of this ten volume series. Michigan State University Press expresses its sincere thanks to each.

A. CRAIG BAIRD DISTINGUISHED PROFESSORSHIP
University of Iowa

COLLEGE OF ARTS AND SCIENCES
Indiana University

COLLEGE OF LIBERAL ARTS
Texas A&M University

DEPARTMENT OF COMMUNICATION
Texas A&M University

DEPARTMENT OF COMMUNICATION ARTS & SCIENCES
The Pennsylvania State University

DEPARTMENT OF COMMUNICATION AND CULTURE
Indiana University

DEPARTMENT OF COMMUNICATION STUDIES
Northwestern University

SCHOOL OF COMMUNICATION
Northwestern University

CONTENTS

INTRODUCTION
The Gilded Age and the New America

Martha S. Watson and Thomas R. Burkholder

A few days before Christmas 1873, a much heralded new novel appeared, a collaboration between Mark Twain and Charles Dudley Warner: *The Gilded Age: A Tale of Today*. Despite the gloomy economic time—the financial crisis of 1873 loomed large—the book sold surprisingly well; within a year over 50,000 copies had been sold.[1] The brisk sales probably reflected the reputation of the authors and their advance promotion of the book rather than the quality of the work itself. Still, the novel, which satirized the excesses of the day, has persisted in American culture as the name of an era, the Gilded Age, stretching roughly from 1870 to 1920.

Although reviewers differed in their assessments of the book, they all acknowledged the force of the satire. The reviewer at the *Literary World* concluded:

> The book is intended to be a satire on our national politics, with special reference to society and legislation at Washington. . . . We have no doubt that the descriptions here given of the methods by which legislation is expedited, by which senators are elected, and by which official opportunities are employed for private ends, are measurably accurate; but there is needed an agency of higher moral tone than this book, to remedy these evils, or even lead the public to serious disapproval of them.[2]

The abuses and practices Twain and Warner satirized were all too characteristic of the last decades of the nineteenth century. Immense accumulations of wealth and power by the few were accompanied by abject poverty and suffering among the poor. The rapid pace of industrialization changed the character of the nation, while tides of new immigrants filled the cities. Further, the lure of jobs and opportunities emptied farms, and the nation moved in a few decades from a largely agricultural country to an industrialized one. In response to the plight of the workers and the abuses of unregulated capitalization, labor unions, reformers, and even revolutionaries agitated vociferously for some mediation of the social, political, and economic ills that beset the country. At the same time, advocates for women's rights, frustrated by the omission of women from the post–Civil War civil rights amendments, stepped up their agitation. Indeed, until they merged in 1890, two separate organizations, the National Woman Suffrage Association and the American Woman Suffrage Association, sought enfranchisement for women as part of a larger fabric of social change.[3]

Perhaps the best metaphor for this tumultuous, conflicted era was the World's Columbian Exposition, the Chicago World's Fair of 1893. Intended to celebrate the 400th anniversary of Columbus's "discovery" of America, the Fair provided an opportunity for the nation in general and Chicago in particular to extol their accomplishments for the world. As Andrew Wood observes in his analysis of the Woman's Building at the Fair: "In the popular press, the WCE [World Columbian Exposition] epitomized the inevitable betterment of humankind that would follow the embrace of civilization and science, the twin gods of progress."[4] That depiction suggests clearly the popular imagination of the day: society was steadily progressing, guided by intelligent citizens.

Despite its intended message, as James Gilbert argues in this volume and elsewhere, the Fair was, in effect, many things to many people.[5] Historians have seen it either as "the achievement of the hegemonic powers of corporate capitalism or imperialism" or as the "palpable failure of a conservative and outdated architectural vision."[6] Close looks at the Fair reveal the racism so prevalent in the nation at the time as well as attempts to control and manage the rising tide of women's rights agitation.[7] On the site itself, the somewhat raucous, very commercial midway contrasted sharply with the intended "planned high culture" of its exhibit areas. In short, the Fair that sought to typify and commend American culture at this juncture reveals the same tensions and conflicts as the era itself.

Not surprisingly, the tumultuous if largely peaceful era produced public discourse as disparate as the forces that were reshaping the country. Understanding that discourse and the essays that follow requires some sense of the tremendous changes that gripped the nation in the Gilded Age.

The Changing Face of America

The last three decades of the nineteenth century and the first two decades of the twentieth century were a period of dramatic, sometimes traumatic change in the United States. Seas of immigrants, migrations to cities, rapid industrialization, and social upheavals all helped transformed the nation at a rapid rate. As historian Charles Calhoun notes:

> During that time [the nineteenth century] the central fact of American life was the evolution of the nation from a largely agricultural, rural, isolated, localized and traditional society to one that was becoming industrialized, urban, integrated, national, and modern. The process began before the 1870s and continued after 1900, but the last third of the century—roughly known as the Gilded Age—saw a rapid acceleration in the country's transformation.[8]

The Civil War helped to alter the United States not only politically but economically as well. According to John Tipple, "war needs created almost insatiable demands for goods—arms, munitions, clothing—and offered some manufacturers unsurpassed opportunities to make fortunes. More important, the stimulus of massive military demands alerted entrepreneurs to new concepts of the power and possibilities of large-scale enterprise."[9]

Many eagerly pursued those possibilities. For example, in 1860 the United States lagged behind western Europe in virtually all measures of industrialization; by 1890 it had soared ahead.[10] One indication of this growth was the burgeoning production of the raw materials needed to support industry. From 1860 to 1900 the production of anthracite coal increased 525 percent, bituminous coal 2,358 percent, steel more than 1,100 percent, and pig iron more than 1,700 percent.[11] In real terms, for example, steel production zoomed from 77,000 tons in 1870 to 11.2 million tons in 1900.[12] Production increased, in part, because of technological advances on many fronts. Between its founding in 1790 and 1860, the U.S. Patent Office issued 36,000 patents; between 1860 and 1900 it granted as many as 440,000.[13]

At the same time, dramatic improvements in the ability to communicate quickly over long distances, primarily through the expansion of the telegraph system and more consistent mail delivery, facilitated business growth on an unprecedented scale. As Glenn Porter explains: "Once advanced transport and communications systems were in place for the first time a firm could effectively operate and integrate many different economic functions and processes throughout a region, across the whole country, and, for a few concerns, around the world."[14] Business activity quickly reached levels unimagined prior to the Civil War.

Although innovations in science and technology were widespread, the impact of the railroads on American life was especially profound. In 1865 the United States had 35,000 miles of steam railways; by 1900 it had almost 200,000 miles. If these railroads transported agricultural goods back from the West, they also stimulated iron and steel production. If they knit the nation together, the concentration of control of their operations produced great wealth and extensive abuses.[15] Perhaps more than any other commercial or industrial development of the era, the railroads defined the changing face of the United States. "Not only were they the most potent symbol of the new industrial age and its technical achievements," notes Porter, "but they also pioneered in the organizational means through which Americans came to have access to the improved transportation and communications that permitted the coordination of an enormous volume and range of economic activities across vast distances."[16] Supporting further expansion of the West, the transcontinental railroads dramatically influenced settlement patterns.

This rapid rise of industrialization produced sweeping changes in the social and political landscape. In 1870, 52 percent of all workers were agricultural, and agricultural production exceeded industrial production by about $500 million; by 1900, 60 percent were nonfarm workers, and industrial production was almost three times agricultural output.[17] At the same time, agriculture expanded dramatically without corresponding increases in the prosperity of farmers. So, for example, from 1860 to 1910 the number of farms and the amount of improved land increased threefold, but by 1900 the proportion of the nation's wealth in the hands of farmers had dropped to below half of what it had been in 1860.[18]

Despite technological and scientific advances, the last years of the nineteenth century did not constitute a "Gilded Age" for farmers. Certainly advances like the reaper and the Oliver plow were labor saving; however, at the same time, they displaced workers and forced farmers to make substantial investments in equipment. If westward expansion offered new land for cultivation, it also meant that farmers were dependent on railroads for the transportation of their produce. Increasingly in competition with international markets, farmers found that the rising costs of transportation often consumed much of their profit.[19] Rising costs, unfortunately, were met with falling prices for crops. For example, Samuel Eliot Morison, Henry Steele

Commager, and William E. Leuchtenburg report that "wheat which netted the farmer $1.45 a bushel in 1866 brought only 49 cents in 1894. Corn which brought 75 cents in Chicago in 1869 fell to 28 cents in 1889."[20] The result of these changes was economic upheaval for thousands of farmers. Sean Dennis Cashman reports:

> Farms failed, mortgages were foreclosed, and farmers were put out of house and home. In the four years from 1888 to 1892 half of the population of western Kansas moved on, as did 30,000 people from South Dakota. . . . By 1890, 25 percent of farmers in Kansas were tenants or sharecroppers, in Nebraska, 17 percent; in South Dakota 11 percent. Farm tenantry in the country as a whole increased as the century drew to a close from 25 percent in 1880 to 28 percent in 1890 to 36 percent in 1900.[21]

These events, H. Wayne Morgan explains, "baffled the farmer. He worked hard, produced more, yet received a declining share of the national income." Moreover, farmers "increasingly grumbled at excessive government support to industry, without apparent aid to agriculture."[22] Aside from their obvious economic plight, "what seemed especially worrisome about these events [for farmers] was that they meant the gradual and seemingly relentless decline of agriculture's place in American life."[23] Their discontent led them to a new political activism. According to Porter, "industrial and financial elites became, in the eyes of many farmers and their families, evil conspirators winning a growing place in American life through underhanded and secretive means. Such concerns fed the growth of farmers' organizations, including the Grange and the Populist Party."[24] In the 1880s various farmers' organizations banded together in the "Alliance Movement" that "attacked railroad discrimination, mortgage combines, interest rates, and low prices." Their political efforts, driven by their fiery oratory, aimed to "even out man-made inequalities of opportunity, not destroy the prevailing system. Railroad regulation, currency inflation, and price supports would reduce 'special privilege.'"[25] The cause of their own misfortunes, many farmers believed, was in the East generally and in the cities in particular. Porter concludes:

> To many in the countryside, cities were simply sinkholes of sin overrun with unwelcome foreigners, Jews, and Catholics. Although the heartland's values retained remarkable and disproportionate force despite the shifting economic realities, America's cultural tune was in fact gradually coming to be called more by the urban and industrial sectors and less by the rural and agrarian ones.[26]

Nevertheless, as farmers faced social and economic decline, growing cities also confronted a myriad of challenges. In 1870 only twenty-five cities had a population of 50,000; by 1900 seventy-eight did, including three with more than one million people.[27] The rapid growth of cities was due, in part, to the influx of immigrants. Between 1880 and 1910 almost eighteen million immigrants entered the United States.[28] These numbers are impressive, but as Roger Daniels notes, they must be placed in context:

> What is too often forgotten . . . is that the best single indicator of the incidence of newcomers, the percentage of foreign born recorded in the census, did not change significantly for seven censuses. From 1860 through 1920 each and every census showed that approximately one-seventh of the population had been born abroad. In 1870 that one-seventh amounted to some 5.7 million persons; by 1900 it amounted to more than 10.3 million persons.[29]

What is probably more telling than the sheer numbers of immigrants are their ethnicities and their patterns of settlement. The immigrants who entered the country between 1890 and 1914 were largely from Italy, Greece, Austria-Hungary, Russia, Rumania, and Turkey, in sharp contrast to earlier waves of immigration, which were largely western European.[30] From 1820 until 1860 immigrants from Germany, Britain, Ireland, and Scandinavia accounted for 95 percent of total immigration; during the Gilded Age they accounted for only 40 percent.[31]

Further, settlement patterns were uneven. Cashman explains that 80 percent of the immigrants "settled in a north-eastern quadrilateral between Canada, the Atlantic, Washington, D.C. and St. Louis, Missouri."[32] According to Daniels, the 1870 census revealed that foreign-born persons "were just about one-third of the population of the fifty-two American cities with more than twenty-five thousand people. In nine of those cities—New York, Chicago, San Francisco, Cleveland, Detroit, Milwaukee, Scranton . . . , Lawrence . . . and Fall River, Massachusetts—the immigrant population was more than 40 percent."[33]

Although extensive efforts from various fronts encouraged immigration throughout the 1870s and 1880s, the influx of people soon created a reaction. Increasingly, Cashman observes, native-born Americans regarded immigrants "not as a source of strength, but as a drain on American resources. This was especially true of the East, where most immigrants arrived and where the social system was already hard and fast."[34] Because they lacked the resources to invest in land, equipment, and livestock for farming, the immigrants from southern and eastern Europe tended to choose cities. Further, their different language, culture, and religion led them to cluster together in enclaves in the cities rather than in small towns or on farms. Many who were unskilled and poor crowded into tenements.[35] Racial and ethnic stereotypes and prejudices abounded.[36] As Cashman notes:

> Immigration was now beginning to divide American society. A great gulf was opening between a predominantly native-born plutocracy and a predominantly foreign working class. The United States was becoming two nations separated by language and religion, residence and occupation alike. Not only was the new tide of immigration depressing wages, but also the closing of the frontier and settlement of available land in the West had sealed off the traditional escape route for discontented easterners. Thus, Americans were beginning to lose confidence in the process of assimilation. The outcome was nativism.[37]

Nativist agitation stemmed from three groups—labor unions, social reformers, and Protestant conservatives.[38] Labor unions, usually committed to the craft principle, made only limited attempts to recruit the immigrant workers. American Federation of Labor (AFL) president Samuel Gompers, for example, urged restrictions on the poor immigrants who were thronging to the United States, arguing "the country that kept out pauper-made goods should also keep out the paupers."[39] Since 55 percent of the immigrants in 1873 identified themselves as unskilled, his ungenerous proposal had some appeal for labor union members.[40] Ethnic and religious tensions further inhibited labor unions from trying to organize these workers. In the end, unions, along with other groups, began to favor restrictions on immigration.[41]

Some social reformers and intellectuals were concerned that the immigrants from southern and eastern Europe were the "wrong" sorts of people to sustain a democracy. Daniels states that "eugenicists and sociologists argued that of all the many 'races,' only one—variously called Anglo-Saxon, Aryan, Teutonic, and Nordic—had superior innate characteristics."[42] The founder of the Immigration Restriction League, Prescott F. Hall, put the issue bluntly: Did Americans want their country "to be peopled by British, German, and Scandinavian stock, historically free, energetic, progressive, or by Slav, Latin and Asiatic races, historically down-trodden, atavistic and stagnant?"[43] In the U.S. Senate, Henry Cabot Lodge secured passage of a literacy test bill to assure ethnocultural balance on five occasions, with Senate approval on all but the first bill. The bill was vetoed by various presidents until the veto was overridden in 1917.[44]

Even groups with roots in broad human rights issues felt the impact of anti-immigrant sentiments. For example, the women's rights movement began with a commitment to lofty principles of human rights. After the uniting of the two major suffrage groups into the National American Woman Suffrage Association (NAWSA) in 1890 and their focus almost exclusively on suffrage, the antisuffrage forces argued against extending the franchise in part because they feared the potential radicalism of immigrant women.[45] At the same time, a younger generation of woman suffrage advocates, less connected to the broad egalitarianism of the cause, sometimes expressed their concerns with an expansion of the franchise to immigrants and African Americans.[46]

Protestant conservatives, of course, worried about the impact of immigrants from southern and eastern Europe for a still different reason. In their view, Roman Catholics from Italy and Jews from eastern Europe threatened their social as well as political power. Religious differences exacerbated tensions arising from other sources. According to Cashman:

> Whatever measure one might apply, the nation that entered the twentieth century was vastly different from the one that had emerged from the Civil War. Between 1870 and 1900 the nation's population nearly doubled, reaching just under 76 million in the latter year. Much of that growth was due to the influx of immigrants; in the same thirty year span, the number of foreign-born persons in the population rose 86%. The number of all Americans engaged in gainful employment increased by 132%, while the number of women who held paying jobs jumped 190%.[47]

In this era of profound social and economic upheaval, native-born Americans and immigrants alike confronted both great opportunities and great perils. Many amassed immense fortunes, while thousands more suffered in squalor.

The Great Barbecue

Appalled by what they saw as "a time of spectacular excess, of brass-knuckled business and shady politics on a grand scale," reformers and historians often "gave the times such labels as . . . the Era of Excess and the Great Barbecue."[48] For those invited to the party, times were good. Following the Civil War, government was increasingly willing to foster business expansion. Tipple concludes:

> Through political alliances, principally with the Republican Party, the big businessman consolidated his economic triumphs. Although in the past the commercial and manufacturing interests of the North had received favors from the federal government in the form of bounties to fisheries and protective tariffs, after the defection of the South they were in the envied position of a pampered child. With almost incestuous concern, a dotingly partisan Congress bestowed upon them lavish railroad subsidies, new and higher tariffs, and a series of favorable banking acts.[49]

Moreover, favorable changes in the tax structure gave business and industry huge advantages. In 1870 the inheritance tax expired, the income tax ended in 1872, and no corporate taxes yet existed. Government revenue came exclusively from taxes on consumers—customs duties and taxes on such products as liquor and tobacco. "Under such conditions, stock market volume attained the million-share mark in December, 1886, and industrial capital almost doubled itself every ten years."[50]

The age of the "Robber Barons," so called because of widespread belief that their fortunes were a product of their own ruthlessness, had begun. By 1892 John D. Rockefeller's personal worth reportedly exceeded $815 million; Andrew Carnegie's steel enterprises turned profits of over $7.5 million a year between 1889 and 1899.[51] Entire industries came to be identified by the names of individual entrepreneurs, not just Rockefeller in oil and Carnegie in steel but also "Cornelius Vanderbilt, E. H. Harriman, and James J. Hill in railroads, Cyrus McCormick in reapers, . . . J. P. Morgan in finance, James B. Duke in tobacco, [and] Gustavus Swift and Philip Armour in meatpacking."[52] The roster of the wealthy was not limited to these familiar names. In 1892 the *New York World* newspaper published a list of 3,045 millionaires in the United States. Not to be outdone, the *New York Tribune* published its own list of 4,047. By 1900 there were 25 millionaires serving in the U.S. Senate.[53]

But not everyone was invited to the party, and public outcry ensued. Tipple observes that "the feeling was general that the great fortunes of all the big business magnates . . . represented special privilege which had enabled them to turn the abundant natural resources and multitudinous advantages offered by a growing nation into a private preserve for their own profits."[54] Those feelings were not unfounded. The federal government, dominated by Republicans since the end of the Civil War, became increasingly active in fostering industrialization through granting special favors.[55] Shady business practices and outright fraud were rampant. "The inequity of Wall Street was not merely legendary, but had firm basis in fact," writes Tipple. "Many corporations, although offering huge blocks of stock to the public, issued only the vaguest and most ambiguous summary of assets and liabilities. While this was not iniquitous in itself, secrecy too often cloaked fraud."[56]

This is not to say that all successful industrialists and businessmen of the era were dishonest or even unethical; many who were not simply took advantage of the climate and the flood of innovations in technology, transportation, and communication. But as the great gulf between those who were invited to the barbecue and those who were not grew even wider, public sentiment often turned against big business. Tipple concludes: "While from a corporate point of view the conduct of the money-makers was often legal, the public often felt cheated. Puzzled and disenchanted by the way things had turned out, they questioned the way every millionaire got his money, and were quite ready to believe that a crime was behind every great fortune. While its exact nature escaped them, they felt they had been robbed."[57]

Adding to this discontent was the fact that the very nature of work had changed. The workforce, once composed largely of self-employed individual craftspeople, artisans, and farmers laboring in relative isolation, went to work for someone else. Eric Arnesen comments that "the emergence and consolidation of the new industrial order meant . . . that America was becoming a nation of wage earners for the first time."[58] By 1900 there were six million manufacturing jobs, four times the number of factory workers in 1860. That growth was accompanied by a sixfold increase in the gross national product between 1870 and 1900. The United States surpassed even Great Britain, birthplace of the Industrial Revolution.[59] Moreover, in the view of workers, new attitudes toward business management further degraded their position. "By the 1880s and 1890s," Arnesen comments, "corporations began experimenting with new forms of management aimed at wresting control, or at least more control over the labor process from craftsmen. Toward that end, industrialists sought to divest workers of their skills, knowledge, and power and to invest them instead in management's own supervisory personnel."[60]

For many, working conditions were often horrendous. Wages were low, workdays were often twelve hours or more, managers were frequently abusive, and safety measures were few so that accident rates were high. The workers' response was to unionize on an unprecedented scale. Two types of unions formed during this period. Perhaps foremost among the labor organizations was the Knights of Labor, founded by garment cutters in Philadelphia in 1869.[61] By the mid-1880s the Knights, an industrial union that included all workers within an industry, had become the largest labor organization in the United States. According to Arnesen, "Every state, major city, and sizable town boasted local assemblies [of the Knights of Labor]. Between 8 and 12 percent of the industrial labor force were members of the roughly fifteen thousand assemblies across the country."[62] Such industrial unions, notes H. W. Brands, "were big and often rowdy, drawing from the bottom as well as the top of the labor pool."[63]

But the Haymarket riot in 1886 built public opinion against the Knights. In Haymarket Square in Chicago, the Knights took part in a strike for the eight-hour workday. Someone threw a bomb into the protest meeting, killing seven people and injuring sixty more.[64] Public outrage was fanned by the press. For example, the *Chicago Tribune* of 6 May ranted: "These serpents have been warmed and nourished in the sunshine of toleration until at last they have been emboldened to strike at society, law, order and government."[65] Although the Knights were not responsible for the violence and although their leader, Terance V. Powderly, tried to dissociate the Knights from the eight-hour movement, public reaction against the radicals affected the order. This event, coupled with Powderly's inability to control unauthorized strikes and to hold skilled and unskilled workers in a single union, undercut the Knights. "By the end of the decade, membership in the Order had dwindled to about 100,000, and the Knights had soon all but disappeared."[66]

The primary competing union of the time, one that continues to the present, was the AFL, which emerged in 1886 and was headed by Samuel Gompers.[67] A trade union that focused on workers in a particular craft, the AFL tended to be more conservative and less involved in larger social and political issues. Rather, it concentrated on improving the welfare of its members.[68] Although the two organizations differed in philosophy and organizational structure, they were emblematic of a growing militancy on the part of workers.[69] As Arnesen observes:

> The closing decades of the nineteenth century were marked by a degree of class conflict, much of it violent, as great as any in the industrialized world. During the 1880s, according to the Bureau of Labor Statistics, the United States experienced almost ten thousand strikes and lockouts. In 1886 alone, a year that earned the title "The Great Upheaval," roughly seven hundred thousand workers either went out on strike or were locked out by their employers. Even larger numbers would participate in the titanic clashes of the early 1890s.[70]

If working conditions and the social changes wrought by industrialization were sufficient to drive the traditionally white male labor force to such extreme militancy, the situation was even more bleak for ethnic minorities, primarily African Americans.

In the decades following the Civil War, the "race question" dominated all other issues in the South and affected life throughout the nation. Leslie H. Fishel notes that after the debacle of Reconstruction, "southern white leaders had to confront, be confronted by, and control the African-American presence. While the question of how to handle the black multitude learning to live in freedom was only one of many economic and political problems that dogged the white South in the final two decades of the century, it clung like a leech to almost every issue."[71] The problems were political, economic, and social.

White political leaders in the South, exclusively Democrats, were alarmed by growing numbers of newly enfranchised African American voters who were overwhelmingly Republican and in many districts outnumbered whites. Intimidation, fraud, and legal maneuvering suppressed the African American vote.[72] Calhoun explains:

> To take the two most egregious examples, in Louisiana the black population grew by 33 percent between 1870 and 1880, but from the presidential election of 1872 to that of 1880 the number of Republican votes decreased by 47 percent. In Mississippi the black population growth was 46 percent, and the Republican vote decline was 59 percent. Because of this denial of the suffrage, by 1880 the conservative, white Solid South had emerged, assuring the Democrats of a large bloc of electoral votes that year and in future presidential elections.[73]

Nationally, Republicans seemed to lose interest in African American voters after Reconstruction. President James A. Garfield supported African American education but died before any gains were realized. He was succeeded by Chester A. Arthur, who largely ignored the problem.[74] Former friends abandoned the African American cause. According to Fishel:

> Prominent Republicans, such as former Cabinet member and Senator Carl Schurz, George William Curtis, editor of *Harper's Weekly*, E. L. Godkin, editor of *The Nation*, and former abolitionist and Civil War veteran Thomas W. Higginson, came out as Mugwumps, arguing against continuing Republican support of southern black officeholders. The 1884 election victory of Grover Cleveland, a Democrat disinclined to offend the white South, contributed to the diminishing enthusiasm for racial equality.[75]

Political powerlessness made African Americans vulnerable economically and socially.

Following the Civil War and through much of Reconstruction, "African Americans . . . remained, for the most part, a southern rural and agricultural people."[76] Former slaves became tenant farmers working either for cash, to pay off credit, or for a share of the crop. In any case, they were hardly better off economically than they had been as slaves. Fishel comments: "The cash system required the tenant to pay rent, while the credit system advanced a loan to him for seeds and other necessities, using the unplanted crop as collateral. Sharecropping split the crop's return into shares for landlord and tenant. All three systems exploited the tenants and kept them debt-ridden and cash poor."[77] Moreover, most farm jobs, such as raising tobacco or cotton, were seasonal and thus unreliable sources of income. In response, African American workers migrated in significant numbers, both within the South and into other regions, in search of more stable, higher-paying jobs. In the South, "blacks generally went south and west from the border states, with Alabama, Arkansas, Georgia, Louisiana, Mississippi, South Carolina, and Texas registering large gains." In addition to farming, they often found employment "building railroads, mining coal and phosphate, making turpentine, and lumbering. Black workers often contracted for short-term jobs, moving on when the contract was up."[78] As men wandered in search of work and women remained behind to raise children and tend the home, whites increasingly viewed African Americans—especially males—as an indolent, disloyal lot who shirked their responsibilities.[79]

Like their white brothers and sisters in the Midwest and West, African American agricultural workers in the South sought to improve their condition by organizing but were frequently rejected by the established groups within the farmers' movement. Fishel notes that "facing the issue of black members, the Wheels, Alliances, and Knights [of Labor] initially welcomed them, but, as the Farmers Alliance grew to become the dominant agricultural organization, it yielded to white majority pressure and spurned black members."[80]

Eventually, African Americans migrated from the South in significant numbers. Between 1870 and 1890, for example, the number of African Americans in the North and West grew from approximately 460,000 to more than 910,000, and nearly half of that growth was due to migration.[81] Unlike their southern counterparts, they tended to settle in cities. By 1900, 90 percent of African Americans in New England and 60 to 75 percent in midwestern and western states lived in metropolitan areas.[82] As they sought employment in factories, mines, and warehouses, they again confronted the power of prejudice. "Reflecting and refining the racial ideology of the larger white society, some white unionists actively campaigned to keep their unions and their trades white. Numerous unions within the [AFL] . . . barred nonwhites explicitly or in practice," writes Arnesen.[83]

Bad as economic conditions during the era were for African Americans, social conditions were worse. In 1883 the U.S. Supreme Court invalidated the Civil Rights Act of 1875, ruling that individuals' access to public accommodations was not protected against racial discrimination by the Thirteenth and Fourteenth amendments to the Constitution. Some states, including Massachusetts, New York, Kansas, Ohio, and New Jersey, attempted to fill this void by passing their own civil rights legislation, but the laws were frequently weak and lacked enforcement provisions. In 1896 the Supreme Court ruled in *Plessy v. Ferguson* that Louisiana's laws requiring separate railroad cars for blacks and whites were likewise constitutional, thus clearing the way for the "separate but equal" doctrine.[84]

In the South, racially motivated law enforcement officials often filled the jails with African American prisoners. Wardens at these overcrowded institutions devised a "convict lease system" to cope—and possibly to fatten their own wallets. As Fishel explains, "the law enforcement system trapped more blacks, prisons expanded, the number of black inmates multiplied, and costs escalated. To offset expense and occupy prisoners' time, states and counties began leasing convicts to railroad builders, planters, and mine owners for a pittance."[85] Convinced that growing incarceration rates reflected general African American lawlessness, white citizens either endorsed or ignored the convict lease system and its attendant abuses.

Charged—almost universally without merit—with murder, rape of white women, or other heinous crimes, and unable to defend themselves in a corrupt and racist judicial system, African Americans were lynched by the thousands—2,500 between 1882 and 1899, almost half of that number between 1889 and 1899. The antilynching campaign launched by Ida B. Wells in 1892 barely stemmed a slaughter that continued through World War I.[86]

The implications of the race question extended into other reform movements. Women, who had worked side by side with abolitionists throughout most of the nineteenth century, were deeply disappointed when the post–Civil War amendments failed to affirm their rights along with those of freed slaves. The Fourteenth Amendment, pushed to adoption by a majority Republican Party eager to secure the votes of African American males newly freed from slavery, introduced the word "male" into the Constitution and particularly rankled woman suffrage advocates. Women slowly realized that their old alliances were over and that the "Negro hour" would take precedence over their concerns for women's rights.[87] Women recognized the need to organize to advocate for their own rights but disagreed sharply about how broad the agenda for change should be; two groups organized with differing agendas. Despite the differences between the two groups, Eleanor Flexner and Ellen Fitzpatrick note, "during the decade of 1880–1890 it was becomingly increasingly evident that the factors which had brought about the existence of two separate suffrage associations were steadily diminishing in importance."[88] Thus the two competing women's rights organizations joined in 1890 to become the

NAWSA, under the leadership of Elizabeth Cady Stanton until 1892, when Susan B. Anthony assumed the presidency.[89]

Opponents of the movement launched stiff resistance to the women's cause, often introducing racism and anti-immigrant sentiments. Antisuffrage forces decried the implications of broader enfranchisement on society. On the one hand, they argued that women occupied a special, elevated role that would only be diminished by being involved in politics.[90] On the other hand, some antisuffragists, particularly those from the South and those who feared the potential power of enfranchised immigrants, were blatantly racist and classist in their objections. One inspector for the Commission on Immigration averred: "The immigrant woman is a fickle, impulsive creature, irresponsible, very superstitious, ruled absolutely by emotion and intensely personal in her point of view. In many things much resembling a sheep. She would be as capable of understanding just about as much of political matters as a deaf man and blind would of the opera."[91] In response to these arguments, suffrage supporters sometimes expressed the same reservations. For example, Carrie Chapman Catt noted in her 1901 president's address to the NAWSA convention: "'the aggressive movement that with possibly ill-advised haste enfranchised the foreigner, the negro and the Indian' [is] detrimental to the suffrage cause."[92] Not surprisingly, radicals like Emma Goldman saw suffrage as a "fetish" of elite white women, a cause completely divorced from the substantial and significant issues facing workers.[93]

From its beginning at the first women's rights convention in Seneca Falls, New York, in 1848, through the reunification of the two suffrage associations in 1890, and to the ratification of the Nineteenth Amendment to the U.S. Constitution in 1920, the women's rights movement was first and foremost a *rhetorical* movement. Almost totally without political, economic, or social power, women necessarily employed rhetorical means to attain their goals. Leaders of the movement were arguably among the most talented—and subsequently the most frequently overlooked—orators of the era. Not only Stanton, Anthony, and Catt, but others such as Lucretia Coffin Mott, Angelina Grimké, Ernestine Potowski Rose, and Anna Howard Shaw delivered thousands of speeches to millions of listeners in support of women's rights and woman suffrage. Others, most notably Frances E. Willard, linked the cause of woman suffrage to prohibition in an effort to overcome the great "social evil," alcohol. Still others, like Ida B. Wells and Mary Church Terrell, worked for the cause of women's rights and woman suffrage, but primarily campaigned for civil rights for African Americans. Taken together, their rhetorical efforts were unsurpassed by male orators of the Gilded Age, friend and foe alike.

Public Discourse in the Gilded Age

If an idea can define an era—and especially the discourse of that era—social Darwinism was that idea for the Gilded Age. Used to justify the status quo and attacked by reformers, this misapplication of oversimplified Darwinian principles to social issues exerted a powerful influence on the discourse of the Gilded Age. In muted form, it underlay arguments for social change such as woman suffrage that envisioned a gradual evolution of a species toward greater perfection. At the same time, its principles were educed, at least implicitly, to justify Jim Crow laws and to oppress African Americans, who were not, in the eyes of many whites, as highly "evolved" as others. Whether explicitly stated or implicitly used to ground arguments, social Darwinism and the simplistic interpretations of evolution associated with it shaped the public discourse in subtle, but profound, ways.

The key principle of social Darwinism, at least in its popular development in the United States during the nineteenth century, according to Edward Caudill, was relatively simple: "the survival of the fittest in human society."[94] The idea found currency in a society searching to explain the rapid changes that followed the Civil War. As Robert Crunden observes, "Between the Civil War and American entry into World War I, the country went through a profound change. The religious ideas that had been so central to the nation's identity could not survive in their original form." Americans "had to face the traumas of the war, then the brutalities of the rapid industrialization after the war, and they had to do so in the face of the skepticism generated by science, most obviously what became known as Darwinism."[95]

Initiated by Herbert Spencer in England and popularized by William Graham Sumner and others in the United States, social Darwinism provided what amounted to a scientific extension of traditional Puritanism. Arnesen notes that

> Darwinism seemed to have an immediate applicability to social and political life. Puritanism had left a deep legacy of ideas with which Darwinism seemed compatible. The Puritans had instructed men to labor in their callings and assured them that if they were dutiful then God would reward them with wealth in this world and salvation in the next. Secularized over the years . . . these ideas no longer appeared especially religious, but rather the common sense of democracy. If a decent man had a sober set of habits, if he worked hard and fulfilled his responsibilities, then the way to wealth was open to him. All men were equal in America, and most of them had a reasonable chance at success. Puritan ideas of election thus took on secular meaning, and wealth became emblematic of divine approval.[96]

The ideas of social Darwinism accorded well with long-established American beliefs. The individualistic spirit of the nation insisted that anyone could succeed in this great democracy if only she or he worked hard enough. Although linked to and perhaps undergirded by Puritanism, this belief was part and parcel of the common understanding of a democratic state that promised its citizens the inalienable rights of life, liberty, and the pursuit of happiness. Moreover, capitalism, despite its obvious abuses during this era, emphasized the possibility of economic success if one worked diligently. In the public imagination, rags-to-riches stories, including that of Andrew Carnegie, helped sustain the link between individual effort and surefire reward.

The question of the applicability of Darwin's theory of natural selection to human social phenomena became unimportant, at least in the popular mind. Rather, as Mike Hawkins explains:

> There was a need to show that the social order in some way mirrored the natural order. This created a potential for the production of a whole range of equivalences, analogies, images, and metaphors: that societies are equivalent to biological organisms or that races represent biological species; individuals are akin to cells; that war is a manifestation of the struggle for existence; that women and children occupy the same position as "savages" in the scale of evolution, and so on. Metaphors and images were thus central to any Social Darwinist enterprise.

In short, Hawkins concludes, social Darwinism became "a powerful *rhetorical* instrument."[97]

The successful could tout the status quo as evidence of its accuracy. The captains of industry, assailed as "Robber Barons" and accused of gaining their fortunes through devious deeds, seized upon social Darwinism to justify not only their own success but also the perceived failure of the impoverished masses. In their view, if wealth was a sign of divine approval, then they were the chosen of God. Poverty must likewise be a sign of God's contempt; any effort to alter social or economic conditions was contrary to both the laws of nature and the will of the Almighty. "It was those who wished to defend the political status quo, above all the laissez-faire conservatives," argues Richard Hofstadter, "who were first to pick up the instruments of social argument that were forged out of the Darwinian concepts." Further, he concludes, "they suggested that all attempts to reform social processes were efforts to remedy the irremediable, that they interfered with the wisdom of nature [and] that they could lead only to degeneration."[98] Reformers, however, could couch calls for change in language of evolution and human progress. Indeed, such reformers could argue that evolution had moved humankind to a place where the raw laws of nature could be resisted. The progress gleaned from evolution, from the survival of the fittest, meant that society could be more enlightened and more committed to the common good. For both sides, the arguments gained force because of their grounding in the perhaps misunderstood and misapplied scientific theory.

The English philosopher Herbert Spencer, not his naturalist countryman Charles Darwin, introduced the phrase "survival of the fittest" to the world. A social determinist, Spencer believed in a gradual progression of society to its full potential. Government intervention could either aid or impede the process, but the progression was inexorable.[99] Thus, as Hofstadter explains bluntly: "Spencer deplored not only poor laws, but also state-supported education, sanitary supervision other than the suppression of nuisances, regulation of housing conditions, and even state protection of the ignorant from medical quacks. He likewise opposed tariffs, state banking, and government postal systems."[100] In short, Spencer opposed virtually any form of government intervention into what he saw as the natural progression of society.

Spencer's theories were propounded in the United States by a variety of individuals, perhaps most notably Yale professor of political and social science William Graham Sumner. Viewed by many as the founder of sociology as an academic field, Sumner advanced social Darwinism in the classroom, in public lectures, and in the popular press. Among his most widely read tracts was his essay "The Forgotten Man," first published in 1883. The "Forgotten Man," Sumner states:

> is the simple, honest, laborer, ready to earn his living by productive work. . . . He wants only to make a contract and get his living out of the capital of the country. The larger the capital is, the better living he can get. Every particle of capital which is wasted on the vicious, the idle, and the shiftless is so much taken from the capital available to reward the independent and productive laborer.[101]

Sumner clearly echoed Spencer's message, and he obviously appropriated Darwinian language. "Whatever capital you divert to the support of a shiftless and good-for-nothing person is so much diverted from some other employment," he argued. For Sumner, "vice is its own curse. If we let nature alone, she cures vice by the most frightful penalties." Hence, "a drunkard in the gutter is just where he ought to be. Nature is working away at him out of the way, just as she sets up her processes of dissolution to remove whatever is a failure in its line."[102]

Outside of academia, one of the leading voices of social Darwinism was none other than steel magnate Andrew Carnegie, who befriended Herbert Spencer and became one of his leading benefactors. In the June 1889 issue of the *North American Review*, Carnegie published an article entitled "Wealth," which Hofstadter regards as one of his best writings.[103] Caudill notes the impact of the article:

> The use of Social Darwinism may have reached its zenith in Andrew Carnegie's 1889 article . . . in which the author linked individualism, social divisions, and economic competition. But Sumner and Spencer reached a conclusion unlike

Carnegie's, because their goal was to elaborate a coherent world view which might both explain society and establish an agenda for further sociological inquiry. Carnegie [was] . . . only defending the status quo.[104]

Similarly, Russell H. Conwell, the popular lecturer, Baptist preacher, and founder of Temple University, enthusiastically advocated Spencer's theories to popular audiences. Conwell traveled the lecture circuit delivering his "Acres of Diamonds" speech, which Crunden calls "the longest cliché in history," an estimated 5,000 times.[105] The speech consisted largely of a series of extended examples that moved listeners toward Conwell's thesis: through sufficient individual effort, anyone could become wealthy. Conwell—like Spencer, Sumner, and Carnegie—drew upon familiar Darwinian images and metaphors to extend the traditional Puritan ethic:

> When the traditional Christian attitudes were breaking down, people demanded figures who played the role of the minister: they assured everyone that things were working out, that everything was for the best, and that no matter how confusing the new world seemed to be, some principles were eternal. Contract had replaced covenant, wealth had replaced salvation, the fittest had replaced the saints, but the intellectual processes had not changed all that much.[106]

Despite the leaps in logic required to apply the theories of "natural selection" and "survival of the fittest" to human society, social Darwinism heavily influenced the rhetoric of the conservative defenders of the status quo. That defense, however, was not accepted blindly. The crushing effects of poverty, the horrid working conditions not only for men but for women and children as well, the teeming city slums, and the plight of midwestern farmers were all too visible; they stood in sharp contrast to the opulent palaces of the wealthy. Thus reform rhetoric often took aim, at least implicitly, at social Darwinism.

Among intellectuals, the leading critics of social Darwinsim were the self-educated philosopher Henry George, newspaperman and novelist Edward Bellamy, sociologist Lester Frank Ward, and clergyman Washington Gladden. These critics, Hofstadter remarks, "felt the necessity of refuting the conservative arguments of evolutionary sociology."[107]

According to Crunden, Ward, for example, was a reform Darwinist who "insisted that while Darwinism was true for the animal and vegetable kingdoms, the ideas did not apply to human beings. Men and women had minds, or 'psychic factors,' and they could use them to ward off the effects of natural events." Summarizing Ward's position, Crunden explains that

> society was dynamic and not static, and that both the schools and the state were necessary ways which people used to foster growth and control evolution. The whole practice of medicine was in direct violation of Social Darwinian principles, and only a fool would let someone bleed to death after an accident, or do nothing to prevent the spread of an epidemic. He also pointed out bluntly that the loudest supporters of laissez faire were big businessmen and their pet intellectuals, and that it was intellectually insulting to see them ask for government subsidies in one breath, and then howl with rage in the next at any attempt at exerting control.[108]

Likewise, Gladden declared "survival of the fittest" and "natural selection" as "the law of plants and brutes and brutish men" but not of civilized society. Moreover, Hofstadter writes that Gladden "warned that the weaker classes would unite to attack a competitive system in which they were threatened with annihilation, and that huge warring combinations of capital and labor would be the natural consequence of accepting the law of strife as a norm for industrial society."[109] George, in his book *Progress and Poverty*, and Bellamy, in *Looking Backward*, also assailed what social Darwinists had called the "laws of nature."[110]

Social Darwinism's influence extended beyond the speeches and essays of major figures. The concept of evolutionary progress permeated the public consciousness. Movements as diverse as eugenics and suffrage used the ideas of human evolution, sometimes realized as an endorsement of a romantic, progressive view of human history, to undergird their advocacy. Reformers and advocates of the status quo embraced the notion that human society was moving toward a brighter, more abundant future. The diverse public discourse of the era largely centered on the means to facilitate human progress.

In an era without electronic means of communication other than the telegraph, speeches and printed materials were the only forms of mass communication. "Hence," Calhoun explains, "in the months before elections, hundreds of state and national party leaders took to the hustings, speaking to audiences day after day for weeks on end, laying out their party's doctrines and appealing for support." After addressing literally thousands of listeners, major figures published their speeches in an effort to reach thousands more. "The production and distribution of such speeches and other printed matter played a pivotal role in late nineteenth-century electioneering," says Calhoun. The efforts reached every level of society. In the 1872 campaign, for instance, the Republicans produced a circular three times per week and mailed over seven million tracts to local newspapers. Election textbooks, consisting of documents, speeches, and other materials, were sent out to aid local speakers.[111] Thus the social tensions and upheavals so prevalent in American society of this era permeated public discourse, often becoming central to political campaigns. Speeches, newspapers, pamphlets, and sermons all reflected the forces at work in this turbulent period. That discourse is the focus of this volume.

Preview of the Chapters

This volume begins with Richard Leeman's consideration of African American reform rhetoric in the aftermath of the Civil War. Although the postwar constitutional amendments had ostensibly made dramatic changes in the lives of former slaves, prejudices and oppressions persisted. Even successful and affluent African Americans faced immense challenges in simply living their daily lives. In an attempt to advocate for a changed role for their race in national life, prominent African American spokespersons were forced to confront the tenets of social Darwinism that increasingly permeated the culture. Leeman traces their efforts to co-opt that strain of discourse for their own ends and identifies the costs of that strategy of co-optation.

When the post–Civil War amendments freed and empowered former slaves, white southerners sought legal and extralegal mechanisms for protecting their power. On the slightest pretexts, groups of white southerners began to lynch African Americans in an effort to intimidate and control them. Deeply affected by the lynching of a friend, Ida B. Wells, a young journalist, began to confront the apologists for lynchings who insisted the practice arose to protect the virtues of white womanhood. When her newspaper was burned, she turned to the platform to refute the common defense of lynching and to present the facts of the brutality to the public. In chapter 2, after a brief biography of Wells that highlights the forces shaping her development as a rhetor, Shirley Wilson Logan and Martha Watson carefully analyze her rhetorical practices. Focusing on the obstacles that confronted an African American woman in addressing such a controversial topic, the authors suggest how she adroitly used forceful refutation, buttressed by vivid examples and statistics, to make the issue salient to her audience and to urge them to social action. Although it is impossible to assess her impact directly, the chapter demonstrates that by raising her voice, Wells forced her audiences to confront their own prejudices and preconceptions.

In chapter 3, Cheree Carlson explores the public discourse of one of the most popular and successful public speakers in this era, Russell H. Conwell. Known for his "Acres of Diamonds" address, Conwell attempted to articulate a vision for his contemporaries that transcended the prevailing appeals to amass great wealth. According to Carlson, Conwell attempted to resist dominant social forces, to provide comic transcendence through a vision that insisted true wealth was individual character. Further, Conwell argued that such wealth should and could enable individuals to employ their resources to the betterment of all. In essence, although embedded in the public acceptance of evolutionary and progressive thinking, Conwell sought to offer a vision that would empower his listeners.

Nowhere were the dramatic changes in the United States during the Gilded Age more evident than in the shift from an agrarian-based society to a society based on industry and entrepreneurship. Faced with what they saw as a threat not only to their livelihood but also to their way of life, and convinced that they were the victims of a grand conspiracy of the eastern "Money Powers," western agrarian radicals launched the Populist revolt to regain what they saw as their rightful place in society. In chapter 4, Thomas R. Burkholder uses Kansas Populists as a case study to reveal the mythic appeals that accounted for both the initial success and the ultimate failure of the Populist rhetorical crusade.

No consideration of the rhetoric of this era would be complete without an exploration of one of the most famous men of the time, William Jennings Bryan. Although history has tended to dismiss Bryan and his discourse as mediocre and even simplistic, Sally Perkins takes issue with this interpretation. In chapter 5, she contends that understanding Bryan as a rhetor requires careful analysis of the internal logic of his works. From this perspective, Perkins argues that Bryan's discourse grew out of two grand mythic narratives: the Christ myth and the American foundation myth. Bryan's discourse was governed by the internal logic of these two myths. In this light, Perkins contends, we can see him as a rhetor whose vision of American life reflected and shaped the thinking of his contemporaries.

Among the most notable of reformers during this age was Frances E. Willard, the leader of the Woman's Christian Temperance Union. Subtly and strategically expanding the mission of the organization, Willard used her bully pulpit to advance a host of social causes, but she has nonetheless often been dismissed as too conservative to be of interest to scholars of the women's rights movement. Amy Slagell takes exception to this view in chapter 6. Tracing the concept of the home as a central rhetorical motif in Willard's discourse, Slagell indicates how Willard was able to advance a progressive agenda for social change by tying reforms to the protection of the home. Slagell contends that Willard strategically negotiated the issues of her age by embracing the traditional commitment of women to the home and by using that connection to justify such "radical" notions as companionate marriage. Embedded in Willard's discourse is the view that human society can only progress if women accept a new role in the world and use their power to shape a better world.

In very different contexts and in very different ways, militant female labor organizers also realized the power of certain traditional values in their work. In chapter 8, Mari Boor Tonn traces the careers of two of the most prominent radical activists, Mary Harris "Mother" Jones and Elizabeth Gurley Flynn, to highlight the similarities and differences in their attempts to organize workers. Although sometimes seen as difficult to organize, women workers often became the most radical of labor sympathizers. In this essay, Tonn explores how these two women, distinctively different in style and separated in time, employed appeals to maternity to argue for an expansive agenda of reform. Tonn maintains that Jones and Flynn sought to privatize the public and publicize the private in their attempt to secure not just "bread" but "roses" for workers.

During this period, attempts to organize workers to confront the immense powers of owners took many forms. Ultimately, the AFL and the Congress of Industrial Organizations (CIO) came to dominate the scene. But between 1870 and 1890 the Knights of Labor pursued a much broader agenda in its efforts to organize all workers into a single union that could not just secure higher wages or shorter working hours but could also improve the lives of workers in a myriad of ways. One man, Terance Powderly, became the leader and chief spokesperson for the group. In chapter 9, Charles Stewart explores how circumstances, including the nature and dynamics of the organization itself, forced Powderly increasingly into a posture of apologetics where he was forced to defend himself, his fellow members, and the organization itself. Stewart argues that Powderly employed an array of apologetic strategies in his attempts to mollify both members of the Knights of Labor and external critics of the Knights. Ultimately, however, Powderly and the Knights were unable to overcome public perceptions of them as radicals and to compete with the more conservative and thus palatable approaches of competing labor organizations.

As mentioned earlier, the World's Columbian Exposition, held in Chicago in 1893, became an opportunity for the organizers to present their vision of the country and society 400 years after Columbus's "discovery" of the New World. From the earliest planning stages, its organizers sought to use the Fair to reveal the superiority of the United States to older nations and to tout the immense progress afoot in this country. In chapter 10, James Gilbert traces how everything—from the choice of Chicago, to the planning of the layout, to the development of guidebooks for the Fair—worked to achieve the rhetorical goals of its organizers. Although many of what Gilbert concludes were between twelve million and thirteen million visitors (official numbers were twenty-seven million) never visited the exhibits that depicted the superiority of this nation, they nonetheless could not escape some of its messages. Despite the attempts to make the Fair speak a single message, Gilbert traces how its diverse and sometimes conflicting messages have continued to excite comment and controversy.

The final chapters of this volume parallel the essay by Tonn in treating more than one rhetor in relation to a movement. These chapters, the first on anarchism and the second on the women's rights movement, help reveal the varied strands of discourse that are typical of complex social movements. Further, they indicate how different styles of leadership and rhetoric function, sometimes effectively and sometimes not, to build support for a social movement.

Three women became active anarchist spokespersons during this period: Voltairine de Celyre, Emma Goldman, and Lucy Parson. In chapter 11, Linda Diane Horwitz, Donna Marie Kowal, and Catherine Helen Palczeski examine the distinctive roles that each played in the movement and the rhetorical strategies each employed. Although joined by a common commitment to anarchism, each woman had her own interpretation of that doctrine. Further, the backgrounds and experiences of the three differed sharply. Horwitz, Kowal, and Palczeski contend that these women constructed distinct rhetorical persona with concomitantly different approaches in their advocacy of anarchism. De Cleyre became the philosopher/poet of the movement, Goldman was the agitator, and Parsons used her widowhood to inform her advocacy. In their discussion of these feminist anarchists, the authors also explore how each presents a distinctive embodiment of the feminine style.

The final essay in this volume explores the leadership of the woman suffrage movement from its origins to its successful culmination. Susan Shultz Huxman treats Elizabeth Cady Stanton, Anna Howard Shaw, and Carrie Chapman Catt, the three major spokespersons for the NAWSA, together because she sees their roles and accomplishments as critically intertwined in the final success of the movement. Drawing on social movement theory, Huxman first explores the challenges that the movement faced at each stage and then delineates how each of the women played a distinctive role in advancing the cause. Stanton, who was the prophetic voice for the movement, became its philosophical leader. Shaw used her considerable talents as a speaker to draw thousands of supporters, providing much needed charismatic leadership during a critical period. Finally, in contrast, Catt served as an organizer and mobilizer, offering pragmatic plans for achieving success. Huxman argues that only such contrastive critiques can help us fully understand the vibrant, diverse tapestry of the women's rights movement in America.

No single volume can do justice to the divergent public discourse of such a tumultuous era. As the chapters suggest, all these rhetors sought to invigorate and motivate their listeners to address the pressing issues of the day. Implicit in their advocacy was a progressive view of history, a notion that people were capable of moving human society forward. The voices chronicled here can only suggest the tenor of American society during this period. What is clear from these discussions, however, is that at the turn of the twentieth century, the United States was caught up with social reform and social change. The changing status of African Americans, the pressures for organizing workers, and the efforts to improve the status of women are exemplary of a nation trying to realize the vision it had sought to present in the Columbian Exposition of 1893.

Notes

1. Bryant Morey French, *Mark Twain and the Gilded Age: The Book That Named an Era* (Dallas: Southern Methodist University Press, 1965), 4.
2. Ibid., 19.
3. See Eleanor Flexner and Ellen Fitzpatrick, *Century of Struggle: The Woman's Rights Movement in the United States* (Cambridge, Mass.: Belknap Press of Harvard University Press, 1996), 136–48, for the details of the split in the woman's movement.
4. Andrew F. Wood, "Managing the Lady Managers: The Shaping of Heterotopian Spaces in the 1893 Chicago Exposition's Woman's Building," *Southern States Journal* 69, no. 4 (Summer 2004): 290.
5. James Gilbert, *Perfect Cities: Chicago's Utopias of 1893* (Chicago: University of Chicago Press, 1991), especially chapter 4, "First City: Form and Fantasy."
6. Ibid., 78.
7. Wood, "Managing the Lady Managers," 300; Gilbert, *Perfect Cities*, 82–84.
8. Charles W. Calhoun, "Introduction," in *The Gilded Age: Essays on the Origins of Modern America*, ed. Charles W. Calhoun (Wilmington, Del.: Scholarly Resources, 1996), xi.
9. John Tipple, "Big Businessmen and a New Economy," in *The Gilded Age*, rev. ed., ed. H. Wayne Morgan (Syracuse, N.Y.: Syracuse University Press, 1970), 14.
10. Sean Dennis Cashman, *America in the Gilded Age: From the Death of Lincoln to the Rise of Theodore Roosevelt*, 3rd ed. (New York: New York University Press, 1988), 8.
11. Ibid., 11.
12. Calhoun, "Introduction," xii.
13. Samuel Eliot Morison, Henry Steele Commager, and William E. Leuchtenburg, *A Concise History of the American Republic*, 2nd ed. (New York: Oxford University Press, 1983), 362.
14. Glenn Porter, "Industrialization and the Rise of Big Business," in Calhoun, *Gilded Age*, 11.
15. Morison, Commager, and Leuchtenburg, *Concise History*, 392.
16. Porter, "Industrialization," 10.
17. Cashman, *America in the Gilded Age*, 10.
18. Morison, Commager, and Leuchtenburg, *Concise History*, 424.
19. Ibid., 433–34.

20. Ibid., 433.
21. Cashman, *America in the Gilded Age*, 314.
22. H. Wayne Morgan, "Populism and the Decline of Agriculture," in Morgan, *Gilded Age*, 151.
23. Porter, "Industrialization," 4.
24. Ibid., 5.
25. Morgan, "Populism," 151–52.
26. Porter, "Industrialization," 5.
27. Cashman, *America in the Gilded Age*, 11.
28. Morison, Commager, and Leuchtenburg, *Concise History*, 383.
29. Roger Daniels, "The Immigrant Experience in the Gilded Age," in Calhoun, *Gilded Age*, 64.
30. Cashman, *America in the Gilded Age*, 74.
31. Daniels, "Immigrant Experience," 65. As Daniels notes, however, these numbers require careful scrutiny since they may obscure some significant differences in what were assumed to be monolithic groups. See 66–69.
32. Cashman, *America in the Gilded Age*, 84.
33. Daniels, "Immigrant Experience," 72.
34. Cashman, *America in the Gilded Age*, 93.
35. Morison, Commager, and Leuchtenburg, *Concise History*, 386, 387.
36. Cashman, *America in the Gilded Age*, 93–96.
37. Ibid., 96–97.
38. Ibid., 97.
39. Daniels, "Immigrant Experience," 82.
40. Ibid., 73.
41. Morison, Commager, and Leuchtenburg, *Concise History*, 383.
42. Daniels, "Immigrant Experience," 82.
43. Ibid., 46. According to Daniels, "Asiatic" referred to Jews rather than Chinese or Japanese.
44. Ibid., 83.
45. Sara Hunter Graham, *Woman Suffrage and the New Democracy* (New Haven, Conn.: Yale University Press, 1996), 17–18.
46. Graham, *Woman Suffrage*, 22.
47. Calhoun, "Introduction," xi–xii.
48. Porter, "Industrialization," 2.
49. Tipple, "Big Businessmen," 15.
50. Ibid., 15–16.
51. Ibid., 16.
52. Porter, "Industrialization," 9.
53. Tipple, "Big Businessmen," 16.
54. Ibid., 29.
55. Charles W. Calhoun, "The Political Culture: Public Life and the Conduct of Politics," in Calhoun, *Gilded Age*, 190.
56. Tipple, "Big Businessmen," 28.
57. Ibid., 30.
58. Eric Arnesen, "American Workers and the Labor Movement in the Late Nineteenth Century," in Calhoun, *Gilded Age*, 41.
59. Ibid., 41.
60. Ibid., 52.
61. Ibid., 44, 47.
62. Ibid., 47–48.
63. H. W. Brands, *The Reckless Decade: America in the 1890s* (New York: St. Martin's Press, 1995), 145.
64. Morison, Commager, and Leuchtenburg, *Concise History*, 377.
65. Cashman, *America in the Gilded Age*, 116.
66. Morison, Commager, and Leuchtenburg, *Concise History*, 377.
67. Arnesen, "American Workers," 52.
68. Brands, *Reckless Decade*, 145.
69. Arnesen, "American Workers," 52–53.
70. Ibid., 44.
71. Leslie H. Fishel Jr., "The African-American Experience," in Calhoun, *Gilded Age*, 137.
72. Ibid., 141–42.

73. Calhoun, "Political Culture," 189.

74. Fishel, "African-American Experience," 141.

75. Ibid.

76. Arnesen, "American Workers," 45.

77. Fishel, "African-American Experience," 139.

78. Ibid., 138.

79. Ibid.

80. Ibid., 143.

81. Ibid., 138.

82. Ibid.

83. Arnesen, "American Workers," 54.

84. Fishel, "African-American Experience," 140, 141, 153.

85. Ibid., 147.

86. Ibid., 146.

87. Flexner and Fitzpatrick, *Century of Struggle*, 138–39.

88. Ibid., 208, 212.

89. See Ellen Carol Dubois, *Feminism and Suffrage: The Emergence of an Independent Women's Movement in America 1848–1869* (Ithaca, N.Y.: Cornell University Press, 1978), for a full discussion of advocacy for women's rights in the aftermath of the Civil War.

90. See Graham, *Woman Suffrage*, 12–21, for a full discussion of what she perceives as the two strains of antisuffrage rhetoric, the traditionalist and the tory. The traditionalists focused on the family and the implications of suffrage on that critical social unit. Often these antisuffragists argued for different but coequal roles for the sexes. In contrast, tories acknowledged and embraced class distinctions. This group "favored rule by a paternalistic elite" (Graham, *Woman Suffrage*, 16).

91. Ibid., 18.

92. Ibid., 22.

93. Martha Solomon, *Emma Goldman* (Boston: Twayne, 1987), 69–77.

94. Edward Caudill, *Darwinian Myths: The Legends and Misuses of a Theory* (Knoxville: University of Tennessee Press, 1977), 77.

95. Robert Crunden, *A Brief History of American Culture* (New York: Paragon House, 1994), 129.

96. Ibid., 131–32.

97. Mike Hawkins, *Social Darwinism in European and American Thought, 1860–1945* (Cambridge: Cambridge University Press, 1997), 17, 34–35.

98. Richard Hofstadter, *Social Darwinism in American Thought*, rev. ed. (New York: George Braziller, 1959), 5, 7.

99. Caudill, *Darwinian Myths*, 67, 68.

100. Hofstadter, *Social Darwinism*, 41.

101. William Graham Sumner, "The Forgotten Man," in *Social Darwinism: Selected Essays of William Graham Sumner* (Englewood Cliffs, N.J.: Prentice-Hall, 1963), 119.

102. Ibid., 119, 122.

103. Hofstadter, *Social Darwinism*, 45.

104. Caudill, *Darwinian Myths*, 77.

105. Crunden, *Brief History*, 133.

106. Ibid.

107. Hofstadter, *Social Darwinism*, 110.

108. Crunden, *Brief History*, 134.

109. Hofstadter, *Social Darwinism*, 109.

110. Ibid., 109–11.

111. Calhoun, "Political Culture," 201–2.

Fighting for Freedom Again: African American Reform Rhetoric in the Late Nineteenth Century

Richard W. Leeman

1

The whirlwinds of change that African Americans experienced during Reconstruction were followed by a period in which the change was not as immediately apparent, but far more momentous. It is true that the Reconstruction era (1865–1876) was not the time of freedom and power for African Americans as is often depicted. The attitudes and practices that had enabled slavery to thrive in the United States did not disappear during Reconstruction. White Southerners were hostile to black political influence; stuffed ballot boxes and harassment at the polling place were common tactics designed to reduce the black vote. The Reconstruction era also saw periodic violence, including White Leagues, the Ku Klux Klan, and other white "militias" whose purpose was to discourage African American advancement in politics and business. Although blacks wielded some political power, they never controlled a single Southern legislature, and the only African American governor of the era assumed that position for forty-one days after the sitting white governor was removed from office. Although there were some notable exceptions and some broad economic gains, most blacks, North and South, remained poor during Reconstruction. Discrimination, lack of capital, and the economic depression of 1873 conspired to keep them poor or return them to the poverty from which they had temporarily emerged.

Still, Reconstruction was a time of sharp contrast with the institutional slavery that had preceded it, and African Americans experienced some tangible changes during the era. By 1867 forty-six hospitals had been organized and staffed by the Freedmen's Bureau. By 1870 some 250,000 students were attending over 4,000 schools.[1] During Reconstruction, twenty-two African Americans served in the U.S. Congress, and there were many black representatives and senators at the state level.

John R. Lynch, for example, served as Speaker of the House in the Mississippi legislature and as a U.S. congressman for three terms.

The most significant gains, however, were legislative. Although primarily passed for partisan purposes, the Thirteenth, Fourteenth, and Fifteenth amendments to the U.S. Constitution ended slavery and guaranteed full citizenship rights to blacks. The Reconstruction Act of 1867 forced the Southern states to ratify the Fourteenth Amendment and to rewrite their constitutions to include universal manhood suffrage. The resulting documents, write Franklin and Moss, were "the most progressive the South had ever known."[2] The Civil Rights Act of 1866 guaranteed equal economic rights; the Civil Rights Act of 1875 provided for equal rights in public accommodations. Although these laws were hardly enforced to their fullest, by 1877 the framework had been nominally laid for African Americans to take their rightful place in the community. Even those who were realistic about the present condition of African Americans had reason to be hopeful about the future given the advancements that had occurred in the twelve years following the war.

But however promising Reconstruction might have appeared, the remaining twenty-three years of the nineteenth century—the post-Reconstruction era—were marked by a steady decline of African American rights and liberties, particularly in the Southern states. In public accommodations, Tennessee passed the first post–Civil War Jim Crow law in 1875, the same year Congress voted for the countervailing Civil Rights Act of 1875. In 1883 the Supreme Court overturned the latter, and in the following years Southern states adopted more and more Jim Crow laws. Most Southern states had segregated school systems by 1885, and in 1896 "separate but equal" became nationally sanctioned in *Plessy v. Ferguson*.[3]

Voting rights, too, eroded steadily during this time. In 1890 Mississippi became the first Southern state to rewrite its Reconstruction-era constitution, with the sole purpose of incorporating a poll tax and literacy test to discourage black voting. These taxes and tests, plus the invention of the grandfather clause, had the desired effect. In 1898 Louisiana had 130,344 registered black voters. In twenty-six parishes, blacks constituted the majority of registered voters. Two years later, after the adoption of a new state constitution, the entire state had 5,320 registered black voters.[4]

Economic statistics are sketchier, but African Americans' economic position declined with the loss of civil and political rights. The sharecropping system begun immediately following emancipation kept an economic stranglehold on black farmers. Skilled black laborers, originally recruited by some labor unions, were increasingly locked out of jobs previously open to them in both the North and South.[5] White-collar employment became unavailable, and self-employed African Americans could only count on the patronage of other blacks.

The available statistics about lynching tell a similar story. Using only reports in the *Chicago Tribune*, Ida B. Wells's figures provide conservative estimates of the total number of lynchings that occurred in any given year, but they are probably accurate in the trend they depict. In 1882 the *Chicago Tribune* reported 52 blacks lynched; by 1887 that number was 70; and in 1892 the paper reported 241.[6]

Thus, although the Reconstruction era did not bring African Americans fully into the larger community, it had provided some important legislation and opportunities for blacks. These were the beginnings of freedom and equal citizenship, beginnings that were swept away during the post-Reconstruction era. White Americans' assault on blacks' liberties posed a significant rhetorical challenge to African Americans, which a wide array of speakers and writers attempted to meet.

African American rhetors of this period have been typically categorized into four groups: assimilationists, accomodationists, integrationists, and separationists. Assimilationists believed that ultimately the two major races in the United States, black and white, would amalgamate, or combine into one. Wrote George L. Ruffin: "The negro must go, his fate is sealed; he must be swallowed up and merged in the mass of Southern people. . . . This thought will not now be well received by the negro; his hope has been to build up his race, to vindicate his people . . . but, nevertheless, the merging . . . is inevitable." Because ethnic merging was inevitable, these African Americans argued, blacks should consider themselves *Americans* first, as should all ethnic groups, and that fact was more important than any racial consideration. Laws should be written to allow the full assimilation of blacks into American society, and blacks should take advantage of those laws to do so.[7]

Accomodationists accepted the status quo of political and cultural relations between blacks and whites in America, arguing that as their race "matured" and proved its worth, whites would naturally come to accept blacks as equals in all regards. Accomodationists wanted integration eventually, but they believed that peaceful relations and time were necessary to achieve full legal equality. These rhetors preferred economic achievements over political ones. An 1890 editorialist in the *AME Review* averred that African Americans "have turned their attention to accumulating property, and so unjust treatment has proved a blessing in disguise. Christianity, morality, courage, and industry are sure to produce wealth, and any people who become strong in these qualities are sure to move upward among men."[8]

Integrationists demanded complete political integration—but not cultural assimilation—into American society. They wanted the full rights of citizenship immediately, contending that the Declaration of Independence and Constitution required nothing less. They argued for citizenship rights on both moral and pragmatic grounds. Blacks were, by virtue of natural rights, entitled to all citizenship rights and protections. Political rights were also necessary for blacks to protect themselves physically, politically, economically, and socially. Because blacks were being denied their basic and entitled rights, it was incumbent on both the leaders and the citizenry to protest actively against the status quo. J. C. Price, the president of the Afro-American League, wrote to his organization: "If we do not possess the manhood and patriotism to stand up in the defense of these constitutional rights, and protest long, loud and unitedly against their continual infringement, we are unworthy of our heritage as American Citizens and deserve to have afastened on us the wrongs which many of us are disposed to complain." Most African American leaders of the post-Reconstruction era espoused integration in some form, urging blacks to protest against the continued confiscation of their rights.[9]

Finally, separatist orators held that blacks should keep themselves apart from both the white culture and its government. Some separatists preached emigration back to Africa, others focused on the promise of Pan-Africanism, and still others argued for a black nationalism within the geographic confines of the United States. Bishop Henry McNeal Turner, an ardent advocate of emigration, wrote that he wished the United States "nothing but ill and endless misfortune, wish I would only live to see it go down to ruin and its memory blotted from the pages of history. A man who loves a country that hates him is a human dog and not a man."[10]

The usual conclusion is that this era was marked by a conflict between the integrationists and accomodationists, with the amalgamationists and separatists as lesser players in the drama. The integrationists were strongest during the Reconstruction era, but as the historical tide of segregation overwhelmed them, accomodationists, led by Booker T. Washington, emerged as the dominant rhetors. While such a characterization has some truth to it, a fuller appreciation of the period's rhetoric can only emerge when the role of Social Darwinism is considered. As a major intellectual presence, and one whose principles forcefully pronounced itself regarding race relations, Social Darwinism was a rhetorical constraint that affected audience perceptions regardless of whether an individual rhetor specifically addressed that philosophy. Further, Social Darwinism influenced virtually every facet of American intellectual life, including that of African Americans. Some of its assumptions would be found in the discourse of African American reform rhetors;

in other instances language not intended to be understood against the background of Social Darwinism would still be heard as reinforcing or denying its principles. Social Darwinism was such a pervasive belief system in the nineteenth century that African American reform rhetoric of that era cannot be fully understood without first understanding the rhetorical context that Social Darwinism provided.

Social Darwinism

In 1859 Charles Darwin published his theory of evolution in *On the Origin of Species*. As early as 1865 the Social Darwinist movement had begun applying Darwinian theory to the study of sociology.[11] Arguing that human beings are subject to the same biological laws as other living organisms, sociologists found in the Darwinian principle of natural selection an objective lens by which to understand human behavior. Life, for the Social Darwinist, is a struggle for existence against the forces of nature. Through our inheritance from our parents, wrote Professor William Graham Sumner, a major American populizer of the theory, "the human race keeps up a constantly advancing contest with Nature. The penalty of ceasing aggressive behavior toward the hardships of life on the part of mankind is, that we go backward. We cannot stand still." As set out in the theory of natural selection, those who are weak will fail. Social economist Walter Bagehot, a leading British theorist, argued that "nature disheartened in each generation the ill-fitted members of each customary group, and so deprived them of their full vigor or, if they were weakly, killed them." Conversely, as captured in the phrase "survival of the fittest," Social Darwinists held that those who are ablest among us will succeed the most. "Only the elite of the race," wrote Sumner, "has yet been raised to the point where reason and conscience can even curb the lower motive forces. For the mass of mankind . . . the price of better things is too severe, for that price can be summed up in one word—self-control."[12]

Social Darwinists typically argued that there were two arenas in which humans competed and from which the fittest emerged victorious. The most obvious arena was war, but there was a second, more ubiquitous battlefield: economic competition. The wealthiest individuals were, by definition, the fittest. Sumner's argument was representative of how Social Darwinists treated this proof that success equaled fitness, and of the advantages that resulted from this natural order of things:

> If Mr. A. T. Stewart made a great fortune by collecting and bringing dry-goods to the people of the United States, he did so because he understood how to do that thing better than any other man of his generation. . . . It was for the benefit of all; but he contributed to it what no one else was able to contribute—the one guiding mind which made the whole thing possible.[13]

Using de facto reasoning, Sumner could conclude that Stewart was the only man who had the tremendous ability to create his dry goods empire because Stewart was the only man who *had* created it. Stewart's superior success was the "proof" of his superior fitness.

What was true in the case of individuals, Social Darwinists argued, was also true in the case of race. The Aryan race, for example, had succeeded because it possessed a "good aptitude—an excellent political nature" for the forms of government needed to sustain economic and military superiority. "*Intellectual* progress" and "*moral* quality" were the "preliminary" virtues needed to succeed in war and the economy, because "those kinds of morals and that kind of religion which tend to make the firmest and most effectual character are sure to prevail, all else being the same." In contrast to the Aryans, other races were "lesser," some considerably so. Professor John Fiske, another prolific American advocate of Social Darwinism, traced the difference back to the nature of each race's brain:

> If we take into account the creasing of the cerebral surface, the difference between the brain of a Shakespeare and that of an Australian savage would doubtless be fifty times greater than the difference between the Australian's brain and that of an orangoutang [sic]. In mathematical capacity the Australian, who cannot tell the number of fingers on his two hands, is much nearer to a lion or a wolf than to Sir Rowan Hamilton, who invented the method of quaternions. In moral development this same Australian, whose language contains no words for justice or benevolence, is less remote from dogs and baboons than from a Howard or a Garrison.

Other writers did not pinpoint the "cerebral surface" as the cause of inferiority, but their conclusion was the same. Other races were lesser races, and the proof of this lay in those races' military, economic, and literary inferiority.[14]

Moreover, this lesser ability of other races could not be quickly or easily altered. Evolution had created the differences, and only the slow tide of evolution could change them. Bagehot argued that the "differences as exist between the Aryan, the Turanian, the Negro, the red man, and the Australian are differences *greater altogether than any causes now active are capable of creating in present men.*" Further, such change would also be essentially uncontrollable by outside forces. As Sumner characterized it: "Social improvement is not to be won by direct effort. It is secondary, and results from physical or economic improvements." Again, Social Darwinists argued that this natural order was desirable. The self-control needed to succeed economically, they argued, produced benefits in literature, religion, morals, and government.[15]

Social Darwinism quickly permeated and influenced much of American thought in the late nineteenth century. Richard Hofstadter writes that the United States during the last three decades of the nineteenth century and at the beginning of the twentieth century was *the* Darwinian country. Social Darwinism was seized upon as a welcome addition, perhaps the most powerful of all, to the conservative thought that dominated this period of rapid and striking economic change. Social Darwinism validated America's natural inclination toward rugged individualism and laissez-faire government. It appealed to a growing affinity for scientific explanations, and it helped justify the extraordinary rise of industrialism. It also justified the principle of manifest destiny and the unequal treatment of America's citizens of color. It was, historian August Meier notes, a racist philosophy. A pervasive, almost omnipresent force in that era's intellectual landscape, Social Darwinism was the lens through which most white Americans viewed any discourse by African Americans. In addition, many African Americans subscribed to its basic tenets. Any rhetoric of the era that addressed the issue of race would be understood within the context of Social Darwinism.[16]

"Let Him Alone"

With the exception of the separatists, who believed that white America would never change, most of the rhetors of the Reconstruction and early post-Reconstruction period constructed their discourse around the demand that African Americans be given "a chance." Emphasizing the need for legal equality, such discourse has been classified as integrationist or amalgamationist, depending on the rhetor's stance vis-à-vis cultural assimilation. However, this common theme of equal opportunity, a chance to run the race of life, not only reflected the prevalent emphasis on liberty and rugged individualism, it also participated in the developing discourse of Social Darwinism.

Representative Richard Cain, speaking on behalf of the Civil Rights Act of 1875, gave voice to this theme of a chance: "What we desire is this: inasmuch as we have been raised to the dignity, to the honor, to the position of our manhood, we ask that the laws of this country should guarantee all the rights and immunities belonging to that proud position, to be enforced all over this broad land." "All that we ask," he continued, "is equal laws, equal legislation, and equal rights throughout the length and breadth of this land." Throughout this era, other African Americans repeated that call: give us an equal chance, and we will show you what we can do. During that same 1875 debate, Representative James T. Rapier summarized the argument vividly:

> I have always found more prejudice existing in the breasts of men who have feeble minds and are conscious of it, than in the breasts of those who have towering intellects and are aware of it. Henry Ward Beecher reflected the feelings of the latter class when on a certain occasion he said: "Turn the Negro loose; I am not afraid to run the race of life with him."

Nor, Rapier was clearly implying, were African Americans afraid to run the race of life with Beecher, or anyone else.[17]

This narrow call for legal equality had its historical roots in the abolition and Civil War experiences. The most salient fact about slavery was that it legally controlled the destiny of another group of human beings; "give us a chance" had been another way of saying "make slavery illegal." Then, too, the declaration of African Americans' "manhood" was critical for making the natural rights argument; the argument that legal equality would provide an equal "chance" helped buttress that declaration. For that reason Frederick Douglass and others extended the argument during the Civil War, as they focused a great deal of effort on persuading the Union to employ black troops in combat.

Indeed, Frederick Douglass is representative of the abolitionist influence on late-nineteenth-century reform rhetoric. In the antebellum and Civil War eras, Douglass had been the preeminent African American orator. An escaped slave who was self-taught, Douglass had burst on the scene in 1841 at the age of twenty-three. He toured New England and the British Isles as an abolitionist speaker, until his freedom was purchased by the donations of supporters. Back in America, he pursued abolition through the spoken word as an orator and through the written word as the publisher of the Rochester *North Star* and other abolitionist papers. During the Civil War, he lobbied Lincoln and the Republicans to declare the Civil War a battle against slavery and to open up the army ranks to African American combatants.

Douglass remained an influential and active reformer in the postwar period until his death in 1895. He did, however, encounter increasing opposition to his stands within the black community, especially for his support of the Republican Party and his criticism of the Exoduster migration of Southern blacks to the Kansas area. Still, he was a vocal supporter of equal rights for women as well as African Americans, and vigorously attacked the rise of lynching as a tool for racial intimidation. While one can find a variety of strains in the thirty years of Douglass's postwar rhetoric, his lecture "Self-Made Men," delivered on numerous occasions between 1859 and 1893, is typical of the "let him alone" rhetoric.

"Self-Made Men" articulated the qualities that allowed self-made men to succeed.[18] Douglass postulated that life was a "race" or "struggle" governed by the laws of nature. "The natural laws for the government, well-being and progress of mankind," he said, "seem to be equal and are equal; but the subjects of these laws everywhere abound in inequalities, discords and contrasts." These "inequalities, discords and contrasts" were, Douglass argued, due to the willingness of the subject to work: "We may explain success mainly by one word and that word is WORK! WORK!! WORK!!! WORK!!!!" "Nature has no use for unused power," he warned, and "admits no preemption without occupation." Exertion improves the talent used in the exertion, and labor develops fortitude and perseverance. He summarized, "My theory of self-made men is that they are men of work." Douglass allowed that other qualities could play a part, but they were "subordinate" to the willingness to work.[19]

That willingness to work was, it was assumed, within the individual's prerogative. "Everyone may avail himself of this marvelous power, if he will," Douglass asserted. "Every man," he declared, "has his chance." Self-made men were thus the "architects of their own good fortunes": "When we find a man who has ascended heights beyond ourselves; who has a broader range of vision than we and a sky with more stars in it than we have in ours, we may know that he has worked harder, better and more wisely than we." Moreover, America was singular in its encouragement of self-made men. "America is said," he argued, "and not without reason, to be preeminently the home and patron of self-made men." There were many reasons for this, Douglass claimed: the respectability of labor, especially now that slavery was abolished; the restless "sea" of activity that marked the society; and, first and foremost, "the principle of measuring and valuing men according to their respective merits." "Our national genius," Douglass concluded, "welcomes humanity from every quarter and grants to all an equal chance in the race of life."[20]

Twice in the speech Douglass addressed himself to the question of how this theory of self-made men related to African Americans. In the first instance, Douglass raised the question explicitly, and initially provided a laissez-faire response that echoed Rapier's passage above: "My general answer is 'Give the negro fair play and let him alone. If he lives, well. If he dies, equally well. If he cannot stand up, let him fall down.'" Shortly after, however, Douglass hinted at a problem with a narrow definition of "fair play":

> It is not fair play to start the negro out in life, from nothing and with nothing, while others start with the advantage of a thousand years behind them. He should be measured, not by the heights others may have obtained, but from the depths from which he has come. . . . Should the American people put a school house in every valley of the South and a church on every hill side and supply the one with teachers and the other with preachers, for a hundred years to come, they would not then have given fair play to the negro.

Douglass followed his initial prescription for fair play with another: "throw open to him the doors of the schools, the factories, the workshops, and of all mechanical industries." Once given this kind of "fair play," the African American should be left alone: "For his own welfare, give him a chance to do whatever he can do well. If he fails then, let him fail! *I can, however, assure you that he will not fail*."[21]

This confidence in African Americans' ability to succeed, if left alone, had been a prominent feature of abolitionist discourse. The second time Douglass related his theme to African Americans, he elaborated on the idea of success. After several examples of white self-made men, Douglass turned to the examples of Benjamin Banneker, surveyor of Washington, D.C.; William Dietz, architect, inventor, and bridge designer; and Toussaint L'Ouverture, the liberator of Haiti. The life of each of these men provided proof of the ability of African Americans to succeed.

This common appeal to "let the Negro alone" did, however, lead to some curious concessions in the rhetoric. The most significant of these was in regard to voting qualifications. Time and again, African American rhetors stated that literacy qualifications were not only acceptable but also desirable, as long as those qualifications were equally applied.[22] Time and again, however, Southern states passed literacy laws that looked equal, but were unequally applied. Beyond these tangible losses, however, the "let him alone" rhetoric was overwhelmed—co-opted and subsumed—by the full blossoming of Social Darwinism.

An Ambivalent Rhetoric

Social Darwinism and its laissez-faire philosophy of letting each person rise or fall according to his or her ability neatly fit the existing ideology of white America, but Social Darwinism also complemented the minimalist appeal of "let the Negro alone." Because many of its principles repeated long-held American beliefs, it was enticing not only to white Americans but to many African Americans as well. In the 1880s and early 1890s many African American rhetors, especially the leading intelligentsia, found themselves attacking Social Darwinism's conclusions even as they adopted much of its language and assumptions. The result was an ambivalent rhetoric for which the integrationist and accommodationist labels are not particularly helpful. It was a rhetoric that traveled in both directions, neither fully rejecting nor fully accepting the doctrine of Social Darwinism. Alexander Crummell and Anna Julia Cooper, two African American leaders who were staunch integrationists, provide instructive examples of this ambivalent discourse.

Alexander Crummell

Born a free black in 1819 and educated at several American institutions as well as at Queen's College in England, Alexander Crummell, an Episcopal clergyman who spoke on behalf of abolition, chided his denomination's prejudice as well as white Americans' prejudice generally. In the antebellum era, he strongly advocated separate black institutions, racial self-improvement, equality in the eyes of the law, and a Christian message of hope. Leaving America for England in 1848, five years later he moved to Liberia, where he worked as a missionary and educator. There he pursued his goal of black nationalism, becoming embroiled in Liberian politics until, his party defeated and Crummell certain that the Liberian experiment would fail, he returned to the United States in 1873.[23]

In the United States, he soon became rector of St. Luke's Church in Washington, D.C., a position that provided him with national visibility. He was a well-traveled and well-known speaker, calling for integration even as he also preached economic improvement. He advocated both industrial education for those less able and liberal arts studies for the capable elite. In support of the latter, he helped found and was elected the first president of the American Negro Academy in 1897, a scholarly organization of black intellectuals.[24] Although Crummell never enjoyed wide popularity, Meier writes that he was "generally regarded as the leading nineteenth century Negro intellectual," and he was certainly a figure of national importance.[25] In his wide-ranging post-1873 speeches, Crummell exemplified the difficulty that many African American leaders encountered as they struggled to find a voice that disputed the claims of Social Darwinism even as they remained true to the earlier "let him alone" discourse.

In his rhetoric, written and spoken, Crummell adopted many of the principles of Social Darwinism. Human society is, first of all, subject to the laws of nature.

The "law of nature" is "universal," Crummell argued, a "great principle manifested in every sphere" that defines what is and is not possible. Of the discernible laws of nature, the first important one regarding race relations was the principle that some human societies had evolved into higher civilizations and that this evolution was based on the accumulation of wealth through the productive and efficient use of labor. "The kernel of this higher cultivation is labour," argued Crummell. "Go back in the history of mankind . . . [and] [t]he very first step from savage life to grand civility, is the throwing off the disorganized, irregular toil of the uncivilized man; and turning sharply, into the ways of systematic, orderly, regulated labour."[26]

The second important principle was that in this process of evolution, some races had succeeded better than others. Races possessed, first of all, varying characteristics. The Irish, for example, "are mercurial, poetic and martial," while the French have "fervor, gallantry, social aptitudes, and religious loyalty." The German immigrants bring with them "that steadiness and sturdiness, that thrift and acquisitiveness, that art and learning, that genius and acumen, which have given . . . depth to philosophy, and inspiration to music and to art." While Crummell held that circumstances could encourage or retard the development of a people, he also declared that the foundation for change lay within the nature of a race. "You can't take the essential qualities of one people and transfuse them into the blood of another people, and make them indigenous to them. The primal qualities of a family, a clan, a nation, a race are heritable qualities. They abide in their constitution. They are absolute and congenital things." African Americans also possessed race characteristics. An aptitude for the aesthetic, for example, was "constitutional to the race, and it cannot be ignored." "We are still a tropical race," Crummell averred, "and the warmth of the central regions constantly discovers itself in voice and love of harmonics, both those which appeal to the eye by color, and those which affect the sensibilities through the ear."[27]

Not only did differences in race characteristics exist, but these characteristics comprised the elements of "fitness" that determined whether, in the evolutionary process, a given race would succeed or fail. "In Ireland," said Crummell, "sterility has been a conspicuous feature of their intellectual life. The mind of the whole nation has been dwarfed and shriveled by morbid concentration upon an intense and frenzied sense of political wrong. . . . And commerce, industry, and manufactures, letters and culture, have died away from them." In contrast, Crummell approvingly cited the writings of Tacitus, and the "testimony he bears to the primitive virtues of the Germanic tribes . . . which have proven the historic basis of their eminence and unfailing grandeur." These two Social Darwinist conceptions—the inherent nature of race characteristics and the influence of those characteristics upon success—were suggested in Crummell's declaration that "race is the key to history."[28]

These natural principles were instructive, of course, to the specific circumstances in which African Americans found themselves, and Crummell's espousal of them was most often found in his discourse aimed at African American audiences. First, in his view the qualities of the race would determine its success. "You are not to make the mistake," Crummell instructed the graduating class of Storer College, an African American institution, "that it is *external* forces which are chiefly to be brought to bear upon this enormity. No people can be lifted up by others to grand civility. The elevation of a people, their thorough civilization, comes chiefly from *internal* qualities." In various speeches, Crummell enumerated the same general characteristics as the requisite internal qualities: "moral elevation," "arduous labor," "rugged endurance," "skilled and enlightened labor," and the accumulation of some capital. In rugged individualist tones consonant with the principles of Social Darwinism, Crummell concluded in his "Dignity of Labour" speech that "there is no danger about your [blacks'] progress and success; if you are patient, industrious, vigilant, and aspiring."[29]

Second, the changes needed to be moral as well as economic. Crummell held that African American moral elevation had suffered during slavery in concert with the economic deprivation of African Americans. "We have suffered, my brethren," he declared, "in the whole domain of morals. We *are* still suffering as a people in this regard. . . . And these qualities are the grandest qualities of all superior people." "What we need," he told his Storer College audience, "is a grand *moral* revolution which shall touch and vivify the inner life of a people . . . which shall bring to them a resurrection from inferior ideas and lowly ambitions; . . . which shall put them in the race for manly moral superiority." Again, however, such moral improvement could only be nurtured internally by the race itself. "A revolution of this kind is not a gift which can be handed over by one people, and placed as a new deposit, in the constitution of another. . . . The revolution I speak of is one which must find its primal elements in qualities, latent though they be, which reside *in* the people who need this revolution, and which can be drawn out of them, and thus secure form and reality."[30]

Finally, because such race characteristics had been formed by evolution, reform would also be evolutionary, and therefore slow. "No new people leap suddenly and spontaneously into Senatorial chairs or Cabinet positions," warned Crummell. Although "the black man of this country can eventually present [the necessary] racial qualities . . . it is well to remember that they are not the product of a day." Thus, although Crummell called for immediate legal equality for blacks and encouraged those capable to pursue the cultivation of liberal arts study, he also preached a kind of patience consistent with the principles of Social Darwinism.

> Society never, anywhere, leaps into progress, greatness or power. The black race in this land cannot leap into might and majesty. It is to reach the higher planes in just the same way all other peoples have, in all the past human history. The same conditions apply to us as to them. And these conditions are, first, humble labour; then, a gradual uprise; and then dogged and persistent effort, unfailing hope, living and undying aspiration, and pluck and audacious ambition, which brooks no limitations in the spheres of enterprise!

The uplift of African Americans would be gradual, therefore, and the work hard. Moreover, it was uniquely *their* work, for success would come by their efforts and their efforts alone. This was a rhetoric of uplift, designed to inspire the audience to work hard at their moral and economic improvement. Its roots could be seen in similar kinds of discourse in the antebellum and Reconstruction eras. But in its particulars, it was also drawing from the leading scientific thought of the day—in this case, Social Darwinism—and the basic principles of Crummell's rhetoric resonated with that philosophy. Confronted, however, with Social Darwinism's de facto conclusions regarding African Americans—that their poverty proved their inferiority—Crummell took a different rhetorical tack.[31]

The clearest and most thoroughly anti–Social Darwinist tract among Crummell's many speeches, sermons, and writings is his essay "A Defence of the Negro Race in America." Crummell wrote this piece as a rebuttal to the Reverend Joseph L. Tucker's paper "On the Relations of the Church to the Colored People," delivered at the 1882 Protestant Episcopal Church Congress. In that paper, Tucker had argued that the Reconstruction-era efforts to uplift African Americans had failed miserably and that blacks had demonstrated themselves as unfit to conduct their own affairs in religious or other matters.[32] Crummell's response advanced two major rebuttals. The first refuted the Social Darwinist assumptions underlying Tucker's paper; the second argued that African Americans had indeed provided evidence of success in the years since emancipation.

Admitting to some "degradation of our race in this country," Crummell accepted Tucker's charge that blacks had not prospered since emancipation as a "hypothesis," but he argued that African Americans were not inherently responsible. They were, rather, a "VICTIM race," victims of the "malarial poison of servitude." Crummell turned to Africa for proof that the problems African Americans faced were environmentally caused, and not genetic. In their continent of origin, Crummell argued, the black race demonstrated a commitment to the marriage bond and maidenly virtue, to honesty, and to the principle of economic acquisition. He allowed that "there is wide-spread demoralization among the Southern black population." But, he asked, "How could it be otherwise? Their whole history for two hundred years has been a history of moral degradation." Turning against Tucker his own argument that slavery had been a "schoolmaster" that acquainted blacks with the blessings of civilization and Christianity, Crummell held slavery accountable for the failures.

> And pray what sort of a schoolmaster has slavery proven? Why, the slave system has had the black man under training two hundred years, and yet never in all this period has it developed *one* Negro community of strength or greatness! Never raised up anywhere an intelligent, thrifty, productive peasantry! Never built up a single Negro institution of any value to mankind! Never produced a single scientific or scholarly or learned black man! . . . "Schoolmaster" indeed! Is it not an abuse of the English language and of common sense to print such verbiage?

Successful blacks could be found, Crummell argued, but "all the black men of conspicuous genius and character South have had to get out of the old slave region and come North for the training and development of their intellect."[33]

To develop the argument regarding the success of blacks, Crummell statistically documented the population increase of blacks, their educational advancement, the growth of black churches, and their increase in material wealth. Through these kinds of measures, Crummell estimated that about one-third of blacks had experienced a decline in their living conditions since emancipation, about one-third were a little above their condition upon emancipation, and about one-third had proven very successful and improved their condition markedly. Rejecting the Social Darwinist assumption that races differ in their talent to succeed, Crummell held that "this same relative loss is discovered in all peoples. It is seen in the white population of this land, notwithstanding all their advantages. . . . [Examine the statistics] and you will see that fully one-third of the white population is constantly going down."[34]

But while Crummell spent the majority of the paper explicitly refuting Tucker's Social Darwinist claims, the ambivalent nature of Crumwell's discourse can be seen in his implicit embrace of Social Darwinist assumptions at certain junctures. First, his statistics that demonstrated the improvement of the race were cast in the typical Social Darwinist terms that the effect proves the cause; that is, that black success proved the race's possessions of the needed race qualities. For example, Crummell began his argument with statistics on population growth, grounding that presentation squarely on a key Social Darwinist assumption. "Nothing is more established than the fact that a people given up to concubinage and license lose vitality and decline in numbers. . . . [E]verywhere on earth the integrity and advance of a people's population have been conditioned on the growth and permanency of the family feeling." African Americans' increase in population since emancipation thus demonstrated their adherence to moral virtue and "family feeling." Second, Crummell portrayed the attainment of civilization as an evolutionary trend, a series of slow but continual advances won through the efforts of the "fit." "Society everywhere," he argued, "advances only by the force and energy of minorities. It is the *few* who lift up and bear the burdens and give character to the many. But nevertheless, it is advance; and the human race in civilized countries is ever going upward." Finally, in his conclusion Crummell returned to his familiar Social Darwinist theme that African Americans needed some fundamental change, some moral uplift in order to secure "civilization." "The Negro in the South," he wrote, needed to be "re-fashioned, enlightened, and lifted up to the very highest planes of civilization, grace, and manhood." In a final affirmation of both his anti–Social Darwinist arguments and his pro–Social Darwinist assumptions, Crummell again asserted that the race possesses the needed qualities to succeed.

> The Negro race is a living, not a dead race—alive in several respects of industry, acquisitiveness, education, and religious aspiration. . . . Its leaders, everywhere, conscious, indeed, of deep, radical defects within, and most formidable hindrances without, have, notwithstanding, but few misgivings as to the future. They have very great confidence, first of all, in certain vital qualities inherent in the race! . . . They [also] look with no uncertainty to the large and loving BROTHERHOOD of countless Christians. . . . And they repose in quiet confidence upon the marvelous mercy and loving-kindness of a divine DELIVERER and SAVIOUR.

This embrace of the core assumptions of Social Darwinism, coupled with assigning blame upon white Americans, characterizes the ambivalence of Crummell's reform rhetoric, as well as much of the African American rhetoric of the period. Anna Julia Cooper, a rising voice at the time Crummell was nearing the end of his career, provides another example of that ambivalent stance toward Social Darwinism.

Anna Julia Cooper

Anna Julia Haywood was born in 1858, the daughter of Hannah Stanley Haywood, a North Carolina slave, and George Washington Haywood, Hannah's white slave owner. Anna had little to no contact with her father, nor did she seem to wish for any. Widowed after two years of marriage at the age of twenty-one, Cooper enrolled at Oberlin College. She refused to take the "Ladies Course" of study, however, insisting instead on the classical education of the "Gentleman's Course." After earning a B.A. and M.A. at Oberlin, she went on to teach in the Washington, D.C., school district. In 1906, when conflict with the all-white Board of Education cost Cooper her position as principal of the M Street High School, she left for a position at Lincoln University in Missouri. In 1910 she returned to the M Street High School, where she continued teaching until 1930. In 1915 she adopted her half-brother's five orphaned grandchildren. In 1925, at the age of sixty-seven, Anna Julia Cooper became the fourth African American woman to earn a Ph.D., receiving her degree from the University of Paris in France.[35]

In 1892 Cooper published her most famous work, a collection of essays entitled *A Voice from the South by a Black Woman of the South*. Across her essays, Cooper is sensitive to the issue of race: how it is defined, how differences are constructed, and what the effects of those discursive constructions are. In "Woman versus the Indian," for example, Cooper displayed a keen sensitivity to the rhetorical treatment of Native Americans, arguing that woman suffragists needed to be careful not to make their case for equal rights by contrasting their lack of rights with the bestowal of rights on Native American men. Cooper understood that by feeling slighted that Native American men had received their rights before white women, suffragist speakers implied that white women were entitled, by virtue of their race, to have received their rights before Native American men.[36]

Despite such racial sensitivity, and her intellectual prowess generally, Cooper, like Crummell, constructed an ambivalent rhetoric in regard to Social Darwinism. In *A Voice from the South*, Cooper included two essays that directly address the question of race relations in America. "Has America a Race Problem; If So, How Can It Best Be Solved?" gave a thoroughly Social Darwinist answer to the essay's question, and echoed the "let the Negro alone" rhetoric of "Self-Made Men."

Early in the essay, Cooper surveyed the history of civilization, relying heavily on François Guizot, a French historian writing in the Social Darwinist tradition. Civilizations stagnated, Guizot had argued, when there was only one race either present or dominant. The Egyptian, Greek, Roman, and Hindu civilizations had all declined because of race monopoly. In contrast, Cooper quoted Guizot as saying that modern Europe was the beneficiary of "continual struggle" between the races, thus yielding the "promise of perpetual progress." After discerning these same lessons in the histories of China and England, Cooper applied the principle to America. The United States was founded as a "seething cauldron of conflicting elements," a state of affairs that would ensure the highest evolution of human civilization: "But of one thing we may be sure: the God of battles is in the conflicts of history. The evolution of civilization is His care, eternal progress His delight. As the European was higher and grander than the Asiatic, so will American civilization be broader and deeper and closer to the purposes of the Eternal than any the world has yet seen." In America's "seething cauldron" of competing interests—competing classes, races, and religions—Cooper saw hope for African Americans. There was hope because the fact of conflict had led to the protection of conflict. Here in America, she argued, the feeblest interest, women, and laboring classes could be heard, because no single race, class, or religion had monopolized the culture as it had in India, China, Egypt, or elsewhere. Emphasizing the responsibility of the individual, she proclaimed that "here races that are weakest can, if they so elect, make themselves felt."[37]

The result was a laissez-faire approach to solving the issue of race, one that relied on individual effort, and not governmental intrusion. "Has America a Race Problem?" Cooper asked rhetorically. "Yes," she answered simply. "What are you going to do about it?" she then queried. The reply: "Let it alone and mind my own business. It is God's problem and He will solve it in time." Individual merit and effort, expended in the seething cauldron of competition, would consistently move the race toward success. Responsibility was thus divided. Government needed to ensure a competitive environment that gave no race or individual an advantage. Even in the absence of a perfectly fair environment, however, success still lay largely within the grasp of each individual. Thus each individual should put forth the maximum effort, and by extension so should each individual race.

> *Imprimis;* let every element of the conflict see that it represents a positive force so as to preserve a proper equipoise in the conflict. No shirking, no skulking. . . . The day is coming, and now is, when America must ask each citizen not "who was your grandfather and what the color of his cuticle," but *"What can you do?"* Be ready each individual element,—each race, each class, each family, each man to reply *"I engage to undertake an honest man's share."*

Cooper then rejected the ideas of race amalgamation and emigration to Africa. They were, she thought, the kind of social engineering her sociology had rejected. Both suffered the same two flaws: they represented wasteful meddling into the natural state of affairs, and, more gravely, they represented efforts to eliminate competition from America by removing from it a prime source of competition: the African American race.[38]

By the end of the essay, Cooper had redefined the idea of a "race problem." The "problem"—the competition between the races—was in the larger view a positive good. "It is," she wrote, "a guaranty of the perpetuity and progress of [America's] institutions, and insures the breadth of her culture and the symmetry of her development." The African American race was "ballast" for white America. The African American provided "tropical warmth" and "spontaneous emotionalism," an "instinct for law and order, his inaptitude for rioting and anarchy, [and] his gentleness and cheerfulness as a laborer." "The historian of American civilization," Cooper concluded, "will yet congratulate this country that she has had a Race problem and that descendants of the black race furnished one of its largest factors."[39]

Although the title of a second chapter, "What Are We Worth?," posed a question with Social Darwinist undertones, Cooper's answer contains a mixture of Social Darwinist and non–Social Darwinist elements. Significantly, however, the former elements formed the basis of the chapter's beginning and its conclusion.

Cooper began by framing the question "what are we worth?" in economic terms. The world is "intensely practical," Cooper argued: "[I]n the final reckoning, do you belong on the debit or credit side of the account? . . . It is by this standard that society estimates individuals; and by this standard that finally and inevitably the world will measure and judge nations and races." In language that echoed the "clear-eyed" economic philosophies of the Social Darwinists, Cooper held that there is "no room for sentiment." Admitting that sentiments were at work in the world, she condemned them. After chastising whites for their prejudice against blacks, she also condemned the African American prejudice of "the blacker the better" as "idealized theory" and "sentiment." But while Cooper allowed that prejudice existed in some people, such sentimental feelings were "impervious to reason." Only time would cure the prejudiced person. Cooper thus attempted to differentiate between the idiosyncratic, prejudiced individual and an abstract, reasonable world: "Sentiment and cant, then, both being ruled out, let us try to study our subject as the world finally reckons it—not certain crevices and crannies of the earth, but the cool, practical, business-like world."[40]

In this "business-like world," one's value could be determined in the same economic fashion as one might price a watch. First, the cost of the raw material. Then, the value added to the product through labor. Next, one considered the beauty and utility of the product, and finally, the demand for the product would also influence the value. The remainder of Cooper's chapter was organized around the first, second, and fourth principles, blending the content of the third economic principle with her discussions of the second and fourth.

What was African Americans' raw material worth? Here Cooper struck a mixed tone. Like a Social Darwinist, she argued that the raw material is formed long before birth, as each succeeding generation is, even at birth, a product of those that preceded it. But she did not go back as far as a true Social Darwinist might. Quoting an axiom, she reached back only a few generations: "To reform a man, you must begin with his great grandmother." While the axiom's time period could be poetic license, Cooper's discussion of the specific case of African Americans literally placed the origin of their condition with their forced emigration to America. Speaking metaphorically, she said that "certainly the original timber as it came from the African forests was good enough." The "two hundred and fifty years of training here," environmental conditions of impoverishment, ill treatment, and forced servitude have created, at birth, the present-day "warping and shrinking . . . of the sturdy old timber." In this construction, the degree to which Cooper saw African Americans' poverty as passed on from generation to generation because of environment or because of heredity is unclear.[41]

Yet into this mix Cooper inserted one distinctly Social Darwinist element. In discussing the sturdy timber of Africa, Cooper said that "no race of heathen are [sic] more noted for honesty and chastity than are the tribes of Africa," and she treated these as inherited characteristics when she wrote that the "black side of the stream with us is pretty pure, and has no cause to blush for its honesty and integrity." In contrast, alluding implicitly to the low character of white slave owners who raped their female slaves, Cooper noted that "from the nature of the case the infusions of white blood that have come in many instances to the black race in this country are not the best that race afforded." To add further ambivalence, Cooper's second statement was both Social Darwinist and non–Social Darwinist in nature. Considering questions of character as inheritable reflected Social Darwinism, while not treating all members of a race, in this case whites, as generally sharing the same characteristics did not. Ironically, most white Social Darwinists argued that the black gene pool was improved, even when combined only with an inferior class of whites, because even the "lower" members of a "higher" race would improve the genetic pool of a "lower" race.[42]

But whether the causes were environmental, hereditary, or both, Cooper's viewed some important African American traits—the "raw material" of the present day—in negative terms. "We find [among African Americans] the contempt for manual labor and the horror of horny palms, the love of lavish expenditure and costly display, and—alas, that we must own it—the laxness of morals and easy-going consciences inherited and imitated from the old English gentry of the reigns of Charles and Anne." How, then, to add value to this less-than-valuable raw material? The answer, Cooper wrote, lay in arduous and diligent labor.[43]

Cooper then inventoried the "labor," or efforts toward improvement, already being made in the African American community. She recounted, for example, the amount of money spent on educating blacks and the number of schools and colleges in the South devoted to the education of the race. She also discussed some handicaps that hampered the efforts of education—for example, unsanitary living conditions. Continuing her economic formulation, Cooper argued that these conditions created "waste," by causing premature infirmities and death before an individual could make full use of the education supplied. Significantly, Cooper pointed out that white prejudice caused such living conditions. Using Washington, D.C., as her case study, she noted that affordable, sanitary housing was available for poor whites, but poor blacks were consigned to living in the alleys.[44]

A similar waste of education's efforts could be found in the restrictions whites placed on blacks in terms of job opportunities. In the South, Cooper argued, the sharecropping system was another form of "slavery." "Do you ask the cause of their persistent poverty?" Cooper queried. The answer echoed Douglass's discussion of "fair play."

> It is not found in the explanation often vouchsafed by the white landlord—that the Negro is indolent, improvident and vicious. Taking them man for man and dollar for dollar, I think you will find the Negro, in ninety-nine cases out of a hundred, not a whit behind the Anglo-Saxon of equal chances. . . . Indeed it would not be hard to show that the white man of his chances does not exist.

The "Crackers" and "poor-whites" were never slaves, were never oppressed or discriminated against.

African Americans' poverty "can at least be partially accounted for" by the "past oppression and continued repression which form the vital air in which the Negro lives and moves and has his being." Nor was the North any better. There the prejudice of the labor unions—whose membership was, ironically, largely foreign-born—relegated African American men to the occupations of waiter and barber, and African American women to the job of washerwoman.[45]

Yet throughout this account Cooper periodically returned to her theme of laissez-faire economics. Black capitalists should assume the responsibility of building affordable housing for poor blacks. Life insurance companies should not be blamed for charging higher prices to blacks, or for refusing to sell them life insurance at all, for those companies were simply "recognizing facts." "The individual is responsible," she argued, "not for what he has not, but for what he has; and the vital part for us after all depends on the use we make of our material." Cooper finished her discussion of education and use of education by berating those who would emphasize classical learning to the exclusion of all else.[46]

Cooper's argument in this regard was similar to Crummell's, and was representative of many African American rhetors at this time. She urged industrial training for most and a classical education for the "one mind in a family or in a town" that displayed the talent to make use of it. What is important, she argued, was the suitability of the education for helping the individual make the best use of his or her abilities and the resultant accumulation of wealth. Applying to the individual the same economic principles Bagehot used for society, she argued that "work must first create wealth, and wealth leisure, before the untrammeled intellect of the Negro, or any other race, can truly vindicate its capabilities." "It is leisure," she said, "the natural outgrowth of work and wealth," that "must furnish room, opportunity, possibility for the highest endeavor and most brilliant achievement." Thus in her view the accumulation of capital permitted for the advancement of an individual, or of a race.[47]

As Cooper began the third and final section—will there be a demand for the appropriately educated African American—she started by placing the responsibility squarely with the individual. Will each individual be a net consumer or a net producer for society? She answered: "The question must in the first place be an individual one for every man of whatever race." Like Crummell's statistical recitation in "A Defence of the Negro Race," Cooper proceeded to characterize the race as net producers, and supported that claim through a statistical accounting of its assets. Observing that these financial gains were brought forth in the face of general societal prejudice, Cooper then described examples of individual contributions, by an inventor, an electrician, the poet Phyllis Wheatley, two rose-growing brothers in South Carolina, and the sculptor Edmonia Lewis. She brought her list to a climactic conclusion by describing in vivid detail the Louisiana Native Guards, two black regiments, and their heroic charge in the battle of Port Hudson. Each of these contributors to society had "paid their debt"; they had produced more than they had consumed.[48]

Yet in the middle of this recitation Cooper paused to discuss the economic "character" of African Americans. She used the discussion to make the transition from enumerating contributions of monetary worth to those "highest gifts," which "are not measureable in dollars and cents." The African American "does not always show a margin over and above consumption; but this does not necessarily in his case prove that he is not a producer." Blacks work very hard, Cooper argued, but an African American

> labors for little and spends it all. He has never yet gained the full consent of his mind to "take his gruel a little thinner" till his little pile has grown a bit. . . . He must eat, and is miserable if he can't dress; and seems on the whole internally fitter every way to the style and pattern of a millionaire, rather than to the plain, plodding, stingy old path of common sense and economy.

Cooper concluded ominously, in terms consonant with Social Darwinism: "This is a flaw in the material of the creature. The grain just naturally runs that way." A perceptive reader might have remembered that in Cooper's discussion of the "material" characteristics of African Americans, she seemed to attribute most such properties to "environmental" factors. Few white readers were likely to be that discerning. The "grain just naturally" running that way would more likely be read as an inherited racial characteristic than an environmentally induced one.[49]

Cooper followed the Civil War story with one more example of an individual who had produced more than he had consumed: Booker T. Washington. She made an accounting of Washington's efforts by enumerating the size and growth of the Tuskegee Institute, the number of its graduates, and the kinds of vocations those graduates had entered. Washington was the paragon of a producer because he had produced producers. Tuskegee had accumulated "assets," which in turn enabled its graduates to further accumulate "assets."

As she segued into her conclusion, Cooper allowed that not all could be a Washington, but "we can at least give ourselves. Each can be one of these strong willing helpers—even though nature has denied him the talent of endlessly multiplying his force." With each responsible for himself or herself, the "mists" of prejudice would eventually "clear away," and "the world—our world, will surely and unerringly see us as we are." Cooper concluded with a paean to hard work that was thoroughly compatible with Social Darwinism.

> Our only care need be the intrinsic worth of our contributions. If we represent the ignorance and poverty, the vice and destructiveness, the vagabondism and parasitism in the world's economy, no amount of philanthropy and benevolent sentiment can win for us esteem; and if we contribute a positive value in those things the world prizes, no amount of negrophobia can ultimately prevent its recognition. And our great "problem" after all is to be solved not by brooding over it, and orating about it, but by living into it.

Cooper thus finished the essay with a Social Darwinist formulation: that fitness, in this case as measured by monetary and other "value," would not long be discriminated against because the world would employ that which was of value. It was a principle that Booker T. Washington would reiterate three years later in his famed "Cotton States Exposition Address." Thus, while in her personal life Cooper confronted prejudice vocally and loudly, and while her writings displayed much sensitivity to issues of race, ethnicity, and class, like Crummell and many others of the time, her rhetorical stance vis-à-vis Social Darwinism was ambivalent. Although she rejected its conclusions about the African American race, she found it difficult to abandon or avoid many of its fundamental assumptions.[50]

The Co-optation of Social Darwinism

From the "let him alone" rhetoric of the Reconstruction period had emerged the ambivalent post-Reconstruction discourse that focused on legal equality and self-help. In the course of the 1890s, one rhetor became the dominant voice of that group: Booker T. Washington. Known today for his accommodationist stance and his advocacy of industrial education, at the turn of the century Washington was the best-known and most influential African American. What is less appreciated, however, is that he moved the rhetoric of reform from one of ambivalence toward Social Darwinism to one of co-optation. For many ministers and educators of the day, his rhetoric was representative.

Born on 5 April 1856 in Franklin County, Virginia, Booker T. Washington was the son of a plantation cook and an unidentified white man. After emancipation, he went to work in a salt mine at the age of nine. He managed to attend elementary school and in 1872 enrolled at Hampton Institute. Founded by General Samuel C. Armstrong, Hampton provided an industrial education for African Americans, one that taught the student a trade in industry or agriculture, and it was here that Washington became a devotee of that philosophy. After graduation, Washington taught for three years and also began some study of the law and the ministry, but in 1879 he returned to Hampton as a teacher and graduate student. In 1881 he accepted an appointment to head the Tuskegee Institute in Alabama. From 1881 until 1895 he devoted his efforts to building a national reputation for Tuskegee, doing considerable traveling to proclaim its accomplishments and raise funds for its operation and endowment.

On 18 September 1895 Washington gained national prominence when he delivered a speech at the Cotton States and International Exposition in Atlanta. Following that address, Washington became the most influential African American of the era. He garnered the support of white philanthropists such as John D. Rockefeller, George Eastman, and Andrew Carnegie, and became an informal adviser to Presidents Theodore Roosevelt and William Taft. Tuskegee became the most prominent institution of higher learning for African Americans, with an endowment fund of $2 million. In 1900 Washington founded the National Negro Business League. Although he faced increasing opposition from some African Americans as the twentieth century unfolded, even at his death in 1915 Washington was considered *the* African American leader by most white and many black Americans.[51]

Prior to his Cotton States Exposition Address, Washington's speeches and writings focused primarily on advocating industrial education for African Americans and on raising funds for Tuskegee. Indeed, as rhetorical scholar Stephen Lucas notes, Washington frequently repeated the same stories and used the same sentences in his speeches, even while "tailoring his general message to specific audiences."[52] In these pre-1895 speeches, Washington's general message had five points: (1) although some African Americans had made progress, the large majority remained deeply mired in poverty; (2) their poverty resulted from having become enmeshed in the sharecropping system, a system in which they fell increasingly into debt every year; (3) no significant intellectual and moral progress could be made until African Americans had learned the lessons of accumulating wealth; (4) an industrial education offered them the best opportunity for doing so; and (5) equal treatment would follow once African Americans had accumulated wealth, because "there is no color . . . in business."[53]

From the standpoint of raising funds for Tuskegee, Washington's arguments were strategic. The growth of Tuskegee—the building of buildings, the acquisition of property—proved that the accumulation of wealth was possible. Stories about Tuskegee graduates demonstrated that moral and mental uplift followed from the lessons of economy. The Tuskegee community proved that if blacks had "something" that whites wanted—as customers, suppliers, or investors—equal treatment in business and the law would follow. As a philosophy and an institution, Tuskegee was a success, Washington argued, and merited further "investment" from the audience.

But while successful for fund-raising, his discussion of the causes of African American poverty was problematic. In his speeches and essays, Washington often described the evils of the sharecropping system in clear-sighted terms. While waiting on their crops, blacks were forced to go into debt for their food, paying 25 percent to 40 percent interest on a loan of six months or less.[54] Washington implied that these landowners and lenders had taken advantage of the newly emancipated slaves, but he also refrained from castigating the white lenders too vehemently. Instead, by focusing on blacks' lack of education, Washington seemed to place greater responsibility for their poverty with African Americans themselves. "The trouble is," he argued, "that they [African Americans] do not know how to use the results of their labor." "Four-fifths [of African Americans] are to day in debt," he said, "because of their own ignorance, their lack of economy."

As a race, our people have a great deal of feeling. I believe we can feel more in five minutes than a white man can in a day. You can beat us thinking, but we can beat you feeling. We feel our religion, and when a black man becomes converted, and does not jump and shout, we say he has the white man's religion. . . . [But] in our school work at Tuskegee, and at the Negro Conference, we teach that the way to have the most of Jesus, and to have him in a substantial way, is to mix in some land, cotton and corn and a good bank account.

It was too much ignorance of economy, too much feeling without some "thinking" mixed in, that prevented African Americans from escaping poverty and the sharecropping system.[55]

In this formulation, race prejudice did not prevent success. Although discrimination was an important and immoral obstacle that African Americans faced, the Tuskegee model proved that proper economy by the individual led to the accumulation of wealth, and that the accumulation of wealth created equality of treatment. Ultimately, success belonged to the person who achieved it, because "the American dollar has not an ounce of sentiment in it." "It is in the South as all over the world," Washington proclaimed, "success will only come to those who win and deserve it." If African Americans have not succeeded, then they have not yet acquired the mental and moral talents to win success and therefore do not deserve it. Washington had constructed a useful argument for raising money for education, but from a larger perspective it contained a troubling message. By blaming African Americans, it suggested the Social Darwinist's de facto reasoning that the fact of the poverty indicated the weakness, or unfitness, of the impoverished person.[56]

Washington's Cotton States Exposition Address marked the end of this purely fund-raising era, even as it continued many of the same themes. Often called the Atlanta Compromise Address, it was wildly applauded by Northern and Southern whites, and generally praised by the African American community as well. The proffered "compromise" was that Southern blacks would cease agitating for the "privileges of the law" in exchange for educational and economic opportunities.[57]

Washington began the speech by recounting a story of a ship lost at sea, in desperate need of freshwater. Hailing a passing ship for help, the sailors were told to "[c]ast down your bucket where you are," for they had sailed out of the ocean and into a freshwater estuary. Washington repeated this aphorism first to the black community, and then to the white. As a people, he averred, African Americans had so far ignored that advice. "We began at the top instead of the bottom," Washington said, and did not see that it was in real estate, industrial skill, dairy farming, and truck gardening that African Americans should cast their bucket. "We shall prosper," he declared, "in proportion as we learn to dignify and glorify common labour, and put brains and skill into the common occupations of life." Prosperity would come because the laws of economics were immutable, regardless of race prejudice: "Whatever other sins the South may be called to bear, when it comes to business, pure and simple, it is in the South that the Negro is given a man's chance in the commercial world." If African Americans were to capitalize on this "man's chance," they must embrace the "useful," eschew the "ornamental gewgaws of life," and learn the lesson that "no race can prosper till it learns that there is as much dignity in tilling a field as in writing a poem." Washington concluded that "it is at the bottom of life we must begin, and not at the top."[58]

For the white race, Washington said that casting their bucket down meant providing African Americans with the education and the economic opportunities that he had just asserted already existed. They should hire black workers instead of the new wave of foreign immigrants. African Americans were, after all, deeply experienced with the workings of the Southern economy, and had already demonstrated themselves to be "the most patient, faithful, law-abiding, and unresentful people that the world has seen." Economically, Washington said, the interests of the two races were as one. He then captured the essence of the "compromise" with a metaphor that would become famous: "In all things that are purely social we can be as separate as the fingers, yet one as the hand in all things essential to mutual progress." Washington followed this conciliatory metaphor with a warning about the consequences that would follow if Southern whites did not accept his offer.

> Nearly sixteen millions of hands will aid you in pulling the load upward, or they will pull against you the load downward. We shall constitute one-third and more of the ignorance and crime of the South or one-third its intelligence and progress; we shall contribute one-third to the business and industrial prosperity of the South, or we shall prove a veritable body of death, stagnating, depressing, retarding every effort to advance the body politic.

Significantly, because the warning was oriented toward the future, it did little to blame white Americans for the current status of blacks. This future possibility of blame contrasted sharply with the past and immediate responsibility he had assigned to African Americans.[59]

Washington began his conclusion by calling attention to the products exhibited in the African American hall of the exposition. Those products, he said, were indicative of what African Americans had to offer economically, albeit with the "help" of the Southern state governments and Northern philanthropists. Washington then returned once more to the theme of the speech.

> The wisest among my race understand that the agitation of questions of social equality is the extremist folly, and that progress in the enjoyment of all the privileges that will come to us must be the result of severe and constant struggle rather than of artificial forcing. No race that has anything to contribute to the markets of the world is long in any degree ostracized.

Finally, Washington pledged the goodwill and aid of all African Americans as white Americans strove to "work out the great and intricate problem which God has laid at the doors of the South."[60]

Although later pilloried for its accommodationist stand, the Cotton States Exposition Address was initially praised by almost all, Northerners and Southerners, blacks and whites. James Creelman, reporting for the *New York World*, wrote that the speech "marks a new epoch in the history of the South" and that "it electrified the audience." "I have heard the great orators of many countries," Creelman claimed, "but not even Gladstone himself could have pleaded a cause with more consummate power." Clark Howell, editor of the *Atlanta Constitution* concurred: "I do not exaggerate when I say that Prof. Booker T. Washington's address yesterday was one of the most notable speeches, both as to character and the warmth of its reception, ever delivered to a Southern audience." Like Creelman, Howell characterized the speech as "epoch-making." African Americans, too, praised the speech highly. William Still, veteran of the Underground Railroad and the abolitionist movement, wrote to Washington that it was a "noble speech" and that "in my judgement our cause was absolutely advanced many degrees." Echoing Washington's themes, the Reverend Burwell T. Harvey, from Antioch Baptist Church in Atlanta, congratulated Washington by writing that "leadership along the vital lines which you so earnestly and manly advocate will carry the race up the sure road to success in all walks of life." W. E. B. Du Bois, then teaching at Wilberforce University, cabled simply that "it was a word fitly spoken."[61]

Propelled to stardom by the force of this speech, Washington became a much-sought-after speaker. Although he raised considerable donations for Tuskegee, his speeches at the close of the nineteenth century acquired a larger character, focusing on the "Negro question" broadly rather than making specific appeals for Tuskegee. Still, Washington advocated industrial education and accommodation with many of the same arguments, stories, and language as the pre-1895 speeches. His "Address before the National Education Association," delivered on 10 July 1896, typified the continuity of his message. However, his Harvard University address, given the preceding month, best illustrates the continued adherence to the Social Darwinist principles that had been rooted in his pre-1895 discourse and matured in the Atlanta speech. Washington's oration was given to mark his receipt of an honorary master's degree from Harvard, the first such award bestowed upon an African American. On this significant, nationally publicized occasion, Washington dispatched with his usual stump speech, but, as Lucas notes, the new product was still "perfectly in tune with the Social Darwinist assumptions of the age."[62]

The speech was a brief one, beginning with a statement of the interdependence of the two races: America's most vital question was "how to bring the strong, wealthy and learned into helpful touch with the poorest, most ignorant, and humble and at the same time, make one appreciate the vitalizing, strengthening influence of the other." This question, Washington said, Harvard was helping to answer. He next thanked Harvard for its role in the Civil War, through such veterans as Robert Gould Shaw, and declared that "the sacrifice was not in vain," because the emancipated African American is "crawling up, working up, yea, bursting up." Although he briefly noted the "oppression, unjust discrimination and prejudice" that faced African Americans, he quickly inserted a vow that was fully consonant with Social Darwinism: "with proper habits, intelligence, and property, there is no power on earth that can permanently stay our progress." He then proceeded to elaborate upon that vow. "In the economy of God," he averred, "there is but one standard by which an individual can succeed—there is but one for a race." He reiterated the point by "defining" that standard: "This country demands that every race measure itself by the American standard." Washington concluded this discussion of universal truths by dispatching with the relevance of prejudice, or "sentiment" as he termed it: "By [this one standard] a race must rise or fall, succeed or fail, and in the last analysis mere sentiment counts for little." Washington then said that "during the next half century or more," African Americans would be meeting this standard. He returned to the theme of the racial interdependence in similar terms as his Exposition Address, and finally concluded the speech by saying that, while the "main burden and center of activity" lay with the African American, "we shall need . . . the help, the encouragement, the guidance that the strong can give the weak." Interestingly, although he asked for the help and encouragement of whites, he lay the ultimate responsibility squarely on the shoulders of African Americans. If fit, they would survive (and thrive); if not, they would fall.[63]

A little over two years later, on 16 October 1898, Washington delivered what is commonly perceived as his strongest public statement challenging white Americans to abandon their racial prejudice. The occasion was the National Peace Jubilee in Chicago, a celebration of victory in the Spanish-American War. Washington opened the speech by praising the military contributions of African Americans in war: the Revolution, the War of 1812, the Civil War, and the Spanish-American War. In the most recent conflict, he said, "we find the Negro forgetting his own wrongs, forgetting the laws and customs that discriminate against him in his own country, and again we find our black citizen choosing the better part." "The only request that has come from the Negro," Washington reported, "has been that he might be permitted to replace the white soldier when heat and malaria began to decimate the ranks of the white regiment, and to occupy at the same time the post of greatest danger." But on the heels of these marvelous victories, he declared, there is one victory left to win: against the divide that separates the races in "our business and civil relations."

In the most ominous section, Washington issued a warning that was not unlike the one he included in the Exposition Address, but he used a vivid metaphor to capture the urgency. "Until we thus conquer ourselves, I make no empty statement when I say that we shall have, especially in the Southern part of our country, a cancer gnawing at the heart of the Republic, that shall one day prove as dangerous as an attack from an army without or within." But Washington then qualified his categorical call for equality. Although he avoided placing the burden fully upon African Americans, he reiterated familiar themes. "We shall make the task easier for you," he vowed, "by acquiring property, habits of thrift, economy, intelligence, and character, by each making himself of individual worth in his own community."[64]

In Chicago, the audience was moved. The *Chicago Times-Herald* reported that it was "one of the most powerful appeals for justice to a race which has always chosen the better part," and that "the applause given him made the very columns of the massive building tremble."[65] The Southern press, however, led by the *Atlanta Constitution*, attacked the speech vigorously, until Washington returned to the rhetoric of the Exposition Address.[66]

And so Washington's "Lincoln Memorial Address," delivered in Philadelphia less than four months later, made no mention of a cancer of prejudice, and issued no warnings about the future of America if the cancer were not removed. Instead, Washington declared that the slaves were emancipated "without the requisites for intelligent and independent citizenship," and that "the mere fiat of law could not make a dependent man independent; it could not make an ignorant voter an intelligent voter; it could not make one man respect another man." Achieving independence, intelligence, and respect was once again framed as the responsibility of African Americans: "It is only as the black man produces something that makes the markets of the world dependent on him for something, will he secure his rightful place." Washington's Social Darwinist principles, from which he had never strayed very far, were firmly in place again.[67]

Confronting Social Darwinism

There were, of course, some rhetors of the era who avoided the issue of Social Darwinism entirely. Ida B. Wells's attacks on lynching, for example, did not directly address the question of racial equality or superiority and its origin in evolution. The women's club rhetoric, another important voice in the rhetoric of the late nineteenth century, accentuated education. Some of its rhetoric focused on the prejudice and discrimination of the day, but much of it, like the discourse of ambivalence, exhorted African Americans to greater achievements. It rarely, however, directly addressed Social Darwinist assumptions, whether to validate or deny them.[68]

A smaller group of African American rhetors directly challenged Social Darwinism's assumptions as well as its conclusions. In doing so, they typically advanced two central arguments. The first was that distinctions of race were immaterial. Second, any perceived racial differences were due not to genetic or evolutionary causes, but to the immediate environment, and specifically to white discrimination against blacks. Bishop Henry McNeal Turner, a rhetor who often espoused separatism, and W. E. B. Du Bois, an intellectual who argued for integration, provide two apt examples of the rhetoric of confrontation.

Henry McNeal Turner

Henry McNeal Turner was born in 1834 in Columbia, South Carolina, to free African American parents. During colonial rule, his family's ancestry had been traced to royal lineage, and his grandfather had been freed under a provision of British law. Despite his status as a free black, Turner grew up under the strict segregation and antiblack laws of the antebellum South, including the proscriptions against education. After some self-education and some surreptitious tutoring in the law office where he worked, he turned to itinerant preaching. He began in the Methodist Episcopal Church, but, tiring of that denomination's discrimination, he joined the African Methodist Episcopal (AME) Church. He was appointed by the bishops to a mission in Baltimore, and after some continued education there, was placed in charge of Israel Church in Washington, D.C. During the Civil War, he became the first African American chaplain in the U.S. army. Following the war, he moved to Georgia to organize the AME church in that state. There he was elected to the state legislature during Reconstruction.

In 1868 Bishop Turner addressed the Georgia legislature as the white Democratic-controlled body debated expelling Turner and twenty-seven other African American senators and representatives. In ringing language, Turner attacked the principles of Social Darwinism as they regarded race relations in the United States. First, he denounced the claim that the races were distinct. Even as he did so, he framed the question with language that echoed the abolitionist legacy.

> The great question, sir, is this: Am I a man? If I am such, I claim the rights of a man. Am I not a man because I happen to be of a darker hue than honorable gentlemen around me? . . . A certain gentleman has argued that the Negro was a mere development similar to the orangutan or chimpanzee, but it so happens that, when a Negro is examined, physiologically, phrenologically and anatomically, and, I may say, physiognomically, he is found to be the same as [a] person of different color. . . . If you know nothing of this, I do; for I have helped to dissect fifty men, black and white, and I assert that by the time you take off the mucous pigment—the color of the skin—you cannot, to save your life, distinguish between the black man and the white.

With no inherited differences save color of skin, no significant characteristics prescribed by race, the differences that existed, such as poverty and ignorance, could be categorically assigned to the effects of discrimination. He continued:

> These colored men, who are unable to express themselves with all the clearness and dignity and force of rhetorical eloquence, are laughed at in derision by the Democracy of the country. It reminds me very much of the man who looked at himself in a mirror and, imagining that he was addressing another person, exclaimed, "My God, how ugly you are!" These gentlemen do not consider for a moment the dreadful hardships which these people have endured, and especially those who in any way endeavored to acquire an education.

What differentiated Turner's discourse from that of Crummell, Cooper, and Washington was the absence of ambivalence, and that Turner did not deviate from his central message. In his address, he made no pronouncements about what African Americans needed to do to better their condition. He had no language about the race's ability or the necessity to flourish by its own efforts; nothing was said about struggle being necessary to grow and proper. Instead, he remained focused on the evil being perpetrated by the white majority. After denouncing the two key tenets of Social Darwinism, Turner condemned the white Democrats as hypocrites interested only in power, and he enunciated the legal and natural right of the African American legislators to be seated. No other topic diverted his discourse.[69]

In later speeches, Turner elaborated on his reasons for dismissing the principles of Social Darwinism. The fullest extant explication of his argument was provided in "The Negro in All Ages," a lecture delivered five years later at the Second Baptist Church in Savannah, Georgia. The title page summary accurately reported the lecture as "being an examination into several abominable, anti-scriptural, and pseudo-philosophical theories, designed as a degradation to humanity, by a few malevolent vampires of the age, reviewed and discussed, ethnologically, scientifically, and historically." In the speech, Turner focused on attacking the premise that races were somehow qualitatively "different" from each other, again concluding at the end of the argument that to the degree that the progress of African Americans had been slowed, the responsibility lay with external, not internal, causes.[70]

In an effective counterpoint to Social Darwinism, Turner began his lecture by featuring the scientific nature of the question. "This might be justly entitled the Laboratory age," he avowed, for even the "most attenuated film," the "most ethe-realized fancies," are being subjected to scientific study. His introduction suggested that his remarks, too, would be grounded in science. More, the search for scientific truth participated in the larger struggle for God's truth, and "the forces for error," he warned, "have been marshaled against the most palpable teachings of nature, as ferociously as against the simple revelations of the Holy Writ." An example of the "palpable teachings of nature" that the "forces for error" had attacked was the conclusion that the African American race was somehow unlike the other races of humanity, and it was to that question that Turner addressed his discussion. He stated it plainly: "The question I propose to deal with, is the negro like other people, and are other people like the negro? Does he belong to the same stock, or in other words is he an emanation of the same source?" "I shall assume he does," Turner said, and he then elaborated on the bases for that assumption.[71]

Despite beginning his speech by grounding it in science, Turner's first argument was theological. Tracing the stories of Adam and Noah, interspersed with scriptural texts, Turner held that, biblically, the Christian must conclude with the apostle Paul that God "hath made of one blood all nations of men." Only when this religious argument was firmly enunciated was Turner comfortable in proceeding to the scientific heart of the speech. That part began with an appeal to definitions. Let us examine "what constitutes man," he suggested, "and see if the negro can stand the test." Humans could be distinguished from animals by their ability to reason and their power of speech. Simple observation revealed that African Americans met this definition. They calculated courses of conduct based on conceptions of the past, present, and future; they worshipped God and factored eternity into their moral equations; they possessed articulate speech and artificial language. "No ridicule, abuse, or contemnation," Turner concluded, "can disrobe him of the dignity, with which he was clothed by his creator when he received the image of his maker."[72]

Turner then arrived at the first scientific part of his argument. Are there anatomical or physiological differences between the races? As with his speech to the legislature, he turned first to his own experiences, but in this address he elaborated on them. He had spent several years visiting a medical university, he said, where two or three nights a week he had participated in the dissection of cadavers. Besides the mucous membrane and a few minor shape differences, the bodies were indistinguishable based on race. "I found the same number of bones, muscles, veins arteries," he reported, and "the heart, lungs, stomach, intestines, and the whole machinery were the same in all respects." Moreover, the chemical properties of the bodies were the same. In fact, he pointed out, doctors treated illnesses the same regardless of race. They prescribed the same medicines in the same amounts, and the same compounds that were poisonous for one race were poisonous for the other, and in exactly the same amounts. "All that is peculiar to one man," Turner said, "is peculiar to another." He continued in the same vein in nonmedical areas. The schoolteachers, he declared, had reported that there were no differences in "mode and time of mastering a lesson," and that while some of every race were studious and peaceful, others of both races were "idlers" and "block heads." Phrenologists told a similar story. Here Turner named several of the "pioneers and masters of this science" as authorities who had recorded no differences among the races. "The whole organic composition" was identical, as were the passions that may be aroused and the causes of those passions. There was no difference between the races.[73]

Turner then took an interesting rhetorical tack, striking at the root of Social Darwinism by attacking the theory of evolution itself. The theory was unbiblical, he argued, as well as unscientific. He described in some detail the differences between other primates and human beings, but ultimately he arrived at the rhetorical heart of the matter. "Those wise timber heads who trace man's origin to the monkey tribe, invariably identify the negro race with him especially," he noted. "Well," he continued, "let us see how that position will stand the test." Contrasting the African American with the orangutan, "one of the highest order of the monkey tribe," Turner's evidence became particularly specific. Orangutans have 228 bones; blacks, like all humans, have 245. Orangutans have twenty-four teeth; blacks, like all humans, have thirty-two. And so it went. Turner contrasted the hair, skin, heel, hands, feet, walking stance, height, duration of gestation, life expectancy, lips, legs, arms, and even the modes of disciplining their young. "And thus we might continue to show their dissimilarity, in hundred other instances," he concluded, "but what would be the use?"[74]

But why, then, the skin-deep differences between the races? Here Turner suggested that the yellow skin of the Asians and the brown color of the Semitic tribes reflected more the natural skin color of humans. The black and white hues of those of African and European descent, respectively, were the "extremes." Quoting extensively from scientific authorities, Turner argued that while a precise reason was not yet ascertainable, it was clear that skin pigment was based on geography and climate. He quoted a Professor Moore as saying that skin pigment was a "peculiarity," a fairly typical instance of variety occurring within a species, and he read extensively from the work of a Dr. Good, who described the purpose of skin pigment and its production in the human body. Turner followed this extended scientific discussion with a religious exegesis that eliminated the "curse of Ham" as an explanation for the differences in pigmentation.[75]

Finally, Turner turned to biology for proof of the unity of the races. The evidence, he said, is from the ability of the races to "amalgamate, or inter-propagate their offspring." There were "impassable barriers" that prevented different species from commingling, he argued, and to the degree that they could be forced to interbreed, then "the hybrid is barren and cannot perpetuate its kind." "Dr. Morton," he reported, "to appease his prejudices against the negro, has most elaborately discussed this subject, and labored hard to prove out the hybrid races." But, he said, "Dr. Bachman, a far more able naturalist, has taken up his arguments seriatim, and utterly demolished them." Further, while forced hybrids in the animal kingdom produced less vital offspring, Turner argued that "different races everywhere not only amalgamate, but reproduce their amalgamated offspring for ever, raise up new races, larger in size, more robust, stalwart, and invariably more beautiful." He concluded, "So, if one man came from Adam—all did; but if one man came from a monkey—all did; for we're all of one species."[76]

After thoroughly examining the question of race differences, and concluding that all are members of the same human family, Turner described the history of the black race. Africa had been the seat of civilization, he argued. There was no "kingdom found upon the map of nations, that can lay such an antique claim to art and science" as Africa. Black civilizations created the first national police, and erected tremendous architecture in the obelisks and pyramids. "Eighteen Ethiopians were at separate times monarchs of Egypt," he noted, and it was to Egypt that Plato, Solon, Pythagoras, and other Greek scholars came "to learn the laws and principles of science, statesmanship and religion." Over the centuries, he declared, members of the black race had contributed to every branch of learning, including military science, medicine, philosophy, linguistics, mathematics, and poetry.[77]

And today, Turner held, African Americans still displayed the same talents and abilities. African Americans were distinguishing themselves in Congress and the state legislatures, in the governor's seat in Louisiana, and in the field of jurisprudence. He reminded his audience of the scientific contributions of Benjamin Banneker, the eloquence of Henry Highland Garnet and Frederick Douglass, and the theological gifts of Bishops Payne, Brown, and Ward. His discussion here echoed Douglass's and Crummell's remarks, but the rhetorical tone was qualitatively different. He never argued that these past successes proved the race's ability to survive the struggle of the fittest, or that the ability to succeed thus warranted an "even chance." Instead, these proofs were tied directly to his central claim: that the races were unified in their essential humanity. Immediately following this recitation, he concluded his speech: "I think I hear the voice of God and reason say: Hold! hold! hold your peace, enough has been said! The negro is a human being, the negro has capacities susceptible of eternal evolutions—he too, is a man bearing the undoubted impress of his maker." The human race was a unity. There was no survival of the fittest race, there was no evolutionary process that sorted out the higher from the lower races. There was thus no ambivalence in Turner's rejection of Social Darwinism. The poverty of African Americans was the result of white prejudice, not inherited racial weaknesses.[78]

Throughout his public life, Turner directly assaulted the prejudices and discrimination of white Americans. When asked in 1902 to write an essay addressing the question "Will it be possible for the Negro to attain, in this country, unto the American type of civilization?" he argued that to be civilized "comprehends harmony, system, method, complacency, urbanity, refinement, politeness, courtesy, justice, culture, general enlightenment and protection of life and person to any man, regardless of color or nationality." Although the United States had "books and schools" and other trappings of civilization, such was the "barbarous condition of the United States, the low order of civilization which controls its institutions where right and justice should sit enthroned, I see nothing for the negro to attain unto in this country." But in his discourse, Turner did not simply attack the discrimination and persecution evidenced by white Americans' actions. He squarely confronted the prejudicial conclusions of Social Darwinism and the principles that yielded those conclusions. However, as he himself noted in his introductory remarks to the Georgia state legislature in 1868, his rhetorical choices were not always the ones selected by others. "Some of my colored fellow members," he stated, "in the course of their remarks, took occasion to appeal to the sympathies of members on the other side, and to eulogize their character for magnanimity. It reminds me very much, sir, of slaves begging under the lash." Turner would have none of that appeal: "I am here to demand my rights and to hurl thunderbolts at the men who would dare to cross the threshold of my manhood."[79]

As the twentieth century opened, the rise of rhetoric imitated Turner's strategy. Perhaps the clearest and most interesting exposition of this rhetorical shift came in 1903, from the pen of W. E. B. Du Bois, the man who eight years earlier had congratulated Booker T. Washington on "a word fitly spoken." As the twentieth century began, Du Bois embarked on a prolific rhetorical campaign attacking the premises and the conclusions of Social Darwinism. "On Mr. Booker T.

Washington and Others," the third essay in Du Bois's landmark *The Souls of Black Folk*, is particularly noteworthy. An early example of Du Bois's anti–Social Darwinist work, this essay directly critiqued Washington's political accommodationism and his emphasis on industrial education. What is most interesting, however, is how central Du Bois's attack on Social Darwinist principles was to his case against Washington.[80]

Early in the essay, after expressing his appreciation for Washington's achievements and the rhetorical difficulties that surrounded them, Du Bois began his critique by aiming directly at the Social Darwinist principles so central to Washington's rhetoric.

> This is an age of unusual economic development, and Mr. Washington's programme naturally takes an economic cast, becoming a gospel of Work and Money to such an extent as apparently almost completely to overshadow the higher aims of life. Moreover, this is an age when the more advanced races are coming in closer contact with the less developed races, and the race-feeling is therefore intensified; and Mr. Washington's programme practically accepts the alleged inferiority of the Negro races.[81]

Du Bois recognized that Washington's discourse started by privileging work (that is, struggle for "survival") and money (that is, the gauge by which the "fittest" are measured), and he recognized the prejudicial conclusion that these criteria yielded: African Americans were inferior.

Throughout the essay, Du Bois wove three recurring demands: the right to vote, civic equality, and education of youth according to ability. After criticizing Washington for failing to advance these three causes, Du Bois returned to the issue of African American inferiority, placing responsibility for the race's condition squarely upon its environment, that is, white discrimination.

> Is it possible, and probable, that nine millions of men can make effective progress in economic lines if they are deprived of political rights, made a servile caste, and allowed only the most meagre chance for developing their exceptional men? If history and reason give any distinct answer to these questions, it is an emphatic *No*. . . . [The other class of Negroes who cannot agree with Mr. Washington] know that the low social level of the mass of the race is responsible for much discrimination against it, but they also know, and the nation knows, that relentless color-prejudice is more often a cause than a result of the Negro's degradation.

Du Bois argued that only with political rights and civic equality did blacks stand a chance of successfully battling the everyday discrimination, while "permanent legislation [that puts us] into a position of inferiority" would be "inevitable seeds . . . sown for a harvest of disaster for our children, black and white."[82]

At the close of the essay, Du Bois criticized Washington's discourse for giving the "distinct impression"

> first, that the South is justified in its present attitude toward the Negro because of the Negro's degradation; secondly that the prime cause of the Negro's failure to rise more quickly is his wrong education in the past; and, thirdly, that his future rise depends primarily on his own efforts.

Significantly, it was for giving this last impression, the most directly Social Darwinist of the three, that "Mr. Washington is especially to be criticized," because Du Bois recognized the attitude that resulted.

His doctrine has tended to make whites, North and South, shift the burden of the Negro problem to the Negro's shoulders and stand aside as critical and rather pessimistic spectators; when in fact the burden belongs to the nation, and the hands of none of us are clean if we bend not our energies to right these great wrongs.

Du Bois closed the essay by calling on his readers, black and white, to fully bend their energies in the right, and rightful, direction.[83]

What is most striking about Du Bois's essay was that he did not solely criticize Washington for preaching accommodation, nor did Du Bois simply make a natural rights argument and a pragmatic argument on behalf of black suffrage. Instead, he directed his strongest attack towards the Social Darwinist principles contained in Washington's discourse. Those lay at the root of the problem, Du Bois argued, and it was those principles that needed to be exorcized. It was not enough to call for legal equality, Du Bois was saying, the rhetoric of equal rights must also provide a means of enacting that solution. To do so required that one first identify correctly who and what were responsible for the present state of inequality; only then could the problem be remedied.

The Costs of Co-optation

Some scholars have argued that the co-optation of Social Darwinism by some African American leaders was rhetorically astute. Lucas, for example, holds that Washington had little choice. His retreat from his National Peace Jubilee speech was "strategic," Lucas writes, because of "how little margin for error he had for dealing with the white south. It is easy to find fault with him today for not mounting a frontal assault against the Southern racial system, but he had little to gain and much to lose by such a course."[84] Robert L. Heath goes further, claiming that, in the case of Crummell, his adaptation of Social Darwinism was not simply a strategy of final resort, but in fact an effectual one. Heath observes first that the same Social Darwinist principles used by white Americans to justify racial inequality were fundamental to Crummell's rhetoric of "racial pride and even black superiority."

> Central to [Crummell's] analysis was the notion that regardless of the racist attitudes of society, the objective and impartial judgment of God and the biological struggle for survival not only allowed for the equality of black people, but also provided neutral standards for concluding that the members of the race were in certain ways superior. This doctrine obviously contradicted the belief of Anglo-Saxon superiority, but nevertheless, these criteria, used by the Anglo-Saxon supremacists, justified his conclusions.[85]

In what Heath terms a strategy of "adaptation," Crummell employed black population growth and the measurable success of some to demonstrate the presence of superior qualities in the race.

But was that rhetorical advantage worth validating the principles of Social Darwinism? The contradiction presented by the increase of population (that is, survival) among the "lower classes" (that is, the less fit) has never bothered Social Darwinists unduly. Instead, survival of the species has quickly been redefined to mean "survival of the *progress* of human beings," and such progress was actually threatened by the population increase among the lower classes. In the hands of the slippery Social Darwinist, Crummell's documentation of black population increase thus became another appeal to fear about the "threat" posed to white "civilization" by the "lower" race. Neither was it particularly effective to argue that successful African Americans proved the race's superiority. Successful African Americans were commonly dismissed, as Professor E. D. Cope did, by calling them the "exceptions [who] tend to prove the rule, for it is generally conceded that in whatever proportion his blood may be mixed . . . his development is superior to that of the pure negro." Worried that his readers might conclude that his rationale thus justified race amalgamation, Cope quickly noted that "the hybrid is not as good a race as the white, and in some respects it often falls below the black especially in the sturdy qualities that accompany vigorous physique."[86]

In exchange for arguments that did not sway white Americans, black rhetors, like Washington, who co-opted Social Darwinism had helped validate criteria that justified unequal treatment. They had agreed, for example, that different races possessed different characteristics. While most African Americans held that such differences were environmental, that argument often became lost in the discussion. What generally stood out were the claims about differences that were labeled "natural" or "characteristic." Washington and Crummell, for example, had described African Americans' Christianity as inherently emotional. Wrote George Stetson, a white education official with the federal government:

> The negro in America has by no means outgrown the feebleness of the moral sense, which is an inheritance from his ancestry, and which is common to all primitive and partially developed races. He is still too much in bond to the superstitions which enslaved his ancestors, and cannot fully comprehend the moral and spiritual basis of a highly developed, unemotional, non-imaginative and impersonal religious faith.

In the late nineteenth century, blacks were especially characterized by whites as "imitative" and "peaceable"; people who were "anxious to live at the cost of the least work possible."[87]

Few white Americans, however, believed only that the races were distinct. Once that distinction was made, most, like Stetson, made the easy transition to judging blacks as the inferior race. Caucasians were typically characterized as the "higher" civilization or the "highest race of man." African Americans were typically characterized as "inferior" or "degraded." The particular nature of their inferiority was much debated. For example, Wardon Allen Curtis, in the *American Journal of Politics*, argued that blacks' "laxity of morals" was not due to "innate depravity," but was rather "the fault of their very low grade of intelligence, of their ignorance, their servility, of the laxity bred in their race by the frequent family separations and new marriages of the days of slavery, [and] of a lack of that foresight and prudence which so often passes for virtue." After such a catalog of ills, one might almost wish it had been attributed to innate depravity.[88]

Had not prejudice, slavery, and discrimination created these characteristics? No, responded Cope, noting ominously that "this assertion has enough truth in it to make it dangerous." He continued: "What the negro may become after centuries of education, the present writer does not pretend to say. But he has had as much time in the past as any other race, and he has not improved it, or been improved by it, as the case may have been." Indeed, argued Kemper Bacchic, "at present nine-tenths of the colored people are only too well satisfied" with their lot in life; there was little that outside forces could do to change that inherent lack of drive. In classic Social Darwinist fashion, the fact that African Americans had not as a class "risen" since emancipation was de facto evidence of their inferiority. The post–Civil War amendments were designed to "protect the freedmen from caste," wrote T. B. Wakeman, and have "by their failure tended to justify and establish the very caste they were passed to prevent."[89]

But should not the ethics of humanity, natural rights, or morality dictate a principle of equality? It was here that Social Darwinism was especially vehement, defending inequality on the grounds of pragmatism and nature. Inherent racial differences would *cause* social separation and legal inequality, the Social Darwinists argued, regardless of outside attempts to force equality. Wakeman posited that "it will be found that two castes cannot exist together without one being dominant over the other, especially where the smaller is distinguished by color and menial labor." In rhetoric reminiscent of Washington's Exposition Address, he continued: "It is childish and useless to say that this ought not be so, that it must not be so,— but so it is, and so it will remain." Thus Cope claimed that suffrage for blacks was "folly," because African Americans had demonstrated their "unfitness to exercise these privileges" or any others connected with American citizenship. Unequal treatment before the law simply acknowledged these "facts" and the nature of the case. George Stetson made a similar argument in regard to industrial education: it was the only sort of education for which African Americans were suited. "The comparative failure of our attempt to properly educate the negro," Stetson claimed, "is in great part due to the obstinacy with which a majority has blindly maintained the theory of his equality in mental endowment with the race with which he is in contact." Never mind that this was indeed an invisible majority, or that the "theory" had never been tested with any significant investment of resources. Social Darwinism showed that the "theory of his equality" was wrong, and so the other conclusions logically followed. These were practical matters, these writers averred, but more, they were matters of gravest concern. "Is our own race on a plane sufficiently high, to render it safe for us to carry eight millions of dead material in the very centre of our vital organism?" Cope asked rhetorically. Nature had dictated that the races be unequal, and nature demanded that they be treated so. In this perspective, to ignore nature was to invite catastrophe.[90]

It is important to note that the writers cited above were not demagogues; they were not "Pitchfork" Ben Tillmans set to agitate a mob and garner votes. These were professors in disciplines such as political economy and anthropology, and professionals in the field of education, publishing essays in the respected opinion magazines and academic journals of the day. Yet Social Darwinism became for them a set of prescriptions for keeping the races separate, and a scientific formula that justified the existing social order. Moreover, even the occasional author who wrote in defense of equal rights, such as Frederick May Holland and C. Staniland Wake, usually reiterated key Social Darwinist principles such that African Americans were still treated rhetorically as citizens of inferior quality.[91]

A final disadvantage of trying to co-opt Social Darwinism for the message of equal rights was that white Americans typically focused on the familiar principles of Social Darwinism, and not on how those principles had been adapted to demonstrate the need for equality or the competence/superiority of African Americans. The *New York World*, covering Washington's Exposition Address, quoted his famous metaphor that in "all things that are purely social we can be as separate as the fingers." It also quoted Washington's declarations that it was "in the South that the negro is given a man's chance" and that "no race can prosper" until it learns to begin at the bottom. The *New York Times* coverage focused on the last half of the speech, particularly quoting the sections on African Americans' indebtedness to the generosity of Northern philanthropists, that the "wisest among my race understand that the agitation of questions of social equality is the extremist folly," and Washington's concluding pledge that African Americans would put forth their best efforts. Except for two sentences in the *World*, both accounts deleted the section in which Washington challenged Southern whites to work fairly and equitably with blacks. Thus the one appeal for help was lost, while the admonitions against agitation and for African Americans assuming responsibility for themselves were reported.[92]

But perhaps the *Chicago Inter Ocean's* account is most telling in this regard. The *Inter Ocean*, a reform-oriented periodical, was rather progressive. It dismissed the reports that Washington was a "new negro": "He was a revelation to the great majority who heard him. . . . But the awakening was on the part of the white men, not the negro." The *Inter Ocean* congratulated itself on the fact that it had been following and reporting on his work for the past five years. Moreover, toward the end of the story the reporter recounted touring the African American exhibition with Bishop Turner; the writer repeated without comment Turner's criticism of whites and his praise of the achievements of blacks. For the white press of the day, this was an exceptional display of journalism. Yet at the end of the account, the reporter wrote that "Booker T. Washington and Bishop Turner are not so far apart, except on the question as to where *the negro is to work out his salvation.*" What is telling here is not simply that the reporter could so easily reconcile the fundamentally contradictory views of Turner and Washington, but that the reconciliation was attained through a Social Darwinist principle: that it was African Americans who must "work out" the way to salvation. But this principle was actually introduced much earlier in the piece, as the reporter employed a central organizing question to introduce Booker T. Washington's work: "What are the colored people doing for themselves in the South?"[93]

It was a natural enough question to ask, for its roots lay not only in the principles of Social Darwinism but in the rhetoric of abolition and Reconstruction as well. In both eras, the focus of African American rhetors had been, naturally enough, on achieving legal equality in what was an obviously unequal legal system. It was rhetorically strategic to argue that, once provided with laws ensuring equality, African Americans would achieve and prosper. It was also rhetorically important to assert in the strongest of terms the humanity, and thus equality, of the race. "For the present, it is enough to affirm the equal manhood of the Negro race," Frederick Douglass declared in his famous Fourth of July address of 1852, because "man is entitled to liberty." Against this rhetorical backdrop, the co-optation of Social Darwinist principles to the campaign for equal rights was logical enough, even if it was ultimately not rhetorically strategic.

Confronting Social Darwinism

In his essay on Booker T. Washington, Du Bois tried to be careful, clear-sighted, and objective. Although critical of Washington's rhetorical choices, Du Bois also praised Washington for his accomplishments and acknowledged the myriad and often daunting challenges that Washington faced. I hope to strike the same note here. For some African American reform rhetors of the era, Social Darwinism was not an important or relevant issue. But for most post-Reconstruction rhetors addressing the issue of race, Social Darwinism was like the uninvited guest who would not leave. Many rhetors chose a strategy of co-optation, wherein they attempted to adapt Social Darwinism to their own ends. Despite its disadvantages, co-optation was such a natural course of action that the strategy might almost have been unavoidable. The African American rhetors during abolition and Reconstruction—successful in achieving their ends—had stressed the ability of blacks to succeed if given a chance, and had focused almost exclusively on overturning legal and formal acts of discrimination. But the appeal to "let us alone" was quickly subsumed by the rise of Social Darwinism, itself so rapidly integrated into the whole of American thought. That philosophy, however, regularly preached that ability would overcome difficulty; that is, that for those with true ability, there was always "a chance," and it legitimized the use of de facto reasoning regarding the relative qualities of the races.[94] Ultimately, Social Darwinism provided a philosophical justification for discrimination, and it was actively employed for that purpose—thus its later characterization as a racist ideology.[95]

But did African Americans' adaptation of Social Darwinism to their rhetoric contribute at all to the legal and social segregation and discrimination that arose in the latter years of the nineteenth century? It is always difficult to answer that sort of a question, especially when most of the evidence indicates that in the post-Reconstruction era, white Americans would have followed the same historical course regardless of the nature of African Americans' rhetoric. Northern whites would, eventually, have mended fences with their Southern counterparts. Segregation, North and South, would undoubtedly have occurred in one form or another. It is highly questionable whether any rhetorical option would have prevented or reduced the de jure and de facto discrimination that African Americans faced. Regarding the institution of segregation as it arose in the post-Reconstruction era, however, the strategy to co-opt Social Darwinism may have either hastened its implementation or delayed its departure, because Social Darwinism conferred scientific validity to the language of racism. As sociologist Mike Hawkins writes, "What Social Darwinism contributed to race theory was an apparently scientific rationale for racial hierarchy and a mechanism—the struggle for survival—for legitimating the predicted fate of blacks," a prediction that became, unremarkably, a self-fulfilling prophecy. For his part, observing the phenomenon as a contemporary, Du Bois also believed that it had abetted, but not produced, racial discrimination in the United States: "These movements [disfranchisement, segregation, inferior education] are not, to be sure, direct results of Mr. Washington's teachings; but his propaganda has, without a shadow of doubt, helped their speedier accomplishment."[96]

Whether Du Bois was correct is not and may never be a settled question. What is clear, however, is that Social Darwinism presented a tremendous rhetorical obstacle in the late nineteenth century. How African American rhetors attempted to confront, co-opt, and avoid that philosophy is a central issue of the period. Moreover, as we examine that challenge from the vantage point of our own era, one where the laissez-faire economic principle of "let the market decide" has reemerged as a major voice, and where there is a growing claim in the white community that African Americans have now been "given a chance," the rhetorical problems and strategies of the post-Reconstruction era may appear modern indeed.

Notes

1. John Hope Franklin and Alfred A. Moss Jr., *From Slavery to Freedom*, 7th ed. (New York: McGraw-Hill, 1994), 229, 231.
2. Ibid., 238.
3. Ibid., 262.
4. Ibid., 261.
5. August Meier, *Negro Thought in America, 1880–1915* (Ann Arbor: University of Michigan Press, 1963), 20–21.
6. Ida B. Wells-Barnett, "The Reason Why the Colored American Is Not in the World's Columbian Exposition," in *Selected Works of Ida B. Wells-Barnett*, ed. and comp. Trudier Harris (New York: Oxford University Press), 75.
7. George L. Ruffin, "A Look Forward," *AME Review* 2 (July 1885): 29. George T. Downing and William Wells Brown are two others who, at one time or another, espoused race amalgamation and cultural assimilation. Meier, *Negro Thought*, 55, 57.
8. "Editorial: The Outlook," *AME Review* 6 (April 1890): 503–4. William Hooper Councill, Marshall Taylor, and William Still are three other examples of accommodationist rhetors. Meier, *Negro Thought*, 77–79.

9. Joseph Charles Price, *New York Age*, 11 October 1890. See also Meier, *Negro Thought*, 82.

10. Henry McNeal Turner, *AME Review* 1 (January 1885): 246–47.

11. For example, see the work of Darwin's cousin, Francis Galton, including "Hereditary Talent and Character," *Macmillan's Magazine* 12 (1865), reprinted in Russell Jacoby and Naomi Glauberman, eds., *The Bell Curve Debate* (New York: Random House, 1995), 393–409.

12. William Graham Sumner, *What Social Classes Owe to Each Other* (New York: Harper and Brothers, 1883), 73, 75; Walter Bagehot, *Physics and Politics* (1872; reprint, Westport, Conn.: Greenwood Press, 1973), 107.

13. Sumner, *What Social Classes Owe*, 53–54.

14. Bagehot, *Physics and Politics*, 49, 55, 56, 74; John Fiske, *The Destiny of Man: Viewed in Light of His Origin* (Boston: Houghton, Mifflin, 1892), 71–72.

15. Bagehot, *Physics and Politics*, 99; Sumner, *What Social Classes Owe*, 61. See also Bagehot, *Physics and Politics*, 48; Fiske, *Destiny of Man*, 100–101; and Sumner, *What Social Classes Owe*, 30.

16. Meier, *Negro Thought*, 22. See Richard Hofstadter, *Social Darwinism in American Thought* (Boston: Beacon Press, 1955), 170–200; Mike Hawkins, *Social Darwinism in European and American Thought, 1860–1945* (Cambridge: Cambridge University Press, 1997), 104–22, 200–203; and Carl N. Degler, *In Search of Human Nature: The Decline and Revival of Darwinism in American Social Thought,* (New York: Oxford University Press, 1991), 15–16.

17. Frederick Douglass, "Speech at Rochester," 5 July 1852, in *Negro Orators and Their Orations*, ed. Carter G. Woodson (New York: Russell and Russell, 1925), 208; Richard H. Cain, "Civil Rights Bill," in Woodson, *Negro Orators*, 329, 336; James T. Rapier, "Civil Rights Bill," in Woodson, *Negro Orators*, 343.

18. Although the term "men" was frequently employed to indicate persons of both genders, the sense of masculinity—of being "manly"—was frequently introduced in this laissez-faire rhetoric of equal rights and the rhetoric of the Social Darwinists.

19. Frederick Douglass, "Self-Made Men," in *The Frederick Douglass Papers*, vol. 5, ed. John W. Blassingame et al. (New Haven, Conn.: Yale University Press, 1992), 550, 551, 556, 559, 560.

20. Douglass, "Self-Made Men," 550, 554, 556, 569, 570, 572.

21. Ibid., 557, emphasis added.

22. For example, see R. B. Elliott, "The Civil Rights Bill," in Woodson, *Negro Orators*, 320–22.

23. John R. Oldfield, *Civilization and Black Progress: Selected Writings of Alexander Crummell on the South* (Charlottesville: University of Virginia Press, 1995), 2–9.

24. Ibid., 11–13.

25. Ibid., 13; Meier, *Negro Thought*, 42. See also W. E. B. Du Bois's chapter "Of Alexander Crummell," in *The Souls of Black Folk: Essays and Sketches* (Chicago: A. C. McClurg, 1903; reprint, New York: Alfred A. Knopf, 1993), 170–79.

26. Alexander Crummell, *Africa and America: Addresses and Discourses* (Springfield, Mass., 1891), 42, 389–90.

27. Ibid., 16–17, 22, 35, 43, 44.

28. Ibid., 16, 32–33, 47.

29. Ibid., 22, 30–31, 33, 383, 388–89, 403.

30. Ibid., 32, 34–35.

31. Ibid., 21, 22, 402.

32. Oldfield, *Civilization*, 78.

33. Crummell, *Africa and America*, 86, 90, 91, 92–93.

34. Ibid., 112–13.

35. Drema R. Lipscomb, "Anna Julia Cooper," in *African-American Orators: A BioCritical Sourcebook*, ed. Richard W. Leeman (Westport, Conn.: Greenwood Press, 1996), 41–43; Mary Helen Washington, "Introduction," in Anna Julia Cooper, *A Voice from the South* (New York: Oxford University Press, 1988), xxvii–liv.

36. Cooper, *Voice from the South*, 117.

37. Ibid., 159, 162, 166, 167.

38. Ibid., 171–73.

39. Ibid., 173, 174.

40. Ibid., 228–29, 230, 232.

41. Ibid., 235, 238, 239.

42. Ibid., 238.

43. Ibid., 240.

44. Ibid., 250–51.

45. Ibid., 258.

46. Ibid., 240, 249, 250.

47. Ibid., 261, 262.

48. Ibid., 264, 265, 280.

49. Ibid., 271–72, 273.

50. Ibid., 281, 284–85.

51. For example, see Du Bois's characterization of Washington's influence in *Souls of Black Folk*, 38–41.

52. Stephen E. Lucas, "Booker T. Washington," in Leeman, *African-American Orators*, 343.

53. Booker T. Washington, "An Account of a Speech in Washington, D.C., 7 April 1894," in *The Booker T. Washington Papers*, ed. Louis R. Harlan, Stuart B. Kaufman, and Raymond W. Smock, vol. 3 (Urbana: University of Illinois Press, 1974), 400 (hereafter cited as *BTW*).

54. For example, Booker T. Washington, "A Speech Delivered before the Women's New England Club," 27 January 1890, in *BTW*, vol. 3, 25–26; and Booker T. Washington, "A Speech before the New York Congregational Club," 16 January 1893, in *BTW*, vol. 3, 282.

55. Washington, "New York Congregational Club," 284; Washington, "Women's New England Club," 26; Booker T. Washington, "A Speech before the National Unitarian Association," 26 September 1894, in *BTW*, vol. 3, 477–78.

56. Washington, "National Unitarian Association," 478; Booker T. Washington, "An Address at a Mass Meeting in Washington, D.C.," 20 November 1891, in *BTW*, vol. 3, 193.

57. See, for example, the letters and telegrams he received following the address in *BTW*, vol. 4, 17–34. See also "South's New Epoch," *New York World*, 19 September 1895, in Louis R. Harlan, Raymond W. Smock, and Barbara S. Kraft, eds., *The Booker T. Washington Papers*, vol. 5 (Urbana: University of Illinois Press, 1976), 3–15. See also Lucas's discussion in "Booker T. Washington," 384–86.

58. Booker T. Washington, "The Standard Printed Version of the Atlanta Exposition Address," 18 September 1895, in *BTW*, vol. 3, 584, 585–86.

59. Ibid., 584, 586.

60. Ibid., 583–84.

61. James Creelman, "South's New Epoch," *New York World*, 19 September 1895, in *BTW*, vol. 4, 3, 9; Howell, as quoted in *BTW*, vol. 4, 17; Still to Washington, 19 September 1895, in *BTW*, vol. 4, 18; Harvey to Washington, 25 September 1895, in *BTW*, vol. 4, 29; Du Bois to Washington, 24 September 1895, in *BTW*, vol. 4, 26.

62. Booker T. Washington, "Address before the National Education Association," 10 July 1896, in *BTW*, vol. 4, 189–99; Lucas, "Booker T. Washington," 349.

63. Booker T. Washington, "An Address at the Harvard Alumni Dinner," 24 June 1896, in *BTW*, vol. 4, 183–84.

64. Booker T. Washington, "An Address at the National Peace Jubilee," 16 October 1898, in *BTW*, vol. 4, 491, 492. For analyses of the strength of the challenge contained in the speech, see Lucas, "Booker T. Washington," 349–50; and *BTW*, vol. 4, xxi–xxii.

65. Qtd. in Lucas, "Booker T. Washington," 350; and in *BTW*, vol. 4, 492. The *New York Times* account, however, indicates that the greatest applause came when Washington praised President William McKinley for his leadership. "Chicago's Peace Jubilee," *New York Times*, 17 October 1898.

66. *BTW*, vol. 4, 493.

67. Booker T. Washington, "An Abraham Lincoln Memorial Address in Philadelphia," 14 February 1899, in *BTW*, vol. 5, 33–34, 35.

68. See, for example, Ida B. Wells, *A Red Record* (1895; reprint, New York: Arno Press, 1969); Ida B. Wells, *Southern Horrors: Lynch Law in All Its Phases* (1892; reprint, New York: Arno Press, 1969); Mary Church Terrell, "The Duty of the National Association of Colored Women to the Race," in *Quest for Equality: The Life and Writings of Mary Eliza Church Terrell, 1863–1954*, ed. Beverly Washington Jones (Brooklyn, N.Y.: Carlson, 1990), 149; Mary Church Terrell, "First Presidential Address to the National Association of Colored Women," in Jones, *Quest*, 135; Mary Church Terrell, "A Plea for the White South by a Coloured Woman," *Nineteenth Century and After* (July 1906): 70–84; Mary Church Terrell, "Peonage in the United States," *Nineteenth Century and After* (August 1907): 306–22; Mary Church Terrell, "The Progress of Colored Women," *Voice of the Negro* 1 (July 1904): 291–93; Mary Church Terrell, "What Role Is the Educated Negro Woman to Play in the Uplifting of Her Race?" in *Twentieth Century Negro Literature*, ed. D. W. Culp (1902; reprint, New York: Arno Press, 1969), 172–77; Rosetta Douglass Sprague, "What Role Is the Educated Negro Woman to Play in the Uplifting of her Race?" in Culp, *Twentieth Century Negro Literature*, 167–71;

and Sarah Dudley Pettey, "What Role Is the Educated Negro Woman to Play in the Uplifting of Her Race?" in Culp, *Twentieth Century Negro Literature*, 182–85.

69. Henry McNeal Turner, "I Claim the Rights of a Man," in *The Voice of Black America: Major Speeches by Negroes in the United States 1797–1971*, ed. Philip S. Foner (New York: Simon and Schuster, 1972), 358, 360, 363.

70. Henry McNeal Turner, *The Negro in All Ages* (Savannah, Ga.: D. G. Patton, 1873), title page.

71. Ibid., 4, 5, 6.

72. Ibid., 8, 9, 10.

73. Ibid., 10, 11.

74. Ibid., 13, 14.

75. Ibid., 16, 17–18.

76. Ibid., 21.

77. Ibid., 23, 24.

78. Ibid., 31.

79. Henry McNeal Turner, "Will It Be Possible for the Negro to Attain, in This Country, Unto the American Type of Civilization?" *Twentieth Century Negro Literature*, ed. D. W. Culp, 42, 45; Turner, "I Claim the Rights of a Man," 358.

80. For example, see W. E. B. Du Bois, "The Training of Negroes for Social Power," *Colored American Magazine* (May 1904): 333–39; W. E. B. Du Bois, "The Niagara Movement," *Voice of the Negro* (September 1905): 619–22; W. E. B. Du Bois, "The Economic Future of the Negro," *Publications of the American Economic Association* 7 (1906): 219–42; and W. E. B. Du Bois, "Is Race Separation Practicable?" *American Journal of Sociology* 13 (1908): 834–38. In contrast to these attacks on Social Darwinism, and to see the evolution of his thought and Du Bois's style of co-optation, see W. E. B. Du Bois, "The Conservation of Races," in *W. E. B. Du Bois Speaks: Speeches and Addresses 1890–1919*, ed. Philip S. Foner (New York: Pathfinder, 1970), 73–85.

81. Du Bois, *Souls of Black Folk*, 45.

82. Ibid., 46, 47, 49.

83. Ibid., 50, 51.

84. Lucas, "Booker T. Washington," 350.

85. Robert L. Heath, "Alexander Crummell and the Strategy of Challenge by Adaptation," *Central States Speech Journal* 26 (1975): 186, 187.

86. E. D. Cope, "Two Perils of the Indo-European," *Open Court* 4 (1889): 2054; George R. Stetson, "The Developmental Status of the American Negro," *Public Opinion* (21 February 1895): 171.

87. Stetson, "Developmental Status," 171; Kemper Bacchic, "The Southern Social Problem," *Social Economist* 4 (1892): 23, 25; Frederick May Holland, "Shall Colored Citizens Be Banished?" *Open Court* 3 (1889): 2080.

88. Wardon Allen Curtis, "The Ultimate Solution of the Negro Problem," *American Journal of Politics* 3 (1892): 353, 354–55; Cope, "Two Perils," 2054; C. Staniland Wake, "The Race Question," *Open Court* 4 (1890): 2355.

89. Cope, "Two Perils," 2053; Bacchic, "Southern Social Problem," 23; T. B. Wakeman, "Planetary Statesmanship and the Negro," *Open Court* 4 (1890): 2433.

90. Wakeman, "Planetary Statesmanship," 2434; Cope, "Two Perils," 2052, 2053; Stetson, "Developmental Status," 171.

91. Holland, "Shall Colored Citizens Be Banished," 2080–81; Wake, "Race Question," 2355.

92. Creelman, "South's New Epoch," 9, 10; "The Atlanta Exposition," *New York Times*, 19 September 1895.

93. L.W.B., "Is He a New Negro?" *Chicago Inter Ocean*, 2 October 1895, in *BTW*, vol. 5, 35, 36, 40–42.

94. Paradoxically, however, most Social Darwinists also preached laissez-faire economic principles; that is, they recognized that environmental difficulties—for example, government regulation—could in fact defeat ability. This seems to have been an unresolved contradiction, and it was certainly never analogized to the legal and social difficulties that encountered African Americans.

95. Meier, *Negro Thought*, 22.

96. Hawkins, *Social Darwinism*, 203; Du Bois, *Souls of Black Folk*, 42.

"The Clear, Plain Facts": The Antilynching Agitation of Ida B. Wells

Shirley Wilson Logan and Martha S. Watson

2

The years after the Civil War should have been a time of opportunity and progress for freed slaves. The Thirteenth Amendment had abolished slavery, the Fourteenth assured civil rights to all citizens, and the Fifteenth specifically gave black males the right to vote. But the white population did not accede willingly to the social and political changes these amendments promised. Seeking to curtail the freed slaves from practicing their newly acquired rights, southerners quickly turned to legal mechanisms to counteract the intent of the amendments and developed a series of Black Codes. Southerners saw these codes as a way to "manage" the newly freed and, to their mind, decidedly inferior black citizens. As *De Bow's Review* asserted:

> We of the South would not find much difficulty in managing the Negroes, if left to ourselves, for we would be guided by the lights of experience and the teachings of history. . . . We should be satisfied to compel them to engage in coarse common manual labor, and to punish them for dereliction of duty or nonfulfillment of their contracts with sufficient severity to make the great majority of them productive laborers. . . . We should treat them as mere grown-up children, entitled like children, or apprentices, to the protection of guardians and masters, and bound to obey those put above them in place of parents, just as children are so bound.[1]

Black Codes varied in intensity and detail from state to state. All granted freed slaves certain rights: the ability to make a contract or be sued; the right to own and inherit property. But these same codes set limits on the activities of blacks. Mississippi allowed the arrest of any black servant who quit his or her work and set the fine according to the distance between where he or she was arrested and the former workplace. Also, in Mississippi a district judge could find a parent of "notoriously bad character" or derelict in teaching good work habits and apprentice his or her children to local business owners. South Carolina's code required all contracts between the races to refer to blacks as "servants" and to whites as "masters."[2] However they differed, the codes were designed to keep the former slaves in positions with little power and autonomy.

Regardless of the Fourteenth Amendment, segregation had emerged in the South after the Civil War in at least three areas without any formal legislation to enforce it. Churches, schools, and the military all honored segregation, even without official sanction for the practice. Although Jim Crow practices antedated the Civil War, southern states quickly adopted legislation to enforce the notion of segregation legally. In 1865 Mississippi forbade "any freedman, negro, or mulatto to ride in any first-class passenger cars, set apart, or used by and for white persons." In the same year Florida prohibited whites from using accommodations set aside for blacks, and in 1866 Texas required all railroads to set aside cars for "freedmen."[3] Reconstruction legislation ended these practices for a time, but they would reemerge with great force at the end of the century.

In response to the Black Codes, Congress sought to guarantee various specific rights to the freed slaves. Most important were the Enforcement Acts of 1870 and 1871, which empowered the federal government to protect the right to vote; the Ku Klux Klan Act of 1871, which sought to keep the Klan from depriving freed slaves of their civil rights; and the Civil Rights Act of 1875, which insisted freed slaves were "entitled to the full and equal enjoyment of the accommodations, advantages, facilities, and privileges of inns, public conveyances on land or water, theaters, and other places of public amusement; subject only to the conditions and limitations established by law, and applicable alike to citizens of every race and color, regardless of any previous condition of servitude."[4]

State legislation continued, however, to challenge the actions of the federal government on behalf of freed slaves and to create new mechanisms to oppress them. When these statutes were challenged by persons claiming the protection of the post–Civil War amendments, the cases made their way to the Supreme Court. In a series of rulings, the Supreme Court proceeded to eviscerate the guarantee of rights. The *Slaughterhouse* case found that the Fourteenth Amendment did not protect important immunities and rights that were bestowed by the state, while the *Cruikshank* and *Harris* decisions of 1875 and 1878, respectively, restricted the reach of the amendment to actions by the state but not by private groups or agencies.[5] In 1883 the Supreme Court ruled that the Fourteenth Amendment prohibited only government violations of civil rights, not the denial of civil rights by individuals unaided by the state. According to Justice Joseph P. Bradley: "It would be running the slavery argument into the ground to make it apply to every act of discrimination which a person may see fit to make as to the guests he will entertain, or as to the people he will take into his coach or cab or car, or admit to his concert or theatre, or deal with in other matters of the intercourse or business."[6] The 1883 ruling effectively overturned the 1875 Civil Rights Act and ended any attempts by those in power to ensure the civil rights of blacks. Together, these decisions ushered in and in fact legitimized the mass denial of civil rights to blacks and signaled the restoration of white political control. Black journalist T. Thomas Fortune wrote that the 1883 decision made blacks feel as if they had been "baptized in ice water."[7] Further, Rayford Logan noted that "practically all relevant decisions of the United States Supreme Court during Reconstruction and to the end of the century nullified or curtailed rights of Negroes."[8] Frederick Douglass also recognized and deplored the significance of the 1883 decision:

It is said that this decision will make no difference in the treatment of colored people; that the Civil Rights Bill was a dead letter and could not be enforced. . . . That bill, like all advance legislation, was a banner on the outer wall of American liberty. . . . It expressed the sentiment of justice and fair play, common to every honest heart. Its voice was against popular prejudice and meanness. It appealed to the noble and patriotic instincts of the American people. It told the American people that they were all equal before the law; they belonged to a common country and were equal citizens. The Supreme Court has hauled down this flag of liberty in open day, and before all the people, and has thereby given joy to the heart of every man in the land who wishes to deny to others what he claims for himself.[9]

Thus the federal government had abandoned its efforts to protect the freed slaves and had opened the door for the South to "manage" the freed population as it wished.

At the end of the century, with federal efforts to secure equality aborted, the South rushed to create legal systems to disenfranchise and oppress blacks. States established barriers to voting, including property or literacy requirements. Of course, these barriers had loopholes for whites such as the "understanding clause, the grandfather clause or the good character clause." South Carolina (1895), Louisiana (1898), North Carolina (1900), Alabama (1901), Virginia (1902), Georgia (1908), and Oklahoma (1910) all adopted constitutional changes to disenfranchise blacks. Florida, Tennessee, Arkansas, and Texas adopted the poll tax to accomplish the same end. Primaries that did not permit participation by blacks were another ploy to disenfranchise those who could somehow meet the other challenges.[10]

Jim Crow laws expanded into new areas. In 1881 Tennessee had required all railroads to "furnish separate cars, or portions of cars cut off by partitioned walls" for blacks who had paid first-class fares but were not to share the accommodations with whites.[11] Other states soon followed that model. Between 1899 and 1909 almost all southern states had extended the provisions to waiting rooms; between 1901 and 1906 streetcars became another site for forced segregation.[12]

In 1896 the Supreme Court had affirmed the doctrine of separate but equal in *Plessy v. Ferguson*. In considering whether a Louisiana statute that mandated separate accommodations for the races violated the post–Civil War amendments and statutes, with only one dissent the Court held "That it does not conflict with the Thirteenth Amendment, which abolished slavery and involuntary servitude, except as a punishment for crime, is too clear for argument." In his dissent, Justice John Harlan noted with some prescience:

The destinies of the two races in this country are indissolubly linked together, and the interests of both require that the common government of all shall not permit the seeds of race hate to be planted under the sanction of law. What can more certainly arouse race hate, what more certainly create and perpetuate a feeling of distrust between these races, than state enactments which in fact proceed on the ground that colored citizens are so inferior and degraded that they cannot be allowed to sit in public coaches occupied by white citizens.[13]

Of course, although *Plessy v. Ferguson* implicitly sanctioned "separate but equal" facilities, in practice the facilities were always separate but never equal.

In addition to legal constraints, informal and formal violence served to discipline and intimidate freed slaves. As Kirt Wilson notes, "Whites injured or killed African Americans for seemingly slight offenses, especially when the perceived affront reinforced black autonomy."[14] The infamous activities of the Ku Klux Klan, the Knights of the White Camellia, and the White Brotherhood terrorized both individuals and groups in an effort to assure continued white supremacy in the South. These southerners "policed 'unruly' Negroes in country districts, discouraged Blacks from serving in the militia, delivered spectral warnings against using the ballot and punished those who disregarded these warnings."[15]

With the growing racial divisions and legally sanctioned oppression, lynching and murders of African Americans reached staggering heights.[16] Between 1890 and 1920 more persons were lynched than were legally executed. In 1892 alone, the year Ida B. Wells began her antilynching campaign, some 161 blacks were reported lynched, more than for any other single year.[17] Logan estimates that the number of persons—most southern blacks—lynched in the United States between 1882 and 1891 totaled 1,544.[18] The actual number was almost certainly much higher since many lynchings went unrecorded. Blacks could be found floating face down in the river, burned in their homes, or hanging from trees. Testimony before a House of Representatives committee investigating the Memphis riot of 1865, as well as testimony in 1871 related to activities of the Ku Klux Klan, document sustained violence against black women.[19] Black men and boys lived knowing a false step might produce fatal violence. At times, lynchers need no pretext for their actions. Even if they were caught, all-white juries were sure to acquit them.

Born during this turbulent period, Ida B. Wells raised her voice as a journalist and speaker on behalf of her race and against its oppressors. For forty years until her death in 1931, Wells spoke out for her race. Although she opposed all forms of racism, Wells was especially vocal on the issue of lynching, a bloody practice that threatened the lives of all blacks regardless of their social status and irrespective of their guilt. Her advocacy arose in a particularly difficult time for her race. Freed and supposedly empowered by the post–Civil War amendments, blacks posed a threat to the political and social power of their former masters in the South. As noted, the response of whites to this potential shift in power was dramatic and hostile; racism blossomed.

We locate the rhetorical activities of Ida B. Wells within this tumultuous period for African Americans. We begin with a biographical narrative because Wells's personal history shaped her development as the social activist who had more to do with originating and carrying forward the antilynching crusade than any other single person. We attend especially to those activities that influenced her development as a public speaker, along with her development as an activist. We then explore the rhetorical features of her antilynching discourse.

Emergence as a Rhetor

Wells's role as activist-orator had roots in the activism of her parents and her community. She was born in 1862 in Holly Springs, Mississippi to slave parents.[20] Her father, James, a skilled carpenter, and her mother, Lizzie, a cook for a contractor for whom James worked, had relatively privileged positions among the slaves. After emancipation, they legally remarried and were able to become financially independent.[21] When the man to whom her father was apprenticed as a builder learned that James had voted Republican, he locked him out of his shop. In response, James Wells purchased another set of tools and moved his family to a location nearby.[22] In her autobiography, Wells recalls as one of her earliest memories reading current events from the newspaper to her father and his friends:

> I do not remember when or where I started school. My earliest recollections are of reading the newspaper to my father and an admiring group of his friends.

He was interested in politics and I heard the words Ku Klux Klan long before I knew what they meant. I knew dimly that it meant something fearful, by the anxious way my mother walked the floor at night when my father was out to a political meeting.[23]

James Wells was a trustee of Rust College, a school established in 1866 under the auspices of the Freedmen's Aid Society of the Methodist Episcopal Church.[24] He was probably also a member of the Holly Springs branch of the Loyal League, a Republican-supported political organization established by local college officials and by the Freedmen's Bureau primarily to encourage blacks to vote. The league met either at the home of Nelson Gill, local head of the bureau, or at a Baptist church, with "long speakings and demonstrations."[25] Wells remembers her mother's anxiety during times when her father attended political meetings. There was reason for her to worry. One story has it that while the Loyal League was meeting at Gill's house, Klan members hid themselves under the house to shoot Gill, but their plans were foiled.[26] Thus Wells grew up in an environment of active participation in community affairs despite overt intimidation. This environment provided an early model for her subsequent public rhetoric.

In Holly Springs, Wells received her early formal education at Rust College. Officially established in 1866, Rust probably evolved from what one observer described as an already established "native school," operated solely by blacks and common throughout the South.[27] In existence long before emancipation, these schools were sites of rhetorical education black people created for themselves as one form of resistance to oppression. As one of the many schools established by and officially for those formerly enslaved and as the first black college established in Mississippi, Rust initially accepted adults of all ages, as well as children, in an effort to build literacy among the newly freed slaves.[28] In her autobiography, Wells writes that she does not remember when or where she started school but does remember that the children in the family had the "job" of learning all they could there. According to Miriam Decosta-Willis, editor of Wells's diary, Wells attended Rust from the age of two to fifteen and was "forced to leave" before completing normal school training.[29]

The circumstances of her departure are not clear. Decosta-Willis's statement that Wells was "forced to leave" probably refers to the family's economic situation.[30] Another biographer speculates that she was "dismissed sometime in 1880 or 1881."[31] These later dates suggest that she continued to matriculate there irregularly after she started teaching, perhaps until the age of eighteen or nineteen.[32] Portions of her first diary entry suggest strongly that Wells's experiences at Rust were not all pleasant. Returning to the school in 1885, she recalls "the most painful memories" of her life, with some implicit references to a strained relationship with W. W. Hooper, president of Rust.[33]

An 1896–97 Rust catalog lists the following among the typical classes taught: spelling, penmanship, advanced grammar, reading, and civil government in the Grammar School; medieval history, literature, rhetoric, pedagogy, and ethics in the Normal Course; and English Bible, Roman history, Greek, Latin, and French in the College Preparatory Course. Since this list is from at least fifteen years after Wells's attendance there, knowing with certainty what courses Wells took at Rust is impossible. But she undoubtedly had some basic grounding in history and grammar.[34]

Although we do not know why she left Rust, we do know that family tragedy played a part in her decision. Added to the social misery associated with Jim Crow life at the time, annual floods and the rapid spread of yellow fever, cholera, and malaria plagued Mississippi. When her parents and two siblings died of yellow fever in 1878, Wells assumed responsibility for the remaining members of the family, taking her first teaching job to support them. Wells writes in her autobiography, however, that "as a green girl in my teens, I was no help to the people outside of the school-room, and at first, I fear, I was very little aid in it, since I had had no normal training. The only work I did outside of my schoolroom, besides hard study to keep up with the work, was to teach in Sunday School."[35] Despite her limited preparation, she was probably not atypical in pursuing teaching as a form of employment. Indeed, the history of Rust College estimates that in one year early in the college's history, about 1,200 of its students taught in area grammar schools during part of the year.[36]

After one year teaching in Holly Springs, Wells moved to Memphis, where she had greater opportunities to develop her talents.[37] Always a voracious reader, Wells was influenced by the Bible and such writers as Charles Dickens, Louisa May Alcott, Charlotte Brontë, and William Shakespeare. But she wrote that during her early years, she "never read a Negro book or anything about Negroes."[38] In Memphis, her interest in public oral performance led her to take elocution lessons from a Mrs. Thompson at two dollars a session, even when she had little money. This interest was also evident in a passage from her diary in which Wells criticized one minister's preaching style for lacking the reverence required in "dealing with holy things" and for being too similar in delivery to a lecture he had given earlier.[39] This critique marks Wells's clear sense of appropriate rhetorical practices. In describing his performance, she noted:

> I went back last night to hear him *preach* in order to come to a decision and came away doubtful as to his holy zeal & fitness for the work. A constant arraignment of the Negro as compared to the Whites, a burlesque of Negro worship, a repetition of what he did not believe in, and the telling of jokes together with a reiteration of his text "ye must be born again" made up his "sermon." It was in style so closely allied to his "talk" of the morning that I detected little difference between the two.[40]

Riding the train to her teaching job in May 1884, Wells took her usual seat in a ladies car. A conductor tried to remove her forcibly to the smoking car of a train; Wells resisted, and as she remembered it, "the moment he caught hold of my arm I fastened my teeth in the back of his hand."[41] When he was unable to remove her on his own, he summoned two other men to help. In her autobiography, Wells observed: "They were encouraged to do this by the attitude of the white ladies and gentlemen in the car; some of them even stood on the seats so that they could get a good view and continued applauding the conductor for his brave stand."[42] Immediately, Wells decided to pursue legal action. When her first choice for an attorney, an African American, was bribed by the train company, Wells turned to a white attorney to pursue her case. A Memphis Circuit Court judge, an ex-Union soldier, found for Wells. The 25 December headline in the white *Memphis Daily Appeal* read: "A Darky Damsel Obtains a Verdict for Damages against the Chesapeake & Ohio Railroad—What It Cost to Put a Colored School Teacher in a Smoking Car—Verdict for $500."[43] The Chesapeake & Ohio ultimately triumphed, however. The railroad filed an appeal, and in 1887 the Tennessee Supreme Court reversed the decision, holding Wells liable for all court costs.

Upon reflection, Wells realized why the railroad had pursued the case so vigorously. It had been "the first case in which a colored plaintiff in the South had appealed to a state court since the repeal of the Civil Rights Bill by the United States Supreme Court. . . . The success of my case would have set a precedent in which others would doubtless have followed."[44] Nearly ten years later, in 1896, the Supreme Court further sanctioned Jim Crow laws and upheld the doctrine of separate but equal in the landmark case *Plessy v. Ferguson*.

Soon after moving to Memphis, sparked by her family's activism and her own interest in public discourse, Wells joined a Memphis lyceum composed mostly of teachers.[45] Established in 1826 to provide a practical, inexpensive education for youth, information to the community generally, and practical applications of the sciences, lyceums sponsored lectures, plays, and debates in which all sorts of groups could participate.[46] Speaking at a lyceum provided valuable practice for many who later became lecturers for such reform movements as abolition. In the late eighteenth and early nineteenth centuries, often banned from the white lycea, African Americans organized societies, including the lyceum Wells joined, that paralleled but rarely intersected with the development of the predominantly white American lyceum movement.

The lyceum Wells joined met weekly either at LeMoyne Normal Institute or at the Vance Street Christian Church. Wells looked forward to these gatherings, describing them as "a breath of life to me, for this program was like the Friday afternoon oratoricals in school. The exercises always closed with the reading of the *Evening Star*—a spicy journal prepared and read by the editor."[47] When the editor left for another position, Wells was, to her surprise, elected to replace him. She found she enjoyed the work and was apparently skillful at it since, according to her report, the attendance increased "by people who said they came to hear the *Evening Star* read."[48] A local minister favorably reviewed her presentations and soon invited her to write for his paper.

Although she thought she had little training and "no literary gifts and graces," she had "observed and thought much about conditions as I had seen them in the country schools and churches. I had an instinctive feeling that people who had little or no school training should have something coming into their homes weekly which dealt with their problems in a simple, helpful way." Despite her lack of formal training, Wells clearly had instinctive rhetorical sensitivities: "I wrote in a plain, common-sense way on the things which concerned our people. Knowing that their education was limited, I never used a word of two syllables where one would serve the purpose. I signed these articles 'Iola.'"[49] When other African American papers reprinted her columns, she began to receive invitations to write for them as well.

Her work as editor of the *Evening Star* and her writing for other newspapers increased her interest in journalism. Among the newspapers that sought her services was the *Free Speech and Headlight*. Wanting to be on equal footing with the two male owners, she bought a third interest in the paper and became its editor.[50] Of course, she used the paper to critique the racist practices around her. In one editorial, she protested the inferior conditions of black schools. As she recalled, "I felt that some protest should be made over conditions in the colored schools. The article was a protest against the few and utterly inadequate buildings for colored children. I also spoke of the poor teachers given us whose mental and moral character was not of the best."[51] At the time she wrote the article, she feared repercussions and asked her coeditor to attach his name to it. He refused, and the column appeared under her name. The next school term she found herself without a teaching position. Thus Wells was left to devote herself full time to what she loved most—journalism.

Devoting her full-time energy to *Free Speech*, Wells determined "to make a race newspaper pay—a thing which older and wiser heads said could not be done."[52] By traveling extensively to solicit subscriptions, Wells was able to increase the circulation from 1,500 to 3,500; within a year the paper was paying its way.[53] One writer suggests that its growing popularity could be attributed to Wells's "lively writing style."[54] Continuing the use of her pseudonym "Iola," Wells took on all the major political issues facing African Americans—denial of civil rights, mob violence, and equal access, to name a few. In a male-dominated profession, she soon became known as the "Princess of the Press."[55]

During this period of Wells's budding journalistic career, events occurred that catapulted her into still more controversy and changed the direction of her life. As she reported, "While I was thus carrying on the work of newspaper, happy in the thought that our influence was helpful and that I was doing the work I loved and had proved that I could make a living out of it, there came the lynching in Memphis which changed the whole course of my life."[56] In March 1892 three black Memphis entrepreneurs, Thomas Moss, Calvin McDowell, and William Stewart, became victims of mob violence. Wells described the course of events in an article in the *London Methodist Times* in May 1894, two years later. According to her, the three men were "energetic business men, who had accumulated a little money which they invested in a grocery business. The white monopolists did not like their rivalry; there was an altercation, my friends defended themselves, were thrown into the gaol, and bail was refused. The whites thought they were too independent, so they were taken out of gaol and lynched."[57] Upset over the death of her friends, Wells began to investigate lynchings and their causes. She admitted that this event had changed her own perspective. "Like many another person who had read of lynching the South, I had accepted the idea meant to be conveyed—that although lynching was irregular and contrary to law and order, unreasoning anger over the terrible crime of rape led to the lynchings; that perhaps the brute deserved death anyhow and the mob was justified in taking his life."[58] Her research led her to the conclusion that these brutal acts represented not retribution for the rape of women as was often alleged, but rather efforts of whites to dominate and control her race.

In May 1892 Wells wrote a scathing editorial in *Free Speech* in which she railed against the growing number of black men being lynched and called into question the motives of many white women who accused them of rape. She quoted from it in her 1892 publication *Southern Horrors: Lynch Law in All Its Phases*: "Nobody in this section of the country believes the old thread-bare lie that Negro men rape White women. If southern White men are not careful, they will over-reach themselves and public sentiment will have a reaction; a conclusion will then be reached which will be very damaging to the moral reputation of their women."[59] Later in the same section of *Southern Horrors*, she responds to the outcry the editorial created:

> The editor of the "Free Speech" [*sic*] has no disclaimer to enter, but asserts instead that there are many White women in the South who would marry colored men if such an act would not place them at once beyond the pale of society and within the clutches of the law. The miscegenation laws of the South only operate against the legitimate union of the races; they leave the White man free to seduce all the colored girls he can, but it is death to the colored man who yields to the force and advances of a similar attraction in White women.[60]

Two days after the editorial appeared, a "committee" of white citizens destroyed the paper's printing equipment and set fire to the facility. Wells was in Philadelphia attending a church conference when the editorial appeared and was advised not to return to Memphis.

Although Wells had long been an activist for causes in which she believed, this series of events also launched her career as a public speaker and as an antilynching activist. After a brief stay in Philadelphia, Wells relocated to New York City and began writing for the *New York Age*. She used this new journalistic outlet to refute "the southern White man's reason for lynching and burning human beings in this nineteenth century of civilization."[61] Her first submission was a 25 June 1892 front-page, seven-column article titled "Exiled," in which she related the Memphis story. T. Thomas Fortune and coeditor Jerome Peterson printed 10,000 copies of that issue and disseminated them throughout the country, especially in the South. This article evolved into her first antilynching pamphlet, *Southern Horrors*, and served as a template for her subsequent antilynching addresses.[62]

On 5 October 1892, some seven months after the murders in Memphis, Wells delivered her first speech at Lyric Hall in New York City at a gathering that had been organized by a committee of 250 black women to raise money to help Wells reestablish the *Free Speech*. At the time, the affair was considered by many "to be the greatest demonstration ever attempted by race women for one of their number." Of this first speaking experience Wells said, "Although every detail of that horrible lynching affair was imprinted in my memory, I had to commit it all to paper." She also noted it was "the beginning of public speaking for me."[63] For her efforts, Wells was given a gold broach and $500, which she used to publish her first pamphlet, *Southern Horrors*.[64] The women who organized that speaking engagement went on to organize similar events for Wells in Boston, New Bedford, Providence, New Haven, and other cities. These events also resulted in the organization of several women's clubs.[65] The following February Wells gave her first address to a white audience, the meeting of the Monday Club in Boston's Tremont Temple, where she delivered "Lynch Law in All Its Phases." However, moving to the public platform was not without its problems. She later recalled her first presentation in her autobiography: "When the committee told me I had to speak I was frightened. I had been a writer, both as correspondent and editor, for several years. . . . But this was the first time I had ever been called on to deliver an honest-to-goodness address."[66] Reading her speech also reminded her of the problems that had led her to the occasion: the destruction of her newspaper; the dispersion of her friends; and her many struggles. Her emotions overwhelmed her:

> A panic seized me. I was afraid that I was going to make a scene and spoil all those dear good women had done for me. . . . I had left my handkerchief on the seat behind me and therefore could not wipe away the tears which were coursing down my checks. . . . I was mortified that I had not been able to prevent such an exhibition of weakness. It came on me unawares. It was the only time in all those trying months that I had so yielded to personal feelings. That it should come at a time when I wanted to be at my best in order to show my appreciation of the splendid things those women had done! They were giving me tangible evidence that although my environment had changed I was still surrounded by kind hearts. After all these years I still have a feeling of chagrin over that exhibition of weakness. Whatever my feelings, I am not given to public demonstrations. And only once before in all my life had I given way to woman's weakness in public.[67]

Her initial public speech, however, impressed her audience, and she received other invitations to speak. This occasion had thus opened the door for a new career and determined the focus of her advocacy.

In March 1893 Wells was invited to England by Catherine Impey, who had heard her speak in Philadelphia the previous year. Wells had her own reasons for taking her antilynching campaign abroad. For one thing, she had only limited success with her efforts in the United States. She recalled: "Only in one city—Boston—had I been given even a meager hearing, and the press was dumb."[68] She also believed that if she was successful in England, Americans might well attend to their British cousins. In a letter to the editor of the *Daily Post* in Birmingham, England, Wells wrote, "America cannot and will not ignore the voice of a nation that is her superior in civilization. . . . I believe that the silent indifference with which [Great Britain] has received the intelligence that human beings are burned alive in Christian(?) Anglo-Saxon communities is born of ignorance of the true situation; and that if she really knew she would make the protest long and loud." In many cities where she lectured, her speeches stimulated the organization of the Society for the Recognition of the Brotherhood of Man (SRBM), which took as its creed the "promise to help in securing to every member of the human family freedom, equal opportunity, and brotherly consideration."[69]

In addition to arousing the British public's interest in mob violence in America, this first trip abroad provided Wells with valuable experience as a rhetor. The trip gave her the opportunity to speak in front of a variety of audiences and helped increase her credibility as a public speaker, since most of her appearances were favorably reviewed by the foreign press. For example, the *Ladies Pictorial*, a prominent women's publication wrote: "Miss Ida Bell Wells, a negro lady who has come to England on the invitation of Miss Catherine Impey, has been lecturing with great success on a subject somewhat new to British audiences, namely, 'Lynch Law in the United States,' especially as it affects the colored people of the South." The *Newcastle Leader* noted: "Miss Wells, who is a young lady with a strong American accent, and who speaks with an educated and forceful style, gave some harrowing instances of the injustice to the members of her race, of their being socially ostracized and frequently lynched in the most barbarous fashion by mobs on mere suspicion, and without any trial whatever."[70] Other reviews were similarly favorable.

Upon her return to the States, she collaborated with Frederick Douglass, I. Garland Penn, and Ferdinand Barnett to write and publish the eighty-one-page pamphlet *The Reason Why the Colored American Is Not in the World's Columbian Exposition*, which used the exclusion of African Americans from participation in the 1893 World's Columbian Exposition to publicize the unheeded accomplishments of the race. Since the exposition was intended to celebrate the 400th anniversary of Columbus's "discovery" of America, to underscore the recent emergence of the United States as a world power, and to display the achievements of the Americas to the rest of the world, the exclusion of African Americans provided an excellent pretext for a discussion of the race's accomplishments. Wells, Douglass, Penn, and Barnett circulated 10,000 copies and published the preface in French and German as well. With the help of funds raised by prominent black women, the pamphlet was made available at no charge except for three cents to cover postage. The collaborators were clear about their intentions for the pamphlet:

> Those visitors to the World's Columbian Exposition who know these facts, especially foreigners will naturally ask: Why are not the colored people, who constitute so large an element of the American population, and who have contributed so large a share to American greatness,—more visibly present and better represented in this World's Exposition? Why are they not taking part in this glorious celebration of the four-hundredth anniversary of the discovery of their country? Are they so dull and stupid as to feel no interest in this great event? It is to answer these questions and supply as far as possible our lack of representation at the Exposition that the Afro-American has published this volume.[71]

In February 1894 Wells returned to England, this time as a correspondent for the *Inter Ocean*, a Chicago newspaper. She delivered more than 100 speeches and used her success in Britain as fodder for her columns.[72] While in England, she republished her pamphlet *Southern Horrors* under the title *United States Atrocities* and sold it at lectures. Her allies stimulated press coverage during her tour. One, the *Fraternity*, claimed: "Her greatest success has been with the London newspapers. . . . Lynching has never been so strongly condemned by the Press in England as during her visit this year."[73] In her autobiography, she recalled that at the same time many readers did not accept her views: "hardly a day passed without letters in the daily papers attacking and discrediting my assertions."[74]

Returning to the United States in July 1894, Wells undertook a challenging lecture tour that stretched from New York to San Francisco. At first her tour was underwritten by the newly organized Anti-Lynching Association; when those funds were exhausted, she charged a fee for her lectures. After almost a year of unstinting effort, Wells returned to Chicago in June 1895 to marry Ferdinand Barnett, one of her collaborators in producing *The Reason Why*.[75] Although she attempted to retire with the birth of the first of her four children, events intervened to draw her back into public agitation, and she continued her work as a journalist. So, for example, in 1898 when a postmaster was lynched in South Carolina, she traveled with a delegation to Washington, D.C., to urge President William McKinley to intervene for his widow.[76]

Wells continued to write and lecture extensively in her efforts to make the facts about lynching more widely known. In 1895 she published *A Red Record: Tabulated Statistics and Alleged Causes of Lynching in the United States, 1892–1893–1894*, which presented an array of facts and figures about lynching. Wells asserted that her crusade was a test of "the white man's civilization and the white man's government which are on trial."[77] Her *Mob Rule in New Orleans: Robert Charles and His Fight to the Death*, published in 1900, not only provided an account of a week of rioting that ensued when white policemen assaulted two African Americans, but it also listed the lynchings between 1882 and 1899 as chronicled in the *Chicago Tribune*.[78] In 1910 Wells organized the Negro Fellowship League, a settlement organization that "drew on southern Black women's church traditions of home missions as well as on club women's impulse to uplift."[79] Since African Americans were largely excluded from other fellowship and uplift organizations like the settlement houses, the league sought to provide many of the same services.[80] In her autobiography, Wells described her time working with the league:

All I can say of that ten years I spent on State Street is that no human being ever came inside the doors asking for food who was not given a card to the restaurant across the way. No one sought a night's lodging in vain, for after his case was investigated, a card to the Douglass Hotel was given him. And nobody who applied for a job was ever turned away. Very few had the price to pay for the job [referral?], but they always promised to come back. I am sorry to say that very few of them came back, and so we took what satisfaction we could out of the fact that we had helped a human being at the hour of his greatest need and that the race would get the benefit of our action if we did not.[81]

The only person from Chicago at the 1909 organizing meetings in New York for what became the National Association for the Advancement of Colored People (NAACP), Wells sought to get that organization to take up her antilynching crusade. The NAACP did not immediately follow through with efforts in this area. When the names of the Committee of Forty were announced, Wells was stunned that she had not been named as part of that planning body for the new organization. Irritated at the rebuff, she left the meeting and refused pleas to return.[82]

In 1913 Wells formed the Alpha Suffrage Club, the first black woman suffrage club in Illinois, in an effort to find a role for African American women in this important effort. When organizers of a suffrage parade in Washington, D.C., that same year put African American women at the back of the demonstration, she protested. Although some white women joined her protest, they were not heeded. Wells, keenly astute about political statements, stood on the sidelines until the Illinois contingent, which was at the front, passed by; then she stepped from the sidelines to join their march.[83]

Until her death in March 1931, at the age of sixty-nine, Wells remained at the center of political controversy and social action. W. E. B. DuBois wrote on her death: "The passing of Ida Wells-Barnett calls for more than the ordinary obituary. [She] was the pioneer of the anti-lynching crusade in the United States. . . . She roused the white South to vigorous and bitter defense and she began the awakening of the conscience of the nation."[84]

As this discussion has indicated, Wells was unusually prolific both as a journalist and as a speaker. Because many of her speeches became pamphlets or articles, making a distinction between her oral and written efforts is problematic. Her extensive publications include one work of fiction, "Two Christmas Days: A Holiday Story"; a series of political pamphlets, including *Southern Horrors: Lynch Law in All Its Phases* (1892), *The Reason Why the Colored American Is Not in the World's Columbian Exposition* (1893), *A Red Record: Tabulated Statistics and Alleged Causes of Lynching in the United States, 1892–1893–1894* (1895), *Lynch Law in Georgia* (1899), *Mob Rule in New Orleans: Robert Charles and His Fight to the Death* (1900), and *The Arkansas Race Riot* (1922); and many magazine articles, including "Lynch Law in All Its Phases" (1893), "Lynch Law in America" (1900), "The Negro's Case in Equity" (1900), "Lynching, the Excuse for It" (1901), "How Enfranchisement Stops Lynchings" (1910), and "Our Country's Lynching Record" (1913). Her autobiography, *Crusade for Justice: The Autobiography of Ida B. Wells* (1970), which she began in 1928, was published posthumously by her daughter.

Although such an extensive corpus may pose challenges for a rhetorical critic, much of Wells's work was reiterative. Speeches became articles or pamphlets; the same arguments appear, with slight variations, in several places. Our analysis draws primarily on three texts: *Southern Horrors, The Reason Why the Colored American Is Not in the World's Columbian Exposition*, and *A Red Record*. While some overlap exists in the two texts on lynching, they represent responses to different rhetorical contexts. *Southern Horrors* was first given as a speech in New York City on 5 October 1892 and was later reprinted as a pamphlet.[85] It contains what became her standard arguments against lynching. *A Red Record*, her attempt to document the rising prevalence of lynching, advances many of the same points but relies on a slightly different rhetorical approach. The pamphlet on the Columbian Exposition, coauthored with three friends, including one who became her husband, provides an interesting, more general defense of her race.

Understanding Wells's role as a public advocate demands an examination of the challenges she faced in her agitation and of how she marshaled rhetorical resources to overcome them. As she sought to create an audience for her cause, Wells relied on three rhetorical approaches: clear arguments, often involving skillful refutation; strong evidence to support her claims, including both extremely vivid examples and compelling statistics; and a problem-solution format that suggested clear paths of action for her listeners. Throughout her speech and writings, she challenged widely held beliefs about lynching, offered an alternate analysis of the issue, and supported her claims with a variety of statistical information as well as vivid examples. If the results lacked rhetorical finesse and eloquence, her work nonetheless created the possibility of conceptual change by creating what Kenneth Burke calls "perspective by incongruity" to overcome the insensitivity of her listeners.[86] In that process, a rhetor stimulates his or her audience to rethink accepted beliefs by highlighting the discrepancy between those beliefs and new information. The resultant unsettling of established patterns of thought becomes the stimulus for changed attitudes and actions. The discussion below focuses on these strategies, drawing examples primarily from the texts we have indicated.

A Red Record Made Public

In beginning her public advocacy about lynching, Wells faced several significant rhetorical challenges. Her audience, gender, race, and topic all created distinct obstacles to her efforts. Moreover, the obstacles were synergistic: her topic confronted deeply held prejudices in her audience, and her gender complicated the inherent barriers posed by the topic; her race interacted with the topic and her gender.[87]

Wells's focus first had to be on creating what theorist Chaim Perleman calls "presence" for her topic. As he writes in *The Realm of Rhetoric*, "Choosing to single out certain things for presentation in a speech draws the attention of the audience to them and thereby gives them a *presence* that prevents them from being neglected. . . . The techniques of presentation which create presence are essential above all when it is a question of evoking realities that are distant in time and place."[88] Lynching was for most Americans, as it initially was for Wells, distant in both time and place. Further, it was embedded in other complex political and social issues. One key strategy for creating presence, according to Perelman, is aggregation: "we begin by enumerating the parts and end with a synthesis."[89] As we will see, this approach became a thrust of much of Wells's agitation.

Further, potential audience members for her discourse were quite disparate. On the one hand, she had to urge members of her own race in this country to take the actions within their purview to end lynching, including boycotts, resistance, and even armed defiance. Because many middle-class African Americans felt themselves removed from the direct threat of lynching, engaging their efforts on behalf of others was problematic. Indeed, Wells herself had been largely indifferent until the lynching of her friends. Further, in an era when violence against African Americans was commonplace, any actions of resistance posed significant risks to them. On the other hand, because whites held all the legal and political power, Wells had to speak to those capable of orchestrating legal change. But her topic was not salient to many of her listeners and readers, especially those in the North or Britain who saw lynching as a "southern" or an "American" problem. Most sought simply to ignore what was happening or to believe it was a necessary, if regrettable, strategy.

On a theoretical level, Kenneth Burke describes how unpleasant realities like those that Wells sought to present impact potential listeners. According to Burke, we develop a "trained incapacity" when the choices and practices of our lives make us unable to perceive certain facts. As he explains the concept:

> Whenever there is an unsatisfactory situation, men will naturally desire to avoid it. In a complex social structure, many interpretations and ways of avoidance are possible; and some of them are likely to be much more serviceable than others. . . . The problems of existence do not have one fixed, unchanging character, like the label on a bottle. They are open to many interpretations—and these interpretations in turn influence our selection of means. Hence the place of "trained incapacity" in the matter of means-selecting. One adopts measures in keeping with his past training—and the very soundness of that training may lead him to adopt the wrong measures.[90]

In a real sense, Wells's contemporaries had developed a "trained incapacity" in the area of race, especially in regard to lynchings. Even Wells herself had assumed that lynchings were regrettable but perhaps appropriate responses to the crime of rape. Only the murder of her friends forced her to confront the issue more directly. Certainly, articulate southern apologists encouraged the view that the punishment suited the crime. For example, Thomas Nelson Page, a noted apologist of the time, expressed a common view: "The crime of lynching in this country has, at one time or another, become so frequent that it has aroused the interest of the whole people, and has even arrested the attention of people in other countries. It has usually been caused by the boldness with which the crime was committed by lawbreakers, and the inefficiency of the law in dealing with them through its regular forms." He then lays out a seemingly commonsensical, rational thesis: "All thoughtful men know that a respect for law is the basic principle of civilization, and are agreed as to the evil of any overriding of the law. . . . To overcome this conviction and stir up rational men to a pitch where the law is trampled under foot, the officers of the law are attacked, and the prisoner taken for them and executed, there must be some imperative cause."[91] For Americans, the very brutality and extent of the crime prompted an effort to excuse it in some way.

Believing that lynchings were punishments for the crime of rape provided a convenient way to avoid confronting the difficult questions surrounding the lynchings. Southerners who took part in these abuses and those who supported them erected a series of untenable defenses of this brutal practice. For example, the prevailing argument that lynching was a crime perpetrated against black men suspected of raping or attempting to rape white women was clearly false. Less than 25 percent of those reported lynched between 1882 and 1946 were accused of rape. Further, many of those lynched were women. From 1884 to 1903 some forty black women, charged with such crimes as murder, "well poisoning," "race prejudice," arson, or theft were lynched. Moreover, the invisible victims of rape, particularly during Reconstruction, were black, not white, women. Bringing these kinds of facts to her audience was to become a central strategy in Wells's agitation.

Moreover, in Wells's era public discussion of sexuality was off-limits. Because she had to refute the defense of lynching that traced its roots to the rape of white women by black men, her speeches and pamphlets had to highlight a topic that was, to much of her audience, a cultural taboo. Also, to expose the roots of the crime, Wells had to uncover the facts about sexual liaisons between white women and African American men, relationships that violated the miscegenation statutes in place in many states.[92] Thus Wells was compelled to present her audience with evidence that many white women, the supposed bastions of morality, were in fact violating state laws in establishing sexual relationships with African American men. The rhetorical perils of advocacy on this topic are apparent.

Further, at the turn of the nineteenth century, public advocacy by women was still not fully acceptable. As a middle-class woman, her very visible presence in the public sphere created challenges to her ethos and credibility. Her race and the topic she addressed accentuated that problem. As an African American woman speaking out against crimes perpetrated against her race, she confronted not only strongly held beliefs about African Americans but also prejudices against her as an advocate for her race. An African American woman refuting arguments that rested on a defense of southern womanhood created still more resistance in her listeners.

In her public advocacy, Wells was clear about the directions she needed to take. As a journalist, she believed in the power of the press and realized that to be successful, she had to attract media attention. Through the press, she could reeducate potentially sympathetic whites. In her autobiography, she confesses that although she was sometimes frustrated by her inability to attract attention from the white press, she recognized that "it was the medium through which I hoped to reach the White people of the country, who alone could mold public sentiment."[93] Again, in the conclusion of *Southern Horrors*, she reiterated her belief that reeducation through the press was critical for her cause: "The assertion has been substantiated throughout these pages that the press contains unreliable and doctored reports of lynchings and one of the most necessary things for the race to do is to get these facts before the public. The people must know before they can act, and there is no educator to compare with the press."[94] As we have seen, however, with the destruction of her own press, she was forced to the public platform, where she hoped to gain the press interest that was essential to her success.

CLEAR, PLAIN FACTS

To create an audience for her discourse, to develop presence for her topic, and to overcome the trained incapacities of potential supporters, Wells uses a variety of approaches, but all involve a direct assault on audience preconceptions. She quite literally thrusts unpleasant facts before her audience, forcing them to acknowledge realities they have sought to avoid. She begins her 1895 work, *A Red Record*, by suggesting how blasé the public has been to the problem of lynching. "The student of American sociology will find the year 1894 marked by a pronounced awakening of the public conscience to a system of anarchy and outlawry which had grown during a series of ten years to be so common, that scenes of unusual brutality failed to have any visible effect upon the humane sentiments of the people of our land."[95] The public's ignorance cannot be explained by the scope of the problem.

> Not all nor nearly all of the murders done by white men, during the past thirty years in the South, have come to light, but the statistics as gathered and preserved by white men, and which have not been questioned, show that during these years more than ten thousand Negroes have been killed in cold blood without the formality of judicial trial and legal execution. . . . [T]he same record shows that during all these years, and for all these murders, only three white men have been tried, convicted and executed.[96]

She labels the first section of *Southern Horrors* "The Offense" and turns to a brief dramatic narrative to attract audience attention:

> Wednesday evening May 24th, 1892, the city of Memphis was filled with excitement. Editorials in the daily papers of that date caused a meeting to be held in the Cotton Exchange Building; a committee was sent for the editors of the "Free Speech" [*sic*]. . . . [T]he only reason the open threats of lynching that were made were not carried out was because they could not be found. The cause of all this commotion was the following editorial published in the "Free Speech" May 21st, 1892, the Saturday previous.[97]

The "offense," of course, was that she dared to publish an editorial that questioned the standard defense of lynching as retribution for the rape of white women. The editorial that she reprints ends with a dramatic threat: "If Southern white men are not careful, they will over-reach themselves and public sentiment will have a reaction; a conclusion will then be reached which will be very damaging to the moral reputation of their women."[98]

Like the other texts, *The Reason Why* intended to make the audience aware of issues that they could easily ignore. The preface was addressed "To the Seeker After Truth." Wells described the "creditable little book" in her autobiography: "It was a clear, plain statement of facts concerning the oppression put upon the colored people in this land of the free and home of the brave."[99] After briefly tracing the evolution of arguments in support of lynching, Wells notes: "The mob spirit has increased with alarming frequency and violence. Over a thousand black men, women and children have been thus sacrificed in the past ten years. Masks have long since been thrown aside and the lynchings of the present day take place in broad daylight. The sheriffs, policy and state officials stand by and see the work well done."[100]

As these three examples demonstrate, Wells immediately confronted the trained incapacities of her audience by insisting that lynchings were so extensive and so brutal that they could no longer be ignored. She made no attempt to ingratiate herself to her listeners; rather, she assumed the persona of agitator and critic. To an audience that had, as she knew, grown used to reports of lynchings and had assumed they were necessary to maintain some social order, Wells's approach was

THE ANTILYNCHING AGITATION
OF IDA B. WELLS

51

startling. Her highlighting of the crime was her first step in forcing her audience to acknowledge a problem existed. This was crucial in creating the perspective by incongruity within her audience that might stimulate social change. The next critical step in her advocacy was to refute directly the preconceptions and prejudices of her listeners. To that end, she turned to the resources of argument and refutation.

THE OLD THREAD BARE LIE

Wells focused her arguments on refuting the thesis that lynchings were linked to the rape of white women. In *A Red Record*, she begins by exploring the history of apologies for the practice. Since lynchings were frequently reported in the press, some defense of the extralegal practice became necessary. A variety of apologists arose, defending lynching as vital to maintain order. With typical disdain and sarcasm, Wells ridicules this apologetic approach: "Naturally enough the commission of these crimes began to tell upon the public conscience, and the Southern white man, as a tribute to the nineteenth century civilization, was in a manner compelled to give excuses for his barbarism. His excuses have adapted themselves to the emergency."[101] Wells proceeds to discuss and refute those reasons, relying on an earlier analysis by Frederick Douglass.

In the chapter "The Case Stated," Wells arrives at her central thesis about the real causes of lynching through a process of eliminating alternative answers to the question, "What motivates and sustains the practice of lynching?" As one reason southerners proferred became untenable, another took its place. First came the claim that lynching was necessary "to repress and stamp out alleged 'race riots.'" But between 1865 and 1872, although "hundreds of colored men and women were mercilessly murdered . . . no insurrection ever materialized; no Negro rioter was ever apprehended or proven guilty, and no dynamite ever recorded the black man's protest against oppression and wrong."[102] This simple fact clearly assaulted her audience's preconceptions and began to create the perspective by incongruity that was necessary for a change in attitudes.[103]

The second excuse emerged during Reconstruction when blacks were enfranchised, and "the Negro's vote became an important factor in all matters of state and national politics." Lynching was necessary to preserve the "white man's government." "No Negro domination became the new legend on the sanguinary banner of the sunny South, and under it rode the Ku Klux Klan, the Regulators, and the lawless mobs, which for any cause chose to murder one man or a dozen as suited their purpose best." Despite the intimidation, the freed male slave "clung to his right of franchise with a heroism which would have wrung admiration from the hearts of savages," but to little avail, because the government that gave him the ballot "denied him the protection which should [have] maintained that right."[104]

However, the total political domination of African Americans by southern whites removed this pretext to defend lynching. So "the murderers invented the third excuse—that Negroes had to be killed to avenge their assaults upon women." This excuse was the most harmful to the race and the most unanswerable:

> Humanity abhors the assailant of womanhood, and this charge upon the Negro at once placed him beyond the pale of human sympathy. With such unanimity, earnestness and apparent candor was this charge made and reiterated that the world has accepted the story that the Negro is a monster which the Southern White Man has painted him. And to-day, the Christian world feels, that while lynching is a crime, and lawlessness and anarchy the certain precursors of a nation's fall, it can not by word or deed, extend sympathy or help to a race of outlaws, who might mistake their plea for justice and deem it an excuse for their continued wrongs.[105]

Wells's goal was to expose this excuse by demonstrating how specious it was. The balance of *A Red Record* and all of *Southern Horrors* focus largely on exploding the claimed link between the rape of white women and lynchings.

In *Southern Horrors*, Wells makes two central arguments to refute the alleged linkage between rapes of white women by black men and lynching. First, she demonstrates that in reality, many alleged rapes were consensual relationships. Second, she notes that rapes of African American women, even children, go unpunished. She begins her refutation by relating the tale of a Montgomery, Alabama, newspaperman who had asked some five years previously: "Why is it that white women attract negro men now more than in former days? There was a time when such a thing was unheard of. There is a secret to this thing, and we greatly suspect it is the growing appreciation of white Juliets for colored Romeos." For daring to suggest such a thing and to impugn the "honah" of white women, the author was forced out of town, and his newspaper was suppressed.[106] Under pressure, he signed a card declaring that he had not intended to slander southern white women, but Wells boldly reiterates his claim: "The editor of the *Free Speech* has no disclaimer to enter, but asserts instead that there are many white women in the South who would marry colored men if such an act would not place them at once beyond the pale of society and within the clutches of the law. . . . White men lynch the offending Afro-American, not because he is a despoiler of virtue, but because he succumbs to the smiles of white women."[107] Clearly this depiction flew in the face of deeply ingrained prejudices and offended accepted social mores.

To buttress this controversial claim, Wells turns to a series of examples, all drawn from the upper reaches of society. She cites a story from the *Cleveland Gazette* of a minister's wife who accused an African American man of rape. Although the man denied the charge of rape and insisted that he had been intimate with her at her invitation, he was tried and found guilty on her testimony. When she recanted later, she confessed that it was she who had encouraged the intimacy. Other examples involve the wife of a physician; a young girl who steals money to send her lover to Chicago; a farmer's wife who, upon giving birth to a clearly biracial child, charged three men with the crime, all of whom "disappeared"; and a woman from the "crème de la crème" of Natchez who had not one but two biracial children before her coachmen fled the city.[108] Here again Wells draws on facts to confront the cherished preconceptions of her audience; in doing so, she highlights the incongruity between the pretexts for lynchings and the truth about them.

Having deftly demonstrated that many charges of rape actually involved consensual relationships, Wells reveals the apparent hypocrisy of southerners, who are outraged when the victims are white but ignore the same act on African American women. Using the same a fortiori strategy as above, she cites cases where white men escape punishment even for the rape of young girls. "At the same time these civilized whites were announcing their determination 'to protect their wives and daughters,' by murdering Grizzard, a white man was in the same jail for raping eight-year-old Maggie Reese, an Afro-American girl. He was not harmed. . . . The outrage upon helpless childhood needed no avenging in this case; she was black." Other examples are of a young girl who is with her boyfriend when she is assaulted and a child who dies of her injuries from a rape by a white man who went unpunished.[109] At this point, Wells has confronted her audience with a strikingly different analysis than the ones to which they had been accustomed. She has disrupted normal thought patterns and rationalizations by laying painful truths in front of her audience.

In constructing her arguments, Wells is astute in her choice of materials. As seen from the preceding examples, she often chooses cases that have particular force: a physician's wife enamored of an African American man, and a child whose rape goes unpunished. In these examples and others, the implication of her argument is

"THE CLEAR, PLAIN FACTS":
THE ANTILYNCHING AGITATION
OF IDA B. WELLS

53

that if these sorts of cases occur, many others must go unnoticed and unreported. For *A Red Record*, she lists case after case to demonstrate the brutality and irrationality of lynching mobs. In one case, the mob, unable to find a young man it deems to be guilty of "outraging" a young woman, lynches the father, a respected member of the community. Another mob lynched a man because a jury had acquitted him. In still another case, she details the brutality of a lynching: thrusting a hot iron down the man's throat, burning his eyes out, and then cremating him. Still unsated, the mob lynches his stepson, against whom no charges had been made.[110] At every point, she assaults the preconceptions of her audience by presenting them with new information; she strives to unsettle their thinking and arouse their moral sentiments.

While her examples are vivid and at times horrifying, Wells also utilizes statistics to buttress her claims. In *A Red Record*, she turns to the *Chicago Tribune* for statistics on the crimes for which people were lynched in 1893. "The purpose of the pages which follow," she insists, "shall be to give the record which has been made, not by colored men, but that which is the result of compilations made by white men, of reports sent over the civilized world by white men in the South. Out of their own mouths shall the murderers be condemned."[111] The data are compelling. Of the 159 lynchings reported, 39 were for charges of rape, 8 for attempted rape, 4 for alleged rape, and 1 for the suspicion of rape. In essence, less than a third involved charges of rape. The data reveal that the vast majority of the lynchings were in the South. Wells also includes data for 1892. In that year, 241 persons were lynched, of whom 160 were African American, and, again, the vast majority were in the South. She singles out a particular case, a boy (age fourteen) and girl (age sixteen), who were lynched apparently because of a crime their father was alleged to have committed.[112] The source of the data and the data themselves establish beyond doubt the prevalence of the crime and the fact that most cases were not linked to rape.

In combination, Wells's use of argument, especially point-by-point refutation, and her skillful use of supporting materials create compelling indictments of the southern apologists. She has addressed directly and forcefully the pretexts offered to defend lynching as an understandable action. Drawing on the resources of argument and a rich variety of supporting materials, Wells has held up to her audience a new analysis on lynching, one that she hopes will create the perspective by incongruity to motivate their actions. Realizing the resistance of her audience, questions about her own ethos, and the controversial nature of her topic, Wells shrewdly and adroitly constructs powerful chains of reasoning to support her claims.

THE REMEDY

While reeducation was important to Wells, in the last analysis she also sought social change. Thus, in addition to elucidating the problem and exposing the fallacies used to justify lynchings, she needed to suggest courses of action for her audiences. For her African American listeners, she provided an array of approaches to combat the problem. For her white listeners, she hoped to encourage them to put pressure on the recalcitrant South. For both audiences, having highlighted an exigency, she proposed a solution. This problem-solution structure provided clear directions for the future.

In *Southern Horrors*, Wells encouraged her African American audiences to employ a variety of strategies to change the behaviors of the dominant white audience. She insisted that "in the creation of this healthier public sentiment, the Afro-American can do for himself what no one else can do for him."[113] Self-help was the key to success. Perhaps the most controversial was her suggestion that armed resistance was one possibility. Near the end of *Southern Horrors* she offers her advice:

The only times an Afro-American who was assaulted got away has been when he had a gun and used it in self-defense. The lesson this teaches and which every Afro-American should ponder well, is that a Winchester rifle should have a place of honor in every Black home, and it should be used for that protection which the law refuses to give. When the White man who is always the aggressor knows he runs as great [a] risk of biting the dust every time his Afro-American victim does, he will have greater respect for the Afro-American life.[114]

Realizing that the white press was unlikely to provide adequate and accurate coverage, Wells also encouraged her African American listeners to support their own newspapers, which might do justice to the story. "The Afro-American papers are the only ones which will print the truth, and they lack means to employ agents and detectives to get at the facts. The race must rally a mighty host to support of their journals, and thus enable them to do much in the way of investigation."[115]

Another alternative she proposes is a mass exodus from the area where such crimes are perpetrated. Because the South is dependent on the labor of African Americans, this course of action might aid the cause. "To Northern capital and Afro-American labor the South owes its rehabilitation. If labor is withdrawn capital will not remain. The Afro-American is thus the backbone of the South." She offers the example of the actions of African Americans in Memphis after the lynchings of her three friends. First urging authorities to take appropriate action and receiving no response, the African American citizens "left the city by thousands, bringing about great stagnation in every branch of business. Those who remained so injured the business of the street car company by staying off the cars, that the superintendent, manager and treasurer called personally the editor of the 'Free Speech,' [sic] asked them to urge our people to give them their patronage again." Pressure mounted, and finally after three months the white citizens passed a resolution to condemn the lynchings. But no punishment ensued.[116]

In *A Red Record*, she lists five distinct actions that her audience may pursue:

1st You can help disseminate the facts contained in this book by bringing them to the knowledge of everyone with whom you come in contact. . . . Let the facts speak for themselves with you as the medium.

2nd You can be instrumental in having churches, missionary societies, Y.M.C.A.'s, W.C.T.U's and all Christian and moral forces . . . pass resolutions of condemnation and protest every time a lynching takes place and see that they are sent to the place where the outrages occur.

3rd Bring to the intelligent consideration of Southern people the refusal of capital to invest where lawlessness and mob violence hold sway. . . .

4th Think and act on independent lines in this behalf, remembering that after all, it is the white man's civilization and the white man's government which are on trial. . . .

5th Congressman Blair offered a resolution in the House of Representatives, August, 1894. The organized life of the country can speedily make this a law by sending resolutions to Congress indorsing Mr. Blair's bill and asking Congress to create the commission.

In answer to the question "'What can I do to help the cause?' The answer is always 'Tell the world the facts.'" Then, she believed, a Christian nation would find a way to stop the outrage.[117]

Wells was less clear in her instructions to her white audiences. Clearly, she hoped to raise their awareness of the scope of the brutality. Also, she hoped that when confronted with the "plain facts," persons of conscience would realize the need for change. She believed that at least some white Americans would understand what must be done. In her preface to the pamphlet *Southern Horrors*, Wells describes the work as "a contribution to the truth, an array of acts, the perusal of which it is hoped will stimulate this great American Republic to demand that justice be done though the heavens fall." She adds: "The Afro-American is not a bestial race. If this work can contribute in any way toward proving this, and at the same time arouse the conscience of the American people to a demand for justice to every citizen, and punishment by law for the lawless, I shall feel I have done my race a service."[118]

Impact of Her Advocacy

Assessing Wells's impact is difficult. In her autobiography, she claims "some little success" in her journalistic career, providing excerpts from contemporary admirers to support her conclusion. She first cites T. Thomas Fortune, editor of the *New York Age*: "She has become famous as one of the few of our women who handle a goose quill with diamond point as easily as any man in newspaper work. . . . She has plenty of nerve and is as sharp as a steel trap. . . . Decidedly Iola is a great success in journalism and we can feel proud of a woman whose ability and energy serve to make her so."[119] Continuing in the same vein, Wells quotes Lucy W. Smith, without identifying her further: "No writer, the male fraternity not excepted, has been more extensively quoted, none struck harder blows at the wrongs and weakness of the race. Her readers are equally divided between the sexes. She reaches the men by dealing with the political aspect of the race question, and the women she meets around the fireside."[120] A contemporary admirer, Gertrude Mossell, quotes Wells herself regarding the response to her oratorical campaign: "The Afro-American has the ear of the civilized world for the first time since emancipation."[121] This evidence suggests that Wells's approach had at least stimulated the thinking of contemporary listeners by exposing the hypocrisies in the defenses of lynching.

Wells was clearly not reticent in evaluating her own impact. In her autobiography, she suggests that her 1892 speech "Southern Horrors" and the pamphlet based on it had several long-range effects. She claimed it stimulated the beginning of organized black women's clubs. Following her speech, the women of New York, Brooklyn, and Boston formed the Women's Loyal Union and the Women's Era Club under the leadership of Josephine St. Pierre Ruffin and others. The organizations formed by black women during this time were united in 1896 as the National Association of Colored Women (NACW), with Mary Church Terrell as its first president.[122] Of course, the speech also launched Wells's own public speaking career, a career that would continue until her death in 1931. As a result of the speech, she met Catherine Impey, from England, who was editor of the *Anti-Caste*, "a magazine published in England in behalf of the natives of India." Because Impey was interested in "the treatment of darker races everywhere," she would later invite Wells to what became a successful speaking tour in England.[123] By giving the issue national and international attention, that tour in turn launched a worldwide campaign against lynching. Before she left England, the British Anti-Lynching Committee was formed, and in Aberdeen, Scotland, the Society for the Recognition of the Brotherhood of Man was created. [124]

In reality, in 1892 most of the white press paid little attention to *Southern Horrors*, with the exception of the jurist and writer Albion Tourgée, who commented frequently in his *Inter Ocean* column on the number of black men being lynched. In *Crusade for Justice*, Wells acknowledges that "only the *Inter Ocean* among the dailies and Judge A. W. Tourgée as an individual, had given any systematic attention and discussion to the subject from the standpoint of equal and exact justice to all the condemnation of lynching."[125]

Recent scholars agree with some of Wells's assessments. Paula Giddings describes the impact of the international campaign launched by the "Southern Horrors" speech:

> The number of lynchings decreased in 1893—and continued to do so thereafter. The decline in the murders can be directly attributed to the efforts of Ida B. Wells. The effect of Wells's campaign was aptly demonstrated in her home city. Memphis exported more cotton than any other city in the world, and Wells's assertions had been especially damaging to its image. So, as a direct result of her efforts, the city fathers were pressed to take an official stand against lynching—and for the next twenty years there was not another incident of vigilante violence there.[126]

Giddings's direct causal linkages seem tenuous, but undoubtedly Wells helped raise public consciousness of the issue. Further, Giddings notes that the speech had more far-reaching consequences: "[It] had not only helped to launch the modern civil rights movement, but it had brought Black women into the forefront of the struggle for Black and women's rights."[127] Bettina Aptheker suggests an important impact of Wells's arguments: "In defending the racial integrity of Black manhood, Wells simultaneously affirmed the virtue of Black womanhood, and the independence of White womanhood. For the dialectics of the lynch mentality required the dehumanization of Black men (as rapists), Black women (as prostitutes), and White women (as property whose honor was to be avenged by the men who possessed them)."[128]

Wells's contribution was to begin to deconstruct the most firmly held beliefs and prejudices supporting the persistence of mob violence against African Americans. Her goal was to begin to force her audience to abandon its facile analyses of lynching, analyses grounded in misconceptions and misinformation. By holding contemporary defenses of the practice up to scrutiny in the light of evidence, Wells began to create the perspective by incongruity that would finally compel social change. As Jacqueline Jones Royster explains:

> Wells' case suggested that lynching encoded several race and gender stereotypes regarding pleasure and desire: White women were pure, virginal, and uninterested in sexual pleasure. They needed and deserved protection. African American women were wanton, licentious, promiscuous. White men . . . could not be accused of raping "bad" women. "Bad," immoral women did not need protection. African American women, as amoral women, were not capable of providing moral influence on African American women or anyone else. African American men were lustful beasts who could not be trusted in the company of "good," white women. . . . Wells' argument declared all this to be false: cover stories designed to perpetuate an evil mythology.

As Royster notes, Wells had to "dismantle stereotypes that were based on both gender and race," no small challenge.[129] But as we have seen, Wells skillfully drew on the resources of argument and evidence to force her audience to see the disparity between their preconceptions about and the facts of lynching. She was adroit in creating the potential for a perspective by incongruity that Burke sees as a path to social change.

Ida B. Wells worked "verbal magic" with her antilynching discourse—heightening consciousness, changing perceptions, stimulating the imagination, and initiating action through tactics of delivery, arrangement, and style. She employed selective description to persuade audiences geographically and emotionally removed from the circumstances to which they were asked to respond. Wells's discourse not only highlighted the act of lynching, making it salient for her listeners, but she also laid bare the motives of the perpetrators and their enjoyment of the brutal practice.

Initially, many white northerners who heard her were probably reluctant to respond because they were being asked not only to question the motives of their fellow citizens in the South, with whom they were attempting to mend the broken fences of the Civil War, but also to question the virtue of the southern woman and to give up some of their own stereotypes about black men. However, the examples Wells uses, the unflinching details she provides about the crimes, and the pictures that sometimes accompany her publications all worked to create an awareness of the issue. If northern whites did not act, they could no longer ignore the lawlessness and brutality.

In his introduction to Wells's autobiography, John Hope Franklin summarizes her contributions: "For more than forty years Ida B. Wells was one of the most fearless and one of the most respected women in the United States. She was also one of the most articulate. . . . By the written and spoken word she laid bare the barbarism and inhumanity of the rope and faggot. Through her visits she became nearly as well known in England as she was in the United States, for she was determined that the entire world should know her native land for what it really was."[130]

Rhetorical Implications

Wells's principal rhetorical challenge lay in her audience, its lack of awareness of lynching, its indifference, and its racial biases. Although reports of lynchings were commonplace in her day, they did not rouse indignation or action in Americans of the time. In many ways, cultural biases and social practices blinded Americans to the issue. Any evaluation of her as a rhetor must, then, take into consideration how she met the challenge of arousing her listeners.

Her extensive use of examples as well as her frequent references to statistical data led virtually inexorably to her conclusions. In her pamphlets, most notably *A Red Record*, she included pictures of actual lynchings as well as drawings to add even greater force to her case. Her evidence was simply too substantial and too coherent to be dismissed. Further, Wells's repetition of a standard slate of arguments in various forums created a rhetorical presence for her topic.

But overcoming the ingrained social biases of her audiences was no simple matter. Wells seemed to understand the challenge in overturning the trained incapacities of her listeners. The description of some brutalities added vividness; the examples of people lynched who had no charges against them highlighted the rampant injustices; the cases of abused African American children whose victimizers went unpunished added poignancy. Wells realized that she needed to unsettle her audience's usual thought patterns by juxtaposing the truth against the preconceptions about lynching.

The alternatives Wells provided for her audience also helped build presence and overcome their trained incapacities. Her African American listeners had a range of options; everyone could at least support an African American paper that publicized lynching. Her white listeners need only insist on the application of existing laws; they need not advocate for dramatic social change. For both groups of listeners, Wells's appeals were grounded in political truths and religious principles. She simply called on Americans to live up to and live out the principles they held dear.

No one could call Wells eloquent. She was impassioned, focused, committed. If her discourse lacks subtlety and even polish, one must remember that her challenge was to rouse those who preferred to remain ignorant. Her rhetorical skill and achievement lie in her ability to understand her challenges and to marshal her resources to address them. Even today one cannot read her pamphlets without being moved to indignation. Her work endures as a model for effective, sustained public advocacy.

In a conversation with Frederick Douglass in Providence, Rhode Island, while both were waiting backstage to speak, Wells explained the contrast between his nervousness and her composure. "That is because you are an orator, Mr. Douglass, and naturally you are concerned as to the presentation of your address. With me it is different. I am only a mouthpiece through which to tell the story of lynching and I have told it so often that I know it by heart. I do not have to embellish; it makes its own way."[131] But, of course, there was art as well as nature in Wells's discourse against mob violence.

This analysis suggest that, in many respects, her art and her strategies were shaped by the experiences of her own life, a life providing a model for resistance. Her resistance was demonstrated in her refusal to move to the smoking car of a train and her subsequent lawsuit against the offending railroad. Her resistance was evident in her decision to publish an article in *Free Speech* criticizing conditions in the black Memphis schools, which resulted in the loss of her teaching job. But her best-known act of resistance was the barrage of editorial appeals in *Free Speech* following the murders of her three friends. Revealing the true motives for lynching, these editorials urged African Americans to leave Memphis and ultimately prevented her from returning to the city for many years.

In light of her history of defiance, it is not surprising that her rhetorical strategies also evince resistance. To some extent, the subject itself, white mob violence, dictated a confrontational stance. As Robert Stepto points out in his study of African American narrative, Booker T. Washington's *Up from Slavery*, written nearly ten years after Wells's first antilynching speech, only "cautiously inveighs against 'the evil habit of lynching.'"[132] In contrast to Washington, Wells was willing to risk condemnation to speak her truth. Her use of statistics, her suppression of emotion, her marshaling of example after example, her admonitions about a course of action, her clear statement of true motivation for lynching—all converge to produce a text that was direct and confrontational, yet factually irrefutable. An obituary in the *Chicago Defender* described Wells as "somewhat intolerant and impulsive."[133] Perhaps a more fitting description is that, true to her convictions, Ida B. Wells spoke out forcefully against conditions that others were willing to tolerate. In a very real sense, she typified William Lloyd Garrison's determination for his own advocacy: she was in earnest; she did not equivocate; she did not excuse; she did not retreat a single inch; and she was heard.

Notes

1. George Fitzhugh, "What's to Be Done with the Negroes?" *DeBow's Review* (June 1866): 578.
2. Kirt H. Wilson, *The Reconstruction Desegregation Debate: The Politics of Equality and the Rhetoric of Place, 1870–1875* (East Lansing: Michigan State University Press, 2002) 13.
3. C. Vann Woodward, *The Strange Career of Jim Crow* (New York: Oxford University Press, 1957), xv, 15.
4. Samuel Eliot Morrison, Henry Steele Commager, and William E. Leuchtenburg, *A Concise History of the American Republic*, 2nd ed. (New York: Oxford, University Press, 1983), 357. See Wilson, *Reconstruction*, for a detailed, complex, and nuanced analysis of this statute.
5. Morrison, Commager, and Leuchtenburg, *Concise History*, 357.
6. Qtd. in Wilson, *Reconstruction*, 357.
7. Rayford Logan, *The Negro in American Life and Thought: The Nadir, 1877–1901* (New York: Dial, 1954), 46.
8. Ibid., 97.

9. Frederick Douglass, "Speech at Lincoln Hall," qtd. in Wilson, *Reconstruction*, 16.

10. Woodward, *Strange Career*, 67, 69.

11. Qtd. in ibid., xvi.

12. Ibid., 82.

13. Qtd. in Morrison, Commager, and Leuchtenburg, *Concise History*, 358.

14. Wilson, *Reconstruction Desegregation Debate*, 13.

15. Morrison, Commager, and Leuchtenburg, *Concise History*, 341.

16. Although the term "lynching" was often associated with a variety of lawless punishments inflicted upon suspected persons, by the end of the nineteenth century it had come to mean summary and illegal capital punishment at the hands of a mob.

17. Lerone Bennett Jr., *Before the Mayflower: A History of Black America* (New York: Penguin, 1962), 505.

18. Logan, *Negro in American Life*, 76. For obvious reasons, determining the exact number of lynchings is impossible. Wells, for example, sometimes claimed that 10,000 lynchings had occurred. The Tuskegee Archives suggests 1,297 whites and 3,446 blacks were lynched between 1882 and 1968. See . The authors appreciate Amy Slagell's drawing our attention to this source.

19. For excerpts from these testimonies, see Gerda Lerner, ed., *Black Women in White America: A Documentary History* (New York: Vintage Books, 1972), 172–88.

20. Patricia A. Schecter, *Ida B. Wells-Barnett and American Reform, 1880–1930* (Chapel Hill: University of North Carolina Press, 2001), 11.

21. Ibid., 11.

22. Ida B. Wells, *Crusade for Justice: The Autobiography of Ida B. Wells*, ed. Alfreda M. Duster (Chicago: University of Chicago Press, 1970), 9.

23. Ibid., 9.

24. Although the college was chartered as Shaw University in 1870 in recognition of a $10,000 gift from the Reverend S. P. Shaw to erect the first building, it was informally called Rust College after Richard Rust, general field superintendent of the Freedman's Aid Society. In 1890 the name was officially changed to Rust University to avoid confusion with Shaw University in Raleigh, North Carolina.

25. William Baskerville Hamilton, *Holly Springs, Mississippi, to the Year 1878* (Holly Springs, Miss.: Marshall County Historical Society, 1984), 43.

26. Ibid.

27. James D. Anderson, *The Education of Blacks in the South, 1860–1935* (Chapel Hill: University of North Carolina Press, 1988), 6–7. For example, a "native school" in Savannah, Georgia, had functioned in secret from 1833 to 1865. Former slaves also recall "pit schools" hidden in the woods, where slaves would gather for reading lessons. See also Ira Berlin, Marc Favreau, and Steven F. Miller, eds., *Remembering Slavery: African Americans Talk about Their Personal Experiences of Slavery and Freedom* (New York: New Press, 1998), 206.

28. For more information about Rust College, see its Web site at www.rustcollege.edu.

29. Miriam Decosta-Willis, *The Memphis Diary of Ida B. Wells* (Boston: Beacon, 1995), 4, 5.

30. Ibid., 4, 5.

31. Linda O. McMurry, *To Keep the Waters Troubled: The Life of Ida B. Wells* (New York: Oxford, 1998), 13.

32. McMurry observes that in T. Thomas Fortune's biographical sketch of Wells in Scruggs's *Women of Distinction* (1893), he writes that Wells continued to attend Rust intermittently for three years while teaching in the area (*To Keep the Waters Troubled*, 342 n33).

33. Decosta-Willis, *Memphis Diary*, 24.

34. Although by the turn of the century Wells was a widely recognized public figure who had been awarded an honorary Master of Arts degree from Rust in recognition of her leadership in the Memphis antilynching initiatives, curiously, the 1924 *History of Rust College* does not list her among its outstanding former students. Lawson Scruggs, *Women of Distinction: Remarkable in Works and Invincible in Character* (Raleigh, N.C.: Author, 1893), 38.

35. Wells, *Crusade*, 22.

36. Ishmell Hendrex Edwards, "History of Rust College 1866–1967" (Ph.D. diss., University of Mississippi, 1994).

37. Mary M. Boone Hutton, "Ida B. Wells Barnett (1862–1931), Agitator for African-American Rights," in *Women Public Speakers in the United States, 1800–1925: A Bio-Critical Sourcebook*, ed. Karlyn Kohrs Campbell (Westport, Conn.: Greenwood Press, 1993), 462.

38. Wells, *Crusade*, 22.

39. Decosta-Willis, *Memphis Diary*, 39.

40. Ibid.

41. Wells, *Crusade*, 18.

42. Ibid., 19.

43. Ibid.

44. Ibid., 20.

45. Ibid., 22.

46. For an intriguing history of the lyceum movement, see Angela Ray, *Lyceum and Public Culture in the Nineteenth-Century United States* (East Lansing: Michigan State University Press, 2005).

47. Ray, *Lyceum*, 22.

48. Ibid., 23.

49. Ibid., 23, 24.

50. Ibid., 35.

51. Ibid., 36. No text of this editorial is available.

52. Qtd. in Hutton, "Ida B. Wells Barnett," 464.

53. Ibid.

54. McMurry, *To Keep the Waters Troubled*, 124.

55. Wells, *Crusade*, 33.

56. Ibid., 47.

57. Qtd. in Hutton, "Ida B. Wells Barnett," 464.

58. Wells, *Crusade*, 64.

59. Ida B. Wells, *Southern Horrors: Lynch Law in All Its Phases* (1892; reprint, New Orleans: Ayer Press, 1990), 4.

60. Ibid., 6.

61. Wells, *Crusade*, 77.

62. Hutton, "Ida B. Wells Barnett," 465.

63. Wells, *Crusade*, 78, 79, 81.

64. Hutton, "Ida B. Wells Barnett," 465.

65. Ibid., 465–66.

66. Wells, *Crusade*, 79.

67. Ibid., 79–80.

68. Ibid., 86.

69. Ibid., 100–101, 128.

70. Ibid., 95, 107.

71. Ida B. Wells, "Lynch Law in All its Phases," in *With Pen and Voice: A Critical Anthology of Nineteenth-Century African-American Women*, ed. Shirley Wilson Logan (Carbondale: Southern Illinois University Press, 1995), 80–105.

72. Hutton, "Ida B. Wells Barnett," 466.

73. Qtd. in Schecter, *Ida B. Wells-Barnett*, 99.

74. Wells, *Crusade*, 190.

75. Hutton, "Ida B. Wells Barnett," 466–67.

76. Ibid., 467.

77. Qtd. in Schecter, *Ida B. Wells-Barnett*, 112.

78. Hutton, "Ida B. Wells Barnett," 467.

79. Schecter, *Ida B. Wells-Barnett*, 212.

80. Ibid., 188–89.

81. Wells, *Crusade*, 333.

82. Schecter, *Ida B. Wells-Barnett*, 135–37. Of course, she saw the omission as strong evidence that some leaders, notably W. E. B. DuBois, did not support her settlement work or her antilynching efforts.

83. Ibid., 198, 200.

84. Qtd. in Hutton, "Ida B. Wells Barnett," 469.

85. Karlyn Kohrs Campbell, *Man Cannot Speak for Her*, vol. 2, (New York: Greenwood Press, 1989), 385. Campbell indicates that Wells gave a similar speech in February in Washington, D.C., with an introduction by Mary Church Terrell. In the pamphlet form, the text was prefaced by a letter from Frederick Douglass.

86. Kenneth Burke, *Attitudes Toward History*, 3rd ed. (Berkeley: University of California Press, 1984), 308–11.

87. "A Red Record Made Public" was the title of a pamphlet first published by Wells in 1895. For this analysis, we will rely on a reprint of the work contained in *Selected Works of Ida B. Wells-Barnett*, ed. and comp. by Trudier Harris (New York: Oxford University Press, 1991).

88. Chaim Perelman, *The Realm of Rhetoric* (Notre Dame, Ind.: University of Notre Dame Press, 1982), 35.
89. Ibid., 37–38.
90. Kenneth Burke, *Permanence and Change* (Berkeley: University of California Press, 1984), 7, 9–10.
91. Thomas Nelson Page, "The Lynching of Negroes—Its Causes and Its Prevention," *North American Review* 178, no. 566 (January 1904): 33, 34.
92. Of course, any application of miscegenation statutes was deeply embedded in the heavily gendered politics of the day. So, for example, these laws were not enforced to punish slaveholders who routinely had sexual relationships with women they owned.
93. Wells, *Crusade*, 86.
94. Wells, *Southern Horrors*, 42.
95. Ida B. Wells, "A Red Record Made Public," in *Selected Works of Ida B. Wells-Barnett*, ed. and comp. Trudier Harris (New York: Oxford University Press, 1991), 140.
96. Ibid., 141.
97. Wells, *Southern Horrors*; Ida B. Wells, "Southern Horrors: The Lynch Law in All Its Phases," in *Selected Works of Ida B. Wells-Barnett*, ed. and comp. Trudier Harris (New York: Oxford University Press, 1991), 16.
98. Wells, "Southern Horrors," 17.
99. Wells, *Crusade*, 117.
100. Ida B. Wells, "The Reason Why the Colored American Is Not in the World's Columbian Exposition," in *Selected Works of Ida B. Wells-Barnett*, ed. and comp. Trudier Harris (New York: Oxford University Press, 1991), 75.
101. Wells, "Red Record," 141.
102. Ibid., 141, 142.
103. Burke, *Attitudes Toward History*, 308–311.
104. Ibid., 142, 143.
105. Ibid., 144.
106. Wells, *Southern Horrors*, 19.
107. Wells, "Red Record," 19.
108. Wells, *Southern Horrors*, 20, 22–25.
109. Ibid., 27.
110. Wells, "Red Record," 173-75.
111. Ibid., 150.
112. Ibid., 150–57.
113. Wells, *Southern Horrors*, 40.
114. Ibid., 23.
115. Ibid., 43.
116. Ibid., 40.
117. Wells, "Red Record," 248–49, 251.
118. Wells, *Southern Horrors*, 14–15.
119. Ibid., 32, 33. The precise source of this citation is difficult to trace in her autobiography. Although she attributes this comment to Fortune, her footnote seems to identify the following as the source: Henry Davenport, Joseph R. Gay, and I. Garland Penn, *The College of Life; or, Practical Self-Educator: A Manual of Self-Improvement of the Colored Race* (Chicago: Chicago Publication and Lithograph Company, 1895), 100.
120. Wells, *Crusade*, 33.
121. Gertrude B. Mossell, *The Work of the Afro American Woman.* (1894; reprint, New York: Oxford University Press, 1988), 45.
122. Wells, *Crusade*, 81–82.
123. Ibid., 82.
124. Ibid., 90, 215.
125. Ibid., 156.
126. Paula Giddings, *When and Where I Enter: The Impact of Black Women on Race and Sex in America* (New York: Bantam), 94.
127. Ibid., 92.
128. Bettina Aptheker, "Woman Suffrage and the Crusade against Lynching, 1890–1920," in *Woman's Legacy: Essays on Race, Sex, and Class in American History* (Amherst: University of Massachusetts Press, 1982), 62.

129. Jacqueline Jones Royster, "Introduction: Equity and Justice for All," in *Southern Horrors and Other Writings: The Anti-Lynching Campaign of Ida B. Wells, 1892–1900*, Ida B. Wells, ed. Jacqueline Jones Royster (Boston: Bedford/St. Martin's, 1997), 30.
130. Wells, *Crusade*, ix ("Editor's Forward").
131. Ibid., 231.
132. Robert B. Stepto, *From Behind the Veil: A Study of Afro-American Narrative* (Urbana: University of Illinois Press, 1979), 39.
133. Emilie Townes, "Ida B. Wells-Barnett: An Afro-American Prophet," *Christian Century* 106 (1989): 285–86.

Finding the Angel's Lily: Redefining American Character in the Rhetoric of Russell H. Conwell

A. Cheree Carlson

3

Russell Herman Conwell (1843–1925), minister, lecturer, lawyer, reporter, is best remembered as a nineteenth-century version of the "one-trick pony." His most popular lecture, "Acres of Diamonds," has been touted as "the Mother of all motivational speeches."[1] Between 1870 and 1925, Conwell earned more than $8 million delivering it over and over to audiences across the country.[2] The speech was, perhaps, too successful. Editors of speech collections still get requests for "Acres," and rhetorical critics continued to analyze it well into the twentieth century.[3] With the exception of Mary Louise Gehring, who wrote both her thesis and dissertation on Conwell, critics have focused on the single lecture to the exclusion of the rest of Conwell's vast body of work. This is unfortunate because, although popular, "Acres" is unquestionably conservative, shallow, and simplistic; focusing on this speech alone has led critics to dismiss Conwell as another in a long line of ministers who put God's stamp of approval on the rising industrial capitalist powers of the United States.[4] Such easy dismissal causes us to lose sight of the fact that throughout his career, Conwell promoted a vision of America that responded ingeniously, if not radically, to the prevailing social forces put into motion by the rapid industrialization of the economy. He attempted to create what Kenneth Burke would term a comic transcendence of the new social order.

Burke's theory of symbolic action is aimed at promoting humane perspectives from which to create new social structures. For Burke, it is a moral imperative that creative communicators use their art as a corrective to whatever extreme directions the social order might be taking, to prevent "a society from becoming too assertively, too hopelessly, itself."[5] If society is becoming too materialistic, then one's symbols should hint at spirituality; if it becomes too religious, counter with the profane. The ethical communicator seeks balance by "leaning" against the majority.

There are, of course, many ways to "lean" depending upon the frame of reference from which the communicator operates. Burke's hope is that rhetorical criticism will discover ways of operating from a "comic" perspective. "Comedy," in this case, is not humor, but simply an open acknowledgment that no social order is perfect, and that people can be mistaken in the strategies they construct to rule their lives. The comic perspective has its eyes wide open to the flaws in a social order, but still recognizes that the order has a right to exist. It seeks to "correct error" in a charitable manner, with the goal of reconstructing social practices as positively as possible, given that no social order, and no member of it, can be perfect. Burke is emphatic about the importance of promoting the comic over the prevailing mode of social change: "[M]ankind's only hope is a cult of comedy. (The cult of tragedy is too eager to help out with the holocaust. And in the last analogy it is too pretentious to allow for the proper recognition of our animality.)"[6]

Conwell's career was largely an attempt to apply such a comic corrective. He was extremely successful at that task. The money garnered through "Acres" was enough to endow an entire university, Temple University, and build a major hospital. As Agnes Rush Burr, Conwell's contemporary, put it:

> Have you or your friends tried to compute the enormous influence of that lecture in *adding to the wealth of our country*? I have seen so many vivid results, and have heard so many, that it seems one of the greatest benefactions of our age. *Enormous* is a conservative word. So many villages have become cities directly in consequence of your lecture; so many individuals and societies started "to do something" for their town; . . . [s]o many reforms made triumphant; indeed, so much good done by that lecture that I stand amazed at the accumulation.[7]

However, Conwell was much more than a single-speech orator. During his successful speaking career, he delivered several other popular lectures that were widely reprinted. As a minister, he prepared and delivered a multitude of sermons that were so well received that his Baptist church in Philadelphia had the largest Protestant congregation in the United States. His sermons and speeches were collected into books, and for good measure, he wrote a few books of entirely new material. He was arguably one of the most influential clergymen of his era. This influence did not entirely die with Conwell; "Acres" is still being reprinted, and in 1985 one wealthy woman inspired by his works donated $5 million to Temple University.[8]

Yet Gehring dismisses Conwell with the claim that "neither in his sermons nor in his lectures is there anything to indicate that he saw deeply into any particular issue of his day. The technical craftsmanship of his lectures is not particularly outstanding."[9] Her attitude is echoed in Robert T. Oliver's history of American public address.[10] Obviously, something is amiss if an orator whom critics judge to be such a poor specimen can have such an impact on audiences.

A more charitable assessment arises if we take the comic road posited by Burke. Conwell was not a merely a shallow "get-rich-quick" preacher, but rather a comic artist doing his best to counter the social tendencies of his time. Although Conwell might not have been a deep thinker about social issues, he was fully aware of the psychological pressure suffered by his audience as the country began to value industrial wealth above all other goals, and sought a remedy. Through his oratory, he was able to transcend the tensions between the old agrarian culture and the new industrial culture that coexisted in the United States at the end of the nineteenth century. He accomplished this through a unique presentation of the fairly standard "gospel of wealth" that borrowed symbols from the concepts of individualism and collectivism that were battling for dominance in the social order. Conwell's strategy was to redefine "wealth" as an individual characteristic that could be developed, rather than as a material good. Money did not matter; personal character did.

Wealth was to be used to help the poor develop the internal resources they needed to succeed. His favorite aphorism was "To help a man help himself is the wisest effort of human love."[11] His goal, then, was to help individuals succeed by creating better individuals.

Conwell pursued this goal in various ways, but his greatest emphasis was on oral persuasion. In a multitude of speeches and sermons, he attempted to inspire people to redefine the meaning of their lives so that they could seek their own individual goals while still accepting the new, more collective order. Thus Conwell sought to change American society for the better through the medium of the platform, an ambitious goal that he approached with great skill. This essay surveys a number of texts created by Conwell during his long career to illustrate how he carefully selected and structured narratives to move audiences toward an acceptance of his vision.

I first lay out the cultural context for the tensions dealt with by Conwell. Then, through an analysis of his body of work, I demonstrate how Conwell responded to these tensions. The analysis is based upon the following texts: four versions of "Acres of Diamonds" as it varied in the decades between 1887 and 1926;[12] two other popular Chautauqua lectures, "The Angel's Lily"[13] and "The Silver Crown";[14] three collections of sermons;[15] and a variety of incidental speeches and writings.[16] After the analysis, I discuss both the strengths and limitations of comic acceptance as a way of dealing with social change.

Conwell's Emergence as a Rhetorical Leader

To understand fully the driving force behind an orator's rhetoric, it is helpful to unearth what Burke calls the "representative anecdote" used by the orator.[17] A representative anecdote is a single compelling event or image that informs and constrains the range of symbolic elements used in the entire body of work. Conwell often served as his own representative anecdote. His life was almost a direct reflection of the dramatic tension existing in the United States in the late nineteenth century. In a sense, every story Conwell told to an audience allowed him to relive the struggle of his own life. He utilized certain moments to set up key tensions that he saw reflected in the lives of others.

One central tenet of Conwell's rhetoric was that people profit most by working to improve their own communities: "Let every man or woman here, if you never hear me again, remember this, that if you wish to be great at all, you must begin where you are and as what you are."[18] Conwell violated that advice from the first. In boyhood, he confessed, "I felt that there were great worlds for me to conquer which I could never find in my native hills."[19] He ran away from home for the first time at thirteen; when he was brought home he tried again. He went to sea for a short time, but was finally forced to return to his father's farm. Eventually, he settled down long enough to work his way through Yale. Although this was no small accomplishment, his strongest memories of those years were of the misery of being poor.[20] Education did not make up for the humiliation heaped upon him by his wealthier classmates. Thus, although Conwell sought his fortune in the outside world, his rewards were small. In fact, some events seemed tailored to make Conwell wish he had stayed on the farm. This period of Conwell's life set up the first tension, between the two contradictory desires of leaving and staying home.

When the Civil War began, Conwell once more became a wanderer, this time as a Union officer. Prophetically, on the verge of building a career, he found himself under court-martial for desertion. He did not flee from battle, he simply went to visit a nearby town without receiving permission. Conwell's biographers defend him on this charge by noting that his motive was to check on a delayed payroll shipment.

Unfortunately, the camp was raided while he was away. His personal aide-de-camp was killed attempting to keep Conwell's ceremonial sword out of enemy hands. When Conwell learned this result of his absence, he collapsed and became dangerously ill. As Conwell later told it, this event converted him to Christianity and gave him the drive to help others, because he had "two lives" to live—for himself and for his fallen comrade. Conwell never tired of telling the story of that fateful decision:

> When I stood beside the body of John Ring and realized that he had died for love of me, I made a vow that has formed my life. I vowed that from that moment I would live not only my own life, but that I would also live the life of John Ring. And from that moment I have worked sixteen hours every day—eight for John Ring's work and eight hours for my own.[21]

This melodramatic tale became the representative anecdote for Conwell's entire life. It focused on the tension between personal ambition and altruism and demonstrated how that tension could be eased. So all-encompassing was this symbolic pair that John W. Stokes even titled a biography of Conwell *The Man Who Lived Two Lives.*[22]

Despite this dramatic conversion, Conwell spent a few more years roaming the world in search of his fortune. He tried his hand at law and had a brief but successful career in journalism as a roving reporter touring Civil War battlefields. Eventually, he decided to go on the lecture circuit with his collection of Civil War stories, but for the most part the rewards came "in the shape of a jack-knife, a ham, a book, and the first cash remuneration was from a farmers' club, of seventy-five cents toward the 'horse hire.'"[23] In 1874 his marriage to a wealthy young widow ended his financial worries. Having retained his ties to the Baptist church during this period, he accepted a call to ministry that same year. He was ordained soon after and became pastor of the Grace Baptist Church in Philadelphia in 1882. There he stayed, after his fashion, for the next forty-three years.

In the church Conwell found the perfect forum from which to pursue his seemingly contradictory goals. Having early discovered a talent for public speaking, he used that talent as a means to personal ends. "Acres of Diamonds," which he had initially delivered as entertainment at a reunion of his old regiment, quickly became one of his most popular fund-raisers. He was soon on the road again and spent the greater portion of each year at speaking engagements. Delivering speeches at churches and Chautauquas across the country allowed him to conciliate his twin needs for travel and security, for he could always return to Philadelphia to see to his flock. What the congregation thought about having an absentee pastor is not recorded. Conwell was lionized as one of the great speakers of his day and almost hailed as a saint. He donated most of his vast earnings to the newly built Temple University. Conwell, at last, seemed to have put his life in order. He then dedicated himself to helping others put their lives on what he believed was the proper road.

Conwell and the Changing Scene

One reason Conwell could call upon his own transformation as a representative anecdote is that it mirrored the lives of many other middle-class Americans of the era. Social historian Michael Kammen calls Americans "people of paradox" precisely because they have traditionally needed to balance many apparently contradictory ideas that infuse their culture.[24] The late nineteenth century was a period of rapid social change. First, the nature of community social life altered. While the early expansion of the frontier had allowed Americans to celebrate the agrarian ideal of the individual farmer who lived and worked in a small communal setting, the closing of that frontier forced an increasing number of citizens to work at industrial labor in large cities. Second, the economic basis of social life was changing. The traditional "American Dream" that prized individual entrepreneurship and offered great wealth to anyone willing to work hard enough was coming to an end. The age of the wealthy industrialist had begun. These changes did not go unnoticed. According to Robert H. Wiebe: "In a manner that eludes precise explanation, countless citizens in towns and cities across the land sensed that something fundamental was happening to their lives, something they had not willed and did not want, and they responded by striking out at whatever enemies their view of the world allowed them to see. They fought, in other words, to preserve the society that had given their lives meaning."[25] The world was changing rapidly, and the resulting tensions made audiences desperate to find a way of resolving the clash between the old and new ways of life.

The first problem was the changing nature of community life that arose from both geographic and economic limitations. Geography dictated a change in culture as the vast frontiers of the continent filled with settlers. Daniel Bjork observes that Americans traditionally valued westward movement: "The meaning of America was entangled in its need to move. A peripatetic society was born in movement from Europe and developed amidst a multitude of wanderings."[26] Once the frontier was settled, however, this need was balanced by the need for collective development, the building of homes and communities that would provide a stable life. Each individual had to decide whether to leave or stay at home. Each had to worry about consequences of that decision. This tension actually worsened as it became more and more difficult for people to move. In 1890 the federal government declared the frontier officially "closed," and ceased offering incentives to settlement.[27] Those who accepted the idea that opportunities derived from expansion found no more symbolic "territory" to explore. Soon economic opportunities were focused upon collective forms of development: one no longer survived by working for oneself, but by working for a company. Even the archetypes began to shift. As James Oliver Robertson notes, the independent frontiersman and yeoman farmer gave way to the cowboy, who was, in the final analysis, someone's employee.[28] Thus the pressure to join the collectivity increased for citizens in a nation built initially on rugged individualism.

Another concept undergoing change was the role of wealth in the social order. Middle-class Americans were richer than they had ever been, yet discontent continued.[29] The Horatio Alger myth still held sway in the popular belief that anyone who worked hard enough could become wealthy, yet less and less evidence suggested that this myth was reliable. Merle Curti notes that as the nineteenth century progressed, fewer opportunities emerged for such material advancement, until the turn of the century marked, for all practical purposes, the end of the dream.[30] Americans widely believed that their declining opportunities were the result of rising industrialism and that "great corporations were stifling opportunity," writes Wiebe.[31] In Michael Kammen's view, this slow change set the stage for another tension "manifest in their wish to succeed, but also in their wish to change the criteria for success."[32] Conwell shared their concern, and quickly moved to ease that tension by redefining the criteria for "success" so that it no longer required accumulating personal fortunes. The balance of this essay will attempt to explain how he accomplished this goal.

Conwell's Rhetorical Transformations

No audience would blithely accept a radical redefinition of cherished values without being brought to it by a skillful manipulation of their symbols. Conwell was a master manipulator. So compelling was he that audience members sometimes nearly bestowed divine status upon him:

> There have been times when he was completely lost in his theme and surrendered himself to the power of an all absorbing emotion, seemingly inspired by supernatural powers. The thunder bolts were but play things in his hands. His eyes flashed, his face was illumined by a strange light, his body quivered, his voice became capable of expressing all shades of feeling, his manner as excited as the rushing waters of the cataract. An unquenchable enthusiasm born of the sublime impulses of a loving heart seizes upon his every nerve, while the enraptured listener holds his breath spellbound.[33]

Conwell did not rely on the supernatural, however, when it came time to harness lightning. His magic was born from the basic human tendency to respond to narratives. He cunningly disguised his transformations as harmless stories, ostensibly used to illustrate his points. The stories, however, *were* his point. Conwell's tales served as "minidramas" that drew the audience into the larger narrative. The lesser stories were arranged so that each series reflected the symbolic transformations Conwell attempted on a grand scale.

The transformation resulted from Conwell's careful manipulation of elements within these stories. Burke recognizes that rhetoric is the main tool through which all such "transformations" are accomplished. All dialectical terms, such as "individual" versus "community" or "wealth" versus "poverty," share a common substance that can serve as a rapprochement. Burke notes that "distinctions, we might say, arise out of a great central moltenness, where all is merged. . . . Let one of these crusted distinctions return to its source, and in this alchemic center it may be remade, again becoming molten liquid, and may enter into new combinations, whereat it may again be thrown forth as a new crust, a different distinction."[34]

The philosopher's stone for this alchemical transformation is the pentad. The pentad is a set of terms derived from the basic elements of the theater, thus it is especially well suited to analyzing a dramatic storyteller such as Conwell. The five key terms of the pentad—scene, act, agent, agency, and purpose—are simply different attributes of any given situation, real or imagined. A speaker creating a dramatic interpretation of such a situation may choose to emphasize certain of these terms and de-emphasize others. These rhetorical manipulations alter the overall meaning given to a particular drama:

> [The pentadic elements'] participation in a common ground makes for transformability. At every point where the field covered by any one of these terms overlaps upon the field covered by any other, there is an alchemic opportunity, whereby we can put one philosophy or doctrine of motivation into the alembic, make the appropriate passes, and take out another.[35]

Conwell's rhetoric played upon those tensions already felt by his audience. This made his stories compelling and lent power to his larger narrative.

Once Conwell discovered his magic formula, he almost never varied it. He distracted the audience from his alchemical manipulations by disguising them as stories. He flooded his stories with details, all the while casually manipulating the pentadic interpretation of the events. These manipulations came in a distinct series. He opened each speech with an apocryphal tale from a mythic past that revolved around a traditional definition of the concept under discussion. He quickly proceeded to tales from recent American history and worked his way around to contemporary examples of the concept. Somehow, by the time the speech was over, the concept was no longer quite the same as in the beginning.

The concept of each speech was usually a "good," material or otherwise, that was desired by the audience. The theme of his most famous lecture, "Acres of Diamonds," was wealth, a goal that recurred often. In "The Silver Crown," he redefined power for the future "Kings and Queens" of America.[36] He also helped his audience in their search for happiness and spiritual growth. In beginning with the desires of his audience, Conwell followed his own advice for success, "This is the whole question: Do you see a need?"[37] Conwell was always stating that giving the audience what they need will never fail to bring in wealth. He neglected to add that it helps if one can convince them that what they need is what you have to offer. By the time Conwell was through with an audience, they were usually convinced that he was giving them what they really wanted, even if they had not known that when they entered the room. Sometimes he did not "give" them anything at all, but merely helped them to discover that they already had what they needed.

Manipulating Scene and Agent

The first set of stories in each performance emphasized scene and agent, primarily the relationship between person and place. Our experience with prior stories creates expectations that constrain new stories. Given a certain scene, one expects to find a certain type of personality abiding there. In other words, the scene demands a certain type of character, one that matches the surrounding circumstances. In all of the stories, the scene itself was a physical reservoir of the quality being sought, and the main character had to recognize and capitalize upon it. Sometimes the character succeeded, sometimes not, depending upon the lesson to be learned.

In his lectures, Conwell frequently used a native guide who apparently did nothing but spin yarns while conducting a tour of the East. He regaled Conwell with stories of a diamond mine, a woodsman who taught a sage, two men who discovered a magical lily, and a peri (fairy) who was entirely too fond of jewels. Despite the "Arabian nights" flavor of the stories, their apocryphal nature made them applicable to any modern topic. Conwell made use of all of these tales, selecting the opening to best fit his audience.

In "Acres," the scene set by the tale was truly apocryphal, for God acts to put material wealth into the soil. In this tale, God sends out a mystical comet,

> and it went rolling through the universe, burning its way through other cosmic banks of fog, until it condensed the moisture without, and fell in floods of rain upon the heated surface and cooled the outward crust. Then the internal flames burst through the cooling crust and threw up the mountains and made the hills of the valley of this wonderful world of ours. If this internal melted mass burst out and cooled very quickly it became granite; that which cooled less quickly became silver; and less quickly, gold; and after gold diamonds were made.[38]

The hero of this story fails to see that these diamonds landed in his own backyard and thus misses his chance at wealth. A wiser fellow stays to dig a diamond mine.

Sometimes, for the sake of variety, the opening story told of a triumph. In one version, the guide tells of a kingdom that sent a wise man out in search of a new king. Along the way the wise man encounters a very unkingly woodsman. But this woodsman is worthy. When he needs water, he knows where to get it. When it gets too cold, he has tricks for warming up. This gauche fellow, through keen observation of the world around him, is able to "control" nature to such a degree that the impressed sage crowns him king, and "he ruled the nation and brought to it a peace and prosperity such as it had never known before." In both cases the person's fortune was in his immediate surroundings; the character who recognized this was rewarded: "*How to observe* should be the motto, not only in the beginning of our life, but throughout our career."[39]

Once the preliminaries were over, Conwell immediately moved the location of his tales to familiar places in the United States. Scene, however, was still the controlling factor. In some cases, scene was so powerful that it overwhelmed the character of the actor. In one sermon, for example, after the myth of the "snake line" (the altitude above which snakes supposedly could not live), Conwell attributed the character of children directly to the circumstances within which they were brought up. He had many negative examples of the evils of the city:

> I remember a widow who was left with five children. She was determined to keep them together, though she could not live in the style her husband maintained. So down in a narrow Alley, a very narrow, dirty Alley, her children were compelled to grow up in, living in the temptations of that awful region. Every single one of the five children went wrong, and one is now serving time for manslaughter, and the poor woman died of a broken heart after she went away from prison doors. Her son is condemned to live a life term in prison. Down below the snake line—God pity the poor that have to live down there amid serpents and sin, surrounded by evil![40]

On the other hand, a good environment produces a superior individual. Conwell attributed William Cullen Bryant's and Henry Wadsworth Longfellow's poetic talent to the lovely hills where they grew up: "They lived where minds were free and hearts were pure, and characters were sound."[41] For the most part, however, the potential of the scene must be grasped by a worthy character. People seeking wealth found it in mines and fields in Sutter's Mill, California; Titusville, Pennsylvania; and Newburyport, Massachusetts. Conwell named millionaires who began poor but grasped their opportunities. Those who found wealth were intelligent and observant. Those who missed their chance were ignorant, or worse, too full of pride to see what their eyes were showing them. In Conwell's story, being too smart for one's own good was just as dangerous as not being smart enough: "There is danger that a man will get so much education that he won't know anything of real value because his useless education has driven the useful out of his mind."[42] As Conwell warmed to each story, he emphasized the foolishness of the person who left home to find wealth, as in this tale of an educated man who sold a silver mine:

> [T]his professor of mines and mining and mineralogy, who would not work for forty-five dollars a week, when he sold that homestead in Massachusetts, sat right there on that stone to make the bargain. He was brought up there; he had gone back and forth by that piece of silver, rubbed it with his sleeve, and it seemed to say, "Come now, now, now, here is a hundred thousand dollars. Why not take me?" But he would not take it. There was no silver in Newburyport; it was all away off—well, I don't know where; he didn't, but somewhere else—and he was a professor of mineralogy.[43]

The moral was clear: The United States is still the land of wealth and opportunity if only one is good enough to seize it. And if you do not get what you want, it is your own fault. Conwell got quite harsh about this truth sometimes, especially when speaking from the safety of his platform in Philadelphia:

> [Y]ou can measure the good you have been to this city by what this city has paid you, because a man can judge very well what he is worth by what he receives; that is, in what he is to the world at this time. If you have not made over a

thousand dollars in twenty years in Philadelphia, it would have been better for Philadelphia if they had kicked you out of the city nineteen years and nine months ago. A man has no right to keep a store in Philadelphia twenty years and not make at least five hundred thousand dollars even though it be a corner grocery up-town.[44]

To this point, Conwell stayed very close to traditional definitions of wealth or power. The gospel of wealth mandated that everyone could and should get rich to manifest God's will. If you were doing your Christian duty, God would see to your success. The only reason not everyone was rich, despite the abundance in the world, was that many people were foolish, or lazy, or ignorant, or had another character flaw. Thus Conwell won the intellectual assent of his audience through his description of the poor. As W. C. Crosby explains, the "smug, thrifty, tightly moral American middle class . . . knew precisely what it wanted to hear," and he gave it to them.[45] At the same time, however, he took advantage of the tensions in their lives to create guilt and increase their desire for change.

This traditional opening is a form of what Burke refers to as "cunning identification," wherein "one can protect an interest merely by using terms not incisive enough to criticize it properly."[46] Conwell encouraged his audience to share with him the disdain for the poor that was common among the well-heeled class. Any criticism was of the individual, not the community. The audience was tricked into identifying with the ruling class, just as it realized that it did not belong to that class. Few, if any, of Conwell's listeners were wealthy. None was of the stature of Abraham Lincoln or William Cullen Bryant. No person could hear these stories without making an implicit comparison. The stories created a strong tension between the audience's middle-class status and the vast wealth that might have been theirs had they applied themselves. No matter how successful these people were, Conwell convinced them that they could have done better. By ostensibly playing into traditional wisdom—that wealth is measured in money, that wealth is an indicator of character, that money buys power, and that power leads to happiness—he made the audience realize they were, by these standards, poor. He made them so dissatisfied with their lives that they would gladly accept his formula for change.

Manipulating Agent and Act

Conwell implied that a lack of success demonstrated a lack of character. His audience was made uncomfortable in the knowledge that they, by implication, lacked character as well. But Conwell did not let his audience languish. The United States was still full of opportunities for the right person, and by taking the proper steps, a person could change her or his character and become the right kind of agent. He admonished the audience to prepare for success, regardless of the scene:

[Y]our future stands before you like a block of unwrought marble. You can work it into what you will. Neither heredity, nor environment, nor any of the obstacles superimposed by man can keep you from marching straight through to success, provided you are guided by a firm, driving determination and have normal health and intelligence.[47]

As Conwell moved through a presentation, he would slowly alter the nature of his stories, until they all told of success rather than failure. The main difference between these and his earlier tales was that in these later cases, the heroes all resembled the archetypal self-made man. Conwell stressed the traditional definition of individualism, which helped obscure the fact that he was altering the definition of success that he just created. Conwell took success for a walk with comedy. The comic frame, Burke says, "admonishes us that social exigencies and 'goodwill' are as *real* a vein to be tapped as any oil deposit."[48] Conwell wrested opportunity from the scene and "de-materialized" it.

In Conwell's earlier works, he tended to place the wealth to be attained in the geography of a place before proceeding with the transformation. In "Acres," for example, his agents first sought education enough that they recognized opportunity. One of his enduring examples was of an unemployed carpenter driven out of the house by his exasperated wife:

> Think of it! Stranded on that ash barrel and the enemy in possession of the house! As he sat there on that ash barrel, he looked down into that little brook which ran through that back yard into the meadows, and he saw a little trout go flashing up the stream and hiding under the bank. . . . [A]s this man looked into the brook, he leaped off that ash barrel and managed to catch the trout with his fingers, and sent it to Worcester. They wrote back that they would give him a five dollar bill for another such trout as that.[49]

The story did not end here, however. When the man sought more trout, he could not find any. He first had to make himself worthy of the opportunity nature had bestowed. After educating himself on the culture of trout, he started a trout farm in his brook. "Since then he has become the authority in the United States on the raising of fish. . . . My lesson is that the man's wealth was out here in his back yard for twenty years, but he didn't see it until his wife drove him out with a mop stick."[50] In this story, the wealth lies hidden in the scene, sometimes for a very long time. Thus opportunity is constantly knocking, and the character who works to be worthy of it answers.

Only after carefully building up the part of the agent did Conwell abandon scene. In "Acres," Conwell's next set of heroes do not wrest success out of any scene, they make it themselves: "It is not so much where you are as what you are."[51] Their good character, improved by hard work and education, is their wealth. He began with a fellow learning to whittle toys and culminated in John Jacob Astor making more money from one hat shop than most people could imagine—simply because he got his hat designs off the street himself instead of letting someone else do the work:

> Out there on that bench in the park he had the most important, and to my mind, the pleasantest part of that partnership business. He was watching the ladies as they went by. . . . But when John Jacob Astor saw a lady pass, with her shoulders back and her head up, as if she did not care if the whole world looked on her, he studied her bonnet. . . . [He] went to the store and said: "Now put into the show-window just such a bonnet as I describe to you," said he, "I have just seen a lady who likes just such a bonnet. Do not make up any more till I come back." . . . He didn't fill his show window with hats and bonnets which drive people away and then sit in the back of the store and bawl because the people go somewhere else to trade. He didn't put a hat or bonnet in that show window the like of which he had not seen before it was made up.[52]

The moral was that anyone can be successful if he or she simply follows two rules: work hard, and give the people what they want. Naturally, a fashionable hat is not a great service to humankind, but Conwell then exhorted his audience to find greater needs and invent new solutions. He asked: "Who are the great inventors? They are ever the simple, plain, everyday people who see the need and set out to supply it."[53] He admitted to no class or sex distinctions. Occasionally, he took pains to inform women that they can do as well as any man:

> When you say a woman doesn't invent anything, I ask, Who invented the Jacquard loom that wove every stitch you wear? Mrs. Jacquard. The printer's roller, the printing-press, were invented by farmers' wives. Who invented the cotton-gin of the South that enriched our country so amazingly? Mrs. General Greene invented the cotton-gin and showed the idea to Mr. Whitney, and he, like a man, seized it. Who was it that invented the sewing-machine? If I would go to school to-morrow and ask your children they would say, "Elias Howe." He was in the Civil War with me, and often in my tent, and I often heard him say that he worked fourteen years to get up that sewing-machine. But his wife made up her mind one day that they would starve to death if there wasn't something or other invented pretty soon, and so in two hours she invented the sewing-machine. Of course he took out the patent in his name. Men always do that.[54]

Conwell's lectures always eventually clarified that success does not depend at all upon scene, if people would only "make up their minds." Some members of the audience actually made up their minds right then and there:

> I was once lecturing in North Carolina, and the cashier of a bank sat directly behind a lady who wore a very large hat. I said to that audience, "Your wealth is too near to you; you are looking right over it." He whispered to his friend, "Well, then, my wealth is in that hat." . . . [H]e drew up his plan for a better hat pin than was in the hat before him and the pin is now being manufactured. He was offered fifty-two thousand dollars for his patent. The man made his fortune before he got out of that hall.[55]

In later lectures, Conwell often moved more quickly to the stories that transform the nature of success, especially when addressing "youth." He stressed that the "Kings and Queens" of the future were not merchants but inventors, and that one only becomes inventive through education. In keeping with the emphasis on individualism, he insisted that the best education comes in the school of "hard knocks:" "A distinct university walks about under each man's hat. The only man who achieves success in the other universities of the world, and in the larger university of life, is the man who has first taken his graduate course and his post-graduate course in the university under his hat."[56]

Conwell's initial thrust was to create a comic attitude in his audience. He stressed self-awareness, keeping one's eyes open and shrewdly capitalizing on any observed opportunity. In fact, he wrote one entire book titled *Observation*. This is the beginning of the comic, training people "*to be observers of themselves, while acting.*"[57] Conwell's ideal agents seek their "own special genius" and then apply it in all their actions.[58]

Of course, cultivating the proper attitude is only the beginning. Conwell then wanted to channel that inspiration in a particular direction. In his vision of the world, the proper first step for all comic agents was to recognize when they needed to rely on themselves and when they needed to rely on the community. From the university "under the hat," one must move to the "school of the world." And this means knowing where to go for the knowledge that one cannot attain on one's own. Obviously, Conwell's own institutionalizing of that vision was the creation of Temple University, founded by profits from Conwell's lecture tours to serve as a blue-collar campus. Tuition was low, classes were held in the evenings so that working students could still attend, and the curriculum was practical. Agents who wished to outfit themselves as future inventors of wealth could achieve that goal by temporarily joining that collective.

Conwell knew, however, that his audience stretched well beyond Philadelphia, so his rhetoric often outlined other paths to the same goal. For example, during World War I soldiers in the trenches obviously could not attend school. Conwell's response was to write a book for them. Like his speeches, it began with stories (this time war stories), before reminding readers that "patents for improvements in many lines were issued to soldiers." Like his speeches, it contained examples of inventors who observed a need and filled it: "The soldier who invented the iron wheel shoe . . . saw the need of that kind of brake when going down hill with a heavy load." He then proceeded to discuss how a person separated from the community could read the right books (of which he provided examples) and become sufficiently prepared to begin the road to success at the moment of discharge. Finally, like his speeches, the book admonished that only worthy characters could grasp the opportunities provided by great books: "And what is needed is that the books shall be read by men who will not only read, but who will train their minds to think, so as to be able to follow up the benefits of the reading."[59]

Conwell here demonstrated his enviable ability to find examples to match every possible audience member. In his previous lectures, the examples involved white male inventors and were intended for white male audiences. When women began to agitate for suffrage, he added white women. When his audience was the U.S. Army in France, he realized that a sizable portion of it was African American. From his plethora of Civil War tales, he pulled in an African American who had moved from slavery to success, serving in the military along the way, and dedicated an entire chapter to him. It was a bit obvious, however, why the man was chosen. Every other chapter was about a soldier identified by rank or job description—for example, "The Lieutenant and His Book" or "The Orderly and His Book." The chapter on the African American was called simply "The Negro and His Book." Still, it demonstrated a comic awareness shrewd enough to realize that race was a factor in the social structure of the United States.

Conwell's stress on education slightly violated the rule of the rugged individual, for it required one to join a collective, at least temporarily, whether intellectual or institutional. The community had resources that modern entrepreneurs needed. That it sometimes offered them through nonprofit institutions such as Temple was just one more reason to be grateful for the American way of life. Burke has noted that collectivism is a natural response to balance an emphasis on individualism, although he adds that Americans have often had to bring it in "by the back door."[60] Conwell would eventually swing open the back door fairly wide.

Education was the first step to success, but it was only the first step. A worthy agent was prepared to grasp opportunity, but must also be prepared to grasp it in the proper way. Conwell began with heroes who were shrewd, but then began to mix in elements of the spiritual. All the intelligence in the world would not help if one's heart was not also well prepared. As a minister, Conwell naturally brought moral elements to his message. The artistry is that he incorporated those elements so deftly as to prepare the audience for further changes in the concept of success.

In many of his stories, the quality of the agents involved soon altered the outcomes of their acts. The most successful people, said Conwell, have "that indwelling spiritual power supporting all their actions" and guiding them so as to prevent "reckless speculation."[61] By implication, a good heart can almost prevent one from buying bad stock. One metaphor that summed it up was "the snake line." Conwell used it concretely at first, then metaphorically, as a "line" between city and country (with the city being below the line). He finally transformed it into a spiritual line: "The minds of men have a snake line. The characters of men have a snake line."[62] Only people who keep their heads above the line prosper.

Naturally, the best way to keep afloat is to be a Christian, although this does not always appear to be sufficient. So powerful became the role of agent that it could completely obliterate the application of wealth. In his sermons, where one might expect Conwell to be his most conservative, he clearly violated the gospel of wealth. Having a great fortune and using it to endow great charities won no praise from Conwell if those actions did not derive from great character. Conwell castigated people whom social convention expected him to praise if their characters did not meet his standards. Conwell offered this unflattering example in a sermon:

> When you visit a library given by Mr. Carnegie, what do you think about the present to your community? It brings you what thoughts? Thoughts of speculation, thoughts of working men who have earned all that money, thoughts of the fact that he has had far more than his share of this world's goods. It brings you to the fact that he gives it, and attaches his name to it. It brings you thought that he is a man of the world who believes this world is all, and says he doesn't believe in the Bible, the Church or Christ. He told me he did not. That library brings you that thought every time you pass it if you know its history. Those books are valuable, the instruction they give is valuable, but are they also associated with such a giver? You can question the value of all such generosity, so-called, to the world because of its association with the giver. If George Washington had given it, or if some saintly man who had lived and sacrificed for the cause of humanity had given it, it might have a far different influence upon human character.[63]

Even Andrew Carnegie, who brought many advances to Conwell's own Philadelphia, was suspect because his spiritual character was bad. If such condemnation seemed an uncharitable act for a churchman, Conwell drove the point home a bit more mildly:

> I use these illustrations only to show that a gift carries with it the character of the giver. You must be careful when you send a gift that you can't send with your self, a noble, upright Christian character, a character that loves the things that are holy and righteous, a character that hates the things that are evil and wrong, a character that stands for the right always, and against evil always. You must send that with your present, or your present will be of little or no value.[64]

The reverse was also true: anything one did with a good heart would probably bring unsuspected good, perhaps even financial rewards. Conwell also told the story of Charlotte Brontë, whom he said learned to write because she was trying to help her brother observe details when he painted. Her writing eventually made her a living. His moral was that "no man ever gives himself for others' good in the right spirit without receiving 'a hundredfold more in this present time.'"[65] Thus the right acts, done by a person of the right character, bring that actor to a successful end.

The importance of character and the internal nature of any outward acts set up the characteristics through which Conwell was able to redefine success in such a way as to make it truly attainable. Conwell eventually surprised his audience with the news that wealth was more than money; success often had nothing to do with power or fame.

Transforming Scene through Actions

With wealth displaced from the scene, and character replacing it as the most important aspect of the pentadic ratio, Conwell prepared his final transformation. Next the stories shifted, so that the newly worthy characters *act* to transform the scene materially, creating new opportunities for themselves and others. Success and happiness come to worthy agents who put success and happiness back into the system, creating an unending supply for all to share. The goal of his rhetoric was not to make people rich, but to remind people that they already were rich and to encourage them to turn their resources toward the proper goals as he defined them. This approach served to reify the social order so as to balance the needs of the new economic community with the values of the old. This move demonstrates how an act can "contain both transcendental and material ingredients, both imagination and bureaucratic embodiment, both 'service' and 'spoils.' . . . A well-balanced ecology requires the symbiosis of the two."[66] Or, as Conwell put it: "Self-help is not selfishness. The duty of helping oneself in the highest sense always involves the duty of helping others."[67]

This duty was illustrated by stories. As usual, Conwell was careful to begin rather traditionally, but he always moved to an entirely new perspective. At first Conwell adhered to principles he had laid out earlier; that is, good deeds arising from money. As he said early on: "Money is power. Love is the grandest thing on God's Earth, but fortunate the lover who has plenty of money."[68] This was a very conservative stance, for it justified business as a roundabout form of social service. Burke has noted that this tactic is excellent for serving capitalistic ends since it enables individuals to pay off their guilt over exploiting the community.[69] And Conwell apparently adhered to this, selecting his examples from among the millionaires who used wealth to serve the community. As he developed his vision, however, his new version of wealth as internal subtly undercuts pure capitalism. For example, in another lecture, "The Angel's Lily," he begins with a new tale, purportedly told by the same Arab guide who provided the theme for "Acres of Diamonds." This apocryphal story was of a rich man and a poor man who are both unhappy. Each man has a dream that he will find happiness in the other's city, and each sets out on a journey.

> They met half-way between the palace and the hovel, half-way between Borzar and Baghdad. . . . They sat down at that spot and were talking in friendly intercourse upon some interesting question that did not touch their personal life, when they saw the opening of the sand and a bright flash of light from the ground. As they watched the increasing light they saw the little green leaves of the lily's stem appear, and as it rose with magic increase of speed it finally unrolled into a beautiful, petaled lily, and the petals rose higher and higher, until they covered the whole horizon like a tent and shut in the Caliph and the beggar under the leaves of the magnificent flower. There they dwelt together in the most perfect peace, absolute happiness, and complete rest; no cares—everything that they needed was supplied and no more, and they dwelt together in loving-kindness; and when the lily disappeared they too were taken into the other world at the same moment.[70]

The moral of the story is that true happiness lies in the middle ground between wealth and poverty. Conwell then questioned whether there is such a thing as too much wealth and concludes that there is:

> How much do you think Mr. Rockefeller knows about his two or three hundred millions? How much does he get out of it? He does not get as much out of it as you do out of what you possess. He cannot enjoy it. No man can enjoy perhaps

over fifty thousand dollars. Fifty thousand dollars furnishes every thing that any healthy man or woman could enjoy, and when a man gets beyond that sum he is going into care; he has passed beyond the place where perfect happiness is found.[71]

In fact, Conwell was even willing to go further, by naming names of millionaires who were actually unhappy, such as Charles Schwab, who once needed fifty cents so badly that he was content when he got it, but "now that he has one hundred million, is discontented."[72] One can have money and be the poorest man in town. If being poor is a bad thing, so is being too rich. Conwell's stories of both rich and poor children coming to bad ends created a dramatic tension between the two extremes. He then balanced that tension by suggesting that the rich should be using their extra money to help benefit the poor. His ideal merchants walked the line between individualism and community:

> They have been satisfied with reasonable profit; they have been willing to turn in and help someone else when they have gotten all they could honorably get from that community. The business that ever takes this middle course of commerce is the business that succeeds; and, anyhow, happiness is success whether you get much money or not.[73]

In this passage, Conwell opened with a straight discussion of profit, but ended by flatly stating that success does not equal money. His middle-class audiences could easily slip into identification with his opening point of view, for who has a more "middling" income than they? But then they were caught when he made the shift to service. If they have not been sharing their wealth, they are still not successful. The guilt rises again, and this tension must be relieved.

Obviously, most members of Conwell's audience were in no position to throw extra money around loosely, either because they were unable or unwilling to part with it. Again, they were ready for Conwell's next strategy. If wealth is really character, then the tool for social improvement is character, not money. The audience was told that they have abundant wealth to share, and they should be sharing. Conwell's many stories about this told of great men, of politicians and of soldiers. They do good deeds and serve their country because they are good; not one of them spends a penny. When the switch has been effected, true wealth is defined as wealth of character. Even a poor person can be a good person, for "men are great only on their intrinsic value, and not on the position that they happen to occupy."[74] All that remained was for Conwell to stress to his audience that they, too, have the character it takes to be great; then he could exhort them to greatness.

Monetary wealth was eventually completely divorced from the equation. For example, in one sermon Conwell spent the entire time talking about how the best deeds ignore money altogether: "No great thing was ever done by a man who was working for pay. None of the great deeds of earth were ever done for a reward in money. That life is a wasted life that is simply lived for wages."[75] The heroes of these stories were men with skills who donated them freely. One lengthy example shows that even a gift of speech could be used well:

> The greatest monumental deeds of the world are those that have been done by men out side of their profession or business, aside from their daily occupation. The great address which made Daniel Webster the idol of America and the admired of the world as a mighty orator, was made at Dartmouth College. . . . He was an unknown lawyer, and had but a few clients, and he was too poor to buy an overcoat when he went. . . . When he was there as a poor man they offered him a fee, and he said, "I will not work for my alma mater for money. I

would have no money in this case. I am here because I love the old college, and because my heart is here. Don't offer me any money, not a penny, not even my expenses."

He then delivered that great oration . . . that magnificent address which gave him a name and fame that lasted even against his faults until the day he was buried, years afterwards. The great thing that Daniel Webster did was that which he did without pay.[76]

While Conwell in this particular example might have exaggerated the role of a single speech in building a career, he could always rely on his own life as an anecdote to back up the claim that a single talent could enrich both the individual and others. His audience would remember the single speech that funded Temple University.

By the end of every speech, Conwell could prove that people could always help others by helping themselves and that the world would be a better place for it. Even "Acres," a paean to wealth, reaches that point:

Greatness consists not in holding some office; greatness really consists in doing some great deed with little means, in the accomplishment of vast purposes from the private ranks of life; that is true greatness. He who can give to his people better streets, better homes, better schools, better churches, more religion, more of happiness, more of God, he that can be a blessing to the community in which he lives tonight will be great anywhere, but he who cannot be a blessing where he now lives will never be great anywhere on the face of God's Earth.[77]

This attitude is a precursor to a full-blown "gospel of service," the idea that communal values are not served entirely by letting capitalism spread the wealth, but by blending capitalism with enlightened "communism." Burke notes this trend was still going strong in the 1940s, and described the tactics used: "One is commending an activity by reason of its *community value*. It is a *collective attribute*. . . . A social service is a way of *paying* something to society. It is the discharging of a *debt*."[78]

Conwell's goal was to bring American society to visit "the Angel's Lily," that point in the middle where individual and community, the power of wealth and of character, are perfectly balanced, "[b]ecause it is, after all, the place where men are happiest, halfway between Borzar, the hovel, and Bagdad, the magnificent palace of the Caliph."[79] The audience never had to choose between the two, which would lead either to enslavement or revolution, both equally negative in Conwell's eyes. Rather, he exhorted his audience to accept the ambivalence and live with it, framing one's acts always with one eye on each half of the dialectic. Conwell created his own comic vision of a world where one always guards against becoming too much like what the new world order demands, while guarding against being oblivious to the weaknesses of the old, creating a third order from that tension. As Burke once put it: "Thus we 'win' by subtly changing the rules of the game—and by a mere trick of bookkeeping, like accountants for big utility corporations, we make 'assets' out of 'liabilities.' And can we, in our humbleness, do better than apply in our own way the wise devices of these leviathans, thereby "democratizing" a salvation device as we encourage it to filter from the top down?"[80]

Conwell and the Comic Frame

Conwell succeeded with his rhetorical balancing act because he was able to create a vision of American life rooted in the comic frame. To appreciate how he accomplished this, we first need to understand what Burke means by "comedy" and how it applies to Conwell.

Burke's grand theory of the role of communication in the creation and maintenance of social structures emphasizes our use of symbols to arrange frames of reference. These "orientations" are a way of ordering the myriad experiences of the physical world so as to make them understandable. Once created, orientations are self-perpetuating: we see the world in a particular way, which dictates our responses to it; these responses in turn reify the perspective. This loyalty to a particular orientation is so strong that, as Burke notes, "One adapts measures in keeping with his past training—and the very soundness of this training may lead him to adopt the wrong measures."[81] An orientation can be so constraining that a person literally will not see a solution to a dilemma if it lies outside the boundaries. There are moments when the realities of a situation may force individuals to alter or adapt a perspective in order to survive. The United States faced such a moment at the turn of the nineteenth century, when new economic realities obviated the traditional modes of economic survival.

Once the necessity of altering the orientation can no longer be ignored, a rhetor must choose a mode of adapting, which Burke would call a "frame," from which to plan for social change. On the broadest level, one can either accept one's prior orientation as still useful and attempt repairs, or one can reject it entirely in favor of a new perspective. Obviously, there is overlap between the two, for every acceptance of one idea inherently involves the rejection of another. However, Burke identifies certain frames as "gravitating" toward one or the other. One frame that stresses acceptance of the old order is the comic.[82] Unlike other acceptance frames, such as the tragic and epic, the comic frame does not unquestionably accept the prior orientation as a state of perfection to be guarded at all costs. Instead, it emphasizes that human beings are, indeed, only human, and will inevitably make mistakes that must be corrected as circumstances demand. Thus social change involves enlightening individuals about the nature of those errors and presenting solutions. It is a difficult perspective to maintain because one is required to remain optimistic yet at the same time stay aware of the pitfalls of optimism. According to Burke, in its ideal form, "the comic frame should enable people *to be observers of themselves, while acting*. Its ultimate would not be *passiveness*, but *maximum consciousness*."[83]

A truly comic perspective is kind and cunning at the same time. It must walk a fine line between the competing forces operating in a social order, trying to avoid both naïveté and cynicism. This balancing act is what gives comedy special favor in Burke's theory, for it is "neither wholly euphemistic, nor wholly debunking—hence it provides the *charitable* attitude towards people that is required for purposes of persuasion and co-operation, but at the same time maintains our shrewdness concerning the simplicities of 'cashing in.'"[84] The comic frame allows social change to proceed without rejection of the old order, but also without blind acceptance of its negative aspects. According to Burke, if a rhetor is going to correct social ills without dismantling the social order, then the best frame is the comic.

While some frames arise naturally from the symbolic condition, the comic frame is maintained only if "coached" by a rhetor. This rhetor must be capable of "reorienting" the symbols of a social order in a way that does not threaten the recipients of the message. Again, this requires a balancing act—this time, a balancing of symbols. The rhetor who "is seeking to adjust a vocabulary to a situation (stressing such ways of feeling as to equip one to cope with the situation)," says Burke, "is necessarily sensitive to both the surviving and emergent factors in the situation . . . [and] will embody a mixture of retentions and innovations."[85]

Conwell's rhetoric embodied that mixture compellingly. He balanced the tensions created by a changing society by transforming their symbolic substance so as to transcend them. Conwell's audience was torn between the quintessentially American drive to move and the material conditions that made moving impossible.

They still revered individualism in a culture that demanded communal effort. Finally, they sought wealth as a sign of God's favor in an economy that had nearly eliminated naive capitalism. Conwell's response was to celebrate the old values while re-creating them. In his vision, movement was still possible, but the adventure was mental rather than physical. One reached individual self-actualization by serving others. Wealth was spiritual, arising from character rather than material, and was available to anyone willing to work for it. When the elements of this vision came together, Conwell had transformed the traditional gospel of wealth into its new incarnation as the gospel of service.

Narratives as Framing Devices

Conwell's successful career illustrates the power of narratives to facilitate the creation of frames of reference from which individuals begin to view the world. Conwell used comic strategies both to alter the social order and to save it by creating a frame that simultaneously accepted principles of the culture and rejected a number of its practices as mistaken. He did this using his "true" stories as vehicles through which to alter those elements of the social order that he viewed as detrimental.

Once Conwell perfected his formula of using carefully chosen examples to alter meanings to fit his worldview, he applied it repeatedly with great success. He even used it when discussing issues "off" the topic of success. In a work about woman suffrage, for example, he stated quite clearly that there was no reason why women should not have the vote if they want it. It was all right with him if women voted. His discussion, however, began with the mythical story of a peri (fairy) who finds a beautiful jewel that is much too big for her, but wears it anyway.

> The name of the rare jewel was Somethingmore. . . . She thought that she only needed this precious Somethingmore in her crown to make her supremely happy. So she commanded the gem to be set in her crown and started in a blaze of light to visit her humbler neighbors. But alas! The new jewel was so bright that its fiery rays melted her diamond robes, blistered her feet, and scorched her wings. Soon, her crown itself was dissolved by the heat, and she herself fell dead of suffocation. When her sisters found her, Somethingmore had scorched the sward around her; and to this day the people of Ormudz show the barren, ashy hillside, burned and crisped so long ago by the fatal Somethingmore.[86]

This gory little tale was followed by more modern discussions of the legal rights of women in various states. By the time he finished with his examples, it was clear, to Conwell at least, that women did not really want the vote, because they already had the legal rights they thought they needed the vote to attain.[87]

Conwell's use of examples demonstrates the power of narratives as instruments of transformation. On the surface, these "true life" stories were functional because examples made his claims believable. Conwell named real people in real cities (Philadelphia, Boston, Sutter's Mill). He described their thoughts and even directly "quoted" their conversations. When discussing tools for success, he named real books to read or mentioned real colleges (Temple, Stanford). He detailed the cut of someone's clothes and occasionally did vocal imitations. These touches made the symbolic transformations offered by the stories salient for the audience. They were not listening to a speech, but participating in reality.

Believing a story and internalizing it, however, are two very different things. For a narrative to function as a transforming agent, it must also be compelling to the audience. One source of such power is the myriad of beliefs already held by the audience. Conwell always began by telling stories that defined social values in traditional ways: wealth was material; rugged individuals helped themselves; rich men donated money to fulfill their debt to society. As he progressed, however, the drama became mutable through the use of symbolic manipulation. Subtly, the values became what Conwell wanted them to be. As a skilled speaker, Conwell used stories to re-create reality in the form he desired without shattering the fragile identification between audience and story.

The goal of this identification is the creation of a reorganized social order, one more "perfect" in the eyes of the rhetor. In Conwell's case, perfection consisted of a reconciliation between old and new values. Such a desire was natural, given that he was born at the precise moment of tension. As Burke observes, humans naturally tend toward a "nostalgic attitude of appreciation towards that which we feel to be *fast receding.*"[88] Conwell capitalized on that nostalgia.

Unfortunately, while Conwell tried to create a new vision of community in changing times, he was, at heart, too naive to recognize the real economic forces that prevented the realization of his vision. He knew that the industrial age was closing off avenues for economic advancement and concentrating wealth into a very few hands. This new capitalist frame encouraged individual exploitation of the community to create increased wealth for a smaller number of citizens. Instead of questioning that premise, however, Conwell saw a world where Christian service would "take up the slack" from the capitalistic drive for individual wealth. This move forced him to redefine wealth in less material terms, because otherwise his audience would not have been able to compete. Conwell prevented disillusion and despair, but only temporarily. Burke claims that a "frame becomes deceptive when it provides too great plausibility" for those "who would *condemn symptoms* without being able to gauge the *causal pressure* behind the symptoms."[89] As long as Conwell treated the symptoms, he and his audience were obliged to walk the comic tightrope continually, a feat that could be maintained only temporarily.

Burke notes that while some frames are self-maintaining, the comic must be continually "coached" to survive. A masterful communicator, Conwell maintained the comic in himself and his audiences throughout his lifetime. His naive treatment for societal tensions, however, guaranteed that his vision would need continual maintenance to survive pressure from the larger culture. The economic changes that created the tensions remained, thus so did the tensions. When Conwell died, no powerful rhetorical heir was at hand to carry on, and the vision soon gave way to external forces. One cynical writer noted that almost as soon as Conwell was buried, the board at Temple raised tuition and started building up its football team in order to resemble other, less blue-collar universities.[90] Conwell's "lily" was forgotten, while his lecture on "diamonds" was reprinted and preserved unto the present. Although his particular vision was flawed, his approach remains a clear example of the power of narrative to create a comic attitude toward social change. Such an attitude still has potential for promoting nonviolent social change. Burke's charge, given only twelve years after Conwell's death, is still pertinent: "Thus, we differ from those who would eradicate 'word magic': we hold that it is not eradicable, and that there is no need for eradicating it. One must simply eradicate the wrong kinds and coach the right kinds."[91] Conwell's magic was a powerful attempt at the sort of magic that is worthy of emulation.

Notes

1. Russell H. Conwell, "Acres of Diamonds," *Executive Speeches* 10, no. 6 (1996): 31–36.
2. Agnes Rush Burr, *Russell H. Conwell and His Work* (Philadelphia: John C. Winston, 1926).

3. Studies of "Acres" include A. Cheree Carlson, "Narrative as the Philosopher's Stone: How Russell H. Conwell Changed Lead into Diamonds," *Western Journal of Speech Communication* 53 (1989): 342–55; Mary Louise Gehring, "Russell H. Conwell: American Orator," *Southern Speech Communication Journal* 20 (1954): 117–24; Phyllis M. Japp, "'A Spoonful of Sugar Makes the Medicine Go Down': Dr. Conwell's 'Feel Good' Cultural Tonic," *Speaker and Gavel* 27 (1990): 2–10; and Richard H. Thames, "A Flawed Stone Fitting Its Nineteenth Century Setting: A Burkeian Analysis of Russell Conwell's 'Acres of Diamonds,'" *Speaker and Gavel* 27 (1990): 11–19.

4. Merle Curti, *The Growth of American Thought* (New York: Harper and Brothers, 1951), 644–49.

5. Kenneth Burke, *Counterstatement*, 2nd ed. (Berkeley: University of California Press, 1968), 105.

6. Kenneth Burke, *Philosophy of Literary Form* (Berkeley: University of California Press, 1973), 20 n2.

7. Burr, *Russell H. Conwell and His Work*, 298.

8. "Temple University Gets $5 Million Gift," *New York Times*, 31 March 1985.

9. Gehring, "Russell H. Conwell," 121.

10. Robert T. Oliver, *History of Public Speaking in America* (Boston: Allyn and Bacon, 1965), 464–66.

11. Burr, *Russell H. Conwell and His Work*, 270.

12. Versions of "Acres" may be found in Burr, *Russell H. Conwell and His Work*; Agnes Rush Burr, *Russell H. Conwell: The Work and the Man* (Philadelphia: John C. Winston, 1905); Russell H. Conwell, *Gleams of Grace* (Philadelphia: J. B Lippincott, 1887); and Robert Shackleton, ed., *Russell H. Conwell: Acres of Diamonds and His Life and Achievements* (New York: Harper and Brothers, 1915).

13. Russell H. Conwell, *The Angel's Lily* (Philadelphia: Judson Press, 1920).

14. Russell H. Conwell, *Observation: Every Man His Own University* (New York: Harper and Brothers, 1917).

15. Russell H. Conwell, *Unused Powers* (New York: Fleming H. Revell, 1922); Russell H. Conwell, *Sermons for the Great Days of the Year* (New York: George H. Doran, 1922); Conwell, *Gleams of Grace*.

16. Russell H. Conwell, "Above the Snake Line," *Christian Century* (29 October 1925): 1335–38; Russell H. Conwell, *How a Soldier May Succeed after the War* (New York: Harper and Brothers, 1918); Russell H. Conwell, *What You Can Do with Your Will Power* (New York: Harper and Brothers, 1917); Russell H. Conwell, *The Romantic Rise of a Great American* (New York: Harper and Brothers, 1924); Russell H. Conwell, *Why Lincoln Laughed* (New York: Harper and Brothers, 1922); Russell H. Conwell, *Woman and the Law* (Boston: B. B. Russell, 1876); Russell H. Conwell, "Fifty Years on the Lecture Platform," in Shackleton, *Russell H. Conwell*, 171–81.

17. Kenneth Burke, *A Grammar of Motives* (Berkeley: University of California Press, 1962), 59.

18. Conwell, "Acres," in Shackleton, *Russell H. Conwell*, 59.

19. Burr, *Russell H. Conwell and His Work*, 68.

20. Conwell, "Acres" in Burr, *Russell H. Conwell and His Work*, 101–5.

21. Conwell, qtd. in Shackleton, *Russell H. Conwell*, 74.

22. John W. Stokes, *The Man Who Lived Two Lives* (New York: Vantage Press, 1973).

23. Conwell, "Fifty Years on the Lecture Platform," 176. The payments eventually became more substantial; Conwell estimated that he averaged $150 per delivery of "Acres." See Shackleton, *Russell H. Conwell*.

24. Michael Kammen, *People of Paradox* (Ithaca, N.Y.: Cornell University Press, 1990).

25. Robert H. Wiebe, *The Search for Order: 1877–1920* (New York: Hill and Wang, 1967), 44.

26. Daniel Bjork, *The Victorian Flight: Russell Conwell and the Crisis of American Individualism* (Washington, D.C.: University Press of America, 1978), 69.

27. Arthur A. Ekrich Jr., *Progressivism in America: A Study of the Era from Theodore Roosevelt to Woodrow Wilson* (New York: New Viewpoints, 1974), 4.

28. James Oliver Robertson, *American Myth, American Reality* (New York: Hill and Wang, 1980), 161.

29. Kammen, *People of Paradox*, 267.

30. Curti, *The Growth of American Thought*.

31. Wiebe, *Search for Order*, 44.

32. Kammen, *People of Paradox*, 264–50.

33. Albert Hatcher Smith, *The Life of Russell H. Conwell* (Boston: Silver, Burdett, 1899), 261.

34. Burke, *Grammar of Motives*, xix.

35. Ibid., xix.

36. Conwell, *Observation*, 17.

37. Conwell, "Acres," in Burr, *Russell H. Conwell and His Work*, 427.

38. Ibid., 407.

39. Conwell, *Observation*, 10, 61.

40. Conwell "Above the Snakeline," 1337.

41. Ibid., 1336.

42. Conwell, *Observation*, 33.

43. Conwell, "Acres," in Burr, *Russell H. Conwell and His Work*, 413.

44. Conwell, "Acres," in Shackleton, *Russell H. Conwell*, 25.

45. W. C. Crosby, "Acres of Diamonds," *American Mercury* 14 (1928): 104.

46. Kenneth Burke, *The Rhetoric of Motives* (Berkeley: University of California Press, 1969), 36.

47. Conwell, *Will Power*, 2.

48. Kenneth Burke, *Attitudes toward History*, 3rd ed. (Berkeley: University Of California Press, 1984), 169.

49. Conwell, "Acres," in Burr, *Russell H. Conwell and His Work*, 428–29.

50. Ibid., 429.

51. Conwell, "Acres," in Burr, *Russell H. Conwell: The Work and the Man*, 330.

52. Ibid., 331.

53. Conwell, "Acres," in Burr, *Russell H. Conwell and His Work*, 426.

54. Conwell, "Acres," in Shackleton, *Russell H. Conwell*, 42.

55. Conwell, "Acres," in Burr, *Russell H. Conwell and His Work*, 426–27.

56. Conwell, *Observation*, 50.

57. Burke, *Attitudes toward History*, 171.

58. Conwell, *Will Power*, 7.

59. Conwell, *How a Soldier May Succeed*, 14, 17, 18.

60. Burke, *Attitudes toward History*, 161.

61. Conwell, *Romantic Rise*, 221.

62. Conwell, "Snakeline," 1336.

63. Conwell, *Sermons*, 221.

64. Ibid., 221.

65. Conwell, *Observation*, 41.

66. Burke, *Attitudes toward History*, 166–67.

67. Conwell, *Observation*, 150.

68. Conwell, "Acres," in Burr, *Russell H. Conwell and His Work*, 414–15.

69. Burke, *Attitudes toward History*, 164.

70. Conwell, *Angel's Lily*, 7.

71. Ibid., 11.

72. Ibid., 8.

73. Ibid., 15.

74. Conwell, "Acres," in Burr, *Russell H. Conwell and His Work*, 431.

75. Conwell, *Unused Powers*, 145.

76. Ibid., 151–52.

77. Conwell, "Acres," in Burr, *Russell H. Conwell and His Work*, 437.

78. Burke, *Attitudes toward History*, 162–63.

79. Conwell, *Angel's Lily*, 7.

80. Burke, *Attitudes toward History*, 171.

81. Kenneth Burke, *Permanence and Change*, 3rd ed. (Berkeley: University of California Press, 1984), 10.

82. Burke, *Attitudes toward History*, 57.

83. Ibid., 171.

84. Ibid., 166.

85. Burke, *Counterstatement*, 108.

86. Conwell, *Woman and the Law*, ix.

87. Ibid. His analysis was again somewhat simplistic, as he believed that if women knew their legal rights and exercised them, social inequality would eventually disappear through the weight of custom.

88. Burke, *Attitudes toward History*, 297.

89. Ibid., 41.

90. See Crosby, "Acres of Diamonds." His is the most cynical view of Conwell's career.

91. Burke, *Attitudes toward History*, 323.

Confronting Evil: Kansas as a Case Study of Nineteenth-Century Populist Rhetoric

Thomas R. Burkholder

4

When asked why he came to Kansas, U.S. congressman Jerry Simpson reportedly said: "The magic of a kernel, the witchcraft in a seed; the desire to put something into the ground and see it grow and reproduce its kind. That's why I came to Kansas."[1] Eloquent as this response was, the speeches of Simpson and his Populist colleagues received scant praise from subsequent commentators. As rhetorical scholar Howard S. Erlich has remarked, "the Populist movement and Populist rhetoric have not fared well at the hands of their rhetorical critics."[2] Their contemporaries and modern critics alike characterized Populist speakers as "calamity howlers," "anarchists and cranks," and "haranguing zealots."[3] Although scholars in other disciplines were also unkind, Erlich explains that "rhetorical analysis of historical Populism has contributed to the generally negative ethos of the American Populist movement of the 1890's, and of the term ['Populist'] itself."[4]

Nevertheless, orators of the Populist crusade were highly effective—for a time—in achieving their political aims. Historian C. Vann Woodward correctly observes, "any political party that aspires to gain power in America must strive for a coalition of conflicting interest groups."[5] In the final decade of the 1800s, agrarian radicals in Kansas built such a coalition with stunning success. Under the banner of the Farmers' Alliance, and later the People's Party, they brought together disgruntled farmers, urban industrial laborers and trade unionists, dissident Republicans and Democrats, prohibitionists, woman suffragists, Greenbackers, Single Taxers, and other reformers of every stripe. Populist successes in the election of 1890, and the success in the election of 1892 of the Populist-Democratic "fusion" ticket, as the cooperative effort of the two parties was called, effectively broke the Republican domination of Kansas politics.[6]

That success alone suggests that reexamination of Populist discourse is in order. Arguably, earlier negative assessments of Populist speechmaking were a product of methods of rhetorical analysis that were inappropriate for the task.[7] Confronted with Populist discourse, rhetorical critics working from traditional, rationalistic perspectives were unable to account for the initial rhetorical success of the movement. However, a more interesting—and potentially more relevant—question is: how could a movement that was at first so successful in building a powerful coalition ultimately fail to sustain itself? By 1894 the Populist orators who had been so successful just two years earlier were routed as the coalition fell apart and Republicans regained control of state government in Kansas. An important answer to that question lies in a careful reexamination of Populist rhetoric.

The aim of this essay is to offer a better accounting of both the initial success and the eventual failure of Populist discourse. The Populists' political successes resulted from a rhetoric that used confrontational strategies grounded in the agrarian myth. Party speakers at all levels appealed to agrarian values in order to transcend ideological differences and form a successful political coalition. Those strategies, however, held the seeds of their own undoing. In their efforts to incorporate ever larger segments of the society into the agrarian ideal, Populist orators reached the limits of transcendence, and the coalition collapsed.[8]

Limits of This Study

The Populist movement was the culmination of agrarian agitation that began with the Grange movement in the 1870s. Diverse groups coalesced into a political force, the People's Party, in 1890. Throughout the nation, Populists enjoyed political success in the elections of 1890 and 1892. In 1894 the party lost the support of dissident Democrats and suffered political losses to the Republicans. Those losses convinced party leaders that "fusion" with Democrats was the key to political success, and in 1896 Populists abandoned their original platform, embraced the cause of "free silver," and supported Democrat William Jennings Bryan in his unsuccessful bid for the presidency. Thus the period between 1890 and 1894 provides the clearest examples of Populist oratory. Consequently, this study is limited to analysis of speeches presented during that period.

Although the party was strongest in the South and on the Great Plains, Populism was a national movement. But nowhere in the nation was the movement as strong as in Kansas. If Kansas was not the birthplace of Populism, it was the nursery. Kansas historian Elizabeth N. Barr, herself a party member, argued that "it was not Populism that distinguished Kansas, but Kansas that distinguished Populism. Neither the conditions nor the proposed remedy was new, but the Kansas method of handling them was novel. It was the Kansas manner that makes the story worth telling."[9] Leaders of Kansas Populism were prominent among leaders of national Populism. Barr continued: "[In 1891] an effort was made, not so much to elect candidates, there being only local elections, as to sow the seed of National revolution. Mrs. [Mary Elizabeth] Lease, Mrs. [Annie L.] Diggs, Jerry Simpson, Judge [William A.] Peffer, John Willits and other leaders spent very little time in this State. They were going North, South, East and West preparing for the campaign of 1892, when they hoped to elect a President."[10] The prominence of these Kansans in the national campaign is evident.

Rhetorical scholars have also concluded that Kansas Populist orators were of national significance. Donald H. Ecroyd argues that "Kansas was the hotbed of Populism as a political movement. . . . The Kansas People's Party manifesto later became the basis of the national platform that was adopted at Omaha in 1892. The Weaver campaign for the presidency [in 1892] was frequently referred to as 'Kansas-izing' the nation." Ecroyd concludes that "Kansas was the source of the movement's greatest strength, and the scene of its greatest triumphs."[11] In his discussion of Populist orators generally, Ecroyd explains the importance of Kansas orators:

> Obviously, not all these speechmakers received or merited equal attention in the press. Consistently, however, mention is made of William A. Peffer, Jerry Simpson, L. D. Lewelling, Mary Elizabeth Lease, and Annie Diggs.. . . Later historians, standard reference works, and articles in contemporary and modern periodicals contain a wealth of material about these five orators though little about the others. In this period these Kansas Populist speakers were probably the best of the group—certainly the most widely known.[12]

Not surprisingly, a significant number of scholarly publications have focused on Kansas Populism.[13] Similarly, this study examines speeches by Kansas Populists who were national leaders of the movement, as well as those active at the state and local levels, as exemplars of Populist discourse generally.

The Historical Context

Historians have argued that the Populist movement arose in protest against oppressive economic and political conditions faced by U.S. farmers in the late nineteenth century.[14] Certainly the economic plight of farmers and other laborers of the era was severe. Their efforts to ameliorate those conditions culminated in the Populist revolt, but to claim that economic conditions were the sole cause of that revolt tells only part of the story. The economic and political problems facing U.S. farmers in the late nineteenth century were only the proximate cause of Populism—a catalyst that came at the end of a series of causal events. Those events are best characterized as two interrelated conflicts, one mythic, the other empirical.

MYTHIC CONFLICT: THE AGRARIAN MYTH ERSUS THE GOSPEL OF WEALTH

According to Richard Hofstadter, "the Populist impulse expressed itself in a set of notions that . . . appeared with regularity in the political literature, [and that] must be examined if we are to recreate for ourselves the Populist spirit." Hofstadter "enumerate[s] the dominant themes of Populist ideology," which included "the idea of a golden age; the concept of natural harmonies; the dualistic [good-versus-evil] version of social struggles; [and] the conspiracy theory of history." He concludes that these themes were "nurtured by the traditions of the agrarian myth."[15]

The Agrarian Myth. "Like any complex of ideas," Hofstadter explains, "the agrarian myth cannot be defined in a phrase, but its component themes form a clear pattern." Those themes, he notes, cast the "yeoman farmer" as hero. The central conception of the myth was "the notion that [the yeoman farmer] is the ideal man and the ideal citizen." Hofstadter writes:

> The yeoman, who owned a small farm and worked it with the aid of his family, was the incarnation of the simple, honest, independent, healthy, happy human being. Because he lived in close communion with beneficent nature, his life was believed to have a wholesomeness and integrity impossible for the depraved populations of cities. His well-being was not merely physical, it was moral; it

was not merely personal, it was the central source of civic virtue; it was not merely secular but religious, for God had made the land and called man to cultivate it. Since the yeoman was believed to be both happy and honest, and since he had a secure propertied stake in society in the form of his own land, he was held to be the best and most reliable sort of citizen.

Accordingly, Hofstadter explains, "agriculture, as a calling uniquely productive and uniquely important to society, had a special right to the concern and protection of government."[16]

This image of the sturdy and happy yeoman farmer may not have been reflected in actual events. But questions regarding reality, that is, questions regarding whether the agrarian myth had a solid basis in historical fact, miss the point. The myth was real. In his discussion of the American West as myth and symbol, Henry Nash Smith argues that "the words ['myth' and 'symbol'] . . . designate larger or smaller units of the same kind of thing, namely an intellectual construction that fuses concept and emotion into an image." Smith writes that "myths and symbols . . . have the further characteristic of being collective representations rather than the work of a single mind. I do not mean to raise the question whether such products of the imagination accurately reflect empirical fact. They exist on a different plane."[17] In the same connection, historian Paul W. Glad explains: "Myth making results from man's efforts to make his experience intelligible to himself. . . . Myths are means of ordering the ordinary facts of life. They are never completely false because without the reality they would never exist."[18] Examination of the agrarian myth reveals its profound influence on both thought and life in the nineteenth century.

The foundation of the agrarian myth was what literary historian Chester E. Eisinger has called the "freehold concept." "This concept," he observes, "based on the legal institution of freehold tenure, is an ideological construct comprised of three propositions which have been extracted from the writings of eighteenth-century authors who interested themselves in the problems of the farmer and the land." Those propositions were: "That every man has a natural right to the land"; "That through ownership of the land the individual achieves status and self-fulfillment. Ownership gives him dignity and a place in society"; and "That the good political society must provide for the uninhibited development of the farmer. . . . The freehold concept . . . [demands] that the farmer be made the dominant figure in the state, and that the laws and legislators favor him."[19] These propositions coalesced into the agrarian myth.

Among the most noteworthy proponents of the agrarian myth was Thomas Jefferson. According to Smith: "Jefferson was primarily interested in the political implications of the agrarian ideal. He saw the cultivator of the earth, the husbandman who tilled his own acres, as the rock upon which the American republic must stand." "Such men," Smith concludes, "had the independence, both economic and moral, that was indispensable in those entrusted with the solemn responsibility of the franchise."[20] Through the influence of Jefferson and other eighteenth-century writers, the agrarian ideal gained wide acceptance. Hofstadter comments that "among the intellectual classes in the eighteenth century the agrarian myth had virtually universal appeal. It was everywhere: in tracts on agricultural improvement and books on economics, in pastoral poetry and political philosophy." So strong was that influence that "at first . . . the agrarian myth was a notion of the educated classes, but by the early nineteenth century it had become a mass creed, a part of the country's political folklores and its nationalist ideology."[21] That "mass creed" shaped thought and life in the United States in several significant areas.

By drawing a relationship between agriculture and self-government, the agrarian myth helped to develop the democratic ideal. The proposition that all individuals had a natural right to own land was of primary importance in this relationship.

As political scientist A. Whitney Griswold observes: "Democracy meant self-government. Who would govern himself must own his soul. To own his soul, he must own property, the means of economic security. Private property was therefore a corollary to democracy, and land that produced the means of subsistence was the typical and most valuable form of private property." "Thus," writes Griswold, "we find in Jefferson's construction of the property right another link between his general principles of agrarianism and democracy."[22]

The agrarian myth also fostered a view of government as the defender of agriculture. Eisinger comments: "[A major] proposition of the freehold concept is that the legally constituted government should be dedicated to the interests of the freehold farmer. . . . The champions of the agrarian way of life exerted every effort to fashion a government that would devote itself to the farmer's interest."[23] As the agrarian myth became a mass creed, the notion became ingrained in national thought.

Moreover, the agrarian myth helped foster a sense of U.S. nationalism. According to Smith, the myth projected an image of the nation's interior as the "garden of the world." Within the garden, natural order and harmony prevailed. Outside the garden was chaos. "Neither American man nor the American continent contained . . . any radical defect or principle of evil," Smith concludes. "But other men and other continents, having no share in the conditions of American virtue and happiness, were by implication unfortunate or wicked." This sentiment grew particularly strong whenever order and harmony were threatened. Smith argues: "This suggestion was strengthened by the tendency to account for any evil which threatened the garden empire by ascribing it to alien intrusion. Since evil could not conceivably originate within the walls of the garden, it must by logical necessity come from without, and the normal strategy of defense was to build the walls higher and stop the cracks in them."[24] For those who adhered to the mass creed of the agrarian myth, such logic was flawless. Because the yeomanry was moral and pure, evil could only originate from without. Nationalistic sentiments were a natural result of such logic.

These sentiments came to be applied not only to forces outside the United States but also to those within the country yet outside the garden. Thus the myth served to create an image of the city as the stronghold of evil. Hofstadter comments that "out of the beliefs nourished by the agrarian myth there had arisen the notion that the city was a parasitical growth on the country."[25] The larger the city, the greater the evil. Journalist and historian Carleton Beals writes that "the farmers saw life in black-and-white terms of Everyman simplicity, of innocent bucolic virtue versus city-slicker and handlebar-moustache villains." "Real sin," he explains, "existed only under the lurid gas jets of the nation's greatest metropolis. New York became Babylon, Sodom and Gomorrah, and all other Biblical hot spots combined."[26]

Finally, the agrarian myth helped define the relationship between humans and the environment. "Another traditional idea invoked by Western spokesmen," notes Smith, "was the conception of nature as a benevolent guardian of man."[27] Yeoman farmers were endowed with mythic power, or at least mythic blessing, enabling them to live in peace and harmony with the elements. They were rewarded by nature with the fruits of a bountiful harvest. As the garden of the world spread onto the arid central plains, the agrarian myth even overcame, for a time, the myth of the Great American Desert.[28]

Generally, such cultural myths perform important social functions by drawing relationships between a society's past, its present, and its future. According to James Oliver Robinson, "myths are self-justifying. Because they often carry social ideals, the people who use them and participate in them assume that the ideals justify the past out of which these ideals came."[29] From its past comes society's collective understanding of its present and its vision of the future. "What the myth represents," literary critic Northrop Frye asserts, "is not what happened in the past, but what is said to have happened in the past in order to justify what is in the present. Such myth has the social function of rationalizing the status quo: it explains, not merely why we do the things we do, but why we ought to go on doing them."[30] In short, myth shapes society's worldview. The agrarian myth served that function in nineteenth-century America. But with growing industrialization, the myth was challenged by a formidable new force.

The Gospel of Wealth. As the agrarian myth reached its zenith as a mass creed, a new force that ultimately would challenge it gained strength in the United States. That force was industrialization. Smith explains that "by the 1830's a new calculus and new symbols were required to interpret the new West that was being created by forces wholly foreign to the agrarian assumptions." "The greatest of the new forces," he argues, "was the technological revolution which set loose the power of steam—in boats on the western waters, somewhat later in railways, and eventually in factories."[31] The birth of the Gilded Age, according to Kansas historian O. Gene Clanton, "was influenced profoundly by an entirely unique factor—the emergence of industrial capitalism."[32]

The centers of industrial capitalism were not within the garden. Rather, they were in the developed and developing cities. The effect on society was monumental. Historian James Turner reports: "Between the end of the Civil War and the turn of the twentieth century, the United States underwent what time may demonstrate to have been the most fundamental transformation in its history: the change from a basically rural nation to an urban society."[33] The shift was accompanied by opportunities for amassing great wealth. In his history of Populism, Sheldon Hackney comments that "at the time of the Civil War no more than 400 millionaires existed in the country, but in 1892 the New York *Tribune Monthly* listed 4,047 millionaires by name."[34] These profound social and economic changes quickly began to alter the way much of the nation thought of itself. In Glad's opinion, "as the new, urban industrial society challenged older rural values, another myth began to bulk large in the popular mind. This was the myth of the self-made man, which for a century or more had run parallel to the myth of rural virtue." Eventually, Glad concludes, "industrial growth all but eliminated the way of life portrayed in the agrarian myth."[35]

The new myth was appropriately christened the "gospel of wealth" and was espoused by none other than Andrew Carnegie. The great and growing disparity between rich and poor, Carnegie explained, was "not to be deplored, but welcomed as highly beneficial. It is well, nay, essential for the progress of the race, that the houses of some should be homes of all that is highest and best in . . . the refinements of civilization, rather than that none should be so. Much better this irregularity than universal squalor." He continued to argue that efforts to equalize opportunity, to reduce the imbalance between rich and poor, were dangerous. Those conditions, he said, were the result of a natural "law" under which a talented few must necessarily succeed. That law, he asserted, must not be challenged, because "we cannot evade it; no substitutes for it have been found; and while the law may be sometimes hard for the individual, it is best for the race, because it insures the survival of the fittest in every department." Only "the Socialist or Anarchist," said Carnegie, would overturn that natural order.[36]

Carnegie's endorsement of the "survival of the fittest" was not accidental. Like the agrarian myth, the gospel of wealth found support in writings of the time. Significantly, some of these writings were scientific or scholarly rather than overtly political. In 1859 Charles Darwin's *On the Origin of Species* shook the scientific world, and by the late 1860s Herbert Spencer was expounding the social counterpart of Darwin's theory. Social Darwinism fed the gospel of wealth. Clanton summarizes its influence on the new myth:

Having both a religious and secular base, the Gospel of Wealth reduced to its most simple formulation was a popular faith in material success, one that equated wealth and morality. It contained within it the idea that the American economy should be controlled by a natural aristocracy brought to the top through the competitive struggle of the marketplace; the idea that the state should confine itself strictly to the role of protecting property (which had divine sanction within the gospel) and maintaining order; that poverty was a natural result of inferior abilities, or sin, or both; and that the rich were obligated to do good with the riches they accumulated.[37]

For the few—like Carnegie—who became the captains of industry, the logic of Spencer's theories of social Darwinism and the gospel of wealth was inescapable. In society, as in nature, evolution led to a higher order. All of history demonstrated this progress toward perfection. But as Clanton explains, for the social Darwinists, "this progress took place only under conditions that allowed the economic struggle for existence and the survival of the fittest to work itself out within a system of unrestricted free enterprise." If social evolution was to occur, "the 'fit' had to be left utterly free to overcome the 'unfit.' The massing of wealth and the accompanying attainment of power and success demonstrated 'fitness,' while disease, poverty, and failure to improve one's status in society were evidence of 'unfitness.'"[38]

The gospel of wealth found literary and rhetorical expression as well, most notably in Russell Conwell's immensely popular speech "Acres of Diamonds." Reputedly delivered over 6,000 times between the late 1870s and the mid-1920s, the speech was heavily influenced by Conwell's belief in the gospel of wealth.[39] "Any man can be great," Conwell told thousands of eager self-made-men-to-be.[40] Consisting primarily of a series of narratives that extolled the virtues of entrepreneurship, "Acres of Diamonds" earned Conwell millions of dollars in lecture ticket sales, much of which he used to found Temple University in Philadelphia. The popularity of Conwell's message revealed the rapidly growing social influence of the gospel of wealth.

MYTHIC CONFRONTATION

Developing industrialism, the gospel of wealth, and social Darwinism challenged the very foundations of the agrarian myth. Where the hero of the agrarian myth was the yeoman farmer, the hero of the gospel of wealth was the self-made man, the archetypal image of the talented few who were "fit" for success. Both strove to "succeed" but in ways that differed sharply.

For the yeoman, success was family self-sufficiency on the small farm and within the relatively isolated rural community. For the self-made man, success was the accumulation of wealth and the attainment of power within the society. In practical affairs, the agrarian myth turned the yeoman farmer inward to self-sufficient subsistence farming. The gospel of wealth turned the self-made man outward to commercial dealings with society. For the yeoman, ownership of land was essential for subsistence, status, and the independence necessary for full participation in democracy. Most important, ownership of property was a natural right to be protected by government. For the self-made man, ownership of property was a means of speculation for the accumulation of wealth. And although the role of government was to protect private property, ownership was to be decided not on the basis of rights, but on the outcome of unimpeded struggle in the marketplace, facilitated by government policy, with property going to the fittest.

Obviously, the premises of the gospel of wealth held significant implications for the proper role of government and notions of democracy. According to the gospel of wealth, "men were born unequal," Clanton notes, "and any effort to equalize them

CONFRONTING EVIL: KANSAS AS A CASE STUDY OF NINETEENTH-CENTURY POPULIST RHETORIC

93

by governmental action [such as protection of the 'natural right' to own land] was contrary to the laws of nature." Such efforts were counter to the teachings of social Darwinism and "a violation of 'scientific law' and detrimental to progress."[41]

The agrarian myth fostered genuine democracy in a Jeffersonian sense: if ownership of land was a natural right of all citizens, and if ownership conveyed status and standing to participate in self-government, then all citizens were suited to participate in self-government. The gospel of wealth moved in the opposite direction. According to Clanton, politicians elected by majority vote, after all, "were not subject to rigorous natural selection and therefore could not be trusted to the same degree as the leaders of the business world." Thus, for the self-made man, efforts to improve democracy were contemptuous because "even the peaceful implementation of majority will was contrary to science, progress, and morality."[42]

To argue that neither the agrarian myth nor the gospel of wealth accurately reflected historical fact again misses the point. As Glad observes, "the two myths . . . were real enough in themselves precisely because they did dominate American thought."[43] Consistent with mythic functions described by Robinson and Frye, the agrarian myth and the gospel of wealth battled for the mind and soul of the society. Representing distinct and fundamentally incompatible visions, each sought to define what it meant to be a U.S. citizen. That conflict was the long-term cause of the nineteenth-century Populist revolt, the mythic backdrop against which the economic chaos of the late nineteenth century unfolded.

EMPIRICAL CONFLICT: PROGRESS VERSUS POVERTY

Development of the North American continent was consistent with the images of the agrarian myth. In Europe, and especially in England, the freehold had been limited by the availability of land. Because most of the available land was in the hands of the gentry, common people existed mainly as tenants or urban workers.

The United States was different. Vast unsettled lands existed, and the growing population moved west with hopes of realizing the agrarian ideal, of acquiring livelihood and status through the freehold. The yeoman toiled, and nature was bountiful. Success and abundance fueled national expansion, but they also set the stage for a new era. Smith observes that "the very fertility of the Northwest posed a dilemma with respect to the agrarian ideal. The hardy yeoman came out into the wilderness seeking land, and his search was rewarded: he acquired title to his farm and reared his numerous children amid the benign influences of forest and meadow."[44] So great was the product of the yeoman's toil that it far exceeded the needs of individual families or even of frontier cities. Other markets were sought. "A farmer who wants access to markets becomes interested in internal improvements. He agitates for highways and canals, for improved navigation of the rivers, and later for railways," states Smith. "Developing commerce creates depots like Cincinnati and Louisville—cities in the wilderness. The cities have banks and at least rudimentary manufactures such as the packing industry, and eventually it is they rather than the farming communities that set the tone of the West."[45] Developing cities meant economic opportunity, and when the yeoman sought new markets, the self-made man was waiting.

Progress. Settlement of the West proceeded at a breakneck pace. Between 1870 and 1880, 190 million new acres came under cultivation; the frontier extended far into the arid central plains. Between 1865 and 1890, nine new states joined the Union.[46] Boomtime had begun on the prairie. Eager for profits, self-made-men-to-be leaped at investment opportunities.

The desire to increase western population was almost universal. More people meant more consumers, larger markets, more parties to purchase goods and land. No effort or expense was spared in attempting to lure settlers to the newly opened prairies. Eager for customers, railroad companies launched great advertising campaigns noted for flamboyance if not truthfulness. States, counties, and towns attempted to entice new citizens. Special inducements were frequently offered to manufacturers who would establish plants in the cities.[47] Easterners unwilling to move west themselves were targets for another message: developing states and localities that were unable to finance the boom on their own sought eastern capital. Cities and towns let bonds to finance schools, streets, water facilities, and jails. Mortgages were attractive to small investors; such endeavors did not require large sums, and interest rates were often 6 to 10 percent on real estate loans and 10 to 18 percent on chattel mortgages.[48]

Nowhere was the boom more spectacular than in Kansas. Kansas historian Peter H. Argersinger comments that "from 1880 to 1885 the Kansas population increased by 37 percent or by more than 300,000 individuals, and the value of property more than doubled."[49] In his history of Populism, Lawrence Goodwyn writes that "in the central third of the state, near the thirty-inch rainfall line, more than 220,000 immigrants poured in between 1881 and 1887. Almost half of them arrived in the three-year period between 1885 and 1887."[50] Clanton explains that "most of these settlers were lured out to the Kansas plains to take advantage of her highly publicized resources. For the majority this meant agricultural pursuits. Those who survived the periodic droughts and grasshopper plagues and who managed to make the necessary adjustment for farming the plains soon created an abundant agriculture in Kansas."[51]

The result was all that recently self-made men could have hoped for. Land prices skyrocketed. Historian Louise Rickard reports that in 1881, "good land in some parts of Kansas was still so cheap that it was possible to pay for a farm in one year. Land prices rose so rapidly as settlement proceeded, encouraging speculation in land and further inflating prices. The value of property in the state more than doubled between 1880 and 1885, and more dramatic increases were recorded in some localities."[52]

The most fertile ground for investment and speculation was railroad construction; it was a golden opportunity for self-made men. Because transportation was essential to continued economic development in Kansas, virtually everyone became a railroad promoter. As historian Raymond Curtis Miller argues, "the roads were built largely from grants of land, guaranteed mortgages, gifts, and bonuses, from nation, state, county, township, city and even individuals."[53] According to historian Hallie Farmer, eastern capital purchased municipal bonds at such a rate that "it was estimated that eighty per cent of the municipal debt of Kansas in 1888 had been contracted to aid railroads."[54] In addition to money, railroads received huge land grants for rights-of-way or for sale to raise even more capital. So extensive were these grants of land, Goodwyn reports, "that fully one-fifth of the total acreage of Kansas" was owned by the railroads.[55] Land sales provided tremendous windfalls. In his history of Kansas, Kenneth S. Davis notes that "the railroads still held in the 1870s most of the more than ten million acres of public land that had been given them, yet paid taxes on only that portion they had patented." Upon sale, speculators, not farmers, reaped the benefits. "When they disposed of their holdings," Davis continues, "the railroads . . . often did so in huge tracts to speculators rather than in farm-sized tracts to individuals."[56]

Industrialization and technological development affected agriculture directly. As farming became more mechanized, it became more commercial, and by the 1870s the transition in U.S. agriculture from self-sufficient to commercial farming was nearly complete. Although historical facts may once have coincided with the agrarian myth, that time was quickly coming to an end. "The cash crop," Hofstadter contends, "converted the yeoman into a small entrepreneur, and the development of horse-drawn machinery made obsolete the simple old agrarian symbol of the plow."[57] Markets were no longer only in nearby villages but also in cities far away. Suppliers of implements were in distant urban areas. And of course the capital with which agricultural mechanization was financed was in the hands of eastern bankers. Increasingly, Glad notes, farmers became "more and more dependent on decisions and policies which emanated from the cities and over which they had no control."[58] Forces outside the garden were tightening their grip on rural society.

Moreover, as agriculture experienced profound changes, so did industry and manufacturing. As Glad argues: "Gone were the days when a large number of small manufacturers sold their goods in a local market protected from the outside by high transportation costs. The new industrial order was one in which a smaller number of larger firms struggled for control of larger markets."[59] Self-made men at the head of the new order were, in their own view, the fittest who had survived. To them, competition in the marketplace took on new meaning. As agriculture had moved beyond the agrarian myth, industry moved beyond the gospel of wealth. "To the men responsible for directing the destinies of such firms," Glad continues, "competition did not seem the life of trade. On the contrary, price competition was potentially ruinous to all. Thus the competing firms in many industries sought to avoid the evils of price rivalry by forming combinations and mergers." Although many became alarmed over the threat of monopolies, self-made men, soon to be called "Robber Barons," were firmly in control. "In short," Glad concludes, "it seemed that the economic power which technology, industry, and transportation had created could be most effectively used when concentrated in the hands of a few. Efforts to prevent the growth of big business were generally as effective as fabled efforts to sweep back the sea."[60]

Rapid industrialization, settlement of the plains, and commercialized agriculture wrought tremendous changes for society. Historical reality moved beyond both agrarian myth and the gospel of wealth. Progress produced almost unimaginable fortunes for a few. But speculation—whether in land, railroads, or industry—provided a precarious foundation. Behind progress lurked poverty. The boom was about to collapse.

Poverty. Because the boom was built on speculation rather than sound business practices, prices of everything—land, municipal and industrial development, railroad construction—were inflated far beyond actual value. Eastern capital flowing into the West seemed without limit, and borrowers grabbed it without restraint. Debt grew to staggering proportions. Conditions in Kansas were particularly frightening. Argersinger explains that "the state auditor's *Report* for [1890] set the assessed value of all property in Kansas at $348,459,943 and the total indebtedness, both public and private, at $706,181,627."[61] "The debt of Kansas," Farmer adds, "if divided equally among the inhabitants of the state, would have fastened a debt of $170 upon each citizen."[62]

In short, everything was mortgaged for all, and in many instances more than all, it was worth. The boom was not built on reality and honest value but on speculation and credit. The state, the cities, and individuals piled up debts with the hope of a quick payout from huge profits. But those profits lagged far behind debts. Decreased profits meant decreased ability to repay loans, and eastern lenders grew more cautious. The boom had produced its share of swindlers, and fraud became more common as money became tight. Business confidence declined slowly at first, and eventually, as Farmer explains, "eastern investors refused to place more money in the west and much of the money already invested was withdrawn as the lenders became more frightened."[63]

Moreover, nature itself seemed to turn against Kansas farmers. "The boom rested on the largesse of nature," Goodwyn argues. "The early 1880's experienced a pattern of bountiful rainfall throughout the plains. . . . To the happy participants the rain was not an unusual freak of nature, but rather a permanent feature of Western life."[64] But as Rickard comments, "what the settlers did not understand until too late was the variability and cyclical nature of rainfall in the Great Plains."[65] In 1887 nearly ten years of abnormally high rainfall ended. The effect was felt immediately throughout the region. In Goodwyn's opinion, Kansas suffered most. "The rains stopped in 1887—not only in Kansas, but throughout the Great Plains, from the Dakotas west to Colorado. In western Kansas, Nebraska, the Dakotas, and all of newly settled Colorado a pronounced economic jolt was felt almost immediately. Kansas, where the boom psychology had been most pronounced, felt by far the sharpest retrenchment. Corn production plummeted from 126 million bushels in 1886 to 76 million bushels the next year."[66] Such tremendous crop failure was devastating. Thousands of farm families, pressed between falling income, on one side, and high taxes to repay bonded debt combined with high mortgage payments, on the other, went bankrupt. Eastern investors' fears of widespread default became reality.

"In the late eighties and the early nineties," writes historian John D. Hicks, "foreclosures came thick and fast. Kansas doubtless suffered most on this account, for from 1889 to 1893 over eleven thousand farm mortgages were foreclosed in this state, and in some counties as much as ninety per cent of the farm lands passed into the ownership of the loan companies."[67] Barr reports that "in the first six months of the year 1890, there were 2,650 foreclosures [in Kansas], and a like number of farms were deeded to mortgage companies to avoid the expense of foreclosure." Due to deflation of the currency, those who wanted to make a clean break and begin again elsewhere after foreclosure often found that the amount of their debt exceeded the value of their land. Their property was in the hands of their creditors, and they were still in debt.[68] In the wake of the collapse, thousands left the state; 179,884 people left between 1887 and 1891.[69] According to Clanton, "such laconic phrases as 'In God We Trusted, in Kansas We Busted' were common words as the discontented were swept away."[70] But although many left, many more chose to stand and fight—not with bullets but with ballots. Their fight was political—a conflict between the "people" and the "money power," between the "masses" and the "classes." And although it was brief, the conflict was spectacular. The Populist crusade, Barr exclaims, "can hardly be diagnosed as a political campaign. It was a religious revival, a crusade, a Pentecost of politics in which a tongue of flame sat upon every man, and each spake as the spirit gave him utterance."[71]

OBSTACLES TO RHETORICAL SUCCESS

As both rhetoricians and historians have noted, behind the economic collapse Kansas farmers saw a grand conspiracy of railroaders, industrialists, bankers, and politicians—usually Republicans—working to destroy not only their livelihood but their way of life.[72] These conspiracy theories necessarily grew from the Populists' belief in the agrarian myth. In fact, their trust in the myth made any other explanation of their economic hardship impossible. According to Miller, "[the Kansas farmer] had been taught, and had taught for years, that Kansas was the land of beauty and unsurpassed opportunity, and for a time he had shared in her bounty and had seen her possibilities. If there had been change, the cause was not a natural one, but man-made and external."[73] Because the yeoman was the ideal citizen, because the garden of the world was both peaceful and beneficent, Kansas farmers believed that any disruption could only emanate from evil forces outside the garden. When confronted by the market power of trusts, combines, and monopolies, farmers naturally concluded that the money power had conspired against them. The Populist crusade was launched to overcome that perceived conspiracy of evil.

But to accomplish that task, Populist orators would have to overcome formidable rhetorical problems.

Populist rhetors needed to develop strategies for defending agrarian culture against attack from growing industrialization, the gospel of wealth, and social Darwinism. As Clanton explains, "the primary obstacle to Populist success . . . in Kansas and probably even more throughout the nation, had been what for lack of better terms must be called a negative climate of opinion." "The most antagonistic part of that prevailing attitude," he writes, "would have to be that complex of ideas designated as social Darwinism, which [caused Populism] to be stigmatized as retrogressive."[74] Traditional images of the independent, self-sufficient yeoman farmer ran counter to social Darwinism. As Glad observes: "The struggle in the market, so the social Darwinist argument ran, paralleled the struggle for survival in nature. . . . As in nature, only the best and fittest survived in society so long as government did not interfere to preserve the weaklings."[75] This philosophy created significant obstacles for Populist speakers. According to Clanton, "it was all but axiomatic among the influential, business-minded segment of late nineteenth-century society that nothing progressive could possibly emanate from the laboring classes of the farm or factory." Indeed, Clanton argues that a "negative climate of opinion" fostered by social Darwinism and the gospel of wealth was the "primary obstacle to Populist success."[76] Overcoming the obstacles generated by these images presented Populist speakers with a formidable task.

Disgruntled farmers also knew they could not achieve the political changes they desired on their own. Instead, they needed to overcome ideological barriers to attracting members—many of whom were industrial laborers, shopkeepers, and the like—to a new political party. Ultimately, those members came from diverse backgrounds and adhered to diverse political ideologies. Historian Walter T. K. Nugent examined the prior political affiliations of Kansas legislators elected as Populists in 1890 and 1892. "About four out of seven of the Populist legislators had been Republicans until a short time before," says Nugent. "About one-fifth had been Democrats and just under another one-fifth had been chronic third party adherents. About 6 percent classed themselves as 'independents' by which they may have meant that they too were third-party men, rather than ticket-splitting or fence-setting 'independents' in the more modern sense."[77] Clanton traced the political evolution of the same legislators. "The usual route traveled," he observes, "carried them from the Republican party to the Greenback party, then to the Prohibition party or the Union-Labor party, and then into the Populist party."[78] Drawing those diverse groups into the new political party presented Populist orators with a significant problem. According to historian Oscar Handlin, "Populism drew together many discontented elements in American society—farmers, laborers, social reformers and intellectuals. The very diversity of these groups renders futile the quest for a single ideology among them."[79] Obviously, then, to form a successful political coalition, Populist rhetors needed rhetorical strategies that could transcend diverse ideologies.

As they sought to defend agrarian culture against the perceived conspiracy and to attract members to the cause in numbers sufficient for political success, Populist orators faced these two significant obstacles to rhetorical success. To overcome these obstacles, Populist orators turned to the agrarian myth. Mythic analysis reveals the distinctive nature of their discourse.

Mythic Analysis of Oral Discourse

According to Frye, "the content of a myth relates it to specific social functions." Because rhetoric aims at social influence, the social functions of myth are important for rhetorical analysis. Frye notes that "seen as content, it becomes obvious that myths are not stories told just for fun: they are stories told to explain why rituals are performed; they account for the origin of law, of totems, of clans, of the ascendant social class, of the social structure resulting from earlier revolutions or conquests." Such myths "form the main body of what might be called . . . revelation, the understanding of [a society's] traditions, its customs, its situation in the world, which a society accepts as primary data."[80] Two social—that is, rhetorical—functions of myth are important for analysis of Populist speechmaking: cultural defense and transcendence.

CULTURAL DEFENSE

When cultures and ideologies come under attack—as the agrarian ideal was attacked by growing industrialism, the gospel of wealth, and social Darwinism—myth can be rallied to their defense. Initially, the defense may consist of little more than restating underlying myths. Secure in their view of the world, members of the assailed culture assume the attackers are simply in error and that enunciation of cultural truth will set them right. But if the attacks continue, defenses escalate; malevolence rather than error is attributed to the attackers.[81] In the view of members of the assailed culture, nothing less than survival of their way of life is at issue. In their discourse of cultural defense, cultural history in the form of the dominant cultural myth is reasserted to justify "the way things are." In this fashion, the dominant cultural myth is brought to bear against attack.[82]

For those who adhered to the agrarian ideal, the myth constituted an agreement, a covenant, between the yeomanry and nature—or God: in return for their honest labor, they would be rewarded with prosperity and their "rightful" place in society. In effect, then, the myth served to blind its adherents to their own responsibility for their economic and social condition. If they had borrowed money foolishly, if they had overestimated the capacity of their farms—and the Kansas climate—to produce a consistently bountiful harvest, they could not see their own error. Blinded by the myth, they ignored their own responsibility and saw themselves as victims of evil forces from outside their culture—the industrialists, bankers, speculators, and railroaders. Naturally, then, they turned to the myth to defend their culture against that perceived attack.

Further, cultural defenses grounded in myth polarize and the rhetorical strategies used are confrontational because they tend to draw clear lines between good and evil rather than to unite. Confrontation can be a "totalistic" rhetorical strategy employed by radical or revolutionary groups that challenge society from without. But in the United States in the late nineteenth century, there were two cultures, or more precisely, two dominant cultural myths, competing for control of the society: the agrarian myth and the gospel of wealth. Hence Populist rhetoric was confrontational but not "totalistic" because the Populists were competing for control of society and government, not for their destruction. The Populists' aim was not to destroy society, but to gain access to societal benefits enjoyed by those they confronted.[83]

Confrontation is a rhetorical strategy designed to make it impossible for those confronted to ignore the issues. For this task, conventional rhetoric is ineffective; "reason" allows for "counter reason," debate, and equivocation—in short, for means of ignoring the issues. Ideally, a sense of guilt must be created in those confronted; sides of good and evil are clearly drawn. The formulation is that "we" are good, but "they" are evil, and "they" have conspired to do us harm. Finally, although the parties involved share many values, those who confront seek to supplant those confronted. As long as the "haves" are in power, the "have-nots" will continue to have naught.[84] Thus the rhetoric of confrontation articulates shared values but also employs tactics that divide, deny middle ground, attempt to create guilt in those confronted, and aim at supplanting those in power. The means advocated are political not revolutionary, but the tone is nevertheless combative rather than benevolent.

MYTHIC TRANSCENDENCE

As the earlier discussion of the agrarian myth revealed, myths explain the origin or foundation of society, and from society's past comes its collective understanding of its present and what its future should be. In short, myth shapes society's understanding of itself and the world around it. Accordingly, myth informs a society's political ideology as well. Kenneth Burke explains that myths are the "pre-political" foundation or set of "first principles" upon which ideologies rest.[85] Moving beyond ideology to mythic first principles enables rhetors to transcend political differences and promote identification among disparate groups within a society. By appealing to first principles implicit within the agrarian myth, Populist speakers were able to transcend political ideologies and form the basis for a coalition of diverse groups.

Rarely did the myth appear in Populist oratory in full-blown form. Rather, mythic elements were woven into the fabric of the speeches, where they functioned in an enthymematic fashion. Because Populist audiences believed in and identified with the agrarian myth, subtle uses of the myth by Populist orators were sufficient. Mythic elements were entwined in discussions of political and economic issues. In enthymematic fashion, those mythic elements called forth emotional responses from listeners for whom the agrarian myth was a mass creed. For Populist audiences, the myth served two functions essential to transcending ideological differences and defending agrarian culture.

The myth established core values, or mythic first principles: the natural rights of all citizens; the democratic ideal; patriotism. Populist rhetors extended the myth to develop what can be called a "labor theory" of property. The society that believed in the myth, writes Eisinger, "was in full agreement that labor should be the key to possession. [Its members] . . . held that possession and improvement of the land were tantamount to ownership. Further, the concept of work for its own sake had been so important in the Puritan ethic that the mere idea was sanctified. Americans were quite willing to recognize labor as the legitimate source of property, and thus of material well-being and security."[86] In short, all people had a natural right to own land, and working that land ensured title to it. By extension, the labor theory of property became a labor theory of value. All honest labor was worthy of respect because labor was the source of everything valuable, whether agricultural commodities or industrial products. Thus all laborers were worthy of respect because they were the producers of the wealth of the nation. These values formed the core of the agrarian myth and constituted the shared values to which Populist speakers appealed in order to transcend ideological differences and attract members to the new political party.

Moreover, the myth provided criteria for separating the forces of good from the forces of evil. If those who labored were worthy of respect, then those who did not labor were worthy of disrespect. The "producers" of wealth were the forces of good. Those who did not produce, that is, those who did not labor in a sense familiar to farmers, were the forces of evil. For example, while farmers acquired the right of ownership by working the land, speculators who purchased and sold land for profit deserved no such right.[87] Feelings of sectionalism and nationalism growing from the agrarian myth, outlined earlier, also served to separate good from evil. The

East was the home of speculators, bankers, monopolists. Not only were these forces outside the garden, in the mind of western farmers they had conspired to destroy the agrarian ideal. Moreover, they were in league with European powers that were farther from the garden and therefore even more evil.[88] In Populist rhetoric, the formulation was clear and simple: the East and Europe were evil; western farmers and laborers were good.

The agrarian myth provided both the shared values and the criteria for separating good and evil necessary for transcending ideological differences and for implementing confrontational strategies. Populist speakers drew upon the natural right of all citizens to own land, the democratic ideal, and feelings of patriotism implicit within the myth. Likewise, they polarized the society into forces of good and evil, with the producers on one side and the idle plutocracy on the other. Those appeals were manifest in their speeches.

The Agrarian Myth in Populist Discourse

Examination of nearly seventy speeches delivered by Kansas Populists between 1890 and 1894 reveals that the strategic use of the agrarian myth was commonplace in Populist discourse.[89] Eleven speeches representative of Kansas Populist discourse in general were selected for this study. They provide clear and concise examples of the strategic importance of the agrarian myth. These eleven speeches span the rise and fall of Populism in Kansas in these years. The speakers include both women and men. They range from figures of national repute, such as William A. Peffer, Mary Elizabeth Lease, Lorenzo D. Lewelling, and Jerry Simpson, to individuals active at the local or county level, such as J. L. Hammers, Bertha Mellen, Mrs. T. J. Whitman, Mrs. J. C. Bare, Samuel Reynolds, and Josie Webber. The analysis begins with an examination of a single speech that illustrates the strategic functions of the agrarian myth. Then, these functions are applied in a thematic analysis of multiple texts, which reveals the pervasiveness of the myth in Kansas Populist discourse.

A REPRESENTATIVE EXAMPLE

One characteristic example of the use of the agrarian myth was in a speech delivered on Saturday, 2 April 1892, before the Harper County, Kansas, Alliance by J. L. Hammers.[90] Issues developed in this speech placed Hammers squarely in line with other Kansas Populist orators. The introduction and initial section of the body of the speech outlined in broad terms the oppression of "the people" at the hands of the "money power." This was followed by a litany of typical Populist "demands" designed to end oppression and improve economic conditions: elimination of national banks; establishment of a subtreasury system; expansion of the money supply; free coinage of silver; government ownership of railroads; establishment of a graduated income tax; and direct election of U.S. senators and the president. The conclusion was a traditional Populist call for united political action to initiate reform. Significantly, this county-level speaker addressed national issues. Hence, as analysis of other speeches will subsequently show, this "grassroots" example of Kansas Populist oratory differed little from efforts of "top-level" speakers.

Elements of the agrarian myth were diffused throughout the speech, influencing the development of substantive issues. That influence was sometimes overt, but frequently subtle and well adapted to listeners who adhered to the agrarian ideal. Thus the myth contributed significantly to the very texture of the discourse, and is best observed in extended excerpts.

"To prove that there is a financial depression among the laboring classes of this country," said Hammers, "one only needs to glance around him." He continued, enumerating a series of antithetical pairs that underscored oppression of the people:

Here we see the rich growing richer, and the poor growing poorer. There we see through "class legislation" the wealth of the many congregating into the hands of the few; here we see instances of serfdom and cruelty imposed upon the laboring classes—there we see faces pictured with poverty, want and despair. Here we see beggars, tramps and paupers; there we see in spite of a prosperous period, men, women and children starving and freezing to death. Here we see crime, insanity and intemperance increasing; there we see farmers and merchants alike on the brink of financial ruin, and every week we hear of strong companies going into bankruptcy.

Significantly, those oppressed were identified as the "laboring classes," thus blurring distinctions between farmers and other workers in an effort to transcend differences between farmers and laborers. Consistent with the tenets of the agrarian myth, all who labored, whether in field or factory or mine, were entitled to the fruits of their labor. To deny those benefits was robbery.

Hammers left no doubt regarding oppression of farm families in particular: "The sheriffs in the many counties are kept busy making levies and selling the poor people's property. All kinds of live stock, the farm products, implements and household goods are sold, and in many cases for merely nothing." Here the myth echoes as well. The property sold was that of the yeoman farmer. And the sheriff, a representative of government, was the culprit rather than the defender of agriculture.

Hammers continued to criticize the relationship of the government to the oppressed classes. "Gradually but surely," he said, "the farmers and laborers of this great nation are awakening to their perilous condition. They plainly see that this government has a system which is fast binding upon the farmers and laborers the heavy burdens of oppression." Again, no distinction was drawn between farmers and laborers as oppressed groups. Moreover, for an audience accustomed to viewing the government as the protector of agriculture, the irony of a government "binding upon the farmers and laborers the heavy burdens of oppression" was surely significant. Good and evil were clearly distinguished, with farmers and laborers on one side and the government on the other.

"Our government," Hammers said, "is accomplishing in a few years, what it took ancient governments ages to complete." He continued his comparison to ancient governments. "Egypt was a rich and powerful nation." But "her rulers became oppressive and finally her wealth drifted into the hands of a few until 1 per cent of her people owned her lands and she sank a lost government forever." Listeners were compelled to recall the natural right of land ownership characteristic of the agrarian myth. "Babylon, the mightiest city on earth," likewise crumbled, Hammers said, because its leaders "forgot the millions of laboring people who had toiled through wet and dry to create this beautiful city. She, like Egypt, allowed monopoly to strangle her and she died with two per cent of her people owning her wealth." The examples played on a key element of the agrarian myth, the natural right to own land. Moreover, Babylon allowed "monopoly to strangle her," much as monopoly gripped America.

"Then came Persia," said Hammers, " . . . and she sank with less that 1 percent of the people owning her lands. Then came glorious Greece! the wonder of the world; but she forgot her laboring people and let usury and monopoly rob them, and she sank with 4 per cent of the people owning her lands and the rest were slaves." Next came Rome. Like America, "she was founded on the principle of equality and justice," said Hammers, "and at one time under her generous system of laws, eighty-five per cent of her people had title in land but she contracted her currency, burdened the people with heavy taxes, allowed monopoly to rob her people and she died with less than one per cent of her people owning land." In each instance, causes of ancient oppression reflected Populist criticism of the U.S. government: ignoring the plight of farmers and laborers; usury; monopoly; taxation; currency contraction. And in each instance, economic issues were entwined with the natural right to own land characteristic of the agrarian myth.

Continuing his attack on government, Hammers said:

We believe that the present state of affairs are [sic] similar to the oppressions which were imposed upon our forefathers by England before they bled and died to free this country. We believe they founded this government upon the right principles. Equal rights to all and special privileges to none, which is nothing more or less than a synonym for the golden rule: Do unto others as you would others to do unto you.

Our government is far from what our forefathers intended that it should be "the land of the noble and the free." Monopolies, trusts, combines, etc., have got control of our government and are eating the heart out of the nation. The shackles of oppression have been tightened on us until forbearance has ceased to be a virtue, and we are going to do as our forefathers did; strike for freedom, not with the deadly musket or cannon, but with our powerful ballots—the only vestige of liberty left.

The passage was filled with patriotic appeals grounded in the agrarian myth. Allusions to "our forefathers" who "bled and died to free this country," and who "founded this government on the right principles," called forth images of the "embattled farmer" who left his fields to overthrow British oppression and found a democratic nation. Indeed, Hammers used the very language of the Declaration of Independence, saying "forbearance has ceased to be a virtue" in the face of economic oppression. These images had firm footing in the agrarian myth. Moreover the slogan "Equal rights to all and special privileges to none" drew upon the Jeffersonian and Jacksonian traditions central to the myth.[91] Significantly, these were first principles capable of transcending ideology and unifying farmers and laborers as oppressed people. And images of "monopolies, trusts, and combines" that were "eating the heart out of the nation" and placing "shackles of oppression" on the people delineated good from evil.

Efforts to release the government from control of monopolies, trusts, and combines, Hammers said, would "restore this nation and make this once more a government of, by and for the people." His words were those of Lincoln, the common man, the farmer, the rail-splitter who left the fields to lead the nation in its moment of greatest peril. With the possible exception of Jefferson, no figure could have been more closely identified with the agrarian myth in the mind of the audience.

The "demands" Hammers made were aimed at specific economic reforms and comprised the traditional Populist platform. Yet each drew upon elements of the agrarian myth. Abolition of the national banking system would return control of the currency to the government, that is, to the people. "We the people are the government," said Hammers. Putting the people in control of the government was consistent with the tenets of the myth:

A government that nourishes three thousand and seven hundred banks by providing them with money at one per cent per annum, and gives to them the control of the circulating medium when it knows that these same banks are crushing the very life out of industry and robbing the people by making them pay interest on their own money, I say, a government that will allow such a thing is not a government for and by the people, but a government of traitors and thieves, and is not deserving of support by the honest people.

"Government for and by the people," again echoed Lincoln. But most important, justification for reform of government rested in the agrarian myth. It taught that just government protected agriculture. The "honest people," the yeoman farmers, were not bound to support evil government. Rather, they were bound to supplant forces of evil and return government to first principles of democracy.

Hammers next presented the Populist demand for establishment of a national subtreasury. This plan, under which farmers would be advanced low-interest government loans on nonperishable commodities held in government warehouses, was intended to eliminate speculation that resulted in low prices for farmers at harvest and high prices for speculators later in the year. Hammers acknowledged opposition to the scheme: "From the calamity-howlers of the old parties comes the cry of class legislation, unconstitutional, impracticable, visionary and never will do." His refutation of these charges constituted perhaps the most clear example of the agrarian myth in the speech: "But my dear friends it is not class legislation even though it benefit the farmer, because the farmer is the basis of all classes; that is to say all other occupations are class occupations except farming which is the basis of all classes, and anything that benefits the farmer must benefit all other classes, and all benefits permeate through him to each and every class of society." No precept was more characteristic of the agrarian myth. The freeholder—the independent, self-sufficient yeoman—was the foundation of democratic society. In the Populist view, then, programs to benefit farmers were consistent with the teachings of the myth, and would benefit other laborers as well.

Likewise, demands for expansion of the currency, free coinage of silver, and a graduated income tax were entwined with mythic elements. "Since the demonetization of silver," said Hammers, "the price of property and labor has decreased 33½ per cent, and will continue to do so just as long as the circulating medium is limited to the gold standard alone." Thus the natural right to own property was undermined by the gold standard. "In 1867 the farmers owned 70 per cent of the wealth of our nation and they paid 80 per cent of the taxes; to-day," he continued, "they own less than 20 per cent of the wealth but still are compelled to pay 80 per cent of the taxes." Again, government policy undermined the foundation of society, the farmer.

In his conclusion, Hammers made Populist demands "the means of making this a government for the people because they would bring liberty, justice and equality to all." The language echoed both Lincoln at Gettysburg and Jefferson in the Declaration of Independence. Influence of the agrarian myth was unmistakable.

This extended analysis reveals the influence of the agrarian myth in a single characteristic example of Kansas Populist oratory. In essence, elements of the myth served two functions. Mythic first principles fundamental to natural rights and U.S. democracy minimized distinctions between farmers and other laborers in the mind of the Alliance audience. Farm listeners were encouraged to view themselves and, by extension of mythic first principles, other workers as a single class. At least for the Alliance audience, this function provided a means of transcending ideological differences between farmers and other laborers. Mythic elements also provided a foundation for defense of culture. Listeners were invited to gaze upon images of the yeoman assailed by plutocracy and government. The forces of good confronted the forces of evil. Images of attacks upon the dominant cultural myth, upon the worldview of the audience, provided motivation for political activity to supplant the forces of evil. Those mythic elements pervaded Populist discourse and are evident in the speeches of both women and men who ranged from major figures to county lecturers. Thematic analysis of the remaining texts supports that claim.

THE IDEAL CITIZENS

No image was more fundamental to the agrarian myth than that of the sturdy, self-sufficient yeoman farmer, the ideal citizen and foundation of U.S. democracy. Populist efforts to transcend ideological differences between farmers and laborers were necessarily grounded in values exemplified by that image. In September 1892 Bertha Mellen spoke to those gathered for an Alliance picnic in Anderson County, Kansas. Noting that opposition newspapers frequently classed Populists as "calamity howlers" and "a crowd of lazy, worthless loafers," Mellen rallied images of the yeoman farmer to their defense:

> Notwithstanding all this vilification, I believe today that the farmers of Kansas are the truest—the most honorable—the most chivalrous and heroic people on the earth. Not more so were our patriot fathers under the immortal Washington—not more so those fire-tested and battle-scarred veterans of France, the old guard of Napoleon—and not more so were the legions of ancient Rome, under the martial leadership of the imperial Caesar.
>
> True to principle, true to home, and true to country; honorable in the discharge of all the obligations of life; chivalric in their love of, and devotion to, their wives and children; heroic in their endurance of misfortune, failure, losses, and the oppression and depression of the times, the Kansas farmer stands today the living representative of the noblest and best type of manhood in all the civilized world. It is a true man who stands up for principle in the face of taunts and falsehoods and vilification. It is an honest man who goes without the necessaries [sic] of life that he may keep his word and pay his debts. It is a truly heroic man who battles with the elements and wrests a living from Kansas soil amid the uncertainties of our seasons, the relentless encroachments of capital, the merciless discrimination of class legislation, and the general depression of prices that hangs like a pall over our land.[92]

Thus her listeners were presented with a full-blown portrait of the hero of the agrarian myth, the yeoman farmer.

For Mellen and her Populist audience, yeoman farmers were "the truest—the most honorable—the most chivalrous and heroic people on the earth." They were "[t]rue to principle, true to home, and true to country; honorable in the discharge of all the obligations of life; chivalric in their love of, and devotion to, their wives and children." According to Mellen, farmers were no less honorable that the first agrarian heroes, "our patriot fathers under the immortal Washington." Other historical allusions, to France and especially to Rome, intensified the encomium. Classical images were consistent with the patriotic values implicit in the agrarian myth. Therefore Mellen's language heightened the effectiveness of mythic elements present in the speech.

However, this image of the yeoman farmer was tarnished, Mellen said, besmirched by "taunts and falsehoods and vilification." The sturdy yeoman was oppressed by "the relentless encroachments of capital, the merciless discrimination of class legislation." Thus the sides of good and evil were drawn, with the honest, upright yeoman on the side of good, and capitalists and their legislative servants on the side of evil. Mellen rehearsed the traditional values characteristic of the agrarian myth and necessary for transcending ideological differences. She also separated society into forces of good and evil along lines suggested by the myth. Other Populist orators invoked the same mythic images.

On 26 July 1894 Populist governor Lorenzo D. Lewelling delivered a major campaign address at Huron Place in Kansas City that reasserted his commitment to traditional Populist issues.[93] Like Mellen, Lewelling invoked images of the sturdy yeoman oppressed by the forces of evil, but he did so in the earthy style that often characterized Populist discourse:

> Now our friends have told us that the only trouble about this country and our condition is a "lack of confidence." And I saw an old farmer the other day who said he had been to market with a load of wheat. He said he got $7.50 for the 30 bushels of wheat that he had taken to town, and he bought a couple of pairs of shoes for the children, and a calico dress for his wife, and then he felt confident that he had gone dead broke. He said he felt all played out by the biggest confidence game that had ever been perpetrated on an unsuspecting public. And I sympathized with him because I believe it was true; still he had to pay his mortgage—And when his neighbor sold another load of wheat and still another load, and put his money in the bank and kept on accumulating in order to pay off the mortgage and finally the bank broke and then he said he had lost his confidence, and his patience too, and swore by the Great Horn Spoon, that hereafter he would vote the Populist ticket.[94]

Again, the hard-working yeoman farmer, who sought only to provide for his family, was beset by the forces of evil, the banks and mortgage holders.

Lewelling's repeated pun on "lack of confidence" exemplified the wit of Populist speaking. The old farmer was not "oppressed," but rather, in the language of the common people, he was "all played out" and had "gone dead broke." This style enhanced the image of the yeoman farmer; it heightened the effectiveness of the mythic elements Lewelling employed. Moreover, Lewelling's suggestion that the old farmer would hereafter "vote the Populist ticket" was an invitation to his listeners to join in political action characteristic of nontotalistic confrontation.

However, Populist orators could not expect to form a working coalition of farmers and laborers without extending these values to include other segments of the productive class. Lewelling did just that:

> Now, I am going to say something to you, whether you are a merchant, whether you are a business man or a farmer or a day-laborer. It is my opinion that if you are an honest industrious citizen; if you are frugal, if you are careful of what you earn, that you have a right to enough to eat and drink, and clothe your self and family, and if you do not have it, it is because somebody else has got more than his share. Now, that is anarchy—Talking treason now. But, if that is anarchy my Republican fellow citizen, put it in your pipe and smoke it. I remember what Patrick Henry said many years ago when he stood up before the Virginia Assembly and said "Caesar had his Brutus, Charles the First his Cromwell, and George the Third"—"Treason, Treason!" echoed through the House, "Anarchy, Anarchy! Put him out"—"And George the Third," continued Patrick Henry, in a faltering voice, "May profit by their example. If that be treason make the most of it."
>
> If that be treason, when I state a citizen is entitled to enough to eat and decently clothe himself—if that is treason, my Republican fellow citizen, "Make the most of it."

Honorable qualities characteristic of the yeoman farmer—honesty, industriousness, frugality—were applied to farmers, merchants, small businessmen, and laborers alike. All were oppressed; their natural right to self-sufficiency, to enough to eat and drink and to clothe their families, was abridged because "somebody else has got more than his share."

Quoting Patrick Henry linked the common people with the Revolutionary spirit. They were placed on the side of good with the founders of the nation. On the side of evil were the Republicans. Hence, for Lewelling and his Populist audience, if "somebody else has got more than his share," it was because Republican government was guilty promoting the gospel of wealth and the self-made man and of failing to protect the yeoman. Listeners were invited to confront the forces of evil.

Populist speakers consistently linked the interests of farmers with those of other laborers. On 21 July 1890 Mrs. T. J. Whitman reminded the Norton County, Kansas, Farmers' Alliance: "That the industrial and agricultural classes of society are the real foundations of our government and the support of its institutions has been taught us from our earliest recollection."[95] This teaching was consistent with values implicit within the agrarian myth—that the yeoman was the ideal citizen and the bedrock of true democracy. Moreover, Whitman's speech reflected the Populist effort to extend key provisions of the agrarian myth to encompass industrial laborers and expand the political coalition.

In May 1891 representatives of farm and labor organizations met in Cincinnati and formed the national People's Party. Chairman of the convention was William Alfred Peffer, the Populist U.S. senator from Kansas. Peffer's speech to the convention also linked the interests of farmers and industrial laborers: "Then let all of us, every man whose work adds anything to the wealth of the country, or to the comfort of the people, unite in this movement, with malice toward none, but with charity to all, gathering force as you go along."[96] Like Hammers, Peffer's words echoed Lincoln, the latter-day Cincinnatus. They also embodied the Populist labor theory of value that was essential for extending the boundaries of the agrarian myth to encompass urban industrial laborers.

Once formed, said Peffer, this mighty coalition of farmers and industrial laborers could not be stopped. "You will find that among the first fruits of the marriage which we are celebrating here will be the birth of a child about nine months from next Saturday, and his name will be 'National Party,'" he said. "We will unite the blacksmith and the printer, the carpenter and the tailor, the manufacturer and the farmer, in one, great, army of the people, and we will sweep the country like a cyclone sweeps our western prairies. (Loud applause.)" Peffer linked the interests of all laborers, of all producers of wealth, in the cause of reform. And with the formation of the new party, listeners were once again invited to political action characteristic of totalistic confrontation.

On 15 September 1891 "Sockless" Jerry Simpson, U.S. congressman from Kansas's Seventh District, addressed a party gathering at Wichita. With wit and irreverence, Simpson also separated the interests of producers—yeoman farmers and industrial laborers—from those of evil capitalists:

> They say to us again, "You people are only talking in the interest of one class; you but speak for physical labor; you neglect brain labor. You should protect that." It has been demonstrated that brain labor is usually capable of taking care of itself; it can shift from one occupation to another. If a man is a minister of the gospel and he proves that he is not capable for that position he becomes a railroad conductor. If he shows he is not capable for that, (he can shift from place to place) if he shows an incapacity to fill that position, you make him president of the railroad; if he shows that he has struck the right job and steals the company's money you at once send him to the United States Senate.
>
> You see, brain labor can change from place to place. If he shows that he cannot fill any of these positions, nature has not endowed him in this way, probably you make him editor of a daily paper in your city. (Applause.)[97]

Producers had a good laugh at the expense of nonproducers. But Simpson's joke carried double meaning. It directly confronted the gospel of wealth by ridiculing social Darwinism. Instead of rising through competition to positions of importance,

Simpson said, railroad presidents, senators, and newspaper editors descended through incompetence.

In a paper presented to the Douglas County, Kansas, Farmers' Alliance on 4 October 1892, Mrs. J. C. Bare also separated good from evil along lines suggested by the agrarian myth.

> The ballot is the golden gateway to liberty, and the privilege of use should be guided by reason and the deepest and truest instincts of true loyalty to our nation's prosperity. Now what has been the object of all these agitators in all they have written and spoken? Is it to awaken sympathy and feeling and call the attention of the favored Jew to the neglected classes? Oh, no! It is their great purpose to bring the industrial classes to see the necessity of sympathizing with themselves and their children, and not leave to them slavery as a legacy.[98]

Bare's statement again pitted the industrial classes against the moneyed class. It also revealed the confrontational nature of Populist rhetoric. Her aim was not to "awaken sympathy and feeling" within the enemy. Rather, it was to spur political action through the ballot, "the golden gateway to liberty." She sought not to convince or persuade, but rather to supplant. Bare's statement also revealed what historians have seen as a strain of anti-Semitism in Populist discourse.[99] Significantly, she made the "favored Jew" the symbol of the moneyed class.

Populist orators carried their gospel far and wide. On 2 September 1893 Kansas Populist Mary Elizabeth Lease spoke before a labor audience in Chicago. After enumerating the political and economic ills suffered by the laboring classes, Lease argued:

> The farmers in every conflict that has swept this country from the battle of Lexington down to the great rebellion have always come to the front and have solved the great questions involved successfully. Today they are called on to solve the labor question. You may club down the laborers in the cities and make them the slaves of plutocracy, but you cannot, thank God! starve and club down the farmers of this country who stand ready to save it.[100]

Speaking to an eastern audience at Cooper Union in New York City a year later, Lease echoed her Chicago speech. "We have heard, out on the prairies of the West, the cry of your starving thousands," she said. "But your monopolies and corporations cannot starve down the farmers of this broad, free land. The farmers are the hope of the nation. They are the ones who leaped forward on every occasion to save the country."[101] In this fashion Lease attempted to unite western farmers and eastern laborers in the crusade against the evil money powers.

Populist orators drew upon values implicit in the agrarian myth in an effort to transcend political ideologies that separated farmers and laborers. All producers of wealth were invited to join in the great Populist reform crusade. As evidence that listeners should leave the old parties, Populist speakers frequently offered themselves as examples. Simpson told his Wichita audience:

> I used to be a true blue Republican, but I want to tell you good people I am working, I am working hard that I may undo the wrong I did. I believe in atonement for sins. (Applause.) If God will spare my life long enough, I hope to atone for all the evil I did when I voted the Republican ticket. Looking back as I do I cannot remember a single vote that I cast that was for a good principle. I make that as an open confession. They say open confession is good for the soul.

Peffer's account of his own conversion from Republicanism was equally forceful:

Why, my Republican friends, and I have lots of them . . . they say to me, "Why, Peffer, you were always a strong Republican. Ain't you afraid the course you and your people are pursuing will result in placing the Democratic party in power?" I have two answers to that; the first is, it is not any of our business whether the Democratic party comes into power or not; the other answer is this, My dear old friend, I love you for the good you did. If you really fear the incoming of the Democracy; if you would rather take forty doses of quinine in two hours and a half than to address the President as a Democrat, there is one easy way out of the difficulty—you just turn in with us. (Laughter and applause.) And we won't leave a grease spot of Democracy by the time you and we go for them together. (Applause.) Then you can go and tell your wives and neighbors, "We killed the bear." (Laughter.)

Thus Simpson and Peffer both offered themselves as role models for others to follow in their conversion to Populism.

Lewelling did the same. He told his Kansas City audience: "I am a Republican myself—I am an Abraham Lincoln Republican myself; and I guess I am a Democrat too. I am a Thomas Jefferson Democrat, because those great and good men stood for all that was good and true and noble in the government of men; and I am glad to be classed in that company, if you will permit me to say that I am a Republican and a Democrat." Of course, Lincoln and Jefferson were not only Republican and Democrat, respectively, but both were also exemplars of the agrarian ideal.

Populist orators consistently invited listeners to move beyond political ideologies of the old parties and join the new party of the people. Values implicit in the agrarian myth were the "first principles," in Burke's words, under which all laborers could unite in opposition to the money power. That power had conspired to oppress the people.

A CONSPIRACY OF EVIL

The agrarian myth taught that people had a natural right to the land. "The freemen of this country are entitled to the homes that they have made," said Peffer. "All they ask is to be allowed time in which to pay their debts and save their homes." Simpson echoed the sentiment before his Wichita audience: "What are opportunities? Well, the land is an opportunity. That is the store house [sic] of wealth, where the God that created this earth stored up enough for everybody. They must have access to it to produce wealth. Is not that right my brother?" "Man is a land animal," Simpson continued. "He can neither live under the earth nor in the earth; he must live on top of it, not in the sea. If by granting special laws and legislating special privileges for monopolies you have deprived your brother of a chance to live, he must go back to you and buy the right to live." Simpson's words embodied the most fundamental tenets of the agrarian myth: God had made the land and called the yeoman to cultivate it. In turn, the yeoman would be rewarded with nature's bounty. But government had failed the yeoman, Simpson said, "by granting special laws and legislating special privileges for monopolies."

Thus if the people, the producers of all wealth, did not enjoy the bounty of nature, it was because evil forces outside the garden had conspired against them. Said Simpson:

Now, then, we complain that while we have a great many opportunities for producing wealth, while the Great Creator of the universe has furnished it with boundless resources, enough for everybody, every man, woman and child should have a good living if they would be industrious and saving. We claim that the people have been deprived of this opportunity, that they do not get the necessaries of life, but they have been deprived of their rights by cunning schemes of the legislators, a new and more refined system of robbery.

The people were "deprived" of a "good living" not through their own sloth, as social Darwinists would have it, and not even through fair competition in the marketplace, but by "cunning schemes," by conspiracy. Bare told her Douglas County audience:

> This world, where life ought to be grand, beautiful and joyous, where the hungry ought to find food, the weary rest, and comfortable homes could be provided for all; this world of matchless beauty with fountains of blessings springing up on every hand, so admirably adapted to the needs and highest profits of the human race; this, our native home, has become the abode of selfishness and greed, and mental force is now being substituted for the old time force in planning all sorts of ways for inflicting wrong on the defenseless. By making corners and combines and securing laws for individual advantages, the producer of wealth is forced to see only his daily round of labor become as "a great serial story, continued at the end of each day so long as life shall last." Cruel and unjust legislators with politicians and voters swerving this way and that by tides of self interest and passion have practically placed human rights and liberties in the hands of the minority and have enchained and thwarted the legal rights of the industrial classes.

In the Populist view, only a human-made conspiracy of evil, originating outside the garden of the world, could account for the economic plight of the producers.

For Populists, the guilty parties were easily identified. "We complain that in the last twenty-five or thirty years the laws of the country have not kept pace with the new facilities for producing wealth. . . . We charge both the republican [*sic*] and democratic [*sic*] parties with this neglect; that they have legislated in the interest of the classes and in the interest of a few," said Simpson, "and we think we can maintain our case." And in Kansas City, Lewelling said: "The machinery of government has been arrayed against us. It seems to me that the Courts and Judges of this country have become the mere tools and vassals and jumping-jacks of the great corporations that pull the string while the courts and judges dance." The government, the old political parties, and even the courts had conspired with evil capitalists to oppress the people.

According to the agrarian myth, the proper role of government was protection of the yeoman farmer. Government in league with giant trusts and corporations failed its responsibility and was unworthy of support. In Kansas City, Lewelling made that point clearly to his partisan audience:

> What is government to me if it do not [*sic*] make it possible for me to live! and provide for my family! The trouble has been, we have so much regard for the rights of property that we have forgotten the liberties of the individual. . . . I claim it is the business of the government to make it possible for me to live and sustain the life of my family. If the government don't [*sic*] do that, what better is the government to me than a state of barbarism and everywhere we slay, and the slayer in turn is slain and so on the great theatre of life is one vast conspiracy [in which] all creatures from the worm to the man in turn rob their fellows. That my fellow citizens is the law of natural selection—the survival of the fittest—Not the survival of the fittest, but the survival of the strongest. It is time that man should rise above it.

Lewelling and other Populist orators thus rejected the gospel of wealth and social Darwinism and invited their listeners to join in the great crusade to supplant the forces of evil, to restore the yeoman—the mythic hero of the agrarian ideal—to the preeminent position in society.

CONFRONTING THE DEVIL

Populist speakers sought not to destroy society or government, but rather to supplant the forces of evil from positions of power. Those aims were reflected in Populist oratory. For example, in his speech at Wichita, Simpson clothed his call for political action in a literary allusion undoubtedly familiar to his Kansas audience:

> In Mark Twain's last book, *The Yankee In Rome*, the man that illustrated it has made two very striking pictures. Over here is a long legged, long billed crane standing near a jug with a long neck on it, full of water. Over here is a little short nosed poodle dog. Here is an opportunity; both must drink of it. The crane has a long bill and puts it down into the long necked jug and gets a drink for himself, and the little poodle dog can only stand and look at him. After a little while the crane turns around and says: "Look here, you are thirsty. Why don't you grow a long bill like me?" After awhile the little dog lays down [*sic*] and dies for want of water.
>
> Here is another picture, the same one continued, so to speak: The top is knocked off the long necked jug, and the little dog drinks and the crane drinks; both on an equality. That is what the Alliance proposes to do. We are going to knock the top of this jug off, so that the dog and the crane will get an equal chance, an equal opportunity. (Great Applause.)

The tale illustrated the familiar Populist slogan: "Equal Justice for All, Special Privilege for None." Moreover, Simpson's tone was combative and confrontational, and his language enhanced images of the oppressed yeoman. The story was based upon Aesop's fable of the fox and crane, but Simpson attributed it to the prototypical U.S. writer known for praise of common people and local color, Mark Twain. The four-legged creature was not a fox, suggesting cunning, but a dog, suggesting the common, loyal, and faithful. They drank not from a patrician water vessel, but from a an unpretentious jug. And Simpson suggested not that his audience "demand their fair share of the water," but that they "knock the top of this jug off!"

In Cincinnati, Peffer charged that "money is king in this country, and, like a king, it parcels out its patronage to leaders of clans, relying on them for support in time of need, and the leaders of clans stand at the head of parties and their vassals are the voters." His solution was united political action of the people to supplant evil forces:

> We, the people, have come to the conclusion that it is time for this feudalism to cease. We propose to restore the authority of the people. We propose to place the government of the country in the hands of its rightful inheritors, the people. (Applause.)
>
> This movement then does not mean the wiping out of existence of existing forms of government or any of the present usages of society that are not built up and sustained by the money power. What we mean is that the people shall rule, as they have a right to—that is all. (Applause.)

Peffer's language echoed the Declaration of Independence. But he pledged united political action of the people to supplant evil forces rather than armed revolt.

Mellen employed similar images to inspire her audience. "I believe that the men and women who have wrought from the American desert of the geographers a commonwealth that is the peer of any in the galaxy of states," she said, "can mould from this confusion of financial theories—this Babel of partisan clamor—this chaos of political antagonisms a golden age of justice, of peace and of universal prosperity for every dweller beneath the protecting folds of the flag we love and venerate." Her images were patriotic, not revolutionary; they were consistent with the values implicit in the agrarian myth.

Lewelling invoked divine assistance and exhorted listeners to political action in the coming election:

> I believe that if there is a God in heaven, as I do believe, that he will hear the cry of his suffering children and the giant Despair will yet be slain by the great uprising of this nation. With these great principles of our common cause, we are going forth. We will be fearless as we go forth and we will be able to conquer. We will be able to subdue kingdoms and in time will stop the mouths of liars, out of weakness we will be made strong. We shall wax valiant in the fight, and when November comes will put to flight the armies of the aliens.

Thus did Lewelling and other Populist speakers call the Alliance into political battle against the forces of the devil.

When Populist orators surveyed the economic, political, and social chaos of the 1890s, they looked out from a position grounded in the agrarian myth. The myth taught that all people had the right to own land and to enjoy the fruit of their honest labor. It taught that nature was beneficent and would reward all who were honest, frugal, and diligent. It taught that agriculture was the foundation of the truly democratic society that offered equal rights to all and special privileges to none. But the mythic ideal differed sharply from the farmers' perception of economic reality. As Norman Pollack remarks:

> In place of a society suffused with an equalitarian spirit, a society which is responsive to the growth of all and oppresses none, Populists pointed to the mortgage-ridden farmer, the unemployed worker, and the so-called "tramp" moving from one town to the next in search of work. In place of the free citizen, deriving benefit from his labor on the farm or in the factory, determining the policies under which he is to be governed, and enjoying a sense of dignity in his daily life, Populists found man to be impoverished, voiceless and degraded.[102]

In response, Populists sought not to return to the past agrarian ideal, but to infuse the present with the values implicit in that agrarian heritage. Contrary to the teachings of social Darwinism, Pollack states, Populists contended "that there is nothing inevitable about misery and squalor, nothing irreversible about the tendencies toward the concentration of wealth and the legitimation of corporate power." And they sought to "alter the course of . . . society in a humanistic direction."[103] The means they chose were rhetorical and political, not revolutionary. In their oratory, Populists drew upon fundamental principles implicit in the agrarian myth in an effort to transcend ideological differences and unify producers in a crusade to supplant the forces of evil from power. At least for a time, Populist orators were successful in forming a working political coalition of diverse groups.

The Rhetorical Success and Failure of Populism in Kansas

In the summer and fall of 1890 the common citizens of the Populist Party in Kansas launched a campaign unlike any seen before on the plains. "Never before," said Clanton, "had the ordinary citizen been so engrossed in political matters. From

August to November, 1890, political ferment consumed the state like a prairie fire, as tens of thousands of Kansans flocked to the banner of the People's Party intent on demonstrating, apparently, that the purification of politics was not," as Kansas Republican senator John J. Ingalls had asserted, "an iridescent dream."[104] If, as those who adhered to the agrarian myth believed, the privileged classes had conspired to take control of government from the people, Kansas Populists were determined that the people must take it back.

Their success was stunning. In the November election, the Populists elected five U.S. congressmen, ninety-one members of the state House of Representatives—compared to twenty-six for the Republicans and eight for the Democrats—and came within three percentage points of capturing the governorship. Moreover, with the Populists firmly in control of the House, the retirement of Ingalls from the U.S. Senate was a foregone conclusion; early in 1891 the Populist House replaced him with William A. Peffer of Topeka, editor of the *Kansas Farmer*.[105] Nationally, election results for 1890 indicate that third party candidates were as successful in other states as well. Frederick Emory Haynes, their contemporary, reported that farmers "elected governors in Georgia, Texas, South Dakota, and South Carolina, carried State tickets in . . . Nebraska, and South Dakota, and elected a number of Congressmen."[106] Said Rickard, "the results of the election proved that the Populists had articulated the issues that concerned the voters."[107]

Despite their success in 1890, Kansas Populists approached the 1892 election campaign with caution. Party leaders were distressed by the results of local elections in 1891. In those contests, Goodwyn explains, "the Republicans had won 277 local offices to the Populists' 127, a shocking change from the previous year, when Alliancemen had won 324 to only 71 for the G.O.P." As the campaign of 1892 neared, he continues, "this setback caused a shift in policy. Officeholders, who were rather prominent in Kansas third party leadership, responded to the election returns by sounding out Democrats on the idea of possible cooperation."[108]

Cooperation, or fusion, with the Democrats was not popular with the majority of Populists, but when the Democrats agreed to campaign on the basis of the Populist platform, fusion was achieved. According to Walter T. K. Nugent, "there had been talk in the first Populist campaign, in 1890, of a fusion ticket for state officers, but it had not happened [on a formal basis]. . . . In 1892, however, fusion did take place, as Democrats endorsed Populist candidates for state offices, congressional seats, and the legislature."[109] At the state level, the result of fusion was a sweep. Populist gubernatorial candidate Lorenzo D. Lewelling and the rest of the state ticket were elected. The Populists also took control of the state Senate, but the huge margin they had gained in the House in 1890 had melted away. That fact presaged the political catastrophe that awaited. Sensing potential trouble for 1894, Populists again sought fusion with the Democrats. Together the two parties could again defeat the Republicans, they believed. But two issues stood in the way: woman suffrage and prohibition. For most Democrats and many other members of the Populist coalition, no reforms were more abhorrent.

As political issues, both woman suffrage and prohibition antedated Populism in Kansas.[110] Thus, by the time of the agrarian revolt in the 1890s, the controversy surrounding woman suffrage grew from attempts to grant women "full" rather than "limited" suffrage, and the disagreement over liquor revolved around attempts to "resubmit" the prohibitory amendment to the state constitution to a vote of the people. The issues were tightly linked because the majority of Kansas voters on both sides of the prohibition issue believed that granting women full suffrage would significantly strengthen the antiliquor vote.[111] Moreover, both issues were linked with the People's Party. For example, Argersinger reports that "in the 1891 Kansas House of Representatives, Populists introduced at least two bills to establish woman suffrage." Votes in the House revealed the partisan nature of the issue. Populists "overwhelmingly supported the issue when it came to a vote (56-17 and 65-18); Republicans, on the other hand, were even more united in opposing the question (3-16 and 3-12), as were Democrats (1-16 and 1-4)."[112] Values implicit in the agrarian myth fostered unity among Populists, suffragists, and prohibitionists.

According to political scientist Alan P. Grimes, the social forces that sparked the Populist crusade likewise fueled the drive for woman suffrage, especially in the West. Spreading industrialization and urbanization that threatened the agrarian lifestyle prompted reformers to seek a return to more traditional values. For many, woman suffrage seemed a means to that end. Grimes concludes that an appeal for woman suffrage was an appeal for "the standards of decency and righteousness that had prevailed at home; an appeal to the platitudes, the commonplaces, the little moral aphorisms which had been voiced in the kitchen or at the family table."[113] Such standards of decency and righteousness were virtually identical to those embraced by the simple, honest, self-sufficient yeoman. This ideological affinity between suffragists, prohibitionists, and Populists was manifest in Populist rhetoric.

Attendant to the rhetorical vision of the yeoman farmer as the ideal citizen who possessed a natural right to the land was the belief that all citizens had a natural right to participate in their own governance. The right to participate meant the right to vote. That right, many Populist orators argued, applied to women no less than men. Populists were influenced also by the spirit of individualism and the work ethic that had driven farmers to homestead in Kansas in the first place. Consistent with the tenets of the agrarian myth, that philosophy held that people of proper character and moral strength could succeed and prosper through their own labor, if only given an equal opportunity to do so. Use of alcohol undermined character and independence and eventually destroyed prosperity. Hence it is not surprising that Populist orators extended key values implicit within the agrarian myth to advocate both woman suffrage and prohibition. Temperance was consistent with the yeoman hero's "wholesomeness and integrity" described by Hofstadter. And as "the best and most reliable sort of citizen" in a democracy, the yeoman stood for enfranchisement of all, regardless of sex.

Although many Kansas Populists supported the moral reforms, as woman suffrage and prohibition were called, the sentiment was not unanimous within the coalition that had been so successful in the elections of 1890 and 1892. Most of the state's Democrats were industrial laborers and immigrants who strongly opposed both reforms. Their support was essential if the coalition was to succeed again in 1894. They were willing to compromise on economic issues, but deep-seated, Old World cultural biases made acceptance of woman suffrage and prohibition impossible.[114]

The equal suffrage and prohibition issues forced Populist orators in Kansas to walk a rhetorical tightrope. The trick was to appease suffrage and prohibition groups without alienating industrial laborers and dissident Democrats. Simpson's speech at Wichita illustrated the difficulty of the task. "I went to my prohibition friends," he said. "I approached the subject with awe. I know it is a dangerous subject, for when he votes prohibition he closes the gates of the whiskey traffic. If I had the power tonight I would sweep all the infernal traffic in liquor out of existence. (Great Applause.)" The enthusiasm with which his audience greeted the mention of prohibition only reminded Simpson of the rhetorical feat he must perform. "There is no use talking temperance," Simpson continued, ". . . poverty is the father and breeder of intemperance today. We say we propose to surround those men with purer conditions; we will open up new modes of living to him; give him an opportunity; . . . give him a good home." "The question with us is not whether he goes home tonight drunk or sober," said Simpson, "but the question is shall he have a home to go to. After that we will take the next step and see if we cannot persuade him to quit drinking liquor." Thus did the congressman attempt to work both sides of the prohibition issue. He opposed liquor, but blamed its abuse on the evil forces of economic oppression that were familiar Populist targets. The solution, he said, was not prohibition but an end to the poverty that drove otherwise good people to drink. Even then, the answer was not elimination of liquor but persuasion to end its use.

However, in 1893 the state legislature forced the issue and ended the rhetorical balancing act by placing before the Kansas voters a constitutional amendment providing equal suffrage. As the election of 1894 approached, apprehension grew within the Populist coalition. Both sides knew that the fate of the coalition, and of the party itself, rested on this single issue.[115]

Prosuffrage voices grew increasingly strident. For supporters of the amendment, there could be no compromise; the People's Party must declare for woman suffrage, and against resubmission of the liquor question, or lose their support. In March Josie Webber of Anderson County presented a paper before the Lone Elm Alliance. Unlike Simpson, she made no effort to straddle the issues of suffrage and prohibition. From the beginning, Webber questioned the motives of those Populists who claimed to support woman suffrage:

> One week ago tonight the question of "Woman Suffrage" was brought before the Lodge and ably discussed by a number of our members, and, with but one exception, all agreed that women, being deprived of "suffrage" were . . . being defrauded of their rights. . . . Of course, it is all right for them to think so. We think so ourselves, but, does it not seem a little strange that man, who is proverbially selfish, is for once proving himself so unselfish?[116]

Her answer was not flattering. She admitted that "a great number of men really think it is unjust not to give woman a voice in making the laws of a nation she helps to maintain," but concluded, "a greater number . . . are ready to give her a helping hand because they deem it expedient. They want the women's votes to help their party out, and they think if they help them, they will be grateful enough to return the compliment."

Webber argued that women were willing to support the party. But she made it clear that the party must support both woman suffrage and prohibition in return. Her statement illustrated the dilemma the Populists faced in 1894. Webber continued:

> Don't, magnanimous man, O! don't build a castle in the air to tumble down, about your ears. Since you are so wise as to take that stand [to support woman suffrage], be a little wiser, and go a step farther—put a Prohibition plank in your platform. . . . Why, I am afraid when Woman Suffrage at last wins the day, these parties will be in as bad a strait as the drunken man in London station, who was clinging to a lamp post and looking despairingly after a departing train which he wished to board and saying, "If I let go I'll fall, and if I don't let go I'll get left." And so with them. If they endorse prohibition they will lose the whiskey votes, and if they don't they will lose the women's votes.
>
> They had better let the beer-drinking Germans and whiskey-drinking Americans go and have the votes of honest, upright men, and pure, virtuous women.

Webber's speech illustrated the position of the prosuffrage and prohibition forces in the People's Party; the forces of good were clearly divided from the forces of evil. In her view, those who supported prohibition were good. Those who opposed prohibition by voting "with a party that will not come out against intemperance," and thereby dug their sons "a drunkard's grave," were evil. There was no middle ground; the party must either support both woman suffrage and prohibition or lose the support of women. But her argument also revealed the other side of the dilemma confronting Kansas Populists. Supporting the moral issues meant losing the support of "beer-drinking Germans" and "whiskey-drinking Americans," who were frequently the immigrants, industrial laborers, and dissident Democrats the party had courted since 1890.

Populist advocacy of woman suffrage was not limited to women speakers. In August 1893 county lecturer Samuel Reynolds presented the case for woman suffrage to the Douglas County, Kansas, Farmers' Alliance. Reynolds saw complete harmony between the Populist faith in the agrarian myth and the campaign for woman suffrage. "I believe in the doctrine of 'equal rights to all and special privileges to none,'" he said. "This principle is held by the alliance, it is the shibboleth of every reformer, and is taught, if not in direct terms in spirit by the Sermon on the Mount." "How any one can advocate this principle and at the same time refuse equal rights to woman and accord special privileges to man," he concluded, "is beyond my comprehension."[117]

Nor did prohibition escape Reynolds's attention. Like many voters, he linked the two issues together, saying that woman suffrage would constitute a mighty force against the liquor interests:

> On the question of temperance the woman's vote would be mainly correct. But few women drink liquor. Almost none in the middle walks of life among the great body of the people. The women who drink are found among the wine bibbers of the upper stratum and the beer guzzlers of the city slums. The great body of woman voters would be in favor of temperance and morality.

Unfortunately, Reynolds faced the same dilemma that haunted Simpson, Webber, and other Populist speakers. Consistent with the tenets of the agrarian myth, he portrayed women from the "middle walks of life among the great body of the people" as good; they would vote to prohibit demon rum. On the other hand, he portrayed the female "wine bibbers of the upper stratum" as evil users of alcohol. But classed along with those of the "upper stratum" were "the beer guzzlers of the city slums." Again, those "beer guzzlers" were frequently the industrial laborers the party wanted to attract. Obviously, the People's Party in Kansas was much like Webber's man in London station. Their train was scheduled to depart on 12 June 1894, when the Populist state convention was set to open.

Kansas Republicans were acutely aware of both the political volatility of woman suffrage and of the potential split between Populists and Democrats. Intent on breaking up the Populist coalition, at their state convention in Topeka during the first week of June the Republicans drafted a platform that ignored both woman suffrage and prohibition.[118] The Populist convention opened one week later, also in Topeka, with battle lines drawn over the suffrage amendment and its implications for prohibition. Heated debate continued through most of the first day and until noon on 13 June. At that point the vote was taken, and by a narrow margin the People's Party of Kansas declared for suffrage. A short time later the party adopted a plank opposing resubmission of the liquor question.[119] As Nugent remarks, "a switch of five percent of the delegates would have changed the result, and the resolution was softly worded, but the damage had been done. The chances of fusion had virtually been destroyed."[120] Two weeks later disgruntled Democrats met to nominate their own candidates and draft a platform opposing woman suffrage and calling for resubmission. Fusion died.

With Populists and Democrats officially split, the Republicans rolled to an impressive victory in 1894. The entire Republican state ticket was elected. They won control of the lower house at the state level and beat the Populists in all but one of eight congressional races. By a vote of 130,139 to 95,302, the woman suffrage referendum was decided in the negative.[121] On 13 November 1895 the Republicans met in Topeka and, according to Clanton, "held an elaborate public funeral . . . to celebrate the death of Populism." The funeral was appropriate. As Clanton concludes, "it was a devastating gesture, for only the most impractical Populist could fail to see that Populism in its original form was indeed dead; it might rise again to fight another day but never again in the same form."[122]

Clanton was right. At their 1896 national convention, the Populists nominated William Jennings Bryan, who had already been nominated by the Democrats, for president. Although a separate Populist vice-presidential candidate was also nominated, in effect the party achieved total fusion with the Democrats by drafting a platform resting on a single issue: the free coinage of silver. With that act, the Populist Party was no more. As Hicks remarks, "free silver captured the Populist Party; then the Democratic party, by embracing free silver, captured Populism. When the Populists in 1896 nominated as their candidate for President William Jennings Bryan . . . their day of independence was done."[123] Nationally, Republican William McKinley defeated Bryan. In Kansas, the combined Populist and Democratic ticket was successful. But the party had been stripped of its essence. By reducing the campaign to the single issue of free silver, the Populists forfeited their traditional ground of broad social and economic reform.

The Limits of Mythic Transcendence

Like their successes in 1890 and 1892, the Populist failure in Kansas in 1894 was both rhetorical and political. Without question, the Republicans waged an effective campaign. But Populist advocacy of woman suffrage and prohibition was the decisive factor. Had the People's Party not taken those positions, fusion with the Democrats might once again have been achieved, and Republican success would have been far from assured. According to Rickard, "the Populists ran alone in 1894 because they endorsed woman suffrage by a narrow margin. Since woman suffrage was anathema to stalwart Democrats, fusion was thereby doomed, and the Populists went down to defeat."[124] In 1890 and 1892 Populists were able to transcend partisan ideologies to achieve fusion and political success. But advocacy of woman suffrage and prohibition exceeded the limits of transcendence.

The coalition of Populists, industrial laborers, and dissident members of the old parties was always fragile because the agrarian myth provided an unsteady foundation. Although values implicit in the myth were traditional values, it was, after all, an *agrarian* myth that fostered suspicion of forces outside the garden: industry was suspect; the cities were the strongholds of evil; foreigners were lower class. Kansas Populists certainly felt sympathy for industrial laborers because they believed that both farmers and wage earners were oppressed by a common enemy—the monopolies, the corporations, the money powers. Nevertheless, they also considered themselves to be superior to their political allies.[125]

Given their desire to perpetuate the politically successful coalition, one might wonder why Kansas Populists did not take the expedient course and forsake woman suffrage and prohibition. Indeed, the agrarian myth seemed to be an unsteady foundation for advocacy of woman suffrage, and therefore prohibition as well. Although the myth taught that citizens had a natural right to participate in their own governance, the yeoman was, after all, a *male* image. And the myth comprised the predominant norms for a society that had denied women the right to vote for nearly 120 years.

But in fact the ideological links between Populism and woman suffrage were much stronger than those between Populism and labor. According to Grimes, for the woman suffrage movement in the West,

> at issue was a conflict over styles of life or modes of existence. On one side was the older, conservative, rural, essentially Protestant and Puritan way of life which the native-born liked to think of as typically American; on the other side was the new or "faster" style of life that accompanied late nineteenth-century urbanization, and was ostentatious, crude but sophisticated, and enthusiastically "wet." The former style drew its nourishment from farms, small towns, and a traditional way of life; the latter style was fed by mining, factories, immigrant labor, and the new modes of wealth made possible by burgeoning capitalism.

Thus, Grimes concludes, "it would appear that the Populists and the woman suffrage movement appealed to much the same type of voter."[126] As actions at the 1894 Populist state convention attest, those appeals ultimately drove Kansas Populists from the expedient course and toward defeat.

Moreover, just as the agrarian myth served to blind its adherents to their own responsibility for economic and social conditions, it likewise constrained their ability to adapt their rhetoric to the larger audience of industrial laborers and dissident Democrats. Assured by the myth of their own rightness—and righteousness—agrarian radicals found it difficult to understand how that audience could reject the "moral reforms" of woman suffrage and prohibition.

For a time, Kansas Populists were able to form a working political coalition to confront a common enemy, the "large corporations" and "monopolies," the evil forces of the "money power." Farmers, laborers, and dissidents from the old parties were united on the side of good against bankers, railroaders, and industrialists on the side of evil. On the issues of woman suffrage and prohibition, however, the sides of good and evil were redrawn. In effect, the somewhat vague and elastic boundaries of the agrarian myth were stretched in one direction to encompass Democrats and industrial laborers. When those boundaries were stretched in another direction in an effort to encompass advocates of woman suffrage and prohibition, they snapped. Factions once united in opposition to the evil forces of capitalism were split, with those supporting woman suffrage and prohibition on the side of good, and those opposed on the side of evil. The fragile coalition came apart, and the Populist movement in Kansas was dead.

Political ideologies and the dominant cultural myths on which they rest are, after all, human—that is, rhetorical—constructs. They are abstractions, "first principles" to which their adherents turn for answers to concrete questions. But because they are the rhetorical products of the cultures that embrace them, they are as imperfect as their creators.[127] The danger, as illustrated by this analysis, is that although rhetorical appeals grounded in myth are powerful for adherents, they are limited in their capacity to transcend cultural diversity.

Despite the failure to maintain their political coalition in support of woman suffrage and prohibition, however, the speeches of Kansas Populists reflected the essentially moral character of the frontier farmer, and their dedication to principles of fairness and equal justice was consistent with the teachings of the agrarian myth and the traditional values that continue to guide the society. Although Populist discourse expounded conspiracy theories that were often factually inaccurate, it quite accurately reflected the mythic conflict between the agrarian myth and the gospel of wealth, a conflict that significantly influenced U.S. society in the late nineteenth century. And Kansas Populist speakers were successful, at least for a time, in building a powerful political coalition because they skillfully grounded their rhetoric in the overlapping worldviews and political ideologies of diverse, frequently discordant, groups. That their advocacy of prohibition and especially woman suffrage reached the limits of mythic transcendence was no more a sign of rhetorical failure than an illustration of an idea whose time, unfortunately, had not yet come. Faced with an unprecedented and unimaginable change in the very nature of their society, a change that threatened not only their individual lives but also their collective way of life, Kansas Populists sought to reassert the old morality and the traditional democratic values on which the nation had been founded. That their oral discourse occasionally carried the tone of a "calamity howl" was not surprising. As Jerry Simpson proclaimed to his audience in Wichita: "Oh yes! We are calamity howlers. There are a good many calamity howlers. I pride myself I am a considerable of a calamity howler myself; I rather enjoy it because the other fellows are contributing the funds for me in this new revolution. I feel pleased that I have the opportunity to howl calamity; I am feeling well, draw my salary with promptness and regularity and am enabled to do a good deal of howling. (Applause.) I am going to keep on howling calamity as long as the national evils exist in this country."

Notes

1. Qtd. in Annie L. Diggs, *The Story of Jerry Simpson* (Wichita, Kans.: Jane Simpson, 1908), 55–56.

2. Howard S. Erlich, "Populist Rhetoric Reassessed: A Paradox," *Quarterly Journal of Speech* 63 (1977): 141.

3. Robert Gunderson, "The Calamity Howlers," *Quarterly Journal of Speech* 26 (1940): 401; Donald H. Ecroyd, "The Agrarian Protest," in *America in Controversy: History of American Public Address*, ed. Dewitte Holland (Dubuque, Iowa: Wm. C. Brown, 1973), 179; Kenneth G. Hance, H. O. Hendrickson, and Edwin W. Schoenberger, "The Later National Period, 1860–1930," in *A History and Criticism of American Public Address*, ed. William Norwood Brigance, vol. 1 (New York: Russell and Russell, 1960), 136.

4. Erlich, "Populist Rhetoric," 140.

5. C. Vann Woodward, "The Populist Heritage and the Intellectual," *American Scholar* 29 (1959–60): 68.

6. For detailed accounts of these events, see Peter H. Argersinger, "Road to a Republican Waterloo: The Farmers' Alliance and the Election of 1890 in Kansas," *Kansas Historical Quarterly* 33 (1967): 443–69; Peter H. Argersinger, "The Most Picturesque Drama: The Kansas Senatorial Election of 1891," *Kansas Historical Quarterly* 38 (1972): 43–64; and O. Gene Clanton, *Kansas Populism: Ideas and Men* (Lawrence: University Press of Kansas, 1969).

7. See, for example, Erlich, "Populist Rhetoric"; Gunderson, "Calamity Howlers"; Ecroyd, "Agrarian Protest"; and Hance, Hendrickson, and Schoenberger, "Later National Period."

8. Portions of this analysis were published earlier in Thomas R. Burkholder, "Kansas Populism, Woman Suffrage, and the Agrarian Myth: A Case Study in the Limits of Mythic Transcendence." *Communication Studies* 40 (1989): 292–307. That article and this chapter are based on my doctoral dissertation completed in 1988 under the direction of Wil A. Linkugel. See Thomas R. Burkholder, "Mythic Conflict: A Critical Analysis of Kansas Populist Speechmaking, 1890–1894" (Ph.D. diss., University of Kansas, 1988).

9. Elizabeth N. Barr, "The Populist Uprising," in *A Standard History of Kansas and Kansans*, William E. Connelley (Chicago: Lewis, 1918), 1116.

10. Ibid., 1152.

11. Ecroyd, "Agrarian Protest," 176.

12. Donald H. Ecroyd, "The Populist Spellbinders," in *The Rhetoric of Protest and Reform, 1878–1898*, ed. Paul H. Boase (Athens: Ohio University Press, 1980), 137.

13. For example, see Peter H. Argersinger, "Pentecostal Politics in Kansas: Religion, the Farmers' Alliance, and the Gospel of Populism," *Kansas Quarterly* 1 (1969) 24–35; Peter H. Argersinger, *Populism and Politics: William Alfred Peffer and the People's Party* (Lexington: University of Kentucky Press, 1974); Argersinger, "Road to a Republican Waterloo," 443–69; Peter H. Argersinger, "The Most Picturesque Drama: The Kansas Senatorial Election of 1891," *Kansas Historical Quarterly* 38

(1972): 43–64; Karel D. Bicha, "Jerry Simpson: Populist without Principle," *Journal of American History* 54 (1967) 291–306; Michael J. Broadhead, *Persevering Populist: The Life of Frank Doster* (Reno: University of Nevada Press, 1969); O. Gene Clanton, "Intolerant Populist? The Disaffection of Mary Elizabeth Lease," *Kansas Historical Quarterly* 34 (1968): 189–200; Katherine B. Clinton, "What Did You Say, Mrs. Lease?" *Kansas Quarterly* 1 (1969): 52–59; Raymond Curtis Miller, "The Background of Populism in Kansas," *Mississippi Valley Historical Review* 11 (1925): 469–89; Walter T. K. Nugent, *The Tolerant Populists: Kansas Populism and Nativism* (Chicago: University of Chicago Press, 1963); and Donald E. Press, "Kansas Conflict: Populist versus Railroader in the 1890's," *Kansas Historical Quarterly* 43 (1977): 319–33.

14. See Walter T. K. Nugent, "Some Parameters of Populism," *Agricultural History* 40 (1966): 270; and Argersinger, "Road to a Republican Waterloo," 443.

15. Richard Hofstadter, *The Age of Reform: From Bryan to F.D.R.* (New York: Alfred A. Knopf, 1955), 61–62.

16. Ibid., 24–25

17. Henry Nash Smith, *Virgin Land: The American West as Symbol and Myth* (New York: Vintage Books, 1957), v.

18. Paul W. Glad, *McKinley, Bryan, and the People* (Philadelphia: J. B. Lippincott, 1964), 34.

19. Chester E. Eisinger, "The Freehold Concept in Eighteenth Century American Letters," *William and Mary Quarterly*, 3rd ser., 4 (1947): 44–45.

20. Smith, *Virgin Land*, 144.

21. Hofstadter, *Age of Reform*, 27, 28.

22. A. Whitney Griswold, "The Agrarian Democracy of Thomas Jefferson," *American Political Science Review* 40 (1946): 672.

23. Eisinger, "Freehold Concept," 53–54.

24. Smith, *Virgin Land*, 218.

25. Hofstadter, *Age of Reform*, 35.

26. Carleton Beals, *The Great Revolt and Its Leaders: The History of Popular American Uprisings in the 1890's* (New York: Abelard-Schuman, 1968), 10.

27. Smith, *Virgin Land*, 198.

28. See Ibid., 202–13.

29. James Oliver Robinson, *American Myth, American Reality* (New York: Hill and Wang, 1980), 19.

30. Northrop Frye, "Literature and Myth," in *Relations of Literary Study*, ed. James Thorpe (New York: Modern Language Association of America, 1967), 27–28.

31. Smith, *Virgin Land*, 179.

32. Clanton, *Kansas Populism*, 2.

33. James Turner, "Understanding the Populists," *Journal of American History* 67 (1980): 370.

34. Sheldon Hackney, ed., *Populism: The Critical Issues* (Boston: Little, Brown, 1971), xiii.

35. Glad, *McKinley, Bryan, and the People*, 14, 35.

36. Carnegie, "Wealth," 653, 655, 656.

37. Clanton, *Kansas Populism*, 8.

38. Ibid., 9.

39. Ronald F. Reid, *Three Centuries of American Discourse: An Anthology and a Review* (Prospect Heights, Ill.: Waveland Press, 1988), 575.

40. Russell Conwell, "Acres of Diamonds," in Reid, *Three Centuries of American Discourse*, 586.

41. Clanton, *Kansas Populism*, 9–10.

42. Ibid., 11.

43. Glad, *McKinley, Bryan, and the People*, 49.

44. Smith, *Virgin Land*, 178.

45. Ibid., 178.

46. Hackney, *Populism*, x.

47. Hallie Farmer, "The Economic Background of Frontier Populism," *Mississippi Valley Historical Review* 10 (1924): 409.

48. Farmer, "Economic Background," 410–11.

49. Argersinger, "Road to a Republican Waterloo," 443–44.

50. Lawrence Goodwyn, *Democratic Promise: The Populist Moment in America* (New York: Oxford University Press, 1976), 96.

51. Clanton, *Kansas Populism*, 19.

52. Louise E. Rickard, "The Impact of Populism on Electoral Patterns in Kansas, 1880–1900: A Quantitative Analysis" (Ph.D. diss., University of Kansas, 1974), 39.

53. Miller, "Populism in Kansas," 470.

54. Farmer, "Economic Background," 413.

55. Goodwyn, *Democratic Promise*, 96.

56. Kenneth S. Davis, *Kansas: A History* (New York: W. W. Norton, 1984), 139.

57. Hofstadter, *Age of Reform*, 38.

58. Glad, *McKinley, Bryan, and the People*, 45.

59. Ibid., 39.

60. Ibid., 39–40.

61. Argersinger, "Road to a Republican Waterloo," 445.

62. Farmer, "Economic Background," 420.

63. Ibid., 419.

64. Goodwyn, *Democratic Promise*, 96.

65. Rickard, "Impact of Populism," 70.

66. Goodwyn, *Democratic Promise*, 97.

67. John D. Hicks, *The Populist Revolt* (Minneapolis: University of Minnesota Press, 1931), 84.

68. Barr, "Populist Uprising," 1139.

69. Farmer, "Economic Background," 421.

70. Clanton, *Kansas Populism*, 29.

71. Barr, "Populist Uprising," 1148.

72. See Erlich, "Populist Rhetoric," 144; Hofstadter, *Age of Reform*, 70; and Oscar Handlin, "Reconsidering the Populists," *Agricultural History* 39 (April 1965): 72.

73. Miller, "Populism in Kansas," 489.

74. Clanton, *Kansas Populism*, 242.

75. Glad, *McKinley, Bryan, and the People*, 35–36.

76. Clanton, *Kansas Populism*, 63, 242.

77. Nugent, "Parameters of Populism," 260.

78. Clanton, *Kansas Populism*, 65.

79. Handlin, "Reconsidering the Populists," 71.

80. Frye, "Literature and Myth," 27.

81. V. William Balthrop, "Culture, Myth, and Ideology as Public Argument: An Interpretation of the Ascent and Demise of 'Southern Culture,'" *Communication Monographs* 51 (1984): 344.

82. Balthrop, "Culture, Myth, and Ideology," 344.

83. Robert L. Scott and Donald K. Smith, "The Rhetoric of Confrontation," *Quarterly Journal of Speech* 55 (1969): 1–8.

84. Scott and Smith, "Rhetoric of Confrontation," 2–3.

85. Kenneth Burke, "Ideology and Myth," *Accent* 7 (1947): 201.

86. Chester E. Eisinger, "The Influence of Natural Rights and Physiocratic Doctrines on American Agrarian Thought during the Revolutionary Period," *Agricultural History* 21 (1947): 17.

87. Smith, *Virgin Land*, 196.

88. Ibid., 214.

89. With the exception of Governor Lorenzo D. Lewelling's campaign speech at Huron Place in Kansas City (see note 95 below), all texts analyzed in the course of this study were published in newspapers identified as affiliated with, or sympathetic to, the People's Party and the Farmers' Alliance in Kansas between 1890 and 1894. These texts were discovered through systematic examination of ninety-five such newspapers. Microfilm copies of these newspapers are available at the Kansas State Historical Society Library in Topeka. For a complete explanation of the collection, authentication, and preparation of these texts, see Burkholder, "Mythic Conflict," vol. 2, 1–9. All texts analyzed for this study are included in that volume.

90. J. L. Hammers, "Our Demands," *Weekly Bulletin* (Anthony), 8 April 1892. Subsequent quotations from this speech are from the same source.

91. See Norman Pollack, "Fear of Man: Populism, Authoritarianism, and the Historian," *Agricultural History* 39 (April 1965): 59–60.

92. Bertha Mellen, "Calamity Howlers," *Kansas Agitator* (Garnett), 15 September 1892. Subsequent quotations from this speech are from the same source.

93. Clanton, *Kansas Populism*, 163–64.

94. Lorenzo D. Lewelling, speech at Huron Place, Kansas City, July 26, 1894, paragraph 1. A typescript of the speech is on file at the Kansas State Historical Society Library in Topeka. Subsequent quotations from this speech are from the same source.

95. Mrs. T. J. Whitman, "Importance of Correct Education," lecture delivered before the Norton County Alliance, 21 July 1890, *Topeka Advocate*, 6 August 1890.

96. William A. Peffer, speech to the Cincinnati Convention, *The American Nonconformist and Kansas Industrial Liberator* (Winfield), 28 May 1891, 1, 4, 5. Subsequent quotations from this speech are from the same source. The text of Peffer's speech also appeared in the *Alliance Monitor* (Abilene), 5 June 1891; and the *Central Advocate* (Marion), 12 June 1891.

97. Jerry Simpson, speech delivered at Wichita, 15 September 1891, *Kansas Commoner* (Wichita), 24 September 1891. Subsequent quotations from this speech are from the same source.

98. Mrs. J. C. Bare, "A Call for Continued Action," paper read before the Douglas County Farmers' Alliance and Industrial Union, 4 October 1892, *Lawrence Jeffersonian*, 10 November 1892. Subsequent quotations from this speech are from the same source.

99. For example, see Victor C. Ferkiss, "Populist Influences on American Fascism," *Western Political Quarterly* 10 (June 1957): 350–73; and Handlin, "Reconsidering the Populists," 68–74.

100. Mary Elizabeth Lease, "Speech Before the Labor Congress," delivered at the Chicago Art Palace, 2 September 1893, *Abilene Monitor*, 7 September 1893.

101. Mary Elizabeth Lease, "Address at Cooper Union," New York City, 30 April 1894, *Kansas Agitator* (Garnett), 8 March 1894. Subsequent quotations from this speech are from the same source.

102. Pollack, "Fear of Man," 59.

103. Ibid., 60.

104. Clanton, *Kansas Populism*, 73.

105. Argersinger, "Road to a Republican Waterloo," 468; Miller, "Populism in Kansas," 469; Rickard, "Impact of Populism," 52.

106. Frederick Emory Haynes, "The New Sectionalism," *Quarterly Journal of Economics* 10 (1896): 271.

107. Rickard, "Impact of Populism," 52.

108. Goodwyn, *Democratic Promise*, 317.

109. Walter T. K. Nugent, "How the Populists Lost in 1894," *Kansas Historical Quarterly* 31 (1965): 248.

110. See Wilda M. Smith, "A Half Century of Struggle: Gaining Woman Suffrage in Kansas," *Kansas History* 4 (1981): 76; and Rickard, "Impact of Populism," 21–22.

111. See Nugent, "How the Populists Lost," 252; and Rickard, "Impact of Populism," 97.

112. Peter H. Argersinger, "Ideology and Behavior: Legislative Politics and Western Populism," *Agricultural History* 58 (January 1984): 45–46.

113. Alan P. Grimes, *The Puritan Ethic and Woman Suffrage* (New York: Oxford University Press, 1967), 105.

114. See Clanton, *Kansas Populism*, 95; and Nugent, "How the Populists Lost," 248.

115. Clanton, *Kansas Populism*, 153.

116. Josie Webber, "Woman Suffrage and Prohibition," paper read before the Lone Elm Alliance, *Kansas Agitator* (Garnett), 1 March 1894, 3. Subsequent quotations from this speech are from the same source.

117. Samuel Reynolds, "Equal Suffrage," *Jeffersonian* (Lawrence), 9 August 1894.

118. Clanton, *Kansas Populism*, 151.

119. See Ibid., 155–63.

120. Nugent, "How the Populists Lost," 252.

121. See Clanton, *Kansas Populism*, 167–68; and Goodwyn, *Democratic Promise*, 408.

122. Clanton, *Kansas Populism*, 169.

123. John D. Hicks, "The Farmer Protests: Populism," in *The American Story: The Age of Exploration to the Age of the Atom*, ed. Earl Schenck Miers (New York: Charmel Press, 1956), 224.

124. Rickard, "Impact of Populism," 104.

125. Theodore Saloutos, "The Professors and the Populists," *Agricultural History* 40 (1966): 246; Frank L. McVey, "The Populist Movement," in *Selected Readings in Rural Economics*, ed. Thomas Nixon Carver (Boston: Ginn, 1916), 675.

126. Grimes, *Puritan Ethic*, 89, 95.

127. See Karlyn Kohrs Campbell, "The Rhetoric of Mythical America Revisited," in Karlyn Kohrs Campbell and Thomas R. Burkholder, *Critiques of Contemporary Rhetoric*, 2nd ed. (Belmont, Calif.: Wadsworth, 1997), 204; and Northrop Frye, *Anatomy of Criticism: Four Essays* (Princeton, N.J.: Princeton University Press, 1957), 119–22.

William Jennings Bryan: A Modern Disciple with a Political Mission

Sally Perkins

5

The rhetoric of William Jennings Bryan exemplified the Progressive Era and Populist politics of the late nineteenth and early twentieth centuries. Not only did his speeches articulate the Populist political agenda, but they also garnered significant praise and interest from his audiences. People traveled for miles to hear Bryan speak at Chautauquas, and his "Cross of Gold" speech remains an exemplar in American oratorical history. Oddly, despite all the contemporary enthusiasm surrounding Bryan as an orator, biographers and even his own colleagues criticized him harshly for the uninformed and simpleminded ideas laid out in his public rhetoric. On the whole, among scholars his reputation as a politician remains mediocre. Recently, however, some have begun to reexamine his work, challenging the negative criticisms of his discourse. In this essay, I use a rhetorical analysis to contribute to that reexamination, demonstrating that Bryan's oratory was grounded in two mythic narratives that appealed to the commoner whose concerns he represented. I show that when judged by the logic of those narratives, his rhetoric was neither illogical nor simpleminded, but instead firmly and consistently grounded in a mythic logic that guided his thinking.

To accomplish that aim, I examine rhetorical patterns among several prominent speeches representing different dimensions of Bryan's career. Specifically, I position his deliberative political rhetoric against the backdrop of his cultural rhetoric found in two of his Chautauqua speeches. When viewed together, one can see that Bryan's speeches were grounded in a grand, mythic-narrative logic rather than a discursive logic; when judged on those grounds, his rhetoric is highly logical, consistent, and unwavering in principle. In other words, in the past scholars have judged Bryan's rhetoric from the criteria of discursive logic, by which standards Bryan comes up short. But if Bryan's rhetoric is judged from the standards of narrative reasoning, his rhetorical choices must be judged more favorably.

The Rise to Prominence

Born in 1860, Bryan was the fourth child of Silas and Mariah Jennings Bryan, a humble, modest couple from Salem, Illinois. His parents educated him at home until he attended "Old College" in Salem; Whipple Academy in Jacksonville, Illinois; Illinois College in Jacksonville; and finally Union College of Law in Chicago. In addition to his formal education, Bryan was a self-taught biblical scholar.

One year after his completion of law school in 1883, at the age of twenty-four, he married Mary Baird; the first of their three children was born the following year. In their early years of marriage, Bryan established a small legal practice in Jacksonville, helping business owners collect debts from their patrons. But in 1887 he and Mary agreed to move the family to Lincoln, Nebraska, where he could establish a more profitable law practice with his old college friend Adolphus Talbot. Nebraska then became the state in which his political career centered, for by 1888 he had become an active Democrat in the state and by 1890 was elected to Congress by voters in Nebraska's First Congressional District. He served in Congress for two terms, choosing not to seek reelection in 1894.

By 1894 Bryan had become a popular spokesman for both the Populists and the Democrats. In 1896 he was nominated as the Democratic Party's presidential candidate, but lost in the general election to Republican William McKinley. Again in 1900 Bryan was nominated as the Democratic Party's presidential candidate; again he lost to McKinley. In 1908 Bryan made his final run for the presidency as the Democrat nominee but was defeated, this time by William Taft.

Despite his failures as a presidential candidate, Bryan maintained his commitment to progressive, Populist politics and the Democratic Party. In 1912 that commitment brought him the cabinet position of secretary of state under President Woodrow Wilson. However, Bryan resigned in 1915 due to conflict with Wilson about America's position in World War I. Nevertheless, he remained active in the Democratic Party as a loyal spokesman, even stumping on Wilson's behalf in the 1916 election. Bryan made his final mark in 1925 when he participated as a prosecuting attorney in the famous "Scopes Trial," defending the ruling that evolution not be taught in public schools.

Throughout his career, Bryan was a prominent, popular speaker on the Chautauqua circuit. Perhaps in those settings more than any other, he reached the common people whose interests he defended in his politics. Although never a member of the Populist Party (in fact, he declined several requests to be the party's presidential candidate), Bryan was faithful to progressive politics and remained concerned about what many scholars call "the commoners." He advocated: the bimetal standard of coinage; a federal income tax; election of U.S. senators by direct vote of the people; government ownership of railroads; antitrust legislation; anti-imperialism; an eight-hour workday; child labor laws; woman suffrage; a peace treaty plan for resolving international conflicts; and prohibition, among other positions.

Bryan was famous as an orator, and people came for miles to hear him speak, even if they had no interest in voting for him. Biographer Charles Morrow Wilson writes: "In great part he was preaching what his rural listeners wished to hear. Even if he wasn't winning votes, he was winning audiences."[1] Historian Kendrick Clements notes that audiences "returned his affection and respect with unstinting love . . . flocked to hear him by the thousands as he stumped the country and lectured on the platforms of . . . 'circuit Chautauquas.'" Clements claims that "Bryan's supporters loved him because they knew he cared about them more than about anything else, and because he perfectly embodied their attitudes and values. . . . As a diagnostician of the ills that beset the middle border, Bryan had no peer."[2] Many simply marveled at his strong, melodious speaking voice. Wilson describes his voice on one occasion as "clear, without distinguishable bass or tenor, but with a bell-like lilt. Each word, clearly enunciated, seemed to stand momentarily alone, then join in a rhythmic, almost lyrical, current of words."[3]

Bryan's Rhetorical Career

Although Bryan was a popular orator, many accused him of appealing to the heart rather than the mind, and of not having sufficient knowledge of some of the issues he addressed. Scholars have documented well the criticisms made against Bryan's political rhetoric. For example, historian Richard Hofstadter writes: "Politicians cannot be expected to have the traits of detached intellectuals, but few men in any phase of life have been so desolately lacking as Bryan in detachment or intellectuality. While he was eager to grapple with his opponents in the political arena, he was incapable of confronting them in the arena of his own mind."[4] Rhetorical critic Myron G. Phillips claims that Bryan failed to produce valid solutions to the various social problems he identified. "His deficiency lay in the broad scope of argument and in his utter lack of a fecund imagination, in a lack of ability to synthesize a program. He was not constructive or creative, but he was an effective orator."[5] Rhetorical critic Donald Springen, who praises Bryan, notes that many considered him another "emotional, simple-minded hayseed" politician.[6] Clements describes Bryan's rhetoric as an overly simplified moral struggle between right and wrong. "In appealing to the heart, Bryan sought to reach the best in man, but unfortunately it was also possible to tap the worst in the form of unbridled passions."[7] Even Bryan himself acknowledged these attacks on his style and intellect. In his speech "Democracy's Deeds and Duties," delivered at a banquet in his honor, he thanked his audience for what he called their "gross exaggeration" of his worth, humorously commenting, "It is necessary, too, that a man in public life should be overpraised by his associates to make up for unmerited abuse from his opponents; having had my full share of criticism, I need an excess of praise."[8]

Recently, scholars have begun to question these negative interpretations of Bryan and his rhetoric. Springen argues that anyone who believes Bryan was "an emotional, simple-minded hayseed" should read volume 1 of his speeches.[9] Noting that his congressional speeches were much more intellectually sound than the speeches delivered to the public, Springen defends the effectiveness of Bryan's public rhetoric because of his unique ability to appeal to the common people and to speak their language. Explaining the contradiction between Bryan's apparent shift from progressivism to a conservative attack on evolution and defense of Christianity in the Scopes Trial, scientist Stephen J. Gould points out the serious flaws in Bryan's understanding of evolution. But he concludes that Bryan "was right in one crucial way." According to Gould:

> Lord only knows he understood precious little about science, and he wins no medals for logic of arguments. But when he said that Darwinism had been widely portrayed as a defense of war, domination, and domestic exploitation, he was right. Scientists would not be to blame for this if we had always maintained proper caution in interpretation and proper humility in resisting the extension of our findings into inappropriate domains.[10]

Additionally, rhetorical critic Michael J. Hostetler reconstructs Bryan's reputation regarding his position on evolution espoused in the 1925 Scopes Trial. Hostetler analyzes Bryan's last, undelivered speech to argue that Bryan used an intellectually complex, rhetorical, argumentative strategy of "incompatibility" to work through the logic of his position. Hostetler's conclusion calls into question the "popular 'broken man' narrative of the end of the Great Commoner's life."[11]

While the work of these scholars has begun to reconstruct Bryan's rhetorical reputation, it is limited in scope. Hostetler and Gould make compelling arguments about the argumentative soundness and creativity of Bryan's antievolution rhetoric, but they do not examine other rhetorical messages. Springen's rhetorical critique is perhaps the most comprehensive in scope, and while he defends Bryan's extraordinary capacity to appeal to the commoner and describes some of his rhetorical strategies, he does not examine the rhetorical patterns across Bryan's speeches to defend his logic against the popular criticisms. Yet Bryan's historical presence and influence in American Populist politics, international affairs, the Presbyterian church, and late-nineteenth- and early-twentieth-century cultural life justify further critique of his discourse to extend the critical conclusions regarding Bryan as an orator.

Springen and others comment upon Bryan's speeches in chronological order. In that chronology, one notices that Bryan turned his attention more toward religious activity after his second presidential candidacy at the turn of the century. However, the speeches used in this analysis will be examined in a reverse chronology because the later Chautauqua speeches actually provide the philosophical backdrop necessary for understanding the logic of the earlier political speeches.[12] As Bryan aged and matured, his philosophical foundations likely became more clearly defined and therefore are more clearly articulated in his later Chautauqua speeches. Moreover, the rapidly growing influence of modernist thinking and biological and social Darwinism in the early twentieth century may have motivated Bryan to articulate explicitly and to defend the basis of his political philosophy. Additionally, speeches that offered political and religious philosophies were fitting for the Chautauqua setting and its educational agenda, while the campaign trail and legislative context invited deliberative speeches dealing with more immediate political policy debates. For these reasons, it is reasonable and illuminating to examine Bryan's political speeches within the framework of his Chautauqua speeches.

The two Chautauqua speeches to be examined here were selected on two grounds. First, Bryan delivered these speeches more than any others while on the Chautauqua circuit, and they were highly popular. Second, more than any other Chautauqua address, these speeches clearly articulate Bryan's political and religious philosophies, demonstrating his perception of the relationship between these philosophies. "The Prince of Peace" was Bryan's most famous, most repeated Chautauqua address. Millions of people heard the speech, which he revised with each repetition. "It was Bryan's most popular lecture," write Herrick and Herrick, "and week after week and year after year he gave it before vast audiences," which included those in numerous cities on his international tour in 1905.[13] His most widely published lecture, it also contained the mythic foundations for his political rhetoric. Bryan also delivered "The Value of an Ideal" over and again on the Chautauqua circuit. This address completed the mythic narrative established in "The Prince of Peace," connecting the religious mythic foundations from "The Prince of Peace" to a political mythic foundation upon which Bryan's political rhetoric rested.[14]

The four political speeches examined here include "The Cross of Gold" (1896), "America's Mission" (1899), "Imperialism" (1900), and "Democracy's Deeds and Duty" (1916). Three of these speeches ("Cross of Gold," "America's Mission," and "Imperialism") were selected for analysis because, first, each addressed one of two main political issues Bryan fought for over the years. While he spoke on numerous topics of concern to Populist and Democrat audiences, the two issues he spent the most time and energy debating were the gold standard and imperialism. "The Cross of Gold" was Bryan's most famous speech on the gold standard, and "America's Mission" and "Imperialism" broadly outlined his anti-imperialist position. Essentially, these three speeches helped set Bryan's presidential campaign agendas. Second, these three speeches were selected for analysis because they were heard by large audiences and influenced Democratic Party platforms during their respective election cycles. "Cross of Gold" was delivered at the 1896 Democratic Convention in Chicago and won Bryan the presidential nomination. "America's Mission" was delivered in 1899, after an intense congressional debate on the Spanish-American War treaty regarding America's role in the Cuban and Filipino governments. "Imperialism" was delivered at the 1900 Democrat Convention as Bryan's acceptance speech for his second presidential nomination.

The speech "Democracy's Deeds and Duty" differs from the others in that it was delivered somewhat later, in 1916, and not to a large national audience but to fellow Democrats at a banquet in honor of Bryan's contributions to Woodrow Wilson's 1915 presidential campaign. The speech is included in this analysis, however, because it summarized his position on a host of Populist issues and demonstrates the way Bryan linked his position on a wide array of issues to a consistent and small set of political principles. As mentioned, although he focused on the gold standard and imperialism in his presidential campaigns, he spoke on many other topics throughout the years. "Democracy's Deeds and Duty" offers a sampling of Bryan's rhetorical response to those issues, including woman suffrage and prohibition.[15]

The Rhetorical Power of Mythic Narratives

Contemporary scholars of rhetoric commonly draw attention to the role of myth in rhetorical texts.[16] Robert C. Rowland argues that myths provide "true" answers for solving social and personal problems that cannot be solved by other symbolic means.[17] Myth, unlike science, is necessary for solving problems of value, not problems of fact. Susanne Langer argues that ideology emerges from myth.[18] If myth is necessary for the resolving of value problems and if myth is the source of ideology, then myth must play a central role in rhetoric. In fact, Dan Nimmo and James E. Combs argue that myth is central to and pervasive throughout American politics, specifically American presidential rhetoric.[19]

Philosophers from a variety of fields define myth differently. Generally, however, scholars agree that myths are stories that are neither true nor false yet at the same time are absolutely true. They are true not on the basis of their accuracy as historical accounts but on basis that they are believed as true. Mircea Eliade defines myth as a "'true story' and, beyond that, a story that is a most precious possession because it is sacred, exemplary, significant."[20]

In his definition, Eliade narrows the scope of a myth, arguing that myths tell the stories of sacred histories, telling people how supernatural beings brought a reality into existence, whether that reality is a culture, a political system, an institution, a religion, or even a pattern of human behavior. Nimmo and Combs offer a broader definition, suggesting that myths tell the stories not only of origins but also of struggles in the present and visions of the future. Although some scholars insist that myths, by definition, fit a particular dramatic form, others, like Nimmo and Combs, admit that myth is a dramatic form that does not always manifest itself in an explicit narration of events. Rather, it may involve "a dramatic image specific to a political present and only tangentially related to the large-scale myths of the historical-political order."[21] Myths, then, may be evident in dramatic images or symbols that may implicitly or synecdochically make reference to a larger origin myth. Similarly, Roland Barthes defines myth as "a system of communication . . . a message. . . . [M]yth cannot possibly be an object, a concept, or an idea; it is a mode of signification, a form." Myth, then, is a particular way of talking about a subject. Any object, for instance, could be talked about in a manner that is mythic. In fact, Barthes says that "some objects become the prey of mythical speech for a while, then they disappear, others take their place and attain the status of myth."[22] His definition suggests that myth is a matter of how we communicate about any given object at any particular point in time, by endowing that object with power beyond its natural condition, elevating it to the realm of the sacred.

In defining myth, these scholars identify comparable lists of overlapping functions of myth. Northrop Frye identifies three functions of myth: sociological—energizing a society, offering social identity; psychological—helping individuals and societies with crises and solving social (value) problems; and mystical—providing a people with "ultimates," meanings, "perfects" for which to aim.[23] Eliade argues that myths return us to our origins that are, in mythic form, re-created as sacred, primordial, perfect. Thus myths take us back to a time of a perfect order or perfect condition, giving us ideals for which to aim.

Barthes identifies a different set of functions of myths, one of which is to portray their "objects" as historically transcendent, natural, and eternal, as if the objects have never existed outside the natural course of events. The objects of myth are portrayed to have essential characteristics and qualities present because of nature. Myth is ahistorical speech that takes its objects out of their political contexts. The function of myth is not to deny things, but to discuss them: "simply, it purifies them, it makes them innocent, it gives them a natural and eternal justification, it gives them a clarity which is not that of an explanation but that of a statement of fact."[24] Barthes calls this process "naturalization" because myth transforms history into nature. Consequently, myth is experienced as "innocent speech: not because its intentions are hidden—if they were hidden, they could not be efficacious—but because they are naturalized." As innocent speech, myth is rhetorically powerful.[25]

The analysis that follows shows that Bryan makes use of the Christ myth (as developed in social gospel theology) and interfaces that myth into America's foundation myth, urging his audiences to view the latter as an extension of the former.[26] Bryan's speeches do not, in fact, always manifest an explicit narration of events, but they draw upon dramatic images that are synecdochically related to the larger Christ myth and founding fathers myth to provide a consistent and seemingly natural set of "ultimates" for what he sees as the perfect political order. Because the two speeches are analyzed together, a brief description of the Chautauqua setting and an overview of the content and structure of the two speeches precede the mythic analysis.

A Mythic Backdrop Through Chautauqua Speeches

Perhaps one of the most fortunate cultural developments for Bryan in the late nineteenth century was the birth and expansion of the Chautauqua, predominantly in rural America. The original Chautauqua (held in 1874 at Lake Chautauqua, New York) was designed to improve Sunday school teaching by educating teachers through Bible study. The seminars quickly evolved, however, to a broader, "liberal arts"–based education, with lectures on history, music, philosophy, and political science. Eventually, the Chautauqua included performances by traveling musicians in addition to the traveling lecturers. Bryan's wife, Mary Baird Bryan, described the Chautauqua as "something deeper than concerts or inspirational lectures. It is more than the gathering together of great crowds in the interest of civic progress." She went on to characterize the Chautauqua as "the occasion for town unity and village improvement." William Jennings Bryan quickly became one of the most frequently booked and popular lecturers on the Chautauqua circuit. Mary Baird Bryan wrote, "It is not too much to say that Mr. Bryan has remained the most popular Chautauqua lecturer in this country for thirty years."[27] Others have noted that rural Americans "flocked to hear him by the thousands" as he worked the Chautauqua circuit from 1899 until it began to wane around 1915.[28] Typically, Bryan delivered one of several lectures he perfected specifically for the Chautauqua circuit. Two of his most highly acclaimed and best-remembered speeches were "The Prince of Peace" and "The Value of an Ideal."

First delivered in 1904, "The Prince of Peace" stood as a defense of Bryan's religious doctrine and did not concern itself explicitly with political matters. In his *Memoirs*, Bryan justified his choice to turn his oratorical attention to religious matters by lamenting the fact that "some young men seem to think it smart to be skeptical. They regard it as larger intelligence to scoff at creeds and to refuse to connect themselves with churches. I thought that possibly I might reach and influence some young men who avoided the churches."[29] So, as Herrick and Herrick point out, Bryan preferred to deliver this speech to young men, particularly those exposed to the tenets of Darwinism who struggled to find its compatibility with their faith. Charles Morrow Wilson contends that by 1904 many scientists found Darwinian principles to be of interest and use, although not entirely accurate. Nonetheless, Bryan selected Darwinism as a symbol of the general modernist ideologies that he could readily attack.[30] Bryan was deeply concerned that the teaching of Darwinism particularly and modernism generally was causing students to lose their faith in the Bible and, concomitantly, other doctrines stemming from the Christian faith. According to historian Paolo E. Coletta, Bryan was "gravely concerned with the skepticism, infidelity, agnosticism, and even atheism taught in various colleges and universities," and he attempted to refute those ideologies in "The Prince of Peace."[31]

On its face, "The Prince of Peace" appears as a discursive, logically constructed rebuttal of various arguments made against Christianity, though even the most sympathetic of Bryan's biographers observe his "lack of real knowledge" about Darwinism.[32] The speech began deductively with two definitions that served as general premises from which subsequent premises must follow. First, he defined man as an essentially "religious being." Then he then defined religion and morality as fundamentally different but having a natural relationship to one another. Bryan relied upon these definitions to develop four rebuttals to the materialist's system of morality, which, he claimed, is ultimately subjective. By contrast, argued Bryan, a moral system derived from a relationship with an omniscient God is based upon objective authority.

Next, he refuted the evolutionary theories of creation by staking out a position of precedence, placing the "burden of proof" on the proponents of evolution. Bryan addressed the popular disbelief in the "mystery" and "miracles" of the Christian story, acknowledging that science had, in fact, eliminated many mysteries. He then shifted the question of mystery from one of degree to one of type, arguing that if his audience was willing to accept mysteries of nature (for example, how a watermelon seed turns into a watermelon), they also ought to accept the mystery of Christ feeding a multitude with only a few loaves and fishes. Finally, Bryan moved from a defensive to an offensive line of reasoning in which he described the qualities of Christ, the standard of all morality: pure, perfect, forgiving, peaceful, and the demonstrator of an ultimate love beyond what any human can give. He asserted that, by definition, Christ must be divine and that Christ alone can bring peace. He concluded with a plea for young men to recognize the Prince of Peace as their only source of strength and by labeling them as "brave" if they chose to believe.

Equally value laden but less explicitly religious was another popular Chautauqua lecture, "The Value of an Ideal." Where Bryan constructed a somewhat narrow target audience for "The Prince of Peace," in "The Value of an Ideal" he appealed to Americans more broadly. The speech progressed in a parallel structure through which he enumerated general principles ("ideals") to guide individual and collective moral behavior. Each ideal was illustrated through short narratives.

Bryan opened this lecture with a series of rhetorical questions that point directly to his position. "What is the value of an ideal?" he asked. He then answered his question with the first of many stories. As in "The Prince of Peace," early on Bryan established a common definition of his topic, ideals. First, he constructed two negative definitions, telling his audience that false ideals are to measure one's life according to what others have done for oneself rather than what oneself has done for others; and to measure one's life according to one's accumulations. Alternatively, he defined true ideals as goals and measures that are permanent. Bryan then used a series of short narratives, some personal and some from common people he had met, to illustrate the permanent nature of ideals and the positive impact they have when allowed to rule.

Next, Bryan offered a brief refutation of the arguments against miracles and mysteries and of the arguments advocating materialism, using a humorous anecdote to illustrate his point. After characterizing ideals as permanent, transcendent, and life-changing and positioning those ideals in the miracles and mysteries of Christian faith, Bryan counseled his audience to avail themselves of particular ideals and illustrated their positive results. First, he suggested a personal ideal: individuals should want to serve others fully as much as wanting to receive full pay for services. Next, he recommended an ideal for domestic life: that married couples mutually forbear and assist one another, and build a home that becomes an "earthy type of heaven." From the domestic realm, he moved to the business realm, recommending an ideal of integrity and honesty. He then added that those in the professions (for example, physicians, lawyers, judges) also ought to espouse an ideal of working for the benefit of others rather than for the collection of income.

Bryan then shifted from personal to political ideals. Primarily, he advocated the ideal of self-government as the ruling principle for moral practice, noting that the duty of the political party is to develop policies in accord with the desires of the people. Finally, Bryan broadened the contexts of ideals to the nation, arguing implicitly against imperialism by reinforcing the national ideal of self-governance.

Mythic Foundations in the Chautauqua Speeches

According to Coletta, parents and students alike showered Bryan with accolades of praise and gratitude for having kept them on the straight and narrow through "The Value of an Ideal." By contrast, however, those who attended the Chautauqua with an interest in contemporary political/social/economic problems and the many Jews who came to hear him speak were sorely disappointed by his defense of Christianity.[33] Bryan's refutation hardly stood as a logical rebuttal to his opponents' arguments. Rather, he drew upon the mythic Christ story and the mythic founding fathers to establish moral and political principles in the wake of modernist ideology. Eliade notes that myths return us to our origins that are, in mythic form, re-created as sacred, primordial, perfect, giving us ideals for which to aim.[34] In fact, Bryan took his audiences back to the mythic, sacred characters of Christ and the American founding fathers to establish a set of ideals for his audiences to uphold. His strategy was not so much an explicit recounting of the Christ story or the story of the American Revolution, but involved, as Nimmo and Combs suggest, a dramatic imaging of those characters (the heroes) as well as the villainous tempters whom he wanted his audiences to resist.[35]

In both "The Prince of Peace" and "The Value of an Ideal," Bryan depicted his villains as modernists, materialists, greedy corruptors of government, and imperialists, using refutation strategies and anecdotes to make them appear less as evil criminals, but more as men of folly. Bryan used Darwinism as a symbolic representation of modernism generally. For Bryan, Darwinian thought exemplified the modernist, positivistic faith in scientific rationalism and objectivity as the primary source of absolute truth. Armed with the hope of controlling and perfecting the human experience, modernists were interested in objective reality, objective representations of reality, absolute truths, and underlying, universal, deep structures, all of which could be known through disciplined scientific modes of inquiry.[36] Bryan never referred to his ideological villains as "modernists" per se. But he spoke of the "evolutionists" and those contemporary thinkers who doubted the mysteries and miracles of life, seeking to explain them away through science.

In "The Prince of Peace," Bryan condemned the evolutionists for never answering the question of the ultimate place and source of life's origin, and mocked their disagreements with one another as proof that their "subjective" theories had never successfully disproved biblical truth. Though he wisely acknowledged that science had eliminated many mysteries, citing the example that humans know the cause of lightning and thus no longer fear it, he used simple analogies to depict his modernist villains as fools who rejected mystery and miracle (and thus their faith in God) altogether. Miracles, he claimed, are no less mysterious than lightning once was, but they are simply different in type. He explained, for example, that how a watermelon seed turns into a watermelon remains a mystery, but that does not stop one from eating watermelon. However, failing to understand the mystery of Christ feeding a multitude with only a few loaves and fishes stops the modern thinkers from following Christ. He asked his listeners, "And our food, must we understand it before we eat it? If we refused to eat anything until we could understand the mystery of its growth, we would die of starvation. But mystery does not bother us in the diningroom; it is only in the church that it is a stumbling block." Through simple analogies like this, Bryan made his villainous scientific thinkers men of folly. By portraying the work of modernists as merely "subjective," he appealed to the audience's growing faith in objectivity while making the evolutionists appear foolish, an undesirable characteristic in an unfolding age of reason.

Other villains depicted in "The Prince of Peace" were those he called the "materialists," who represented what he saw as a troubling modern system of morality. After defining "man" as "a religious being [who] . . . instinctively seeks for a God," and religion as "the foundation of morality in the individual and in the group of individuals," Bryan critiqued the materialist system of morality. He argued that the moral principles of materialism were established on the basis of a mathematical calculation of whether it "pays to abstain from wrong doing [sic]." Bryan then developed four rebuttals, concluding that materialist morality requires logical, mathematical calculation and reason, which, he claimed, were ultimately subjective because one's calculation of the benefit of abstaining from wrongdoing may be based on "passion" or "selfish interest" as well as reason. In "The Value of an Ideal," Bryan used anecdotal narratives to depict the materialists as fools. Upon asking his audience, "What is the value of an ideal?" Bryan told this story:

If you would know the pecuniary value of an ideal, go into the home of some man of great wealth who has an only son; go into that home when the son has gone downward in a path of dissipation until the father no longer hopes for his reform, and then ask the father what an ideal would have been worth that would have made a man out of his son instead of a wreck. He will tell you that all the money that he has or could have he would gladly give for an ideal of life that would turn his boy's steps upward instead of downward.

This simple hypothetical story featured not a plot but characters: the foolish father who failed to teach his son ideals, modeling only the value of monetary wealth.

Later in the speech, Bryan refuted the modernists' arguments against miracles and mysteries and the materialists' morality. Though he never addressed the specific tenets of either the modernists or the materialists, he concluded that his attempt to follow their logic required faith rather than reason. He mocked, "it requires more faith to accept the scientific demonstrations of materialism that to accept any religion I have ever known," again depicting his villains as foolish, subjective, illogical thinkers. A humorous anecdote about a man who believed that grasshoppers heard through their legs embellished his depiction. The man would not accept his own hypothesis without proof, so he

> took a grasshopper, put it on a board and knocked on the board. The grasshopper jumped, and this he regarded as evidence that the sound traveled along the board till it reached the grasshopper's legs and then went up through the legs to the center of life. But he was not willing to accept it upon affirmative proof alone . . . so he pulled the legs off the grasshopper and put it on the board and rapped again. As the grasshopper did not jump, he was convinced that it heard through its legs.
>
> I say I was reminded of the grasshopper scientist when I read the arguments employed to prove that there is no god, no spiritual life. In the journey from the cradle to the grave we encounter nothing so marvelous as the change in the ideals that works a revolution in the life itself, and there is nothing in materialism to explain this change.

The "grasshopper scientist" was a fool, and the power of ideals was inexplicable without faith in something beyond the objective material world. Bryan's villain was not heinously evil, but a fool whom a person of common sense would not want to emulate.

Another villain Bryan depicted was the greedy politician who was interested in both personal and national wealth. In "The Value of an Ideal," he described such politicians' behavior as "corrupt," lamenting, "Men sell their votes, councilmen sell their influence, while State legislators and federal representatives turn the government from its legitimate channels and make it a private asset in business." So, too, Bryan lamented the national greed of those who advocated imperialism, wanting to "make our flag float everywhere" rather than allowing people to govern themselves. Bryan attributed all this demoralization to the lack of ideals in these men of folly.

In contrast to the foolish villains, Bryan depicted Christ as the perfect mythic hero whose characteristics must be emulated to prevent further demoralization. Bryan's deployment of the Christ myth relied not on the traditional narratives of Christ's miraculous birth, death, or resurrection, all of which focus on sin, redemption, and life hereafter. Instead, he attended to images of Christ's character as emphasized in social gospel theology, popular in Bryan's day. Advocates of the social gospel believed the Protestant institutions had a responsibility to respond to the growing problems arising from industrial development, unequal distribution of wealth, and worsening urban conditions for the poor. They recognized these problems to be systemic, requiring organized social response based on Christian teachings. At the same time, most advocates of the social gospel also emphasized the importance of the rights and responsibilities of individuals.[37] Bryan never explicitly used the term "social gospel" in his discourse, but did use the phrase "applied Christianity" to describe his belief that Christians should not only tell others about Christ but also should do for others according to Christ's model, as recorded in the Gospels. In fact, historians consistently note Bryan's concern for the social application of his faith.[38] Coletta describes Bryan as "a lay prophet of the social gospel."[39] Although Bryan was a leader in the fundamentalist movement, he also had strong connections, socially and theologically, with the social gospel movement.

In "The Prince of Peace," Bryan drew upon a social gospel representation of Christ, pointing to three essential characteristics of Christ that prove his divinity and his status as the source of peace: *pure in thought and deed, peaceful, and compassionate toward the masses (commoners)*. Specifically, Bryan first featured Christ's "purity in thought and life . . . without sin." He admired the purity in Christ's "every thought and deed." He spoke of Christ's forgiving spirit, contrasting it with the revengeful spirit that "seems to be natural with man." Second, Bryan characterized Christ as the embodiment of peace. In fact, he emphasized Christ's title as the "Prince of Peace," describing Christ's self-sacrificial love as "wide as the sea; its limits were so far-flung that even an enemy could not travel beyond its bounds." Finally, according to Bryan, Christ was without selfish ambition, never concerned with self-aggrandizement or accumulation of material wealth, only with the needs of the masses, the commoners, the poor and the poor in spirit. From these characterizations, Christ as pure, peaceful, and compassionate toward the masses, Bryan concluded, "It is easier to believe Him divine than to explain in any other way what He said and did and was." Evil, by contrast, lies in the use of force, the accumulation of wealth for its own sake, the exploitation/hurting of others. Bryan assured his listeners that if they would believe in this Christ, they would experience consolation to the individual soul; peace between individuals; and justice and peace between nations. A belief in the immortality offered by Christ, claimed Bryan, moved individuals to serve others rather than be served and to propagate the truth by overcoming evil with good.

He concluded the speech with a plea for young men to recognize the Prince of Peace as their only source of strength, characterizing them as "brave" if they did. They, too, would become heroes in the mythic drama if they followed the way of the Christ hero, since faith in those mysteries would be transformative, leading an individual to live like the hero and experience the "mysterious change that takes place in the human heart when the man begins to hate the things he loved and to love the things he hated." Similarly, in "The Value of an Ideal" Bryan positioned ideals in the mysteries and miracles of Christ, suggesting that following the ideals of Christ would lead to a "revolution in the life itself." Individuals "will . . . measure life by what they bestow upon their fellows and not by what they receive." So, although the villains were fools, the hero and those who followed him or her were pure, peaceful, and compassionate toward the masses—ultimately wise and brave.

Upon establishing the three Christ-like qualities of purity, peacefulness, and concern for the masses as principles behind both personal and national decisions and policies, Bryan implicitly interfaced the Christ myth and the American heritage myth. In "The Prince of Peace," he claimed that the peace of Christ was the model for resolving all personal, political, even international conflicts. He stated that "a belief in immortality must exert a powerful influence in establishing justice between men and thus laying the foundation for peace." He argued that the model of Christ as Prince of Peace "gives us the only hope that the world has—and it is an increasing hope—of the substitution of reason for the arbitrament of force in the settlement of international disputes. But Christ has given us a platform so fundamental that it can be applied successfully to all controversies." Bryan framed the ideal response of Americans to national and international political conflicts around the three principles modeled by Christ: a spirit of purity (including loving forgiveness), a spirit of peacefulness, and a spirit of concern for the masses. The American story was to be an extension of the Christ story.

In "The Value of an Ideal," Bryan intertwined his social gospel version of the Christ myth with a version of the American foundation myth that Nimmo and Combs refer to as "the patriotic version," in which "giants walked the earth." Nimmo and Combs describe the myth this way:

> The American Revolution was the response of brave men to oppressive tyranny; a successful war of independence yielded . . . to a period of economic and political crisis that, in turn, was vanquished by "the miracle of Philadelphia," an "Olympian gathering of wise and virtuous men who stood splendidly above all faction, ignored petty self-interest, and concerned themselves only with the freedom and well-being of their fellow countrymen" in formulating the Constitution of the United States; finally, men of vision—Washington, Hamilton, Adams, and later Jefferson and Madison—stepped forth to render the new republic a continuing miracle, the world's most perfect self-governing nation.[40]

Bryan's Chautauqua addresses rang of this version of the American heritage myth, applauding the virtuous men who upheld above all else the freedom of others and who rose above self-interest. The "perfect self-governing nation" was the mythic ideal to which Bryan wanted his audiences to return. In "The Prince of Peace," he implicitly portrayed the democratic principle of self-governance as an extension of Christ's peaceful and pure spirit, suggesting that self-governance presupposes peaceful modes of decision making rather than forceful modes imposed by monarchies or aristocracies, and that self-governance presupposes trust (purity of thought and deed) in common people (the masses). In applying the principle of ideals to the political realm, he said:

> But let me speak of the ideals of a larger group. What of our political ideals? The party as well as the individual must have its ideals. . . . In order to formulate a party ideal, we must have a theory of government as a basis, and in this country the fundamental principle of government is that the people have a right to have what they want in legislation.

For support, he drew upon the authoritative mythic voice of the founding fathers, the "giants that walked the earth." In the following passage, Bryan did not recount the traditional narrative of the American foundation myth, but he called upon the dramatic images of the characters that stood for the larger myth.

> Jefferson said that there were naturally two parties in every country—a democratic party and an aristocratic party. . . . Jefferson said that a democratic party would naturally draw to itself those who believe in the people and trust them, while an aristocratic party would naturally draw to itself those who do not believe in or trust the people. Jefferson was right.

The failure to "believe in the people and trust them" stood in contrast to Christ's purely loving, forgiving spirit. Moreover, the failure to trust, argued Bryan, inevitably would lead to (aristocratic) force that stood in contrast to Christ's peaceful spirit.

More explicitly, Bryan connected the principles from the Christ narrative to principles in the American narrative when he lamented the corruption he saw in government practice caused by greedy accumulation of wealth accompanied by exploitation, a thematic evil within the social gospel narrative. In contrast to the villainous politicians who bought votes and sought their own financial gain, he advocated that a Christ-like conscience (purity in thought and deed) must be placed against money. He warned, however, that in adopting such a conscience, one might face persecution, much like Christ. "A conscience is stronger than money.

A conscience that will enable a man to stand by a stake and smile while the flames consume him is stronger than money, and we must appeal to the conscience—. . . to an American conscience and to a Christian conscience." Americans of principle must be willing to suffer on behalf of their purity, peacefulness, and concern for the masses over a concern for their own political success.

Later Bryan turned even more directly to the character of Christ to advocate a national ideal of self-governance. He stated, "The highest ideal of human life that this world has ever known was that furnished by the life of the Man of Galilee, but it was an ideal within the comprehension of the fishermen of his day, and the Bible says of Him that the common people heard Him gladly." After offering the suggestion that an ideal politician ought to listen to and respect the "common people," Bryan advocated a national ideal of self-governance. He claimed that Americans did, in fact, follow this ideal in allowing the Cubans to self-govern. Bryan blended the American story and the Christ story, suggesting that Americans must consciously continue to see the two stories as one.

As Glad notes, "Bryan made it clear that the teachings of Christ applied also to the structure and administration of government as well as to the life and conduct of the individual."[41] Bryan's religion-government connection was rhetorically powerful in part because it allowed him to counter the modernist, Darwinian perspective that suggested knowledge is never fixed, but always tentative. By casting the modernists as those who dwell in the realm of continuous subjective unknowing, Bryan's myths offered an appealing alternative of a truth that is fixed and coherent. Myths offer "dramatic wholes" that convey "the impression of a complete entity in which everything fits comfortably with everything else."[42] As such, myths and their rhetorical components appear to transcend the apparent limitations of modernist ideology. In addition, Bryan drew upon three other mythic rhetorical components to "naturalize" history in Chautauqua addresses: portraying his principles as historically transcendent, natural, and eternal; drawing parable-like analogies; and producing authoritative statements of fact and definition.

Much in the same way that Christ used parables and analogous reasoning to convey his principles, Bryan used parable-like nature analogies throughout his Chautauqua addresses, making his ideals and principles historically transcendent, natural, and eternal. In "The Prince of Peace," for instance, he refuted the resistance of his young audience to accept the mysteries of God by comparing a belief in the mystery of God to a belief in the mystery of a watermelon:

> I was eating a piece of watermelon some months ago and was struck with its beauty. I took some of the seeds and dried them and weighed them, and found that it would require some five thousand seeds to weigh a pound; and then I applied mathematics to that forty-pound melon. One of these seeds, put into the ground, when warmed by the sun and moistened by the rain, takes off its coat and goes to work; it gathers from somewhere two hundred thousand times its own weight, and forcing this raw material through a tiny stem, constructs a watermelon. . . . Who drew the plan by which that little seed works? Where does it get its tremendous strength? . . . How does it develop a watermelon? Until you can explain a watermelon, do not be too sure that you can set limits to the power of the Almighty and say just what He would do or how He would do it.

Later, Bryan refuted his young audience's resistance to the biblical notion of atonement, arguing that the act of suffering on the behalf of another was "one of the most familiar of principles . . . illustrated every-day of our lives." Hence, atonement was portrayed as natural, eternal, and historically transcendent. He used the mother-child relationship as an analogy from nature to prove the logic of atonement.

Take the family, for instance; from the day the mother's first child is born, for twenty or thirty years her children are scarcely out of her waking thoughts. Her life trembles in the balance at each child's birth; she sacrifices for them, she surrenders herself to them. Is it because she expects them to pay her back?. . . [N]o child can compensate a parent for a parent's care. In the course of nature the debt is paid, not to the parent, but to the next generation, and the next—each generation suffering, sacrificing for and surrendering itself to the generation that follows. This is the law of our lives.

The act of atonement was described, by analogy, as part of "the course of nature," the natural "law of our lives." Bryan concluded his refutation of doubts toward the theory of atonement by explicitly naming the biblical "plan of salvation" as being in perfect harmony with human nature. "Instead of being an unnatural plan, the plan of salvation is in perfect harmony with human nature as we understand it." Bryan's analogies naturalized his justification of Christian faith.

Bryan also naturalized his principles and beliefs about faith and ideals through statements of fact and definition. Barthes identifies the statement of fact as a figure of speech common to myth that functions to curtail reflection, invite acceptance without explanation, and universalize subjects.[43] Bryan used statements of fact (or definition) throughout "The Prince of Peace" and "The Value of an Ideal," which gave his narrative greater mythic appeal. In "The Prince of Peace," for example, he began his defense of Christianity by noting that the human "heart instinctively seeks for a God." He also characterized "man" as one who feels "the weight of his sins" and "looks for One who is sinless." Next, Bryan defined the relationship between religion and morality, portraying his distinction as statements of fact. "Religion is the foundation of morality in the individual and in the group of individuals. . . . Morality is the power of endurance in man; and a religion which teaches personal responsibility to God gives strength to morality." In claiming God's capacity to perform miracles, Bryan used an argument from definition, saying, "the power to perform miracles is necessarily implied in the power to create."

Similarly, in "The Value of an Ideal" Bryan laid out definitions and facts in the context of his mythic narratives, making those facts and definitions transcendent, eternal facts of nature. For example, he began the speech by distinguishing between "false ideals" and "true ideals," portraying both as universal facts of nature to be agreed upon by all because of their authority in nature. False ideals included measuring the value of one's life by what others do for oneself and measuring the value of one's life by one's accumulations. True ideals, then, were portrayed as equally factual and universal: "if he [a man] measures life by the contribution which he makes to the sum of human happiness, his only disappointment is in not finding time to do all that his heart prompts him to do." Later in the speech, when arguing that humans must have ideals, he proposed what those ideals ought to be, portraying them as ideals wrought of nature, not historically or politically grounded. For example, he essentialized marriage as "an American ideal of domestic life," saying:

When two persons, drawn together by the indissoluble ties of love, enter marriage, each one contributing a full part and both ready to share life's struggles and trials as well as its victories and its joys—when they, mutually helpful and mutually forbearing, start out to build an American home it ought to be the fittest earthly type of heaven.

He created an essentialized "American home," naturalizing the marital relationship as "indissoluble ties of love."

In reinvoking the traditional mythic narratives of Christ and the American foundation, Bryan called upon his rural audience's epistemological framework of what Walter Truett Anderson identifies as a "social-traditional" worldview "in which truth is found in the heritage of American and Western Civilization."[44] On its face, Bryan's appeal to the social-traditional worldview seems to be a reactionary attack on modernist ideology. After all, he refuted the evolutionary theories of origin, concluding that "one does not escape from mystery . . . by accepting this [Darwinian] theory, or it does not explain the origin of life." But in fact Bryan actually supported the rationalist ideology of modernism by constructing these compatible, underlying grand narratives. He established a need for a social-traditional source of truth by casting the truth claims of materialism's rationality as subjective and relative, and by citing the disagreement among scientists on the question of life's origin as an indication of their subjectivity. At the same time, he accepted the contributions of science to an understanding of the body (through X-ray technology) and of nature (through the development of technology). "Science," he claimed, "has taught us so many things that we are tempted to conclude that we know everything, but there is really a great unknown which is still unexplored and that which we have learned ought to increase our reverence rather than our egotism."

Bryan did not fully reject the modernist project. Rather, he voiced the social-traditional narratives so that they might provide direction and meaning to the truths of modernism. Historically, the modernist project has relied upon grand narratives, or "metanarratives," to support its new systems of logic. Jean-François Lyotard argues that the metanarratives articulate the primary direction of history because they are big enough to provide a unified meaning to discoveries of science.[45] Anderson posits that scientific-rationalists and social-traditionalists work in conjunction with one another "in an occasionally quarrelsome coexistence" to ensure a belief in the stability of some truth.[46] If, indeed, social-traditional metanarratives are employed to support the modern systems of knowledge, Bryan was the voice of those narratives, keeping valued cultural truths intact.

Although Bryan's use of the traditional mythic narratives in his Chautauqua speeches appears conservative, perhaps even reactionary in his response to scientific rationality, in his political speeches those myths manifest themselves in a progressive political ideology. And while his political rhetoric appears to rely on logical, discursive structures, a closer examination suggests that these speeches, too, follow the narrative logic of his two grand, mythic stories of the social gospel and the American heritage. Specifically, he used the social gospel to characterize political decisions and players in the American foundation myth as "good" or "evil."

A Mythic Backdrop for Political Speeches

Although Bryan delivered hundreds of political speeches throughout his career, four will be examined here. His most famous address, "Cross of Gold" (1896), which won him the Democratic nomination for the presidency, makes exceedingly clear the consistency of his narrative logic in interfacing the social gospel and American heritage myths. His two speeches on imperialism, "America's Mission" (1899) and "Imperialism" (1900), voiced the anti-expansionist, anti-imperialist attitudes of many Americans and most explicitly connected principles derived from the social gospel with the democratic principle of self-governance. Finally, his later speech "Democracy's Deeds and Duty" (1916) summarized the progressive reforms instituted by the Democratic Party, many of them due to his influence, providing apparent proof of his narrative logic, and offering a basis for two additional reforms: woman suffrage and prohibition. While not his most famous speech, "Democracy's Deeds and Duty" exemplified Bryan's politics and their relationship to his fundamental religious beliefs.

Based on an isolated reading of these four political speeches, one could describe Bryan's political prowess as naive, simplistic, and underinformed. In fact, many critics dismissed Bryan as a politician, arguing that he lacked sophistication in his understanding, for example, of the complex economics of the gold standard issue, foreign policy, and tariff legislation. However, when the logic of these speeches is considered against the backdrop of the principles revealed in his religious and moral speeches delivered on the Chautauqua circuit, Bryan's political reasoning was, at the very least, consistent within the logic of his mythic grand narrative of the social gospel and, by extension, the myth of America's foundation.

CROSS OF GOLD

A common misconception about Bryan was that he was an unknown young delegate to the 1896 Democratic Party Convention who emerged out of nowhere to deliver in a loud, vibrant voice an emotionally appealing speech that won him the Democratic presidential nomination. Many historians today refute that conception, providing evidence to support the fact that Bryan's campaign was long and deliberate, his support widespread, and his success widely anticipated.[47] During his final season as a U.S. representative in Nebraska in 1893, Bryan decided to alter the course of the Democratic Party primarily by making it the party of currency reform in support of silver coinage in addition to the existing gold coinage. The Populists and some Democrats fervently advocated this "bimetal standard," believing that the coinage of gold alone would contract the circulation of currency, driving up prices, making trade more difficult for the common person, and bringing the silver-mining industry to a close. Despite his wife's misgivings about his aspirations for the presidency, Bryan launched an active public-speaking and writing campaign, advancing his progressive agenda, focusing specifically on the currency issue. By the time of the Democratic Convention in Chicago in July 1896, Bryan was well connected in the party, especially among the Nebraska delegation. He was a member of the Bimetallic Democratic National Committee, helping to craft its platform. Historian David Nordloh notes that "the formal, legitimate National Committee was in the hands of the Gold Democrats, and Bryan was clearly at best a dark-horse candidate, placing no higher than fifth in pre-convention polls of several newspapers." Others, however, acknowledged that "he could become the nominee only if the silver forces captured control of the convention."[48] In fact, Bryan set out to position himself to "capture control of the convention." He participated in the platform construction but intentionally chaired no committees, strategically positioning himself to orchestrate the sequencing of events so that he could deliver his nomination speech at the ideal time. He managed to schedule himself to be the final speaker in support of the majority platform that favored "bimetallism," the coinage of both gold and silver. He followed Governor William E. Russell of Massachusetts, who spoke in defense of the gold standard, and Bryan delivered his speech to an audience already enthusiastic about his presence. Bryan's description of the response to his speech, found in his *Memoirs*, is entirely consistent with that of historians':

> The excitement of the moment was so intense that I hurried to the platform and began at once. My nervousness left me instantly and I felt as composed as if I had been speaking to a small audience on an unimportant occasion. From the first sentence the audience was with me. My voice reached to the uttermost parts of the hall. . . .
>
> I shall never forget the scene upon which I looked. I believe it unrivaled in any convention ever held in our country. The audience seemed to rise and sit down as one man. At the close of a sentence it would rise and shout, and when I began upon another sentence, the room was still as a church. . . .

The audience acted like a trained choir—in fact, I thought of a choir as I noted how instantaneously and in unison they responded to each point made.

The situation was so unique and the experience so unprecedented that I have never expected to witness its counterpart.

At the conclusion of my speech the demonstration spread over nearly the entire convention.[49]

At that point, Bryan's nomination was nearly assured.

"The Cross of Gold" speech began with an expression of Bryan's humility before his audience. He then made clear whose interests he represented: the commoners'. Having established his goodwill in his introduction, Bryan laid out a series of logical refutations of his opponents' positions on several issues—their opposition to the income tax and a national bank currency, and their advocacy of congressional representatives having life tenures in office. His fourth refutation constituted the longest section of the speech dedicated to his defense of bimetallism and his attack on the gold standard. The discussion of the gold standard contained two primary sections. The first was a set of three rebuttals to those within the Democratic Party who favored the gold standard. Then, after refuting the opposition within his party, Bryan built an affirmative case, explaining why so many Democrats recently developed a conviction for free coinage. Primarily, he reasoned that free coinage was most consistent with the principles of self-governance. The conclusion used metaphors and analogies to cast his bimetal positions as manifestations of the social gospel and American heritage myths. Finally, he ended the speech with his well-remembered metaphor: "You shall not press down upon the brow of labor this crown of thorns, you shall not crucify mankind upon a cross of gold."

Any careful observer would be hard-pressed to deny that the logic of Bryan's refutations in "The Cross of Gold" was weak. Never, for example, did Bryan provide an expediency argument for how free coinage would benefit the farmers, the laborers, and the working class he represented. Never did he explain the economics of the gold and silver standards. When he asked why, within three months, so many more Democrats had come to support free coinage, he assumed that the answer was evident and said, "Is not the reason for the change evident to any one who will look at the matter?" Yet his only explanation for the sudden shift was that Democrats and others suddenly realized that they would surrender their right of self-government if they elected McKinley. Bryan offered no proof or reasoning to explain this sudden realization. Similarly, when inoculating his audience against further attacks from his opponents, he stated:

> If they tell us that the gold standard is a good thing, we shall point to their platform and tell them that their platform pledges the party to get rid of the gold standard and substitute bimetallism. . . . I call your attention to the fact that some of the very people who are in this convention today and who tell us that we ought to declare in favor of international bimetallism—thereby declaring that the gold standard is wrong and that the principle of bimetallism is better—these very people four months ago were open and avowed advocates of the gold standard, and were then telling us that we could not legislate two metals together, even with the aid of all the world.

According to Bryan, to advocate bimetallism internationally was to declare the gold standard as "wrong." Throughout the speech, Bryan used arguments that pointed to the logical inconsistency, hence hypocrisy, of his opponents (though he did not assess their reasoning accurately), but never articulated an affirmative position as to why bimetallism would be better for the masses.

Such flaws in Bryan's argumentation give support to the belief of many that he lacked intellectual depth in his consideration of economic issues.[50] Coletta reports, for example, that Illinois governor John Peter Altgeld believed Bryan never understood the fundamentals of the coinage question.[51] However, "The Cross of Gold" speech accomplished something else rhetorically, despite its argumentative blunders. The speech refocused the metal debate away from expediency questions (that were extremely complex and perhaps difficult for the average citizen to understand) toward common principles derived from the prevailing grand mythic narratives of the social gospel and the American heritage. Bryan moved the debate out of what rhetorical scholar Walter Fisher refers to as the "rational world paradigm" that requires participants in a public debate to be qualified, learned, and able to speak rationally on the matter at hand—in this case, the economics of coinage. Given the complex economics surrounding this issue, the rational world paradigm precluded the commoner from participating in this all-important debate.[52] By relying on a mythic, narrative logic, however, Bryan enabled the commoner to participate in the dialog. "The materials of narrative [myth]" argues Fisher, "are symbols, signs of consubstantiation, and good reasons, the communicative expressions of social reality," materials accessible to Bryan's implied audience, unlike the inaccessible expert knowledge of economics. Furthermore, while the rational paradigm requires self-conscious learning, narrative rationality "presupposes the logic of narrative capacities that we all share"; thus Bryan's common audience was capable of reasoning, even in sophisticated ways, within his narrative framework.[53]

"The Cross of Gold" hearkened primarily to two principles derived from the Christ myth and the American heritage myth. First, it iterated the social gospel concern for the masses. As noted above, in "The Prince of Peace" Bryan laid out his foundational narrative, deriving several ideals from the social gospel version of the Christ story: concern for the masses, purity of thought and deed, and peacefulness. As in his Chautauqua addresses, "The Cross of Gold" invoked the dramatic images of these myths through character development rather than a reiteration of those mythic narratives. The predominant characters in this speech were the commoners who were to be served and protected from the wealthy, greedy, powerful upper-class conservatives. Bryan appealed to the Democrats to take on the characteristic of compassion for commoners, a characteristic that he said in "The Prince of Peace" came only from Christ. Implicitly, then, in "The Cross of Gold" he drew upon the images of the Christ figure, whose perfection he asked his audience to model. Because of the political context for this speech, Bryan emphasized the character of the commoner (the victim) and the opponents of bimetallism (the villains) in a manner that implied the larger social gospel myth rather than referring to it explicitly.

The characterization of the masses or commoners was most evident in Bryan's opening paragraphs in which he established his persona as a holy warrior for the masses he represented, saying, "I come to speak to you in defense of a cause as holy as the cause of liberty—the cause of humanity." Naming the bimetal cause a "holy cause" made the implicit connection to the Christ myth more apparent. Bryan even assured his opponents that the "silverites" were not tyrants but crusaders against organized wealth that served only a few at the expense of the many. The term "crusaders" aligned the bimetalist Democrats with Christ rather than with tyranny. After establishing the bimetalist Democrats as holy heroes, Bryan characterized the victims, or the "masses," for whom they must have compassion, broadening the typical definition of a businessman to include the laborer, the farmer, and the miner.

We say to you that you have made the definition of a business man too limited in its application. The man who is employed for wages is as much a business man as his employer; the attorney in a country town is as much a business man as the corporation counsel in a great metropolis; . . . the farmer who goes forth in the morning and toils all day—who begins in the spring and toils all summer—and who by the application of brain and muscle to the natural resources of the country creates wealth, is as much a business man as the man who goes upon the board of trade and bets upon the price of grain; the miners who go down a thousand feet into the earth, or climb two thousand feet upon the cliffs, and bring forth from their hiding places the precious metals to be poured into the channels of trade are as much business men as the few financial magnates who, in a back room, corner the money of the world. We come to speak for this broader class of business men.

Ah, my friends, we say not one word against those who live upon the Atlantic coast, but the hardy pioneers who have braved all the dangers of the wilderness, who have made the desert to blossom as the rose—the pioneers away out there [pointing to the West], who rear their children near to Nature's heart, where they can mingle their voices with the voices of the birds—out there where they have erected schoolhouses for the education of their young, churches where they praise their Creator, and cemeteries where rest the ashes of their dead—these people, we say, are as deserving of the consideration of our party as any people in this country. It is for these that we speak.

In these paragraphs, Bryan emphasized that he speaks for the masses, for the average working Americans (particularly the underrepresented westerners) who work the land, educate their children, worship their God, and ultimately die just as those in the East to whom he spoke.

By contrast, the villains were the opponents of bimetallism, whom Bryan characterized as hypocrites, and wealthy bankers who wished to protect their own financial interests. For example, Bryan characterized his opponents as hypocrites when he claimed that they would propose to add to the bimetal platform a provision that bimetallism shall not affect existing contracts intended to be paid in gold. This provision was unnecessary and suggested that the lenders (bankers) needed to be protected if the silver standard was used. Equal consideration, he claimed, was not given to the debtors when the gold standard was established in 1873, hence the hypocrisy. Bryan then asserted that his opponents proposed to add a clause to the platform that would allow them to suspend free coinage if parity was not maintained within a year. Again he characterized his opponents as hypocrites since such an "out" clause was not typically included in a platform. He told them that if it was applied in this case, it should also be applied in the case of other platform planks to protect the people. In many respects, Bryan sounded like Christ speaking to the common people, unveiling the hypocrisy of the Pharisees and Sadducees who performed religious rituals for selfish gain rather than genuine service to others.

Finally, Bryan characterized those who dominated and oppressed the masses as villains. He ultimately bifurcated the gold standard debate for the Democratic Party, requiring Democrats to decide whether they would fight for "idle holders of idle capital" (the wealthy eastern bankers and investors) by siding with the gold standard, or for the masses by siding with free coinage. He told his listeners that the gold standard struggle was between 'the idle holders of idle capital' and 'the struggling masses, who produce the wealth and pay the taxes of the country'; and, my friends, the question we are to decide is: Upon which side will the Democratic party fight; upon the side of 'the idle holders of idle capital' or upon the side of 'the struggling masses?'" He also polarized the principles of government that would support either decision. The former, he suggested, stems from a "trickle down" principle of government in which legislation was designed to make the upper class prosper, assuming that prosperity then trickled down to the middle and lower classes. The latter stemmed from a "bottom-up" principle, where legislation was designed to make the masses prosperous and, in turn, upwardly affect the smaller upper class.

Bryan again invoked the ideals of Christ in protecting the masses when he justified his support for term limits, saying, "What we oppose by that plank [that declares against life tenure in office] is the life tenure which is being built up in Washington, and which excludes from participation in official benefits the humbler members of society." His concern for the "humbler members of society" rang of the mythic Christ who concerned himself with the poor and needy.

In addition to the concern for the masses, Bryan's speech also drew upon the American foundation mythic principle of self-governance that implied peacefulness. He established a presumption that even those who opposed free coinage actually must support it since they advocated waiting until other countries adopted bimetallism. Waiting for other countries was then redefined as relinquishing the right of self-government, allowing other countries to dictate what was best for America, and failing to govern the self. By characterizing his opponents as passive, he made them appear weak and hypocritical. Bryan also compared the metal debate to the independence debate of 1776, arguing that the current debate was equally important in determining the extent to which America would be a self-governing nation. By implication, his opponents, he suggested, would have opposed American independence. By pointing to the hypocrisies of his opponents, Bryan drew upon one of the logical demands of narrative rationality: narrative probability, the question of whether a narrative is internally consistent, structurally coherent, and characterologically coherent.[54] He insisted that the Democratic Party play out the American heritage narrative consistently.

Not only did "The Cross of Gold" recall the underlying narratives found in Bryan's Chautauqua addresses, but it also relied upon the rhetorical strategies of myth identified by Barthes. For example, in "The Cross of Gold" Bryan used "neither-norism," a rhetorical strategy commonly found in myths. Barthes writes,

> By this ["neither-norism"] I mean this mythological figure which consists in stating two opposites and balancing the one by the other so as to reject them both. (I want *neither* this *nor* that.) . . . [R]eality is first reduced to analogues; then it is weighed; finally, equality having been ascertained, it is got rid of. . . . [B]oth parties are dismissed because it is embarrassing to choose between them.[55]

Bryan posed a "neither-norism" by suggesting that the Democratic Party could neither wait to uphold free coinage until other countries did so (because waiting meant relinquishing the right to self-governance, thus violating the mythic narrative principles) nor uphold the gold standard in full (because denying free coinage meant abandoning responsibility to the masses, thus violating the mythic narrative principles). The speech's topical structure also constructed a "neither-norism" form of mythic logic. He identified argument upon argument from the opponents of bimetallism, refuting each one as he went, suggesting neither this argument nor that one was a worthy reason to oppose the bimetal standard. Although his refutations were not evidence-based counterarguments but loosely reasoned characterizations of his opponents as hypocrites, the enumerative structure within the narrative logic of the Christ myth and American heritage myth gave the refutations rhetorical appeal, leaving the audience member ashamed to align with the opponents in any way.

In addition to "neither-norism," Bryan deployed another rhetorical strategy Barthes sees frequently in myths: tautology. "Tautology is this verbal device which consists in defining like by like ('Drama is drama'). . . . [O]ne takes refuge in tautology as one does in fear, or anger, or sadness, when one is at a loss for an explanation."[56] Barthes uses the illustration of the parent who replies to a child who continues to ask for explanations by saying, "Because that's how it is." Bryan resorted to tautology toward the end of the speech after refuting his opponents. Rather than providing an explanation for how free coinage would benefit the masses, he used a bandwagon appeal, saying that the opponents might claim that if the gold standard is the standard of civilization, then, as a civilized people, Americans should use it. Bryan said:

> If they [the opposition] come to meet us on that issue we can present the history of our nation. More than that; we can tell them that they will search the pages of history in vain to find a single instance where the common people of any land have ever declared themselves in favor of the gold standard. They can find where the holders of the fixed investments have declared for a gold standard, but not where the masses have.

So, because the masses had never stood in favor of the gold standard, it must not have been desirable. Bryan's logic here is easily refutable, but the rhetorical strategy fits within the mythic frame from which his discourse operates.

On its surface, "The Cross of Gold" appears as a simplistic, emotional defense of free coinage, particularly with the memorable final phrase of the speech, delivered by a man with limited understanding of the complex economic principles behind the debate. But when considered within the mythic moral framework revealed in Bryan's Chautauqua addresses, "The Cross of Gold" reflects a narrative logic that meets the standards of probability and fulfills the ideological functions of grand mythic narratives.

"AMERICA'S MISSION" AND "IMPERIALISM"

Bryan vowed to keep the currency issue at the forefront of national politics and of central concern to the Democratic Party. But in 1898 his focus shifted when a U.S. battleship, the *Maine*, was sunk in the harbor at Havana, Cuba, costing the lives of 250 Americans. The event shifted American attention to the three-year struggle between Cuban rebels and Spanish troops. Once he conceded to the inevitable involvement of American troops in defense of Cuban rebels, Bryan took up the Cuban cause. "War is a terrible thing," he wrote, "and cannot be defended except as a means to an end."[57] Though a pacifist in principle, Bryan believed by this time that war was the only means left to liberate the Cubans from Spanish injustice. After war was declared against Spain on 25 August, Bryan wrote a letter to President McKinley offering his services in the armed forces. On 13 July 1898 he became colonel in the Third Nebraska Regiment, U.S. Volunteers. By December he was actively involved in the debate over the ratification of the peace treaty. The matter of imperialism became most contentious during the treaty deliberations; Republicans favored the treaty, and Democrats opposed it. The treaty included provisions for the liberation of Cuba, allowing Cubans to establish their own form of government, but it also yielded to an offer by Spain to hand over the entire Philippine Islands for $20 million. The Filipinos responded by preparing to resist annexation by force, while McKinley suddenly proclaimed American sovereignty over the islands on the basis of military conquest. Although the treaty included imperialist overtones, Bryan argued in its favor in order to end the war. He intended, however, to persuade Congress to pass a resolution granting the Filipinos their independence.

On 22 February 1899, after intense debate in Congress about the role the United States was to play in the Philippines, Bryan delivered his speech "America's Mission," promising to make imperialism his central issue if the matter was unresolved at election time. In November 1899 the Democratic Party announced that silver would be the primary issue for the election of 1900, but by the time of the convention in July, the unresolved questions of expansion and imperialism had grown increasingly salient. The Platform Committee at the convention in Kansas

City declared imperialism to be the paramount issue of the campaign. On 5 July 1900 Bryan was nominated as the party's presidential candidate. Instead of delivering the typical acceptance speech, on 8 August in Military Park in Indianapolis he delivered an extensive speech devoted solely to the matter of imperialism. Coletta describes the speech, now entitled "Imperialism":

> Lofty in spirit and captivating to its hearers, the speech gave evidence of intellectual power; it combined ardor without intemperance, argument without abuse, and fire without fanaticism. Its tone was moderate except for the charge that the Army built forts near large cities in order to intimidate the workers therein. Like Cleveland in his famous tariff message of 1887, he had dealt with one subject alone in an eloquent and dignified manner. . . . The speech became a major campaign document and won Bryan many friends in the East.[58]

Many critics and historians considered his anti-imperialist rhetoric to be more carefully reasoned than his bimetallism speeches. Nonetheless, a careful examination of "America's Mission" and "Imperialism" reveals a close alignment between Bryan's foreign policy, his second presidential campaign discourse, and his guiding moral myths.

"America's Mission" was a compact, carefully crafted speech that began with a description of the pro-expansionist argument that imperialism was America's destiny. After admonishing his audience of the dangers of assuming to know a destiny, Bryan posited a deductive argument in which he first defined destiny and then defined the purpose of the nation so he could refute, on principle, the act of imperialism. Once he established the general premise that the purpose of the United States was to protect the principle of self-government, he moved to his particular premise of the Filipino case, cautioning the audience against the temptation to impose the U.S. system of government on the Filipinos. Bryan then set forth a brief expediency appeal, arguing that annexing the Philippine Islands would not necessarily make the United States a world power since the United States already was a world power. Finally, Bryan concluded the speech by comparing the American and Anglo-Saxon civilizations. He explained that the union of the Anglo and the Saxon formed what had evolved as the most civilized of people, but that the American people must maintain yet higher standards of civilization.

Although built upon the same basic premise that anti-imperialism was the only acceptable position consistent with the principle of self-government, Bryan's "Imperialism" speech unfolded differently. Like "America's Mission," "Imperialism" began with a deductive argument that characterized the issue of imperialism as a contest between democracy and plutocracy. He then attacked the Republican Party for its inconsistencies and abandonment of American ideals. After illustrating the failures of the Republicans, he explained his support for the treaty that ended the Spanish-American War, which failed to give independence to the Filipinos. From there, Bryan began a series of arguments refuting the imperialist policy toward the Filipinos. Next, Bryan differentiated expansionism from imperialism, arguing that imperialism relied upon the force of one government over another. He then refuted the pro-imperialist argument that America's duty was to hold the Philippines. Bryan demanded consistency in U.S. policy toward foreign nations, arguing that the same freedoms granted to the Cubans after the Spanish-American War be granted to the Filipinos. He also refuted the argument that the Filipinos were incapable of self-governance, claiming that such a belief inevitably would lead to force. Finally, Bryan identified and refuted the four arguments most commonly used in support of American colonization of the Philippine Islands: that the United States must improve its opportunity to become a world power (he argued it already was a world power); that the country's commercial interests made it necessary to hold the islands (he argued that money was never a reasonable justification of force); that the spread of Christianity would be facilitated by colonization (he argued that Christianity must be spread by examples of love, never by force); and that fate had put the United States in this position, and no honorable retreat was possible (he argued that since the United States allowed Cubans to self-govern, there was no reason it could not respectfully do the same for the Filipinos). Bryan ended the speech by stating his desire that the United States restore the Filipinos' freedom of self-governance and classifying as "lazy" the argument that the United States was destined to rule the Philippine Islands.

Both "America's Mission" and "Imperialism" relied heavily and explicitly on dramatic character images derived from the social gospel interpretation of the Christ myth and the American foundation myth. In "America's Mission," the villains were, as in his Chautauqua addresses, once again fools. In the opening paragraphs, Bryan mocked the pro-expansionist argument that imperialism was America's destiny, representing this argument as one of folly. He mimicked his opponents: "'Suppose it [imperialism] does violate the Constitution,' they say; 'suppose it does break all the commandments; suppose it does entail upon the nation an incalculable expenditure of blood and money; it is destiny and we must submit.'" Bryan characterized this assertion as "helpless despair" and then questioned his opponents' qualifications to predict America's future and declare its destiny. He cited several examples from his mythic references—beginning with Old Testament stories, moving through Western history, and ending with the story of the American Revolution—to demonstrate the dangers of assuming to know destiny. Many historical figures who claimed to be following destiny were proven wrong. Bryan illustrated:

> History is replete with predictions which once wore the hue of destiny, but which failed of fulfillment because those who uttered them saw too small an arc of the circle of events. When Pharaoh pursued the fleeing Israelites to the edge of the Red Sea, he was confident that their bondage would be renewed and that they would again make bricks without straw, but destiny was not revealed until Moses and his followers reached the farther shore dry shod and the waves rolled over the horses and chariots of the Egyptians. When Belshazzar, on the last night of his reign, led his thousand lords into the Babylonian banquet hall and sat down to a table glittering with vessels of silver and gold, he felt sure of his kingdom for many years to come, but destiny was not revealed until the hand wrote upon the wall those awe-inspiring words, "Mene, Mene, Tekel Upharsin." . . . When the redcoats of George the Third routed the New Englanders at Lexington and Bunker Hill, there arose before the British sovereign visions of colonies taxed without representation and drained of their wealth by foreign-made laws, but destiny was not revealed until the surrender of Cornwallis completed the work begun at Independence Hall and ushered into existence a government deriving its just powers from the consent of the governed.

Again Bryan called forth imagery of the villains (fools) in the Judeo-Christian myth and the American foundation myth, thereby deriving a kind of truth to his claims.

In "Imperialism," the villains were the imperialists who acted from greed to exploit the commoners for their own wealth and political self-interest. In "America's Mission," Bryan identified the imperialist policy as "criminal aggression" in contrast to a "standard of morality." Similarly, in "Imperialism" he vividly characterized the imperialists invading the commoners of the Philippine Islands: "A colonial policy means that we shall send to the Philippine Islands a few traders, a few taskmasters and a few officeholders and an army large enough to support the authority of a small fraction of the people while they rule the natives." A large standing army, he pointed out, was the "personification of force" and inevitably would lead to discord rather than a security of self-governance among the Filipino people.

To further dramatize his characterization of imperialists, Bryan metaphorically compared the United States to King George III, arguing that if the United States were to colonize the Philippines, it would be behaving as King George III did in response to the American colonies. Bryan asked, "If, in this country where the people have a right to vote, republican [*sic*] leaders dare not take the side of the people against the great monopolies which have grown up within the last few years, how can they be trusted to protect the Filipinos from the corporations which are waiting to exploit the islands?" Bryan admonished against the treatment of the Filipinos as "possessions," arguing that the American title to the Philippines, if Americans did colonize the Philippines, must not be held by conquest or purchase if they were to remain consistent with their principles of government. "If governments derive their just powers from the consent of the governed," he argued, "it is impossible to secure title to people, either by force or by purchase."

In contrast to these foolish and exploitative villains, Bryan offered an anti-imperialist position that exemplified "perfect" characteristics of the mythic Christ and mythic founding fathers: peacefulness, self-governance, and concern for the masses. First, these two speeches hearkened back to the social gospel narrative in their call for peace over force. In "America's Mission," he opposed "forcible annexation of the Philippine Islands," arguing that a democracy was built upon the peaceful force of ideas rather than the force of weapons. He stated, "In the growth of democracy we observe the triumphant march of an idea—an idea that would be weighted down rather than aided by the armor and weapons proffered by imperialism." Bryan also drew directly from the gospel text of the mythic Christ in elevating the standards of Americans over those of the Anglo-Saxons, claiming that while "Anglo-Saxon civilization has taught the individual to take care of himself, American civilization, proclaiming the equality of all before the law, will teach him that his own highest good requires the observance of the commandment: 'Thou shalt love thy neighbor as thyself.'" He then held American civilization to a higher standard of civility, that of the perfect mythic hero. "Anglo-Saxon civilization has, by force of arms, applied the art of government to other races for the benefit of Anglo-Saxons; American civilization will, by the influence of example, excite in other races a desire for self-government and a determination to secure it."

Like "America's Mission," Bryan's "Imperialism" speech also called to mind the principle of peace derived from social gospel Christ myth, as he applied that ideal to the narrative of the American heritage. Throughout the speech Bryan expressed his opposition to force. In refuting the argument that the colonization of the Philippine Islands would aid in the spread of Christianity, Bryan maintained that conversion was not successful (or appropriate) if accomplished through force. "If true Christianity consists in carrying out in our daily lives the teachings of Christ," he asked, "who will say that we are commanded to civilize with dynamite and proselyte with the sword?" "Imperialism finds no warrant in the Bible," he claimed. Referring directly to the gospel, he added:

> The command "Go ye into all the world and preach the gospel to every creature" has no Gatling gun attachment. When Jesus visited a village of Samaria and the people refused to receive him, some of the disciples suggested that fire should be called down from Heaven to avenge the insult; but the Master rebuked them and said: "Ye know not what manner of spirit ye are of; for the Son of Man is not come to destroy men's lives, but to save them." Suppose he had said: "We will thrash them until they understand who we are," how different would have been the history of Christianity! Compare, if you will, the swaggering, bullying, brutal doctrine of imperialism with the golden rule and the commandment "Thou shalt love they neighbor as thyself."

Here Bryan drew explicitly from the Christ myth to justify his opposition to force. That principle was applied to his telling of the American foundation myth, which he again constructed as an extension of the Christ story. For Bryan, Christ defied the use of force, and the country's founders followed that command when establishing their principles of government. He quoted the mythic hero Thomas Jefferson as saying, "'If there be one principle more deeply rooted than any other in the mind of every American, it is that we should have nothing to do with conquest.' And again he said: 'Conquest is not in our principles; it is inconsistent with our government.'" Later, Bryan made the case that the annexation of the Philippine Islands would require the presence of an army. "The army," he claimed, "is the personification of force, and militarism will inevitably change the ideals of the people and turn the thoughts of our young men from the arts of peace to the science of war." Thus the necessary presence of an army in the Philippines was an invitation to forcefulness rather than peacefulness. In these comments, Bryan interfaced his two underlying mythic narratives, providing clear moral standards and consistent narrative logic for his anti-imperialist position.

In addition to the principle of peacefulness, Bryan also called upon the principle of self-governance, derived from the American foundation myth and, ultimately, from the social gospel principle of peacefulness. For example, in "Imperialism" Bryan argued that to deny self-governance to the Filipinos was to weaken self-governance in the United States. Again, he invoked images of the American mythologized characters, noting that "Lincoln said that the safety of this nation was not in its fleets, its armies, or its forts, but in the spirit which prizes liberty as the heritage of all men, in all lands, everywhere, and he warned his countrymen that they could not destroy this spirit without planting the seeds of despotism at their own doors." Bryan then tapped into the foundation myth by citing the Declaration of Independence, arguing: "[W]e believe in the principles of self-government and reject, as did our forefathers, the claims of monarchy. If this nation surrenders its belief in the universal application of the principles set forth in the Declaration of Independence, it will lose the prestige and influence which it has enjoyed among the nations as an exponent of popular government." Since the United States had supported the independence of other countries, Bryan suggested, it must consistently apply its principle of self-governance to the Filipinos.

Bryan pitted hero against villain when he compared the imperialist policy to the acts of King George III in 1776:

> In what respect does the [imperialist] position of the Republican party differ from the position taken by the English government in 1776? Did not the English government promise a good government to the colonists? What king ever promised a bad government to his people? Did not the English government promise that the colonists should have the largest measure of self-government consistent with their welfare and English duties? . . . The republican [sic] party has accepted the European idea and planted itself upon the ground taken by George III, and by every ruler who distrusts the capacity of the people for self-government or denies them a voice in their own affairs.

In "America's Mission," Bryan again invoked the American heritage myth, identifying the purpose of the historic heroes' actions. He stated, "The main purpose of the founders of our Government was to secure for themselves and for posterity the blessings of liberty, and that purpose has been faithfully followed up to this time. Our statesmen have opposed each other upon economic questions, but they have agreed in defending self-government as the controlling national idea." By comparing the proponents of imperialism to King George III, Bryan depicted them as the antagonist in his unfolding narrative of the American story. Here he relied on what Fisher identifies as the "fidelity" of his narrative to appeal to his opponents' sense of guilt. In addition to the criterion of narrative probability, Fisher believes that humans, as storytellers, apply the criterion of "fidelity" in their judgment of narratives. "Fidelity" refers to the truthfulness of a story.[59] Since the story of King George III would, in fact, ring true for his opponents, Bryan was able to demand that Americans apply the principles of self-governance consistently, relinquish their role as King George III, and thus remain consistent in their actions.

A third principle Bryan employed in his anti-imperialist rhetoric was the principle of concern for the masses, derived from the Christ myth. In "Imperialism," Bryan expressed his concern that both the Filipinos and the working class of America would be exploited by the colonization of the Philippine Islands. He asked,

> If secret influences could compel a disregard of our plain duty toward friendly people [Puerto Ricans], living near our shores, what treatment will those same influences provide for unfriendly people 7,000 miles away? If, in this country where the people have a right to vote, republican [sic] leaders dare not take the side of the people against the great monopolies which have grown up within the last few years, how can they be trusted to protect the Filipinos from the corporations which are waiting to exploit the islands?

Bryan echoed Christ's concern for the welfare of the masses, expressing his own concern that any economic gain from trade with the Filipinos would be enjoyed by a few, but the expense borne by many:

> Imperialism . . . would be profitable to those who would seize upon the franchises, and it would be profitable to the officials whose salaries would be fixed here and paid over there; but to the farmer, to the laboring man and to the vast majority of those engaged in other occupations it would bring expenditure without return and risk without reward.
>
> Farmers and laboring men have, as a rule, small incomes and under systems which place the tax upon consumption pay much more than their fair share of the expenses of government. Thus the very people who receive least benefit from imperialism will be injured most by the military burdens which accompany it.
>
> In addition to the evils which he and the farmer share in common, the laboring man will be the first to suffer if oriental subjects seek work in the United States; the first to suffer if American capital leaves our shores to employ oriental labor in the Philippines.

Bryan not only expressed a concern for the masses, but he also identified as "evil" those forces leading to the exploitation of laborers and farmers. So, too, in "America's Mission" he challenged Americans to take up arms to aid a neighboring people struggling to be free, to set a "silent example" that would do more to extend self-government and civilization than anything else. Here he echoed the mythic Christ telling and enacting the story of the Good Samaritan who silently helped a struggling neighbor. The proponents of imperialism were the villains who saw but walked past the one in need.

The two myths merged again in "America's Mission" when Bryan described the debate over the Philippine Islands as "the hour of temptation." "The hour of temptation has come, but temptations do not destroy, they merely test the strength of individuals and nations; they are stumbling blocks or stepping stones; they lead to infamy or fame, according to the use made of them." By characterizing the debate as the "hour of temptation," Bryan framed this policy issue as a public moral dilemma that was easily answered if considered within the context of his guiding myths. The temptation metaphor signified the grand narrative of the social gospel and brought to mind Christ's purity of mind and deed, his self-restraint from the temptation of wealth and acquisition.

Throughout both speeches, Bryan pleaded for consistency—that the Filipinos be treated as the Cubans were and that Americans consistently uphold the principles of democracy. By grounding his arguments in a mythic narrative logic, and by viewing the imperialist question as a continuation of the mythic stories of Christ and the American foundation, Bryan positioned himself to demand principled consistency, to be determined by the future actions of the nation. Bryan's grand narratives were not simply myths of the past. For him, the Christ myth was enacted in the myth of America's foundation, which in turn was to be played out by the policies of the twentieth century.

As in "The Cross of Gold," in both of Bryan's anti-imperialist speeches his rhetorical power came, in part, through the mythic qualities of his rhetoric. Two strategies were especially potent in "America's Mission" and "Imperialism." As explained above, myth makes its subject innocent, giving it a natural and eternal justification, transforming history into nature. A rhetorical strategy that transformed the historical and political nature of the imperialist debate into a natural phenomenon appeared in the introduction of "Imperialism" when Bryan laid out, as a statement of fact, the "proper relation which should exist" between the dollar and man. "Man, the handiwork of God, comes first; money, the handiwork of man, is of inferior importance. Man is the master, money the servant, but upon all important questions today Republican legislation tends to make money the master and man the servant." Bryan opposed the practices of the Republican Party by stating as fact what he perceived to be the natural order of things.

Similarly, in "America's Mission" he refuted the argument that America was destined to colonize the Philippine Islands, arguing that "destiny is not a matter of chance; it is a matter of choice; it is not a thing to be waited for, it is a thing to be achieved." His argument from definition coupled with his linguistic scheme of antithesis functioned to convey his perspective as the way things essentially are, by nature. Bryan frequently relies on schemes of antithesis, bifurcation, and proverbial phrasing as well as metaphors, all of which supported the naturalization of his ideas. In "Imperialism," for example, he stated: "Rights never conflict; duties never clash;" and "Love, not force, was the weapon of the Nazarene; sacrifice for others, not the exploitation of them, was His method of reaching the human heart." In "America's Mission," he crafted phrases like an Old Testament proverb. "Unexpected events may retard or advance the Nation's growth, but the Nation's purpose determines its destiny." "Whether a man steals much or little may depend upon his opportunities, but whether he steals at all depends upon his own volition." Phrasing reminiscent of the book of Proverbs reinforced the mythic power upon which his discourse relied.

As in "The Cross of Gold," Bryan's anti-imperialist rhetoric in "America's Mission" and "Imperialism" is best understood against the backdrop of his Chautauqua rhetoric. Perhaps more than his other speeches, these two explicitly interfaced the individual moral standards derived from the Christ myth with national moral standards derived from the American foundation myth. The mythic undertones in these political speeches were, in fact, the source of their internal logic.

"DEMOCRACY'S DEEDS AND DUTY"

Bryan entered his final presidential race in 1908, again winning the Democratic nomination but not the presidency. He continued his participation in politics, however. He served as Woodrow Wilson's secretary of state between 1912 and 1915, but resigned due to conflicting opinions with Wilson regarding America's involvement in World War I. Despite his disagreement with Wilson, he vigorously campaigned on Wilson's behalf during the 1916 presidential election. Many historians agree that without Bryan's endorsement and rhetorical contributions to the campaign, Wilson would not have been nominated or elected.[60]

On 6 December 1916 in Washington, D.C., Senator Thomas J. Walsh of Montana hosted a victory dinner to thank Bryan for his help and influence on Wilson's campaign. Though the president himself was unable to attend, he sent his words of praise. After the dinner, many speakers lauded Bryan. Because so many wanted to express their praise, Bryan himself was unable to begin speaking until nearly midnight. Although the speech, "Democracy's Deeds and Duty," lasted nearly one and a half hours, ending at 1:25 A.M., the audience was riveted. The structure of "Democracy's Deeds and Duty" was quite simple compared to other Bryan speeches, following a past-future pattern. In the first half of the speech, Bryan enumerated the successes of the Democratic Party. The second half posed two additional issues for the party to mount: woman suffrage and, more controversial, prohibition. In enumerating the recently passed "remedial legislation," Bryan recalled the constitutional amendment providing the election of U.S. senators by direct vote; the income tax constitutional amendment; the tariff laws; currency reform, including the shift to gold *and* silver standards; the rural credits law; and two antitrust laws. He mentioned a shipping law, child labor laws, and eight-hour-day laws. All this legislation he attributed to Democratic effort. Finally, he praised the party for its support of independence to the Filipinos and its support of his treaty plan through which international conflicts would be resolved with permanent treaties, mediated by other countries, rather than armed forces.

Bryan then set forth a six-plank agenda for the party. First, he described the need to inform voters of voting issues, advocating a government publication that would evenly represent Congress or requiring newspapers to give a percentage of their space to inform voters of issues they would be voting on in return for the postal privileges they have. Second, he expressed his support of the electoral system. Next, Bryan recommended that the party push for an amendment making the Constitution easier to amend. Bryan then proposed a constitutional amendment that would require all declarations of war to be submitted to a referendum for the vote of the people, except in the case of an actual invasion of the country. Fifth, he advocated the passing of woman suffrage. Finally, he urged the Democratic Party to support prohibition. In the conclusion of his speech, Bryan expressed gratitude to the Democratic Party. He then returned to prohibition, arguing that the party that took on prohibition first would lose drinkers to the other party, but if that was the Democratic Party, it would benefit by losing the drinkers who were, more often than not, "bad men."

Both in rehearsing the party's successes and in envisioning its future, Bryan constructed the Democrats as heroes who lived according the heroic model of Christ. Bryan's praise and direction centered around three principles derived from the Christ myth and American foundation myth: self-governance, peacefulness, and protection of the masses. The principles of self-governance and peacefulness were explicitly evident—for example, as Bryan applauded the Democrats for their support of Filipino independence. He quoted the Declaration of Independence as one of two theories of government: "governments derive their just powers from the consent of the governed." The only other theory of government, he claimed, was that of monarchies and empires, which stood "sixteen inches in diameter, round in shape and fired out of a cannon. It is the theory that governments rest on force; that a government can be thrown, like a net, over a helpless people, and those people compelled at the point of the bayonet to obey laws in the making of which they have had no voice. That is the policy of emperors and kings."

Here he invoked the foundation myth, suggesting that the American story was one of peace and concern for the "helpless people," just as Christ was concerned for the helpless. Similarly, he invoked the principle of self-governance and concern for the commoners when arguing that voters needed to be more informed about issues because "[t]he value of government by the consent of the governed depends largely upon the information those have whose consent is required." Self-government, then, would be enhanced when voters were informed. Moreover, his argument for making the Constitution more easily amendable was grounded in his belief "that time has come when we ought seriously to consider making our constitution reflect the spirit of confidence that we today have in the intelligence of the people."

Finally, in proposing that all declarations of war be submitted to a referendum of the people, Bryan stood upon the principle of self-governance, arguing that those who must give of their lives in war (and who bear the burden of taxation) should have a strong voice in the decision to use national force. Bryan developed his argument further by alluding to his two prevailing myths, which he portrayed as still being constructed in American politics. In congruence with the Christ myth and the American foundation myth, he upheld the desirability of peace over "brute force" and depicted the Europeans as having "worshiped force," as they had been "writing their history in blood." These European characters needed America to bring them the social gospel of peace, to "lift them to a higher [moral] level." He then asked:

> And how shall we lift them? There is only one way to lift, and that is the way that is given us by the Author of our religion, "And I, if I be lifted up, will draw all men unto me." It is the drawing power of example. That is the difference between the philosophy of force and the philosophy of love. Love is a drawing power; force is a coercive and compelling power. . . . If we can convince the world that the individual citizen who must give his life upon the battlefield has a right to a voice in the declaring of war, we will do more to protect the people of Europe from the ambitions of their monarchs than we can do in any other way.

In this passage, Bryan made his proposed referendum for declaring war part of the larger mythic narrative that America must live out the law of Christ to "love thy neighbor" and the American heritage story of the triumph of democracy over monarchies and empires. For Americans to pass this constitutional amendment, he implied, was to play out their role in the grand master narrative.

In addition to the interconnected principles of self-governance and peacefulness, Bryan's speech echoed Christ's compassion for the masses. Bryan reinforced the recently passed income tax amendment by stating that the law "transfers a considerable percentage of the burden that was formerly borne by the over-taxed masses to the backs of those who have large incomes, but who had escaped their just share until the income tax law was passed." He noted that the "Democratic Party has justified the faith of the common people in it." He praised the Democrats for their concern for the masses, specifically laborers, farmers, and children, demonstrated in currency reform, the rural credits law, antitrust laws, shipping laws, and the child labor law that they passed. Regarding the child labor law, he stated, "I rejoice that the Democratic Party has put itself at the head of the movement for social justice in this country. This law says to the money-mad employer, 'You shall not dwarf the body of a child; you shall not stunt the mind of a child; you shall not coin the blood of a child into illegitimate dividends.'" By depicting those in industry as the "money-mad employer" and the Democratic Party as "head of the movement for social justice," he created characters in keeping with his grand narrative. Even his concluding argument for prohibition alluded to the pure, self-disciplined Christ of the social gospel who concerned himself with the poor and needy, as Bryan pleaded, "I appeal to you to put the Democratic Party on the side of the mother, the child, the home and humanity, and not allow it to be made the champion of the most mercenary, the most tyrannical, group that ever entered politics for the purpose of debauching parties and corrupting government." Thus one more political argument was advanced through the logic of Bryan's master narratives.

The mythic quality of Bryan's rhetoric was especially apparent in the transition between his description of the successes of the past and his outline for the future. As Barthes notes, the purpose of myth is not to deny things, but to discuss them simply so as to represent them as statements of natural, eternal fact rather than complex explanation. In the transition section of "Democracy's Deeds and Duty," Bryan posed the question of why certain reforms had come about. He answered not with an explanation, but with a statement of fact and a metaphor that naturalized what were actually historical, political events:

> If a surveyor says that the extension of an established line a certain distance in a certain direction will reach a certain point, it is not a prophecy, it is merely a statement of fact. The laws that govern human progress are just as clearly defined. . . .
>
> When a few years ago, my wife and I visited South America, we crossed the Andes in Southern Peru. We left the ocean at Mollendo and followed a mountain road up three thousand five hundred feet; there we came to a level plain, a sort of bench. . . . When we reached this plain, we saw innumerable dunes of white sand; they differed in size, but were uniform in appearance. . . . *And those sand dunes moved with the precision of an army two hundred feet a year, from the edge of this shelf to the mountains.* . . . For hours after we crossed that plain I could think of nothing but those sand dunes; and when, that evening, we reached the city of Arequipa, I consulted an encyclopedia to find out the cause. The explanation given was that at that point there is a constant trade-wind blowing from the west; that it carries the fine sand from the shore up the mountain ravines to this plain, and there forms the sand into these dunes, and then moves the dunes across the plain.
>
> And so, my friends, there is a force as constant and unvarying, that forms reformers into groups, and carries forward these reforms. *It is the spirit of democracy* that is at work. You will find these reforms differing in magnitude and in importance, but all moving in the same direction; and back of them is this constant force. It is that force that has impelled us to act, and when our brief day is past, it is that force that will compel those who come after us to continue the work in the same direction. . . . It is not prophecy, it is not prediction, it is merely a statement of fact when we say that these same forces, working on the hearts of men like ourselves, will produce certain results.

Bryan's metaphor cast the party's reform efforts as the result of natural forces, not as historical, political events. He predicted more reforms, as the narrative continued, not because of some prophecy or because he understood how the political system would work, but because progress was a "simple fact of nature."

Although Bryan endorsed most of the reforms through the principles derived from his driving narrative, prohibition required that he use his narrative differently. Prohibition could not be justified on the grounds of self-governance or protection of the masses per se (although he did argue for the protection of women and children). In fact, supporters of prohibition argued for the denial of a right to choose and govern one's own behaviors. To escape this apparent contradiction, Bryan first naturalized prohibition by telling his audience that "the time has come to take up the prohibition issue," that "you cannot escape the logic of it" (making the prohibition position appear logical and thus morally right), and that the Democratic Party must "take the moral side of this question." "I present it to you as the gospel of right; it is also the gospel of expediency." Thus Bryan used language that presented prohibition as the naturally moral, logical, timely position. Instead of refuting the question of individual rights, Bryan set a standard for individual moral behavior that was modeled in the self-controlled, self-sacrificial behavior of Christ. Bryan established his standard not through direct references to the social gospel, which may not have appealed to his audience, but through indirect references found in short vignettes about those who gave up liquor or those who came to see its potential damage to society. For example, he told the story of a man who, after many years of opposition, changed his position on the prohibition issue. When asked why, stated Bryan, the man explained, "'I have not a son who is worth anything. Drink has ruined them all, and in my old age I am left alone.' What an awful punishment for God to visit on a father who had thrown his influence on the side of the saloon until it has robbed him of his own flesh and blood!" Bryan's vignettes pointed not to the Christ figure who demonstrated concern for the masses or peace, but to the Christ figure who lived purely. But again, the narrative was clearly mythic, as it ignored the sociocultural customs that might have led even Christ to consume alcohol. Bryan's implicit twist of the myth to justify his position was, as Barthes describes, "depoliticized speech."[61]

Narrative Criteria for Judgment

The criteria for judging a mythic or narrative discourse differ from the criteria for judging traditional, logical, scientific discourse. Jean-François Lyotard defines narrative as the "quintessential form of customary knowledge" in a culture. He views narrative as the source of "traditional knowledge." "Scientific knowledge," by contrast, is that produced by those willing to speak a language separate from the language forming the larger social bond. It is impossible, therefore, to judge the validity of "narrative knowledge" on the basis of "scientific knowledge." The criteria simply are different. For example, Lyotard identifies five characteristics (criteria) of scientific knowledge that are irrelevant to traditional, narrative knowledge. First, scientific knowledge "requires that one language game, denotation, be retained and all others excluded." Those participating in the knowledge must ultimately make denotative statements; that is, true, verifiable statements about a referent. Second, scientific knowledge is "set apart from the language games that combine to form the social bond." The relationship between this type of knowledge and society is one of "mutual exteriority." Third, competence is required only by the sender, not by the addressee. Fourth, the fact that scientific knowledge has been reported is an insufficient indicator of its validity. Fifth, the current sender of scientific knowledge is supposed to be acquainted with previous statements concerning the subject.[62]

In contrast, narrative knowledge operates on different assumptions. First, narratives "allow the society in which they are told . . . to define its criteria of competence and . . . to evaluate according to those criteria what is performed or can be performed within it." Competence is assumed to reside within the addressee as well as with the sender of such knowledge, and narrative knowledge is produced by those willing to speak the language of the larger social bond. Second, narrative "lends itself to a great variety of language games." The denotative claims of scientific knowledge may be present in narrative knowledge, but narrative knowledge might also produce prescriptive statements, interrogative statements, and evaluative statements. Third, the right to occupy the post of "sender" of narrative knowledge is based on "having occupied the post of addressee," and "having been recounted oneself, by virtue of the name one bears, by a previous narrative." Furthermore, the validity of narratives is based, in part, on the fact that the narrator heard the story. Authority is gained simply by listening to the narrative before telling it. So, not only the speaker but also the addressee can participate with competence in discourse about the referents in narrative knowledge. Fourth, narrative form follows a rhythm, as with proverbs, maxims, musical properties, and so forth.[63]

Walter Fisher distinguishes the rational world paradigm from the narrative paradigm via similar criteria and characteristics. "Actualization of the rational-world paradigm," he argues, "depends on a form of society that permits, if not requires, participation of qualified persons in public decision making." Like Lyotard's "scientific knowledge," the rational world paradigm requires a certain competence in the senders based on their participation in the common language of a community of other experts. The linguistic materials of the rational world paradigm are "self-evident propositions" (denotative statements), "the verbal expressions of certain and probable knowing." By contrast, narrative rationality is "determined by the nature of persons as narrative beings—their inherent awareness of narrative probability, what constitutes a coherent story, and their constant habit of testing narrative fidelity, whether or not the stories they experience ring true with the stories they know to be true in their lives." As the means by which public moral decisions are made, narratives function more broadly than to posit only denotative statements, and because the addressees are "narrative beings" with an "inherent awareness of narrative probability . . . and . . . narrative fidelity," they can participate in the narrative knowledge.[64]

As this essay has demonstrated, if judged on the standards of "scientific knowledge," Bryan's rhetoric fails, but it succeeds if judged on the standards of "narrative knowledge." His discourse was morally driven, and thus made morally prescriptive and morally evaluative statements more often than denotative statements. In "The Cross of Gold" especially, he refused to use the exclusive language of the scientific, economic experts, but instead used a language that was part of the social bond—a language derived from two cultural myths with which many in his audiences were familiar. His narrative knowledge authority was gained by the fact that he "listened" carefully to these myths that he told. As evidenced by "The Prince of Peace" and "The Value of an Ideal," as well as by the biographical records of his careful study of the Bible and Jeffersonian politics, Bryan listened well to the stories he told. When he wrapped his political policies in these myths, he could do so with a certain authority, at least for some audiences.

Bryan's concern for the masses and common people was evident not only in his policies but also in his use of myth. He trusted the common people to participate in the political discourse of any issue, no matter how complex. From his discussions of the gold standard to his discussions of international politics, Bryan used the language of the masses, trusting them to engage in the discourse not in a technical manner, but in a manner accessible through the myths that were familiar and sensible to them. In "Democracy's Deeds and Duty," he called for the Democratic Party to be "a party that believes in discussion, is the champion of free speech, and an advocate of intelligence among the voters." He believed the voters could engage intelligently in the mythic narrative. Finally, Bryan's rhetoric followed a certain rhythm and poetic quality, as demonstrated in his extensive use of antithesis and metaphor. He will, in fact, always be remembered for the final line of "The Cross of Gold," "You shall not press down upon the brow of labor this crown of thorns, you shall not crucify mankind upon a cross of gold."

As this essay demonstrates, Bryan's use of mythic images and their derivative principles were applied consistently throughout his speeches, making his story coherent. And while those myths may not have rung true for his entire audience, they did ring true for many who shared these cultural foundations.

A Mythic Gesture Gone Awry

The rationality of William Jennings Bryan's discourse was underestimated by some of his critics, who saw him appealing only to the hearts and not to the minds of his audiences. His work, in fact, can be considered quite rational when held against the narrative logic of the grand myths that are woven throughout his speeches. This perspective, nonetheless, should not function as an excuse for the occasionally weak lines of refutation or absence of factual evidence scattered throughout Bryan's speeches. Robert C. Rowland cautions that the logic of the narrative paradigm not be misused to justify the logic of any and all narratives. Sometimes, he argues, "good" stories that meet the criteria of fidelity and probability do not necessarily add up to good social policy. Rowland cites the narrative discourse of Adolf Hitler, and others, as examples, saying, "Yes, the Greeks relied on traditional stories to teach their children about virtue. But so did the Nazis. Christ told parables to make his point, but Jim Jones and Charles Manson also told stories. The problem facing any narrative theorist (or any other student of values) is to discover a means of distinguishing between the good stories and those that do not lead to virtue."[65]

In the case of Bryan, one can conclude with some certainty that his narrative logic was highly consistent (probability) throughout his oratory. But one is still able to argue that his stories did not ring true with all Americans, such as Jewish audiences or those of other religious faiths, and that not all of his progressive policies were the most desirable for America—for example, prohibition. And one legitimately could still hold him to the standards of traditional logic where, in some instances, he would fail. Therefore, using the standards of narrative in this analysis primarily has explanatory power in demonstrating that Bryan's discourse was not without reason and in explaining that his popular appeal stemmed from more than his use of common language and his powerful, melodic voice.

Although Bryan reacted against the emerging modernist ideology of his time, his rhetoric was appealing to many because he drew upon the grand mythic narratives alive in a modernist culture, even though that culture was moving rapidly toward the hegemonic legitimation of scientific knowledge. Of course, Bryan's definition of modernism featured only the developments in science regarding theories of evolution. Nonetheless, he was able to use two dominant mythic narratives, still commonly accepted by the general public, to advance his progressive political agenda. At the same time, however, others in his audiences likely were unable to identify with the Christ myth and the American foundation myth because modernism itself debunked those myths. Nimmo and Combs argue, for example, that the Industrial Revolution and modernist thought led to widespread suspicion about the past and a willingness to revise historical constructions of what happened in the founding of America. The "realist version" of the American foundation myth began to compete with the "patriotic version."

> The modern, educated, and informed version of the founding fathers was to view them not as altruistic, disinterested patriots bent upon expanding popular rule, but as self-serving, hard-fisted conservatives protecting special interests at the expense of the rabble and riffraff. . . . For [noted historian Charles A.] Beard, the motivation for a new constitution in the 1780s was not patriotism or a commitment to popular government, but selfish economic interest.[66]

Views like Beard's were not widely accepted without question. Nonetheless, his perspective represents an air of critique pervasive in the early twentieth century, an air that made it difficult for some to accept Bryan's mythic heroes.

In fact, a liberal politician today with a similarly progressive agenda surely could not rely on similar rhetorical strategies. A postmodern culture rejects the grand narratives in favor of local narratives that do not presume to have universal appeal. Thus, although narrative knowledge is legitimated in postmodernity, the universality of any narrative is called into question. Truett Anderson writes:

> People in premodern, traditional societies had an experience of universality but no concept of it. They could get through their days and lives without encountering other people with entirely different worldviews. . . . People in modern civilization have had a concept of universality. . . . Now, in the postmodern era, the very concept of universality is, as the deconstructionists say, "put into question."[67]

Bryan's use of the Christ myth and American foundation myth, his use of statements of fact, and his use of analogies based in natural phenomena likely would be put into question in today's world by a larger proportion of Bryan's audience. Principles that drive his policies are based in essentialist beliefs drawn from narrative premises that would not work with contemporary audiences. We are left, then, to wonder upon what principles contemporary progressive politics can be based or whether such policies can only be drawn from immediate, expediency arguments that respond to the needs of local audiences at particular points in history.

William Jennings Bryan was a gifted orator who developed a carefully considered strategy for appealing to the layperson in his audience. Understanding that strategy gives us pause to consider whether we will ever know such an orator again.

Notes

1. Charles Morrow Wilson, *The Commoner: William Jennings Bryan* (Garden City, N.Y.: Doubleday, 1970), 124.
2. Kendrick A. Clements, *William Jennings Bryan: Missionary Isolationist* (Knoxville: University of Tennessee Press, 1982), 21.
3. Wilson, *Commoner*, 123.
4. Richard Hofstadter, "The Democrat as Revivalist," in *William Jennings Bryan and the Campaign of 1896*, ed. George F. Whicher (Boston: D. C. Heath, 1953), 94.
5. Myron G. Phillips, "William Jennings Bryan," in *A History and Criticism of American Public Address*, ed. William Norwood Brigance (1943; reprint, New York: Russell and Russell, 1971), 901.
6. Donald Springen, *William Jennings Bryan: Orator of Small-Town America* (New York: Greenwood Press, 1991), 12.
7. Clements, *Missionary Isolationist*, 10. Also, it should be noted that although by today's standards Bryan's language, and that of many of his early critics, is considered sexist (for example, the use of "man" to refer to men and women), he and his critics are quoted accurately throughout this essay. Further, any paraphrase of a passage in Bryan's speeches referring to "mankind" also uses the male term to be consistent with the flavor of Bryan's speech.
8. All references to "Democracy's Deeds and Duties" are drawn from a reprint of the speech in Springen, *William Jennings Bryan*.
9. Ibid., 12.
10. Stephen J. Gould, "William Jennings Bryan's Last Campaign," *Natural History* 96 (1987): 16, 20, 22, 24, 26.
11. Michael J. Hostetler, "William Jennings Bryan as Demosthenes: The Scopes Trial and the Undelivered Oration, 'On Evolution,'" *Western Journal of Communication* 62 (1998): 176.
12. One political speech delivered later in his career, "Duty, Deeds and Democracy" (1916), will be examined with the earlier political speeches. Chronology was not the criterion for speech selection. Rather, it is important in considering the order in which the speeches will be analyzed in this essay. Also, it is worth noting that Bryan's forensic discourse on evolution, from the Scopes Trial, while important to his career, is excluded from this discussion because Hostetler ("Bryan as

Demosthenes") has conducted a thorough analysis of this discourse in his essay that accomplishes a similar end of restoring Bryan's reputation.

13. Genevieve Forbes Herrick and John Origen Herrick, *The Life of William Jennings Bryan* (Chicago: Grover C. Buxton, 1925), 255.

14. All references to "The Prince of Peace" are drawn from William Jennings Bryan, *The Prince of Peace* (London: Funk and Wagnalls, 1915). All references to "The Value of an Ideal" are drawn from *Speeches of William Jennings Bryan*, 2 vols. (New York: Funk and Wagnalls, 1909).

15. All references to "Cross of Gold" are drawn from a reprint of the speech found in *William Jennings Bryan's "Cross of Gold" Speech July 9, 1896, at the Democratic National Convention, Chicago*. All references to "America's Mission" are drawn from a reprint of the speech in Springen, *William Jennings Bryan*. All references to "Imperialism" are drawn from a reprint of the speech found in *Imperialism*, ed. Jim Zwick (1995), www.boondocksnet.com/ailtexts/bryanimp.html.

16. The following sample of essays illustrates the scholarly recognition of myth in rhetorical texts: Janice Hocker Rushing, "The Rhetoric of the American Western Myth," *Communication Monographs* 50 (1983): 14–32; Janice Hocker Rushing, "Mythic Evolution of 'The New Frontier' in Mass Mediated Rhetoric," *Critical Studies in Mass Communication* 3 (1986): 265–96; Janice Hocker Rushing, "*E.T.* as Rhetorical Transcendence," *Quarterly Journal of Speech* 71 (1985): 185–203; Martha Solomon, "The 'Positive Woman's' Journey: A Mythic Analysis of the Rhetoric of Stop ERA," *Quarterly Journal of Speech* 65 (1979): 262–74; Robert C. Rowland, "On Mythic Criticism," *Communication Studies* 41 (1990): 101–16; Sally J. Perkins, "The Myth of the Matriarchy: Annulling Patriarchy through the Regeneration of Time," *Communication Studies* 42 (1991): 371–83.

17. Rowland, "On Mythic Criticism."

18. Susanne Katherina Knauth Langer, *Philosophy in a New Key: A Study in the Symbolism of Reason, Rite and Art* (Cambridge, Mass.: Harvard University Press, 1957).

19. Dan Nimmo and James E. Combs, *Subliminal Politics: Myths and Mythmakers in America* (Englewood Cliffs, N.J.: Prentice-Hall, 1980).

20. Mircea Eliade, *Myth and Reality*, trans. Willard R. Trask (New York: Harper and Row, 1963), 1.

21. Nimmo and Combs, *Subliminal Politics*, 25.

22. Roland Barthes, *Mythologies*, trans. Annette Lavers (New York: Hill and Wang, 1957), 142–43.

23. Northrop Frye, *Anatomy of Criticism: Four Essays* (Princeton, N.J.: Princeton University Press, 1957).

24. Barthes, *Mythologies*, 142–43.

25. Ibid., 131.

26. In this essay, the phrase "Christ myth" is used to refer to Bryan's reliance on the New Testament mythic Christ figure as the basis for his guiding spiritual principles that then shaped his political principles. The more common references of the "Christian myth" or the "Judeo-Christian myth" are not used because the broader Christian story is not included as the religious basis for Bryan's thinking. For example, his discourse did not feature the following principles from the broader Judeo-Christian story: sin, death, resurrection, heaven/hell, grace, the early Christian church, or "Pauline" church doctrine. These elements of the Christian myth are more commonly emphasized in evangelical interpretations than in the sort of "social gospel" interpretation adopted by Bryan and explained further in this essay.

27. William Jennings Bryan and Mary Baird Bryan, *The Memoirs of William Jennings Bryan* (Chicago: John C. Winston, 1925), 286–87.

28. Clements, *Missionary Isolationist*, 21.

29. Bryan and Bryan, *Memoirs*, 451.

30. Wilson, *Commoner*, 402.

31. Paolo E. Coletta, *William Jennings Bryan: Political Evangelist, 1860–1908*, 3 vols. (Lincoln: University of Nebraska Press, 1964), 200.

32. Wilson notes that "although Bryan insisted he 'owned' all of Darwin's works, he soon demonstrated that he had not read them all" (*Commoner* 402).

33. Coletta, *Political Evangelist*, 200.

34. Eliade, *Myth and Reality*.

35. Nimmo and Combs, *Subliminal Politics*.

36. The perspectives on modernism in this essay are derived from the following works: Jean-François Lyotard, *The Postmodern Condition: A Report on Knowledge*, trans. Geoff Bennington and Brian Massumi (Minneapolis: University of Minnesota Press, 1993); Walter Truett Anderson, introduction to *The Truth About the Truth*, ed. Walter Truett Anderson (New York: G. P. Putnam's Sons, 1995); Steinar Kvale, "Themes of Postmodernity," in Anderson, *Truth About the Truth*, 18–25; and

Maureen O'Hara and Walter Truett Anderson, "Psychotherapy's Own Identity Crisis," in Anderson, *Truth About the Truth*, 1–11.

37. For a more detailed explanation of the various social gospel positions, see Robert T. Handy, ed., *The Social Gospel in America* (New York: Oxford University Press, 1966). Handy's book is particularly useful because it contains both summative explanations of the social gospel movement by Handy and writings by three prominent theologians in the social gospel era: Washington Gladden, Richard T. Ely, and Walter Rauschenbusch.

38. See, for example, Paul W. Glad, ed., *William Jennings Bryan: A Profile* (New York: Hill and Wang, 1968), 87–108.

39. Coletta, *Political Evangelist*, 387.

40. Nimmo and Combs, *Subliminal Politics*, 34. Nimmo and Combs draw their quote from Stanley Elkins and Eric McKitrick, "The Founding Fathers: Young Men of the Revolution," in *Myth and the American Experience*, vol. 1, ed. Nicholas Cords and Patrick Gerster (New York: Glencoe Press, 1973), 112.

41. Glad, *William Jennings Bryan*, 99.

42. Nimmo and Combs, *Subliminal Politics*, 18.

43. Barthes, *Mythologies*, 153.

44. Walter Truett Anderson, "Four Different Ways to Be Absolutely Right," in Anderson, *Truth About the Truth*, 111. See also Lyotard, *Postmodern Condition*, 37; and Kvale, "Themes of Postmodernity," 18–24.

45. Lyotard, *Postmodern Condition*, 33–34.

46. Anderson, "Four Different Ways," 113.

47. See, for example, David J. Nordloh, *William Jennings Bryan* (Boston: G. K. Hall, 1981), 82; and Coletta, *Political Evangelist*, 109–10.

48. Nordloh, *William Jennings Bryan*, 72.

49. Bryan and Bryan, *Memoirs*, 114–15.

50. See a thorough example of the critiques of Bryan in Robert W. Cherny, *A Righteous Cause: The Life of William Jennings Bryan*, ed. Oscar Handlin (Boston: Little, Brown, 1985), 185.

51. Coletta *Political Evangelist*, 117.

52. See Milton Friedman's essay "The Crime of 1873," *Journal of Political Economy* 98 (1990): 1159–94, for a thorough analysis of the gold standard debate. This essay provides excellent perspective on the complexity of the economics surrounding the gold standard question.

53. Walter R. Fisher, *Human Communication as Narration: Toward a Philosophy of Reason, Value, and Action* (Columbia: University of South Carolina Press, 1987), 60–66.

54. Ibid., 47.

55. Barthes, *Mythologies*, 153.

56. Ibid., 152–53.

57. Qtd. in Coletta, *Political Evangelist*, 222.

58. Ibid., 267.

59. Fisher, *Human Communication*, 47.

60. Springen, *William Jennings Bryan*, 52.

61. Barthes, *Mythologies*, 143.

62. Lyotard, *Postmodern Condition*, 25–26.

63. Ibid., 21-22.

64. Fisher, *Human Communication*, 60, 64.

65. Robert C. Rowland, "The Value of the Rational World and Narrative Paradigms," *Central States Speech Journal* 39 (1988): 215.

66. Nimmo and Combs, *Subliminal Politics*, 35.

67. Anderson, *Truth About the Truth*, 6.

"Making the World More Homelike": The Reform Rhetoric of Frances E. Willard

Amy R. Slagell

6

> For love of the dear homes whose watchfires are as beaconlights of heaven; for love of you, heartbroken wives, whose tremulous lips have blessed me; for you, sweet mothers, who in the cradle's shadow kneel tonight beside your infant sons; and for you, sorrowful little children, who, with faces strangely old, listen tonight for him whose footsteps frighten you, it is for love of you that I have dared to speak.
>
> —Frances E. Willard, address before the House Judiciary Committee, 1 February 1878

Frances E. Willard did dare to speak, and when she spoke she reached the ears of thousands. Like many nineteenth-century reformers, Willard exercised her greatest influence through the public platform. Her efforts as a speaker while president of the Woman's Christian Temperance Union (WCTU) helped establish that organization in every state and territory. With membership lists swelling to nearly a quarter of a million, the WCTU became the largest organization of women in America up to that time. As a spokesperson for this mostly white, middle-class, Protestant organization of women and for reform in general, she traveled extensively, addressing crowds that ranged in number from 20 to 13,000. In an 1894 interview she claimed that "during the last twenty years I have been perpetually on the road, going 15,000 to 20,000 miles a year, holding a meeting once a day on an average throughout the period."[1]

Through her reform work as a speaker and writer, Willard's stature as a public figure was nearly unmatched among women. At the time of her death in February 1898, she was already known as "St. Frances" and "the uncrowned queen of America."[2] No less a spokesperson for the nineteenth century than Henry Ward Beecher called her "the best known and best beloved of women."[3] A Los Angeles paper commented: "Miss Willard is the Lord's Anointed this day as the ancient Monarchs of Israel were—not simply as leader of the WCTU, but to be the greatest conqueror and sovereign of history."[4] At the height of her influence in 1889 she was introduced to a Mississippi audience with the statement: "There are two women on whose dominions the sun never sets. One is Victoria Queen of Britain and Empress of India, and the other is Miss Frances E. Willard."[5]

Such accolades emerged after decades of work in the fields of education, evangelism, temperance, and reform. Willard began her career as a teacher and school administrator. She rose to the rank of president of the Evanston Ladies College and soon became dean of women and professor at Northwestern University when it absorbed the Ladies College and became a coeducational institution in 1873. After leaving the university over several disagreements with the administration (perhaps complicated by the fact that the new Northwestern president was her ex-fiancé, Charles Fowler), Willard dramatically altered her path to work on behalf of the newly invigorated woman's temperance movement. She was a delegate at the founding meeting of the WCTU at Cleveland in November 1874, at which time she was elected corresponding secretary. In this capacity, she traveled to hundreds of communities, urging women to organize local branches of the WCTU and to work on behalf of temperance. As president of the Chicago WCTU, she spoke frequently in churches in the area and conducted evangelical meetings for those living in the impoverished downtown area. By 1877 her activities as a temperance speaker and evangelist had come to the attention of Dwight Moody, who asked her to join him in his Boston revival meetings. Willard's association with the famous evangelist, though brief, increased her stature nationally. In 1879 she was elected president of the national WCTU, a position she held until her death in 1898. She also served as president of the World's Woman's Christian Temperance Union from 1888 to 1898, making her influence felt around the globe.

During her reign as queen of the woman's temperance movement, Willard advocated a "Do Everything" policy. First conceived as a policy encouraging women to do anything possible to bring about the success of the temperance movement, "Do Everything" soon evolved into a much broader reform agenda including temperance, woman suffrage, dress reform, woman's rights, peace and arbitration, labor reforms, and Christian socialism. "Everything is not in the Temperance Reform," she said in her 1893 annual address to the WCTU, "but the temperance reform should be in everything."[6]

Stepping well beyond traditional notions of women's work for benevolence, Willard carried her reform work into politics. Early on she recognized that women needed the ballot to have their say about issues such as school policy, saloon licensing, treatment of women in the courts, and laws governing prostitution. She believed the surest road to woman's ballot was through the support of a political party. After being rebuffed by the Democrats, Greenbacks, and Republicans, she became a prominent figure in the Prohibition Party and gained for it the support of a large number of women. In the 1890s she played a major role in efforts to create a unified reform party made up of prohibitionists, populists, and unionists.[7]

Though much of Willard's reputation was built through the platform, she was also a prolific writer, authoring nine books and coauthoring two others. These included commemorative volumes honoring her sister and mother, a history of the woman's temperance movement, a 700-page autobiography (the first 50,000 copies of which sold out within a matter of months), a polemic calling for the ordination of women, a work encouraging young women to discover their ambitions and to prepare for occupations that fit their desires and abilities, and even a book on women and bicycling.[8] She also composed numerous pamphlets such as *Should Women Vote?* and *Temperance and the Labor Question* and magazine articles such as "Man in the Home" and "Women in Journalism."[9]

As a platform speaker, Willard was a pioneer. She was the first woman to address the Illinois Senate and the first to speak on a subject other than Sunday school at the famous New York Chautauqua. She spoke before the National Education Association, three U.S. congressional committees, and audiences of thousands at the Moody revivals in Boston. She spoke at national Prohibition Party conventions, at the pivotal 1892 St. Louis Industrial Conference that founded the People's Party, and before the committee on resolutions of the Republican Party. At the height of her popularity in the late 1880s and early 1890s, Willard reached a broad spectrum of women through addresses to the other major women's organizations of the period whose participants were more diverse than the WCTU, such as the International Council of Women, the National Council of Women, and the Chicago Woman's League. She also spoke at camp meetings, religious conferences, churches, and public meetings all across the country, and she capped off her career with several speaking tours through Great Britain. In all, she addressed well over 7,000 audiences during her public career.

Moreover, Willard consistently had a powerful impact on listeners. A newspaper account of one of her speeches reported:

> Last evening Plymouth Church was crowded full to hear Miss Frances E. Willard speak on the subject of Temperance, and what a speech it was! As the crowd dispersed at the close, such exclamations as these were heard on every hand: "What a wonderful woman!" There was nothing ranting in her speech, nor did it contain any of the sentimental stuff some temperance orators try to make use of, but it was a practical common-sense view of the question in all its newest phases, so adorned by the poetic imagery of the speaker, that every listener sat entranced to the end.[10]

Such comments were typical. "She is an unqualified success as a speaker," wrote an Ohio paper in an article entitled "Frances Willard: The Modern Joan of Arc." "She spoke with remarkable ease; for two solid hours the words came unhesitatingly, always pleasantly. Entertaining at all times, she often rose to the domain of the purest eloquence."[11] "While Miss Willard talks she is supreme; she captivates, she fascinates," claimed an Iowa newspaper, which further declared that "all people, no matter how they view the question under discussion, leave Miss Willard's presence charmed and pleased."[12] Another paper declared: "That she is an orator, and a great one, cannot be doubted by anyone who considers what she accomplishes. At her first word the vast audience was hushed to absolute silence, and remained so during the whole address, hanging upon her words with an interest which excluded all perception of surrounding objects or of the flight of time."[13] The *Chicago Evening Journal* deemed Willard the "best female lecturer of this era of woman's intellectual progress."[14]

Despite her extraordinary influence and visibility in the late nineteenth century, Willard's contributions have attracted only limited attention.[15] Her fame was perhaps buried in the dust of Prohibition and the repeal of the Eighteenth Amendment. While texts of Willard speeches now appear in several collections,[16] only recently have public address scholars begun rediscovering her contributions to the temperance crusade as well as to the nineteenth-century woman's rights movement. Still, only a handful of essays attempt any sustained examination of her discourse, and these essays offer a mixed assessment of Willard's virtues as an orator.[17] Karlyn Kohrs Campbell and Bonnie Dow agree that Willard embraced nineteenth-century notions of "true womanhood" and used this ideology in order to justify women's entry into the public sphere. While applauding Willard's short-term accomplishments, these leading scholars conclude that Willard's discourse was at its heart conservative and tended to undermine rather than advance the feminist cause. Because

Willard grounded many of her appeals for change in women's special nature or women's interest in the traditional sphere of the home, they argue, she "never firmly established woman's *natural* right to the ballot," and she "closed down opportunities for any form of persuasion other than reinforcement of existing belief."[18]

These assessments, however, apply modern feminist criteria to the late nineteenth century. Nancy Cott reminds us that "the radical feminist move of one generation may become the conventional move of its successors."[19] In the nineteenth century, woman's rights ideology was inherently radical. A conservative woman's rights advocate, a nonradical feminist, an acceptable public woman—all were oxymoronic. Willard, perhaps more than any other nineteenth-century woman, embodied these oxymorons. Her public discourse revealed her progressivism, but at the same time it maintained her womanliness. She was adamant in her belief that every human deserved the right to develop fully his or her potential, but her appeals for change were self-consciously clothed in the language of traditional images of men and women. She recognized the power of naming: "Words have souls, nay, what is worse, they have ghosts," she wrote in 1892. "Men are more frightened by words today than by ideas. If one can but couch his thought in acceptable forms it will be received in quarters where, did he utter it squarely, he would be cast out as evil."[20] Willard's self-conscious concern about such issues can clearly be seen within the pages of her private journals. In the years before she embarked on her public career as a reformer, she mulled over her desire to play a public role and the risk involved with such a break from traditional roles for women. In a journal entry from 1869, she noted her resolve to speak on behalf of "evolution, not revolution;—for *womanly* liberty, not . . . wild license."[21] As a result of this resolution, Willard typically worked to couch her ideas in "acceptable forms" in order to adapt her appeals to the largely white, middle-class, Protestant audiences she addressed. Nevertheless, she lived as a model of a successful public woman and so exposed the myth of female domesticity. At the same time, she maintained an aura of womanliness that brought her accolades from conservative audiences before whom speakers such as Elizabeth Cady Stanton and Susan B. Anthony could never dream to gain a hearing.

It was in fact the public perception of her "womanliness" that set Willard apart among the leaders of the late-nineteenth-century woman's movement. In 1871 the *Galena (Illinois) Evening Gazette* reported, "It was a real treat to hear a woman lecture, without the constant scold, scold, scold, that one must listen to in hearing Annie Dickinson and Susie Anthony."[22] This difference between Willard's persona and that of the handful of other prominent women platform speakers persisted throughout her career. An 1896 review claimed: "Those who have been accustomed to regard a coarse, repulsive mannishness as a necessary accompaniment of feminine oratory have only to hear Miss Willard once in order to have all their ideas on the subject revolutionized. A more perfect specimen of womanliness can not be found."[23]

Indeed, in contemporary accounts of Willard's speeches the most frequent comment is that she was, above all, womanly. Reviewing her spring 1887 speaking engagement in Washington, D.C., one writer said: "Miss Willard's addresses here were well received; indeed, the one on prohibition was listened to by an immense audience, which often gave vent to its high appreciation in most animated applause. She is a wonderfully gifted woman, and is accomplishing great good. Her language is always refined, and she never forgets that she is a woman."[24] In 1891 a Maine newspaper thought Willard "an imminently pleasing speaker" and concluded that "no finer example of speaking in a manner forcible yet marked by feminine grace and modesty is presented in the country."[25] Following Willard's tour of Scotland in 1893, a paper there offered this commentary: "Miss Willard is a woman of unique character and gifts. Her voice and a marvelous power of administration are all equally at her command. As a speaker she is fervent, forcible, and withal most womanly."[26]

In her series "Noble Women," for the *Presbyterian Messenger*, Jessie Ackerman wrote: "As a speaker, Miss Willard's greatest strength and force lies [sic] in the fact that *she never ceases to be one's highest ideal of a woman.*"[27] Time and again, year in and year out, observers commented on Willard's womanliness and its appeal to her listeners. As the *Boston Post* stated:

> There is no woman in the wide world who holds a place so close to the hearts of good women, young and old, as does Miss Willard. It is not only the great ideas for which she stands a prominent representative; it is not only advancement she has given to great reforms through her efforts; it is not her lofty intellectuality alone which gives her this prominence. It is more than all these, her tender and kindly womanliness, her sympathy, her sincerity.[28]

Though there are many rhetorical strategies involved in Willard's conscious choice to become the embodiment of the oxymoronic womanly public speaker, none is more central to her appeal than her use of the home. One of the main constituents of the "true womanhood" ideal explored in Barbara Welter's now famous essay is that of woman's domesticity.[29] However, an interest in domestic issues and the home is not necessarily a mark of conservatism. The divergent conceptions of domesticity that emerged from three of the daughters of Lyman Beecher offer a good reminder that the concept is more complex than is often thought.[30]

The pages to follow investigate Willard's use of the home as the central feature of her reform thought and discourse. Willard's interest in the home is clear from one of her earliest publications. In this essay, published in 1859 as the winner of a contest sponsored by the Illinois State Agricultural Society for the best essay addressing the topic "On the Embellishment of a Country Home," we catch a glimpse of the young Willard's conception of the ideal home.[31] The influence of the culture of domesticity in which Willard came of age is clear; issues of decor and arrangement as experienced by sight, sound, and smell are paramount, but in the conclusion Willard revealed that a true home required something more. Noting that this essay had not aimed beyond the "'outward seeming' of embellishment," she nevertheless wanted to clarify her belief that the "the beauty of a pure life and honest purpose" is "more needful to the attainment of perfection in a home than anything we have mentioned." She closed by comparing the relationship between a ship and its harbor to a man and his home and then declared, "as 'Heaven' is the watchword for Eternity, so is 'Home' the watchword for Time."[32] Such sentimental discourse suggests that Willard's early conception of home was wholly in keeping with mainstream middle-class Victorian culture. But throughout her reform career Willard used the "home" both literally and figuratively to accomplish a variety of strategic, and sometimes radical, goals.[33] Among these goals are those that will be explored in this chapter: the home as a justification and motivation for women's activity in the realm of civic affairs; the home as a model for reforms in education and politics; and, perhaps most important, the need for an evolution in the structure and nature of the private home itself, in order to bring it closer to the ideal home that could stand as the model for a homelike world. Careful examination of Willard's use of the term and concept of home reveals that she did not simply work within the "true womanhood" tradition hoping to expand women's roles, but also directly challenged the doctrine of spheres for both men and women. Willard's singular effort to collapse the dichotomous separate spheres doctrine, while acknowledging gender differences, accounts for her continued relevance today.

The Home as Justification for Public Action

Willard's most straightforward and well-recognized argumentative strategy is embodied in her call for "home protection." She first heard the phrase in August 1876 when Letitia Youmans, a Canadian temperance worker, used it at camp meeting. Youmans had adapted the phrase from debates over tariffs in Canada. Willard saw the potential in the phrase. It contained "our best argument," she noted, and fit nicely with the WCTU motto, "For God and Home and Native Land."[34] According to her autobiography, it had been a few months earlier when, in prayer, "there was borne in upon my mind, as I believe from loftier regions, the declaration, 'You are to speak for woman's ballot as a weapon of protection to her home and tempted loved ones from the tyranny of drink.'"[35] Putting together this line of argument with the title "Home Protection," she addressed the Association for the Advancement of Women meetings in Philadelphia in October 1876 with a speech supporting the home protection or woman's temperance ballot. At the start Willard used the phrase "home protection" to encapsulate her argument that women should have a voice in whether the sale of alcohol should be licensed in the towns and cities where they lived. In her home state of Illinois in 1879, Willard led an extensive "Home Protection" petition campaign, garnering 175,000 signatures of men and women in an effort to establish this practice as a state law. Though unsuccessful, the petition campaign demonstrated its persuasive effect when, during the next year, 645 of the 832 Illinois communities that voted on the licensing issue voted against granting licenses.[36] For the next two decades, Willard repeated speeches with the "Home Protection" title all around the country. The text of the speech, however, did not remain static. As time passed, the slogan "home protection" became less a reference to the specific issue of woman's temperance ballot and more a powerful ideograph containing the heart of Willard's broad appeal for women's social and political action. At its heart was the argument that the home, which the culture widely regarded as women's special province, was threatened by alcohol, and women therefore had a duty to take action to protect it. Presenting the home as a threatened site was the necessary first step Willard took with her conservative audiences.

HOME PROTECTION RESPONDS TO THREATS TO HOME AND NATION

The stereotype of the "temperance tale" is contained in sentimental narratives detailing the ravages of drink such as those presented in T. S. Arthur's *Ten Nights in a Barroom*, pathetic tales such as "Married to a Drunkard," or picture stories like "The House that Rum Built" and "The Easy Road and Its End," which illustrated the downhill journey from moderate and sociable alcohol use to drunkenness and death. These moralistic tales that presented the threat of alcohol to the home and the family were the stock and trade of many temperance speakers, but Willard rarely offered this kind of narrative. In her earliest temperance speech, a text that rhetorical critic Richard Leeman has judged relatively immature and largely derivative, Willard used the tale of the man of "dissolute life" as the opening allegory to establish the dangers of drink.[37] In his pocket the worn man carried a picture of himself as a young, handsome man, and as he showed it to a temperance worker he confessed that it was taken before he took to drink. But such pathetic scenes had little place in Willard's discourse within a few months of her entry into temperance work on the national stage. Instead, Willard often invoked subtler, and more powerful, visualizations of domestic violence prompted by alcohol use. For example, with passages such as "for you, sorrowful little children, who listen at this hour, with faces strangely old, for him whose footsteps frighten you; for love of you, have I thus spoken," she made emotionally stirring references to the relationship between alcohol and child abuse.[38]

Much of Willard's primary audience—middle-class white Protestants—had been steeped in decades of temperance tales and, more important, often could readily supply a real instance of the negative impact of alcohol use. Historian Ruth Bordin notes that throughout the nineteenth century, Americans were heavy drinkers, heavier "than they have ever been since."[39] Even a casual look at nineteenth-century newspapers reveals the problems linked to alcohol use. When Willard assured audiences that the vast majority of women could be counted on to stand against alcohol because it "nerves, with dangerous strength, arms already so much stronger than their own," and puts men out of their right minds, such "that they strike down the wives men love and the little children for whom, when sober, they would die," she was building on beliefs many members of her audience already shared about the effects of alcohol abuse.[40] Evidence of the domestic violence and economic distress suffered by families due to alcohol use provided a sure foundation on which Willard could construct her case that alcohol had a negative impact on the Republic as a whole and on women in particular. Once this was established, it was a relatively small step to argue that women ought to be at the forefront of the public battle to combat the use of alcohol.

In order to establish the case that alcohol threatened the nation, Willard sometimes used the standard temperance statistics represented in "The Nation's Annual Drink Bill," "with its nine hundred millions for intoxicating liquors, to five millions for the spread of Christ's gospel."[41] At other times she reviewed the additional costs to the nation. In a lecture in Iowa during the campaign for a state constitutional prohibition measure, she argued that the liquor industry was responsible for "60 percent of the insanity in America; 75 percent of our criminals become such when crazed by alcohol; 80 percent of our worthless youth are schooled in dram shops," and added that "90 percent of our paupers emerge from drunkards' homes."[42] At times she waxed more poetic on the threat to the nation. Her 1886 address before the Michigan WCTU envisioned "a frightful leak in America's grand ship of state; the tawny, seething, nauseous, foaming tide of rum and beer and wine threatens to draw us down to death."[43]

More often, however, Willard used the image of the threatened home to both heighten the seriousness of the problem and to establish the warrant supporting women's action in the face of the threat. Suzanne Marilley argues that Willard's arguments are an example of the liberalism, or feminism, of fear. Distinguished from the liberalism of rights that gives priority to "guarantees of equality," the liberalism of fear "focuses first on the elimination of violence" and aims to guarantee protection. Though critical of Willard's intolerance, claiming that she assumed middle-class white women's moral superiority over and against the moral status of men and of immigrants, Marilley concedes the value and necessity of Willard's protectionist appeal. It was this appeal that supported Willard's success in the mass political mobilization of temperance women. Since Willard's appeal for protection was grounded both in alcohol's threat to the state and its threat to relationships, Marilley associates Willard's argument with Carol Gilligan's notion of woman's different voice, "a voice that speaks from inside relationships, rather than as self-interested individuals."[44] In this way, Willard was able to speak in what was heard as a womanly voice and co-opt the moral high ground as justification for women's activism. The threat to the home was the central vehicle for making this case.

The primary cause of decay in the home was the saloon; "snugly sandwiched" among the schoolhouse, the church, and the home, "the saloon is the open Pandora's box of every evil that flesh is heir to."[45] As the source of the threat to the home, the saloon became the first target of women's protest. Willard and the WCTU celebrated the exploits of the participants in the Woman's Crusade of the winter of 1873–74. The crusaders rose up within dozens of towns and cities, where they sang and prayed inside saloons or on the streets around them in an effort to discourage customers from entering and to persuade saloon keepers to give up their harmful trade.[46] When the hundreds of saloons women were able to shut down during the crusade began to reopen in the months following the protests, the temperance women realized the need to add legal means to their moral suasion efforts. In her earliest "Home Protection" addresses, Willard continued to refer to the saloon as the enemy, calling it an "abomination" or "cancerous excrescence," but she clearly demanded a governmental solution. She built her early arguments explicitly on audience beliefs that women were "the sweet and pleasant sunshine of our homes" and "the beams which light the larger home of social life." They even sent a "gentle radiance" into "the great and busy world." But Willard saw the potential for greater significance and power in these scattered beams. Through "that magic lens, that powerful sunglass which we name the ballot," they could "be made to converge upon the rum-shop in a blaze of light" with explosive results.[47]

Willard believed that her focus on the sentimental side of the threat to the home was the easiest way to reach what she called "the average woman." She "does not care a farthing" for the "abstract principle of justice on which the woman question is really based," Willard declared in a particularly revealing explanation of her rhetorical strategy in her 1894 Presidential Address. "Devoted and good and conventional," the average woman had little exposure to progressive literature, shied away from politics, and had been socialized by male voices in the press, pulpit, and home to be suspicious of women's activism, especially woman suffrage. Yet the average woman could be educated and wakened to a desire for political agency. The key was to focus on how the average woman would benefit from the "practical politics" of reform. "There is no lever so long by which to lift the Average Woman above her prejudices," Willard declared, "as that of the reforms that tend to safeguard those to whom she has given birth and being." Though uneducated about "the relations of cause and effect in politics and law," the average woman staunchly agreed that no one has the right to build saloons, gambling dens, or brothels "along the streets in neighborly nearness to her home."[48] Once a woman had an arrest of thought and realized the need to protect her home and loved ones, Willard was confident that she would grow to develop a wider sense of justice and of her own power. A vast array of reforms would result from women's new status and focused energy.[49]

In fact, as Willard pushed her reform efforts beyond temperance into social purity reforms that urged a deep revision in public policies and attitudes concerning prostitution, age of consent laws, the sexual double standard, and even treatment of unwed mothers, she continued to sound the protectionist theme. She denounced the current system under which "the ravisher usually got off scot free," and fumed, "thus considerately have men from time immemorial legislated for woman. Their laws have shown the mercy that a wolf shows to a lamb."[50] In these later texts she exposed the inefficacy of the sexual contract that presumed male protection of women's interests.[51] Women must be granted the power to protect their own interests. Furthermore, since women have long been accustomed to recognizing the needs of those around them, Willard believed that their newly gained power would be wielded in the best interest of the community at large.

HOME PROTECTION MOVES WOMEN TO POLITICAL AGENCY

Significantly, home protection was not only needed to guard women from the saloon or from men's power to dominate women in sexual matters, it was also needed in order to grant women the opportunity to be fully occupied and developed individuals. Willard believed that the secret "of a happy life" was to be found in "working *somewhere*," so even if the threat of the saloon to the home was resolved, she would continue to advocate women's public agency. For this reason, once she was firmly established as the leader of the WCTU and the national organization had endorsed full enfranchisement for women, Willard developed a lighthearted and optimistic line of argument that justified woman's entry into what was seen as man's sphere of action on the grounds that man's inventiveness threatened woman's traditional functions in the home. The argument was most fully developed in her address "Woman and Philanthropy," delivered before the conservative Presbyterian Social Union of Chicago in 1887 during its annual "Ladies Night," the only meeting each year when women were welcome to attend its sessions.[52] Though she shared her view that the world is "bewildered and broken hearted" and in need of "mothering" (399), and she commemorated the Woman's Crusade as a time when women "routed the liquor traffic" (402), she did not address at length the threat of alcohol to the family or the home. Instead, the introduction to the speech identified the cause of women's new philanthropic and political engagement as emanating directly from male interference. There seemed to be, she acknowledged, a "'woman's sphere,' the exact dimensions of which men seemed to know and women were dutiful to learn." But men in their "curious inconsistency" had "steadily encroached upon" the occupations of women in the home, and thus women found themselves with less and less to do (399). Specifically, Willard charged:

> They took away their mothers' spinning wheel and loom, and transformed them into the flying spindles of great factories worked by steam; they have changed the "stitch, stitch, stitch" of the old-fashioned seamstress over to the "click, click, click" of the swift sewing machine; and they bid fair, by reason of their witty inventions, to turn the stove out of the kitchen along with its time-honored associate, the washtub. More than this, they have even gone so far as to snatch the hallowed knitting work from the trembling fingers of industrious old ladies. My own dear mother, at eighty-two, has been obliged to seek for herself a new occupation, and, rather than to sit idle, she makes temperance scrapbooks! Indeed, time would fail me to tell of the ruthless encroachments made by men upon our "sphere"; and we had no earthly redress open to us except to capture some of the territory over which they had thus far exercised undisputed control, or else to spy out a new world. Being versatile in the spirit of our minds, we have done a little of both and a good deal of one. From about thirty industrial pursuits open to women thirty years ago, we have risen to three hundred, and still the good work goes swiftly on (399).

The argument is perhaps disingenuous from one who, during her teen years, had confided to her journal, "I'm fonder of anything *out* of my sphere, than of anything *in* it," and had vowed to "make up for this hermit-a-cy—*never you mind!*"[53] Nevertheless, it was artfully constructed and classic Willard. Targeting the conservative male members of the audience, the argument combined the ingratiation implicit in the recognition of man's inventiveness with a celebration of the culture of progress. Adopting the optimistic tone of the Gilded Age, Willard characterized women's movement into the male sphere of action as inevitable. Even her eighty-two-year-old mother, who no longer needed to knit for the family but who wanted to stay active, had turned her perspective outward and had begun keeping scrapbooks on the events and arguments involved in the temperance movement.[54] Taken out of context, some of the word choices may seem accusing or aggressive. Men "took away their mother's spinning wheel," they "snatch[ed]" the knitting from old women's "trembling fingers" and made other "ruthless encroachments," while women "capture" territory and "spy out a new world." Nevertheless, though the text of the address as printed in the *Christian Union* does not mention the audience's response, from what we know about Willard's winning ways with audiences, we can be confident that she carried off the lighthearted tone with its hyperbolic style. By the end of this introduction, the audience was likely poised to listen charitably to hear more about the "good work" women were doing.

Confidence in the probable success of this argumentative strategy is bolstered by the knowledge that Willard used the same argument about a year later in her high-profile role during the 2 April 1888 day of testimony before the U.S. Senate Suffrage Committee. Sharing the table with other women from the Woman's International Council—including Elizabeth Cady Stanton and the moderator of the group, Susan B. Anthony—Willard offered the closing argument for that day's hearing. Once again she used men's "incursion" on the home and women's sphere "by the power of invention" as justification for women's growing interest in political action. She avoided granting serious legitimacy to the doctrine of spheres, noting that "women have been obliged to seek out a new territory and to pre-empt from the sphere of our brothers, *as it was popularly supposed to be*, some of the territory they have hitherto considered their own."[55] At the same time, however, she offered her assurances that women would "retain that womanliness" so admired by her listeners. Willard's approach was entirely disarming: women simply needed "more occupation," and they thought it would be "desirable" for the men to let them "lend a hand in the affairs of government" (448). She spoke in support of woman suffrage, yet aligned herself with her target audience, calling herself a "conservative woman" who was nevertheless "one in heart with all these good and true suffrage women" (449). At the close of her remarks, Willard returned to her traditional home protection appeal and argued for support of women's political action because of the threat of legalized "snares" set out to harm the people women love best (449). Since children "will not come back again to the home" once they have entered the wide and dangerous world, she appealed to the senators to let women "go forth and make a home, and make that home in the State and in Society" (450).

Consistent in all of Willard's home protection arguments was the emphasis on activity. Far from endorsing popular notions of true womanhood that insisted on submissiveness and tended to limit activity to realms in keeping with women's piety and domesticity—namely, the church and home—Willard aimed to call women to new worlds of action. In the most widely circulated version of the "Home Protection" address, published in the *Independent* and in a pamphlet titled *Home Protection Manual*, Willard celebrated the quick growth of the WCTU: "Every day brings fresh accessions of women, translated *out of the passive and into the active voice* on this great question of the protection their homes." The motivating power of the home protection cry was strong. "Not rights, but duties; not her need alone, but that of her children and her country; not the 'woman,' but the 'human' question," Willard argued, was powerful enough to overcome the average woman's fear and prejudice concerning women's public agency.[56]

The Protestant core of Willard's WCTU audience had long been bombarded with messages about the inappropriateness of women's public agency. In the pages of one of the leading religious journals for women in the mid-nineteenth century, the *Ladies Repository*, even essays advocating new careers for women by opening "more numerous and remunerative avocations to female industry" still argued strenuously against woman's civic involvement, fearing that she would become man's "rival and competitor in public strife." By usurping male "spheres of action," such essays argued, woman "ceases to be a woman and becomes only another man."[57] Critics were especially concerned with women speaking in public. Willard herself faced public criticism for her efforts on the platform. During one of her early speaking tours through the southern states, she read the following response to her lecture in a Denison, Texas, newspaper:

On Saturday evening the people of Denison listened to the lecture of one of God's creatures who had stepped out of the sphere in which her Creator placed her and taken upon herself duties belonging solely to a man.

Of this particular woman we know nothing; but we suppose that her character is irreproachable, as she was chaperoned by some of the leading ladies in Denison; but we have no word to say in her praise, as we are opposed to strongminded women, weak-minded men, and codfish balls, on general principles.[58]

Willard worked hard to overcome such prejudice and was often successful. In 1881 a Charleston, South Carolina correspondent wrote to the *Evanston (Illinois) Index*: "One night last week we had a new experience. We heard a woman 'speak in public upon the stage,' and there were probably five hundred persons present to whom the experience was as new as to us." Sympathetic to temperance work but unsure of the appropriateness of women taking on public roles, the correspondent was surprised to find himself "persuaded that it is not necessarily an unwomanly thing for a woman to be a public speaker." He applauded Willard's "deportment," tasteful dress and bonnet, and earnest delivery style. Tellingly, he observed, "she seemed the very sister of every man among us."[59] Willard was no doubt pleased by this observer's brotherly response.

Although aware of the risks taken by women who approached the public platform, Willard aimed to persuade many women that the dire crisis facing the home justified the risks. She took special pains to encourage women to speak in public to protect their interests. Willard's first handbook for temperance workers, *Hints and Helps for Temperance Work*, confronted this idea directly: "Let not any woman whose heart is in the work imagine that she cannot 'talk temperance' to public audiences. The truth is that the nimble tongue so long employed in utterances less noble has a power not easily excelled, when the high themes of human destiny engage it."[60] Throughout her career she reinforced the message that women must be willing to exercise public agency through public speech. In her 1883 history of the WCTU and its workers, *Woman and Temperance*, she advised WCTU leaders to use *Robert's Rules of Order* for meetings and to urge women to make and to second motions. When it is time for a vote, she suggested, the leader should claim to be tired of her "own voice and anxious to hear theirs." Ask those in favor of the motion to say "aye," she continued, and be sure to call for the vote with "a rising circumflex." In this way, she suggested, the leader can encourage even "the timid" to respond out loud. She objected strenuously to the "dumb show of 'the lifted hand'" and argued that by calling for "that most inspiring response, the human voice divine," the leader would "educate women out of the silence which has stifled their beautiful gifts so long."[61] Part of Willard's call to move women from the passive to the active voice, then, was to be taken quite literally.

At times Willard advocated steps to protect the home using militaristic language. In an early presidential address before the national WCTU, Willard noted that some women resisted the WCTU's call to arms. Nevertheless, she argued, their services were mandatory. "In a military exigency recruiting is not enough," she declared. In this crisis a "commander is obliged to order a draft including those ordinarily exempt from service." It is time, she said, to call "out the *Home Guards*, the gentle, soft-voiced creatures who are afraid of guns and gunpowder, but who, upon a moral battleground, can march side by side with the gallant and the strong."[62] In her widely circulated *Home Protection* pamphlet, she called the crusade women, who had once marched in the streets to protest the presence of saloons in their communities, to enter the fray once again. But this time, she said, they would do their work not "with trembling lip and tearful eye," but with "devout hands" as they "grasp the weapon of power" and shout, *The sword of the Lord and of Gideon!*"[63] The imagery speaks to the empowerment of women through possession of the ballot and clearly illustrates Willard's martial theme. The home, she said in her 1891 presidential address, should be "protected by two votes instead of one," and the ballot would then transform women so that they could stand, like "Minerva, with helmet, shield and a spear, full panoplied against the foes of her helpless little ones."[64] Willard's vision is not of woman standing guard in the doorway to her home; rather, she gave the WCTU its marching orders so that women might enter "into the thickening battle." "Let us live the life of action," she implored, because it "is the only true and happy life."[65]

The ideology encapsulated in Willard's call to women's political action under the banner of home protection was built on the widespread belief that the home was the special province of woman. Casting the saloon and alcohol as threats to the home and to the relationships among the people who lived there, Willard hoped to move women to act. James Kimble has demonstrated how Willard, an unmarried woman who traveled so much that she did not live in her home in Evanston, Illinois more than a few weeks a year, used her autobiography to tell the stories of the home of her youth as an anchor to demonstrate the source of her commitment to the home and as an image of the idyllic home that the temperance movement was committed to saving.[66] Willard's own domestic vision often seemed to echo the cult of domesticity so prominent during the Gilded Age. She used the growing belief that the home and the relationships of mother to child and husband to wife were the primary concerns of one's life in order to strengthen the community and to move it toward action. In Colorado in 1883, she said that although "the poet has said that the hand that rocks the cradle moves the world," the current crisis proved that this simply was not true. "For mankind doesn't stay in the cradle," she continued, "it comes out of the cradle, out of the home, to see and feel the corruption of the world and the snares of the grogshop." Because of the inevitable movement of children beyond the confines of home, she argued, there must be new strategies "to protect the home." She noted that "America is a great country for protection. Protection for industry, subsidies for railroads and steamships, but while protecting so much besides we have neglected to protect the home."[67] While she called for the ballot as the strongest means to home protection, she also argued more abstractly that "what the world most needs is mothering."[68] In 1888 Willard helped launch the National Council of Women a kind of women's shadow government formed to legislate on behalf of women and children until women were included as full partners in the state. She argued that at the local level the Woman's League's affiliated with the NCW should "in the interest of mothering . . . seek to secure for women admission to all school committees, library associations, and boards entrusted with the care of the defective, dependent, and delinquent classes; all professional and business associations; all colleges and professional schools that have not yet set before us an open door of ingress."[69] Women's role as mothers provided a wedge which Willard used to argue that women's activity in the public realm could be seen as necessary and appropriate.

HOME PROTECTION TAKES A RADICAL TURN

Karlyn Kohrs Campbell has noted that Willard had the "ability to fuse traditional values to proposals for social change."[70] Nowhere is this ability more visible than in her pursuit of the home protection argument. Although Campbell maintains that Willard's reliance on traditional values led to mere "reinforcement of existing belief,"[71] adapting one's persuasive message to the audience is one of the most common strategies of reformers and cannot be dismissed as ineffective. Such value-grounded appeals signal a major difference between the discourse of agitators and that of reformers, and rare indeed is the social movement whose goals are accomplished by agitators alone. Furthermore, Willard did not appeal simply to what people already believed, but rather to their ideal selves. One of her most remarkable traits, as one newspaper noted, was her "constant appeal to what is best and noblest in men—her brothers—and her unwavering faith in them, that they will, seeing what is right, do what is right."[72] Willard appealed to what Lincoln called the "better angels" of human nature, in much the same way that Martin Luther King Jr. would later ask white Americans to live up to the ideals of the Constitution and the Declaration of Independence.

Although Willard's protectionist argument was built on an idyllic vision of the home, she did not seek to reinforce the popular doctrine of spheres. At the heart of her appeal was an effort to create a nonthreatening way to expose the current system with its "unnatural two worlds in one."[73] Instead of separate spheres, Willard envisioned men and women working together in all aspects of life in order to create a homelike world for everyone. In 1886 she noted that the foremothers of the American Revolution "did not see that if a man and woman are stronger together than either can be separately in the home, by the same law of mind they are stronger together than either can be separately in literature and science, in business and professional life, in Church and State." The lives of men and women were indissolubly linked in all areas of life, and, working together, they could wield enough power to change the world. "By the laws of being," Willard argued, "men and women must go hand in hand if they would not go astray; that equally do man and woman need, not an echo, not a shadow, not a lesser nor yet a greater self, not 'like with like, but like with difference,' so that when these two, with their individual outlook upon destiny, shall together set their heads to any problem, or their hands to any task, they shall unite in that endeavor the full sum of power that this world holds."[74] Although Willard admitted differences between men and women, she fought the notion that these differences necessitated different spheres of action. Men and women had different needs to which the home protection movement responded. Willard claimed that "the supreme object of the W.C.T.U. is to elevate the home and to protect its members, one and all—the stronger from legalized temptation, the gentler from oppression."[75] Willard's vision of the idyllic home grounded her vision of the ultimate goal of the reform movements she advocated—to make the "world more homelike." At the same time, however, her call to uplift the home in order to relieve women's oppression involved a dynamic re-visioning of the home itself. In this new home, the new woman and new man of the next century would live in an equal partnership aided by the new technologies of the coming age.

The Home as the Model for the Goals of Reform

Willard used the home to justify women's entry into reform and political work, but she also used it to provide a model for the society that this work aimed to create. Within her Protestant worldview, the proper end of all of life's activities was the improvement of the world. All Christians, she believed, were called to do their part to make the world a better place to live in order to establish the reign of Christ on earth. In her 1887 presidential address, she predicted "the day when the nations shall form one universal brotherhood," and declared that "the kingdom of Christ is no poetic fancy with us white ribboners; no mystic dream. It is a solid piece of fact—a realm in which dwell neither alien nor native, neither bond nor free, neither male nor female, but all are equal integers in the working out through Christ-like laws and customs of a Christ-like destiny."[76] There is certainly a perfectionist and millennial spirit at the heart of Willard's reform thought that must be recognized in order to appreciate her rhetorical choices.

The path to this millennial world was to remake the world into a larger home for everyone. The home was not only a justification for women's activity in the public world but also was a model whose characteristic traits ought to be woven into the warp and woof of society. The vision was, of course, grounded in her faith that the home was the best place on earth. We have already noted Willard's early writing that saw the home as heaven on earth.[77] The ideal home was a place of love and nurture. Marked by safety, it encouraged the growth of individuality within the context of a caring family. Abundant in religious sympathy, affection, and intellectual stimulation, Willard's childhood home often stood as the prime example of what a home could be and, implicitly, what kind of individual such a home could produce. James Kimble has argued that one of the two central purposes of Willard's autobiography was to establish the appropriateness of her interest in protecting the home by concretizing the home through the rehearsal of the idyllic memories of her girlhood.[78] More than that, this concretized ideal home also reveals the outcome of Willard's entire vision of reform. In the introduction of her 1884 presidential address, Willard declared that if she were asked to state the "thought and purpose" of the WCTU in a single sentence, she would offer: "*It is to make the whole world HOMELIKE.*"[79] This goal is the heart of Willard's reform rhetoric across social movements.

THE IDEAL HOME OFFERS PATTERNS FOR CHANGE IN EDUCATION, REFORM, AND GOVERNMENT

Willard's most detailed presentation of the home as the model for public institutions was articulated in her 1873 address on women's education presented at the first Woman's Congress of the Association for the Advancement of Women.[80] Willard's analysis of the salient issues facing women's education identified three central questions. The first, "Should we teach women?," she said, had been answered affirmatively by all of the people gathered at the Woman's Congress. The second, "What should we teach?," was an issue under debate, but she believed that the "bill of fare" ought to be identical for boys and girls, and together they should sit "at the Banquet of Truth" (151). Answering the third question, "Where and in what surroundings ought we to learn?," was the focus of Willard's presentation. Her answer was that women should be educated somewhere between the "cloister" and the male "assembly room" where "women are admitted but not provided for" (152). The model for this middle-ground institution, she declared, was the home.

Making the analogy explicit, she advised college leaders to "look into the truest, purest HOME of your own neighborhood" to find inspiration. In this home there were "sons and daughters" under the "joint guardianship of men and women" whose different perspectives "bring the subjects which they look at into stereoscopic clearness." These guardians "consult together" about all of the plans for the family. Similarly, the best college would be coeducational and would have equal numbers of men and women who work together in the classroom, in administration, and on the board of trustees. This variety in the "angles of vision" would provide a depth and clarity for the school just as it did for the home (153).

"To carry out still further the fundamental idea of home," Willard continued, "I would assign to the especial care of each teacher a small number of students—who should go to him or her as a parent" (154). In fact, she argued that the "students and teacher should be associated in families." Though the men and women would sleep in separate facilities, "there should be a common dining hall" where students should sit in family-sized groups of no more than eight. Rather than living in large dormitories, the students should be grouped in tenements with "one teacher and the pupils under his or her care, or better a teacher's family, besides a convenient number of students" (155). In this way Willard hoped to re-create the interpersonal relationships and support systems students were used to finding in their homes in order to best foster the development of their intellect as well as their character.

Willard's vision, however, was more extensive than that suggested by the traditional in loco parentis doctrine in higher education, for she also called on teachers and students to make their school a home by developing links to the community in which the school is located. Specifically, she suggested that they join a community church and participate in other social activities of the town and so divest the university of its long-standing "monastic character" (155). Willard recognized that this integration into the community would require greater freedom of movement than was seen in most women's colleges. She anticipated this concern by suggesting that the goal of the home and the school was the same, since they both aimed to produce individuals of strong character who are capable of self-government. In the ideal home the parents knew their children and what kind of responsibilities and challenges they could handle; even so, the school should have as few formal rules as possible and should instead adapt to individual students according to "the disposition they display" (155). She believed that students, like children, would rise to meet the high expectations of their elders, thus an honor system, rather than an arbitrary system of rules and curfews, would be a successful disciplinary program.

Willard's address on this occasion was not grounded in theory, but was the result of her experience at the Evanston Ladies College as it collaborated with Northwestern University. The "home idea" she presented was the vision she was building on the shores of Lake Michigan. At the time of this address she had every reason to regard her plan a success. However, her home idea with its honor system plan became controversial soon after the college's official merger with Northwestern. The economic stresses in the Chicago area, resulting from the Great Fire, created insurmountable challenges. The lack of resources meant that Willard's vision of "homelike" housing was not brought to fruition, and male and female students were both farmed out to boardinghouses in town. This led to public scrutiny of Willard's jurisdiction over the female students. As Willard biographer Ruth Bordin points out, during the resulting conflict, which involved public debate in the Chicago papers, "Willard, the innovator, the opponent of arbitrary rules," was labeled as the conservative. The new president of the university, Charles Fowler, Willard's ex-fiancé, cast himself as the liberal and claimed to support "complete freedom" for all students of the university.[81] Thus Willard's vision of the homelike school was not fulfilled, though the idea has been given new life in recent years through the creation of learning communities as well as service learning initiatives on many university campuses.

Willard saw the home as the ideal model not only for reforms in higher education but also for more radical reforms of society. In 1887, addressing the conservative Presbyterian Social Union, she claimed that not only was the "hearthstone" the "chief cornerstone of the State," but that "the model home is Heaven's own type of the ideal government," and the "State should be a larger home, and not, as now, a monastery or a camp."[82] Willard often expressed her vision of the homelike world by extending the relationships found in the home to the larger society. In a White House ceremony at which Willard presented a portrait of temperance heroine "Lemonade" Lucy Hayes to President James Garfield, she claimed, "'Where is thy brother?' is today the central question in that larger home which we call social life, answered by a thousand kindly charities." Willard seized upon the popular understanding of God's query of Cain about his brother, Abel, with its implication that we ought to "keep" our "brothers" from harm and transferred its meaning to the temperance movement.[83] She believed that the success of the Prohibition Party could usher in this new age since the party aimed to outlaw liquor traffic and protect the home, and promised "to make us one family, with firm clasped hands and loving hearts."[84]

The central figure in the home was the mother, and Willard argued that the role women played in their homes provided a good model for the duties and responsibilities of women in the larger world. "What the world most needs is mothering," she declared on more than one occasion. The need arose out of men's efforts to take on more than they could handle. Men have, Willard lamented, "vainly" attempted "to play the mother's part to a half-orphaned world."[85] As a result of women's lack of involvement in public life, politics had become increasingly corrupted. That very corruption, Willard believed, had become an argument to continue to exclude women on the grounds that they are "not suited to such politics" (383). Willard responded by turning that argument on its head; agreeing that the current system was corrupt, she then denied that this was "politics as it must be." She noted that women were equally ill suited to "the style of housekeeping that prevails in a bachelor's hall" and declared that the first step they would take in the bachelor's hall and in politics was "that of vigorous housecleaning" (383). Elsewhere she argued that women had entered "into the college and humanized it, into literature and hallowed it, into the business world and ennobled it," and similarly would cleanse government and politics. "For woman," she pronounced in a favorite aphorism, "will make home-like every place she enters, and she will enter every place on this round earth."[86]

Though Willard sometimes invoked these kinds of housekeeping images and often spoke in essentialist-like language of the "mother-hearted woman" whose "mother love" would work miracles for humanity, she had a firm grasp on the power of socialization to shape men and women to meet their role expectations. In her presidential address of 1887, she envisioned the new age emerging where "man and woman shall map out home as the one true state, and *she who, during centuries of training, has learned how to govern there*, shall help man make the great, cold, heartless state a warm, kind and protecting home."[87] If men and women have different angles of vision and different skills to offer the world, those differences can, in large part, be explained by the distinctiveness of their life experiences. In fact, when pressed, Willard disavowed any belief that woman was "inherently better than man (although his voice has ten thousand times declared it)" and instead attributed the apparent differences in their moral behavior to "her more favorable environment."[88]

THE IDEAL HOME RESHAPES PUBLIC SPACE

The home, within which women developed the skills necessary to have a positive influence on the larger world, provided not only a blueprint for profound changes in social structure, but in Willard's evolved world it also offered a model for less dramatic social evolutions. For example, she argued that the physical space of the home could be profitably imitated by institutions such as offices and the public platform. In her presidential address of 1883, Willard suggested that the WCTU create a national headquarters. The facility, she said, "must be made of parlors as well as offices." It should have copies of "every temperance paper in Christendom" as well as every temperance speech on file and be decorated with up-to-date statistics "not in dry tabulated statements but speaking to the eye in form and color, by chart, map, and diagram." With these features this headquarters could become the "beloved and sacred Home of the reform that seeks Home's purity and peace."[89] In addition, in her *Do Everything* handbook, Willard told temperance women who spoke from the public platform that they should avoid speaking in a space bearing the "forlorn aspect of a Lyceum stage." Instead, Willard suggested, the platform should be "beautified by plants and vines," with ice water set out "upon a handsome table . . . while easy chairs and warm rugs [give] the place a homelike look." Re-creating the home on the public platform accomplished two significant tasks: first, each listener would be reminded of the home that alcohol threatens, thus increasing the persuasiveness of the speaker's appeal; second, women speakers themselves would also be put at ease by the comforting surroundings of home. Temperance conventions should also bear the marks of the home and be "free from the distinctive features of large Conventions conducted by men." Sporting "clear light, graceful ferns, flowers, fruits, pictures, mottoes, banners, bannerettes, and flags," the convention platform should "present the aspect of a parlor."[90] In this way Willard remade the public space of the platform into an extension of the home.

Presentations given upon this homelike platform should also imitate the patterns of home life, with speakers adopting conversational speaking styles. Willard herself cultivated a conversational style often commented upon in newspaper reports of her speeches. "The idea of impropriety in her so appearing and speaking before us," one listener noted in 1881, "could not have been more distant if she had been talking to each one of us alone in a drawing-room."[91] A New Jersey observer wrote, "[S]he is easy and self-possessed in manner, her style of speaking is colloquial, and her gestures are few, but quiet and expressive. Her entire deportment is refined and womanly—of the drawing room, and not of the public platform."[92] A Texas newspaper accounted for her success as follows: "Miss Willard is not what is usually called an orator. There being none of the gestures, tone and tricks of the fourth of July [sic] orator about her. Her style is that of the conversationalist. She impresses you with the idea that she has a message to deliver, something to say and goes about it."[93] Reports from Great Britain echoed the Americans' assessments: "What a delightfully unaffected platform style she had! Indeed it was not a 'platform style'; it was her own sweet, witty and winning conversation in a slightly louder but never a harsh key."[94]

Willard encouraged other women to adopt a similar conversational style. She advised speakers to avoid an authoritative tone. "Teach without seeming to do so. Carefully skip around all such 'hard words' as 'take notice,' 'I call your attention.' . . . Put yourself in the attitude of a learner along with the rest."[95] Her advice was grounded in her success in approaching audiences in this manner, and it also reflected the precepts she had learned during an intense speech-training session she had undergone in the late 1870s.[96] Under the direction of Robert McLean Cumnock, professor of rhetoric and elocution and director of the School of Oratory at Northwestern, Willard learned an approach to speaking with an "elevated conversational voice." Set forth formally in his *Choice Readings for Public and Private Entertaining*, Cumnock's approach was a departure from most elocution texts because of its emphasis on a natural style. Presentations should be made, he adjured the reader, *"as though you were talking in the most direct way to your hearers."* One should speak in order *"to impress the truth in as earnest and natural tones as you would use in uttering the same precepts to your personal friends."*[97] It appears as if Willard took Cumnock's directive to heart and made an effort to encourage others to adopt similar homelike styles. Women who spoke as though they were talking to friends and family in a drawing room could help transform the public space into a space inviting enough to encourage everyone's participation.

THE IDEAL HOME MODELS A NEW PARTNERSHIP FOR PUBLIC LIFE

Willard's use of the home as a model for various reforms was tied to her belief that men and women ought to be partners in all aspects of life. At times she exploited her middle-class Protestant audiences' sentimental beliefs about the necessity of having women present in order to make a house a home and attempted to transfer that feeling to her belief in the necessity of having women engaged in public life. "'A community without woman's equal social action, a church without her equal ecclesiastical action and a state without her equal political action,'" she echoed in 1886, "'is very much what a home would be without a mother, wife, sister, daughter or friend.'"[98] Though a mother's place in the home was important, in Willard's model home the most essential feature was that men and women were in it together. She celebrated the marriage bond as "the sum of human weal or woe of both man and woman equally," and she honored relationships where men and women were partners in the home.[99]

Once audiences were reminded of this quality of the model home, Willard would urge them to accept her vision of men and women working as equals everywhere, thus making the world a larger home. Building on the passage from Genesis 2:18, "it is not good for man to be alone," Willard constructed a case arguing that the very separation of man from woman in the public sphere was the source of man's moral "deterioration" and, implicitly, woman's deterioration in that she remained infantalized.[100] At the International Council of Women in 1888, she declared that whatever came "out of the aggregation of men by themselves, always comes to harm," while "out of the coming of men and women into true, and noble, and high conditions, side by side, always comes good."[101] Willard supported her position that the separation of spheres was evil by arguing that it was the result of the sins of Adam and Eve: "under the curse, man has mapped out the state as his largest sphere, and the home as woman's largest." Under the new dispensation of the Christian gospel, however, men and women are "steadily traveling back to Eden—that is, they have been slowly learning that they were created to live in one world—not two." Under the curse, she argued, man ventured out to fight battles and then returned home to find woman "waiting." But now, "under the blessing, man and woman go hand in hand wherever they are called to go at all." Willard proclaimed that WCTU women were "tired of this unnatural two worlds in one, where men and women dwell apart; they would invade the solitude of the masculine intellect; break in upon the stereotyped routine of the masculine hierarchy in church and state," and together, men and women would "re-make the world." Her millennial vision was that of "one world of men and women side by side, God's home for all humanity."[102]

Willard's approach to reform, then, elevated the ideal home as the model for society to follow. Higher education would be more successful, she argued, if it became a more homelike environment where men and women in a family-like setting taught boys and girls. The public platform, too, could be improved by adopting the look and the speaking conventions of the homelike parlor. Even public life, she believed, would be improved when men and women worked as partners in the way they do in ideal homes. The only way to divest the world of the consequences of what Willard saw as centuries of sexual division was to remake it, and the blueprint for that makeover should be the home, since in the ideal home men and women function as equals, bringing their individual talents to the table for the betterment of the whole.

Whether Willard's advancement of the home as a model is a radical or a conservative move may be a debatable question, but there are reasons to view her position as radical. By arguing that the creation of separate spheres of influence and action for men and women was the result of God's curse and, at least given current levels of civilization, produced more harm than good, she was clearly calling for far-ranging social changes. The specific homelike reforms she suggested for building coeducational institutions also called for changes in every aspect of the existing male educational system. She insisted that educational institutions had to adapt to their new female constituents and rid themselves of "the last trace of monastic character." She announced her agreement with the statements of Erastus Haven, the first president of Northwestern University, that "to give ladies an 'equal chance' with gentlemen, means something more than to control a college wholly by men, arrange its surroundings solely for men, give the instruction entirely by men, and then, forsooth! open the doors alike to both sexes."[103] Here

Willard foreshadowed more recent feminist arguments, including those made in the academy concerning the literary and rhetorical canons. To truly rethink women's contributions to literary and rhetorical history, many have argued, we must do more than simply include women authors and speakers selected according to the qualities they hold in common with great male writers and orators. We must also continue to consider the possibilities of alternate standards of literary and rhetorical artistry and significance.[104] Willard was ahead of her time in recognizing the need to reconsider the implications of including women in the public sphere.

Willard's call to redesign public spaces and institutions to better fit women's needs eventually grew to an inspired critique of the doctrine of spheres.. Since children inevitably leave the cradle and leave the home she argued, women must follow men into the world and "bring the home to them."[105] The entry of women into civic life, she believed, would create significant change: "We want this to be no longer Atilla's world, or Alexander's, or Napoleon's, struck off to the highest bidder. . . . We want it no more to be the world where the harem makes women but the sport and [t]oy of men." Instead, she envisioned "a homelike world, the world of Barak and of Deborah, of Albert and Victoria, of Robert and Elizabeth Browning, of Daniel and Mary A. Livermore, of Henry Blackwell and Lucy Stone," a world where men and women worked as equals at home and in the larger home of the world. Her goal was to improve the living conditions of all people "until society, through industrial reform, universal education, parental (not *paternal*) government, and everyday religion, should become simply a larger home in which no human being should be any longer forgotten or forlorn."[106]

The idea of home Willard used as a model for reform may be idyllic, but unlike many early-twentieth-century woman's rights advocates, she also recognized that in order for her reform vision to be carried to fruition, the inner workings of the home and the roles of man and woman within it must undergo serious change.

The Home as Site for Evolutionary Change

In her analysis of Willard's discourse, Karlyn Kohrs Campbell, recognizing the differences between Willard's goals and those of other woman's movement leaders, concludes that the work of Willard and the WCTU, while significant for feminism in that it created broader opportunities for women, was essentially "independent of" the feminist movement itself.[107] While Willard's theologically grounded vision may separate her from Stanton's humanistic feminist ideology, her work and discourse were critical to the creation of a growing feminist consciousness in the closing years of the nineteenth century and beginning of the twentieth. Furthermore, by actually addressing the quotidian issues of heterosexual marriage and offering a new vision of life in the home and relationships among family members, Willard began to address the central issues that shadowed the feminist movement throughout the twentieth century. Some argue that the greatest failure of second-wave feminism was its inability to address what were the living issues for the vast majority of women, such as: Who will take care of the children? Who will take care of the house? Scholarly interest in Willard's call for political change and for the entry of women into all walks of life in church and state has, by and large, overlooked her attention to reshaping the domestic sphere itself.[108] Although her vision was impaired by her persistent optimism and constrained by Victorian mores, Willard often addressed the very issues that contemporary feminists have only recently succeeded in bringing to the forefront.

RESHAPING THE HOME THROUGH CHANGING
THE MARRIAGE RELATIONSHIP

Willard's overhaul of the home began with her attention to new marital relations, including the foundations of the marriage partnership, as well as her call for changes in sexual relations and in parenting. She also advocated some basic economic reforms for work within the home and articulated a vision of the home transformed by new technologies. Furthermore, all of these changes in the home went hand in hand with her vision of a new understanding of manhood and womanhood.

Willard believed that the transformation of the home needed to begin with the transformation of heterosexual marriage. In her first formal lecture, "The New Chivalry," an address that she repeated many times throughout the 1870s as she began her public speaking career, she announced her call for changes in marital relations even as she celebrated the progress of the institution of marriage in America.[109] The text of the speech is built around her observations of the lives of the women she saw during her two and a half years traveling abroad. In journals Willard kept during her travels through the Middle East, Europe, and England, she carefully documented the scenes and stories of women's lives in the Old World and reflected on the differences between the treatment of women abroad and in America. These stories served as the basis for the speech that contains her earliest ideas about how the home was evolving and progressing in the United States due to Americans' rejection of the ideas about women's place and women's duty that she found so common abroad. Willard placed American ideals of marriage in stark contrast to the practices of other cultures: Egypt, where she saw a woman who had been sold into marriage "before the age of ten, by her own father's hand"; Rome, where a woman must avoid gaining much education, for marriage and the cloister were her only choices, and too much learning spoiled her for the former; and even England, where she saw the "marriage markets" of Hyde Park. Under the system of the "New Chivalry" in America, Willard argued, a new sense of equality was emerging due to advances in women's education (129, 130, 139). A new home would emerge as a result of this change in women's training, and it would "be the gift of this Better Age to the New America, in which a *threefold tie* shall bind the husband to his wife, the father to his daughter, the mother to her son" (140). In addition to the traditional ties of religion and affection, Willard envisioned a new tie, "intellectual sympathy." When men cease to simply drink to women's health and instead "invite us to sit down beside them at the banquet of truth," women would have access to knowledge and to a new sense of self that would reform them, the home, and the whole of society (140).

The need for "intellectual sympathy" as a new part of the ideal marriage bond was central to Willard's view of the new home. Even into the 1890s she continued to argue that a common bond forged through education was the third "cable that anchors man's adventurous heart to home." She also celebrated the fact that 40,000 young women were attending colleges as evidence that "this age is weaving" this new bond.[110] Willard's faith in the transforming nature of education, no doubt encouraged by her years spent teaching, was pervasive in her discourse. She considered many of the evolutions of the nineteenth century to be the result of increased access to learning. In her presidential address of 1886, she contrasted the homogeneity of the "mothers and sisters of the old-time Revolution" in early America with the "great variety," not only in dress but also in occupation, profession, and purpose, among the women of the WCTU. The change, she argued, could be attributed to the fact that the contemporary woman's "educational advantages have been without restriction."[111]

Education was so transformative that a marriage between a man and woman who shared a common educational background would result in radically reshaped possibilities in the home founded by the couple. To illustrate this point, Willard offered her audiences a history of the emergence of the home. The first move, she noted, was "to separate one man and one woman from the common herd, into each home." There the woman would remain "in grateful quietness, while the man stood at the door to defend its sacred shrine with fist and spear." However, these conditions, she argued, proved the root of many evils since they encouraged man to legislate "first for himself, and afterward for the physically weaker one within 'his' home."[112] She theorized that patriarchy emerged from man's sense of ownership of woman grounded in the ancient chieftain's wish that his son would "inherit his prowess and the prerogatives" he had earned but risked losing with age. Thus emerged the "cruel expedients" visible across cultures to control women's sexuality. Willard hypothesized that the binding of women's feet in China, the veiling of Mohammedan women, and the right of men to physically discipline and control women in many cultures were all rooted in this sense of ownership.[113] While some contemporary feminists may take this same analysis of patriarchy and conclude that women's liberation is to be found in unleashing women's sexuality and granting women the same sexual freedoms permitted to men, Willard took a different turn.

As women learned to rethink the oppressive roots of male commemoration of womanly virtue, Willard hoped that they would begin to demand a similar standard of morality from men. Women's oppression came not from the suppression of her sexuality, argued Willard, but from her position of subservience to a male sexuality that is unrestrained in large part because of women's economic dependence. Young men, she argued, are easily tempted to lead dissolute lives when even the most respectable women in their class seemed to have no choice but to accept their proposals of marriage because the women had no other means of financial support. "Not one girl in a hundred has been endowed with the talent and the pluck that make her independent of him," but as soon as coeducation equalized access to opportunity and women could have careers, Willard claimed, this would change. Women would rise "to the plane of perfect financial independence" and from there could "dictate the equitable terms" that demand an equal measure of purity and respect from men.[114] Part of the work of the WCTU, Willard announced in her first presidential address, was dedicated to deepening "in the thought of girlhood the truth that Home, if it is to be the shrine we love to call it, requires not only a pure priestess but a *pure priest* to keep its altars fair and bright."[115] Certainly, the radical implications of women's education were not lost on Willard. Education would reform "the question of life companionship" so that it could "be decided on its merits, pure and simple," and not be complicated with questions of expediency such as, "'Did she get a good home?' 'Is he a generous provider?'"[116] Education would give women power through creating the opportunity for them to make freer choices about marriage.

The coeducation of girls and boys would also enable the emergence of the true "American home, with its Christian method of a dual headship." This new model of the home, Willard believed, would root out "all that remains of the monastic, the French, and the harem philosophies" concerning relations between men and women and put an end to the notion of women's legal invisibility in marriage.[117] Acknowledging the power of language to construct reality, Willard also argued that the marriage ceremony itself be reformed to reflect the new ideal of dual headship in marriage: "Because language is one of life's greatest educators," she argued before the National Council of Women in 1891, "let us now attack the phrase 'man and wife' (still standing in the odor of sanctity upon the pages of Catholic and Episcopal ritual) because it incarnates all the serfdom of woman's past, exaggerates sex out of its due subordination to personality, and is false to the facts of the case." The minister could just "as properly pronounce them man and woman," Willard noted ironically.[118] Repeatedly, Willard asserted, "husband and wife are one, and that one is husband and wife."[119]

Willard's notion of the new marriage was in keeping with that espoused in Tennyson's poem "The Princess." As Tennyson scholar James Kincaid notes, the struggle the poet contemplated in this work was the challenge of creating a marriage that accomplished a merging, a oneness, but that at the same time preserved difference. Willard had long maintained that through differences in training (if not biology), men and women look at the world from different angles. When they looked at issues together, she believed, their vision was improved by the "stereoscopic clearness" that resulted. When men and women were given the opportunity to look on the issues of the public world together, this clearer vision would bring the human family greater insight into understanding that world and solving its problems.[120] Willard often quoted (or paraphrased) lines 170–75 from Tennyson's poem:

> Two heads in council, two beside the hearth,
> Two in the tangled business of the world,
> Two in the liberal offices of life,
> Two plummets dropt for one to sound the abyss
> Of science, and the secrets of the mind:
> Musician, painter, sculptor, critic, more.[121]

Many thinkers celebrated this model of the companionate marriage during the second half of the nineteenth century; Willard was among those who explored its ramifications quite thoroughly. Altering the balance of power within marriage had serious ramifications for male privilege and for women's responsibilities. Willard insisted that marriage was "the sum of earthly weal or woe to both" men and women.[122] The home may even be of more importance to men than women, Willard speculated, since they, "with all the world to choose from, *choose* home."[123] Willard believed the home had "already done more for man than any other member of its favored constituency," and yet she marveled at the fact that women's lives and options had changed dramatically, while "man in the home" had not yet undergone "the faintest evolution."[124] She knew that the companionate marriage she championed must be built on terms of equality and would demand changes from both sexes.

Some of these changes would affect legal privileges. In a lengthy address for the National Education Association in 1890, Willard explored the needed legal reforms.

> It will not do to give the husband of the modern woman power to whip his wife, "provided the stick he uses is not larger than his finger"; to give him the right to will away her unborn child; to have control over her property; to make all the laws under which she is to live; adjudicate all her penalties; try her before juries of men; conduct her to prison under the care of men; cast the ballot for her; and, in general, hold her in the estate of a perpetual minor.[125]

Elsewhere she suggested that the states should reform inheritance laws so that the wife would always receive at least "half and not one-third of the estate."[126] And before the National Council of Women she declared her support for the Knight's of Labor demand, "'Equal pay for equal work.'"[127]

Although legal changes would affect marriage and the home, Willard more often addressed the need to transform attitudes. In her 1890 presidential address, for example, she introduced an analogy between the consciousness-raising about justice and human rights that had taken place during the antislavery movement and the current awakening to the rights of women.

"Each age," she declared, "develops a new conscience—becomes just concerning a class to which before it had considered itself generous. For instance, a charitable master thought well of himself because he took good care of his slave, but a just master liberated him that he might care for himself; an 'indulgent husband' as the phrase is, thinks well of himself because he permits his wife to do as she chooses, but a just husband perceives that to do so is her right which he can neither give nor take away." The recognition of women's equality within the home was necessary, she argued, for the continued progress of humanity. Although "[m]an's greatest pride is in his sons," she argued, those sons are handicapped when they are raised in a home where the father "is unspeakably degraded by his desire to rule" his wife.[128] Instead, the emerging consciousness would create a new man who "recognizes himself as her comrade, not her master, and rejoices in their joint partnership in all this world affords."[129]

Not only men needed to reform their attitudes toward marriage; many women also needed to rethink their roles in life. Willard herself had been inspired by Margaret Fuller's statement, "No woman can give her hand with dignity, or her heart with loyalty, until she has learned *how to stand alone*."[130] In her 1886 book, *How to Win: A Book for Girls*, Willard shared this notion with thousands of girls and women while she encouraged them to cultivate their own specialty, to develop a wage-earning profession, and to rethink the institution of marriage. She warned young women considering marriage that their attitudes must change if they think their husband's "role in their new drama is to be that of the money-maker and hers of money-spender" (118). The emerging ideal of marriage Willard championed demanded that the "firm steady, even clasp of a pair of bread-winners ought to be realized when you obey the minister's instructions to 'join hands' at the altar" (119). Women would be empowered to retain a sense of self in marriage, Willard believed, when they first prepare to live a full life, to be someone, with or without marriage. This sense of selfhood should be maintained, Willard recommended, again foreshadowing contemporary feminism, by altering the tradition of women giving up their names in marriage. "The ideal woman," she insisted, "will not write upon her visiting card, nor insist on having her letters addressed, to Mrs. John Smith . . . but if her maiden name were Jones, she will fling her banner to the breeze as 'Mrs. Jones-Smith'" (53).

Perhaps the most important change to emerge in Willard's vision of equality in the home was a new perspective on women's right to control reproduction. For Willard, the first step toward reforming women's sexual power in marriage was the same as that needed to reform the institution of marriage as a whole, education. There needed to be room within each home, she argued, for the discussion of sexuality. "To be forewarned ," she declared to an audience in 1886, "is the only way to be forearmed."[131] At WCTU-sponsored mothers' meetings held throughout the nation, women were encouraged to talk to their children about sex, offering appropriate information along with the American middle-class's reverential perspective of sexuality. Such education, WCTU leaders hoped, would inoculate children from the deleterious effects of coarser perspectives of sexuality shared in the schoolyard. In her 1889 presidential address, Willard asserted the right of women to control their own bodies; even within marriage, women should not be asked to "barter their personal liberty." As women's attitudes shifted due to the effects of sex education, so would men's: "to-morrow men will learn that it was their sense of absolute possession which robbed them of their wives' most potent charm." Reforms in sexual practices within and outside of marriage were needed, Willard argued, to end "the sexual pandemonium" that had allowed children "to come into the world by accident, or against the will of either parent." Willard maintained that in the coming peaceful age that was the necessary consequent of the reform spirit of the time, women would no longer provide the quantities of children demanded under an Alexander or a Napoleon as "bullet meat" for his plans of conquest. Instead, attention would switch to quality and the right of "children to be well born." Marriage, itself, she claimed, would then come to be viewed as a "sacrament" rather than "as a resource."[132]

RESHAPING THE HOME THROUGH SHARING PARENTING AND CHANGING HOUSEWORK

New attitudes toward reproduction and the rights of children, Willard hoped, would carry over into changed attitudes concerning parenting duties and roles. Seeing marriage as a union of two people equal on the planes of intellect and sexual purity would enhance the likelihood that fatherhood would take its rightful place next to motherhood and men would come to be an "equal sharer in the cares" that have helped to shape womanhood's often celebrated character traits.[133] This vision revealed the breadth of Willard's comprehension of the implications of the multitude of reforms she championed. She recognized the fact that as mothers moved to take a larger place "in the constantly more home-like world," fathers would become "a hundredfold more magnified." In other words, Willard had a ready response for those objectors to woman's rights who wanted to know "who would care for the children" if women participated more broadly in public affairs. The equality Willard envisioned in the reformed and homelike state would be mirrored by equality in tending to the needs of the private home and family. This was a win-win plan according to Willard. The addition of "childward care" to societal expectations of men's roles would help men to add "unselfish devotion" to the virtues of intellectual development and courage that society already inculcates in them.[134] In her autobiography, Willard wrote about this new man in concrete terms, reminiscing about the home life of a Dr. Foster, whose willingness "to relieve his wife from the care of a fretful child," soothing the child to sleep, gave her a vision of the new home and gave her "a more exalted opinion of Dr. Foster than of any other living man."[135]

More was necessary, however, to truly reform the home in such a way that women would not be constrained by its demands as they sought a more public life. Willard anticipated by nearly a hundred years the "second shift" phenomena that saw middle-class women adding work outside the home to their responsibilities without dropping many of their responsibilities to the family.[136] Her central response to this quandary was to argue for the financial recognition of women's labor within the home and to propose the use of technological advances to reduce the labor required to maintain the home.

In the 1880s Willard began her call for a serious reconfiguration of an economy that failed to recognize women's labor in the home. These issues, she insisted, lie at "the core of the woman question." Not only must girls be trained to work outside the home to establish a path to economic independence, but society should also "put a money value upon a wife's industry in helping to build up and maintain a home." This money should "be hers out of the common income and collectable by law."[137] As Willard moved further toward advocating an economy grounded in a beneficent Christian socialism, she embraced Edward Bellamy and argued that women should "'share and share alike'" in a "national income with the noblest Roman of them all."[138] Her long association with the labor movement in the 1880s and early 1890s encouraged her to develop a critique of any agitation for an eight-hour workday that failed to consider women's unpaid labor. "In all this agitation," a frustrated Willard declared in her presidential address of 1890, "it astounds me to hear so very much about the eight hour husband and so very little about the sixteen hour wife!" The eight-hour workday, she believed, would be a part of a healthful system of life where every day saw eight hours devoted to sleep, eight to work, and eight to recreation, intellectual development, or community development.[139] But any such sea change must include women in the picture. The eight-hour workday, she insisted, "ought to apply to men and women equally and to the home as well as to the shop." How this evolution might come about, she admitted, was not entirely clear, "but when women share the power as well as the burdens of the State we will find or make a way to disprove the old adage that 'a woman's work is never done.'"[140]

One possible solution to the problem of women's sixteen-hour workday could be found in technology. Willard often celebrated scientific and industrial advances and in an 1888 address given at the Chicago Woman's League, she took a detailed look at the role of technology in working out a solution to routine housework. The speech, entitled "The Dawn of Woman's Day," was widely circulated through *Our Day*, a popular reform journal of the period.[141] In the speech, Willard argued that "organized womanhood" could solve the "problem of the modern home" through sharing resources and applying technology (473, 476). Willard noted that "hot water and steam-heated air" were already supplied to every house. On a similar basis, women could devise "a public laundry system, so complete as to drive the washtub out of every kitchen, banishing forever the reign of a steamy, sudsy, indigo-blue Monday." Furthermore a kind of "caterer's system" could be implemented so that the cookstove itself would be rendered obsolete (476). In fact, the home of the future could be modeled after the innovations of George Pullman's rail cars. Pullman might suggest that we have "house porters who would come around regularly and set everything to rights, build fires in the open grate, just for the beauty and coziness thereof, and clear up the house generally." The problem of meals could be solved with "pneumatic tubes" through which meals, "ordered by telephone," were sent. Waiters would be available "so many to the block, to serve and gather up the fragments" of the meal. The end result of these technological advances would be "a proportionate increase in the health and happiness of the families thus served." These "material inventions" would relieve a woman "from the drudgery of daily toil" and free her for other work (477).

The overhaul of the home, however, would not only apply modern technologies but also innovations in labor management. Home specialists trained in the specific duties required in the home would replace the current system that relied on a "maid-of-all-work" to carry on an "infinite variety of industries." The image of these specialists moving up and down the street suggested a kind of assembly line approach to housekeeping. Development of such expertise would allow home workers to "command respect" akin to that of specialists in the corporate world. Willard envisioned a transformation of the home supported by a community network of specialists. She also noted, in the words of an unknown reformer, the economic principle behind such a transformation, for these services, once "'attainable only to the man of large wealth'" would soon be available to all, since "'the all can collectively afford a better service than the few'" (478). Applying principles based on economies of scale, these changes would not only permit middle- and upper-class women to enter into greater participation in public life but also would also make the comforts of home available to members of the lower class.

The home, then, would be transformed through the education of women that would justify a dual headship within the home even as women began to share leadership roles in the state. Recognition of women's equality within the home would create a better balance between men's and women's sexual and economic power within marriage. Supporting these transformations, Willard called for rethinking the value of women's labor in the home and for applying scientific principles to create a technological revolution that would solve the challenges of housekeeping. Underlying all of these changes were alterations to the roles of men and women in society. Women were called to see themselves as active agents, to "'be not simply good, be good for something' . . . not a drone in the great hive of humanity, but a happy, humming, honey-gathering bee, not a croaker, but a persuasive voice."[142]

Both men and women were changing, she declared in her 1887 presidential address. "In an age of force," Willard suggested, "woman's greatest grace was to cling," but the modern woman "has strength and individuality, a gentle seriousness; there is more of the sisterly, less of the siren; more of the duchess, and less of the doll." "To meet the new creation," she continued, "how grandly men themselves are growing; how considerate and brotherly, how pure in word and deed!"[143] Unleashing women's powers to play a central role in the state required an equivalent elevation of fatherhood and the celebration of men's equal stake in the success of the home. As noted earlier, the overlapping of men's and women's roles that Willard envisioned was accompanied by changes in the underlying worldview that had once sustained the separate spheres ideology. Looking more closely at how her reform of the home took aim at the very heart of the nineteenth-century doctrine of spheres indicates the breadth of the consequences of her reform vision.

RESHAPING THE HOME BY ELIMINATING SEPARATE SPHERES

In her 1888 presidential address, Willard announced that women's reform work "contemplates as its highest object the harmonization of men and women into one circle of worth, work and winsomeness."[144] Maintaining her effort to speak for evolution rather than revolution, Willard retained the metaphor of the circle while rejecting the separation of men and women into spheres. While Willard's ultimate interest for the middle-class woman's reform movement was to push women who had stood still too long as statues "upon the pedestal of 'woman's sphere'" into "the common world about them to act a mother's part to thousands worse than motherless," she knew that the reform of the world outside the home was dependent on reform of the world within it.[145] Holding up the ideal home as motivation for women's activity in the public sphere and as a model for reform within that sphere, Willard also considered the need to reshape the private home to bring it closer to the ideal she envisioned. All these reforms were based on a rethinking of the separate spheres doctrine that maintained that God had assigned men and women predestined roles within society. Even thinkers moving toward a more secular worldview saw support for maintaining separate spheres in Darwinian notions of evolution. The specialization of tasks that was part of the separate spheres doctrine seemed to agree with the popular understanding of Darwinism that evolution involved relentless progress toward specialization of the species. Willard's notion that there was "one circle of worth" within which men and women should develop their individual specialties ran against both the theologically grounded and Darwinian-supported doctrine of separation of spheres.[146]

Willard knew that confronting and altering these deeply held beliefs required a long-term commitment. Simply exposing the inconsistencies of the separate spheres doctrine was insufficient. An early presidential address attempted such a strategy by showing the inconsistency of women's exclusion from the ballot on the grounds of women's difference, when it was ludicrous to imagine an "assessor, who should ignore women in making up his estimates," or a "judge who should declare their sphere so different, the dear, delightful creatures, that penalties and prisons were not for them."[147] Revealing this inconsistency might draw a few converts to the cause, but the real way to change society's ideas about men's and women's spheres, Willard knew, was to change the way children were socialized. This would help to elide the differences between the sexes that seemed to be so evident in nineteenth-century America. The result would be a complementary equality between men and women who would then bear equal responsibilities in the home as well as the state.

The home and the parents and children within it must undergo transformation if the wider world is to change, Willard argued. Before a British audience in 1895, she called for breaking down "the middle wall of partition between parent and child, between the boy's heart and the heart of the mother from which his first caught its rhythm." And the father should "become the closest friend of the son." Within the household itself, sisters should be given a "larger place." But most important, she declared, is the need to "tune the lives of boys and girls to the same key, teaching them the same sports, the same books, the same standards of purity."[148] On several occasions she called for less sexist use of toys, insisting that boys should be encouraged to play more with dolls to encourage development of "the fatherly instinct." Moreover, the time girls spent playing with dolls should be limited, since too much such play dulled "their curiosity concerning the mechanism of the world," and thus interfered with their comprehension of how the real world works.[149]

More similar experiences when growing up would better prepare all children to take on equal roles in the world. In *How to Win*, Willard aimed to retrain young women who had missed the chance to develop a strong sense of self in their early years. She argued that young women had been handicapped by a culture that expected little from them and provided no encouragement for them to dare to do more than to meet conventional expectations for women. As noted earlier, the book encouraged women to consider themselves as potential wage earners, but to support this re-visioning, young women needed to adopt some of the purposeful behaviors and focus they often saw in their brothers. While new opportunities were opening up for women to participate in society outside the confines of their homes, Willard acknowledged that some fundamental changes in self-concept had to occur before women would be ready to make new choices. The first task, she said, was to encourage young women to develop their strengths, their specialties, rather than to develop a generic level of accomplishments. A girl should take time to discover what she is good at and develop that gift and use it to give her life direction. "In place of aimless reverie," Willard wrote, develop "a resolute aim." Having a goal, she argued, "is where your brother has had his chief intellectual advantage over you," for he had been trained to set his sights and to be somebody, "while you have been just as sedulously taught that the handsome prince might whirl past your door 'most any day,' lift you to a seat beside him in his golden chariot and carry you off to his castle in Spain".[150] But daydreaming about such a plot had led to vagueness in direction, Willard decried, and few women were outfitting themselves with the necessary skills to have an impact on the world. Throughout the rest of the book, Willard used slogans such as: "It is not so much *what comes to you as what you come to*, that determines whether you are a winner in the race of life," as she continued the theme of developing a sense of self as key to a successful and happy life for both boys and girls (39).

Willard's call for a similarity of ambition and equal support for self-development for boys and girls was kept from falling either into girlish self-indulgence or into a call for girls to become mannish by her demand that both boys and girls also receive an equal emphasis on moral training. "There are not two sets of virtues," she declared before the National WCTU in 1893; "there is but one greatness of character." The crown of virtue rests upon those who combine "the noblest traits of man and woman in nature, words, and deeds." This character will be most likely to develop if we teach our girls "*to be brave*" even as we instruct our boys "*to be gentle*."[151] Once again Willard acknowledged the significance of nurture over nature. Continuing to raise boys with the traditional virtues of boyhood while adding to their training the traditional virtues of girlhood, and vice versa, would produce men and women who share common values and who are prepared to work together in both the private and the public world.

Of course, Willard maintained that the first place to offer such moral instruction was within the transformed home itself. It is the home, she had declared to her constituents some years earlier, "which brings human beings into closest relations of interdependence, each upon the other, for highest and most enduring happiness."[152] Other living arrangements failed to provide this kind of training. "Living in hotels and boarding-houses, what develops most, interdependence or segregation? unselfishness or self-seeking? community of interest or isolation?" Willard queried her audience (86–87). "At home," she argued, the older members set their needs aside "for the little ones," while "at hotel and boarding house, all claim the best . . . and are a unit in complaints" (87). Within a home shared with one's nuclear family, or in some home shared with others in a family-like setting, these virtues would be most able to flourish. Even if one missed the most opportune time of childhood to develop the virtues most often celebrated in the opposite sex, changes in the roles of parents within the home would create opportunities to develop character in adulthood. Willard noted that when the home changes as "woman goes more into the world," the responsibilities "of the father and mother will be equalized to his great advantage in tenderness, and to hers in equipoise and continuity of thought" (87). Once again, the push was toward equal responsibilities for men and women, equal education, and living together in one shared sphere.

Although the best moral training would take place in the home, Willard recommended that when boys and girls must leave the home for school, that parents "send them out hand in hand to schools where men and women shall teach our youths and maidens in the larger home, . . . [the] co-educational colleges."[153] At the coeducational institutions Willard had championed early in her career, even as she called on them to reaffirm the comforts and teachings of home, "we are beginning to train those with each other who were formed for each other." Equality of education in the home and in the schools supported a world where men and women were "being set side by side in school, in church, in government, even as God sets male and female everywhere side by side throughout His realm of law, and has declared them one throughout His realm of grace."[154]

Willard believed that breaking down separate spheres and placing men and women side by side in every aspect of life both within and outside the home would encourage a rethinking of supposed sex differences. She declared "that the noblest way in which to think of men or women is to think first of their more enduring nature."[155] With a religious perspective analogous to the secular view presented by Elizabeth Cady Stanton in "The Solitude of Self," Willard encouraged her listeners to think about people first in terms of their spiritual nature, since "it is the most enduring, it is the most godlike." By reverencing that nature, which they held in common, Willard believed her listeners would treat one another more nobly. From this vantage point, it would become obvious that people ought to "legislate for a woman first of all as a being endowed with intellect, sensibilities, and will," and that "to educate her because she has these characteristics is the noblest way in which to give her an education." Like Stanton, Willard asserted that recognition of humanity's common nature provided a sure basis to just treatment. Unlike Stanton, Willard talked less about men's and women's ultimate isolation from one another and more about their interconnectedness. In this way she assuaged the fears raised in the minds of her audiences concerning the changes she advocated. She asserted that "the whole intention of the woman movement is not to declare the rights of women, or to usurp power, or to alienate men, but on the contrary it is to unite men and women on the most enduring plane; to study the harmonies between them; to prove that their interests are indissolubly linked; and it is a far more scientific, sensible, and Christian way of dealing with one half of the human race, because it is equally in the interest of the two halves" (715).

Willard argued that only conservatives supported separate spheres and the role specialization of the sexes. In response, she declared that "the progressive" answered, "'Let each add to those already won the virtues of the other.' Man has splendid qualities, courage, intellect, hardihood; who would not like to possess all these? What woman would not be the nobler and the greater if they were hers? And what man would not be grander, happier, more helpful to humanity, if he were more patient, gentle, tender, chaste?" (715). Like the children who must be raised to value bravery and gentleness simultaneously, so must men and women seek to develop within themselves the virtues associated with the opposite gender. In particular, Willard noted, women must learn "the greatness and sacredness of power" and acknowledge "that there is nothing noble in desiring not to posses it" (715–16). To increase women's comfort level with wielding power, Willard defined power as simply grasping one's right "to evolve the utmost mastership of one's self and the elements around one's self." This evolution, this self-development that was common to man and woman, became "the highest possible attainment" in Willard's millennial vision, when the self thus created adopted a purpose "to bless all other lives" (716).

Although Willard devoted most of her life to working in segregated women's organizations and focused on unleashing women's power upon the world, her reform vision clearly included a call to men to share the moral purposes seen throughout women's work for benevolence in the nineteenth century. Willard's discourse most often addressed women's new roles in the public sphere, but she was equally committed to the need to address men's new roles in the private as well as the public sphere.[156] All people were called to develop themselves fully and to work to make the world a better place. Within that vision there was no need or justification for maintaining the separate spheres doctrine.

Making the Whole World Homelike

Frances Willard made significant contributions to the reform movements of the Gilded Age. Addressing issues ranging from education to the eight-hour workday, from temperance to woman suffrage, from Christian socialism to the institution of marriage, she left her mark on the closing years of the nineteenth century. While some might view her octopus-like reform activities as dilettantish, she saw the movements as deeply interrelated.[157] One central bond that held together her reform mission was the home. Her explicit goal *to make the whole world HOMELIKE,"* was the driving force in her ideology and in her discourse.[158] Though some current interpretations of Willard critique the fact that she treated reforms such as woman suffrage as means rather than ends and so compromised her feminist stance by never establishing a natural right to the ballot, all of Willard's reform work can be seen as means rather than ends[159]; for her, the end of all reform is the creation of a homelike world. Other critics, such as Karlyn Kohrs Campbell, note Willard's emphasis on the home and argue that she reinforced elements of the true womanhood ideology and so assured audiences that "they could have it all: femininity and reform, successful female leadership which affirmed true womanhood and separate spheres."[160] By contrast, I have argued that Willard's use of the homelike world as the end goal of reform work was in many ways an effort to elide the division of the separate spheres for men and women. Even as Willard vehemently criticized the sexual double standard and argued that there ought to be one standard of moral behavior governing both men and women, so, too, she critiqued the dualistic notion of separate spheres. She may have granted differences between men and women, but she recognized the role of socialization in creating those differences and, more important, argued that those differences did not change the nature of men's and women's responsibilities to one another, to the community, to the nation, or to God.

With shared education, shared virtues, and shared purpose, Willard believed that men and women would evolve to a level where they would share responsibilities for the whole world rather than for half. Although Willard first gained the attention of her middle-class, Protestant, and female audience motivating them to become politically active through elaborating on the threat to the home as the traditional province of women, she was soon using the home to encourage much more radical reform. Moving from the commonly held Victorian notion that "the woman's view of home affairs is the needful complement of man's view," to the more radical position of complementary equality, holding that the same principle "applies equally to [the need for] woman's view of State affairs," Willard argued that the fully developed skills of both men and women were needed in all realms of life.[161] Only through combining the talents and powers of both sexes would humanity unleash the strength to remake the world.

Such unity presented a win-win situation because division into separate spheres oppressed women by limiting their economic and personal independence and threatened men because wherever man "goes alone, he falls into deterioration." Willard's goal was to change the world, to do the work of reform to create a better environment in which all people could thrive. Through a conglomeration of reforms the world "should become simply a larger home in which no human being should be any longer forgotten or forlorn."[162]

In these ways Willard's push for reform came full circle. The vision of a reformed society, including changes in governmental as well as educational institutions, was modeled on the ideal home. However, to make the ideal home a reality, that home itself had to undergo reforms that would increase the domestic involvement of men in the home while increasing opportunities for women to contribute more to the community outside the doors of the home. Willard was clearly optimistic about the possibilities. In response to protests from labor elements that the movement of women into the industrial workplace threatened men's job security, she declared,

> This is one of those catastrophes that are always expected but never occur. The true position is that men and women shall be perfectly free to apply their energies to the world of work, to professions, art, government, in accordance with their own will and pleasure, and shall together carry on the affairs of the home and train little ones. By these means man will gain incalculably in all those gentle qualities which have made woman the admiration of the world; and by sharing his outdoor pursuits in the genial garden that they make and till together, she will gain intellectual power.[163]

The common ground in the natures of men and women precluded any need to persist in separate spheres. Soon, she predicted, "the disabilities of women shall be reduced to their last analysis, and will be found to melt away into a single one: women have not been, and never will be, the fathers of the race." "But this unchanging condition," she continued, "is offset by the fact that men will never be the mothers of the race, so that the practical equality of the two integers in the unit of humanity will yet be demonstrated."[164]

Willard's reform vision, then, meant that from the newly re-formed home where separate spheres had dissolved, men and women could walk out into the world to reshape it as an extension of the home. The ideal home would be grounded in a new reverence both for individuality, in terms of development, and for community, in terms of putting the needs of others before the needs of the self. With that new ethic in place for both men and women, both the home within and the larger home without would approach the promise of the millennium.

Notes

1. Unidentified clipping in *Temperance and Prohibition Papers (Microfilm Edition)*, Woman's Christian Temperance Union National Headquarters Historical Files, Ohio Historical Society and Michigan Historical Collections, WCTU series, roll 41, frame 55.

2. These encomiums are expressed in a number of sources. See Elizabeth Shafer, "St. Frances and the Crusaders," *American History Illustrated* 11 (1976): 33; Anna Gordon, *The Beautiful Life of Frances E. Willard* (Chicago: Woman's Temperance Publishing Association, 1898), 314; George M. Hammell, ed., *The Passing of the Saloon* (Cincinnati: F. L. Rowe, 1908), viii, 154; and August Fehlandt, *Century of Drink Reform in the U.S.* (Cincinnati: Dennings and Graham, 1904), 246.

3. *Weekly Censor*, 5 May 1887, in WCTU series, roll 39, frame 55.

4. *Weekly Censor*, 13 January 1887, in WCTU series, roll 36, frame 82.

5. *Meridian (Mississippi) News*, 17 April 1889.

6. Frances Willard, *Address before the Second Biennial Convention of the World's Woman's Christian Temperance Union, and the Twentieth Annual Convention of the National Woman's Christian Temperance Union* (Chicago: Woman's Temperance Publishing Association, 1893), 2.

7. For excellent biographical material, see Ruth Bordin, *Frances Willard* (Chapel Hill: University of North Carolina Press, 1986); and Carolyn DeSwarte Gifford, "Frances E. Willard," in *Women Building Chicago, 1790–1990: A Biographical Dictionary*, ed. Rima Lunin Schultz and Adele Hast (Bloomington: Indiana University Press, 2001), 969–74.

8. Frances Willard, *Nineteen Beautiful Years* (New York: Harper and Brothers, 1864); Frances Willard, *A Great Mother* (Chicago: Woman's Christian Temperance Publishing Association, 1894); Frances Willard, *Woman and Temperance* (Hartford, Conn.: Park, 1883); Frances Willard, *Glimpses of Fifty Years: The Autobiography of an American Woman* (Chicago: Woman's Christian Temperance Publishing Association, 1889); Frances Willard, *How to Win: A Book for Girls* (New York: Funk and Wagnalls, 1886); Frances Willard, Helen Winslow, and Sallie White, eds., *Occupations for Women* (New York: Success, 1897); Frances Willard, *A Wheel within a Wheel: How I Learned to Ride the Bicycle* (New York: F. H. Berell, 1895). For sales information, see Bordin, *Frances Willard*, 116. For a more complete list of Willard's publications, see Amy Rose Slagell, "A Good Woman Speaking Well: The Oratory of Frances E. Willard" (Ph.D. diss., University of Wisconsin, 1992), 688–94.

9. Frances Willard, *Should Women Vote?* (Chicago: Ruby Gilbert, n.d.); Frances Willard, *Temperance and the Labor Question* (Chicago: Ruby Gilbert, n.d.); Frances Willard, "Man in the Home," *Chautauquan* (February 1887): 279–81; Frances Willard, "Women in Journalism," *Chautauquan* (July 1886): 576–79.

10. *Leavenworth (Kansas) Daily Press*, 16 May 1880, in WCTU series, roll 32, frame 108.

11. *Chillicothe (Ohio) Daily News*, 24 October 1890.

12. *Muscatine (Iowa) Daily Journal*, 2 May 1890.

13. Unidentified clipping in WCTU series, roll 33, frame 166.

14. *Chicago Evening Journal*, 22 March 1871, in WCTU series, roll 30, frame 79.

15. The two standard biographies are Mary Earhart, *Frances Willard* (Chicago: University of Chicago Press, 1944); and Bordin, *Frances Willard*. Other works, such as Barbara Epstein, *The Politics of Domesticity* (Middletown, Conn.: Wesleyan University Press, 1981), and Carol Mattingly, *Well-Tempered Women* (Carbondale: Southern Illinois University Press, 1998), offer engaging interpretations of Willard's contributions.

16. Patricia Kennedy and Gloria O'Shields, eds., *We Shall Be Heard* (Dubuque, Iowa: Kendall/Hunt, 1983), 146–54; Karlyn Kohrs Campbell, ed., *Man Cannot Speak for Her*, vol. 2 (New York: Praeger, 1989), 317–40; Richard Leeman, *"Do Everything" Reform: The Oratory of Frances E. Willard* (New York: Greenwood, 1992), 111–19, 121–36, 159–71; Judith Anderson, ed., *Out-Spoken Women: Speeches by American Women Reformers, 1635–1935* (Dubuque, Iowa: Kendall/Hunt, 1983), 221–26; James Andrews and David Zarefsky, eds., *American Voices: Significant Speeches in American History, 1640–1945* (New York: Longman, 1989), 225–33; Carolyn De Swarte Gifford and Amy Slagell, eds., *"Let Something Good Be Said": Speeches and Writings of Frances E. Willard* (Urbana: University of Illinois Press, 2007).

17. Leeman, *"Do Everything"*; Bonnie Dow, "Frances E. Willard: Reinventor of 'True Womanhood,'" in *Women Public Speakers in the United States, 1800–1925*, ed. Karlyn Kohrs Campbell (Westport, Conn.: Greenwood Press, 1993), 476–90; Bonnie Dow, "The 'Womanhood' Rationale in the Woman Suffrage Rhetoric of Frances E. Willard," *Southern Communication Journal* 56 (1991): 298–307; Slagell, "Good Woman"; James Kimble, "Frances Willard as Protector of the Home," in

Lives of Their Own: Rhetorical Dimensions of Autobiographies of Women Activists, ed. Martha Watson (Columbia: University of South Carolina Press, 1999), 47–62; Campbell, *Man Cannot Speak for Her*, vol. 2, 121–32; Amy R. Slagell, "The Rhetorical Structure of Frances E. Willard's Campaign for Woman Suffrage, 1876–1896," *Rhetoric and Public Address* 4 (2001): 1–23. Leeman, Slagell, and Kimble draw the most enthusiastic conclusions concerning Willard's rhetorical success, while Campbell and Dow are restrained. See also William O'Neill, *Everyone Was Brave: A History of Feminism in America* (Chicago: Quadrangle Books, 1969), 34–35, whose devastating analysis of social feminism undergirds Campbell's argument.

18. Dow, "'Womanhood,'" 305; Campbell, *Man Cannot Speak for Her*, vol. 1, 129.

19. Nancy Cott, "What's in a Name? The Limits of 'Social Feminism'; or Expanding the Vocabulary of Women's History," *Journal of American History* 76 (1989): 823.

20. Frances Willard, "The Woman's Cause Is Man's," *Arena* 5 (1892): 724.

21. Frances Willard, 3 December 1869, in Carolyn DeSwarte Gifford, *Writing Out My Heart: Selections from the Journal of Frances E. Willard, 1855–1896* (Urbana: University of Illinois Press, 1995), 323.

22. *Galena (Illinois) Evening Gazette*, undated clipping, in WCTU series, roll 30, frame 143.

23. *Christian Advocate*, 5 March 1896, in WCTU series, roll 43, frame 98.

24. *Christian Advocate*, 6 April 1887, in WCTU series, roll 39, frame 103.

25. *Calais (Maine) Times*, 23 June 1891, in WCTU series, roll 38, frame 49.

26. *Life*, 18 February 1893, in WCTU series, roll 40, frame 161.

27. *Presbyterian Messenger*, 6 April 1894, clipping in WCTU series, roll 42, frame 377.

28. Undated clipping in WCTU series, roll 42, frame 377.

29. Barbara Welter, "The Cult of True Womanhood," *American Quarterly* 18 (Summer 1966): 151–74.

30. See Jeanne Boydston, Mary Kelley, and Anne Margolis, *The Limits of Sisterhood: The Beecher Sisters on Women's Rights and Woman's Sphere* (Chapel Hill: University of North Carolina Press, 1988). This volume carefully traces the divergent positions taken by Catherine Beecher, Harriet Beecher Stowe, and Isabella Beecher Hooker. All could be called proponents of women's domesticity, yet their positions range from conservative to radical when examined closely.

31. For a discussion of this contest, see Willard, *Glimpses*, 500.

32. Frances Willard, "On the Embellishment of a Country Home," in *Transactions of the Illinois State Agricultural Society*, ed. S. Francis (Springfield, Ill.: Baihache and Baker, 1859), 471.

33. The term "radical" is, of course, relative. While I argue that Willard ought to be read as much more radical than she is typically, her goals and tactics are certainly evolutionary rather than radically revolutionary. As will be made clear, she wants to reform much of middle-class white culture, but she does not advocate its overthrow. She is, then, properly viewed as a less radical social reformer than figures such as Victoria Woodhull or even Ernestine Rose. For a discussion of Willard at her most radical(critiquing capitalism and proposing serious economic reform)see Gifford and Slagell, eds., *"Let Something Good Be Said,"* xxxiv–xlv, 192–206, and 217–230.

34. Willard, *Glimpses*, 401; Bordin, *Frances Willard*, 100.

35. Willard, *Glimpses*, 351.

36. Frances Willard, *Woman and Temperance* (1883; reprint, Chicago: Woman's Temperance Publishing Association, 1897), 365.

37. Willard, "Everybody's War." A stenographic report of Willard's speech is available at the Willard Memorial Library, WCTU Headquarters, Evanston, Ill. The text is also available in Slagell, "Good Woman," 160–74, and in Leeman, *"Do Everything,"* 111–20. Leeman's critique of this as a weak speech is on 24–32.

38. Frances Willard, "Home Protection Address," in WCTU series, roll 30, frames 269–70. The text in this unidentified scrapbook clipping is marked "New Jersey, 1876"; see also "Home Protection," rpt. in Slagell, "Good Woman," 184–97; the quote is from Slagell, "Good Woman," 197. Versions of nearly identical "Home Protection" addresses can also be found in Willard, *Woman and Temperance*, 452–59; and Anna Gordon, *The Beautiful Life of Frances E. Willard* (Chicago: Woman's Temperance Publishing Association, 1898), 116–25. The same line is found in "Address before the House Judiciary Committee," 1878, in WCTU series, roll 30, frame 406, rpt. in Slagell, "Good Woman," 235.

39. Bordin, *Frances Willard*, 7.

40. Willard, "Home Protection," rpt. in Slagell, "Good Woman," 190.

41. Willard, "Address to the Committee on Resolutions of the Republican National Convention," 4 June 1884, in the *Patriot*, 26 June 1884, rpt. in Slagell, "Good Woman," 344.

42. Frances Willard, "Personal Liberty," 11 June 1882, rpt. in Slagell, "Good Woman," 322.

43. Frances Willard, "Address to the Michigan State WCTU," 10 June 1886, in WCTU series, roll 36, frame 207, rpt. in Slagell, "Good Woman," 379.

44. Suzanne M. Marilley, "Frances Willard and the Feminism of Fear," *Feminist Studies* 19 (1993): 123–46.

45. Willard, "Address to the Michigan State WCTU," rpt. in Slagell, "Good Woman," 379–80.

46. For a history of the crusade, see Jack Blocker, *American Temperance Movements: Cycles of Reform* (Boston: Twayne, 1989); and Annie Wittenmyer, *History of the Women's Temperance Crusade* (Philadelphia: Office of the Christian Woman, 1878).

47. Willard, "Home Protection," rpt. in Slagell, "Good Woman," 191.

48. Frances Willard, "Presidential Address," in *Minutes*, 1994, 123–124, rpt. in Gifford and Slagell, "Let Something Good be Said," 200–201.

49. Willard, interview, in *Great Thoughts* (February 1893), 343, in WCTU series, roll 40, frame 156. See also Slagell, "Willard's Campaign for Woman Suffrage."

50. Frances Willard, "Social Purity: The Latest and Greatest Crusade," 22 April 1886, *Voice Extra*, in WCTU series, roll 35, frames 161–66, rpt. in Slagell, "Good Woman," 353–72, quote is from Slagell, "Good Woman," 361. See also Willard, "Woman's Cause," 717–24, where she expresses anger about the unequal treatment of unwed mothers.

51. For further discussion of related issues, see Carole Patemen, *The Sexual Contract* (Palo Alto, Calif.: Stanford University Press, 1988); and Marilley, "Feminism of Fear," who concludes that Willard did not "condemn the sexual contract; she aimed to salvage it" (139).

52. Willard, "Woman and Philanthropy," 9 May 1887, *Christian Union* 35, no. 25, rpt. in Slagell, "Good Woman," 395–406. Page references to the version in Slagell, "Good Woman," are given in the text.

53. Willard, 7 August 1855. Willard's journals are housed in the Willard Memorial Library at the national WCTU Headquarters in Evanston, Ill. A complete transcription of the journals prepared by Carolyn De Swarte Gifford is also available.

54. Mary Hill Willard's temperance scrapbooks are housed in the Willard Memorial Library at WCTU Headquarters in Evanston, Ill. They offer an invaluable collection of temperance materials, most of them related to the work of her daughter and of the WCTU.

55. Frances Willard, "Address before the Senate Committee on Woman Suffrage," in *Miscellaneous Documents of the Senate of the United States*, 1st session, 50th Congress, II, document no. 114 (Washington, D.C.: Government Printing Office, 1888), 19–21, rpt. in Slagell, "Good Woman," 445–50; quote is from Slagell, "Good Woman," 448, emphasis added. Additional page references from the Slagell version are given in the text.

56. Frances Willard, "Home Protection," in *The Home Protection Manual* (Broadway, N.Y.: Independent Office, 1879). The pamphlet contains a slightly revised version of the text published in the *Independent* on 10 July 1879. Quotes are from the text in Slagell, "Good Woman," 252, 262.

57. "Female Suffrage," *Ladies Repository* 27 (1867): 504–6.

58. *Democrat*, 12 February 1882, in WCTU series, roll 32, frame 467.

59. *Evanston (Illinois) Index*, 16 July 1881, in WCTU series, roll 30, frame 289.

60. Frances Willard, *Hints and Helps in Our Temperance Work* (New York: National Temperance Society and Publication House, 1875), 64.

61. Willard, *Woman and Temperance*, 624.

62. Willard, "Presidential Address," in *Minutes*, 1881, lxxviii.

63. "Home Protection," rpt. in Slagell, "Good Woman," 257.

64. Willard, "Presidential Address," in *Minutes*, 1891, 162.

65. Willard, "Presidential Address," in *Minutes*, 1890, 96–97.

66. Kimble, "Frances Willard as Protector of the Home."

67. Frances Willard, "Address at the Colorado State WCTU Convention," 10 August 1883, in the *Denver Daily News*, 11 August 1883, in WCTU series, roll 33, frame 147, rpt. in Slagell, "Good Woman," 335–40. Quotes are from the text in Slagell, "Good Woman," 338.

68. Willard, "Presidential Address," in *Minutes*, 1888, 48.

69. Frances Willard, "The Dawn of Woman's Day," 4 October 1888, in *Our Day* 2 (November 1888): 345–60, rpt. in Slagell, "Good Woman," 466–83. Quote is from the text in Slagell, "Good Woman," 482.

70. Campbell, *Man Cannot Speak for Her*, vol. 1, 123.

71. Ibid., vol. 1, 129.

72. *Saint Peter (Minnesota) Tribune*, 24 November 1886, in WCTU series, roll 35, frame 386.

73. Willard, "Presidential Address," in *Minutes*, 1887, 72.

74. Willard, "Presidential Address," in *Minutes*, 1886, 70.

75. Willard, "Presidential Address," in *Minutes*, 1890, 25.

76. Frances Willard, "Presidential Address," in *Minutes*, 1887, 71.

77. Frances Willard, "On the Embellishment of a Country Home."

78. Kimble, "Frances Willard as Protector of the Home."

79. Frances Willard, "Presidential Address" (1884) in *Minutes*, 1885, 50.

80. Frances Willard, "A New Departure for Woman's Higher Education," 17 October 1873, in *Papers and Letters Presented at the First Woman's Congress of the Association for the Advancement of Women* (New York: Mrs. Wm. Ballard, 1874), 94–99, rpt. in Slagell, "Good Woman," 147–59. Though Willard was unable to present the speech herself, it was published in the proceedings of the congress. Quotes that follow are from Slagell, "Good Woman," with page references given in the text.

81. Bordin, *Frances Willard*, 62. Evidence that these labels were misapplied can be seen in the next conflict between Willard and Fowler. At the 1888 Methodist General Conference, Fowler was among the Methodist leaders who prevented Willard and the four other women who were elected from their conferences from being seated as lay delegates.

82. Willard, "Woman and Philanthropy," rpt. in Slagell, "Good Woman," 405.

83. Willard, "Address to President Garfield," 8 March 1881, in Willard, *Woman and Temperance*, 281.

84. Willard, "Presidential Address," in *Minutes*, 1885, 93.

85. Willard, "Address to the Michigan State WCTU," rpt. in Slagell, "Good Woman," 382. Quotes that follow are from Slagell, "Good Woman," with page references given in the text. See also Willard, "Presidential Address," in *Minutes*, 1888, 48.

86. Frances Willard, "Presidential Address," in *Minutes*, 1884, 51.

87. Willard, "Presidential Address," in *Minutes*, 1887, 72, emphasis added.

88. Willard, "Woman's Cause," 718.

89. Willard, "Presidential Address," in *Minutes*, 1883, 55.

90. Frances Willard, *Do Everything: A Handbook for the World's White Ribboners* (Chicago: Woman's Temperance Publishing Association, 1895) 80, 146.

91. *Evanston (Illinois) Index*, 16 July 1881, in WCTU series, roll 30, frame 289.

92. *Monmouth (New Jersey) Democrat*, 10 February 1887.

93. *Our Brother in Red*, 19 March 1896, in WCTU series, roll 43, frame 113.

94. Qtd. in Gordon, *Beautiful Life*, 414.

95. Willard, *Woman and Temperance*, 622.

96. Cumnock to Anna Gordon, 2 April 1898, in WCTU series, roll 27, frame 53. Exactly when Willard's training took place is not clear from this letter or from any other clues. My guess is that it was sometime in 1877 or in 1878. Cumnock also commented on Willard's persistence in overcoming a "naturally frail body." At times it seemed she would never "acquire the physical vigor essential to successful public speaking." One day when she was particularly discouraged, she sighed, "Oh, these abominable muscles." Her humorous reference "to the abdominal muscles," Cumnock wrote, remained "a current joke in our school."

97. Robert M. Cumnock, ed., *Choice Readings for Public and Private Entertaining*, rev. ed. (Chicago: A. C. McClurg, 1898), 63, 92.

98. Willard, "Address to the Michigan State WCTU," rpt. in Slagell, "Good Woman," 382. Willard is quoting from an unknown source here.

99. Frances Willard, "White Life for Two," 1 August 1891, in *Chautauqua Assembly Herald*, 3 August 1891, in WCTU series, roll 31, frame 533, rpt. in Slagell, "Good Woman," 582; see John B. Finch, "Eulogy to John Finch," 30 November 1887, rpt. in Slagell, "Good Woman," 430–31; and Willard, "Woman's Cause," 718.

100. Willard, "Presidential Address," in *Minutes*, 1884, 51.

101. In Frances Willard, *Report of the International Council of Women* (Washington, D.C.: Rufus Darby, 1888) 286–89, rpt. in Slagell, "Good Woman," 441.

102. Willard, "Presidential Address," in *Minutes*, 1887, 71–72, 86.

103. Willard, "New Departure," rpt. in Slagell, "Good Woman," 158.

104. See, for example, Campbell, *Man Cannot Speak for Her*, vol. 1, ix–xxviii; Diane Helene Miller, "From One Voice a Chorus: Elizabeth Cady Stanton's 1860 Address to the New York State Legislature," *Women's Studies in Communication* 22 (Fall 1999): 152–89; Kristen Vonnegut, "Listening for Women's Voices," *Communication Education* 41 (January 1992): 26–39; Barbara Biesecker, "Coming to Terms with Recent Attempts to Write Women into the History of Rhetoric," *Philosophy and Rhetoric* 25 (1992): 140–61; and Rita Felski, *Beyond Feminist Aesthetics: Feminist Literature and Social Change* (Cambridge, Mass.: Harvard University Press, 1989).

105. Willard, "Presidential Address," in *Minutes*, 1884, 51.

106. Willard, "Woman's Cause," 716.

107. Campbell, *Man Cannot Speak for Her*, vol. 1, 131.

108. Epstein, *Politics of Domesticity*, is the only work that gives extended attention to this issue. She reads Willard's reform of the home as a conservative effort to control male sexuality.

109. Slagell, "Good Woman," 125–26. The entire speech is available in Slagell, "Good Woman," 128–41; the page references in the text refer to this version. The speech can also be seen in Willard, *Glimpses*, 576–89.

110. Willard, "Woman's Cause," 717.

111. Willard, "Presidential Address," in *Minutes*, 1886, 71.

112. Frances Willard, "White Cross in Education," 9 July 1890, in *National Education Association Journal of Proceedings and Addresses* (Topeka, Kans.: Clifford Baker, Kansas Publishing House, 1898), 159–78, rpt. in Slagell, "Good Woman," 502–28; quotes are from Slagell, "Good Woman," 510.

113. Frances Willard, "Social Purity: The Latest and Greatest Crusade," in *Voice Extra* (June 1886), in WCTU series, roll 35, frames 161–66, rpt. in Slagell, "Good Woman," 353–72; quotes are from Slagell, "Good Woman," 362–63. For one of the most comprehensive discussions of this history, see Gerda Lerner, *The Creation of Patriarchy* (New York: Oxford University Press, 1986).

114. Willard, *How to Win*, 63–64.

115. Willard, "Presidential Address," in *Minutes*, 1880, 15.

116. Willard, "White Cross," rpt. in Slagell, "Good Woman," 508.

117. Willard, "Presidential Address," in *Minutes*, 1887, 89.

118. Frances Willard, "Women and Organization," 23 February 1891, in *Transactions of the National Council of Women of the United States* (Philadelphia: J. B. Lippencott, 1891), 23–57, rpt. in Slagell, "Good Woman," 529–74; quotes are from Slagell, "Good Woman," 563–64.

119. Willard, "White Cross," rpt. in Slagell, "Good Woman," 511.

120. Willard, "New Departure," rpt. in Slagell, "Good Woman," 153. For more on the "stereoscopic view" see Gifford and Slagell, eds. "Let Something Good Be Said," xxxiv,49, 55, 69.

121. See, for example, Willard, "Presidential Address," in *Minutes*, 1883, 67. For an analysis of the poem, see James Kincaid, *Tennyson's Major Poems* (New Haven, Conn.: Yale University Press, 1975), chapter 4.

122. Willard, "White Cross," rpt. in Slagell, "Good Woman," 503.

123. Frances Willard, "Man in the Home," *Chautauquan* 7 (1887): 279–81.

124. Willard, "Presidential Address," in *Minutes*, 1888, 56.

125. Willard, "White Cross," rpt. in Slagell, "Good Woman," 511.

126. Willard, "Presidential Address," in *Minutes*, 1886, 78.

127. Willard, "Woman and Organization," rpt. in Slagell, "Good Woman," 550.

128. Willard, "Presidential Address," in *Minutes*, 1890, 59, 76.

129. Willard, *How to Win*, 59.

130. Ibid., 39. Further page references are given in the text.

131. Willard, "Social Purity," rpt. in Slagell, "Good Woman," 360.

132. Willard, "Presidential Address," in *Minutes*, 1889, 121, 123. A similar notion was propagated in the early 1870s by Elizabeth Cady Stanton in a series of speeches titled "For Women Only": "The new Gospel of fewer children and a healthy, happy maternity is gladly received," she wrote to her friend Martha Coffin Wright. See Carol DeBois, *Woman Suffrage Women's Rights* (New York: New York University Press, 1998), 103.

133. Willard, "Presidential Address," in *Minutes*, 1885, 73.

134. Willard, "Man in the Home," 281.

135. Willard, *Glimpses*, 110.

136. See Arlie Hochschild, with Anne Machung, *The Second Shift: Working Parents and the Revolution at Home* (New York: Viking, 1989).

137. Willard, "Presidential Address," in *Minutes*, 1886, 78.

138. Willard, "Woman and Organization," rpt. in Slagell, "Good Woman," 553.

139. Willard, "Presidential Address," in *Minutes*, 1890, 77.

140. Willard, "Presidential Address," in *Minutes*, 1886, 86–87.

141. Frances Willard, "Dawn of Woman's Day," in *Our Day* 2 (November 1888), 345–60, rpt. in Slagell, "Good Woman," 466–83. Later page references to the text in Slagell, "Good Woman," are given in the text.

142. Willard, *How to Win*, 125.

143. Willard, "Presidential Address," in *Minutes*, 1887, 90.

144. Willard, "Presidential Address," in *Minutes*, 1888, 56.

145. Willard, "Presidential Address," in *Minutes*, 1883, 48.

146. See Aileen Kraditor, *The Ideas of the Woman Suffrage Movement* (1965; reprint, New York: Norton, 1981), esp. chapter 2.

147. Willard, "Presidential Address," in *Minutes*, 1883, 51.

148. Frances Willard, "Address before the World's WCTU," 19 June 1895, in *Address by Frances E. Willard President of the World's Woman's Christian Temperance Union at its Third Biennial Convention* (London: White Ribbon, 1895), 27.

149. Willard, "Presidential Address," in *Minutes*, 1888, 57; similar passages about doll play can be found in Willard, "White Cross," rpt. in Slagell, "Good Woman," 524.

150. Willard, *How to Win*, 27–28. Subsequent page references are given in the text.

151. Frances Willard, "Presidential Address," in *Minutes*, 1893, 87.

152. Willard, "Presidential Address," in *Minutes*, 1887, 86. Later page references to this speech are given in the text.

153. Willard, "Address at the World's WCTU," 1895, 27.

154. Willard, "White Cross," rpt. in Slagell, "Good Woman," 504.

155. Willard, "Woman's Cause," 715. Page references for quotes that follow from this article are given in the text. For an excellent discussion of the ideas and implications of this essay, see Carolyn DeSwarte Gifford, "'The Woman's Cause Is Man's'? Frances Willard and the Social Gospel," in *Gender and the Social Gospel*, ed. Wendy Deichmann Edwards and Carolyn DeSwarte Gifford (Urbana: University of Illinois Press, 2003).

156. See, for example, Willard, "Man in the Home"; and Frances Willard, "The Coming Brotherhood," *Arena* 6 (1892): 323.

157. In her introduction to Willard's autobiography, Hannah Whitall Smith refers to Willard as "my beloved Octopus." Willard, *Glimpses*, x.

158. Willard, "Presidential Address," in *Minutes*, 1884, 50.

159. Dow, "Frances E. Willard," 483.

160. Campbell, *Man Cannot Speak for Her*, vol. 1, 130.

161. Willard, "Presidential Address," in *Minutes*, 1886, 70.

162. Willard, "Woman's Cause," 718.

163. Willard, "Address at the World's WCTU," 1895, 12.

164. Ibid., 13.

"Lifting as We Climb": Race, Gender, and Class in the Rhetoric of Mary Church Terrell

Martha S. Watson

7

This is the story of a colored woman living in a white world. It cannot possibly be like a story written by a white woman. A white woman has only one handicap to overcome—that of sex. I have two—both sex and race. I belong to the only group in this country which has two such huge obstacles to surmount.

—Mary Church Terrell, *A Colored Woman in a White World*

Mary Church Terrell's autobiography, *A Colored Woman in a White World* (1940), was, in one reviewer's opinion, "a notable story of a notable life."[1] The publishers Church Terrell approached, however, did not share this perspective. They found the book too long, or they questioned its potential audience. When Church Terrell approached Carrie Chapman Catt for an endorsement for its publication, Chapman Catt observed the "difficulty in getting feminist books published."[2]

Church Terrell's difficulty in securing a publisher is, in a sense, a suitable representative anecdote for her life. As her book reveals, she constantly confronted barriers that reflected the intersection of prejudices based on race and gender. Her autobiography highlights her struggles as a middle-class African American woman in Jim Crow America. In her advocacy, she drew on her personal experiences, along with those of friends, to construct an indictment of racial and gender prejudices in a society allegedly committed to egalitarian, open democracy.

Church Terrell was not alone in exploring the intersection of racial and gender prejudices. Another contemporary forceful African American female advocate, Ida B. Wells, highlighted the horrors of lynching for African American men, particularly those on the lower rungs of the socioeconomic ladder, refuting the arguments of its supporters with an array of powerful examples drawn usually from newspapers.

Church Terrell's focus was on the middle class; she explored the daily frustrations and humiliations of middle-class African Americans, often women, who, whatever their accomplishments and background, were often second-class citizens. As Karlyn Kohrs Campbell suggests, both women explored the intersections of race, gender, and class on African Americans in early-twentieth-century America.[3] However, their emphases were markedly different. Although Wells in her antilynching advocacy suggested that socioeconomic class did not deter the lynch mobs, Church Terrell was almost entirely concerned with middle-class African Americans and the obstacles they confronted. In contrast to Wells, Church Terrell sometimes highlighted class cleavages in her enthusiasm for securing more equitable treatment for the upper-class African Americans who were her peers.

This essay examines Mary Church Terrell's discourse around the issues of gender, class, and race. In part, I argue that her enthusiasm for her own social class sometimes led her to accede to the stereotypes of her race that were advanced by apologists in her era. Further, I contend that in seeking to build identification with her middle-class audiences, especially those composed mostly of Caucasians, Church Terrell disparaged some members of her own race in ways that lent support to socially sanctioned discriminatory practices. To establish this thesis, I first briefly trace her biography before summarizing her philosophical views on how to advance her race. Then I analyze three texts by Church Terrell that highlight her rhetorical strategies and skills in contesting the obstacles of gender, race, and class.

A Colored Woman in a White World

Born in 1863 in Memphis, Tennessee, Mary Church was the child of a former slave, who later became one of the first African American millionaires in the South.[4] Realizing the limitations of the schools in that area, her parents sent her north to school when she was about six years old, but not before she had firsthand experiences of racism. In particular, she recalls a train trip with her father when he, like many middle-class African Americans of the time, declined to go to the car designated for them. When he left her to go to the smoking car, a conductor grabbed her and asked, "Whose little nigger is this?" Upon his return, her father quickly confronted the conductor; as she remembered, a scene ensued that "no one who saw it could ever forget." Her father would not discuss the incident; her mother simply said that "sometimes conductors on railroad trains were unkind and treated good little girls very badly." For her part, in adulthood, Church Terrell concluded: "Seeing their children touched and seared and wounded by race prejudice is one of the heaviest crosses which colored women have to bear."[5]

Living happily with a family in Yellow Springs, Ohio, Church Terrell attended a model school, which she later described as the "forerunner of the kindergarten in the United States."[6] When she transferred to the public schools, Church Terrell came to a startling realization:

> While we were reciting our history lesson one day, it suddenly occurred to me that I, myself, was descended from the very slaves whom the Emancipation Proclamation set free. I was stunned. I felt humiliated and disgraced. When I had read or heard about the Union army and the Rebel forces, I had never thought about my connection with slavery at all. But now I knew I belonged to a group of people who had been brutalized, degraded, and sold like animals. This was a rude and terrible shock indeed. "Here you are," said a voice ironically, "measuring arms with these white children whose ancestors have always been free. What audacity." I was covered with confusion and shame at the thought,

and my humiliation was painful indeed. When I recovered my composure, I resolved that so far as this descendant of slaves was concerned, she would show those white girls and boys whose forefathers had always been free that she was their equal in every respect. At that time I was the only colored girl in the class, and I felt I must hold high the banner of my race.[7]

Other experiences exacerbated this sense of her difference and of the devaluing of her race by society. Once she was offered a role in a school play which she declined since it would have required her to "take the part of a servant who made a monkey of himself and murdered the king's English." On another occasion, when she attempted to join the fun of a group of girls who were primping and admiring their "wonderful tresses" and "rosebud" mouths, one compatriot observed, "You've got a pretty black face," and pointed at her derisively.[8] These and other experiences cemented Church Terrell's determination to be a credit to her race.

Despite these hurtful events, her life at the model school and in the public schools of Yellow Springs was largely happy and fruitful. During this period, she discovered her talent for public speaking, happily memorizing and reciting poems. Also, she realized that she had received a far better education there than had she remained in the South. She later reflected: "I owe much to the instruction given me during the two years in the model school and the two years I attended the public schools of the little village. My training there was excellent and I was started on the right track."[9]

Her enthusiasm for learning and her considerable academic ability led her to enroll in Oberlin College, a place noted for its openness and tolerance. There she defied the advice of her friends and enrolled in the "gentleman's course" of study that had a classical focus. Her friends tried to dissuade her, asking sarcastically: "Where will you find a colored man who has studied Greek?"[10] Accustomed to such unthinking prejudice, Church Terrell excelled at the more demanding course of study. But even there she confronted the racism prevalent in society of the time. When Matthew Arnold was a guest of the school, Church Terrell's instructor asked her to read aloud and then translate a Greek passage. Later Arnold commended her reading. When the instructor revealed that she was of African descent, "Arnold expressed the greatest surprise imaginable, because, he said, he thought that the tongue of the African was so thick he could not be taught to pronounce the Greek correctly."[11]

Although her life at Oberlin was relatively free of racial prejudice, she confronted the issue in other places. While visiting her mother in New York, she was denied the summer employment she had sought and for which she was well qualified when the woman learned she was African American. This was, Church Terrell recalled, her "first bitter experience of inability to secure employment on account of her race." Despite these incidents, Church Terrell had a remarkably successful career at Oberlin. She received numerous honors and invitations, tried all sorts of activities, and concluded years later: "I do not see how any student could have enjoyed the activities of college life more than I did."[12]

After graduation, despite her desire to find a way to help her race, she agreed to her father's request and returned to Memphis to keep house for him. When he remarried a year later, she took at job at Wilberforce University, over his stern disapproval. In his eyes, women of means did not work. Taking the job at Wilberforce produced a painful breach with her father, but Church Terrell did not regret making a commitment to use her skills to help others. For two years at Wilberforce she was incredibly busy, teaching five diverse classes, serving as secretary to the faculty, and playing the organ at her church. Although she had few idle moments at Wilberforce, she found the experience gratifying. But an opportunity for a teaching job in Washington, D.C., lured her there, although she was tempted by an offer to tour Europe with a wealthy friend.[13]

The next summer Church Terrell had her opportunity to see Europe with her father, who had become reconciled to his daughter's ambitions. After three wonderful months, she decided to stay to study French. She spent a year in Lausanne, Switzerland, before moving on to Germany to study German. Throughout her travels, she enjoyed relative freedom from prejudice, in striking contrast to her life in the United States. She was tempted to remain in Europe, but her desire to serve her race prevailed. As she recalled, "I knew I would be much happier trying to promote the welfare of my race in my native land, working under certain hard conditions, than I would be living in a foreign land and where I would enjoy freedom from prejudice, but where I would make no effort to do the work which I then believed it was my duty to do. I doubted that I could respect myself if I shirked my responsibility and was recreant to my trust."[14]

She returned to teaching in Washington, perhaps because of the urgings of a fellow teacher, Robert Terrell. The next year she received an offer to become registrar at Oberlin, which would have been a first for her race. Although she was tempted by the opportunity and saw the significance it might have for others, she opted to remain in Washington to marry Terrell. Since marriage disqualified her from continuing to teach, she assumed the role of wife of a young man with a rapidly advancing career. Eager to have a child, she endured the loss of three babies in five years. These losses came near the time her friend, Thomas Moss, was lynched. Moss, who had been a childhood friend, was lynched in Memphis because his store posed competition for one owned by a white man across the street.[15] Together, these events put her into a deep depression. But during this period she also met Frederick Douglass, whose son was to influence her to consider using her talents for public advocacy. According to Church Terrell's account, her mother's bragging about her daughter's jelly-making skills to Lewis Douglass produced an unexpected response: rather than devoting herself to housewifery, he urged Church Terrell to use her talents to advance her race.[16]

Church Terrell followed his advice. She served six years on the Board of Education of the District of Columbia, became active in the woman suffrage movement, and became involved with woman's club work. In 1896 she was elected the first president of the National Association of Colored Women(NACW), an organization formed by the merging of two other groups. Her ambitious agenda for the NACW included both mothers' clubs to enhance women's child-rearing skills and kindergartens to better prepare young children.[17] Reflecting her long-standing commitment to the advancement of African Americans, Church Terrell proposed the motto for the club, which it adopted: "Lifting as We Climb."[18]

Throughout her life, Church Terrell lent her voice to various causes and advocated to diverse audiences. For example, she joined the campaign against lynching, responding strongly to Thomas Nelson Page's defense of the practice published in such journals as the *North American Review* and *McClure's*.[19] To members of the NACW, she urged the necessity for outreach to those at the bottom of the socioeconomic ladder, insisting that the fate of the race depended on lifting all African Americans.[20] She sought to establish day-care centers and kindergartens with an eye to helping the young get the foundation necessary for their future success. A strong proponent of woman suffrage, she was an ardent advocate for the passage of the Nineteenth Amendment.

In her later years, Church Terrell joined demonstrations to force integration of stores and restaurants in Washington, D.C.[21] The final chapter of Church Terrell's autobiography bore the title "Carrying On." Published when she was seventy-seven, the final chapter indicates her determination to continue in her activities in behalf of her race. She persisted in her efforts to secure an antilynching law and worked to secure a memorial in Washington, D.C., to "give tangible evidence of their [African Americans'] contributions to the growth and prosperity of this country as well as furnish proof of the marvelous progress which they have made themselves."[22] Even in these latter years, she eschewed her family's advice to slow down, instead taking on new causes and issues that attracted her attention. She spoke out on issues as diverse as housing conditions for poor African Americans and intermarriage. She spoke frequently in schools and colleges, always urging her listeners to be proud of their heritage and to work to advance their race.

Despite her prominence and her many accomplishments, Church Terrell continued to confront the obstacles and barriers that she had long striven to demolish. For example, she yearned to belong to a particular literary society where she "would have derived great benefit from the discussions in which these women have engaged and from the methods of doing their work which they have used." But she lacked one key qualification: as she explained, "I am not white."[23] Proud of her own accomplishments and those of her race, Church Terrell was keenly aware of the challenges African Americans continued to confront in this country. Her struggles were, in some senses, a representative anecdote for the struggles of her race.

Although her rhetorical career was unusually long and active, Church Terrell has not been as widely recognized as other advocates of the time. Perhaps her reputation has been eclipsed by the prominent, highly visible conflict between Booker T. Washington and W. E. B. DuBois. Still, her influence was substantial, in part because of the scope of her activities. As Kohrs Campbell concludes:

> She spoke all over the nation to diverse audiences, including church groups, college students, chautauquas, and lyceums, for over forty years, and she published articles in journals of opinion and in white and African-American newspapers throughout her life. To her fellow African-Americans, she preached the gospel of self-esteem, self-confidence, and self-help, sometimes through organized protest. To whites, she was an educator. She had an unshakable belief that if whites, particularly northern whites, knew and understood the plight of African-Americans, they would act to reaffirm the nation's fundamental values, to remove obstacles to African-Americans, and to create condition of equality of opportunity for all. Her lifelong commitment to the efficacy of persuasion and to the ultimate rightness of the workings of democracy is her eternal monument.[24]

Because her rhetorical career was so extended and because she addressed such a variety of issues, choosing representative texts for analysis is challenging. To present a broad overview, I selected three distinctly different texts directed to three diverse audiences. The first is her presidential address to the NACW, delivered in 1896. One of her earliest texts, this speech to her peers suggests her aspirations for their efforts and her race. The second text is "Lynching from a Negro's Point of View," published in June 1904 in the *North American Review*.[25] This essay, written in response to an article by southern apologist Thomas Nelson Page, reveals Church Terrell's skills as a rebuttalist and her adaptations in speaking to a largely white audience. Finally, I examine "What It Means to Be Colored in the Capital of the United States," published in the *Independent* in 1907 after being delivered at the United Women's Club in October 1906.[26] In this text, Church Terrell is addressing white women of her same social class. Thus, by examining three texts targeting different audiences, this essay highlights her strategies for building identification across racial boundaries.

Striving to Reach the Highest

Although Church Terrell ranged widely in the topics she discussed, in every case they were related to her aspirations for her race. In writing a creed for the Delta

Sigma Theta Sorority at Howard University, Church Terrell encapsulated her philosophy of life, which she tried to use as the guide for her actions.[27] She wrote: "I will take an active interest in the welfare of my country, using my influence toward the enactment of laws for the protection of the unfortunate and weak and for the repeal of those depriving human beings of their privileges and rights. I will never belittle my race, but encourage all to hold it in honor and esteem."[28]

As the creed indicates, Church Terrell was deeply committed to advancing her race. A contemporary of both Booker T. Washington and W. E. B. DuBois, Church Terrell also wrestled with how best to move African Americans forward. Although she became increasingly supportive of Washington's accomplishments at Tuskegee, at the core she agreed with DuBois on the necessity of supporting the potential leaders among African Americans so that they could help others rise as well. Understanding her perspective requires a consideration of the views of Washington and DuBois about advancing the race.

Perhaps the most concise and well known statement of Washington's perspective on the relationship between the races is contained in his "Cotton States Exposition Address." In that speech, he urges mutual understanding, encouraging African Americans to pursue the opportunities open to them. In what has become a famous metaphor, he exhorts African Americans to cast down their buckets "in agriculture, mechanics, in commerce, in domestic service, and in the professions." He adds:

> Our greatest danger is that in the great leap from slavery to freedom we may overlook the fact that the masses of us are to live by the productions of our hands, and fail to keep in mind that we shall prosper in proportion as we learn to draw the line between the superficial and the substantial, the ornamental gew-gaws of life and the useful. No race can prosper till it learns that there is as much dignity in tilling a field as in writing a poem. It is at the bottom of life that we must begin, and not at the top.[29]

He cautions the "Gentlemen of the Exposition": "You must not expect overmuch," noting that the advancement of his race depended in large part on the "constant help" from northern philanthropists as well as from people in the southern states. He concludes: "The wisest among my race understand that the agitation of questions of social equality is the extremest [sic] folly, and that the progress in the enjoyment of all the privileges that will come to us must be the result of severe and constant struggle rather than of artificial forcing." His accommodationist stance emphasizes that "in all things that are purely social we can be as separate as the fingers, yet one as the hand in all things essential to mutual progress."[30]

For Washington, the approach to uplifting the race lay in industrial and technical education to make students competent to start at the bottom of the economic ladder. Developing practical skills would, he thought, teach students valuable lessons for life. As he recalled about the building of Tuskegee, "Almost from the first I determined to have the students do practically all the work of putting up the buildings. . . . [T]he lesson of self-help would be more valuable to them in the long run than if they were put into a building which had been wholly the creation of the generosity of some one else."[31]

The reasons for Washington's insistence on vocational training for African Americans were complicated and highly pragmatic. First, realizing the economic and industrial growth in the South, Washington surmised that providing skilled workers was "the wave of the future."[32] Thus vocational training would help prepare students for participating more fully in the economic growth of the region. As Frederick Dunn observes, Washington "strongly felt that African Americans could best develop a strong economic base through the acquisition of utilitarian skills."[33] At the core, Washington was resigned to and pragmatic about what he saw as the conditions of the time. He thought that the white power structure would only tolerate vocational education for African Americans. His strategy was to build on the willingness of whites to support that focus and help students gain economic power through lucrative employment. Indeed, as Dunn concludes:

> It is this last point—Washington's ability to read the societal landscape, avoid the pitfalls, and achieve his objectives, limited though they were—that gained him the title "the Wizard of Tuskegee." When Washington coupled his educational ideas of manual training with his social philosophy of accommodationism, or acceptance by African Americans of second-class citizenship and legally mandated segregation, he was widely endorsed by southern and northern White philanthropists and politicians.[34]

For his part, Washington also believed that "economic self-reliance and the habit of thrift would open avenues of social mobility."[35] Knowing the strong prejudices of southerners, he realized that any argument for education of any sort for his race would have to be grounded in gains for the society as a whole. Industrial education thus had the double virtue of producing added value to the South without broaching the topic of social equality. In addition, such education "provided a means of achieving racial solidarity against political and social repression. Industrial education held out for a cessation of racial antagonism, even while it afforded blacks a measure of control over their destiny."[36] Not surprisingly, Washington's approach garnered widespread approval, especially among progressive educators, and built his political power.

W. E. B. DuBois would have none of this. In his *The Souls of Black Folk: Essays and Sketches*, DuBois developed his critique of Washington at length. Commending Washington's ability to gain "place and consideration in the North," he added that "there is among educated and thoughtful colored men in all parts of the land a feeling of deep regret, sorrow, and apprehension at the wide currency and ascendancy which some of Mr. Washington's theories have gained." DuBois castigates Washington for developing a "gospel of Work and Money to such an extent as apparently almost completely to overshadow the higher aims of life." He adds: "Mr. Washington's programme practically accepts the inferiority of the Negro race." According to DuBois, Washington "asks that black people give up, at least for the present, three things,—First, political power, Second, insistence on civil rights, Third, higher education of Negro youth—and concentrate all their energies on industrial education, the accumulation of wealth, and the conciliation of the South."[37] DuBois urges that his fellow African Americans reject the accommodationist stance of Washington, repudiates this implicit acceptance of the inferiority of the race, and insists on their full and appropriate civil rights.

Although he agreed with Washington that education was the key, DuBois had a distinctively different perspective on the kind of education that was appropriate. In an essay written for the *Atlantic Monthly* in 1902, DuBois provides an overview of the evolution of education for freed African Americans in the aftermath of the Civil War.[38] He contends that the industrial revolution that developed in the South between 1885 and 1895 presented new challenges as well as new opportunities for those interested in education for African Americans. However, the hastily constructed educational system of the time was ill-equipped to meet this new need: "The Negro colleges, hurriedly founded, were inadequately equipped, illogically distributed, and varying efficiency and grade; the normal and high schools were doing little more than common school work, and the common schools were training but a third of the children who ought to be in them, and training these too often poorly." At the same time, racial prejudices had hardened, making life increasingly difficult. "The industrial school springing to notice in this decade, but coming to full recognition in the decade beginning in 1895, was the proffered answer to this combined educational and economic crisis, and an answer of singular wisdom and timeliness."[39]

By raising industrial training to a new prominence, these schools, "in direct touch with the South's magnificent industrial development . . . reminded black folk that before the Temple of Knowledge swing the Gates of Toil." Although these schools had enjoyed some success, DuBois is concerned with their focus on material advancement and questions whether "after all the industrial school is the final and sufficient answer in the training of Negro race."[40] DuBois contends that while such training is good for many of his race, the more academically talented demand and need more. To prove his point, he identifies the many graduates of northern colleges and universities who clearly "thirst" for more. He asks rhetorically: "by refusing to give this Talented Tenth the key to knowledge, can any sane man imagine that they will lightly lay aside their yearning and contentedly become hewers of wood and drawers of water?"[41] If the South is to continue to advance, he insists, there must be appropriate educational opportunities available to this group.

DuBois returned to this theme in the 1903 book, *The Negro Problem: A Series of Articles by Representative American Negroes of Today*, edited by Washington.[42] In a chapter with a more extended discussion of the Taletned Tenth, he begins with his premise: "The Negro race, like all races, is going to be saved by its exceptional men. The problem of education, then, among the Negroes must first of all deal with the Talented Tenth; it is the problem of developing the Best of this race that they may guide the Mass away from the contamination and death of the Worst, of their own and other races." To explore this issue, DuBois examines three interrelated themes: the history of this Talented Tenth as leaders of their race, their education and preparation for leadership, and their role in relation to the "Negro problem."[43] In his discussion, he provides examples of exceptional leaders as well as statistics about the occupations of the group as a whole. "These figures illustrate vividly the function of the college-bred Negro. He is, as he ought to be, the group leader, the man who sets the ideals of the community where he lives, directs its thoughts and heads it social movements. It need hardly be argued that the Negro people need social leadership more than most groups; that they have no traditions to fall back upon, no long established customs, no strong family ties, no well defined social classes. All these things must be slowly and painfully evolved."[44] The fact that virtually all college graduates of his race had become teachers and other types of professionals bolstered DuBois's confidence that his race could itself provide the leadership for advancement.[45]

One key role of this Talented Tenth was to invigorate and improve the entire educational system for African Americans. In his view, "the main question, so far as the Southern Negro is concerned, is: What under the present circumstance, must a system of education do to raise the Negro as quickly as possible in the scale of civilization? The answer to this question seems to me clear: It must strengthen the Negro's character, increase his knowledge and teach him to earn a living."[46] DuBois believed firmly that the so-called common schools could provide one aspect of the needed training, a sound educational grounding and character development; the industrial school could provide another important aspect, preparation to earn a living. However, broadly trained university and college graduates were necessary to train the teachers for these institutions.

In every area of social life, the race needed the leadership that could only be provided by its most gifted and accomplished members. With some passion he asks rhetorically:

Do you think that if the leaders of thought among the Negroes are not trained and educated thinkers, they will have no leaders? On the contrary a hundred demagogues will still hold the places they so largely occupy now, and hundreds of vociferous busy-bodies will multiply. You have no choice; either you must help furnish this race from within its own ranks with thoughtful men of trained leadership, or you must suffer the evil consequences of a headless misguided rabble.[47]

Although Church Terrell was a representative of the Talented Tenth that DuBois sought to empower, she nonetheless had strong sympathies for Washington's self-help doctrine. She initially disagreed with his heavy emphasis on industrial training, but an invitation to speak at commencement at Tuskegee altered her view. "After I had seen Tuskegee with my own eyes I had a higher regard and greater admiration for its founder than I had ever entertained before. I realized what splendid work he was doing to promote the welfare of the race, and that he was literally fulfilling 'a long felt want.'"[48] Despite her admiration for Washington and his work at Tuskegee, she enthusiastically became a charter member of the National Association for the Advancement of Colored People (NAACP), which was widely perceived as having been formed to circumvent his power. For Church Terrell, the decision to join was complicated by the friendship of her husband and Washington. Indeed, some believed that Washington's influence with Theodore Roosevelt had secured a federal judgeship for her husband.[49]

As the discussions below indicate, Church Terrell focused her concern on the advancement of the race by removing the obstacles that confronted its most talented members. She was certainly concerned about the plight of the less privileged, but like DuBois, she believed that the intellectual and social leaders of her race had both the potential and the responsibility to work for advancement of the group as a whole. Central to her concerns was the insistence that middle- and upper-class African Americans be accorded the respect and opportunities they merited.

The Role of Women

In 1896, at age of thirty-three and pregnant with her third child, Mary Church Terrell was elected the first president of the NACW, which had just been created by a merger of two clubs. The goal of the new organization was to bring the considerable energy and strengths of women to bear on elevating the status of the entire race. As Church Terrell explains: "The work which we hope to accomplish can be done better, we believe, by the mothers, wives, daughters, and sisters of our race than by the fathers, husbands, brothers, and sons." That work was to encourage their race to acquire "the attributes of mind and grace of character that claims the real man."[50] This ambiguous, nonthreatening goal was certainly well suited to her audience.

Before the NACW was created, self-help organizations for African American women had proliferated as the realities of Jim Crow legislation became apparent. As northern whites lost interest in the fate of African American citizens after Reconstruction and middle-class African American women faced growing social difficulties, the women organized themselves in the hopes of bringing concerted actions that would benefit themselves and their race. One black club woman and activist recalled, "the club movement among colored women had grown out of the organized anxiety of women who have only recently become intelligent enough to recognize their social condition and strong enough to initiate and apply the forces of reform."[51] In 1892 the Colored Women's League was formed with the goal of becoming a truly national organization of African American women. Its preamble read, in part:

Resolved, That we, the colored women of Washington, associate ourselves together to collect all the facts obtainable, showing the moral, intellectual, and social growth and attainments of our people; to foster unity of purpose; to consider and determine methods which will promote the best interests of the colored people in any direction that suggests itself.

Resolved, That we appeal to the colored women of the United States, interested in the objects set forth, to form similar organizations, which shall cooperate with the Washington League, thus forming a National League in which each society shall be represented.[52]

Just three years later an incident occurred that renewed the interest in a more powerful and visible national association. In a letter dated 6 March 1895, James W. Jacks, president of the Missouri Press Association, wrote Florence Belgarnie, the honorable secretary of the Anti-Lynching Society of England, that "the Negroes of this country were wholly devoid of morality, the women were prostitutes and were natural thieves and liars."[53] Copies of the letter circulated widely in African American circles, and the Women's Era Club called a national conference of women to meet in Boston in July 1895. The call for that meeting read in part:

Although this matter of a convention has been talked over for some time, the subject has been precipitated by a letter to England, written by a southern editor, and reflecting upon the moral character of all colored women. This letter is too indecent for publication, but a copy of it is sent with this call to all the women's bodies across the country. Read the document carefully and discriminatingly and decide if it be not time for us to stand before the world and declare ourselves and our principles.[54]

In her opening comments, Josephine Pierre Ruffin, the president of the Women's Era Club, averred:

Years after years, Southern [white] women have protested against the admission of colored women into any organization on the ground of the immorality of our women and because our reputation has only been tired by individual work, the charge has never been crushed. . . . It is "most right," and our boundless duty to stand forth and declare ourselves and principles to teach an ignorant suspicious world that our aims and interests are identical with those of all aspiring women.[55]

With the Colored Women's League not represented at the meeting, a new organization emerged, the National Federation of Afro-American Women (NFAAW), with almost identical goals. But recognizing the advisability of an immediate merger, the organizers appointed a committee to facilitate that process. Thus the following year two separate but consecutive national meetings of women were held in Washington, D.C., with both groups recognizing the need for a single organization.[56] A joint committee from the two organizations recommended on 21 July 1896: "That we do consolidate under the name of the National Association of Colored Women."[57] After several tied ballots between representatives of the two merging organizations, Church Terrell, who had dropped out of the running earlier, was nominated and elected president.[58]

On assuming the presidency of the NACW, Church Terrell faced two distinct sets of rhetorical challenges. First, she needed to find a common ground that the members of both organizations, as well as other women of her race, could embrace. It was well and good to call for the elevation of the race; the mechanisms and approaches to bring that about were less clear. Church Terrell's challenge was to find a compelling and acceptable agenda for pursuing this dramatic social change.

On the other hand, Church Terrell had to respond at least indirectly to the immediate rhetorical exigency, the Jack letter. Although such charges were not new, middle-class African Americans felt a need to respond to the allegations if only to assert their self-respect, especially since the author was an educated and supposedly open-minded newspaper editor. As the call for the national meeting that produced the NFAAW suggested, the time had come for a public declaration and concerted actions to assert the dignity, accomplishments, and potential of the race. She and the women who formed the NACW were fully aware of the barriers they confronted. In an announcement in the *Woman's Era* of August 1896, Church Terrell sounds the tone of optimism and determination that were to characterize her presidency:

> Having overcome as a race and a sex so many obstacles that to the fainting, faltering heart seemed insurmountable in the past, we shall neither be discouraged at the temporary failures of our friends, nor frightened at the apparent success of our foes. . . . Forgetful of the past, hopeful for the future, let us work in the present with undaunted courage and untiring zeal. With so many heads that are thoughtful and hearts that are true enlisted in our service, how impossible is failure, how inevitable success! . . . The magnitude of the work to which we seem divinely called and are solemnly pledged, far from affrighting and depressing us, inspires to greater effort.[59]

Church Terrell's first presidential address set the tone and direction of her leadership and the association's efforts. Typical of what Kohrs Campbell notes are her skills in adapting to diverse audiences, Church Terrell chooses two rhetorical strategies that enabled her to unite and motivate her audience.[60] First, she establishes a compelling need for action. She explains both the reasons for the foundation of the NACW and its agenda for change. Within this pattern, Church Terrell is able to present an optimistic future for her fledgling organization and lay out an appealing, doable agenda. She proceeds first to explain the critical need for the organization itself and then to analyze the central problem it confronted. In the first case, she creates a mandate for the group, and in the second, she energizes them to action. In each case, Church Terrell is able to appeal to the gender stereotypes of her day by adapting the rhetoric of the social gospel. In particular, she suggests that the nature of the work, uplifting the race by improving families, was ideally suited to women.[61] The strategies she proposed were both achievable by her audience and in line with dominant cultural values of the time.

First, Church Terrell insists that the need for the NACW was "questioned by no one conversant with our peculiar trials and perplexities, and acquainted with the almost insurmountable obstacles in our path to those attainments and acquisitions to which it is the right and privilege of every member of every race to aspire." The association must be of "colored" women only because "our peculiar status in this country at the present time seems to demand that we stand by ourselves in the special work for which we have organized. For this reason it was thought best to invite attention of the world to the fact that colored women feel their responsibility as a unit, and together have clasped hands to assume it." These women had "uttered the cry of alarm" not because they were discouraged by the progress of their race. Indeed, as she avers, "But thirty years ago, we have advanced so far in the realm of knowledge and letters as to have produced scholars and authors of repute. Though penniless as a race a short while ago, we have among us today a few men of wealth and multitudes who own their homes and make comfortable livings." She concludes: "We therefore challenge any other race to present a record more creditable and show a progress more wonderful than that made by the ex-slaves of the United States and that too in the face of prejudice, proscription, and persecution against which no other people has ever had to contend in the history of the world." The need for the NACW was to continue that progress and elevate others because the women were "painfully mindful of our weaknesses and defects [in] which we know the Negro is no worse than other races equally poor, equally ignorant, and equally oppressed."[62] The first problem was, then, how to elevate the balance of the race. The answer was the efforts of the NACW.

On a second level, Church Terrell traces some of the persistent problems among her race to the wretched situations in which many of their youth were raised: "Crowded into alleys, many of them the haunts of vice, few if any of them in a proper sanitary condition, most of them fatal to mental and moral growth, and destructive of healthful physical development as well, thousands of our children have a wretched heritage indeed." The answer to elevating the race, then, begins with "[h]omes, more homes, purer homes, better homes. . . . So long as the majority of people call that place home in which the air is foul, the manners bad, and the morals worse, just so long is this so called home a menace to health, a breeder of vice, and the abode of crime."[63]

To solve these problems, Church Terrell adopts the rhetoric of the social gospel to call for free kindergartens "in every city and hamlet." In those kindergartens, leaders could inculcate children with "correct principles, and set good examples" to offset the "thorny paths of prejudice, temptation, and injustice" the children were forced to tread. To assist the mothers of these children, Church Terrell proposes "Mother Congresses" that could teach simple housekeeping skills such as sweeping, dusting, and washing. "Let us have heart to hear talks with our women that we may strike at the root of evil." She recommends advocating against "brutal methods of punishment" on the grounds that such approaches crushed self respect and pride. She urges practicing and preaching "race unity, race pride, reverence, and respect," as well as insisting on the "dignity of labor" and "a desire to work."[64]

Church Terrell acknowledges that this progressive agenda requires money: "Money we need, money we must have to accomplish much which we hope to effect." But real social change, she insists, does not come through the mere expenditure of money. Rather, "It is the silent, though powerful force of individual influences, thrown on the side of right, it is by arduous persistence and effort to keep those with whom we come in daily contact, to enlighten the heathen at our door, to create wholesome public sentiment in the communities in which we live, that the heaviest blows are struck for virtue and right."[65]

Church Terrell's decision to establish a compelling need for action grounded in prevailing cultural and religious themes that privileged the moral role of mothers was well suited to her rhetorical situation in several ways. By explaining the need for the organization itself and the reason for limiting it to "colored" women, she implicitly refuted Jack's attacks on the group she represented. If these women could organize and commit themselves to the advancement of their race, his depiction of them as "prostitutes . . . natural thieves and liars" was demonstrably groundless. By claiming as their province the improvement of the welfare of children, she allowed her listeners to align themselves with dominant cultural views of women. In essence, her speech associated "colored" women with widely accepted cultural values and reaffirmed their moral uprightness.

In addition, her use of a logical organizational pattern demonstrated the competence of the group she represented. As she explained the rationale for the formation of the organization and laid out a clear-cut agenda, she demonstrated that she and other women of her race had the skills and aptitudes to help solve persistent social problems. Her analysis of the issues, then, once again belied Jacks's depiction of them.

For her audience, her rhetorical choices also opened for them possibilities for action that were both doable and laudable. Calls for petition drives or direct political actions might have seemed too daunting or inappropriate for the middle-class women in her organization. But they could envision themselves offering advice to other mothers or working to establish kindergartens. Her audience could, then, remain safely inside social stereotypes while advancing their race.

Finally, Church Terrell offered an appealing, optimistic picture to her audience. By emphasizing the accomplishments of her race, she outlined the potentials for change. By acknowledging the persistent problems, she showed an awareness of the realities of her time. By offering solutions, she opened the possibility of constructive change and further progress.

During her tenure as NACW president, Church Terrell moved forward on the agenda she outlined in her presidential address. By the time of the second national convention, she could tout the successes NACW members had enjoyed, even with limited funds. She pointed to the kindergartens they had established, their work with the women of Alabama, and mothers' meetings in various places. At the same time, she urged the middle-class members to study "the labor question in relation to our race" to understand the plight of working African American women, to reach out to the "masses of our women," and to set "a high moral standard." Despite the need for renewed and extended efforts, she declared: "An infant of but three years is this organization, over which I have had the honor to preside, ever since it first saw the light of day in the Capital of the Nation, and yet in those short years it has accomplished a vast amount of good."[66]

These early rhetorical activities reveal traces of both Washington and DuBois and reflect what was to become Church Terrell's characteristic synthesis of their divergent views. Her aspirations for the members of NACW are consonant with DuBois's insistent views about the impact of the Talented Tenth. The members of the NACW, as they lived out the goal of "Lifting as We Climb," were enacting exactly the role that DuBois had seen for the elite of his race. Their focus on helping their less-fortunate sisters learn the rudiments of domestic science to improve their homes reverberates with Washington's notions that African Americans must start at the bottom to elevate themselves. Those less fortunate than the members of the NACW might not aspire to the same lofty roles, but they could evince the mastery of basic life skills and, by improving their homes, contribute to the advancement of their race. As we shall see, much of Church Terrell's later rhetoric acknowledges sharp social cleavages, as does this early rhetoric, and depicts a particularly important role for the elite of the race.

The Lawless South

The January 1904 issue of the *North American Review* carried an article by Thomas Nelson Page entitled "The Lynching of Negroes—Its Causes and Its Prevention." The son of a Confederate officer and himself a lawyer, Page was a well-known author, lecturer, and apologist for the South.[67] The article, written in response to calls for the outlawing of lynching, attempted to analyze the cause of such acts and to propose a remedy. In Page's eyes, lynching arose because a new generation of African Americans had arisen in the South who had been seduced with talk of racial equality that produced strong racial antagonisms.[68] Lynching was a response to the increasing "ravishings" of white women and sometimes young girls by some of this new generation who had no respect for human life or normal standards of decency. Indeed, the increasingly brutal forms of lynching (for example, burning at the stake) arose when white protectors of women were unable to staunch the rising tide of rape through mere hanging. As he writes: "For a time, a speedy execution by hanging was the only mode of retribution resorted to by lynchers; then, when this failed of its purpose, a more savage method was essayed, born of a savage fury at the failure of the first, and a stern resolve to strike a deeper terror into those whom the other method had failed to awe." Page's solution was to call on "influential" African Americans to become outraged at the behaviors of some of their race and to be "held accountable for the good order of their race in every community."[69]

Church Terrell was outraged. She wrote to the magazine: "In the 1904 January number of the *North American Review* Thomas Nelson Page had an article on Lynching which was one of the most scurrilous attacks upon the colored men of this country which has ever appeared in print. It was full of misleading statements from beginning to end. When I read it I thought I could not survive if something were not done to correct the impressions that Mr. Page's article had made."[70] But getting the opportunity to respond was a challenge. Despite repeated letters, the editor of the magazine was unresponsive.[71] Church Terrell turned to her friend William Dean Howells, asking him to intervene. Howells responded quickly but insisted he was only a contributor, with little influence. Nonetheless, soon thereafter she received a letter from the editor, asking her to write the response. However, he was quite clear "that if he wanted to publish it, he would; and if he didn't, he wouldn't."[72]

Church Terrell responded to Page's exposition in the June issue of the same magazine.[73] The title of her essay, "Lynching from a Negro's Point of View," seems directly related not only to Page's January essay in the *North American* Review but also to the first of a series of essays on race relations he had published that year, entitled "The Negro: The Southerner's Problem: Slavery and the Old Relation Between Southern Whites and Blacks."[74] In writing her response, Church Terrell faced two interrelated rhetorical challenges. First, she had to make a thorough, convincing rebuttal of Page's points. If one can judge by the acceptance of his essays, Page had established himself as an effective defender of southern practices. While the substance of his articles may be offensive to modern readers, his discussions are marked by clear organization and appeals to reason. Church Terrell had the opportunity, then, to take on one of the most articulate southern apologists who also iterated the dominant stereotypes of his day. Her challenge was to mount an effective refutation.

Second, Church Terrell needed to establish her own ethos since she could well be perceived as biased on the subject. As an African American woman, she needed to present herself and her ideas in ways that would overcome resistance to her views. In short, she needed to build the basis for identification with her largely non–African American audience.

In meeting these challenges, Church Terrell demonstrates her rhetorical virtuosity. Her rhetorical approach in this text differs sharply from her speech to the NACW. Reacting explicitly and strongly to Page's excuses for lynching, Church Terrell adopts the stance of rebuttalist, answering Page's arguments point by point adroitly and effectively. At the same time, she attempts to educate her audience by offering her own analysis of the issue.[75] In advancing her ideas, she speaks articulately as an educated, well-informed member of her race. Her style and tone implicitly help refute Page's attacks on African Americans.

In his essay, Page had insisted that analysis must precede solutions: "In discussing the means to put an end to this barbarity, the first essential is that the matter shall be clearly and thoroughly understood."[76] Church Terrell adopts a similar stance: "But means of prevention can never be devised, until the cause of lynching is more generally understood." She calls Page's views into question, at least by implication, when she notes that "those who live in the section where nine-tenths of the lynchings occur do not dare to tell the truth, even if they perceive it."[77] As a southerner, then, Page was likely to be blind to the real issues surrounding lynching.

The starting point of Page's argument was that the existence of lynching was evidence that reasonable people (the lynchers) had been forced to extreme responses:

> All thoughtful men know that respect for law is the basic principle of civilization, and are agreed as to the evil of any overriding of the law. All reasonable men know that the overriding of law readily creates a spirit of lawlessness, under which progress is retarded and civilization suffers and dwindles. This is as clearly recognized at the South as at the North. To overcome his conviction and stir up rational men to a pitch where the law is trampled under foot, the offices of the law are attacked, and their prisoner taken from them and executed, there must some imperative cause.[78]

The "imperative cause" was the "ravishings" of women and young girls. Page's strategy, then, was to suggest that lynchings were understandable, if regrettable, responses to serious crimes.

Since rape had been relatively unknown even during the Civil War when women were left largely unprotected, Page surmised that social changes since that time were responsible for the growing numbers of "ravishings" and the subsequent lynchings:

> During the whole period of slavery it [rape] did not exist, nor did it exist to any considerable extent for some years after Emancipation. . . . Then came the period and process of Reconstruction, with its teachings. Among these was the teaching that the negro was the equal of the white, that the white was his enemy, and that he must assert his equality. The growth of the idea was a gradual one in the negro's mind. This was followed by a number of cases where members of the negro militia ravished white women; sometimes in the presence of their families.[79]

When whites resumed some political control, the outbreak of rape abated. But the doctrine of equality persisted, and the "'New Issue' with the new teaching took its place; the crime broke out again with renewed violence."[80] In Page's analysis, lynchings were the direct consequence of the rape of white women; the rapes were so offensive that they provoked outrage among "reasonable" men, forcing them to acts of violence.

Again, without mentioning Page by name, Church Terrell sets out to correct the "four mistakes [that] are commonly made," all of which are claims Page makes in his essay. Church Terrell begins by insisting that "it is a great mistake to suppose that rape is the real cause of lynching in the South."[81] She continues: "It is easy to prove that rape is simply the pretext and not the cause of lynching. Statistics show that, out of every hundred negroes who are lynched, from seventy-five to eighty-five are not even accused of this crime, and many who are accused of it are innocent."[82] These statistics, incidentally, are from Page's own data and observations.[83] She offers a graphic description of the brutal torture and lynching of a man and his wife to refute Page's claim that brutal rapes prompt brutal lynchings.[84]

In response his second argument, that notions of social equality had stimulated African American men to crimes of sexual violence, Church Terrell draws sharp class distinctions:

> It is a mistake to suppose that the negro's desire for social equality sustains any relation whatsoever to the crime of rape. According to the testimony of eye-witnesses, as well as the reports of Southern newspapers, the negroes who are known to be guilty of assault have, as a rule, been ignorant, repulsive in

appearance and as near the brute creation as it is possible for a human being to be. It is safe to assert that, among the negroes who have been guilty of ravishing white women, not one had been taught that he was the equal of white people or had ever heard of social equality. And if by chance he had heard of it, he had no clearer conception of its meaning than he had of the principle of the binomial theorem. In conversing with a large number of ignorant negroes, the writer has never found one who seemed to have any idea of what social equality means, or who expressed a desire to put this theory into practice when it was explained to him.[85]

Church Terrell continues to defend her own social class, noting that "negroes who have the 'convention habit'" are not part of the criminal class, although they are "always held up by Southern gentlemen as objects of ridicule, contempt and scorn." Instead of cultivating this more sophisticated class of African Americans, southerners "coddled and caressed" the lower class and held them up as examples to others of "what a really good negro should be": "The dictionary is searched in vain by Southern gentlemen and gentlewomen for words sufficiently ornate and strong to express their admiration for a dear old 'mammy' or a faithful old 'uncle' who can neither read nor write, and who assure their white friends they would not, if they could." She contends that "social equality" is a strawperson for the South, used to "explain its unchristian treatment of the negro and to excuse its many crimes."[86] She also notes that in the North, the only region that "accords the negro the scrap of social equality," accusations of rape against African Americans are rare.

In the next stages of his argument, Page alleged that the "better" class of African Americans tended to identify with the members of their race who were accused of rape rather than condemning the crime; thus they failed to assume the proper leadership roles in their community. To the first point, Church Terrell declares fervently: "only those who are densely ignorant of the standards and sentiments of the best negroes, or who wish willfully to misrepresent and maliciously slander a race already resting under burdens greater than it can bear, would accuse its thousands of reputable men and women of sympathizing with rapists, either black or white, or of condoning their crime." She notes that teachers and preachers as well as other leaders of her class "are continually expressing their horror of this particular crime" and exhort others to do everything possible "to wash the ugly stain of rape from the race's good name."[87] Their sympathies may be roused, she notes, for the cases where evidence of guilt is weak or where clear injustice is present. Too often, she observes, more careful examination of cases reveals that innocent men have been lynched without any chance to present facts in their defense.

Church Terrell also highlights the difficulties in finding the facts of any case in newspaper accounts. She provides examples to bolster her claim that newspapers are at best unreliable sources and at worst instigators of violence. She concludes: "Instance after instance might be cited to prove that facts bearing upon lynching, as well as upon other phases of the race problem, are often garbled—without intention, perhaps—by the press."[88]

Having dispatched of Page's arguments about the causes of lynching, Church Terrell provides her own analysis. Succinctly, she contends: "At last analysis, it will be discovered that there are just two causes of lynching. In the first place, it is due to race hatred, the hatred of a stronger people toward a weaker who were once held as slaves. In the second place, it is due to the lawlessness so prevalent in the section where nine-tenths of the lynchings occur." For her, lynching is an aftermath of slavery in that the people who perpetrate the crime are the sons and daughters of former slaveholders who had "little, if any compassion, on the race when it was enslaved." Further, she suggests that these people, secure in families of their own, "looked with unpitying eye and adamantine heart upon the anguish of slave mothers whose children had been sold away, when not overtaken by a sadder fate." If Page castigated middle- and upper-class African Americans for their lack of concern about the "ravishings" performed by some of their race, Church Terrell takes on the "best citizens" of the South, who, she asserts, make up the lynch mobs and own the papers that propagate race hatred. These people were predictably "brutalized" into insensitivity by their slaveholding environment. Members of her race cannot, however, depend on the courts to protect them. "With the courts of law entirely in the hands of the white man, with judge and jury belonging to the superior race, a negro could no more extricate himself from the meshes of the law in the South than he could slide from the devil-fish's embrace or slip from the anaconda's coils. Miscarriage of justice in the South is possible only when white men transgress the law."[89]

Lynchings are, in her view, only one example of the South's "determination to wreak terrible vengeance on the negro." She indicts the peonage system where, in her example, six children from ages six to sixteen were working barefoot in the snow for the man who had killed their father a few years earlier. The denial of educational opportunities to children who are forbidden to go above the sixth grade is another example. She concludes passionately: "Instance after instance might be cited to prove that the hostility toward the negro in the South is bitter and pronounced, and that lynching is but a manifestation of this spirit of vengeance and intolerance in its ugliest and most brutal form."[90] She turns to statistics to disprove the claim that rape is primarily a crime of African Americans. Even if her race were as responsible for rapes as critics contend, Church Terrell explains that their experience under slavery would explain it. She points to the debauching of African American women by their white masters and the preying of white men on young African American women in the current day to suggest that the "superior" race has set a poor example for those they see as inferior. The spread of lawlessness occasioned by lynchings, she opines, impacts the entire society and raises concerns internationally.[91]

After this thoroughgoing refutation of Page's claim and her own analysis of the problem, Church Terrell sees only two solutions. First, the masses of ignorant whites in the South must be educated and "uplifted." She quotes the *Atlanta Constitution* to note that the number of illiterate white men over the age of twenty-one in the South has not diminished in over fifty years. In contrast, her own race has dramatically reduced its illiteracy level. Second, she avers that all classes of white people in the South must come to respect the rights of all human beings and obey the law. She does not fault Americans for being cruel or callous; rather, she points to the efforts of the South to denigrate and libel her race as the cause for the lack of outrage over the problem of lynching. She perceives a weariness with hearing about the plight of African Americans, but she is clear that such attitudes cannot be reconciled with the principles of liberty and equality on which the country was founded.[92]

Throughout the essay, Church Terrell's diction and syntax reflect her education and sophistication. While the materials quoted above indicate her mastery of syntax, her diction is equally sophisticated. She ridicules the notions of "diabolical assaults" by men of her race on white women; she argues that white men had "perpetuated" a special form of social inequality in forcing their sexual attentions on slave women; and she avers that public opinion is one obstacle to "extirpating" lynching.[93] In every respect, her style in the essay builds her ethos and identification with her educated, largely white audience as she implicitly refutes Page's depiction of her race.

In contrast to her speech to the women's club, this essay is also marked by strong sarcasm. Referring to statistics that indicate that most lynchings do not involve accusations of rape, Church Terrell comments: "And yet, men who admit the accuracy of these figures gravely tell the country that lynching can never be suppressed, until negroes cease to commit a crime with which less than one fourth of those murdered by mobs are charged." Later in refuting the claim that desires for social equality underlie rape, she responds: "Of whatever crime we may accuse this big, black, burly brute, who is so familiar a figure in reports of rape and lynching-bees by the Southern press, surely we cannot truthfully charge him with an attempt to introduce social equality into this republican form of government, or foist it upon a democratic land."[94] These and other flashes of sarcasm throughout the essay convey her impatience with the specious arguments offered by apologists and her clear conviction that reasonable people like her readers will share her disdain.

Although her arguments against Page seem devastating to the modern reader, her contemporaries may have been less convinced. Church Terrell does not share the editor's reactions to her essay, which of course took a highly confrontational approach; apparently he published it in close to her submitted form. She does note that he rejected a subsequent essay, after expressing enthusiasm for proposed focus on "A Plea to the White South by a Colored Woman," "not because of its mediocrity or inferiority, but because of the indisputable facts presented by it which the magazine would not print."[95] Her conclusion is based on his recommendation that she submit the completed essay to another reputable journal. She does cite a later review in *Harper's Weekly* that commends her writing: "And yet, when Colonel Harvey, who differed with me on several points, reviewed it in *Harper's Weekly*, he began by saying: 'It is in respect to diction a remarkable article on "Lynching from a Negro's Point of View" which is contributed in the June number of the *North American Review* by Mrs. Mary Church Terrell, and scarcely less striking in form.'"[96] Another reader urged her to write a novel on the same theme to expand her readership.[97] Despite these favorable reviews, Church Terrell's frequent obstacles and frustrations in getting her work accepted by the mainstream white-dominated press were, to her, further evidence of the barriers all her race confronted.

Although Church Terrell raised many of the same arguments about lynching that Ida B. Wells did, their rhetorical styles contrasted sharply. Grounding her persona in her middle-class status, Church Terrell sought to educate white audiences with careful arguments and strong evidence. She used statistical data rather than specific examples to support her claims about lynching. If she was sometimes sarcastic, she was primarily assertive and firm. In contrast, Wells sought to instigate resistance among her fellow African Americans. Rather than reasoning with white Americans, she excoriates them. She is militant and scolding. The details of particular cases add poignancy and force to her arguments. Ironically, despite their shared concerns for their race, the women were not friends. Two of the most articulate spokespersons against lynching make no mention of each other in their discourse.

The Colored Man's Paradise

On 24 January 1907 an unsigned essay appeared in the *Independent*, entitled "What It Means to Be Colored in the Capital of the United States." A note from the editor, however, identified the author as "a colored woman of much culture and recognized standing." He also noted that the essay depicted conditions in Washington, D.C., "a city governed solely by the United States Congress. It is our only city which represents the whole country."[98] The unidentified author was, of course, Church Terrell, and the text was a written version of a speech she had delivered to the United Women's Club in October of the previous year.[99] Speaking as a middle-class woman and resident of Washington, D.C., Church Terrell presented in bold relief the daily humiliations and barriers respectable African Americans faced in a city that should have been a model for enacting American values.

Church Terrell's invitation to address the group was a mark of the respect they had for her. Nonetheless, she recognized that she faced significant challenges in presenting her case to them. Campbell quotes an unpublished document by Church Terrell in which she reflects on this challenge:

> It is a dangerous thing to tell the truth about the injustice and barbarism inflicted upon the colored people in the U.S. at the present time. . . . No matter how tactfully one discusses the painful and revolting conditions under which thousands of my race live, the individual who discusses the subject is accused even by those who say they want to know the facts of exaggerating them and being so bitter and biased himself as to be incapable of telling the truth. This is particularly true when a colored person refers to the hardships and humiliations to which his race is subjected and urges redress of wrongs.[100]

Because much of what she would present could challenge her audiences' preconceptions both about her race as a whole and about American society, she needed to be strategic in how she advanced her arguments. Further, since she was an African American speaking in behalf of her race, she had to overcome the presumption of bias on her part.

Typically, Church Terrell adapts her strategies to her rhetorical context. Rather than advancing a series of carefully crafted and well-supported arguments as she had in the response to Page, she argues implicitly with a series of dramatic, compelling examples. Church Terrell begins with sharp irony.

> Washington D.C. has been called "The Colored Man's Paradise." Whether this sobriquet was given to the national capital in bitter irony by a member of the handicapped race, as he reviewed some of his own persecutions and rebuffs, or whether it was given immediately after the war by an ex-slave-holder who for the first time in his life saw colored people walking about like freemen, minus the overseer and his whip, history saith not. It is certain that it would be difficult to find a worse misnomer for Washington than "The Colored Man's Paradise" if so prosaic a consideration as veracity is to determine the appropriateness of a name. For fifteen years I have resided in Washington, and while it was far from being a paradise for colored people, when I first touched these shores it has been doing its level best ever since to make conditions for us intolerable.[101]

She explicates her claim with a series of personal hypothetical examples. She portrays herself as a woman entering the city "any night, a stranger in a strange land" unable to find "a place to lay my head" and thus obliged "to spend the entire night wandering about"; "ravenously hungry with abundant money," unable to find a restaurant to serve her unless she sits behind a screen; forced to sit in the Jim Crow section of a streetcar to travel to visit George Washington's tomb; if she refuses to be "humiliated," imprisoned for violating Virginia's laws; denied seating in a church except in the Jim Crow section; unable to find suitable employment, regardless of her "intellectual attainments," except as a trained nurse or dressmaker or, with exceptional difficulty, a teacher in a segregated school; and excluded from public places like theaters.[102] If one remembers that initially Church Terrell laid out these examples as she stood, well attired and distinguished, before women who had invited her to address them, the power of these personal examples in her initial forum becomes evident. In some senses, Church Terrell's speech sought to create a "perspective by incongruity" by juxtaposing her physical appearance and demeanor with the demeaning treatments she described as typical for one of her race and gender in Washington.[103]

Church Terrell expands her discussion by developing a string of concrete examples of the discriminatory practices in the nation's capital. Her examples serve as enthymemes to substantiate her observation at the beginning: prevalent practices and policies make life in Washington virtually intolerable for middle-class African Americans. Her examples are noteworthy because they span a variety of situations and issues. She begins by focusing on education, with examples from the frustrations of securing access to educational opportunities in art and law, noting that Catholic University is the only institution in the area that will admit African Americans; other doors are shut despite the individual's abilities, ambition, character, and thirst for knowledge. The next pair of examples reveals blatant discrimination in employment. The first is the story of a young woman, overqualified for a position, who is turned away because of her color; the second is that of a woman dismissed from a position for which she is well qualified because her coworkers discover her race. As customers, African American women are treated no better, denied service, and embarrassed regardless of their merits.[104] One of her most poignant examples is of a group of young African American girls, escorted to a theater, where only one is challenged away because of her darker skin color. Only the ruse of insisting she is from the Philippines secures her admission. Later the young girl asks her mother plaintively: "'What is the matter with me this afternoon? mother,' asked the little brown girl innocently when she mentioned the affair at home. 'Why did the man at the theatre let my two sisters and the other girls in and try to keep me out?'"[105] Church Terrell's final examples focus on the inability of skilled laborers to join unions, regardless of their employment history.[106]

Having surveyed the indignities and discrimination to which middle-class African Americans are subjected in Washington, D.C., Church Terrell suggests the impact on aspiring young people of her race. "Early in life many a colored youth is so appalled by the helplessness and the hopelessness of his situation in this country that in a sort of stoical despair he resigns himself to his fate. 'What is the good of our trying to acquire an education? We can't all be preachers, teachers, doctors, and lawyers. Besides those professions there is almost nothing for colored people to do but engage in the most menial occupations, and we do not need an education for that.'" If her examples have built identification with her audience, Church Terrell concludes by highlighting the distance between members of her race and her listeners: "It is impossible for any white person in the United States, no matter how sympathetic and broad, to realize what life would mean to him if his incentive to effort were snatched away." This denial of incentive is, to her mind, the source of many problems with youth of her race: "To the lack of incentive to effort, which is the shadow under which we live, may be traced the wreck and ruin of scores of colored youth."[107]

Church Terrell's examples from Washington, D.C., have been, in fact, a sustained a fortiori argument. If these situations exist in the capital, an area under the control of Congress, which has supposedly assured equal treatment of former slaves in the post–Civil War amendments, then the situations in other areas must be even grimmer. Church Terrell makes this point in her closing statement: "And surely nowhere in the world do oppression and persecution based solely on the color of the skin appear more hateful and hideous than in the capital of the United States, because the chasm between the principles upon which the Government was founded, in which it still professes to believe, and those which are daily practiced under the protection of the flag, yawns so deep and wide."[108]

As this brief analysis has shown, Church Terrell deftly adapts to her audience. The issues she raises—education, employment, religion—as well as the concrete examples she provides—well-qualified women for the most part—build identification with her target audiences. If her focus is limited to the challenges of middle-class African Americans, she nonetheless builds a powerful case for her claims of discrimination. By relying on concrete examples, she makes the issues vivid and compelling to her listeners and, subsequently, to her readers. As mentioned above, by using Washington, D.C., as the source of her examples, she is able to suggest not only the scope of the problem but also its intensity throughout the country. Further, once again her style, including her syntax and diction, provides ample evidence of her own accomplishments and distinction. Her skillful rhetorical performance as a speaker and writer becomes strong evidence for the unwarranted discrimination she castigates.

Carrying On and Carrying Over

At the age of eighty, in an article published in *Negro Digest* in 1943, Church Terrell reflected on the course of her life and on her accomplishments: "If I had my life to live over again, I am sure I would do exactly what I have been trying to do for nearly fifty years. I have been trying to present the colored man's case clearly, strongly and tactfully to people of the dominant race."[109] If one uses this standard to assess her rhetorical activity, she was remarkably successful. Hers was an articulate voice for her people.

Whatever the specific issue, she was adept at choosing and executing rhetorical strategies that were appropriate for her topic, the audience, and the occasion. As Kohrs Campbell notes, to her own race Church Terrell was optimistic and encouraging.[110] She often cited their accomplishments, which were particularly remarkable in light of the history of slavery. She also expressed great conviction that by working together they could advance their race. Her accomplishments as a leader of the NACW supported her claim. To others, she was an educator and advocate. She had a keen sense of using arguments and examples that would reach the audience she had targeted. By any account, she was a powerful advocate.

As the opening of her autobiography indicates, Church Terrell was clear about her position at the intersection of issues of race and gender. But understanding her rhetorical skills as well as her limitations involves taking her distinctive class position into consideration. She was clearly sympathetic to the plight of poor African Americans. Indeed, she wrote with outrage at the "peonage" embodied in the convict lease system and defended those men, often unlettered and poor, who were lynched for alleged rapes.[111] However, the solutions to the problems she perceived, especially racial discrimination, lay squarely in the hands of the upper middle class, people capable of educating and persuading members of the "dominant" race about the abuses. Her ability to reach the members of the "dominant" class lay in part in her position as an upper-middle-class African American woman. Her educational background and sophistication enabled her to build identification with audiences who did not share her racial background. Pictures of her indicate that her physical bearing and dress reinforced her class background. Each photograph reveals a dignified, well-dressed, and impressive woman with impeccable posture and bearing.

Utilizing her class position as a rhetorical advantage, however, was not without problems. At times, she emphasized class cleavages in ways that dismissed at least implicitly many of her own race. For example, in her efforts to mobilize members of the NACW, Church Terrell established a clear social hierarchy, urging her listeners to realize their responsibility to the children of the "lower" classes. She urged the "purification of the home" by "telling and reading stories, teaching kindness to animals, politeness to elders, pity for the unfortunate and weak," clearly implying that their own parents were unable to provide these valuable lessons.[112] Through women's clubs, she hopes her members will teach others "how to clothe children neatly, how to make, and especially mend garments, how to manage households economically, what food is the most nutritious for the money, how to ventilate as thoroughly as possible the dingy stuffy quarters which the majority are forced to inhabit, all these are subjects on which the women of the masses need more knowledge."[113] While she does not fault poor women for the conditions their families confront, her condescension toward them evinces the noblesse oblige often typical of members of the upper middle class. In adopting this position, she emphasizes the social distance between her associates and the women they seek to improve.

Similarly, in her rebuttal to Page's defense of lynching, Church Terrell reveals her class bias. Responding to his claim that a desire for social equality motivated rapes of white women and that middle-class African Americans ignored the problem, she cites southern newspapers to demonstrate "the negroes who are known to have been guilty of the assault have, as a rule, been ignorant, repulsive in appearance and as near the brute creation as it is possible for a human being to be. . . . In conversing with a large number of ignorant negroes, the writer has never found one who seemed to have any idea of what social equality means, or who expressed a desire to put his theory into practice when it was explained to him."[114] Church Terrell was quick to note that the status of such people had roots in slavery. But still in defending her own middle class African Americans from the allegation that they were insensitive to the crimes that excused lynching, Church Terrell was willing to speak disparagingly of a whole segment of her race.

Church Terrell's class and gender complicated her views on women. As noted above, she was an ardent supporter of woman suffrage because she perceived that, like suffrage for African Americans, it was an issue of fundamental civil rights. She saw a close link between women's rights and her aspirations for her own race. In an essay on woman suffrage, she asked rhetorically: "What could be more absurd than to see one group of human beings who are denied rights which they are trying to secure for themselves working to prevent another group from obtaining the same rights? For the very arguments which are advanced against granting the right of suffrage to women are offered by those who have disenfranchised colored men." She continues with some disdain: "To assign reasons in this day and time to prove that it is unjust to withhold from one-half of the human race rights and privileges freely accorded the other half, which is neither more deserving nor more capable of exercising them, seems almost like a reflection upon the intelligence of those to whom they are presented."[115] She was friends with and respected by many of the suffrage leaders of the day. Her class and social status accorded well with many leaders of the movement. While woman suffrage was only one cause among the many she addressed, she saw it as intricately connected to gaining dignity and respect for her race, especially for women of her social class.

She also espoused the view that women should seek appropriate paths for their talents. In an address to students of a prominent African American high school in Washington, D.C., as she lists the accomplishments of its alumni, she points to female graduates who have won prestigious scholarships, have been educational leaders, or have been politically active. While her list of successful male graduates is longer, it is clear that she fully supports the accomplishments of the women as well.[116] Having been a teacher until forced to resign when she married and became pregnant, she continued to endorse women's efforts in the professions. For herself, for example, she opined late in life that she wished she had studied law. Her reason was simple: that training might have facilitated her work in behalf of her race.[117]

Despite her progressive views on women, her appeals to members of the NACW are grounded in gender stereotypes. If she advocated suffrage, she still embraced the dominant gender stereotypes of her day. Women, she insists, are suited to the moral uplift of the race in ways men are not. Further, she focuses the attention of the women on the home: "Believing that it is only through the home that a people can become really good and truly great, the N.A.C.W. shall enter the sacred domain to inculcate right principles of living and correct false views of life. Homes, more homes, purer homes, better homes, is the text upon which our sermons to the masses must be preached."[118] Preaching this kind of social gospel connected her to her white audience. Her values accorded with theirs, and they shared a common viewpoint. Further, she insisted: "The duty of setting a high moral standard and living up to it devolves upon us as colored women in a peculiar way."[119] Again with noblesse oblige, she contends that

> so long as the majority of people call that place home in which the air is foul, the manners bad, and the morals worse, just so long is this so called home a menace to health, a breeder of vice, and the abode of crime. Not alone upon the inmates of these hovels are the awful consequences of their filth and immorality visited, but upon the heads of those who sit calmly by and make no effort to stem the tide of disease and vice will vengeance as surely fall. . . . It is, therefore, into the home, sisters of the Association, that we must go, filled with all the zeal and charity which our mission demands. To the children of the race we owe, as women, a debt which can never be paid until herculean efforts are made to rescue them from evil and shame, for which they are in no way responsible.[120]

She firmly believed that successful, prosperous, advantaged African Americans had a duty not only to serve as models for others of their race but also to work for their betterment and uplift. As we have seen with her agenda for the NACW, part of their role was to enhance the practical skills of the lower classes. In this sense, she shared Washington's views about the necessity for her race to build from the ground up, mastering the basics without losing their aspirations for something better. With Washington, she had great faith in education as a panacea for racism and saw the future of her race as resting with its children. Her ardent support for free kindergartens stemmed from her belief that early interventions could counterbalance early environmental influences. But she also saw education as necessary for much of white America, especially in the South. In a 1905 essay, she argued the need for a special kind of "missionary" work to that region. Although she acknowledge the deplorable conditions that many of her race faced in the South, she saw the white citizenry as in need of substantial help:

> Briefly stated, this service consists in freeing the white South from the thralldom of its prejudices, emancipating it from the slavery of its petty, narrow views which choke the good impulses and throttle the better nature of even its worthiest citizens, teaching them the difference between the highest, purest patriotism and a harmful sectional pride, instilling into the people as a whole a sense of justice which will prevent them from either inflicting or withhold penalties for wrongdoing and crime according to the color of a man's skin, finally, breathing into the hearts of all a compassionate and a Christian charity which shall extend even to the despise and oppressed.[121]

Later in this same article, she repeats an explanation from the *American Missionary Magazine* for the growth of prejudice against African Americans in the North to "'the constant iteration on the part of the dominant South that the Negro is a failure.' . . . [that] secures attention by virtue of its repetition."[122] As with the uplifting of her own race, Church Terrell insisted with DuBois that education, carried out by people like her, was the only way to dispel ignorance and create a basis for greater racial harmony.

As this discussion has indicated, Church Terrell attempted to negotiate the tensions among issues of race, gender, and class. At times one or another of these factors posed obstacles or opened opportunities for her as an individual. Which was most salient in her life and in her advocacy? The introduction to her autobiography suggests the answer to that question: she was a "*colored* woman living in a *white* world." Her ability to live out common gender stereotypes and to share certain matriarchal values with white women often opened doors for her. In contrast, the color of her skin provided no advantages. Her essay on the treatment of African Americans, many of whom were clearly middle class, in Washington, D.C., confirms this perspective. While she sometimes deplored the activities of others in her race, she realized that neither her gender nor her class could protect her from discrimination on the basis of race. In the end, she remained "a *colored* woman in a *white* world."

To modern ears, Church Terrell's discourse sometimes seems condescending to those less fortunate than she. However, she saw the limitations of some in her race as the consequences of the social injustices they had and continued to suffer. She had great compassion for them and equally great indignation at the forces that oppressed them. A woman of considerable means and talent, Church Terrell committed herself to working for justice. She drew on all assets, including her social class, to speak as clearly and as persuasively as she could for those who often had no voice of their own. As a "colored woman in a white world," she left her mark on her age and provided a notable legacy to her race. Her rhetorical heritage lies in her ability to draw on all her many resources to sound a call for social justice for her race. Understanding the obligations of the privileged to those less fortunate, Church Terrell lived out the motto of the NACW; she devoted her energies and advocacy to lifting others as she sought to surmount the barriers of race and gender. With great dignity and sophistication, Church Terrell sought to model what others in her race could become. Speaking to white audiences, she exemplified the possibilities of African Americans in a more just America.

Notes

1. *Christian Century*, 30 October 1940, 1346.
2. Carrie Chapman Catt to Mary Church Terrell, 19 January 1939, Mary Church Terrell papers in the Library of Congress.
3. Karlyn Kohrs Campbell, *Man Cannot Speak for Her: A Critical Study of Early Feminist Rhetoric*, vol. 1 (New York: Praeger, 1989), 145–56.
4. Karlyn Kohrs Campbell, "Mary Church Terrell," in *Women Public Speakers in the United States, 1925–1993: A Bio-Critical Source Book*, ed. Karlyn Kohrs Campbell (Westport, Conn.: Greenwood Press, 1994), 108–19.
5. Mary Church Terrell, *A Colored Woman in a White World* (1940; reprint, New York: Arno Press, 1980), 16, 18. Apparently, Tennessee had no Jim Crow laws at the time.
6. Ibid., 18.
7. Ibid., 20–21.
8. Ibid., 22.
9. Ibid., 28.
10. Ibid., 32.
11. Ibid., 41.
12. Ibid., 46, 48.
13. Ibid., 56–67.
14. Ibid., 99.
15. Ibid., 105. Moss was also friends with Ida B. Wells. The impact of his death led her to begin rigorous antilynching advocacy.

16. Ibid., 101–12, 125.

17. See Beverly W. Jones, "Mary Church Terrell and the National Association of Colored Women, 1896 to 1901," in *Church and Community among Black Southerners 1865–1900* (New York: Garden, 1994), 350–63, for an excellent discussion of Church Terrell's accomplishments in this role.

18. Mary Church Terrell, "The Duty of the National Association of Colored Women to the Race," *AME Church Review* (January 1900): 340–54, rpt. in Beverly Washington Jones, ed., *Quest for Equality: The Life and Writings of Mary Eliza Church Terrell, 1863–1954* (Brooklyn, N.Y.: Carlson, 1990), 144.

19. Campbell, *Women Public Speakers*, 111.

20. Terrell, "Duty," 26.

21. See Terrell, "Duty," 71–86, for a full discussion of her participation in demonstrations.

22. Terrell, *Colored Woman*, 408–9

23. Ibid., 421.

24. Campbell, *Women Public Speakers*, 109.

25. See Mary Church Terrell, "Lynching from a Negro's Point of View," *North American Review* (June 1904), rpt. in Jones, *Quest for Equality*, 167–82. Throughout the discourse of this period, the word "negro" is used by authors to refer to African Americans. Sometimes it is capitalized; other times not. I have decided to honor the original versions of the author and thus have not standardized the capitalization.

26. Karlyn Kohrs Campbell asserts that the only extant copy of this address is the version printed in the *Independent* (see *Man Cannot Speak for Her*, 155). However, Beverly Washington Jones (*Quest for Equality*, 283) suggests a handwritten copy exists in Church Terrell's papers at Howard University.

27. The first statement in the creed was: "I will strive to reach the highest educational, moral, and spiritual efficiency which I can possibly attain." Terrell, *Colored Woman*, 426.

28. Terrell, *Colored Woman*, 426.

29. Booker T. Washington, "Cotton States Exposition Address," 18 September 1895, rpt. in Ronald F. Reid, *American Rhetorical Discourse*, 2nd ed. (Prospect Heights, Ill.: Waveland Press, 1998), 565.

30. Ibid., 566–67.

31. Booker T. Washington, *The Booker T. Washington Papers*, ed. Louis R. Harlan (Urbana: University of Illinois Press, 1972), 38.

32. Frederick Dunn, "The Educational Philosophies of Washington, DuBois, and Houston: Laying the Foundations for Afrocentrism and Multiculturalism," *Journal of Negro Education* 62, no. 1 (1993): 27.

33. Ibid.

34. Ibid.

35. Michael Dennis, "The Skillful Use of Higher Education to Protect White Supremacy," *Journal of Blacks in Higher Education* 32 (Summer 2001): 117.

36. Ibid.

37. W. E. B. DuBois, "On Mr. Booker T. Washington and Others," in *The Souls of Black Folk: Essays and Sketches*, rpt. in Reid, *American Rhetorical Discourse*, 569, 570–71, 573.

38. *Atlantic Monthly*, 90 (September 1902), rpt. in Eugene F. Provenzo Jr., ed., *DuBois on Education* (Walnut Creek, Calif.: AltaMira Press, 2002), 51–63. A slightly changed version of this became chapter 6 in *The Souls of Black Folk*.

39. Ibid., 53-54.

40. Ibid., 54.

41. Ibid., 60–61.

42. Booker T. Washington, ed., *The Negro Problem: A Series of Articles by Representative American Negroes of Today* (New York: James Pott, 1903).

43. W. E. B. DuBois, "The Talented Tenth," rpt. in Provenzo, *DuBois on Education*, 76.

44. Ibid., 84–85.

45. Ibid., 85.

46. Ibid., 86.

47. Ibid., 87.

48. Terrell, *Colored Woman*, 192.

49. Ibid., 193–95.

50. Mary Church Terrell, "First Presidential Address to the National Association of Colored Women," rpt. in Jones, *Quest for Equality*, 134, 135.

51. Fannie Barrier Williams, qtd. in Beverly W. Jones, "Mary Church Terrell and the National Association of Colored Women, 1896 to 1901," in *Church and Community among Black Southerners 1865–1900* (New York: Garden, 1994), 351.

52. Mary Church Terrell, "The History of the Club Women's Movement," *Aframerican Woman's Journal* (Summer–Fall 1940): 34–38, rpt. in Jones, *Quest for Equality*, 316.

53. Qtd. in Jones, "Mary Church Terrell," 352–53. Jones misidentifies Belgarnie as the secretary of the Anti-Slavery Society; Church Terrell ("History") provides the correct organization, 320.

54. Qtd. in Terrell, "History," 321.

55. Qtd. in Jones, "Mary Church Terrell," 353. I am confused by the phrase "'most right,' and our boundless duty." It resembles a phrase from the *Book of Common Prayer* of the Episcopal Church (1892), "it is very meet, right and our bounden duty," which would make sense here.

56. Terrell, "History," 323. The two groups were National League of Colored Women, the outgrowth of the Colored Women's League, and the National Federation of Afro-American Women.

57. Ibid., 324.

58. Jones, "Mary Church Terrell," 23; Terrell, "History," 324–25.

59. Mary Church Terrell, "N.A.C.W. Department Announcement," *Woman's Era* 1896, 3–4, rpt. in Jones, *Quest for Equality*, 132.

60. Campbell, "Mary Church Terrell," 116.

61. See Jones, "Mary Church Terrell," 354–56.

62. Terrell, "First Presidential Address," 134-35.

63. Ibid., 135.

64. Ibid., 136–37.

65. Ibid., 138.

66. Terrell, "Duty," 340–54.

67. Campbell, "Mary Church Terrell," 111. See this work for another, similar analysis of Church Terrell's response. I am indebted to Campbell for the sources of Page's essays.

68. Thomas Nelson Page, "The Lynching of Negroes—Its Cause and Its Prevention," *North American Review* 178, no. 566 (January 1904): 44.

69. Page, "Lynching," 39, 48.

70. Terrell, *Colored Woman*, 224–25.

71. Church Terrell identifies the editor with whom she corresponded only as "Mr. Munro." My research indicates that the editor at the time was George Harvey. I have been unable to determine the full name of the person to whom she refers.

72. Terrell, *Colored Woman*, 224

73. Terrell, "Lynching From a Negro's Point of View," 167–81.

74. *McClure's* 22, no. 5 (March 1904): 548–45. Subsequent articles were: "Second Paper: Some of Its Difficulties and Fallacies," *McClure's* 22, no. 6 (April 1904); and "Third Paper: Its Present Condition and Aspect, as Shown by Statistics," *McClure's* 23, no. 1 (May 1904): 96–102.

75. Again, see Campbell, "Mary Church Terrell," 111–13.

76. Page, "Lynching," 34.

77. Terrell, "Lynching From a Negro's Point of View," 167.

78. Page, "Lynching," 34.

79. Ibid., 36. Page consistently does not capitalize "Negro," although Church Terrell and others do. The variation is practice is undoubtedly linked to racial bias and a distinct lack of respect for the people he is addressing.

80. Ibid., 37.

81. Terrell, "Lynching From a Negro's Point of View," 167.

82. Terrell, "Lynching From a Negro's Point of View," 168.

83. Page, "Lynching," 35.

84. Terrell, "Lynching From a Negro's Point of View," 168

85. Ibid., 169.

86. Ibid., 170

87. Ibid., 171.

88. Ibid., 172–73, 174.

89. Ibid., 174–75, 176.

90. Ibid., 176–77.

91. Ibid., 178.

92. Ibid., 180, 181.

93. Ibid., 168, 170, 181.

94. Ibid., 168, 170.

95. Terrell, *Colored Woman*, 226.

96. Ibid., 231.

97. Ibid., 234. Church Terrell identifies the writer as Bruce Porter from San Francisco but gives no other information about him.

98. Mary Church Terrell, "What It Means to Be Colored in the Capital of the United States," *Independent*, 24 January 1907, 181–86, rpt. in Jones, *Quest for Equality*.

99. Campbell, *Man Cannot Speak for Her*, vol. 2, 421.

100. "The Effects of Disenfranchisement Upon the Colored Women of the South," 13 typed pages, Library of Congress, ms. 16976, reel 23, container 32, 385–97, qtd. in Campbell, *Man Cannot Speak for Her*, 2:152.

101. Terrell, "What It Means," 283.

102. Ibid., 282–84.

103. For a discussion of "perspective by incongruity," see Kenneth Burke, *Permanence and Change: An Anatomy of Purpose*, 3rd ed. (Berkeley and Los Angeles: University of California Press, 1984), 71–97.

104. Terrell, "What It Means," 285–88.

105. Ibid., 288–89. Church Terrell narrates similar instances in her autobiography. See especially 246–49.

106. Ibid., 290.

107. Ibid., 290, 291.

108. Ibid., 291.

109. Mary Church Terrell, "Needed: Women Lawyers," *Negro Digest* (September 1943): 57–59, rpt. in Jones, *Quest for Equality*, 327.

110. Campbell, "Mary Church Terrell," 114–15.

111. Mary Church Terrell, "Peonage in the United States: The Convict Lease System and the Chain Gangs," *Nineteenth Century* (August 1907): 306–22, rpt. in Jones, *Quest for Equality*, 255–73; and "Lynching from a Negro's Point of View," *North American Review* (June 1904), rpt. in Jones, *Quest for Equality*, 167–82.

112. Terrell, "Duty," 143.

113. Terrell, "First Presidential Address," 137.

114. Terrell, "Lynching from a Negro's Point of View," 169.

115. Mary Church Terrell, "The Justice of Woman Suffrage," *Crisis* 4 (September 1912): 243–45, rpt. in Jones, *Quest for Equality*, 307, 308.

116. Mary Church Terrell, "Graduates and Former Students of Washington Colored High School," *Voice of the Negro* (June 1904): 221–27, rpt. in Jones, *Quest for Equality*, 159–66.

117. Terrell, "Women Lawyers," 327–28.

118. Terrell, "First Presidential Address," 135.

119. Terrell, "Duty," 148.

120. Terrell, "First Presidential Address," 135.

121. Mary Church Terrell, "Service Which Should Be Rendered the South," *Voice of the Negro* (February 1905): 182–86, rpt. in Jones, *Quest for Equality*, 206.

122. Terrell, "Service," 207–8.

Radical Labor in a Feminine Voice:
The Rhetoric of Mary Harris "Mother" Jones and Elizabeth Gurley Flynn

Mari Boor Tonn

8

Prior to the second wave of feminism, to mention "women" and "labor" in the same breath often conjured images of childbirth, an event that long circumscribed the reigning cultural view of woman's prescribed domestic care-taking roles. Paid labor, by contrast, commonly evoked masculine public sphere associations, impressions magnified by adding the word "unions." And in conspicuous ways, both public employment and the militant coerciveness of common labor union practices initiated in the industrial labor movement violated the cardinal virtues of domesticity and submissiveness prescribed for True Women since the onset of the Industrial Revolution.[1] So, too, the raw bawdiness of some mining camps and factory towns seemed at the farthest remove from genteel Womanhood's remaining tenets of purity and piety.

Yet in recent years scholars not only have begun documenting the broad scope of women's long history as wage-earners but also unearthing their pivotal presence as active rank-and-file union members and highly influential champions of the workers' cause. In fact, prior to the Civil War roughly half of all women actually performed paid labor in some form, through piecework, as domestics, or in stints in various burgeoning industries.[2] In the early textile mills, women workers outnumbered men two to one, and by midcentury women composed a quarter of all factory employees generally.[3] Swelling the percentages of female industrial workers were largely invisible "permanent part-timers," including women who often substituted temporarily for others during emergencies to safeguard their positions.[4]

Despite widespread participation by women in the paid workforce, various factors rendered unionization of female employees particularly challenging. Because some younger, single women viewed employment as a temporary hiatus before marriage, they opted to forego what they perceived as the "unsexing" political dimension of union membership.[5] Many working wives and mothers, on the other hand, lacked both the energy and time for union meetings and job actions given the demands of performing essentially two full-time shifts: ten- or twelve-hour days on factory floors plus a full slate of household and child-rearing chores. The markedly lower wage-scales of women also handicapped both single women and female heads of households as prospective dues-paying union members. And even if such difficulties were surmounted, female workers still faced explicit exclusion from the vast majority of male-dominated unions in mixed-sex industries. Thus it is not surprising that women made up only between 3 percent to 5 percent of union membership around the turn of the century.[6]

The distinctive culture of women also contributed to a paradox regarding their labor activity: although vastly underrepresented in sheer numbers as union members, many women nonetheless often met or even eclipsed their male counterparts as labor radicals. Beyond transferring their domestic skills to paid professions such as garment making, the earliest women workers also brought into the workplace their expectations for control, creativity, and communal care cultivated in their work in the home. Moreover, with the escalation of feudal-like practices in early industry—including speedups, wage cuts to below-subsistence levels, and the proliferation of job-site health hazards—women confronted the mounting threats to the physical survival of their families with protective maternal ferocity. Similar to politicized mothers in other reform campaigns,[7] women labor activists vehemently asserted their "right" as caretakers to adequate food, shelter, and safety for children and other dependents. Beyond catalyzing women and galvanizing their resolve, the pronounced relational emphasis of traditionally female care-giving roles also led women to embrace an enlarged view of the "collective" and its interests beyond what many unions conceived and operationalized. As a result, women often made more thoroughgoing demands on employers, forced earlier governmental involvement and reforms, enjoyed greater success in forging solidarity both among workers of diverse backgrounds and with community members, capitulated and compromised less readily, and frequently employed more extreme tactics. As early as the 1840s, women were at the forefront of labor militancy in the United States,[8] and this radical streak figured prominently in key labor struggles well into the next century.[9] Emblematic are the massive walkouts by textile workers in Lawrence, Massachusetts, in 1882 and 1912. Largely conducted by women, these strikes were among the most militant in labor history.

Many of the industrial labor movement's most devoted and radical voices were women. Some translated, wrote, or edited Socialist or Marxist publications. Florence Kelley issued the first English translation of Frederick Engels's *The Condition of the Working Class in England,* and Meta Stein Lilienthal translated a second version of August Bebel's *Women Under Socialism.* Charlotte Perkins Gilman authored *Women and Economics* and published the magazine the *Forerunner.* Popular pamphlets such as *Shop Talks on Economics, From Fireside to Factory,* and *A Woman of the Future* all were penned by a woman's hand. Editors of Socialist newspapers included Kate Richards O'Hare of the *National Rip-Saw,* Ida Crouch-Hazlett of the *Montana News,* Lena Morris of both the Alaska *Labor News* and the Seattle *Daily Call,* Mary Marcy of the *International Socialist News,* and Josephine Conger-Kaneko of the *Socialist Woman.*[10]

Other women were among the movement's most tireless, courageous, and compelling labor agitators. Scores of women gave countless stirring speeches, constantly courted danger and imprisonment, engineered dramatic and coercive tactics—such as parades, strikes, boycotts, sitdowns, or sabotage—and otherwise helped to mobilize the movement's constituency. Included among them are Kate Richards O'Hare, Mary Halley, Annie Welsenback, Leonora O'Reilly, Clara Lemlich, Jeannie Bateman, Pauline Newman, Josephine Lis, Ella Reeve Bloor, Sarah Bagley, Rose Pastor Stokes,

Mary Skubitz, Leonora Barry, Bessie Hillman, Rose Pesotta, and Dorothy Bellanca. Some, such as Fannie Sellins, were killed for their efforts.[11]

Two women in particular, Mary Harris "Mother" Jones and Elizabeth Gurley Flynn, earned stature as labor movement legends. Jones persists as an icon for contemporary champions of progressive causes.[12] Separated in age by nearly six decades, both gained reputations for their "leather-lunged" and militant oratory, their disarming fearlessness, and their uncanny talent for captivating the minds and hearts of audiences regardless of sex or ethnicity. Some observers have linked the pair through what Marx termed "the feminine ferment" of the movement. "The fiery example of Mother Jones had one conspicuous follower," notes Lloyd Morris, "Elizabeth Gurley Flynn."[13]

To some degree, Jones and Flynn are anomalous as women labor movement leaders. Unlike the short-lived careers or sporadic involvement of many female labor activists, both women committed half a century of their lives fully to their political causes.[14] Although many female labor advocates divided their time among an array of causes, Jones and Flynn remained relatively focused on economic reforms. Both have escaped the historical "invisibility" of many other key female agitators, each gaining a notoriety that has generated biographies;[15] anthologies of their speeches, writings, or correspondence;[16] and autobiographies.[17] Their public renown no doubt resulted not merely from their extraordinary rhetorical talents and effectiveness but also from their unconventional affiliations with more recognized male-exclusive or male-dominated unions and labor causes.

Remarkably enough, the closest and the most famous of Jones's many alliances was with the United Mine Workers of America (UMWA), which hired her as a paid organizer sometime in the 1880s when its locals closed membership and even meetings to women. Despite initial male hostility, her ability to persuade impoverished coal miners to risk starvation, imprisonment, and even death to join the union became unrivaled in the movement's history.[18]

Flynn gained prominence fighting in the Industrial Workers of the World's (IWW) free speech battles in the Northwest and upper Midwest, participating in various labor strikes throughout the country during the first three decades of the century, and by defending indicted unionists and other political dissenters, such as those opposed to the entry of the United States into World War I. During her ten-year stint as an IWW or Wobbly "jawsmith," she earned star billing as "the ablest speaker on the IWW platform,"[19] an open-door organization nonetheless so dominated by men that Wobbly songwriter Joe Hill once characterized it as "a kind of one-legged freakish animal of a union."[20] For several of her final years, Flynn was embroiled in various challenges to the right to membership in the Communist Party of the United States, an organization that elected her its first female chair.

Although the longevity of their vocations, their celebrity, and certain of their political alliances were somewhat atypical of female labor reformers, their radicalism and the contours of their pronounced militancy were not. In many respects, the rhetorical and philosophical approaches of these two women reflect key influences of female culture that have been hallmarks of women's labor union involvement. Thus, despite their distinctly different persuasive styles and the alternate paths of their respective careers, Jones and Flynn are useful case studies to explore the assorted ways women *as women* helped to shape the rhetorical and radical texture of the industrial labor movement. The purpose of this essay is to place Jones and Flynn within the philosophical, strategic, and militant tradition of radical female labor union activists, many of whom drew upon female experiences as both a motivation for their activism and also a tactical resource.

In what follows, I first provide a brief overview of the activities of women as labor unionists. I next discuss certain similarities and differences between Jones and Flynn in terms of their life experiences, philosophies, and rhetorical styles.

The bulk of the essay then treats salient ways in which Jones and Flynn reflect key dimensions of radical labor unionism by females: their approach to political activism and reform; their demands to broaden the labor agenda beyond the "bread" of wages to include various workplace "roses;" their commitment to an expansive, inclusive solidarity; and their reliance on maternal and other female experiences and strategies as both catalyzing and informing their militancy.

Because Jones's career centered solely on union organizing, the texts analyzed here primarily are the surviving complete speeches given extemporaneously at public organizing meetings of coal miners and national and international labor union conventions between 1901 and 1922. Augmenting these texts is testimony given during congressional hearings into mining conditions in 1914, her 1926 autobiography, extended fragments of public speeches reported in various newspapers, and select interviews, all of which provide further glimpses into Jones's motivations and philosophy. From Flynn's debut as a teenage labor activist in 1906 until her death in 1964, she was prolific as both a speaker and writer in various labor-related causes. Some of Flynn's numerous speeches and writings have been anthologized, although a much more extensive body of rhetorical documents are housed at the Tamiment Library in New York City. The texts examined for this analysis include complete transcripts and detailed outlines of speeches, radio addresses, essays and columns in various outlets such as the Communist newspaper the *Daily Worker*; statements surrounding her expulsion from the board of the American Civil Liberties Union (ACLU) in 1940 and during her 1953 trial and conviction for violating the Smith Act, which criminalized Communist Party membership; her public speaking teaching notes; and two books—her autobiography, the first edition of which chronicled her career from 1906 to 1926, and her account of her imprisonment at Alderson penitentiary.

Women as Labor Radicals

Although cultural distinctions between home and work had constrained most women as paid employees and potential unionists, many nonetheless readily rejected the private/public boundaries as artificial. Almost from the outset of their involvement with labor, women used their domestic experiences, sensibilities, and obligations to expand the parameters of union philosophy, objectives, and strategies. The "bread and roses" campaigns of women that began as early as the 1820s, for example, often made more far-reaching claims on employers than male unions had considered or dared by broadening the critique of capitalist development beyond the "bread" of wage disputes to include expectations for the "roses" of autonomy, human justice, and personal dignity, qualities many women perceived they had enjoyed and fostered as homemakers and mothers. Translated into concrete demands, these "roses" included employee input into factory operating procedures and policies and workers' rights to adequate sanitation, a safe workplace, decent housing, child care, and even time "which belongs to us."[21] As Alice Kessler-Harris explains, "In contrast to the perceptions of skilled male workers, dignity [for women workers] involved not so much the practice of one's craft, as the capacity to retain one's sense of place while earning a living."[22] Illustrative is the first known "turnout" by women workers in 1827 in Paterson, New Jersey, a strike spontaneously precipitated by management's arbitrary change in the lunch hour. Although some credit this early desire for self-sovereignty and self-respect to the Yankee heritage of the first female millworkers,[23] the yearning for such "roses" endured among women workers long after immigrants dominated the ranks of factory operatives. As one woman union member put the matter decades later when discussing her organizing impulse, "There must be something more than the economic issue[;] there must be idealism."[24]

Although female workers first organized around such "self-love" issues, they soon became catalyzed as well by "other-love," a concern for individuals and for families increasingly jeopardized by a rapid mix of declining wages, accelerating work quotas, rising costs, and mounting occupational hazards. Actuated by what Carol Gilligan and Sara Ruddick term an "ethic of care" and "maternal thinking," respectively,[25] women rapidly ensconced themselves as the radical standard bearers of labor-related issues in multiple respects:[26] women pioneered various labor reforms; preached and practiced a more inclusive brand of solidarity; and routinely employed an array of militant, coercive tactics. Following a series of defeats in one-on-one confrontations with industry, women began courting the outside political power of city councils and state legislatures.[27] By the end of the 1840s, the Lowell Female Labor Reform Association had impelled the first governmental investigation into oppressive labor conditions and had engineered the first state laws in the nation limiting daily hours an employer could demand of males or females;[28] later women activists also played pivotal roles in the passage of legislated reforms such as factory inspections and child labor laws.[29] This sense of obligation for the safeguarding of others persists as a key mobilizing force for women involved with labor issues and continues, at times, to exact unprecedented results. In 1982, for example, 20,000 Chinese women garment workers, galvanized by their duties as mothers and family breadwinners, defied potent "old world" cultural prescriptions for female docility and took to the streets in the largest labor strike in the history of New York's Chinatown.[30]

Moreover, given what Ardis Cameron describes as "women's belief in the public nature of individual misfortune,"[31] sympathy emerges as a salient and persistent theme in their conceptions of labor solidarity. Although, by definition, unionism trumpets the collective, women were more likely to strike spontaneously over mistreatment of other workers,[32] to reject settlement offers that failed to accommodate all workers equitably, to guarantee that "everyone" or "no one" be arrested on picket lines,[33] and to form powerful empathetic alliances with individuals of differing ethnic backgrounds, occupations, personal circumstance, or even class standing.[34] More than a quarter of the female activists in the vast 1912 Lawrence, Massachusetts, textile strike, for example, were housewives of various nationalities and social stations rather than mill employees.[35] This sympathetic impulse also emerges in the résumés of many labor activists who frequently divided their energies among union struggles, relief work, defending the rights of the accused and convicted, battling discrimination against blacks and ethnic groups, and woman suffrage.[36]

Additionally, given the inclination of women socialized into maternal roles to view issues of survival as more important than arbitrary "rules" and laws,[37] women often responded to the physical threats inherent in capitalist malfeasance with a pronounced militancy sometimes surpassing their male counterparts. During the 1912 Lawrence strike, for example, the audacious public spectacles and guerrilla tactics of female factory operatives and housewives brandishing red pepper, scalding water, rocks, and razors prompted one mill official to dub them "[r]adicals of the worst sort," an assessment echoed by local media, who concluded the defiance and fierceness of women rendered them "worse than the men."[38] Far from unusual, the highly aggressive texture of the Lawrence uprising mirrors numerous historical episodes in which threats to the survival of literal and fictive kin tapped into a deep reservoir of female militancy. Flour riots by housewives in the 1830s, immigrant food strikes in the early twentieth century, and nationwide meat boycotts before and after World War II are salient examples.[39] Although such protective fury was and is by no means unique to women, many nonetheless often proved to be more willing and earlier militants. In 1902, for example, Orthodox Jewish women mocked the initial reluctance of men to join them in looting overpriced kosher butcher shops, dousing the purloined meat with kerosene, and burning it in public demonstrations.[40] Similarly, contrary to conventional wisdom, women in the Lawrence strike were far from puppets of the controversial IWW, labor's most radical wing; rather, as Cameron argues, women proved markedly more militant than Wobbly official Bill Haywood and the organization's other male leaders, who "frequently found themselves pressing strikers to curb their emotions, to practice nonviolence, and . . . to accept [an early] settlement, an act that infuriated large segments of the [majority female-inhabited] neighborhoods, especially its most militant women."[41] In 1881 Knights of Labor leader Terence Powderly applauded the combative grit of the female Knights, concluding they ranked as the "best men in the Order."[42]

Not all male unionists, however, were as enamored as Powderly of the tenacity and belligerence of women comrades, especially their propensity as institutional mavericks. The president of the union of boot and shoe workers lamented the uncompromising inclination of the female rank and file to "hold out to the bitter end." Indeed, in 1899 women cigar makers stood fast while male unionists abandoned the strike. A decade later, some 20,000 New York female shirtwaist makers walked out in defiance of male union leaders who feared retaliatory job dismissal.[43] Similarly, in 1912 the willfulness and recalcitrance of Lawrence women initially both unsettled and frustrated Wobbly leaders brought in to govern the massive walkout of 25,000 workers. In the end, the IWW adapted to the informal organizational structure favored and practiced by the female rank and file and who, Haywood eventually conceded years later, "won the strike."[44]

This clear interface between domestic care-taking practices and philosophies and the public militancy of radical labor unionism is acknowledged in the maternal sobriquets attached to women labor agitators such as Ella Reeve "Mother" Bloor, Leonora "Mother" O'Reilly, Mary "Mother" Skubitz, and, the most notable, Mary Harris "Mother" Jones. Even the young and sensual beauty Flynn, sometimes called "Girlie" by her early male Wobbly comrades,[45] in time became characterized periodically as "Mother Flynn."[46] More than a mere strategy to bolster the ethos of such women leaders, motherhood as the chief principle and practice of female domestic culture thoroughly infused female approaches to the labor movement, both constraining and catalyzing women to act, influencing their specific demands on management and government, informing their conceptions of solidarity and methods of mobilization, and fueling their militancy.

Biographical, Thematic, and Stylistic Comparisons and Contrasts

Illuminating the rhetorical careers of Mary Harris "Mother" Jones and Elizabeth Gurley Flynn as well as placing both women within the larger militant tradition of female unionists requires exploring the life experiences that catapulted them into labor activism and influenced their respective philosophies and rhetorical styles. Although the approaches of both women to their missions reflect key characteristics of radical female unionists generally, Jones and Flynn were not replicas of each other or their militant sisters. Even so, an examination of their personal experiences, guiding principles, and strategic choices can shed light not only on each one's unique contribution to the industrial labor movement but also on significant commonalities they share with other female labor union radicals.

Mere acquaintances, Jones and Flynn lived lives ideologically parallel in certain respects; in other important ways, however, their personal, political, and rhetorical histories followed nearly polar paths.[47] Although both typically spoke extemporaneously several times a day,[48] Jones, a former schoolteacher with diploma and debate credentials, preferred a loose, inductive storytelling style she enlivened with dramatic visual stunts, exchanges with audience members, caustic wit, mild profanity, and creative ad hominem attacks. Denouncing enemies of labor in the coarse vernacular of "blood-sucking pirates," capitalist "parasites," and "corrupt, rotten, decayed piece[s] of humanity,"[49] she also occasionally berated male coal miners with withering indictments of their cowardice, arguing in a 1903 speech near Toledo that "the bullets which should be sent into your own measly, miserable dirty carcasses, shoot down innocent men [instead]."[50] In ironic contrast, Flynn, a high school dropout, often argued with a seasoned debater's deductive precision, a skill that reflected her early desire to be a constitutional lawyer and one well suited to and continually honed in the legal defense work that became her "specialty."[51] Indeed, in her later years as a public-speaking instructor, she warned against insulting and alienating audiences by the kind of vulgar language that had become a Jones trademark.[52] Moreover, although Jones believed in the force of written arguments, even helping to launch the most well known Socialist newspaper, the *Appeal to Reason* in 1895,[53] she only rarely plied her rhetorical trade in such media. Flynn, however, frequently augmented her frequent speaking with essays in an array of political organs including *Solidarity*, *New Masses*, and *International Socialist Review*; was an early editor of the *Industrial Worker*;[54] and during the last twenty-six years of her life contributed multiple weekly columns to the Communist newspaper, the *Daily Worker*.[55]

Similarly, whereas Jones would answer only to "Mother," the most salient of her strategic personae, Flynn bristled at this maternal tag.[56] In some measure, this difference may have been rooted in their diverse experiences with domesticity. For Jones, labor agitation filled a void left by the deaths of her unionist husband and four children to yellow fever in her middle years; in contrast, Flynn gave her first major speech at the age of fifteen and later sacrificed her marriage, other romantic liaisons, and the rearing of her only surviving child to career commitments.[57]

To some extent, they likewise differed in certain of their political loyalties and philosophies and approaches to institutions. An incorrigible renegade, Jones abandoned the IWW only six months after signing its manifesto and also split bitterly from the Socialist Party, the forerunner of which she helped found more than a decade earlier.[58] Conversely, Flynn devoted a full decade of her life to the Wobblies, and earned leadership roles in various political organizations including the International Labor Defense Union Fund, the ACLU, and the American Communist Party, which elected her its first female chair. The pair also diverged on crucial issues such as the importation and unionization of Chinese laborers and the United States' entry into World War I.

The two also parted company on certain means to induce capitalist capitulation. At least once, Jones's "bloody shirt" rhetoric moved beyond the figurative, igniting violence as the frenzied crowd waved the blood-soaked bits of a wounded mine-guard's coat she tossed them.[59] Yet, at the same time, she roundly criticized worker sabotage as a self-defeating coercive tool. Preserving rather than destroying machinery and mineshafts protected the workers' self- interests, she argued in a West Virginia speech in 1912, given that factories and mines are "our property. It is inside where our jobs are."[60] For her part, Flynn harbored more aversion to violence, a reluctance other radicals occasionally criticized.[61] Still, she never completely repudiated her infamous 1917 speech and essay defending and advocating worker sabotage, remaining philosophically conflicted throughout her lifetime over the method's ethics and efficacy.[62]

Nonetheless, the two agitators shared several personal, rhetorical, and political affinities. Each descended from Irish rebel stock and ended their lives on soil outside their native countries on the eve of pivotal U.S. ideological change. The eldest child of poor tenant farmers active in and exiled during the Irish Revolution, Jones was born around 1830 in Cork, Ireland, and died in Maryland in 1930 just prior to sweeping New Deal economic reforms. A Concord, New Hampshire, native, Flynn was born in 1890 to a "shanty Irish" socialist father and "lace curtain Irish" feminist mother and died during her second political pilgrimage to the Soviet Union in 1964 just as U.S. political winds regarding race and gender began their dramatic shift. Both also came of age in poverty, buried all of their children prematurely, and lost intimates to revolutionary violence.[63]

Their most conspicuous and significant commonality, however, was unwavering and undiluted devotion to the class struggle. For both women, this commitment not only dominated virtually every aspect of their lives for more than fifty years, but their thorough conflation of the personal and political was mirrored in their ideology and their rhetoric. In Jones's case, coal camps and factory towns literally became her "home" and "family," leading the peripatetic agitator purportedly to quip to a Congressman during hearings on Mexico in 1910, "My address is like my shoes. It travels with me."[64] For her part, Flynn refused to allow even pregnancy to slow an exhausting speaking schedule that she once estimated resulted in some 10,000 speeches in her lifetime.[65] And like many of their militant labor sisters, each also was galvanized by the intensely human dimension of their crusade. "I spoke at the funerals of men and women shot down on the picket line," Flynn wrote in notes for her autobiography, "and the iron entered my soul."[66] In Jones's case, preservative maternal love catalyzed her and grounded her philosophy, as suggested in her poignant and poetic recollections in her autobiography of the massive 1919 steel strike:

Human flesh, warm and soft and capable of being wounded, went naked up against steel; steel that is cold as old stars, and harder than death and incapable of pain. Bayonets and guns and steel rails and battleships, bombs and bullets are made of steel. And only babies are made of flesh. More babies to grow up and work in steel, to hurl themselves against the bayonets, to know the tempered resistance of steel.[67]

Hence, both women also had little tolerance for theoretical political abstractions that ignored the particulars of personal circumstance, and Jones's interactive, narrative, and highly intimate rhetoric, in particular, was devoid of intellectual analyses. In an oblique critique of IWW leadership in a 1914 public speech in Seattle, Jones remarked, "I have no patience with those idealists and visionaries who preach fine spun theories and cry down everybody but themselves. Let us keep our feet on the ground."[68] Although certain of Flynn's early speeches bordered on the esoteric, she nonetheless recognized the centrality of actual people in any political principle. Responding to critics within New York City's circle of intellectual radicals concerning her handling of the Paterson, New Jersey, silk strike, Flynn argued in a 1914 speech before the New York Civic Club Forum that theories must be applied "as the people, the industry, the time, and the place indicate," concluding that astute agitators "realize that we are dealing with human beings and not with chemicals."[69] Similarly, in a speech published in *Political Affairs* during the last year of her life, the labor union veteran couched her disagreements with other Communist officials this way: "I may not have the clearest conception of Marxism, but as I learned it *from experience in movements of the masses* . . . it was based on class struggle, on the conception of organizing the workers, as the basic power in the progressive movement."[70]

The pair's unflagging allegiance to the class struggle also led each of them to controversial tactics and associations, which landed both behind bars many times. Beyond her numerous incarcerations for violating court injunctions, Jones spent several months in a West Virginia military prison following her murder conspiracy conviction; Flynn's ten experiences with the corrections system included a two-year term in the Alderson penitentiary for violating the Smith Act.

Moreover, the careers of both women reveal pronounced streaks of willful political and institutional autonomy, a trait male labor union officials often criticized in female unionists in general. Although Jones and Flynn at times openly embraced alternative political parties–Socialist, and Socialist and Communist, respectively–each periodically and concurrently supported traditional party platforms or candidates. Likewise, both women occasionally fired harsh broadsides against union officials for corruption or cowardice, and their penchant for insubordination and political independence prompted their ouster from various organizations. On at least two occasions, Jones's notoriously stormy formal association with the UMWA crumbled under the weight of officials' frustration with the maverick, and in 1911 the Socialist Party reportedly expelled her for publicly accusing the national secretary of dishonesty.[71] Similarly, the IWW terminated Flynn in 1916 for defying the directives of Wobbly leader Bill Haywood.[72] Most ironic, in 1940 Flynn staunchly refused to resign from the ACLU because of her Communist membership, leading her fellow board members to vote her removal from the free-speech organization she had cofounded two decades earlier.[73]

Finally, in some measure, the philosophies, behaviors, and strategies of both women reflect their experiences and sensibilities as women, especially working-class women, pledged to economic reforms. Given the loss of their own children, both keenly empathized with maternal concern for the physical survival of children across circumstances. In a 1915 interview recounting the treatment of imprisoned unionists, herself included, Jones described the maternal experiences and anguish that propelled mothers such as herself to sacrifice their own interests for a labor "family": "I remember it was raining," she recalled.

> Rain never means green grass to me; it always means wet babies and pneumonia. And then, again, I remember how they drove the boys out of their cells in to snow without their clothes at the point of the guns. . . . [B]ut worst of all, I had to watch [their mothers] that stayed behind. . . . [O]utside [my cell] Mary was calling to me, "Did you see my Johnny?" and I stood there and I knew that children are a terrible thing to have, but a more terrible thing to lose.[74]

The death of Flynn's last son as a young adult in 1940 likewise caused her to "feel deep sympathy now for mothers in wartime, who must part with sons; whose nights are anguished with uncertainty and whose days are dimmed with anxiety and fear."[75] Even decades earlier, she understood that the factors that drove women to "be the most militant or most conservative element in a strike" were often rooted in the same maternal impulse.[76] Given that "all the instincts of maternity are aroused to protect her little ones," she wrote in an essay in 1911, women often "exhibit exceptional courage" in their demands for food and safety or, conversely, adamantly resist job actions that threaten to compound economic hardships on their families.[77]

Despite their sensibilities to the peculiar experiences of females, economic reform was the foremost priority of both Jones and Flynn, leading each to exhibit ambivalence about the intersection of female political equality and labor union issues. On the one hand, Jones firmly believed that the moral tenor of genuine "maternal thinking" and an "ethic of care" held promise to transfigure the political public sphere. Yet she also was deeply disaffected by the woman suffrage movement's class stratification; appeared to resent the time, money, and energy that it and other crusades siphoned away from labor politics; was bitterly disappointed that Colorado women who had won the vote in 1893 had not used it to better conditions of workers in their state; and possessed deeply conflicted faith in the ballot to effect radical reform or to provide immediate relief to threatened families. While Flynn, who had won her first grammar school medal arguing for woman suffrage, continually conceded the ballot was a fundamental right of citizenship, her public comments during her Wobbly years even further developed some of Jones's reservations. In a detailed outline for a 1909 speech devoted entirely to the suffrage question, Flynn echoed Jones's views and presented a litany of reasons why working women, who were more sorely in need of a revised economic system, should not agitate for suffrage.[78] Emblematic of conflicts between her egalitarian principles and her abiding economic concerns was her adamant opposition to the Equal Rights Amendment (ERA). Although Flynn generally favored women's political equality and even advocated military conscription for women, she feared the ERA would invalidate protective legislation for female employees and laws requiring males to compensate current or former wives for the wageless work of mothering.[79]

Despite certain and expected idiosyncrasies, much of the militant texture of their agitation nonetheless bore significant likenesses to the efforts of the other and also of their radical working-class labor sisters. Both fought ferociously for "roses" as well as "bread"; defined "family" as a kinship of class and class consciousness unrestricted by gender, ethnicity, race, or occupation; and generally favored relational integrity, loyalty, and power over institutional authority. At times, both women championed, used, and cooperated with traditional political processes and players to accomplish their ends just as many of their foremothers effectively had done; but like many other women in labor, they also resorted to militant, coercive tactics when argument failed. Obviously, some members of both sexes in the labor organizations and political parties with which they affiliated also exhibited certain of these traits. Even so, key aspects of both women's labor agitation appear nonetheless "gendered," influenced in their direction, emphasis, and form by experiences common to female culture.

Political Activity and Pioneering Reforms

The lengthy careers of both Jones and Flynn mirror key philosophies and tactics that were and continue to be salient aspects of labor union activity by women. Similar to many other female labor reformers, each operated both within and outside of conventional political systems; framed the labor question more broadly than mere wage disputes; viewed labor as an inclusive, extended "family" linked by common class interests rather than specific occupation, gender, or race; and drew upon skills, strategies, and philosophies rooted and cultivated in domestic life experiences.

Just as early women labor sympathizers appealed to government as a means to achieve labor reforms, both Flynn and Jones believed the battle for labor had to be fought on various fronts, including the traditional political system. In fact, Flynn often noted that she greatly admired pioneers such as Sarah Bagley, president of the Lowell Association, who spearheaded both the first governmental labor investigations and the first state law limiting work hours.[80] Despite her typically negative stance on woman suffrage, Jones argued to a UMWA gathering in Columbus, Ohio, in 1911, "We must realize that the woman is the foundation of the government; that no government is greater or ever can be greater than its women." She also noted the significance of maternal influences in political affairs.[81] Although neither Jones nor Flynn regarded the ballot or political lobbying as sufficient, each nonetheless keenly appreciated the potential leverage of the franchise, law, and legislation in effecting long-term changes in industrial conditions.

Flynn, in particular, grew increasingly committed to inserting labor issues into elections and other political processes, particularly after women had gained the vote. Following the ratification of the Nineteenth Amendment, she vigorously courted women as a political bloc, arguing in a radio address in Newark, New Jersey, in the 1940s, "Intensive election activity can be the medium for women to best further their special interests as women," especially as connected to their roles as paid and unpaid laborers.[82] During her Communist years, she campaigned strenuously against the ERA and for various political hopefuls, including President Franklin Roosevelt, and many of her radio addresses and columns during this period reflected a deep-seated concern with political process and political efficacy. For example, a decade and a half before the explosive "Freedom Summers," in a 1947 radio address in Washington, Pennsylvania, Flynn lamented poll taxes and literacy tests that effectively denied southern blacks, among the nation's most impoverished, a right of citizenship inscribed in law.[83] Moreover, like Jones, Flynn was keenly aware of the power of the courts to enforce, ignore, or strike down hard-won rights and labor-related reforms; thus she kept a watchful eye on judicial appointments, testifying in Congress, for example, against the confirmation of Tom Clark to the Supreme Court. His nomination, she declared in a 1949 document, was "an affront on specific counts to the Negro people, the labor movement, and to all Americans who stand by the Bill of Rights."[84] In more general terms, she tirelessly worked to mobilize and influence voters—especially women—on a myriad of issues and candidates, occasionally taking radio listeners down the names on a ballot one by one. Flynn even launched two unsuccessful bids for political office in New York, following in the footsteps of numerous female labor radicals whose involvement in conventional political activities she applauded in several essays and columns.[85]

While equally spirited, Jones's political approach was sometimes less orthodox. In 1903 she orchestrated a dramatic parade of impoverished and disfigured mill children across three states to pressure President Theodore Roosevelt for child labor reform. To a great extent, Kate Richards O'Hare modeled the 1922 Children's Crusade to see President Harding on Jones's effort; O'Hare's march from St. Louis to Washington, D.C., showcased families of less well known political dissidents still imprisoned after World War I, and she termed these walking dependents and loved ones "living petitions."[86] Between 1907 and 1910, Jones engineered a telegram and petition-writing campaign to state and federal officials demanding new trials for Mexican revolutionaries imprisoned and convicted in Arizona, and she later was a key witness in the ensuing congressional inquiry.[87] Forever pledged to the power of the personal, she routinely requested and gained individual audiences with governors, members of Congress, and every president but Theodore Roosevelt. In 1915 Flynn copied this tactic, winning a meeting with President Wilson in a failed effort to stay the execution of Wobbly songwriter Joe Hill.[88]

Jones also preached and practiced more standard political actions. She pushed for and testified in multiple labor-related congressional investigations, attended roll-call votes in Congress on labor legislation, occasionally campaigned for political aspirants she deemed labor-worthy, and often advised and reported to union audiences on pending legislation, political candidates, or voting records of elected officials. Possibly because she had no vote, Jones frequently chastised male audiences for foolishly squandering their precious franchise, as illustrated in a speech to the Central Federated Union in New York City in 1904: "If a mule had a ballot, he would exercise more sense in voting than you do," she exclaimed.[89] And these critiques sometimes contained nods to female political savvy, leaving her genuine attitude toward woman suffrage open to dispute as suggested in a speech before the Central Labor Council in Cincinnati in 1902:

Men will work together, will go to jail together, will defend each other, will trust each other, will support each other. Why is it that they cannot stand together at the ballot box? No bayonet, no injunction can interfere there. You pay Senators, Governors, Legislators, and then beg on your knees for them to pass a bill in labor's protection. You will never solve the problem until you let in the women.[90]

Like other women labor activists, their efforts were occasionally successful. Flynn's 1909 essays in the *Industrial Worker* exposing sexual fraternization between prostitutes and male prison guards in Spokane, Washington, for example, led city officials to pass legislation for women prison matrons.[91] Most notable, perhaps, was Flynn's role as a pioneer in legal defense. Beyond developing the Workers Defense Union, the first united front defense group in the movement, she co-founded the ACLU, an organization whose expansive work continues to cross various political and class boundaries. Although Jones's 1903 Children's March failed to persuade Roosevelt even to grant the agitator a personal hearing, the public outcry engendered by the spectacle ushered in child labor protections in Pennsylvania, New York, and New Jersey.[92] In various ways, their key roles in organizing workers and in gaining acceptance in male-dominated institutions contributed to reshaping the lives of all working-class, men, women, and children.

Fighting for "Roses" as well as "Bread"

In the tradition of their radical foremothers, Flynn and Jones conceived of labor concerns as an inescapable conflation of "bread" and "roses". Indeed, in the minds of both women, the aptness of the "slavery" analogy they employed to describe the conditions of their unskilled constituencies lay both in inadequate compensation and in oppressive practices that denied workers key prerogatives of citizenship, ordinary experiences of self-governance, and some semblance of control over their destiny. The great horror of racial slavery, after all, rested as much if not more in physical violence and the denial of human liberty and dignity as it did in the hardships occasioned by the bare minimum of food, shelter, and clothing. Similarly, in the case of coal miners in particular, "industrial slavery" resulted from a mix of starvation-level "scrip" wages; paternalistic control of overpriced but substandard housing, medical care, and company stores; a litany of special assessments for tools and materials; speedups such as "cribbing";[93] and physical and psychological intimidation. Union sympathizers were usually terminated and blacklisted, frequently beaten, and sometimes even murdered.[94]

As a result of such feudal-like conditions, the UMWA often demanded improved sanitation in company housing, the end to blacklisting of unionists, and rights of all miners to free speech and assembly, to cash wages, and to choice in trading outside of company-owned stores.[95] To Jones, the significance of ending the "pluck-me stores" and "soup-ticket" system lay not merely in increasing miners' purchasing power but in allowing the self-governance necessary for "self-respect."[96] Absent such experiences, workers, she often said, were reduced to mere "brutes" and "mules." Comments from a 1915 speech at Cooper Union in New York City typify her conflation of "bread" and "roses" concerns:

For ten years the C.F. & I and the rest of them have starved and hammered down my boys out there. They have lived like dogs. The companies haven't only underpaid them, but they have taken away the little they got through company stores, and company saloons. My boys and their families had no more rights in Colorado than animals. . . . [W]hen they tried to help themselves they were blacklisted and beaten or shot down.[97]

Jones's commitment to "roses" sometimes overreached the standard union line, and she frequently justified her position on grounds of familial experiences and obligations and personal enrichment and dignity. Unlike most unions' official posture on reducing ten- and twelve-hour workdays to a standard eight, she sometimes advocated a six-hour maximum and occasionally even four,[98] echoing the claims of other female labor radicals to the right to time "which belonged to us."[99] Shorter workdays, she claimed, freed workers to enjoy their families and nurture children, allowed them to read and "study our affairs,"[100] and granted them "the privilege of seeing the color of their children's eyes by the light of the sun."[101] So, too, she took particular offense at company practices that withheld from miners, unlike other rent-paying citizens, sovereignty in the privacy of their own homes. Coal companies, invoking their authority as private owners of industry-held housing, routinely evicted families who harbored union sympathizers or leaders such as Jones. Such actions, she told West Virginia coal miners in 1912, effectively denied them the taken-for-granted "right to invite who you please to your table."[102]

Flynn, like Jones and many of her sister radicals, believed that "economic freedom is not an all inclusive term [but] presupposes *political and social* freedom," sentiments expressed in handwritten speaking notes dating from the earliest years of her career.[103] As such, she and Socialist women such as Margaret Higgins Sanger expanded "bread" and "roses" concerns to include access to birth control. Because smaller families reduced the supply of workers and spread parental wages across fewer family members, limiting procreation was a "proletarian necessity" and therefore germane to the labor movement. According to a 1915 handwritten speech, a "birth strike," Flynn believed, was "woman's strongest protest." But beyond this bread-and-butter component, voluntary motherhood granted women personal autonomy, "the right to choose life in all phases," "to say 'I am the master of my fate.'" Moreover, such freedoms strengthened the family generally: children in smaller families benefited from more parental time and affection, and the elimination of the fear of pregnancy reduced marital friction over sexual relations.[104] This more radical and thoroughgoing vision is explicit in Flynn's 1916 response to the often tepid support, indifference, or resistance to birth control by male comrades (including Flynn's lover, Carlo Tresca). Published in the first women's edition of *Solidarity*, the essay argues:

> Masculine opposition [to birth control] is theoretical, not practical, since few can understand the hopeless, hapless lot of involuntary maternity. . . . Our men should realize that the large family system rivets the chains of slavery upon labor more securely . . . I am besieged by women for information on the subject and avenues of assault upon the [illegal] system, yet whenever the subject is selected by a local it is always amazing how few I.W.W. members bring their women folk to the meeting. *It is time they realized that the I.W.W. stands for a larger program than mere wages and shorter hours and the industrial freedom we all [are] awakening to will be the foundation upon which a different world for man and woman will be reared.*[105]

Jones's views on contraception were not clearly articulated, although she occasionally argued, as she did at a UMWA convention in 1909, that if women such as herself were in Congress, they "would tell Teddy [Roosevelt] to shut his mouth, not [to] be lecturing women about race suicide."[106] Her frequent ridicule of the president's preoccupation with race suicide no doubt lay partly in its inherent anti-immigrant and class and race prejudice. But comments in a 1912 speech in West Virginia also suggest some sympathy with Flynn's perspective about the oppression large families visited on women: "Teddy, the monkey-chaser . . . was blowing his skull off his carcass about race suicide. God Almighty, bring him down [to] the C&O [in West Virginia] and he will never say another word about race suicide. The whole population seems to be made up of 'kids.' Every woman has three babies in her arms and nine on the floor. So you will see there is no danger of race suicide."[107]

Beyond the issue of birth control, Flynn, like many other of her labor foremothers, sisters, and descendants, viewed other aspects of "home" and "work" as largely inseparable. Following in the path of Charlotte Perkins Gilman, Flynn advocated child-care programs for working women and various maternity provisions throughout her life.[108] Indeed, the need for working women to reconcile domestic duties with their economic familial obligations has a long and continuing tradition of radicalizing women, as illustrated more recently by female Chinese textile workers whose hard-fought campaign for industry day care in the 1970s preceded their later massive walkout.[109] Flynn likewise acknowledged the economic value of women's work in the home long before second-wave feminists made such claims commonplace. "Housework is far more useful than lots of jobs for which good money is paid under capitalism," she wrote in a 1941 essay. "To free the individual mother from a twenty-four-hour job, and put it on a professional basis, to have collective nurseries . . . is a belated recognition of just how socially necessary and useful is all the work she has performed so long and laboriously."[110]

Both Flynn and Jones vigorously defended the rights to due process and freedom of speech and assembly for all citizens as "ideals," "roses" central to labor's economic struggle for "bread." Nearly all of Jones's surviving speeches contain tales of her defying injunctions against organizing efforts and the punishments she incurred and reminders to audiences of the First Amendment rights they possess. In a 1912 public organizing speech on the capitol steps of Charleston, West Virginia, she argued that "a state of industrial peonage" exists when corporations are allowed to "beat, abuse, maim and hold up citizens without process of law, deny freedom of speech, a provision granted by the Constitution, deny the citizens the right to assemble in a peaceable manner for the purpose of discussing questions in which they are concerned."[111] Such issues, as much or more than any others, consumed Flynn's time and energies throughout her entire career, beginning with her IWW apprenticeship in the twenty-six free speech battles between 1909 and 1916; covering her years defending imprisoned war dissidents, labor leaders, and other purportedly "undesirable" elements; and peaking in trials of Communists, herself included, during the 1940s and 1950s. At no time was Flynn's trademark irony more apt than in her statements challenging her ouster from the board of the ACLU in 1940 for her political beliefs: "If this trial occurred elsewhere it would be a case for the ACLU to defend!"[112] Similarly, during her Smith Act trial in 1952 and 1953 in New York City, Flynn dryly noted the hypocrisy of President Truman, who had ordered her political arrest: "The President of the United States said the other day at the ceremonies dedicating the new Archives Building where the Bill of Rights is now on public view: 'It is the only document of its kind in the whole world that protects a citizen against his Government.' That protection should be our shield against prosecutions such as this."[113]

Many male-dominated labor unions embraced free speech to refute charges of radicalism, but they nonetheless often viewed women who exercised such public rights for themselves, even on labor's behalf, as militants. Thus, for women such as the 900 textile strikers in Lynn, Massachusetts, in 1862, merely asserting publicly "their need of protecting our rights and privileges as free born women and *our interests as working women*" compounded the radical dimension of this labor action.[114] In Jones's view, not only the Constitution but also women's experiences and duties as wives and mothers afforded them the "right" to speak publicly. In her earliest preserved complete speech at a UMWA convention in Indianapolis in 1902, for example, she countered common objections by her male audiences to women ascending the platform by connecting that public duty with experiences in the home:

> My friends, it is often asked, "Why should a woman be out talking about miners' affairs?" Why shouldn't she? Who has a better right? Has she not given you birth? Has she not raised you and cared for you? Has she not struggled along for you? Does she not today, when you come home covered with corporation soot, have hot water and soap and towels ready for you? Does she not have your supper ready for you, and your clean clothing ready for you? She doesn't own you though, the corporations own you, and she knows that well.[115]

Expanding Solidarity

Although all labor unions preached worker solidarity, Flynn and Jones embraced a more expansive view of the collective than the bulk of their male comrades. Their continual emphasis on relational integrity and responsibility not only reflected a striking and recurrent theme in female labor union activity but also more generally reflected what some theorists see as a common characteristic of female culture. Carol Gilligan, Ann Wilson Schaef, and Nancy Chodorow, for example, argue that developing and maintaining relationships are central to many substantial female experiences and thus define a large part of identity for them, especially for mothers.[116] Although such a focus would seem to be a self-evident priority for any organization self-described as a "union," Jones constantly battled territorial attitudes of union officials and rank-and-file members who sought to exclude women, Latino and black workers, and certain trades both from the larger movement and from specific local and national organizations, and who sometimes criticized her work with other "competing" union organizations. "I am accused of helping the Western Federation of Miners," she said in a Colorado speech in 1903, "as if that were a crime, by one of the National board members. I plead guilty. I know of no East or West, North nor South when it comes to my class fighting the battle for justice."[117] In a 1909 speech at the UMWA national convention in Indianapolis, Jones contrasted her view of labor as an extended, inclusive, and cooperative labor "family" with her male audience's more exclusionary, competitive outlook:

> Some of the delegates took exception to what I said here the other day, [when] I said that Joplin [Missouri] belongs to the Western Federation of Miners. There must be no line drawn. Whenever you organize a man bring him into the United Mine Workers, bring him into the Western Federation of Miners, bring him into the Carpenters' Union–bring him into any union. Whenever you do that you have taken one away from the common enemy and joined him with you to fight the common enemy. . . . I try to bring the farmers with us also, because the stronger we grow numerically the weaker the other fellow grows. I have got no pet organization. Wherever labor is in a struggle with the enemy, the name of the organization cuts no figure with me.[118]

Jones's comments illustrate traits both Patricia Hill Collins and Ardis Cameron attribute to "othermothers" in oppressed black or working-class communities where survival depends on developing a "family" structure constituted from all manner of "fictive kin."[119] Such women treat biologically unrelated individuals as if they were blood children, aunts, grandparents, or other family members, rejecting separateness, individual difference, or individual interest as bases for community organization or for personal self-actualization. Individuals become bound, not by bloodlines, but by shared goals, mutual interests in, and common threats to group survival. As a symbolic union "othermother," "Mother" Jones recognized only the separation between her extended working family and their "common enemy" and explicitly refused to privilege her UMWA "bloodlines" by regarding her own UMWA "boys" and "children" as "pets."

Much of Jones's and Flynn's rhetoric contained properties that Elizabeth Stone contends are common to talk in natural families:[120] defining membership in the labor "family"; outlining its relationship to the larger world; and providing "ground rules" for its duties and its preservation, including the expectation that individual interests be subordinated to the needs of the group. Between them, this labor "family" defined only by class extended beyond all unions to include housewives, prostitutes, farmers, child laborers, Mexican revolutionaries, Japanese revolutionaries, Southern blacks living under Jim Crow laws, prisoners, and occasionally even militia and guards hired to police workers. "I don't want one single man in the State militia hurt," Jones warned West Virginia miners in 1912. "[There] are many workingmen in the militia."[121] Although Jones was not entirely devoid of the racism plaguing mining and factory towns and impeding solidarity efforts, she claimed, "The iron heel feels the same to all flesh. Hunger and suffering and the cause of your children bind more closely than a common tongue."[122] She often framed her vigorous resistance to importing Chinese labor as opposing exploitation of hungry men willing to work, as she said to a UMWA gathering in 1911, "for eight cents and ten cents a day."[123] Indeed, Jones urged UMWA delegates in Indianapolis in 1909 to notify the Japanese consul formally of their defense of "twenty-one brave [Japanese] men [scheduled] to go to the scaffold [in their homeland] . . . for a principle in which they believe, the principle of right and justice."[124] So, too, she viewed the defense of imprisoned "brother" Mexican revolutionaries as a "grave and mighty question" with "importance to the labor movement," compelling her strenuous work on their behalf.[125]

Although the IWW and the Communist Party publicly were less parochial than the UMWA and other national unions about membership, Flynn nonetheless often alluded to discrepancies between their theories of inclusiveness and their actual practice. A 1916 essay in *Solidarity*, "Problems Organizing Women," which invokes a familial metaphor, illustrates:

> Women and foreigners have been step-sisters and [step-]brothers in the AFL. The IWW must be capable, large-spirited, all-inclusive. . . . If women are to be active, however, their ability should not be disparaged. I know a local where members forbid their wives speaking to an IWW woman "because they get queer ideas!" I heard a member forbid his wife, who had worked nine hours in a mill, from coming to the meeting "because she'd do better to clean the house." When I suggested an able woman as secretary of a local, several men said, "Oh, that's a man's job!"[126]

The familial emphasis on deferring self-interest to the larger group welfare underlay both Jones's and Flynn's appeals to the working class in World War I and World War II, respectively. Each advocated temporarily setting aside individual discomforts and struggles to present a united front in fighting the common international enemy. "We are in a war today, and the nation is facing a crisis," Jones told miners in Indianapolis in 1918, "and you must not look at it with indifference. . . . What we must do is to settle down to one thing—no more strikes in the mines, not a single strike. Let us keep to one strike, a strike to strike the Kaiser off the throne."[127] In 1943, Flynn likewise reminded Communist women who "selfish[ly]" left their wartime factory jobs to be near stationed husbands that "we have duties and responsibilities, to set an example of how women should behave in wartime, no matter how hard it is to do.

We talk considerably about 'our vanguard role.' This is it. . . . We are at war. We must strain every effort to win the war [against fascism]."[128]

Although individual interests become subordinated to larger group interests in a familial perspective, the welfare of jeopardized individuals does not. Thus both women, particularly Jones, decried the abuses of child labor. "Fifty years ago," Jones said in 1903 in Brooklyn during her march of the mill children, "there was a cry against slavery, and the men of the North gave up their lives to stop the selling of black children on the block. To-day the white child is sold for $2 a week, and even by his parents, to the manufacturer."[129] Similarly, Flynn framed child labor as "a relic of barbarism,"[130] detailing the respective physical and moral degeneracy such widespread practices engendered in exploited children and exploitive adults. Because Jones viewed labor as a family particularly responsible to its most vulnerable, she continually found herself at odds with locals and union officials who advocated separate local settlements in strike actions, thereby "betray[ing]" often weaker "brothers," as she said in Colorado on 1903 during a particularly contentious and bitter episode.[131] During this Colorado strike, UMWA president John Mitchell advised miners in northern fields to reach a settlement that excluded the fewer, more isolated, and largely immigrant locals in the southern fields. Also alarmed by Mitchell's increasing conservativeness and coziness with corporations as a member of the controversial National Civic Federation—a group of labor leaders and business top-executives convened under the guise of ameliorating labor disputes—Jones encouraged miners to defy Mitchell's directive, igniting a feud that festered for years. At a 1911 UMWA convention in Columbus, Ohio, suggestions for dual organizations in the state prompted Jones to revisit the conflict. Her scathing comments not only reject separateness as a familial principle but also allude to Mitchell's collusion and the extremely self-interested histories of the proposal's backers. The passage thus treats several of the class family's black sheep she often excoriates: compromised or corrupt union officials, self-absorbed or cowardly rank-and-file unionists, and inhuman "scabs."

> When I heard those fellows talking about a dual organization here on this floor I was disgusted—it was enough to make a dog sick! Let me tell you that *the only real dual organization there is in the country is the Civic Federation* and the gang of robbers on Wall Street. . . . I happened to be in the central [Colorado] field a long time ago, before those fellows who are blowing off hot air here were in the union— they were scabbing. I am glad you are in the union [now], however. I know how a scab is made up. One time there was an old barrel up near heaven, and . . . God Almighty said, "What is that stuff that smells so?" He was told it was some rotten chemical down there in a barrel and was asked what could be done with it. He said, "Spill it on a lot of bad clay and maybe you can turn out a scab." . . . [O]nce in a while we get hold of one of [those scabs] and lick him."[132]

Flynn likewise saw the protecting the interests of all as not merely pragmatic but moral. In reflections on the Paterson, New Jersey, textile strike, she describes to a New York audience in 1914 how even the willingness of the local strike committee to consider a shop-by-shop settlement encouraged management and "broke the solidarity" of workers, which ultimately lost the strike.[133] So, too, she sometimes sharply pointed out ways in which labor union leaders, called in to manage the spontaneous solidarity occasioned in female workers' walkouts, often squelched the female impulses for the larger collective. Reflecting in 1911 on various East Coast textile strikes, she wrote:

> A spontaneous revolt, a light with glowing enthusiasm and ardor that kept thou-sands of underfed and thinly clad girls on the picket line, should be productive of

more than a "contract." Contracts binding dressmakers in one union, cloak makers in another, shirtwaist makers in another, and so on . . . contracts arranging separate wage scales, hours, dates of expiration, etc., mean no more spontaneous rebellions on the East Side of New York. Now union leaders arbitrate . . . [with a] new concept of "victory," and if you dare to strike under the contract you will be fired from both shop and union for violation of it. [134]

For Flynn, the ethical aspects of caring eclipsed the practical. For example, the IWW's slogan "an injury to one is an injury to all" notwithstanding, the IWW and the Communist Party frequently resisted Flynn's efforts to defend accused or imprisoned members, arguing such efforts depleted economic resources and distracted the organizations. In a 1950 speech entitled "The Political Significance of Defense Work," which she gave at a Communist Party convention in New York City, Flynn reminded her comrades of the many celebrated and more anonymous lives defense work had saved, thus concluding, "To work for [defense] is not a diversion or a demotion." Moreover, she explicitly rejected the individualist paradigm for the relational familial model, "We must reject any go-it-alone attitude. Attacks on us are attacks on all progressive peace-loving Americans." [135] A speech given two years earlier in a similar venue, following the arrest of twelve Communist leaders, acknowledges both apathy and open resistance to such a perspective by her Communist contemporaries and her former Wobbly comrades:

I was frankly surprised that so few [previous] speakers dealt with [the twelve's] defense. This is our Party. These are our leaders. No one else will defend them unless we do . . . I re-emphasize what [others] said about the danger of submerging our Party in defense. Comrade Foster has repeatedly warned us, this was one of the large contributing factors to the collapse of the I.W.W. . . . But, camrades [sic], this does not mean that we, as a Communist Party . . . forget it. . . . [W]e [cannot] abandon our comrades who fall in the line of [the] march or who are captured by the enemy. No—we must fight every inch of the way—not only for our leaders, [but also] for any other member. . . . In their successful fight—we and the entire working class win. [136]

Like Jones, Flynn had little tolerance for anyone who betrayed the working-class family, whether they were strikebreakers, union leaders, or other union members. In her description of early free speech battles in Montana, she notes with alarm that Carpenters' Union and Clerks' Union jury members voted to convict their working-class IWW brothers. [137] And although her critiques of "scabs" and corrupt union officials fell somewhat short of the picturesque name-calling of Jones's diatribes, she gave nothing away to her acid-tongued elder in conviction. Equally enraged by Mitchell's selling-out of the at-risk southern Colorado miners, for example, she describes labor leaders consorting with the National Civic Federation as "'yellow' . . . Janus-faced double-deal[ers]" who "have constructed an engine with themselves at the throttle, that they may turn on just enough steam to command attention but never enough to smash either their own graft or the bulwark of capitalism." In the undated, handwritten document, she asks, "Is it not strange Mr. Mitchell sports a $5,000 diamond presented by the mine owners?" and "Do you want failure? Trust your fate to a labor leader whose mind, soul, and body belongs to your employers?" [138]

Although both women preached inclusiveness and criticized officials guided by their own personal advantage, neither woman rejected hierarchy out of hand. Similar to talk in natural families, Jones's union rhetoric always favored certain behaviors—those she regarded as fostering the union family—and certain individuals, namely herself. Mothering is far from a democratic process, [139] and in

Jones's case it occasionally became authoritarian. Because internecine squabbling weakened solidarity and subsequent power in defeating the enemy, the self-styled matriarch of labor often treated malcontents as miscreant children, even forcing feuding national officials to shake hands publicly at the 1916 UMWA convention in Indianapolis so as not to "give [the owners] the satisfaction of seeing you have a row."[140] At times she pulled maternal rank to silence debates and democratic procedures she deemed unproductive: "Mother don't permit the contrary [vote]" she told West Virginia miners in 1912.[141] Flynn was less far less dictatorial, but she, too, appreciated the need for pecking orders in labor's "family." At times, including in her autobiography, she expressed concerns over the excessive "rank-and-filism" of the IWW, impulsiveness by the less experienced in labor battles that sometimes led to self-defeating behaviors.[142]

Maternal Strategies and Female Militance

In important and clearly identifiable respects, many of the strategies, militant and otherwise, that Flynn and Jones employed as organizers and strike leaders reflect key influences of female culture. Given the collective identity and interests inherent in a "familial" perspective on labor, any individual resources become joint or "family" property, an orientation Jones and other female unionists clearly embraced. Jones repeatedly demanded that male unions dip into their treasuries to assist their "brother" revolutionaries in Mexico, their "sisters" striking in mills or breweries, or even other miners in different locals. At a 1916 UMWA convention in Indianapolis, she responded to bickering over the parceling out of expenditures with the reminder of "familial" class identity and duty, "[Y]ou haven't got one dollar in your treasury that belongs to Illinois. It belongs to the miners of this country; every dollar of it belongs to the working men, whether they are miners, steel workers, or train men. That money belongs to *us*, the working class, and we are going to use it to clean hell out of the robbing class."[143] Similarly, in the massive 1912 Lawrence strike in which Flynn participated as a key leader, women of various occupations and ethnic backgrounds pooled food, clothing, money, and domestic chores such as child care, laundry, and cooking to sustain both individual strikers and the larger cause. Such efforts, however, were but exaggerated forms of existing networks and practices these women had developed to survive in an oppressive environment on a daily basis. As Cameron explains:

> [N]eighbors and kin converted the familiar and the routine into powerful weapons of protest and resistance. . . . An outgrowth of traditions of female reciprocity and mutual exchange, female networks were especially effective [in the strike] . . . for they accentuated the interconnectedness of individual lives in ways unavailable to unions or political parties. Based on relationships rather than memberships, female networks spun alliances that also breached the divide that otherwise might have separated workers from nonworkers, store owners from strikers, and shopkeepers from consumers. Cross-ethnic cooperation between women in the grocery stores, the streets, the children's boarding houses, at courtyard festivals, and in the swapping of food . . . combined with a rich associational life to concretize solidarity and forge a unity of purpose.[144]

For many of these women, Cameron continues, actions such as sharing picket duty, employing subversion or solidarity to guard each other from solitary arrest, and using interpersonal techniques and appeals to pressure recalcitrant neighbors, grocers, landlords, and merchants grew out of attitudes and skills acquired in their daily lives that were often beyond the view and sometimes the approval of their male family members. In important respects, factory towns like Lawrence, Lowell, and Paterson mirrored key features of female culture in mining communities, camps that anthropologist Jane Nash refers to as the "affair of the tribe" given the dependency on reciprocity and cooperation for day-to-day survival.[145] And to varying degrees, both Jones and Flynn appreciated, promoted, and used persuasive properties from this intimate, relationally oriented female sphere. In the midst of wholesale roundups of Communists, Flynn often reminded comrades during party conventions of the potency of interpersonal connections, arguing in 1948, for example, that victories over suppression of individual human rights "are won outside not inside of courts. . . . Go to the trade unions, locals, knock on doors, [hold] street meetings. . . . Let us popularize our leaders . . . who, when they walk down the street are greeted by workers by their first names."[146]

To an even greater degree than Flynn, Jones appreciated the allure of intimate, human contact, not simply in converting and empowering oppressed workers suffering from low self-esteem but also in gaining sympathy from shopkeepers, politicians, militia, and occasionally even enemy forces such as John D. Rockefeller Jr. As "Mother," she always spoke directly to her "boys," often calling audience members by their given names. In so doing, she provided audiences hungry for emotional attention the opportunity to feel noticed and cared for as individuals. And time and again, she told tales of winning over hungry strikebreakers, lonely or exhausted jailers, struggling merchants, or even the powerful by various acts of motherly kindness. Comments before West Virginia miners in 1912 illustrate Jones's articulation of her faith in the power of intimate compassion, specific calls for audience emulation of this strategy, and evidence of its persuasiveness both on an individual in a tale and on audience members themselves:

> I am going some day [soon] to take dinner with [the militia], and I will convert the whole bunch to my philosophy. . . . I want to tell you another thing. These little two-by-four clerks in the Company stores, they sell you five beans for a nickel, sometimes three beans for a nickel. I want to tell you, be civil to those. Don't say anything. . . . A fellow met me on the street one day—he had asked half a dozen people for a drink. He said, "Give me ten cents, I want a drink." I said, "Here is fifty cents, get a couple of good drinks." I said, "You haven't had anything to eat, here is fifty cents, go get a bed and supper." . . . Eight years afterwards that man came up to me on the train and said "I believe your name is Mother Jones." I said, "Yes, sir, it is. What about it?" He said, "I want to grasp your hand, I would have died that night but for you, I am in business, I am worth over seven hundred thousand dollars today," said he, and he handed me money for the Mexican refugees. . . . Stand by the militia, stand by the boys. Don't allow no [hired] guards to attack them. (Cries of, "That is right." "That is right."). Stand shoulder to shoulder with them .[147]

Jones's rhetoric also exhibited key types of communication forms that women socialized into mothering roles have favored to connect to their offspring emotionally, foster desired behaviors, and encourage them to reason independently and to forge links between their lives and the surrounding world. For example, like many mothers who use linguistic mergers (for example, "*I* want *us* to finish *our* vegetables so *you* will grow bigger"), Jones frequently blended her voice with those of her listeners to create identification and induce miners to act, as illustrated in a UMWA district meeting in Pittsburg, Kansas, in 1914: "I will give them a fight to the finish and all *we* have to do is to quit being moral cowards, rise up like men and let the world know that *you* are citizens of a great nation and *you* are going to make it great."[148]

Moreover, Jones's rhetoric often contained "scaffolds," highly structured language routines involving repetition and imitation whereby caregivers assist children in "reaching" beyond their present cognitive capacity.[149] Because her coal-mining audiences had been denied ordinary personal choices necessary to cultivate mature decision making, her use of scaffolds, such as simulated dialogue and what Deborah Tannen terms "constructed dialogue,"[150] were critical tools by which cognitive dialectical processes could be modeled and miners' crippling dependency checked. Her use of simulated dialogue in Joplin, Missouri, in 1915 illustrates this process: "Don't blame the mine owners. I'd skin you, too, . . . if you'd let me. They combine, don't they? Sure. Why? Because they realize that as individuals they could not do anything."[151] Even Jones's often harsh criticism of her audiences reflects practices used by some mothers in oppressive circumstances to cultivate "essential survival skills" in their young, including learning self-defense, self-control, awareness of when and how to speak up, and the strength to fight if necessary.[152] The transfer of such private-sphere communication skills into the public domain contributes to a rhetorical style that Karlyn Kohrs Campbell terms "feminine," and that she argues is particularly well suited for audiences inexperienced in public deliberation.[153]

Beyond her use of question-answer patterns and her movement among narrative voices, Jones also relied heavily upon other "feminine style" features to create identification with, stimulate personal judgment in, and model behavior for her audiences: personal experience, personal testimony, and enactment; inductive reasoning based upon series of examples; and fictional or real-life stories that encouraged audiences to draw comparisons between their individual circumstances and the larger external world. Like wisewomen known in many primitive and advanced cultures as "mothers" and "grandmothers," she appreciated the force of intellectual engagement required of legends, fables, parables, and myths that contain implied rather than explicit morals.[154] In the vast bulk of her stories, she used reported dialogue between a protagonist and an adversary, a thematic motif Stone contends typifies stories told in any family struggling with some sort of essential survival. "Whatever or whoever the enemy," Stone writes, "the family stories offer an approach to survival . . . [with] application beyond the particular dramatic moment."[155] In Jones's mind, survival hinged on audiences using their wits. In fact, in the coda to one parable she told in 1920 about a small boy who had used his "gray matter" to unmask an authority figure's dubious claims, she explicitly acknowledges to her Williamsburg, West Virginia, audience that her maternal goal was facilitating her audience's intellectual independence, a trait all mothers encourage: "I wouldn't free you tomorrow if I could. You would go begging. My patriotism is for this country to give to the nation in the day to come highly developed human citizens, men and women."[156]

Although Flynn's more deductive and far less intimate rhetorical style could not be characterized as "feminine," in her later life she nonetheless developed a keen appreciation for the use of biblical parables, cultural stories, personal examples, and other "humanized" comparisons to challenge powerful premises and practices that oppressed the underclass and various political dissidents. In her 1953 summation at her own trial in New York City for violating the Smith Act, for example, she used the following story to debunk legal charges that Communist membership in itself constituted a government conspiracy:

I don't know if you recall a poem by Rudyard Kipling in Tomlinson. He died in London and he went to the gates of Heaven, and he was asked by St. Peter what were his qualifications for admission, and the aristocratic British clubman replied: "This I read in a book," he said. "And this was told me. And this I heard that another man thought of a Prince of Muscovy." But St. Peter wrathfully replied, "Ye have read. Ye have heard. Ye have seen," he said, "and the tale is yet to run. By the fate of the body that once ye had—give the answer—what have ye done?" That is the question, the real question, ladies and gentlemen—not what we [Communists] read in a book or what the Government read out of a book, not what somebody heard or made up or said in Oshkosh or St. Louis or Kalamazoo or someplace else, but what have we done? That is the question that the Government's attorney has failed to answer.[157]

Similarly, to point out the logic in her rejection of an offer by the trial judge of exile to the Communist Soviet Union rather than imprisonment, she employed the following religious analogy: "The point is that we do not want to leave our country. It is like the proposition made to Christians who believe in Heaven. 'Well, do you want to go there right away?' Certainly no one of them would want to answer yes to that question although their belief in Heaven would be great."[158]

The pair's extraordinary effectiveness also lay in the fact that the two women shared an acute understanding of familial pressures and personal fears that often inhibited organizing efforts or kept even committed members isolated. Because mobilization depends as much on favorable interpersonal contact as on a remote and abstract ideological appeal,[159] both strove to make union promises to protect, sustain, and improve the physical existence of workers immediate and real, even after they pledged union allegiance. "These men [coal miners] are aggravated to death at times," Jones explained in congressional testimony in 1914, "and it takes someone who understands the psychology of this great movement we are in to take care of them when they are annoyed and robbed and plundered and shot."[160] Thus, as "mother," she fed them, nursed them, as well as their sick wives and children, and confronted any enemy who threatened their safety. For her part, Flynn's exhausting crusades to save individuals such as Hill, Nicola Sacco and Bartolomeo Vanzetti, and Tom Mooney and Warren Billings led her benefactors to worry occasionally for her health. As chair of the defense committee for the first eleven Smith Act victims, Flynn set up numerous committees to raise funds from, involve, and gain support from the public as well as maintain key social bonds with the indicted. One technique occasioning the most resistance from male party members was the committee for families created to provide funds to send the children of defendants to camp, to underwrite family visits to imprisoned family members, and to purchase birthday and Christmas gifts for the accused to reduce their sense of personal separation.[161] Like Jones, Flynn also often spoke and wrote of the "psychology" of organizing and of strikes, noting, in 1916, for example, that the IWW "must . . . adapt our propaganda to the special needs of women," which "[S]ome of our male [IWW] members are prone to underestimate." One result of this failure to adjust, she confessed years later in her autobiography, was that most Wobblies "were wonderful agitators but poor union organizers."[162] In her 1914 speech about the Paterson, New Jersey, textile strike, for example, she explained the rationale for planned Sunday activities for strikers, the bulk of whom were women:

> Monday is the day that a break comes in every strike. . . . If you can bring the people safely over Monday they usually go along for the rest of the week. If on Sunday, however, you let those people stay at home, sit down at the table where there isn't very much food, see the feet of the children with shoes getting thin, and the bodies of the children where the clothes are getting ragged, they begin to . . . lose that spirit of the mass and the realization that all are suffering as they are suffering. . . . You have to keep them busy every day of the week, and particularly on Sunday, in order to keep that spirit. . . . That's why the IWW has these great mass meetings, women's meetings, children's meetings.[163]

Because the psychological factors peculiar to women included male resistance to female attendance and talk in meetings, Flynn and Haywood held special sessions in Lawrence for women and for children to remove certain psychic barriers to female participation.[164] In addition, Flynn, Sanger, and local female leaders sought to quell maternal fears for children by organizing a series of "children's exoduses" in which huge numbers of Lawrence's working-class community's young would be evacuated to the homes of strike sympathizers throughout the country.

The violence this "children's exodus" provoked from authorities who beat women, some of them pregnant, as they attempted to place children on trains helps to explain the militancy of these Lawrence women and many other female labor activists throughout history. As mothers in myth, slave mothers, and even animal mothers evidence, maternal love entails the fierce protection of offspring often at any cost, and this need for maternal protectiveness is most pronounced when oppressive practices, such as those common in early industry, threaten the physical and psychological survival of children and other intimates. In Lawrence, for example, the coupling of speedups and deep wage cuts eventually catalyzed women who already had been struggling to feed dependents. Several women, in fact, termed the uprising as "the strike for three loaves," the exact material price of the wages they had been shorted.[165] Not surprisingly, both Flynn and Jones occasionally framed militant preservative impulses in primal imagery. In an early handwritten outline for a speech entitled "Jungle Law," presumably given around 1908, Flynn defined this tenet as "might behind right," arguing that all animals, including humans, always struggle for "self-preservation" and species "preservation" and "against those who would thwart these two instincts."[166] In another outline for a speech about women's political activities to be given a few months later, she supported her claim that female political "Methods [are] always militant" with a maternal illustration: "witness [the] kidnapping [of a] child for [the] mother which law declared belonged to [the] father"[167] Similarly, Jones bowed only to the tenets of maternal law, a code she viewed as natural, governing all species, and encompassing fierce resistance as well as tender nurturing. "The brute mother," she said in 1913, "suckles and preserves her young at the cost of her own life, if need be."[168]

Militant tactics practiced by women in textile strikes in Paterson and Lawrence bore many resemblances to maneuvers sometimes championed by Flynn and Jones in these and other labor battles. In the 1912 Lawrence strike and its 1882 predecessor, women protected each other from individual arrest in various ways: creating confusion over the instigator of an action; linking arms in huge long queues to prevent individuals from being torn from the group; and ensuring mass rather than individual arrest. Most controversial was that women engaged in rampant sabotage, slashed tires, brandished red pepper, scalding water, rocks, and clubs, stripped and struck male police officers in public, accosted strikebreakers, and "marked" unsympathetic homes, businesses, and individuals, even hanging photographs of turncoats in public places. As Cameron writes, "For those [women] whose primary concern was familial survival and welfare, issues of the shop floor were difficult to separate from home and neighborhood."[169]

At least early in her career Flynn also advocated and defended worker sabotage in various forms: slowing down the rate of work; following time-consuming regulations faithfully; alerting customers to inferior food and textile products; immobilizing machinery; spoiling goods; and deliberately confusing consumers' orders. Among her various justifications for these coercive practices was the argument that spoiling already tainted or inferior goods was an ethical, responsible action taken in the public's best interests: "Any exposure of adulteration or over-adulteration that makes the product unconsumable [sic] is a lot more beneficial to the consumer than to have it tinctured or doctored so that you can use it but so that it is destructive to your physical condition at the same time," she wrote in an infamous essay published by the IWW in 1917.[170] Her larger relational concern, however, lay with workers rather than the general public, and ensuring their survival eclipsed for her more pedestrian legal prohibitions and "finespun moral objections."[171] Using an ethical lens Gilligan argues is common for women, Flynn wrote that if workers believe that sabotage is necessary for their survival, "that in itself makes sabotage moral. And for us to talk about the morality of sabotage would be as absurd as to discuss . . . the morality of the class struggle itself."[172] Even though Flynn preferred nonviolent methods, she argued that "Everybody believes in violence for self-defense." And at times, she conceded, "violence is of course a necessity and one would be stupid to say that either in Michigan or West Virginia or Colorado the miners do not have the right to take their guns and defend their wives and their babies and themselves."[173]

For Jones, the domestic world of the family provided both the resources and rationale for militant actions. She often explicitly coached striking wives to arm themselves with mops, brooms, red pepper, and hatpins to deter strikebreakers, to clang pots and pans to spook mine shaft mules, and, when arrested, to sing loudly and ensure crying babies to preclude their jailor's sleep. Like Flynn, Jones also advocated industry-wide as well as more local boycotts of products and merchants. Repeatedly, harm to families, and especially to children, provided the warrant for the violence she occasionally advocated. A 1915 speech at the Labor Temple in Pittsburg, Kansas, illustrates a grim litany of slaughter that drove her and some other radical mothers to militant conclusions and bloodletting ends:

> Over in West Virginia they murdered the babies before they were born; they hired gunmen and they kicked the babies to death before they were born—the gunmen did.
>
> In Colorado they burned them to death in the holes into which they ran to save themselves. They threw oil on them to be sure that they were murdered; babies were murdered; women were murdered; women, when their sides were burned off, and their arms, they were carried to the morgue, and gave birth to the coming generation when they were two days dead. . . . Buy guns, yes. And I will borrow or steal it to buy guns for my boys, and I will not only do that, but I will make them use them . . . [because the operator] hires murderers [and] pays them with the money I ought to feed my children with.[174]

Such passages illustrate why mothering often assumes a militant face, a fierce other side to the warm and gentle nurturing of dominant maternal images. Given the embattled conditions in which Jones and other working-class women often operated, motherhood not only included the nurturing of children but also pronounced resistance against the forces that threatened them, thereby necessarily broadening the maternal "ethic of care" beyond its genteel moorings to include aggressive confrontation and occasional bodily risk. Both Jones and Flynn firmly believed in peaceful measures if they were viable. Indeed, Flynn's aversion to violence and war compelled her ardent opposition to nuclear proliferation in her later years. Yet as working-class women in a time when industrial peonage was both commonplace and tolerated, they both understood and embodied what Ruddick terms the paradox of maternal thinking. Although maternal thinking is conducive and committed to a "politics of peace," its protective maternal goal frequently and inescapably renders it "militaristic." "The sturdiest suspicion of violence," she writes, "is of no avail to threatened peoples who do not have alternative nonviolent ways of protecting what they love."[175]

In sum, Flynn's and Jones's continual campaigns for both "bread" and "roses" bear significant resemblances to radical women labor activists generally. Like their pioneering sisters, they worked within and outside of traditional political processes, conceived of labor as a "family" bound by class, and relied heavily on skills, methods, and philosophies acquired in the experiences of domestic life. Moreover, in so doing, they and other female labor radicals debunked received wisdom that conflated the domestic and the docile or that perceived of nurturing and militancy as antithetical qualities. Although these militantly maternal traits at times brought them into conflict with their predominately male comrades, the careers of both women illustrate the ways in which such skills and strategies could be adapted to audiences regardless of gender.

Foreshadowing "The Personal is Political"

Like the labor movement itself, female participation in it was and is not monolithic. Obviously, many early women workers eschewed labor activity due to personal or family disapproval, discouragement or exclusion by male-dominated labor unions, fear, and sheer fatigue. Nor did all female labor activists, including radicals like Jones and Flynn, conform completely in philosophy, political methods, and rhetorical form and style. Still, despite undeniable differences, these two women provide a glimpse into the catalyzing forces, general outlook, and strategic choices that generated what Helen Marot termed in 1910 "a trade union truism, that 'women make the best strikers.'" Although women were more reluctant unionists, she writes, "when they reach the point of striking they give themselves as fully and as instinctively to the cause as they give themselves in their personal relationships."[176] In fact, as Cameron points out, the radical tenor of female labor activity led mill owners to view conventional trade unionism as a more moderate and acceptable alternative to the more unorthodox "bread and roses" campaigns undertaken largely by women.[177] In far-reaching ways, Flynn, Jones, and other radical women in the movement embraced and embodied the belief that the "personal is the political" long before second-wave feminists ensconced the controversial slogan in the public imagination. At the same time that all these women were politically and culturally constrained by divisions between public and private, they at once privatized the public and publicized the private, ultimately rejecting boundaries between the domestic sphere of familial interaction, experiences, and obligations and the public In this regard, radical women in the U.S. labor movement have not been unique. Women in various countries and in a myriad of causes, both progressive and conservative, have shifted the sensitivities and strategies acquired in or associated with the home into public campaigns. As Alexis Jetter, Annelise Orleck, and Diana Taylor point out in the introduction to their edited volume, *The Politics of Motherhood*, maternity in particular has proven itself to be both a potent catalyst and an effective tactic for politicized women across the globe, both for mothers and childless women. "Some sincerely believed," they write, "that motherhood conferred upon them special insights and responsibilities to solve the problems plaguing their families and communities." Others, however, used motherhood to ennoble their political cause and bolster themselves, "aware that speaking out as mothers would give them more credibility in sexist societies than they would have as individual women."[178]

To differing degrees, both Jones and Flynn conflate these philosophical and tactical patterns. The protective maternal zeal they displayed in their battle for "bread" was genuine, even though both clearly recognized ways in which maternal appeals made that struggle more sympathetic and palatable. Although Jones's appropriation of and appeals to motherhood are the most salient, motherhood was a common topic for Flynn even at the outset of her career.

At the same time, however, although both women and many other radical labor women clearly demonstrated the self-sacrifice typically associated with idealized "good" mothers, they likewise exhibited healthy concern for the "roses" of personal autonomy, not only for other members of their extended working family but also for themselves. No slaves to convention or decorum, radical women in the labor movement proclaimed their desire and asserted their rights in to determine directions of their lives. Hence, in various ways most seemed to concur with a teenage Flynn, who declared in public appearances as early as 1909, it is "free mothers [who] will have free children."[179]

Notes

1. Barbara Welter, "The Cult of True Womanhood: 1820–1860," *American Quarterly* 18, no. 2 (1966): 151–74.
2. Ardis Cameron, *Radicals of the Worst Sort: Laboring Women in Lawrence, Massachusetts, 1860–1912* (Urbana: University of Illinois Press, 1955), xii.
3. Rosalyn Baxandall, Linda Gordon, and Susan Reverby, eds., *America's Working Women: A Documentary History–1600 to the Present* (New York: Vintage Books, 1976), 41; Cameron, *Radicals*, xiii.
4. Cameron, *Radicals*, 43.
5. Françoise Basche, "Introductory Essay," in *The Diary of a Shirtwaist Striker*, by Theresa S. Malkiel, ed. Francoise Basche (1910; reprint, Ithaca, N.Y.: ILR Press, Cornell University, 1990), 19.
6. Basche, "Introductory Essay," 19; Ronald L. Filippelli, *Labor in the USA: A History* (New York: Alfred A. Knopf, 1984), 97.
7. Alexis Jetter, Annelise Orleck, and Diana Taylor, eds., *The Politics of Motherhood: Activist Voices from Left to Right* (Hanover, N.H.: University Press of New England, 1997), 87.
8. Baxandall, Gordon, and Reverby, *America's Working Women*, 66.
9. Filippelli, *Labor in the USA*, 97–98.
10. Rosalyn Fraad Baxandall, *Words on Fire: The Life and Writings of Elizabeth Gurley Flynn* (New Brunswick, N.J.: Rutgers University Press, 1987), 169–74.
11. Sellins, an organizer for coal miners, was murdered during strike violence. According to Flynn, Stokes died from complications following a clubbing during a demonstration, although her interpretation is open to question. See Baxandall, *Words on Fire*, 179. Women strikers occasionally were killed in strike violence, such as the killing of Annie LoPizzo during the 1912 Lawrence, Massachusetts, uprising, an incident that led to the arrest of IWW leaders Joseph Ettor and Arturo Giovannitti, even though neither man had been on the scene at the time of the shooting. See Helen C. Camp, *Iron in Her Soul: Elizabeth Gurley Flynn and the American Left* (Pullman: Washington State University Press, 1995), 28.
12. Jones's stature as an icon of progressive causes is most salient in the use of her name for the left-leaning magazine *Mother Jones*, which includes a photo and short biography of her on its contents page.
13. Lloyd Morris, *From Postscript to Yesterday* (New York: Random House, 1947), Elizabeth Gurley Flynn Papers, Tamiment Library, New York University, n.p. Flynn's papers contain early essays, speeches, speech outlines, and teaching notes, in addition to news clippings, diary entries, and personal memorabilia. Many early speeches, essays, and speech outlines are handwritten, and only in some cases do the title, date, and page numbers, if any, appear to have been supplied by Flynn. Certain dates apparently supplied by archivists are approximate, and a few seem to be incorrect given the content of the speech. Typed addresses by Flynn are also heavily edited in her hand, and several do not include page numbers. I have not added page numbers to these materials. Baxandall, *Words on Fire*, includes a number of Flynn's speeches and essays, although a number of speeches, in particular, have been heavily edited. In some cases, particularly when the original is in poor condition, I refer to Baxandall.
14. Flynn's career began in 1906 when she delivered her first major speech at the age of fifteen and ended with her death in 1964, although she spent nearly a decade convalescing during the 1920s and 1930s. The exact beginning of Jones's speaking career is unknown, occurring sometime between 1871 and the late 1880s. Although Jones's advanced age slowed down her speaking during the last decade of her life, she remained involved with labor until her death in 1930. For the most thorough biographies of Flynn and Jones, respectively, see Camp, *Iron in Her Soul*, and Dale Fetherling, *Mother Jones, the Miners' Angel: A Portrait* (Carbondale: Southern Illinois University Press, 1974).

15. See, for example, Linda Atkinson, *Mother Jones, the Most Dangerous Woman in America* (New York: Crown, 1978); Camp, *Iron in Her Soul*; Fetherling, *Mother Jones*; Priscilla Long, *Mother Jones, Woman Organizer* (Cambridge, Mass.: Red Sun Press, 1976); Irving Werstein, *Labor's Defiant Lady: The Story of Mother Jones* (New York: Thomas Y. Crowell, 1969).

16. See, for example, Baxandall, *Words on Fire*; Philip S. Foner, ed., *Mother Jones Speaks: Collected Speeches and Writings* (New York: Monad Press, 1983); Edward M. Steel, *The Correspondence of Mother Jones* (Pittsburgh: University of Pittsburgh Press, 1985); and Edward M. Steel, ed., *The Speeches and Writings of Mother Jones* (Pittsburgh: University of Pittsburgh Press, 1988). Steel's anthology of Jones's speeches contains only complete texts; Foner's volume also includes some lengthy fragments of her speeches reported in newspapers and magazines.

17. Elizabeth Gurley Flynn, *I Speak My Own Piece: Autobiography of "The Rebel Girl,"* rev. ed. (New York: International Press, 1973); Mary Harris Jones, *The Autobiography of Mother Jones*, ed. Mary Field Parton, 3rd ed. (Chicago: Charles Kerr, 1980).

18. Eugene V. Debs, "To the Rescue of Mother Jones!" *Appeal to Reason*, 3 May 1913, 1.

19. Qtd. in Audrey Perryman Olmstead, "Agitator on the Left: The Speechmaking of Elizabeth Gurley Flynn, 1904–1964" (Ph.D. diss., Indiana University, 1971), 68.

20. Qtd. in Camp, *Iron in Her Soul*, 65.

21. Cameron, *Radicals*, 3.

22. Alice Kessler-Harris, "Problems of Coalition-Building: Women and Trade Unions in the 1920s," in *Women, Work, and Protest: A Century of U.S. Women's Labor History*, ed. Ruth Milkman (Boston: Routledge and Kegan Paul, 1985), 114.

23. Baxandall, Gordon, and Reverby, *America's Working Women*, 41.

24. Qtd. in Kessler-Harris, "Problems of Coalition-Building," 119.

25. Carol Gilligan, *In a Different Voice: Psychological Theory and Women's Development* (Cambridge, Mass.: Harvard University Press, 1982); Sara Ruddick, *Maternal Thinking: Towards a Politics of Peace* (New York: Ballantine Books, 1989).

26. Baxandall, Gordon, and Reverby, *America's Working Women*, 66.

27. Filippelli, *Labor in the USA*, 47.

28. John Andrews and W. D. P. Bliss, *History of Women in Trade Unions*, vol. 10 of *Report on the Condition of Women and Child Wage-Earners in the United States* (Washington, D.C.: Government Printing Office, 1911), rpt. excerpts in Baxandall, Gordon, and Reverby, *America's Working Women*, 64; Baxandall, *Words on Fire*, 168.

29. Filippelli, *Labor in the USA*, 81.

30. Xialon Boa, "Chinese Mothers in New York City's New Sweatshops," in Jetter, Orleck, and Taylor, *Politics of Motherhood*, 128.

31. Cameron, *Radicals*, 113.

32. Ibid., 112; Mary Frederickson, "'I Know Which Side I'm On': Southern Women in the Labor Movement in the Twentieth Century," in *Women, Work, and Protest: A Century of US Women's Labor History*, ed. Ruth Milkman (Boston: Routledge and Kegan Paul, 1985), 164–66.

33. Cameron, *Radicals*, 139, 161.

34. Basche, "Introductory Essay," 222–23.

35. Cameron, *Radicals*, 55.

36. Anna Whitney, for example, was second vice president of the National Equal Suffrage Association, an executive committee member of the NAACP, and a former social worker and relief worker who later was indicted for membership in the Communist Party. Kate Richards O'Hare was a social worker, Socialist editor, prison reform activist, suffrage campaigner, labor advocate, and antiwar dissident whose imprisonment for her criticism of World War I led to her campaign for amnesty for other dissenters.

37. Gilligan, *Different Voice*, 44, 74–76.

38. Cameron, *Radicals*, 134.

39. Ibid., 111; Jetter, Orleck, and Taylor, *Politics of Motherhood*, 87.

40. Baxandall, Gordon, and Reverby, *America's Working Women*, 184–85.

41. Cameron, *Radicals*, 135.

42. Filippelli, *Labor in the USA*, 81.

43. Ibid., 97–98.

44. Cameron, *Radicals*, 126, 135.

45. Camp, *Iron in Her Soul*, 17.

46. Baxandall, *Words on Fire*, 69.

47. For a more thorough discussion of each woman's personal and professional histories, see Mari Boor Tonn, "Mary Harris 'Mother' Jones (1830?–1930), 'Mother' and Messiah to Industrial Labor," in *Women Public Speakers in the United States, 1800–1925: A Bio-Critical Sourcebook*, ed. Karlyn Kohrs Campbell (Westport, Conn.: Greenwood Press, 1993), 229–41; and Mari Boor Tonn and Mark S. Kuhn, "Elizabeth Gurley Flynn (1890–1964), Advocate Who Merged Feminism and Radical Labor Organizing," in Campbell, *Women Public Speakers*, 221–37.

48. Jones always spoke extemporaneously, occasionally even constructing her text based upon topics initiated by audience members or other kinds of comments and responses from listeners. See Mari Boor Tonn and Mark S. Kuhn, "Co-constructed Oratory: Speaker-Audience Interaction in the Labor Union Rhetoric of Mary Harris 'Mother' Jones," *Text and Performance Quarterly* 13 (1993): 1–18. Flynn occasionally spoke from complete prepared texts, most often during radio broadcasts, or from detailed outlines. She claims, however, that of the estimated 10,000 speeches she gave throughout her lifetime, most were delivered without the luxury of notes. See, "Hoarse," *New Yorker*, 26 October 1946, 23.

49. Steel, *Speeches and Writings of Mother Jones*, 63, 102.

50. "Mother Jones Fiery," *Toledo Bee*, 24 March 1903.

51. Baxandall, *Words on Fire*, 23; Flynn, *I Speak My Own Piece*, 109.

52. Elizabeth Gurley Flynn, "Public Speaking Notes," holograph, in Flynn Papers.

53. Fetherling, *Mother Jones*, 23–24.

54. Camp, *Iron in Her Soul*, 23.

55. Baxandall, *Words on Fire*, 47.

56. Ibid., 58.

57. Camp, *Iron in Her Soul*, 283.

58. Fetherling, *Mother Jones*, 23–24, 76–78; Foner, *Mother Jones Speaks*, 283; Steel, *Correspondence of Mother Jones*, xxix.

59. Howard B. Lee, *Bloodletting in Appalachia* (Morgantown: West Virginia University Library, 1969), 29.

60. Foner, *Mother Jones Speaks*, 204.

61. Elizabeth Gurley Flynn, "The Truth about the Paterson Strike," 31 January 1914, New York Civic Club Forum, New York City, in Flynn Papers.

62. Mari Boor Tonn, "Elizabeth Gurley Flynn's *Sabotage:* 'Scene' as Both Controlling and Catalyzing 'Acts,'" *Southern Speech Communication Journal* 1 (1995): 59–75; Camp, *Iron in Her Soul*, 56.

63. Jones's paternal grandfather was hanged for insurgency in the Irish Rebellion, whereas Flynn's lover, Tresca, was assassinated, most likely by agents of Mussolini.

64. Jones, *Autobiography*, 136.

65. Flynn, *I Speak My Own Piece*, 98; "Hoarse," 23.

66. Qtd. in Camp, *Iron in Her Soul*, 123.

67. Jones, *Autobiography*, 224. For an analysis of the ways in which Jones's philosophy and discursive and non-discursive practices reflect primary maternal aims, see Mari Boor Tonn, "Militant Motherhood: Labor's Mary Harris 'Mother' Jones," *Quarterly Journal of Speech* 82 (1996): 1–21.

68. Foner, *Mother Jones Speaks*, 249.

69. Flynn, "Paterson Strike," 72.

70. Elizabeth Gurley Flynn, "Speech by Elizabeth Gurley Flynn, *Political Affairs*, 615, in Flynn papers, emphasis added.

71. Steel, *Correspondence of Mother Jones*, xxix.

72. Flynn, *I Speak My Own Piece*, 208; Olmstead, "Agitator," 72–75.

73. For a detailed account of this incident, see Corliss Lamont, ed., *The Trial of Elizabeth Gurley Flynn by the American Civil Liberties Union* (New York: Horizon, 1968).

74. Jones made this statement during an interview included in Djuna Barnes, *Interviews*, ed. Alyce Barry (Washington, D.C.: Sun and Moon Press, 1985), 101–2. Barnes's interview with Jones occurred on 7 February 1915.

75. Baxandall, *Words on Fire*, 157.

76. Ibid., 108.

77. Ibid., 94.

78. The extensively detailed handwritten outline for this speech is located in Flynn's papers and bears only the title and date, apparently supplied by the archivist, "Women–This was 1909."

79. Baxandall, *Words on Fire*, 215–17; Camp, *Iron in Her Soul*, 176, 181–84.

80. Baxandall, *Words on Fire*, 168.

81. Steel, *Speeches and Writings of Mother Jones*, 45.

82. This untitled radio address was given in Newark, New Jersey, and dated as 1 November 1948, apparently by an archivist. Content in the speech, however, suggests an earlier date, most likely 1944.

83. Elizabeth Gurley Flynn, "Radio Address," August or September 1947, Washington, Pa., in Flynn Papers; Baxandall, *Words on Fire*, 221.

84. Elizabeth Gurley Flynn, "Opposition to the Confirmation of Tom Clark as Associate Justice of the Supreme Court," 10 August 1949, in Flynn Papers.

85. Camp, *Iron in Her Soul*, 170–71, 290.

86. Baxandall, *Words on Fire*, 176.

87. Foner, *Mother Jones Speaks*, 138.

88. Camp, *Iron in Her Soul*, 63.

89. Foner, *Mother Jones Speaks*, 110.

90. Ibid., 92.

91. Camp, *Iron in Her Soul*, 24.

92. Foner, *Mother Jones Speaks*, 283.

93. Because many coal miners initially were paid on a per-wagon basis, some employers instituted "cribbing," a practice in which the sides of coal wagons were greatly extended, resulting in substantially more mined coal for the same paid wage. Other companies achieved similar results less flagrantly by fixing weight scales or incorrectly logging work credits.

94. See, for example, Lee, *Bloodletting in Appalachia*; Herman R. Lantz, with J. S. McCrary, *People of Coal Town* (New York: Columbia University Press, 1958); and Fred Mooney, *Struggles in the Coal Fields: The Autobiography of Fred Mooney* (Morgantown: West Virginia University Library, 1967). Mooney was a UMWA organizer who often worked closely with Jones.

95. Foner, *Mother Jones Speaks*, 155.

96. Ibid., 77, 92, 296.

97. Ibid., 266.

98. Ibid., 126, 203, 215.

99. Cameron, *Iron in Her Soul*, 3.

100. Foner, *Mother Jones Speaks*, 170, 215.

101. Jones, *Autobiography*, 231.

102. Foner, *Mother Jones Speaks*, 210.

103. Elizabeth Gurley Flynn, "Early Notes," holograph, 1907 or 1908, in Flynn Papers, emphasis added.

104. Elizabeth Gurley Flynn, "Small Families—a Proletarian Necessity," holograph, 1915, in Flynn Papers.

105. Elizabeth Gurley Flynn, "Problems Organizing Women," holograph, 1916, in Flynn Papers, emphasis added.

106. Foner, *Mother Jones Speaks*, 126.

107. Ibid., 197.

108. Baxandall, *Words on Fire*, 169.

109. Bao, "Chinese Mothers."

110. Baxandall, *Words on Fire*, 225.

111. Steel, *Speeches and Writings of Mother Jones*, 89.

112. Qtd. in Lamont, *Trial of Elizabeth Gurley Flynn*, 99.

113. Elizabeth Gurley Flynn, "Summation in the Smith Act Trial," 6 January 1953, in Flynn Papers.

114. Baxandall, *Words on Fire*, 169.

115. Steel, *Speeches and Writings of Mother Jones*, 6.

116. This premise runs throughout Gilligan, *Different Voice*; Ann Wilson Schaef, *Women's Reality: An Emerging Female System in a White Male Society* (San Francisco: Harper and Row, 1981); and Nancy Chodorow, *The Reproduction of Mothering: Psychoanalysis and the Sociology of Gender* (Berkeley: University of California Press, 1978).

117. Foner, *Mother Jones Speaks*, 106.

118. Steel, *Speeches and Writings of Mother Jones*, 33.

119. Patricia Hill Collins, *Black Feminist Criticism: Knowledge, Consciousness and the Politics of Empowerment* (New York: Routledge, 1991), 129–31; Cameron, *Radicals*, 39, 45, 108–10.

120. This premise runs throughout Elizabeth Stone, *Black Sheep and Kissing Cousins: How Our Family Stories Shape Us* (New York: Times Books, 1978).

121. Foner, *Mother Jones Speaks*, 164.

122. Ibid., 106.

123. Ibid., 142.

124. Steel, *Speeches and Writings of Mother Jones*, 34.

125. Ibid., 48.

126. Baxandall, *Words on Fire*, 136–38.

127. Foner, *Mother Jones Speaks*, 294–95.

128. Baxandall, *Words on Fire*, 198–99.

129. Foner, *Mother Jones Speaks*, 102.

130. Baxandall, *Words on Fire*, 108.

131. Foner, *Mother Jones Speaks*, 106.

132. Ibid., 142, emphasis added.

133. Baxandall, *Words on Fire*, 120–21.

134. Ibid., 95.

135. Elizabeth Gurley Flynn, "The Political Significance of Defense Work," Communist Party Convention, New York City, 1950, in Flynn Papers, 8, 14.

136. Elizabeth Gurley Flynn, "On Arrests and Indictments," 6 August 1948, in Flynn Papers.

137. This three-page untitled and undated handwritten text is in Flynn Papers.

138. Elizabeth Gurley Flynn, "Evaluation of Labor Leaders," holograph, n.d., in Flynn Papers.

139. Ruddick, *Maternal Thinking*, 72–73.

140. Steel, *Speeches and Writings of Mother Jones*, 170.

141. Ibid., 105.

142. Camp, *Iron in Her Soul*, 33, 35.

143. Steel, *Speeches and Writings of Mother Jones*, 168, emphasis added.

144. Cameron, *Radicals*, 126.

145. Qtd. in Cameron, *Radicals*, 112.

146. Flynn, "Arrests and Indictments," 3.

147. Foner, *Mother Jones Speaks*, 175, 188–90.

148. Steel, *Speeches and Writings of Mother Jones*, 146, emphasis added.

149. Jerome Bruner, "The Ontogenesis of Speech Acts," *Journal of Child Language* 2 (1975): 1–19; Elinor Ochs, "From Feelings to Grammar: A Samoan Case Study" in *Language Socialization Across Cultures*, ed. Bambi B. Schieffelin and Elinor Ochs (New York: Cambridge University Press, 1986), 5–6.

150. Deborah Tannen, *Talking Voices* (New York: Cambridge University Press, 1989), 98–133.

151. "Mother Jones at Jop[l]in," *Workers' Chronicle* (Pittsburg, Ks.), 17 September 1915, 5.

152. Peggy Miller, "Teasing as Language Socialization and Verbal Play in a White Working-Class Community," in Schieffelin and Ochs, *Language Socialization*, 199–200, 205, 210.

153. See, for example, Karlyn Kohrs Campbell, "The Rhetoric of Women's Liberation: An Oxymoron," *Quarterly Journal of Speech* 59 (1973): 73–86; Karlyn Kohrs Campbell, "Femininity and Feminism: To Be or Not to Be a Woman," *Communication Quarterly* 31 (1983): 101–8; and Karlyn Kohrs Campbell, *Man Cannot Speak for Her: A Critical Study of Early Feminist Rhetoric*, vol. 1 (New York: Greenwood Press, 1989).

154. See, for example, Northrop Frye, *The Critical Path: An Essay on the Social Context of Literary Criticism* (Bloomington: Indiana University Press, 1973), 37–38; Robert Briffault, *The Mothers*, abbrev. ed. G. R. Taylor (New York: MacMillan, 1959), 275; and Aida Hurtado, "Relating to Privilege: Seduction and Rejection in the Subordination of White Women and Women of Color," *Signs* 14 (1989): 848.

155. Stone, *Black Sheep and Kissing Cousins*, 136.

156. Steel, *Speeches and Writings of Mother Jones*, 220.

157. Elizabeth Gurley Flynn, "Summation at the Smith Act Trial" in Flynn papers.

158. Elizabeth Gurley Flynn, "Statement at the Smith Act Trial," in *We Shall Be Heard: Women Speakers in America*, ed. Patricia Scileppi Kennedy and Gloria Hartmann O'Shields (Dubuque, Iowa: Kendall/Hunt, 1983), 243.

159. See, for example, James F. Walsh Jr., "An Approach to Dyadic Communication in Historical Social Movements: Dyadic Communication in Maoist Insurgent Mobilization," *Communication Monographs* 53 (1983): 1–15; and James F. Walsh Jr., "Paying Attention to Channels: Differential Images of Recruitment for Students for a Democratic Society, 1960–1965," *Communication Studies* 44 (1993): 71–86.

160. *Conditions in the Coal Mines of Colorado*, U.S. Cong. House, Subcommittee of the Committee on Mines and Mining, 63rd Cong., 2nd sess., H. Res. 387 (Washington, D.C.: Government Printing Office, 1914), 2927.

161. Baxandall, *Words on Fire*, 57.

162. Flynn, *I Speak My Own Piece*, 138.

163. Baxandall, *Words on Fire*, 117.

164. Camp, *Iron in Her Soul*, 29.

165. Cameron, *Radicals*, 151.

166. Elizabeth Gurley Flynn, "Jungle Law," holograph, approximately 1908, in Flynn Papers.

167. Elizabeth Gurley Flynn, "Woman," holograph, 1909, in Flynn Papers, 4.

168. "Mother Jones, Mild Mannered, Talks Sociology," *New York Times*, 1 June 1913.

169. Cameron, *Radicals*, 163.

170. Elizabeth Gurley Flynn, *Sabotage: The Conscious Withdrawal of the Workers' Industrial Efficiency* (Cleveland: IWW Publishing Bureau, 1917), Wayne State University Industrial Workers of the World Collection, Archives of Labor and Urban Affairs, Box 171, 13. Also in Flynn Papers.

171. Flynn, *Sabotage*, 9.

172. Ibid., 3.

173. Baxandall, *Words on Fire*, 115–16.

174. Steel, *Speeches and Writings of Mother Jones*, 164.

175. Ruddick, *Maternal Thinking*, 139.

176. Helen Marot, "A Woman's Strike—An Appreciation of the Shirtwaist Makers of New York," *Proceedings of the Academy of Political Science of the City of New York* 1 (October 1910), reprinted excerpts in Baxandall, Gordon, and Reverby, *America's Working Women*, 190.

177. Cameron, *Radicals*, 169.

178. Jetter, Orleck, and Taylor, *Politics of Motherhood*, 4.

179. Flynn, "Woman," Flynn Papers, 12.

Terence V. Powderly and the Knights of Labor: A Leader Under Siege

Charles J. Stewart

9

Leaders of reform movements exert control, at best, over the core of a single organization and on occasion influence larger numbers of sympathizers. In reality, they represent movements rather than lead or control them.[1] As Charles J. Stewart, Craig Allen Smith, and Robert E. Denton note, the environment in which leaders operate is "fraught with repressive uncertainty, complex conditions, conflicting demands, pressures from inside and outside the movement, power struggles among movement elements and organizations, disagreements over philosophies and strategies, financial crises, and competition among aspiring leaders."[2] Herbert Simons summarizes the plight of reform movement leaders when he writes: "Shorn of the controls that characterize formal organizations, yet required to perform the same internal functions, harassed from without, yet obligated to adapt to the external system, the leader of a social movement must constantly balance inherently conflicting demands on his position and on the movement he represents."[3] These situational exigencies require movement leaders to employ a variety of apologetic rhetorical strategies to defend themselves and their movement's ideologies, positions, actions, decisions, and associations.

The post–Civil War labor movement encountered these exigencies as it struggled to improve the plight of American workers. America changed during the Civil War years as it experienced rapid development into an urban, industrial nation with a population swelled by millions of immigrants. Massive industrialization necessary for the war effort, fed by a seemingly endless array of mechanical inventions, led to the development of new markets; the creation of giant companies in steel, railroads, shipbuilding, and oil; and the search for cheap, unskilled labor. The fledgling labor movement that formed along craft lines in the decade before the war emerged in shambles with the end of hostilities in 1865.[4] "Monopoly," "trust," and "industrialist" became household words and Gould, Rockefeller, Carnegie, and Vanderbilt household names. Poor working conditions, low wages, and economic depressions led workers into disastrous strikes that destroyed many of their labor organizations and resulted in unemployment and lower wages in part because of cheap, unskilled, immigrant labor.[5] Labor activists were thus forced to seek new approaches to organizing American workers.

Powderly and the Knights of Labor

On 28 December 1869 the garment cutters of Philadelphia dissolved their trade union to form a secret organization they believed could better withstand the attacks of employers who sought to destroy the labor movement. A week later the new Garment Cutters' Assembly of the Noble Order of the Knights of Labor elected its first officers and chose Uriah S. Stephens as its master workman (president). This new union was to enjoy a tempestuous, if dynamic, career.

On 20 October 1870 the Order of the Knights of Labor outlined its principles, which established a distinct sort of union. First, unlike the traditional trade or craft union, the Order opened its membership to all working people, regardless of trade or skill. This decision stemmed in part from the Order's profound fear of the potential jealousy and malice within the movement and among workers. In addition, the determination of industrialists, the press, government, and the church to destroy organized labor and anyone identified with it alarmed those who founded the new Order and led to extreme secrecy. In his autobiography, Terence Powderly wrote that "no one connected with organized labor dared to allow his name to appear publicly as a member. The blacklist would be employed and idleness, poverty, destitution, and perhaps death would be the reward of open identification with a labor union of that era."[6] Members may have exaggerated the dangers they faced, but they took no chances. The name of the Order was never used in documents and correspondence but was identified with asterisks.

Unlike traditional labor unions, the Knights of Labor was reformist in attitude and ideology and went far beyond concerns for hours, wages, and working conditions. Its concern was the general welfare and rights of workers rather "than improvement of specific working conditions."[7] The goal was to organize everyone who worked for a living (excluding only doctors, lawyers, bankers, and those who sold intoxicating drink) into one grand union in which an injury to one would be an injury to all. The Order believed that cooperatives, in which all workers were part owners of enterprises, had to replace the wage system if the lot of labor was to improve. The solution to interminable labor and management conflict was a system of arbitration in which labor and capital would sit down, both from a position of strength, and settle their differences without a strike or lockout. The Knights of Labor and Terence Powderly seemed destined for one another.

Terence Powderly was born on 22 January 1849 in Carbondale, Pennsylvania, to Irish immigrant parents.[8] Some of his earliest memories were of political debates between his father, Terence, a pronounced Democrat, and his mother, Madge, an outspoken abolitionist. He took his mother's side during the Buchanan-Frémont presidential campaign in 1856, and was outraged to learn that his mother could not vote her abolitionist beliefs because she was a woman. Though only seven, he marched to the polling place, asked for and received a ballot, and voted in his mother's place for Frémont. Frémont lost the election, but young Powderly became a lifelong advocate of women's rights and suffrage.

Not unlike his peers of the time, Powderly left school at thirteen to seek employment. He worked first as a guard at a railroad switch and later as a rail car examiner, car repairer, and locomotive brakeman. At seventeen, he became an apprenticed machinist and, upon completing his three-year apprenticeship in 1869, moved to Scranton, Pennsylvania, to work in a locomotive shop.

It was in Scranton that Powderly first experienced the effects of a strike on other workers and was both puzzled and disturbed by the opposition of other workers who saw the striking miners as their enemy rather than fellow workers striving for their rights and better working and living conditions. Powderly became convinced that a strike should be used only as a last resort in labor and management disputes because it inevitably harmed the strikers, led to divisions among workers and unions, and weakened companies to the point where jobs were lost.

In September 1869 Terence Powderly traveled to Avondale, Pennsylvania, to the scene of a mine disaster and heard his first labor speech. Both events were to have profound effects on Powderly's thinking and future. Years later he reported his reactions to this terrible scene.

> When on that September day at Avondale I saw the blackened, charred bodies of over one hundred men and boys as they were brought to the surface, when I saw a mother kneel in silent grief to hold the cold, still face of her boy in hers, and when I saw her fall lifeless on his dead body, I experienced a sensation that I have never forgotten. It was such a feeling as comes to me whenever I read of death in the mines or on the railroad.[9]

That same day John Siney, founder of the Miners and Laborer's Benevolent Association, delivered a moving speech at the sight of this fatal coal mine explosion south of Scranton. Powderly wrote in his autobiography:

> Then when I listened to John Siney I could see Christ in his face and hear a new Sermon on the Mount. . . . I was just a boy then, but I looked at John Siney standing on the desolate hillside at Avondale, with his back to a moss grown rock the grim witness to that awful tragedy of ignorance, indifference, thoughtlessness, and greed, and listened to his low, earnest voice, I saw the travail of ages struggling for expression on his stern, pale face. I caught inspiration from his words and realized that there was something more to win through labor than dollars and cents for self. I realized for the first time that day that death, awful death such as lay around me at Avondale, was a call to the living to neglect no duty to fellow man.[10]

Upon returning to Scranton after his visit to Avondale, Powderly inquired about the existence of a union or brotherhood of workers in the area and learned that none existed. Later he saw a notice in a Philadelphia paper about a moulders union meeting and wrote for information about a machinists union. After learning of the existence of the International Union of Machinists and Blacksmiths of the United States of America, Powderly induced a shop mate to write to the president of the union about forming a local in Scranton. He thought he lacked both the penmanship and ability to write an effective letter. Powderly would soon overcome this early fear of writing and contribute extensively to union correspondence, official orders, circulars, annual addresses, labor publications, and newspapers and write *Thirty Years of Life and Labor, 1859–1889*, published in 1890. His family would later give the editors of his autobiography some 75,000 letters, postcards, and telegrams.

An organizer of the Machinists and Blacksmiths International Union arrived in Scranton a few weeks after receiving Powderly's inquiry and established Subordinate Union No. 2 of Pennsylvania. Unfortunately, Powderly was too young to join, and when he became old enough, the local had disappeared. It was revived a year later, and Powderly became first its secretary and then its president. This was a pattern of leadership he would follow throughout his union career.

Powderly soon learned there was price to pay for union activity in the 1870s. A year after joining the Machinists and Blacksmiths International, he was fired from his machinist position in Scranton and blacklisted because of his position in the union. For nearly two years he "tramped" the railroad lines from New York to Canada, Ohio, and Pennsylvania looking for work. Each time he was hired, however, the employer would discover his previous union activities through the blacklist network and dismiss him. Rather than deter his commitment to organized labor, these experiences made Powderly a firm believer in the necessity of a labor organization that could bring about reforms that would protect all workers and allow them to deal on an equal plane with owners and industrialists.

As Powderly thought about his experiences as a worker and a fledgling union leader, he came to realize "that many of the hurts the workingman suffered from were self-inflicted." The abuse of alcohol topped the list. He determined that "intemperance was a curse of labor" that caused "poverty, loss of self-respect, loss of standing in the community and other evils." When he "dived beneath the surface," Powderly claimed he "discovered that liquor was carried into the mine and drunk there; it was carried out on the railroad and drunk there to the risk and danger of fellow worker and traveling public." Powderly concluded that "strange as it may appear to you, the industrious, faithful, sober workman stood less chance of promotion at that time than the grafter, perhaps I should say graftee, who greased the itching palm of some petty foreman or superintendent for leave to earn his daily bread."[11] He became a lifelong supporter of the temperance movement.

Powderly's experiences from childhood to young adulthood fed his reformist instincts and led him inexorably toward organized labor and the reform-oriented Knights of Labor. His abolitionist mother and her inability to cast a vote for what she believed in so fervently led him to support woman suffrage and the "rights of man." His experiences as a laborer, machinist, and union officer led to his belief in temperance. The ill effects of strikes on all parties involved led him to seek alternatives to strikes in labor-management relationships. And his introduction to a union orator at the scene of death and destruction and his time in the wilderness after being blacklisted because of his union activities convinced him that solidarity of all workers was essential for their protection and ability to negotiate as equals with management. His long tenure with the Knights of Labor was about to commence.

Powderly claims that he was sworn into the Knights of Labor in 1874 but did not join officially until 1876. In 1877 he joined District Assembly No. 5 in Scranton and was elected corresponding secretary, a position that required him to be in contact with the national office and leaders. That same year, the company he was working for in Scranton closed for lack of orders, and Powderly decided to go back to school and devote his spare time to building up his district assembly. Within just two years, 1879, he was elected to his first national office, general worthy foreman. Later that year Uriah Stephens, first leader of the Knights, resigned his position as grand master workman because of poor health, and the general assembly selected Powderly to succeed him. He was now the national leader of the Knights of Labor, and would lead the Order through its greatest triumphs and failures from 1879 to 1893. During Powderly's tenure as grand master workman (later renamed general master workman), the Knights experienced a roller-coaster ride from a small, regional union of a few thousand members, to great victories and prestige with hundreds of thousands of members in several countries, and finally to decline as a significant force in the American labor movement with fewer than 75,000 members.

Powderly's platforms for espousing a variety of reforms did not stop with his rise within the Knights. His reputation as a utopian reformer, particularly in regards to labor, monetary, and temperance issues, led to his election as mayor of Scranton on the Greenback Labor Party ticket in 1878. He was reelected in 1880 and 1882. The party nominated him for lieutenant governor of Pennsylvania in 1882, but he declined.

Although Powderly was known then as, and is considered now, a nineteenth-century reformer, he detested that label. He wrote in his autobiography:

> Nor was I a reformer, for of all the ill-used, ill-fitting, and undeserved terms, reformer, it seems to me, takes rank with the worst. Men claiming to be reformers came to me by the hundred [sic] to enlist my aid, or that of the Knights of Labor through me, in some project that at first seemed worthy, but a half hour, or an hour's talk—for I listened to all of them—disclosed the microbe of personal feeling and ambition, hate or greed, that hoped to grow big and powerful with a little help from me. Whenever I hear a man proclaim himself a reformer I look for a motive. In a majority of cases it may be found rooted in revenge, disappointment, or greed.[12]

He preferred to be called an "equalizer" or "agitator." Under whatever label one might apply, Powderly led the largest labor union of the nineteenth century for nearly fifteen years and was an outspoken champion of numerous reforms of the time.

The Rise and Decline of the Knights of Labor

During the early 1870s, with most members working in the Philadelphia area, the secret Order of the Knights of Labor grew slowly. When strikes and riots in 1877 destroyed many trade unions, new members pushed into the Order partly because it had not taken part in the strikes and had counseled moderation and peaceful means of change.[13] District assemblies formed in six states. The Order's motto, "an injury to one is the concern of all," appealed to workers within a fractured movement who increasingly felt powerless and insecure.

On 1 January 1878 the Knights, with a membership of 9,000, reorganized into the General Assembly of the Knights of Labor of North America and selected Uriah Stephens as grand master workman, the national president. The constitution of the general assembly emphasized organization, education, cooperation, and arbitration and called "upon all who believe in securing 'the greatest good to the greatest number' to aid and assist us."[14] Although Powderly had experienced firsthand the dangers of operating openly as an organization and leader and appreciated why the Knights had opted for absolute secrecy in its early years, he led a faction in 1878 to end secrecy and delete all scriptural passages and quotations. He rightly saw the growing antagonism toward secret organizations, particularly among the press and clergy. Like Powderly, a great many members and potential members in eastern Pennsylvania were Roman Catholic, and the clergy was pressuring them to leave or avoid the Knights. He gave an example in his book on the history of the early labor movement when many workers left or withdrew temporarily following "a scathing denunciation of the association" from the altar of one of the churches in Schuylkill County.[15] A large majority at the general assembly, twenty-two to four, voted with Stephens in favor of Article I of the constitution, which said, "This body shall be known as the General Assembly of the * * * * * and shall be composed of Delegates elected according to Art. II of this Constitution.[16]

As membership grew slowly in the early 1880s, internal dissension mounted. The range of differences was broad and deep. Leaders emphasized cooperatives, arbitration, and monetary, legislative, and temperance reforms, while the rank-and-file members were mostly concerned with wages, hours, and working conditions. Some elements wanted to form a political party; others favored affiliation with the Democratic, Republican, or Greenback Party. The Order found itself increasingly in the middle of the struggle for organizing and representing labor. Socialists wanted to overthrow the capitalistic order; trade unions wanted higher wages and organization along craft lines to solve all troubles; and the Order wanted to form a single inclusive organization and to end the wage system by establishing a cooperative economic system.[17] Disgruntled former members of the Knights created the Improved Order of the Knights of Labor and the Independent Order.[18] According to labor historian Joseph Rayback, the issue of secrecy produced constant internal conflict among members and leaders.[19] In 1881 Powderly determined that secrecy was doing far more harm than good to the growth and stability of the Order and had to end. In his address to the general assembly, he claimed that many locals were anxiously awaiting the results of the general assembly's "deliberations on the question of making the name of the Order public. Many locals were already working under protest, the alternative of leaving the Order or the church in which many of them were born and raised staring them in the face." After much thought, Powderly had come to believe that "we must admit that we want the men of all religions, and to get them we must make concessions to the church, for its influence is too vast to be idly passed over." He reported that during the past year, he had visited clergy in many localities to explain in detail the workings of the Order and why it had maintained secrecy. They understood and accepted his explanations but remained opposed to "the taking of rash oaths."[20] This time Powderly's arguments found a receptive audience, and secrecy ended. All members and publications could now proudly and openly use the name Knights of Labor instead of asterisks.

Events in 1885 catapulted the Order into undisputed leadership of the labor movement. After the Order called a strike against the Missouri-Pacific Railroad, Powderly successfully arbitrated grievances with its powerful owner, Jay Gould. The Order also conducted a number of successful boycotts. For thousands of workers, Powderly had shown the power of arbitration and of the Knights of Labor; he was, in their eyes, the undisputed leader of the labor movement. According to Rayback, "All the bitterness and resentment which had accumulated among workingmen during two years of depression, all the frustration produced by wage cuts, all the fury caused by employer use of Pinkertons, black lists, and yellow-dog contracts suddenly burst forth to create a wild rush to join the ranks of the Knights of Labor."[21] Membership soared to over 700,000 in 1886, a year during which Powderly reported the formation of 4,068 new assemblies.[22] This growth created its own set of problems. Coordinating the training and organization of new assemblies and controlling the huge increase in members and assemblies were impossible. The highly decentralized structure of the Order gave the general officers (general master workman, general worthy foreman, general secretary-treasurer, general executive board) little authority to discipline officers or members of local and district assemblies who violated the Order's principles and instructions from the general officers. The Order quickly became a massive, out-of-control, and undisciplined labor force.[23] Assemblies launched all sorts of unauthorized strikes and boycotts, often the moment an assembly was formed. New members expected moral and financial support once a strike or boycott was under way, but neither was forthcoming. The Order had limited funds available for covering essentials and none available to support thousands of strikers for extended periods. Bitter confrontations between local and district assemblies and the national office were inevitable and frequent.

Two events in 1886 jolted the Order and started its precipitous decline in membership and power. The movement for an eight-hour workday had been gaining momentum for some time, and many labor leaders decided to make a big push for it in the spring of 1886.[24] The leadership of the Knights of Labor wanted a shorter workday, but believed the key demand of ten-hour pay for an eight-hour day would harm companies financially and eventually lead to layoffs and a search for cheaper labor. Powderly wrote a secret circular in March advising Knights to stay out of the eight-hour movement, but members were enthusiastic and joined the campaign for shorter hours with equal pay. They entered into a number of disastrous strikes, including a new strike against the Gould railroad system. Rayback writes that "although Powderly and Gould made an effort to arbitrate, the strikers, influenced by the prevailing 'give no quarter' sentiment, refused to make any concessions."[25] The strike dragged on for two months with hundreds of violent acts, and finally ended in early May with no gains and significant loss of wages and jobs for workers. Striking members and those in the labor movement supporting the eight-hour movement accused Powderly and the Order of betraying them by opposing their efforts.

On 4 May 1886 a bomb was thrown into a group of police during a rally of anarchists at Haymarket Square in Chicago, killing seven police officers, and the ensuing police gunfire killed four civilians and wounded dozens of others. Eight anarchist leaders were arrested and charged with murder; four were hanged the next year. Although the Knights of Labor and the anarchists were bitter enemies in the struggle for the rights of labor and the Order had played no part in the Haymarket Square riot, the public and the press blamed all organized labor for the disorder, particularly the Knights. Rayback writes that "in the public mind, the Haymarket affair was a climax of ten years of labor violence" and proved that "the nation's labor elements were inherently criminal in character: inclined to riot, arson, pillage, assault, and murder."[26] Those who condemned the anarchists and those who praised the anarchists, including some local assemblies of the Order that aided the anarchists financially and morally, assaulted Powderly and the Knights of Labor for what they did and did not do.

Although the Order continued to grow in membership during the early months of 1887, continuing strikes and violence contributed to a decrease in membership from 703,000 to 510,000 by the end of the year. Rayback claims that "the public decided that the Knights—the noisy, tempestuous, strike-happy Knights—were at the bottom of the whole labor upheaval."[27] The Order, as the largest and most threatening organization in the labor movement, and Powderly, as the dominant face of both the Order and the movement, thus became the primary targets of the public, industrialists, state governments, press, and church. These groups saw the aftermath of the Haymarket riot and public fear of organized labor as an ideal time to destroy the movement and the hated Knights of Labor. Opponents not only attacked Powderly and the Order verbally through the press and pulpit but also provoked unwise strikes among workers to rid companies of union leaders and to break local assemblies.

The inevitable war with trade unions and the American Federation of Labor (AFL), primarily because of deep philosophical differences over organizing along craft lines or by industry, began when mixed assemblies, consisting of both skilled and unskilled workers, tried to get trades members to withdraw from their national affiliations. Faced with this choice, trades members left the Order. Samuel Gompers, the leader of the AFL, recognized the opportunity events provided to eliminate his organization's chief rival and the movement's "inferior" element. Refusing to meet with Powderly to discuss their differences or to work in unison, he began to threaten trade unions with expulsion from the AFL if they did not leave the Knights of Labor.[28]

The Order's influence dwindled with urban workers. A system of cooperatives that Powderly had championed as the "way to make every man his own master,— every man his own employer" and the plan that "must one day supersede the present system," had ended in failure.[29] The largely uneducated membership with little or no experience in business affairs proved incapable of running their own businesses and often succumbed to petty jealousies among members of cooperatives and competition from privately owned companies and corporations. In spite of efforts to ally the Order with the Farmers' Alliance and other labor groups, membership declined to 260,000 in 1888, 100,000 in 1890, and 74,000 in 1893, Powderly's final year as general master workman.

The 1880s and 1890s were turbulent years for the nation as well as for organized labor. During most of those years, the Knights of Labor was the largest and most powerful force for reforms that would improve the lives and working conditions of the working men and women of America. It was loved and loathed, respected and scorned, praised and condemned, supported and undermined, feared and ridiculed by members, former members, workers, trade unionists, industrialists, journalists, politicians, and clergy. As undisputed leader of the Order for fourteen years, Terence Powderly became the Knights of labor for many observers. Some critics aimed their attacks at "Powderly & Co."[30] For most of those fourteen years, he was the face not only of the Knights of Labor but of the labor movement as well. As sociologist Joseph Gusfield writes, "It is with leadership that the public identifies in describing and judging a movement. . . . [T]he leader personifies the movement, in cartoon, picture, story, and legend. For much of the public, the leader becomes synonymous with the movement and its adherents."[31] Terence Powderly, as the face and personification of the Order and the labor movement, became their lightning rod. He experienced few quiet times during his long tenure as leader of the Knights of Labor. From his earliest days as grand master workman in 1879 to his final days in 1893, he was a leader under siege. Powderly's task became addressing and surmounting the never-ending obstacles encountered by organized labor in general and the Knights of Labor in particular. He had to satisfy workers and members who wanted immediate solutions for long hours, low wages, and job insecurity. He had to address strikes, nearly all of which he neither initiated nor approved, and their disastrous consequences for all associated with them. He had to reply to the escalating competition and conflicts between trade unions and the Order. And he had to fend off attacks by industrialists, government, the press, and the church, all of whom believed organized labor posed a grave threat to all that was American.

In this chapter, I analyze Terence Powderly's rhetorical efforts to address and overcome the numerous obstacles the Order encountered and the incessant criticism and attacks that came from within and without. Unlike more typical rhetorical situations in which persons or corporations must employ rhetoric to defend themselves against a single crisis, controversy, or charge, Powderly faced multiple obstacles, charges, and attacks. He had to defend himself as a person and as general master workman. He had to defend his fellow general officers. And he had to defend the Knights of Labor and the labor movement. On many occasions, two or more of these targets were intertwined. This analysis centers primarily on Powderly's rhetoric of defense as revealed in his annual addresses to the general assembly as general master workman and his many columns in the *Journal of United Labor* (1880–90) and the *Journal of the Knights of Labor* (1890–93).[32] This chapter reveals the difficulties leaders encountered in attempting to organize, manage, and sustain labor organizations in the nineteenth century, particularly leaders, such as Powderly, who espoused reform principles that conflicted with members' desires for immediate betterment of their lives, superseded the craft union philosophy of traditional trade unions, and challenged the power of industrialists in the age of social Darwinism. Like other reform leaders of the nineteenth century, Powderly began his crusade without the power and financial base or the legitimacy enjoyed by institutional leaders. Rhetoric was the only means available to sustain his leadership, the Order, and the movement in the face of dissension from within, attacks from without, disastrous strikes, the anarchists and Haymarket riot, and the escalating conflict between the Order and trade unions.

Internal Dissension

Although the Knights of Labor grew steadily during the early 1880s, almost as many members dropped out each year as joined.[33] New and old members wanted action and immediate improvements in their lives; many became disillusioned when neither need was satisfied. Naturally, Powderly became the target of their frustrations. Thus handling internal dissension about a variety of issues was an ongoing challenge for Powderly.

ACTIONS AND DECISIONS

Like most utopian reform movements of the nineteenth century, the Knights of Labor had a strong strain of Jeffersonian democracy that "eagerly sought to make all men free and equal."[34] Not surprisingly, it was organized from the bottom up rather than top down. The Order was decentralized, with real control reserved for the local and district assemblies, while the general officers could exert little more than moral, philosophical, and educational influence. Dues arrived at the national office sporadically, which meant that the office was chronically understaffed and underfunded. These limits on the national office and deep suspicion of national officers did not dampen the expectations and demands of members and local Members scrutinized Powderly's actions and decisions early and often in his long leadership of the Order. For instance, members accused him of failing to perform duties such as timely publication of the proceedings of the annual general assembly, to respond quickly to correspondence, and to visit local assemblies. They claimed he showed favoritism toward some assemblies while ignoring communications from others. While criticizing him for not complying with resolutions and amendments passed at general assemblies, members also attacked him for not readily granting dispensations to these actions.

In response to these charges, Powderly often portrayed himself as a helpless, innocent, principled victim of elements beyond his control. On several occasions he related devious actions of members and officers. He reported in his annual address in 1882 that when he refused to grant dispensations to constitutional amendments passed in 1881 because he "had no power to grant" them, a revolt was fostered by "those who were active in exciting members to insubordination" and who "lost no opportunity to blacken me whenever an opportunity presented itself."[35] He also claimed that some assemblies had sent him "one-sided appeals" and withheld "the most important part of the testimony until" he "had rendered a decision. By this means the impression was created that I favored one party more than another, and no amount of argument will remove such impressions."[36] He was obviously the victim of dirty tricks and unethical behavior by members and assembly officers who were attacking him for actions and decisions they did not like or had perpetrated.

Powderly claimed that secretaries of assemblies who disliked the national officers had refused to write to them as instructed by their memberships and, when the time came to report to their assemblies, claimed that they had "written to Headquarters but that no notice was taken of it." "Other Secretaries after receiving communications from headquarters," he said, "have refused to read them, claiming they were of a personal nature."[37] Faultfinding members and devious, unprincipled officers were thwarting his efforts to lead the Order in times of crisis. Powderly contrasted his principled decisions and actions, motivated by the best intentions, with those who would destroy the Order for personal gain, advancement, or animosity.

When members of the Order accused Powderly of being a weak and fearful leader, he turned this criticism upon the whole membership. Powderly argued that if he were a weak leader, the Order was at fault. He recognized that he was called weak because he "discountenanced violence and hasty, ill-advised action."[38] "I have

TERENCE V. POWDERLY AND
THE KNIGHTS OF LABOR:
A LEADER UNDER SIEGE

263

no excuse to offer," he declared, "for if this is an offence let the General Assembly itself offer the apology." After all, he concluded, "My views upon such questions were known to each General Assembly before my election as General Master Workman, and in electing me they endorsed and made themselves responsible for these sentiments." Powderly transferred the apologetic obligation, and the guilt, to the Order and its members, some of whom were his critics. How could readers and listeners criticize him for actions and decisions when they reelected him year after year precisely because they knew how he would act and the decisions he would make? He attempted to turn an alleged weakness, slow and overly cautious leadership, into a strength—avoidance of violence, strikes, and actions that would harm members and the Order.

Powderly differentiated actions, motives, matters, and events, a strategy designed to place what "repels an audience into a new and more acceptable perspective."[39] Rather than denying actions or criticized decisions, for instance, Powderly often said he had no apologies to make, no cause for regret, because the "errors" or "mistakes" he may have made were "of the head, and not the heart," unintentional rather than intentional.[40] He redefined his acts and distinguished them from conscious efforts to do harm or make bad decisions. He had not "pleased all members," he admitted, but distinguished minor matters from "living questions" that involved the principles, safety, or welfare of the Order.[41] To err, after all, was only human. In his 1882 address to the general assembly, Powderly declared, "To all who find fault I have only to say, that until man himself becomes perfect you cannot expect his works to be so."[42] Thus any mistakes or errors he may have made, and he admitted to no specific instances, were minor and excusable because they were merely unintentional, human errors of the head involving insignificant matters. His intentions and motives were pure even if the results were sometimes not.

Powderly frequently defended his actions and decisions by arguing from transcendence. He placed both in larger, higher, or grander contexts and claimed he had become a victim for his lofty motives and actions.[43] When, for example, members asked him why he did not reply to attacks on himself and the Order, Powderly explained that he did not refrain through fear but through reluctance to "lay aside duty to the Order to engage in self-defense."[44] His intentions and motives always transcended what he failed to do to a critic's satisfaction. The membership expected of the general master workman "a faithful performance of his duty, and to do that duty faithfully and well he must waste none of his time in refuting malicious statements which are made with the purpose in view of stopping him in his work."[45] He responded to a higher need and calling, the welfare of the sacred principles of the Order and labor. He assured delegates at the 1889 general assembly that "there never was a charge made against your General Master Workman that he could not successfully refute, and if he did not always lay aside duty to the Order to engage in self-defense it was not through fear." His critics were "not worthy of the time or trouble."[46] Thus he was motivated by duty and loyalty to the Order rather than by fear, and his goals and person transcended the need to reply in kind to unworthy critics concerned about insignificant routine matters.

When members raised questions about the Order's financial state, spending by the officers, and possible corruption, Powderly denied charges of wrongdoing and transferred blame to those with evil motives, particularly critics, the general assembly, and former officers. At the 1888 general assembly, Powderly urged members to

[s]tamp out every effort to create strife if such a thing is attempted; but, above all things, do not leave here until you have carefully revised the laws and until each separate item of expenditure for the past two years has been carefully scanned. Do not allow anyone to have an opportunity to again say that the publication of our expenditures was suppressed. It was that the fullest light might be shed

on this very important matter that I voted to have separate items read at the last session. There is nothing contained in the expense account of this Order that your officers need be ashamed of. There has been no dishonesty or attempt at it, and the Order at large is entitled to a full and complete account of what was done with its money.[47]

He urged members of the general assembly to check every "item of expenditure" and "[i]f extravagance is discovered then fix the responsibility where it belongs, and do not forget that a former session of the General Assembly opened the treasury to the expenditure of more money than those to whom it went were entitled."[48]

In his 1889 address to the general assembly, Powderly transferred blame and distanced himself and current officers from the acts and persons responsible for actions detrimental to the Order. He reported: "Those who entailed the greatest expenditures are no longer in the Order, and the legacy of debt they left had to be met by your present officers. . . . Not a dollar was borrowed, no assessment levied, and we stand to-day the debtors of none outside of our own ranks."[49] The general assembly, evil-minded members, and former officers were to blame for financial misdeeds, not Powderly or other general officers. He was the innocent scapegoat, not the perpetrator; he intimated that he and the general officers had taken appropriate steps by expelling those who were guilty.

While Powderly usually identified people as his victimizers (particularly members and local assembly officers), he sometimes portrayed himself as a victim of a situation not of his making. Under difficult circumstances beyond his control, Powderly had done the best he knew how with the means the Order afforded him. He explained in 1885 that he had not complied with a general assembly resolution requiring the general master workman to visit all assemblies in the country because "the condition of the Order and the disturbed relations existing between labor and capital rendered it impossible."[50] The "many vexatious questions" he had to deal with may "have given offence," Powderly admitted, and he was "willing to apologize for the wound inflicted, but not for the motive that led to it."[51]

The 1886 general assembly resolved an internal conflict between two competing cigar makers' assemblies by expelling the Cigar Makers International Union, thereby creating a disastrous external conflict between the Knights of Labor and the Federation of Organized Trades and Labor Unions, a five-year-old federation of trade unions soon to be reorganized into the AFL. The Cigar Makers Union was the labor home of Samuel Gompers, a past president of the Federation and soon to be elected president of the newly formed AFL. Labor historian Charles Madison claims that "Powderly, ineptly striving for harmony within and without the Order, permitted himself to be maneuvered into siding with the Home Club and thereby gave Gompers the opportunity to call the organizational conference which brought about the formation of the American Federation of Labor." By the time Powderly "became aware of the grievous blunder committed" at the general assembly, the damage had already been done.[52]

At the 1887 meeting, Powderly defended his role in the Cigar Makers Union blunder by explaining that the executive board had been victimized by a situation and organizational exigencies not of its own making. "The Board had no alternative but to obey the will of the General Assembly," he exclaimed. "Its hands were tied, and it was forced to let matters take their course." Now he and the board were attempting to right a wrong by providing a corrective action in the form of ruling the action unconstitutional. The general assembly, not Powderly or the executive board, was guilty of creating a situation that deprived some men of their membership in the Order and caused a conflict with trade unions.[53] Although Powderly was the target of disgruntled members and local officers because he was the general master workman and the Order's most visible leader, he also used this position to defend himself, his actions, and his decisions. He wrapped himself in the protective folds of the Knights of Labor not only by claiming that he acted only when and how the Order directed and approved, and with the highest of motives, but also by referring to himself in addresses and journal articles as "your General Master Workman," "the General Master Workman," "Mr. Powderly," or "he."[54] For example, he wrote in the *Journal of the Knights of Labor* in 1891 that "as T. V. Powderly the individual I can do anything I please," but "[a]s General Master Workman it is my duty to follow out my instructions, and up to the present time I have endeavored to do so."[55] His rhetoric blurred the distinction between Powderly the man and Powderly the general master workman; they became one. This blurring of man and leader legitimized his actions and decisions and permitted him to use the Order and his position as scapegoat and shield.

ONE-MAN RULE

The decentralized, bottom-up leadership tradition of the Knights posed serious problems and created controversy within the Order during the decisively critical years of 1887–88 when it was beginning its steep descent. Someone had to take charge, but when Powderly tried to stem the bleeding of the unwieldy Order through strong leadership and contacts with leaders in industry, government, and the church, unhappy members accused him of striving for one-man rule and becoming a dictator. Powderly addressed these charges in his annual address in 1887: "The air has been filled with a volume of sound for the past year concerning autocracy and usurpation of your General Officers. The promulgation of the Constitution has been charged with evil intentions." He assured members that there was "no cause for alarm" because the constitution could be changed each year by the general assembly and because he had no desire for dictatorial powers.[56] He was merely their elected leader and servant, acting always with their best interests in mind.

In a spring 1888 issue of the *Journal of United Labor*, Powderly addressed a question from a member pertaining to one-man rule. The questioner asked if enforcement of discipline in the Order meant "in accordance with the 'peculiar notions of the General Master Workman'?" Powderly's reply emphasized the democratic checks and balances within the Order and that discipline obliged members and assemblies "to live up to the laws of the Order. Where the law is not plain, the decision of the General Master Workman, approved by the General Executive Board, will be considered law until reversed by the General Assembly."[57] The constitution prevented the general master workman from becoming a dictator even if he possessed such inclinations. The discipline portion of his reply was clearly aimed at the questioner and critics who disobeyed the Order's laws while accusing him of striving to be a dictator. Powderly challenged all Knights to do their duty. "Remember that I have the right to demand the best effort of every member, for it is not for self that I have re-enlisted," he declared, "I have been pressed into service again with these words ringing in my ears: 'We are passing through a crucial test, we need the aid of your experience, your counsel, your knowledge of the Order.'" Members had repeatedly called upon him to lead, so he was now calling upon them to do their part. "You are not organized to uphold Powderly, to worship one-man power, to sustain an idol," he concluded, "you are bound together to assist each other and do good for all, but not combined to injure."[58] He transferred blame and responsibility from himself to individual Knights while deflecting the one-man rule charge.

Powderly used the one-man rule conflict to argue for additional powers necessary to lead the Order and the movement more effectively. "The man at the head of the Order," he pleaded, "should be permitted to exercise his own judgment in many cases not defined by law," should be "permitted to think for the Order," and should not be subjected to "the demagogue's cry" that "he is selling out the labor movement" if he makes a decision or is seen "talking to a capitalist or entering the office of a man of wealth."[59] He insisted that ambition and desire for power played no part in his relationships, decisions, or actions. Most significant, the value of a strong leader who could think, be decisive, and develop links with important elements of society transcended the potential danger of a dictatorship. Hamstringing a democratically inclined leader, often because of evil motives, was not the way to prevent organizational tyranny.

In his annual address for 1888, Powderly complained that if he did not "give an ear to every trifling thing," he was "branded as an autocrat who will not heed the voice of the oppressed, and all of this is believed by thousands who never think for themselves and who can do injury, not to the General Master Workman, but to the Order."[60] He transformed potential harm from himself to the Order while attributing evil motives to his critics and incompetence to those who believed what the critics said.

But instead of using his critics' words to deny their charges, he capitalized on them to open a lengthy case for more, not less, power. He noted that "every act of every officer may be charged to him and yet he has no more power vested in him than the officer who may offend." He added: "We have been treated to many a discourse during the past year on the subject of one-man power. The chief trouble with our Order is because of the lack of one-man power. Our Order has been divided in the past, and it has worked injury to us." He warned of the danger of divided power: "Allow every self-seeker, every knave, every disturber and faultfinder to interpret the laws and we have anarchy pure and simple." Anarchy, he implied, was a graver state than dictatorship. He was censured "for not accomplishing results when the authority to do so was not placed in his hands and when the power to thwart his every move was delegated to others who were supposed to act in unison with him."[61] Powderly turned potentially lethal charges against the leader of a reform-oriented organization—dictatorial tendencies and actions—into a need for the good of the Order and the labor movement, to eliminate organizational anarchy. It was a strategy of both attack and defense. The advantages of delegating real power and authority to the general master workman transcended the potential dangers of vesting too much power in this vital position and provided a corrective to persistent and serious problems in the Order.

Powderly not only defused potentially lethal criticisms but also convinced the general assembly to grant him the one-man powers for which he had recently been severely chastised. He placed responsibility and potential blame upon other officers and members for making certain that the new power arrangement worked for the good of the Order.[62] Only a strong leader in times of severe crisis and with the support of the membership could thwart the actions of demagogues, self-seekers, and perennial faultfinders who victimized the leaders and the Order, hampering the effectiveness of the former and the existence of the latter. Although Powderly was constantly responding to internal issues, external criticism and attacks also demanded his attention.

External Assaults

In one of the first issues of the *Journal of United Labor*, Powderly wrote that "members of the Organization have been obliged to listen to slanders most foul, and read libels of the most villainous character on the Order and its officers." He predicted that "as our Order grows in strength and influence, so will increase the spleen and opposition of the enemies of labor," and assured readers that such attacks were good rather than bad signs for the future of the Order: "the more we are attacked by our enemies the stronger will be the faith of the true and earnest workers of our Order in the eternal justice of its principles."[63] If attacks on Powderly and the Order were signs of strength, then both were strong indeed. Again, a wide variety of issues, from his personal character to derogatory associations, demanded his attention.

CHARACTER

Many groups monitored and criticized Powderly's actions and inactions in an effort to diminish his stature within the Order and the labor movement. Some were jealous of his success and position in the movement, while others opposed his utopian brand of unionism and outspoken stands on issues such as temperance, women's rights, strikes, and government ownership of essential industries. Many would have agreed with labor historian Madison's assessment that Powderly was "[e]ssentially the talker rather than the doer, acutely sensitive to criticism, vain and spiteful as well as kindly and idealistic."[64] His reelection year after year as general master workman indicates that he was supported at least by delegates to the general assembly, but it is apparent from loss of membership and turnover among the general officers that he alienated many inside and outside the Order. Powderly's critics and enemies presented reports through the commercial or labor press or through the rumor mill about actions that were allegedly detrimental to labor or the citizenry.

Powderly often countered accusations by presenting a new version of a situation or event, a counternarrative. For example, in an 1888 issue of the *Journal of United Labor*, Powderly responded to the charge that he had created and sent a special committee to Harrisburg to keep track of legislation pending in the Pennsylvania legislature and then kept the committee's reports secret, a dictatorial action.[65] He denied this charge by claiming that he had created this committee because "I did not feel that it would be proper for me to assume the role of dictator, and therefore called the representatives of the workingmen together that they might examine and pass upon the bills then in the hands of the house and senate of Pennsylvania." And upon creating this committee of workingmen, he left "the convention free to act for itself." He continued:

> My duties ended the moment I laid down the gavel, and from that moment to this I have had nothing to do with the matter. I had no voice in the selection of the committee and have no fault to find with it or its work. Have not been consulted by the committee and know of no reason why it should do so. In short, I have no more to say or do in the affairs of that convention or the committee which it appointed than any other member of the Order in Pennsylvania.

Powderly supported his denial by providing a version of the situation, his actions, and his intent that was diametrically opposite of the charge. He was a democrat, not a dictator. He clearly hoped that if his audience saw the situation through his eyes, they would not judge him adversely.[66]

To answer other charges, Powderly referred to his record in the Order and the movement and long-standing support from the general assembly. Some outside critics accused Powderly of cowardice and fearfulness. In his 1886 address to the general assembly, while the Order was beginning its rapid ascent in membership and power, Powderly addressed accusations that he displayed a "lack of nerve" and a "want of backbone," and was "too weak a man to lead a strong movement." He refused to answer the charges but posed a question to the general assembly:

> I have never replied to these charges, nor will I do so now. I simply point back to a record of seven years of service and ask this question: If, while holding a position such as no man living or dead ever held before, with the full blaze of

public scrutiny shining upon my every action, with public opinion as ready to condemn as to applaud, I have displayed a lack of nerve or backbone, why is it that a million men and women of nerve, backbone and common sense have gathered around the standard which was placed in my hands seven years ago by the founder of the Order himself? If I have been proven a weak man, why do so many strong men support me? I dislike to speak of these matters, but I believe that, in justice to yourselves and me, you should know of them.[67]

He attempted to deflect charges of cowardice by associating his actions with managing a great office of unprecedented importance, withstanding intense public scrutiny, being chosen for leadership by the founder of the Order, and being repeatedly reelected by strong members of good sense. How could he be weak or a coward under these circumstances? If members saw him as either, they were to blame and were weak themselves. Apparently, the general assembly accepted his compliment because it reelected him six more times.

When the Order experienced intense external assault, supporters as well as enemies sometimes questioned Powderly about why he did not defend himself and the Order from attacks by the press, pulpit, former members, and other labor organizations. In response, Powderly tried to exude an image of a long-suffering leader who would absorb attacks for the good of the Order. When he thought the time was right, however, Powderly was well known for his sharp tongue and pen.[68] He did not hesitate to use name-calling and invective in responding to antagonists, often reducing them verbally to animal status. When the Knights of Labor was beginning to attract attention in the early 1880s, Powderly assured readers of the *Journal of United Labor* that attacks were good rather than bad signs for the Order: "Tis the brilliancy of the moon that causes the curs to bark the loudest."[69] He referred to John T. Elliott, a former member who charged the Order with drunkenness, as a "Snarling Cur of Low Degree" who had "attempted to organize a new order while pretending not to like the methods of the old, and from experience could not state anything that took place in the supreme councils of the old Order due to his drunkenness."[70] Elliott was merely one of "a number of yellow dogs yelping at my heels for years," Powderly wrote, "and only when the interests of labor demanded it have I noticed them." When members questioned his silence in face of attacks from within and without, he responded that "if the General Master Workman should lay aside his work for the purpose of wrestling with a skunk he would smell just like the skunk when he finished his job."[71] Powderly employed vituperation to destroy his critics' credibility and the believability of their accusations while establishing his forcefulness and courage expended solely for the good of the Order.

Powderly often replied to critics by attributing evil motives to their charges and actions. Chief among these motives was their determination to harm the Knights of Labor and the labor movement by attacking him as the most visible and powerful leader of both. For instance, when he was criticized for not accepting the nomination for lieutenant governor of Pennsylvania, he argued that if he had accepted the nomination, the Order's enemies would say he had used the Order and "its influence to secure political power." And if he were elected, he "could accomplish nothing, absolutely nothing for the cause of labor."[72] Powderly wrote in the *Journal of United Labor* that "enemies of our Order . . . charge me with cowardice," thus placing him in a lose-lose situation that would do harm to the labor movement.[73] Powderly attempted to deflect personal criticism by claiming it was really aimed at the Order and the labor movement. He was merely a convenient and camouflaged target of those with evil motives, a lightning rod for the Order and labor.

Powderly differentiated his commitment to and experience in the labor movement with those of his detractors. When members and the press attacked him for not accepting the nomination for lieutenant governor of Pennsylvania, he challenged his accusers to "[s]how me your own record on the labor question; place it side by side with mine; let the workers decide whether you can justly accuse me of such a thing." Powderly exhibited his bravery with readers, declaring: "To charge me with that [cowardice] won't change my mind," and "I will not allow a convert of yesterday, to attempt to intimidate me into doing anything against my will." Contrasting his experience and commitment with those of his accusers, Powderly noted his motives, unlike those of the enemies, were honest and for the good of labor rather than dishonest and self-centered. He claimed that he could "do ten times more good for the Order by declining the nomination," and that his platform was "[l]abor first, last and all the time, wherever and whenever I can strike a blow for labor I will do it."[74] These commitments and actions were not those of a coward but of a person totally committed to the cause and possessing motives far superior to those of his critics.

External charges of corruption and dishonesty escalated as the Order struggled to sustain its membership and place in the labor movement during the late 1880s and early 1890s. Powderly denied such charges, not by presenting proof to the contrary, but by attacking the credibility of those who made them. In a *Journal of United Labor* article in 1887, Powderly reported that "the members of the Order are treated each day to a rehash of charges of dishonesty, corruption and villainy on the part of your General Officers. The press of the day is busy with tales of the gross misconduct and incapacity of Powderly."[75] Notice the third-person reference to himself. He attacked those who were making such charges and assured members that the Order's finances were sound and the leadership above reproach. Powderly relegated critics to a crowd of insignificant failures who had no purpose other than trying to cause trouble for the general master workman and the Order to which Powderly was devoting his life. They were traitors, blackmailers, knaves, poltroons; were blind and misguided; and had abandoned "the Order at the hissing of geese."[76] He called editors and reporters "willful and malicious liars" who wanted to destroy organized labor.[77] According to Powderly, his antagonists were determined either to take over or destroy the Order. He exclaimed that "the evilly disposed" were "ever ready to tear down instead of build up." Warning members that charges of dishonesty and corruption were "not made without a cause," he claimed that continual attacks on him kept workers from watching events of real importance: "The eyes of our members, filled with the sands of slander, could not see the work which our common enemy—monopoly—was at."[78] Charges came from "designing men whose chief aim seems to be to disrupt and destroy what they could never build" and from "the evil-minded" who "could misconstrue our actions and create distrust."[79] Attacks on him were in reality multifaceted assaults on the Order and workers.

Powderly attacked the credibility of the critics and the legitimacy of their accusations by labeling these critics as enemies of the oppressed, despisers of the Order's sacred principles, enemies of reform, and those who loved only themselves. In a column in the *Journal of United Labor*, he replied to an editorial in the *Paterson* (New Jersey) *Labor Standard* that accused him of having "no confidence in the efforts of the masses themselves or he would never ask for power exercised only by despotic kings." Powderly attacked the credibility of the editor, whom he identified as an "avowed enemy of the Knights of Labor" who "is not now and never was a Knight of Labor."[80] If Powderly could convince members that attacks on him came from their enemies designed to do them harm, he had little need to refute specific charges.

DEROGATORY ASSOCIATIONS

As Powderly struggled during the late 1880s and early 1890s to defend the Order and stem its decline, critics, particularly the press and clergy, began to associate him with perceived evils that would arouse negative public reactions against the

Order, as well as its longtime leader, and to encourage members to leave in growing numbers. Socialism and Catholicism, both feared and despised by the mostly Protestant citizenry and leaders in government and industry, topped the list of evil associations.

Socialism. Powderly answered allegations about his socialist connections and tendencies in three messages to the Knights. In his 1887 address to the general assembly, Powderly explained in detail his early "connection with socialism, or rather with the men who in former years were the head of the socialistic labor party."[81] Although he distanced himself from socialist organizations, he did not deny connections with socialist individuals. Powderly related in one narrative how he got to know socialist Philip Van Patten. He emphasized his friendship with an honorable man, a reformer, and a former Knight, who had a platform similar to that of the Knights of Labor:

> In 1880 Philip Van Patten, the National Secretary of the socialist labor party, was a member of the General Executive Board of the Knights of Labor. I became very intimate with him, and we frequently discussed the various measures of reform which all men in the movement regarded as of importance. . . . He sent me a slip on which was printed the platform of the party. I said to him, after reading it, that if that was socialism I had no objection to it. . . . My warm friendship for Van Patten, whom I always regarded as an honorable man, and our frequent discussions on the question of labor, made me quite intimate with the platform of the socialist labor party of that day. I saw, however, that the Declaration of Principles of the Knights of Labor contained all of socialism that I cared to advocate. . . . I never cast a vote for the candidates of that party, was never a member of any of its sections, and had no connection with it except in the manner related above.

Powderly associated himself with an honorable friendship while denying potentially negative actions such as voting for socialists or being a member of a section. He reassured delegates that "I owe allegiance to no other organization."[82]

In 1888 Powderly replied to charges in the *Pittsburgh Chronicle-Telegraph* that he had "embraced socialistic doctrines" by opposing the Reading Railroad's efforts to gain control of the anthracite coalfields of Pennsylvania and supporting government ownership of these fields. The editor challenged Powderly to be consistent by proposing government control of all farming. Differentiating farming from coal mining, Powderly argued that "wheat, rye and corn will not grow unless the hand of man plants the seed," and they can be grown in every state. Anthracite coal, on the other hand, can be found only in Pennsylvania. Powderly hoped this distinction demonstrated both that his position was consistent and that he was not espousing socialism. If he were "classed as a socialist," however, then he was "in eminently respectable company, for the men who drew up the 'Bill of Rights' of the State of Pennsylvania were completely in harmony with the doctrine of the socialists also."[83] He cited several sections of the Pennsylvania Constitution that gave important rights to the people, including control over the anthracite coalfields. Thus Powderly distanced himself from socialists while identifying with Pennsylvania's founding fathers, constitution, and people.

In 1890 Powderly responded to an editorial in the *St. Louis Evening Call* that declared, "Two years ago he stated he was a protectionist from the crown of his head to the soles of his feet. A year subsequently he gave his adhesion to the single-tax, free-trade idea, and now he is a socialist. Why not announce himself as an ass and be done with it forever." Powderly denied that he had ever claimed to be a socialist, prohibitionist, or protectionist and attacked the editor in kind. He asserted: "The editorial in question is a deliberate lie, and the editor could have had no foundation for it except it be other lies as told by other editors equally asinine as himself." However, he would not "advise the editor to announce himself an ass, for his editorials show to what length his ears have grown."[84] Powderly often attempted to establish or reestablish his credibility and legitimacy with members and readers by destroying those of his attackers.

Catholicism. Powderly clashed early and often with the Catholic Church during his many years as labor leader and Catholic layman. For instance, he relates in a lengthy chapter in his autobiography, entitled "Ecclesiastical Opposition," that he was barred from entering the Scranton Cathedral in 1871 because his Machinists and Blacksmiths International Union pin looked suspiciously like a Masonic pin.[85] Until the late 1880s, he had to defend himself and organized labor frequently to Catholic priests and bishops, sometimes having to respond to scathing attacks from the pulpit. Secrecy and oaths of allegiance were contentious issues in the early years, but even the word "international" in union names and documents caused friction and confrontations with the Catholic hierarchy. All of organized labor was often associated with the worst of its forces, such as the violent Molly Maguires, who operated in the coal-mining areas of Pennsylvania. Sometimes the issue seemed to be competing social forces and realms of authority. Powderly recalls an incident in 1884 that occurred after he had delivered a series of lectures on the "labor question" in Maine. Bishop James Healy of Portland asked to see him that evening and began their meeting by asking: "Are you a Catholic?" When Powderly replied that he was, the bishop demanded, "Then what right have you to speak in my state without my permission?" Powderly claims he answered in these words:

> I speak only on the labor question, I do not meddle with religion, I do not interfere with the faith or morals of any man, I am a freeborn American, and do not acknowledge your right, or the right of any other man no matter what his religion or position in society may be, to question me for doing that which I have a right to do under the laws of my country. If that is what you wanted me for and you have nothing else to say to me I shall retire.[86]

The meeting degenerated quickly into an ugly confrontation between two strong-willed leaders defending their rights and positions. Powderly claimed that the church's opposition to labor unions lessened after Cardinal James Gibbons of Baltimore espoused the cause of the Knights of Labor in late 1886.

It is ironic that Powderly, who clashed so often with his church, was the target of innuendoes about the influence of his Roman Catholicism throughout his leadership of the Knights of Labor. He generally ignored such charges. In the winter of 1893, Powderly faced a charge he could not avoid because of its virulence and the precarious nature of his leadership and the Knights of Labor. The Reverend J. G. White addressed the Milwaukee Ministers' Association and declared that

> he had proofs of a conspiracy of the Church of Rome against the United States to overthrow its government; that the Pope, Cardinal Gibbons, sixty clergymen and bishops and ten archbishops were backing a man who is endeavoring to raise a revolution in this country; that this man is T. V. Powderly, who, under the pretext of aiding and assisting the laboring men, was plotting with the aid of the Catholic Church to overthrow this country.

Powderly replied in the *Journal of the Knights of Labor* that "in nearly every mail I am requested by our own members to disprove these accusations, and in many of them the intimation is conveyed that there must be something in them or they would not be made."[87] Distrust if not open hostility to Roman Catholicism was widespread in areas where the Order's membership was strongest in 1893.[88] Powderly had to respond.

Here again, Powderly portrayed himself as the victim of outside forces that were determined to destroy the Order and the movement by destroying him. He charged Rev. White with unfairness in creating distrust, suspicion, and jealousy that would cause members to abandon the Order and the movement. "To realize that, no matter what I may say or do," he exclaimed, "the poison has been given, the steel driven home, the fangs fastened so securely that no earthly act of mine can ever tear them away."[89] White had made these charges without giving Powderly an opportunity to explain or providing proof to support charges of treason. Powderly appealed for empathy by asking his audience to "think for a moment of what it means to be charged with conspiracy to overthrow the institutions of my country." He was a helpless victim placed in an untenable situation by an unscrupulous minister with a "black heart and forked tongue" and a "bigot's malice."[90] His defense was both personal, asking readers to imagine being so charged, and organizational, identifying attacks on him as attacks on the Order.

Rev. White's claim of a Roman Catholic conspiracy prompted other clergy to join in the assault. In his final address as general master workman in November 1893, Powderly devoted fourteen pages to anti-Catholic charges, portraying himself as a victim of never-ending charges that he was a puppet of the Catholic Church. "I have not known a week to pass over my head since" the last general assembly, he exclaimed, "when letters of the most villainous and scurrilous nature were not showered upon me."[91] This was one of the few times Powderly asked for sympathy and understanding, indicating perhaps how deeply he felt about these charges.[92] He included abusive letters and newspaper articles to enhance portrayals of himself as a victim of White and others unnamed. He clearly hoped Knights would accept his explanations, reject the venomous attacks on him and the Order, and see him as an innocent victim of bigotry. It would be difficult to regard him as calculating and devious when he included letters of attack and defense in an apparent quest for truth and understanding.[93] Powderly claimed that he was being targeted because he headed the Order, whose enemies were trying to destroy it by destroying him. He urged delegates to realize "[t]hese rumors and this system of warfare have been and are being conducted for but one purpose—the destruction of this Order."[94] His treatment of this issue evolved from addressing it as a personal issue to one involving the Knights of Labor because capitalists and others were determined to destroy what they feared and hated most.

Labor Strife

The Knights of Labor as an organization and Terence Powderly as its leader came under fire for real and imagined actions and reactions that instigated or fueled labor strife. Violence and deaths were frequent companions during strikes and rallies of labor organizations and workers in the 1880s and 1990s, and diverse elements of American society (ranging from strikers, organized and unorganized workers, the general public, industrialists, the press, the church, and government leaders) sought someone to blame. That someone was often Terence Powderly and the Knights of Labor. They became immersed in the controversies surrounding numerous strikes, the Haymarket Square bombing, and activities of anarchist leaders.

STRIKES

No actions and decisions attracted more criticism than those made during strikes both because of and in spite of the Order's leaders, who almost always opposed the strike as a means of bettering the conditions of workers. Powderly condemned the strike as an "old barbarous, clumsy, unyielding, and treacherous system,"[95] and "one of the evils which beset the trades union, and which ever and anon comes to the surface in this organization."[96] Workers were "willing victims of an outrageous system," Powderly declared. "So long as a pernicious system leaves one man at the mercy of another, so long will labor and capital be at war, and no strike can hit a blow sufficiently hard to break the hold with which unproductive capital to-day grasps labor by the throat."[97] Members who disagreed with this assessment launched strikes in spite of the Order's policies and the leaders' wishes.

Because some strikes were inevitable, however, Powderly admitted that while he opposed strikes as a general rule, there were good and bad strikes. He emphasized timing, study, and preparation. "If the strike is the only remedy and the best one then strike by all means," he advised, "but study the situation first and know what is best, instead of striking first and learning afterward that to do so was foolish and possibly criminal." "I do not blame men for striking," Powderly exclaimed, "I blame them for making fools of themselves in not knowing how to strike."[98]

A common rhetorical strategy when addressing a strike was to distance the Order and the general master workman from the strike and the violence that accompanied it. Powderly would issue a denial of involvement and bolster it with a detailed and lengthy narrative of causes, how the Order got entwined in the conflict (through no fault of its own), the course of the event and its highlights, and the conclusion that was often disastrous for members or strikers. Powderly's narratives countered charges in the press and by industrialists, government officials, and angry workers who felt betrayed. For example, he delivered an eight-page account of the New York Central Railroad strike to the general assembly in 1890 in which he detailed its causes, the Order's and his involvement, violence during the strike and those most likely to have committed such acts, and malicious press accounts, all bolstered with letters, telegrams, and assembly proceedings.[99] When addressing the charge that the Order had caused the great southwest railroad strike that had harmed the company as well as the public and that was adversely affecting the Order, Powderly declared that "it would be difficult to get into the same space [in a newspaper report] an equal amount of misrepresentation. The Knights of Labor, aside from the men locally involved, had nothing to do with this matter."[100] He wrote in his autobiography that "fully four-fifths of the strikers belonged to no organization at all."[101] The intent was to disassociate and distance himself and the Order from the events of a labor conflict and any responsibility for starting or supporting it.

Powderly attempted to identify the real culprits behind labor problems and strikes. When attacking press accounts of the Chicago meatpackers' strike, he accused reporters and editors of fabricating interviews with him that created conflict within the Order and generated public opposition to organized labor. When his relationship with the Order's representative in Chicago during the meatpackers' strike worsened, he traced the problem to reports of newspaper interviews with himself. "It was reported that an agent of a New York paper interviewed me on Sunday, and a report of the interview was sent to the Chicago papers. . . . I was not interviewed on Sunday, or any other time by a reporter for a New York paper or for any other paper," he declared. "The report in the Chicago papers of an interview with me was a forgery, or at the very least, a misrepresentation."[102] Powderly designed his narratives to give the full story, set the record straight, and reveal the Order's critics as dishonest and driven to destroy the Order, while maintaining his legitimacy and reputation as defender of the Order and champion of labor.

When Powderly could not deny his involvement in a strike, he attempted to take the moral high ground in defending his actions. For example, he claimed that his actions were never self-centered but Order-centered. In a lengthy discussion of the Order's refusal to aid the Chicago meatpackers' strike, Powderly claimed: "Had the strike been taken up and men refused or denied aid, the cry against me personally might not be so bitter, but the voice of discontent from the stock yards would be loud in denunciation of the whole [Executive] Board and the whole Order for not rendering the expected aid."[103] He had sacrificed himself for the good of the Order. Powderly claimed he had opposed the eight-hour movement's strike because he was "firm in the belief that had I not done so great loss would have been entailed upon vast numbers of our assemblies."[104] Three years later in 1889 he wrote in the *Journal of United Labor*: "It was far better that our members should know the truth than to rush into that movement unprepared, under the impression that the Order, supposed to be millions strong at the time, stood back of them with millions of dollars to support those who suffered loss through the strike."[105] Powderly had acted for the greater good of the Order and its members.

On other occasions, Powderly defended his actions and decisions by arguing that he had acted not only for the good of the Order but for labor and the country as well. His motives were never personal or selfish. For example, his secret circular demanding that workers end the southwest railroad strike of 1886 was issued "only when the threat was made to stop every wheel in the United States and engage the whole Order in the difficulty that I raised my voice in denial. I did that in defense of the Order and the country."[106] Powderly claimed on many occasions that the Order had sustained him in his actions and decisions during strikes. To those who criticized his efforts to end the Southwest strike, he declared, "If the position which I took during the strike was wrong, then the entire Order sustained me in it, for . . . I was most generously sustained, as a reference to the report of the General Secretary-Treasurer will show."[107] He was sharing blame with members, if not transferring blame to the Order, for his actions during strikes. Powderly wrote in his autobiography years after the great strikes of 1886 and 1887: "Individuals criticized me for my views, but the General Order of the Knights of Labor always approved of my position and by an overwhelming majority."[108] The editors of his autobiography and labor historians have sometimes doubted the support Powderly claimed to have for his position on strikes, and thus the distinctions he claimed and the blame he shared or transferred.[109]

HAYMARKET SQUARE AND THE ANARCHISTS

Anarchists were never part of the labor movement but attempted to influence unions and workers through their belief that voluntary groups (syndicates) should replace all political government and profit-making businesses. Syndicates and individuals would exchange goods and services without profit, and each would share equally in the exchange. Some anarchists believed in nonviolent means, while others believed that only violence and terrorism could bring about the desired revolutionary transformation of American society.

When some 340,000 workers, including many members and assemblies of the Knights of Labor, went on strike in early May 1886 to promote legislation for an eight-hour workday, anarchists took advantage of the situation to preach their solution for improving the plight of labor. On 4 May the anarchists held a rally at Haymarket Square in Chicago, and someone threw a bomb into a group of police officers standing nearby. The bomb and ensuing riot resulted in a number of deaths and serious injuries to officers and civilians. The growing fears among the populace and leaders in the church, business, and government toward organized labor and its perceived inclination toward violence escalated instantly. Rayback writes that "the Haymarket affair, which accented anarcho-syndicalist principles drove the terror deeper into the nation's mentality and turned it into hysteria. A violent anti-labor campaign followed."[110] The Knights of Labor and Powderly became the primary targets of this campaign even though they opposed strikes, violence, and anarchism.

In spite of the devastating impact the Haymarket Square bombing and the subsequent conviction of prominent anarchist leaders had on the Knights of Labor, Powderly spoke only once of the event, in his annual address of 1887. He introduced a counternarrative when prefacing his lengthy account of anarchism and the Order, commenting, "I will lay the case before this General Assembly, and after I have done so, will ask this body to say whether I was right or not." He denied the charges against him, asserting, "I have never publicly uttered a sentiment regarding the course of the seven men who are condemned to death in Chicago," and "Before the public I have never said a word concerning these men. I have never felt called upon to say anything, for it is none of my business." He followed up this denial with a hypothetical argument that enabled him to avoid a stand for or against the anarchists:

> If these men did not have a fair trial, . . . then they should be granted a new trial. If they have not been found guilty of murder they should not be hanged. If they are to be hanged for the actions of others it is not just. The man who threw the bomb in Chicago should be hanged and his accomplices should receive the punishment allotted to such offences by the laws of the State of Illinois.[111]

Powderly refuted a host of accusatory letters and newspaper articles, often attributing evil motives to the writers. For instance, he noted that of two clippings sent to him, one was aimed at him and one "at the church to which I belong." He charged that "the height of the anarchists' ambition is to do or say something that will array the church against the Order, so that a denunciation will follow. Then when the conservative element is out of the Order . . . the anarchists' dream of happiness will be realized. He will have destroyed what he could not build, and that is all he ever accomplished." Powderly reported that for weeks after the bombing and trial, "the papers East and West were full of interviews with 'prominent Knights,' in which all manner of threats were made to disrupt the Order and call special sessions for one purpose or another." Although he had "made no public statements, . . . several were made for me by enterprising newspaper men."[112] The obvious motives of attacks and fraudulent accounts were to divide and destroy the Order.

Powderly employed two rhetorical strategies when addressing charges that he had condemned the arrested anarchists. First, as he often did on other topics, Powderly alleged that evil forces had attacked him because of his efforts to protect the Order. By taking "issue with these men in their efforts to make the Order of the Knights of Labor subordinate to the violent element known as the anarchist element," he said, "I have been taken to task more than once" by "prominent members" of the Order who claimed they were speaking only for themselves and "some of their [anarchists] friends have put words of condemnation in my mouth to have me say something in their favor." Apparently Powderly felt some anarchists had victimized him to enhance their martyrs' cause, but he "allowed it to go, as many false reports concerning me went, unnoticed. I felt if they could stand it I could."[113] Second, he defended his actions by differentiating the Knights of Labor from anarchists. Unlike anarchists, the Order was "an army of peace" that never approved or excused violence. Powderly described the relationship between the two elements clearly:

> For years in the City of Chicago the adherents of the anarchists' cause have maligned, opposed and insulted the Order of the Knights of Labor. The meeting-room of the Assembly was abandoned by this class of people for the low beer saloons. None of the teachings that found expression on the streets of Chicago during the first days of May were ever heard in the sanctuary of the Assembly of the Knights of Labor.

Powderly asserted that because the anarchists and their teachings were "in direct conflict with the fundamental law of the Order," district assemblies could not use their funds or pass resolutions in support of the anarchists.[114]

Powderly differentiated rights and actions of the Order and those of individuals. "As individuals we may express our feelings as we please," he told delegates, "but as Knights of Labor we must not commit the Order, or any part of it, to the teachings of the anarchist."[115] In response to a letter accusing him of attacking a leading anarchist who had been condemned to death, he reiterated: "Your members, as individuals, may donate as much money as they please to that or any other fund. That is none of my business." Powderly reminded delegates that "my order extends no further than the limits of the organization. Outside of that you can do as you please."[116] Apart from the Haymarket Square riot, Powderly warned of the dangers of anarchism and defended his relationships with other labor organizations. For instance, when reports circulated that he considered anarchism and socialism to be one and that he "assailed socialism" every time he spoke of anarchism, he contended that "I have never, as has been so often asserted in the press of the land, confounded socialism with anarchy." Instead, he drew "a wide line of distinction between the two, as every reading, thinking man must." He had warned Knights about the dangers of "the presence of a few of the rankest kind of anarchists" within the Order.[117] According to Powderly's version of events, the welfare of the Order and labor was always uppermost in his thoughts, words, and actions.

CONFLICT WITH TRADE UNIONS

Conflict with trade unions was inevitable. From its earliest beginnings, the Knights of Labor saw itself as "something in advance" of the traditional trade or craft union. The founders believed that the day of the trade union was rapidly passing for three reasons: inventions were making old crafts or trades obsolete; the exclusive trade union recognized only the rights of tradesmen rather than the rights of all people; and individual trade unions were impotent when encountering the might of capital. Labor could confront capital effectively only if skilled and unskilled workers united under the banner of one national organization.[118] In his first address as grand master workman to the general assembly in 1880, Powderly compared the Knights of Labor to the steam locomotive of the day and the trade union with the "stage-coach of half a century ago." Workers of "different trades and callings," he declared, have had their eyes opened "to the fact that the organization composed of but one trade or calling does not meet their wants, and must give way for a grander, mightier association, which recognizes the right of every honest man to come within its protecting folds."[119]

The same year the Knights of Labor made its first significant gain in membership, 1881, trade unionists met in Pittsburgh and formed the Federation of Organized Trades and Labor Unions in the United States and Canada, later to become the AFL under the leadership of Samuel Gompers. The Federation and the Knights were on a collision course because of their fundamental philosophical differences: trade unionism restricted to skilled craftsmen versus industrial unionism open to all workers regardless of skill.[120] This division in the labor movement would continue until 1955 when the AFL merged with the Congress of Industrial Organizations (CIO) into the AFL-CIO.

Perhaps because his attitude toward the trade union as a self-centered, outdated, and impotent form of labor organization was well known in the labor movement and trade unions were splintered along craft lines, Powderly apparently felt no need to defend this attitude until his annual address in 1886. By that year, individual trade unions were growing stronger, and the fledgling Federation of Organized Trades and Labor Unions of the United States and Canada was attracting a growing number of affiliates and becoming a force to reckon with. It would be four more years before Powderly would address the AFL directly and acknowledge the growing competition and conflicts between the two labor giants.

The first recognition of conflicts between the Order and trade unions appeared in Powderly's 1886 address to the general assembly, where he attempted to minimize these conflicts by labeling them as "mistakes" that had been "greatly magnified and distorted," and noting that he handled and resolved "over fifty cases of dispute between parts of Our Order and other societies" since the last general session:

> I need not enter into detail further than to say that there were mistakes made on both sides. Some of our Organizers have been so zealous in their way of organizing that they have encroached upon the prerogatives of other associations, and on several occasions the rights of our members have been seriously interfered with by members of trade unions. . . . A few lines in each case was sufficient, and the trouble ended. To dig up past troubles is unnecessary; and, in consultation with prominent men of the trade unions, I was gratified to learn that they had no desire to revive the past.[121]

Powderly also attempted to shift the blame from the officers of competing labor organizations to members of these organizations, asserting that overzealous members and organizers on both sides had precipitated "mistakes" between organizations.[122] In 1887 Powderly wrote that wherever a conflict was in progress between the Order and a trade union, it was "a war between individuals rather than between the organizations."[123] Powderly desired to distance himself, other officers of the Order, and leaders of trade unions from interorganizational squabbles while transferring guilt to the rank and file, who had been irresponsible in their efforts to further their own organizations. He claimed: "More trouble has been caused us by men who profess to be members of the Knights of Labor than by members of trade unions." He recommended that "all matters likely to create a breach of peace between our Order and any other be at once submitted to the executives of both organizations," stating, "[t]his plan has worked well in every new case called to my attention since the Cleveland session, and is worthy of adoption."[124] Powderly was, then, a neutral peacemaker in interorganizational fights; he was above the fray while maintaining loyalty to the Order.

When the differences between the Order and the trade unions grew into major conflicts, Powderly attacked individuals who had failed to seek "the high moral ground" of principle, charging that "those who are directly engaged in this strife have descended to the lowest depths of filth and falsehood."[125] Powderly distanced himself and fellow general officers from these individuals and portrayed himself as the innocent victim of those with evil motives. In his annual address to the general assembly in 1888, Powderly answered the charge that he had accused trade unions of trying to take control of the Knights of Labor. He asserted that his earlier "remarks were twisted and tortured to serve the purpose of designing knaves who attempted to play upon the feelings of Trade Unionists."[126] As with so many issues, Powderly attributed problems to unnamed others who plotted for selfish, evil reasons to destroy his credibility as an effective labor leader and thus destroy the most advanced labor organization, the Knights of Labor.

As conflicts between the Knights of Labor and trade unions escalated, Powderly defended his positions by differentiating labor organizations. In his 1888 address to the general assembly, he contrasted trade unions with the International Workingmen's Association, an organization he had recently attacked. Powderly maintained that the trade unions' "cause and ours are one in the main" and that "thousands of young and enthusiastic members of the trade unions and the Knights of Labor should know something of the past" that tells of the struggles each had fought for the good of labor. Despite his positive attitude toward trade unions, Powderly had few kind words for the International, "which passed resolutions three years ago to secure the election of its trusted agents as General Officers of the Order of the Knights of Labor" and had since worked "secretly and untiringly . . . for the ruin of this Order."[127]

By 1890 the struggle was no longer with trade unions in general but between the Knights of Labor and the AFL. Powderly called for a face-to-face meeting between Gompers and himself at Cooper Union in New York, with members of both organizations in attendance. Accusing Powderly of challenging him to take part in a meeting so Knights would greatly outnumber himself and the Federationists, Gompers refused to attend. In an exchange of letters over the invitation, Gompers attacked Powderly's character, motives, claims, and refusal to meet on terms he had counterproposed. Gompers's replies were reprinted in the *Journal of the Knights of Labor* apparently to show, at least in the eyes of loyal Knights, that Powderly had been wrongfully attacked and accused of deviousness and was an innocent victim of interorganizational hostility and jealousy:

> Let us be frank with each other, Mr. Powderly; at least I propose to be, and say to you that it is my candid opinion that you never expected that I would accept your challenge, or that, if I did, I would be entrapped into a packed meeting for which preparation (I am reliably informed) have [*sic*] been in progress for several weeks. . . . But finding that I am man enough, feel strong and justified enough to reiterate and prove any and everything that I ever said in connection with your Order, you hide yourself behind a subterfuge of words and say it was not a challenge. I direct your attention to the press of this city and of the country for a confirmation of my assertion that your letter was a challenge.[128]

Powderly denied any sentiments against trade unions and the AFL, claiming he had no choice in certain matters. In lengthy columns in the *Journal of the Knights of Labor* in the summer of 1890 about the Cooper Union meeting that had taken place without Gompers, Powderly denied any part in the interorganizational conflict. He asserted that the meeting and the question of differences between the Order and the AFL had "been forced upon" him and that he "would far rather leave it alone, not touch it at all."[129] In the speech at the Cooper Union meeting, reprinted in the *Journal of the Knights of Labor*, Powderly remarked at the outset that "we have a quarrel, a quarrel that is not of our seeking, one that has been thrust upon us by meddlesome individuals." Although he blamed the discord on unnamed others, the target was obviously Gompers:

> My God! To think that men of sense in the ranks of labor should pick a quarrel with others in the same movement in order to draw attention to themselves, when the enemy of both stands facing us all in a thousand forms. Why should men seek for an opportunity to create discord among us when our united efforts should be put forth to destroy the enemy that menaces all of us? Our quarrel is not with the American Federation of Labor, and most certainly not with the trade unionists of America. It is with certain men who claim to represent the Federation, and who will not allow an opportunity to pass without insulting the Order of the Knights of Labor either openly or through innuendo.[130]

In 1891 Powderly sent a special circular to all labor organizations, inviting them to attend an industrial conference to discuss common concerns and then to send a labor platform to all political parties, hoping at least one would adopt it. In a February 1891 column in the *Journal of the Knights of Labor*, he reported that replies had come mainly from local assemblies of the Order but that many labor organizations had not yet voted on the question of attending. However, he cited a New York newspaper article that quoted the executive committee of the AFL saying it felt "slighted" at the circular and that "it would be condoning the slight if they now recognized it." Powderly replied, "How those gentlemen could feel slighted is beyond ordinary comprehension. They received the invitation at the same time that others did, it was couched in the same language, and being general in its tone and character, no reasonable person could imagine a case of slight unless he wanted to."[131] Powderly again presented himself as wrongfully accused by enemies who impugned his motives.

At this point, Powderly no longer denied his opposition to trade unions. He contrasted the democratic nature of the Order, in which general officers had no authority to stifle local assemblies from expressing political opinions, with the AFL, which was trying to deny affiliated trade unions "the right to say whether they should or should not speak jointly with other workingmen, citizens of the Republic."[132] Clearly the Order was more in tune with American values than the Federation. Powderly urged trade unionists to speak for themselves. When addressing the industrial conference he was organizing, Powderly assured readers that he would "embrace representatives from all industrial societies and reform organizations. It will not be a Knight of Labor gathering; a trade-union meeting or a Farmers' Alliance convention. It is intended to represent all." Concerning the conflict with the Federation, he urged Knights and workers to "glance over the record of proceedings of the American Federation of Labor," and they would discern that the "Trade Union of history and that of 1891 cannot be called distant relatives, much less twins, or members of the same family."[133] By differentiating the historical trade union movement and the Gompers-led AFL, Powderly hoped to place guilt for interorganization conflicts upon the AFL, which was far different from and unworthy of its trade union roots and, unlike its predecessors, was bent on destroying its competition within the labor movement.

In June 1892 Powderly wrote about a series of "peace propositions" sent to the AFL that would terminate "the unfortunate and regrettable differences and disagreements which at times have arisen" between the two organizations and avoid "such differences" and secure "harmonious action in [the] future." Following a listing of peace propositions, Powderly warned that if the AFL refused to accept these propositions, "it shall be the duty of the General Officers of the Knights of Labor to issue an address to the workingmen of America setting forth all the facts." Gompers's reply claimed that "the American Federation of Labor has used every effort to end a useless and wasteful struggle . . . but these were at all times rejected by the Knights of Labor." Gompers then addressed the superiority of the trade union. "History justifies the trade Union movement in its present form," he declared, "and teaches that permanent industrial progress can only be achieved by organization on craft lines." The Knights of Labor, Gompers concluded, "can have no legitimate place in the field occupied by Trade Unions." He offered his own propositions, including one that would deny the Knights the right to issue charters to local or national trade assemblies. Powderly reacted angrily: "Reduced to plain language they mean: 'The Knights of Labor have [sic] no right to organize anywhere on top of the earth, and these resolutions may be regarded as a request to disband your Order.'"[134] Thus guilt for interorganizational conflict rested on Gompers alone in his self-centered goals of commanding the labor movement and restricting it to skilled craftsmen.

During 1893, his final year as general master workman of the Knights of Labor, Powderly addressed the conflict between the Knights and the AFL in a conciliatory tone on several occasions. Newspaper editors and reporters, he claimed, were the real culprits responsible for the animosity between him and Gompers, not the leaders of the Knights and the AFL. Powderly was particularly critical of the labor press. In April he charged that the troubles between the two rivals had been fanned "into a flame by our labor papers" and that "in time it created a division that became only too real." He gave as an example a false report in a New York paper that he wanted the clothing cutters trade to rejoin the Order and that he was ready for the "fray" with the AFL. Powderly related stories that continually reported disagreements between Gompers and himself, concluding that he had never entered "in a dispute between the Knights of Labor and a Trade Union of my own volition, never originated the dispute or quarrel." The labor press, not Powderly, was responsible for interorganizational conflicts. He asked readers: "Who elected these editors to act as fault finders and critics?" Some newspapers, Powderly charged, cited alleged comments to attack him personally. The *Cleveland Leader* declared that "Powderly is a failure and a fraud. Only such a blatant demagogue as he is would confess the past acts of the Knights of Labor failures and then ask his dupes to follow him in another scheme which must eclipse all his former fiascoes."[135] Such reports provided evidence for Powderly's claims that he was the innocent victim of the press and enemies of the Order. Though some attacks seemed personal, Powderly inevitably interpreted them as attacks on his leadership position and the Order.

In his final address as general master workman, Powderly admitted that "one year ago there existed a bitter feeling between the American Federation of Labor and this Order."[136] In a conciliatory tone, he declared:

> There is no good reason why the American Federation of Labor and this Order should not co-operate for the good of all who toil, and there are a thousand very good reasons why the future should witness a friendly intercourse between the two. The jealousy which existed between these associations has, in many places, afforded the enemy of both to insert the wedge of discord, and the result cannot be anything but disastrous to organized labor.

And in a rare admission of guilt, Powderly remarked, "Your General Master Workman was not free from bias one year ago when he wrote the following [concerning an alliance with the Miners' Progressive Association] and presented it to the General Assembly. . . . Your General Master Workman has during the present year made an effort to ascertain just where the Trade Union and the Local Assembly differed."[137] Aside from some regulations, he could find "no great differences of opinion" on the emancipation of workers and the "reign of equity." In a move that must have astounded his audience, Powderly proposed:

> The headquarters of all labor organizations should be in the one city and under the same roof. There should be no dividing lines which would keep one from knowing the condition of all. When a blow is aimed at one division of labor he must be a fool who will argue that it is not aimed at all who labor, but when that blow is aimed to-day note how far apart we are in sentiment and action.

Powderly urged the general assembly to appoint a committee to review all of his writings on the interorganizational problems and cooperation and report to the assembly for its approval or disapproval. "I am firm in the belief," he said, "that we should extend an open hand to all organizations of workingmen."[138]

In his early comments on conflicts with trade unions, Powderly blamed the rank and file for all problems and misunderstandings. By 1891, however, he distinguished the rank and file of trade unions, with whom the Knights had no quarrel, from the AFL and "certain men who claim to represent the Federation,"[139] Gompers obviously among them. In his conciliatory messages of 1893 in which he tried to bring peace to the labor movement, Powderly distinguished members from leaders, claiming now that "here and there members, presuming to speak for their organization, publicly declared that there could be no such thing as reconciliation between the two societies, some going so far as to assert that one or the other must die before success would crown the efforts of those who believe in organization."[140] Blame reverted to the rank and file, with Powderly and Gompers presumably innocent of any actions that created interorganizational discord.

Unfortunately for Powderly, the Knights of Labor, and the labor movement, this conciliatory stance came too late. Divisions between Powderly and Gompers and between the Order and AFL ran too deep. Words could not heal the wounds inflicted on both sides. The Order was no longer a force to be reckoned with, and the AFL was in no mood to compromise with a hated and what it viewed as an inferior labor organization. Speaking to the Machinist's Convention (Powderly's early trade union affiliation) in 1901, Gompers declared: "Those who have gone through the movement of the Knights of Labor, which is now happily removed from the path of progress; those who have studied the previous effervescent movements of that character, know the danger with which such movements are always confronted."[141] Many within the Order saw Powderly's conciliatory stance toward the Federation and trade unions and his proposal to bring all unions under one roof as tantamount to treason. J. R. Sovereign was elected general master workman in 1894, and the report of the general executive board reiterated the basic principles of the Order and contrasted them with trade unions:

A mere Trade Union cannot fully protect the industrial interests of the laboring people; a purely political or social organization of laboring people cannot hold together effectively for any length of time, so as to make a successful headway against the force of combined monopoly. Herein lies the essential and vital importance of perpetuating and extending the Order of the Knights of Labor, which is both industrial, social and political in its character, until it shall embrace within its folds the great mass of the laboring people of America. And any action by members of this Order inimical to or in contravention to this principle and this policy is treason to the Order and the best interests of labor.[142]

This position effectively ended any effort to resolve the conflict between the Order and the Federation and to assure a meaningful future for the Order. In 1895 Powderly was accused of refusing to turn over materials to the new officers and leading a conspiracy to regain control. He was expelled from the Order.[143]

A Skillful Defense of a Lost Cause

When Terence V. Powderly was selected in 1879 as the second grand master workman of the Order of the Knights of Labor, it was a secret labor organization with fewer than 20,000 members primarily in Pennsylvania. He was reelected thirteen times and, during that fourteen-year tenure, led the Order to a peak membership of more than 700,000 members in 1887, with assemblies in many states and several foreign countries. Unfortunately for Powderly and organized labor, the Haymarket Square bombing, numerous disastrous strikes, and intramovement squabbles between trade unions and the Order created a public backlash and energized opposition from industrialists, the press, clergy, and government leaders determined to eliminate the threat of organized labor, particularly the Knights of Labor. When Powderly completed his final year as general master workman in 1893, membership stood at fewer than 75,000 members, mostly in small towns and rural areas.

Powderly's long tenure as leader of the Knights of Labor was laced with obstacles from many quarters. Members and former members, competing labor organizations, the labor press and the commercial press, clergy, politicians, industrialists, and the courts made a never-ending array of charges and countercharges against Powderly and the Knights of Labor. He was a leader under siege from all sides. Members and local officers complained that Powderly did not perform routine duties such as publishing proceedings and responding to correspondence in a timely manner, visit local assemblies and attend their events, and accept speaking invitations. They accused him both of not complying with general assembly resolutions and amendments and not granting requested dispensations to these resolutions and amendments. They claimed he and the executive committee ignored communications and showed favoritism toward some local assemblies. And members accused Powderly of seeking one-man rule, of striving to be a dictator. Critics from inside and outside the Order claimed Powderly was a weak and fearful leader, lacking backbone because he did not reply to attacks on himself and the Order. And all questioned the financial state of the Order and spending by the general officers, accusing Powderly in particular of corruption and dishonesty.

External critics, including many former Knights, questioned Powderly's character and accused him of having no faith in the masses. They tried to destroy his credibility as general master workman and major leader of the labor movement by identifying him with socialism, anarchism, and a Roman Catholic conspiracy to destroy America and its democratic form of government. Above all, the press, industrialists, clergy, and government leaders cited Powderly and the Knights of Labor as the forces instigating labor unrest, strikes, and the violence that often accompanied both. Some accused Powderly of abandoning strikers or ending strikes at critical times when victory was near. Critics charged Powderly with calling strikes at particular times to harm companies and the image of the United States. The public identified the Knights of Labor with the Haymarket Square bombing and radical anarchists. Some antagonists attacked Powderly for allegedly supporting the arrested anarchist leaders while others accused him of condemning the anarchist leaders.

Most critical conflicts, such as Haymarket Square riot and the eight-hour-movement strike, were not of Powderly's or the Order's doing, but both became associated with and blamed for the events and their aftermaths. The public and the press made no distinction between anarchists and Knights, trade unions and the Order, thousands of peaceful union members and small violent elements, strikes called by and ones opposed by the Order, or Powderly and members of his decentralized organization whom he could not control.

Powderly's view that trade unions were antiquated and ineffective means of organizing workers and the fundamental philosophical differences between trade unions (organized along craft lines) and the Knights of Labor (organized regardless of occupation or skill level) made interorganizational clashes inevitable. As trade unions grew stronger during the 1880s, clashes occurred between elements of the Order and individual trade unions. Competition and enmity between the Order and the young AFL, fueled in part by personality and attitude conflicts between Powderly and Gompers, grew into highly visible life-and-death struggles in the early 1890s. The Order was declining while the Federation was growing stronger, partly because the Federation represented only skilled workers and partly because the public, industrialists, the press, and the pulpit viewed it as less of a threat to American society.

Powderly skillfully employed a variety of apologetic rhetorical strategies to overcome the obstacles to his leadership, the Knights of Labor, and the labor movement. He portrayed himself as an innocent victim of elements inside and outside of the Order. Members and officers of local assemblies within the Order made unreasonable demands, often over trifling matters, and were irresponsible and devious in both demands and criticisms. Some were guilty of unethical behavior and playing dirty tricks on Powderly and other general officers they did not like.

He identified victimizers outside the Order as anarchists, clergy, trade unionists, and the commercial and labor presses that slandered him and the executive board, grossly misrepresented their statements on issues, and made never-ending charges. He was accused of evil motives by those with evil motives who, among other things, created interorganizational hostility within the labor movement and forced it on him. Elements outside the movement were looking for someone to blame for labor strife in the 1880s and 1890s, so he became their victim. Powderly also portrayed himself as an innocent, helpless victim of situations beyond his control: unscrupulous officers and organizers, general assembly resolutions, strikes, the Haymarket bombing, and intramovement rivalries.

Since Powderly was an innocent victim, he transferred blame and guilt to others, often his accusers. He readily accepted responsibility but rarely blame for anything he did or did not do. Past and present members and officers caused the problems for which they were attacking him, including performance of routine duties, the financial state of the Order, strikes, and compliance with the laws and principles of the Knights of Labor. When they expressed frustration with or opposition to his actions and decisions, Powderly blamed them for reelecting him year after year, literally begging him to continue as general master workman. They were at fault if they did not approve of his leadership. When conflicts escalated and worsened between trade unions and the Order, Powderly first blamed the rank and file, then the leaders, and then the rank and file once again. Discord was never his or the general officers' fault but belonged to unnamed others (such veiled references usually referred to Samuel Gompers and leaders of the AFL) and the labor press, who purposely distorted what Powderly said or made up interviews with him.

Powderly denied many of the charges leveled at him and the Order, sometimes bolstering his denials with letters, newspaper clippings, or references to witnesses. For instance, when he was identified with socialists, anarchists, and protectionists, he denied all connections with and sentiments toward these philosophies and organizations that espoused them. He denied approving strikes and instigating the violence that often accompanied them. And he denied any part in the interorganizational conflicts with trade unions or of ever having a negative sentiment toward Gompers's AFL.

Differentiation enabled Powderly to disassociate and distance himself and the general officers from many charges and conflicts. For example, he defended the performance of his duties by claiming that all mistakes or failures were of the head not of the heart, unintentional rather than intentional. He contrasted his experience and commitment to the Order and movement with those of his accusers. Powderly differentiated the Order from socialism, anarchism, trade unionism and the AFL. He distanced himself from socialism by differentiating individual socialists, particularly former Knights, from socialism. He separated individual rights and actions from those of the general officers and the Order and distanced officers and Order from the growing discord within the labor movement. The quarrels were not of their making.

Powderly often developed narratives to counter those of critics, set the record straight, or give the full story. The goal was to transform perceptions of reality so members would accept new or improved versions of situations and events. Powderly developed elaborate paper trails of letters, newspaper clippings, telegrams, proceedings, and resolutions to bolster these narratives. Sometimes he would present a detailed narrative and ask the general assembly to decide who was telling the truth. In many of his narratives, Powderly effectively distanced or disassociated himself from labor strife, intramovement discord, or the disastrous results of strikes.

Although Powderly was known for his sharp tongue, he used name-calling and invective sparingly in his annual reports and columns in the *Journal of United Labor* and the *Journal of the Knights of Labor*. When he used each, however, he held nothing back, often reducing antagonists to the animal status of snarling curs, yellow dogs, and skunks. Critics were liars, traitors, blackmailers, bigots, and knaves. Powderly seemed intent on preserving his credibility and legitimacy within the Order and movement by destroying the credibility and legitimacy of his enemies.

Powderly's rhetorical defense reveals how a labor reform leader of the nineteenth century employed rather skillfully a variety of apologetic strategies to meet incessant obstacles to his leadership and movement. Perhaps most important historically and theoretically, however, is how he used the Order and labor movement in his rhetorical efforts to sustain and further both the Order and the movement. While Powderly's long tenure as general master workman made him the face and personification of the Knights of Labor and the labor movement, and thus the target of never-ending criticism by those who opposed and feared the Order and movement, his position and association became essential ingredients in his rhetorical defense. He used the Order and the labor movement as a rhetorical cloak and shield. The resultant rhetoric blended personal and corporate (organizational) apologia into a strategic combination.

Powderly attempted to blur a distinction between himself as an individual and his role as general master workman. He rarely referred to himself in the first person, rather as the "General Master Workman," "your General Master Workman," and "Mr. Powderly." His official position and person became one and the same. This blurring allowed him to deflect attacks, regardless of how personal they might be, to the Order and to take the moral high ground as the Order's protector, savior, and martyr.

A frequent theme in Powderly's rhetoric of defense included the idea that he was the victim of criticism and attacks not because of who he was but what he was—the leader of the most powerful and advanced labor organization in the country. As general master workman, he was the defender of the sacred principles of the Knights of Labor and the leading advocate of worker rights. Those intent on destroying the Order, and thus organized labor in the United States, realized that they had to destroy Powderly's credibility and leadership to achieve their goal. All criticism apparently aimed at him was in reality aimed at disrupting and destroying the Order. For instance, when antagonists warned that Powderly was seeking one-man rule, they knew that lack of a strong leader and divided power would harm the Order and weaken efforts on behalf of the oppressed. Similarly, efforts to identify him with socialism, anarchists, and a Roman Catholic conspiracy; to accuse him of corruption; to paint him as a fearful and spineless leader, to blame him for violent strikes; and to fabricate press reports and interviews while twisting his remarks were designed to destroy the Order by destroying him. Powderly presented himself as merely an elected servant who always abided by the wishes and dictates of the Order, an Order that sustained him in his actions and decisions. Metaphorically, he took the bullet intended for the Order and its members by always doing what was in their best interests, regardless of the consequences to him personally. He was their protector and savior while remaining innocent of any negative actions they may have committed. Thus he identified himself with the Order and its members while maintaining a strategic distance from each, the Order serving as a shield against criticism and charges.

Powderly used his position as general master workman to develop a rhetoric of transcendence that placed his actions and decisions in larger, higher, grander contexts. He was the long-suffering leader of the Knights of Labor who was willing to sacrifice health and well-being for a higher need and calling, the welfare of the Order and its members. Powderly claimed his motivation, unlike that of his antagonists, was never personal gain, advantage, or animosity but the protection and furtherance of the Order. The greater good of the Order, its members, the movement, and the country was always uppermost in his mind. If he made mistakes or seemed to be striving for one-man rule, it was for the good of the Order, never for Powderly. When he failed to reply to attacks on himself or the Order, he refrained not through fear or lack of backbone but because he did not want to set aside his duty to the Order. He would not waste valuable time in personal defense. Powderly was the Order's martyr as well as its protector and savior, and the Order was a protective cloak that explained and justified his every action and decision.

Terence Powderly's rhetoric of personal-organizational defense, in which he used his office and the Order as cloak and shield, was often articulate and masterful. It enabled him to retain his leadership through fourteen of the most turbulent years organized labor has ever faced in the United States. Many members apparently saw him as an experienced and spirited defender of the Order and their interests who was unafraid to take on a long list of enemies. Powdery had a plausible and persuasive answer for every criticism or charge lodged against him and the Order. While his sharp tongue and pen may have alienated some, his constituents among laboring men and women were hardly averse to name-calling and invective. He rarely attacked those in his immediate audiences, such as the general assembly or readers of the journals, but those his audiences could blame as well—former members, ex-officers, the press, industrialists, and competing trade unions. Negative reaction in the Order to his conciliatory moves toward the AFL indicates that members of the Knights preferred a general master workman who would fight rather than compromise with the Gompers-led rival. Although Powderly could not stem the Order's decline after 1887, he did provide continuity of leadership and a spirited, articulate defense against forces from inside and outside the Order.

Unfortunately for Powderly and the Knights of Labor, his rhetoric reached only the organized core within a single labor movement organization. His repeated elections as general master workman indicate that his apologetic strategies were effective with members who attended the annual general assemblies and heard his reports and addresses and with members committed enough to read his columns in the *Journal of United Labor* and the *Journal of the Knights of Labor*. Powderly had difficulty reaching and persuading those outside this organized core, particularly those who were sympathetic with the labor movement but not the Knights of Labor and those who heard only the antilabor side from the press and pulpit.

Rhetoric alone, however, was insufficient to overcome the obstacles Powderly and the Order faced in the 1880s and 1890s. The principles of the Knights of Labor were ahead of their time and out of step with both the labor movement and the rank and file. While leaders such as Powderly preached arbitration, cooperatives, education, and social reforms, members who came and went by the hundreds of thousands wanted immediate changes in wages, hours, and working conditions. The fundamental philosophical differences between trade and industrial unionism, in addition to the personal tension between Powderly and Gompers, set the Order and Federation on a collision course, a conflict the Knights could not win. Powerful industrialists were determined not to share control of wages, hours, and working conditions with organized labor or to bargain collectively, particularly with organizations of unskilled workers who could be replaced at any time with cheap immigrant labor. Violence and strikes, often instigated by industrialists to destroy organized labor, frightened the public, the pulpit, the press, and government leaders.

Why did Terence Powderly remain general master workman for nearly fourteen years when he was under continual assault from within and without? Some detractors would say that his ego, arrogance, and thirst for power would not allow him to quit. This belies the fact that Powderly volunteered to relinquish leadership at several general assemblies, and the delegates refused his offers. The answer lies in this complex man's beliefs and commitments. First, he was firmly committed to the Order's philosophy of one grand union of all skilled and unskilled workers in which an injury to one is the concern of all. His early experiences in an isolated trade union and being blacklisted made him a true believer. Second, he was committed to arbitration rather than strikes as the way to resolve labor disputes and to a system of cooperatives that would eliminate the worker-owner relationship he saw as the root cause of labor's miseries and conflicts. And third, the reform-oriented Knights of Labor and Powderly were an ideal fit. Both were more concerned with reforms that would improve society and the lot of workers—temperance, worker's right, women's rights, ballot reform, immigration—than wages, hours, and working conditions. The Order provided Powderly with a "bully pulpit," in Theodore Roosevelt's words, for espousing a wide variety of reforms. For instance, the Knights' oath of temperance became known as the "Powderly Pledge." He could not abandon the philosophy, principles, and reforms in which he believed so strongly.

What happened to Terence Powderly after he was expelled from the Order? Powderly was a survivor. He soon completed the study of law and became a member of the bar in Scranton in 1894, being admitted to practice before the Pennsylvania Supreme Court in 1897 and the U.S. Supreme Court in 1901. One of Powderly's interests throughout the 1880s and 1890s was immigration reform. He had been invited while still general master workman to appear in Washington, D.C., and to take part in discussions of immigration policy, problems, and solutions. In 1897 President William McKinley appointed him commissioner-general of immigration. The Knights of Labor reinstated his membership in 1900, and he joined Local Assembly 4896 in Washington, D.C. In 1902 President Theodore Roosevelt removed him from his federal position because of the behavior of the assistant commissioner of immigration at the port of New York. A few years later, Roosevelt discovered that Powderly was innocent of charges against him and appointed him first as special representative of the Department of Commerce and Labor to study the cause of immigration from Europe and then as chief of the Division of Information in the Bureau of Immigration. Powderly remained in this latter position until 1921, when he was appointed commissioner of conciliation in the Department of Labor. He was now in a government position to foster his beliefs in arbitration. Powderly remained a reformer—or as he would prefer, equalizer and agitator for causes—until he died on 24 June 1924.

What happened to the Knights of Labor after Powderly's tempestuous departure? It continued its crusade for worker rights, social reforms, and union of all workers through the 1890s, but it continued to decline in membership due to the economic and social climate of the time, competition with trade unions, and increasing changes in leadership. The Order suffered through five different leadership changes from 1897 to 1901. Although it held its last general assembly in 1913, a few local assemblies remained intact until the 1930s, at least in name.

What did the Order accomplish in its relatively brief time as the largest and most visible labor union? Rayback claims that "the influence of the Order extended beyond its brief moment of triumph. The unity it fostered among workingmen has remained a labor dream to the present day, and the concept of industrial unionism it produced remained a major goal of large numbers of laboring men and ultimately brought about reorganization of labor unionism in the New Deal period."[144] Many of the founders and leaders of the AFL, which eventually united nearly all trade unions, came out of the Order with the idea of unity along craft lines. Historian Leon Fink writes that "skilled trade unionists played a vanguard role in the rise of the Order."[145] The principles of the Order influenced Eugene V. Debs's efforts to unite all skilled and unskilled railroad workers into the American Railway Union in the 1890s. The Industrial Workers of the World (IWW) in the early part of the twentieth century and the CIO in the 1930s carried on the pursuit of organizing the growing numbers of unskilled or minimally skilled workers in factories, particularly autoworkers. Fink argues that "the choices open to the CIO, it is fair to say, were undoubtedly influenced both by the achievement and failure of their counterparts a half-century earlier."[146] Finally, in 1955 the Order's dream of one grand union came close to fruition with the merger of the AFL and the CIO.

The Knights of Labor was a significant force supporting major reform efforts of the nineteenth century such as temperance, worker's rights, women's rights, land reform, and controls on immigrant labor. Fink notes that "at its zenith the movement around the Knights helped to sustain a national debate over the social implications of industrial capitalism."[147] Fink conducted in-depth studies of the influence of the Order in five selected cities in New Hampshire, Vermont, Kansas, Virginia, and Wisconsin. He concludes that "wherever the Knights of Labor had organized by the mid-1880s, it seemed, contests over power and rights at the workplace evolved into a community-wide fissure over control of public policy as well. Indeed, in some 200 towns and cities from 1885 to 1888 the labor movement actively fielded its own political slates."[148] Terence Powderly and the Knights of Labor are now relegated to brief mentions in history textbooks, but the principles they espoused and the reforms they championed are legacies enjoyed in the twenty-first century.

Notes

1. Herbert W. Simons, "Requirements, Problems, and Strategies: A Theory of Persuasion for Social Movements," *Quarterly Journal of Speech* 56 (1970): 4; Joseph R. Gusfield, "Functional Areas of Leadership in Social Movements," *Sociological Quarterly* 7 (1966): 137.

2. Charles J. Stewart, Craig Allen Smith, and Robert E. Denton Jr., *Persuasion and Social Movements*, 4th ed. (Prospect Heights, Ill.: Waveland Press, 2001), 109–10; Anthony Oberschall, *Social Conflict and Social Movements* (Englewood Cliffs, N.J.: Prentice-Hall, 1973), 158.

3. Simons, "Requirements," 4.

4. Terence Powderly, *Thirty Years of Life and Labor, 1859–1889* (Philadelphia, 1890).

5. Norman J. Ware, *Labor Movement in the United States, 1860–1895: A Study in Democracy* (Gloucester, Mass.: P. Smith, 1959); Matthew Josephson, *The Robber Barons* (New York: Harcourt, Brace, 1934); Milton Metzler, *Bread and Roses: The Struggle of American Labor 1865–1915* (New York: Knopf, 1967); Ian Randle Kingston, *From Chattel Slaves to Wage Slaves: The Dynamics of Labour Bargaining in the Americas* (Bloomington: Indiana University Press, 1995); Charles J. Stewart, "Labor Agitation in America: 1865–1915," in *America in Controversy: History of American Public Address*, ed. DeWitte Holland (Dubuque, Iowa: William C. Brown, 1973), 153–69.

6. Terence V. Powderly, *The Path I Trod* (New York: Columbia University Press, 1940), 24.

7. Charles A. Madison, *American Labor Leaders: Personalities and Forces in the Labor Movement* (New York: Frederick Unger, 1960), 44.

8. Unless otherwise noted, this biographical account comes from Powderly's autobiography, *The Path I Trod*.

9. Powderly, *Path I Trod*, 35.

10. Ibid., 24, 35.

11. Ibid., 37–38.

12. Ibid., 35–36.

13. Joseph G. Rayback, *A History of American Labor* (New York: Macmillan, 1959), 144; Powderly, *Thirty Years*, 114.

14. "Preamble," *Records of a Convention of the *********, 1 January 1878, 28.

15. Powderly, *Thirty Years*, 133.

16. "Constitution of the General Assembly of the ********," *Records*, 1–4 January 1878, 29.

17. Rayback, *History of American Labor*, 158–59.

18. Powderly, *Thirty Years*, 143–47, 291.

19. Rayback, *History of American Labor*, 146.

20. Terence V. Powderly, "Address of the Grand Master Workman," *Proceedings of the General Assembly of the Knights of Labor* (referred to hereafter as *Proceedings*), 6 September 1881, 271–71.

21. Rayback, *History of American Labor*, 162.

22. Terence V. Powderly, "Address of the General Master Workman," *Proceedings* (6 October 1886): 38.

23. Terence V. Powderly, "Address of the General Master Workman," *Proceedings* (October 1887): 1477; Madison, *American Labor Leaders*, 59.

24. Powderly, *Thirty Years*, 240–70; Powderly, *Path I Trod*, 140–62; Rayback, *History of American Labor*, 164–65.

25. Rayback, *History of American Labor*, 165.

26. Ibid., 168.

27. Ibid., 174.

28. Stewart, Smith, and Denton, *Persuasion and Social Movements*, 116.

29. Terence V. Powderly, "Address of the Grand Master Workman," *Proceedings* (7 September 1880): 171; Powderly, "Address," 1886, 41.

30. *Journal of the Knights of Labor* (15 January 1891): 2.

31. Gusfield, "Functional Areas of Leadership," 141.

32. This chapter is informed by a number of studies of personal and corporate apologetic rhetoric, in particular: B. L. Ware and Wil A. Linkugel, "They Spoke in Defense of Themselves: On the Generic Criticism of Apologia," *Quarterly Journal of Speech* 59 (1973): 273–83; Ellen Reid Gold, "Political Apologia: The Ritual of Self-Defense," *Communication Monographs* 45 (1978): 306–16; Robert A. Varatbedian, "Nixon's Vietnam Rhetoric: A Case Study of Apologia as Generic Paradox," *Southern Speech Communication Journal* 50 (1985): 366–81; Susan L. Brinson and William L. Benoit, "Dow Corning's Image Repair Strategies in the Breast Implant Crisis," *Communication Quarterly* 44 (1996): 29–41; Keith Michael Hearit, "'Mistakes Were Made': Organizations, Apologia, and Crises of Self Legitimacy," *Communication Studies* 46 (1995): 1–17; and Susan Schultz Huxman and Denise Beatty Bruce, "Toward a Dynamic Generic Framework of Apologia: A Case Study of Dow Chemical, Vietnam, and the Napalm Controversy," *Communication Studies* 46 (1995): 57–72.

33. Rayback, *History of American Labor*, 148.

34. Madison, *American Labor Leaders*, 52.

35. Terence V. Powderly, "Address of the Grand Master Workman," *Proceedings* (16 September 1882): 276, 278.

36. Ibid., 278.

37. Ibid., 278.

38. Powderly, "Address," 1886, 43.

39. Ware and Linkugel, "They Spoke in Defense of Themselves," 278, 283.

40. Powderly, "Address," 1880, 176; Terence V. Powderly, "Address of the Grand Master Workman," *Proceedings* (5 September 1883): 410.

41. Terence V. Powderly, "Report of the General Master Workman," *Proceedings* (5 October 1885): 26.

42. Powderly, "Address," 1882, 274.

43. For discussions of argument from transcendence, see Stewart, Smith, and Denton, *Persuasion and Social Movements*, 273–77; and Ware and Linkugel, "They Spoke in Defense of Themselves," 280–82.

44. Terence V. Powderly, "Report of the General Master Workman," *Proceedings* (November 1889): 2.

45. *Journal of United Labor* (26 May 1888): 1.

46. Powderly, "Report," 1889, 2.

47. Terence V. Powderly, "Report of the General Master Workman," *Proceedings* (10 November 1888): 4. For discussions of transferring blame, see William L. Benoit, "Sears Repair of Its Auto Service Image: Image Restoration Discourse in the Corporate Sector," *Communication Studies* 46 (1995): 90; and Noreen Wales Kruse, "Apologia in Team Sport," *Quarterly Journal of Speech* 67 (1981): 376.

48. Powderly, "Report," 1888, 4.

49. Powderly, "Report," 1889, 2–3.

50. Powderly, "Report," 1885, 7.

51. Powderly, "Address," 1882, 285.

52. Madison, *American Labor Leaders*, 66.

53. Powderly, "Address," 1887, 1528.

54. See, for example, *Journal of the Knights of Labor* (18 September 1890): 1; Powderly, "Report," 1888, 18; *Journal of United Labor* (14 March 1889): 1.

55. *Journal of United Labor* (12 February 1891): 2.

56. Powderly, "Address," 1887, 1538.

57. *Journal of United Labor* (21 April 1888): 2.

58. *Journal of United Labor* (27 December 1888): 1.

59. Powderly, "Address," 1887, 1539.

60. Powderly, "Report," 1888, 6.

61. Ibid., 7.

62. Ibid., 6–7.

63. *Journal of United Labor* (15 May 1880): 12.

64. Madison, *American Labor Leaders*, 53.

65. *Journal of United Labor* (2 August 1888): 2.

66. Jackson Harrell, B. L. Ware, and Wil A. Linkugel, "Failure of Apology in American Politics: Nixon on Watergate," *Speech Monographs* 42 (1975): 252.

67. Powderly, "Address," 1886, 43.

68. Madison, *American Labor Leaders*, 53.

69. *Journal of United Labor* (15 May 1880): 12.

70. *Journal of the Knights of Labor* (23 October 1890): 1.

71. *Journal of United Labor* (26 May 1888):

72. *Journal of United Labor* (June 1882): 241.

73. Ibid.

74. Ibid.

75. *Journal of United Labor* (26 March 1887): 2330.

76. *Journal of United Labor* (26 May 1888): 1.

77. *Journal of United Labor* (10 September 1887): 2.

78. *Journal of United Labor* (26 March 1887): 2330.

79. Powderly, "Report," 1888, 4; Powderly, "Report," 1889, 3.

80. *Journal of United Labor* (21 April 1888): 2.

81. Powderly, "Address," 1887, 1536.

82. Ibid.

83. *Journal of United Labor* (24 March 1888): 2.

84. *Journal of the Knights of Labor* (17 July 1890): 1.

85. Powderly, *Path I Trod*, 317–82.

86. Ibid., 346–47.

87. *Journal of the Knights of Labor* (30 March 1893): 1.

88. Foner, *History of the Labor Movement*, vol. 2, 166; Madison, *American Labor Leaders*, 67.

89. *Journal of the Knights of Labor* (30 March 1893): 1.

90. Ibid.

91. Terence V. Powderly, "Address of the General Master Workman," *Proceedings* (November 1893): 6–20.

92. Some theorists have noted that American audiences, particularly ones consisting of industrial workers, have little respect for the emotions of pity or sympathy and may have contempt for their users. See, for example, Sherry Devereaux Butler, "The Apologia, 1971 Genre," *Southern Speech Communication Journal* 37 (1972): 288; and Gerald L. Wilson, "A Strategy of Explanation: Richard M. Nixon's August 8, 1974, Resignation Address," *Communication Quarterly* 24 (1976): 17.

93. Edwin Black, *Rhetorical Criticism: A Study in Method* (New York: Macmillan, 1965), 153.

94. Powderly, "Address," 1893, 17–18.

95. *Journal of United Labor* (June 1882): 287.

96. Powderly, "Address," 1880, 169.

97. Ibid., 170.

98. Powderly, "Report," 1888, 18–19.

99. Terence V. Powderly, "Report of the General Master Workman," *Proceedings* (November 1890): 4–12.

100. *Journal of United Labor* (31 December 1887): 2.

101. Powderly, *Path I Trod*, 131.

102. Powderly, "Address," 1887, 1480.

103. Ibid., 1485.

104. Powderly, "Address," 1886, 39.

105. *Journal of United Labor* (14 March 1889): 1.

106. Powderly, "Address," 1886, 39.

107. Ibid.

108. Powderly, *Path I Trod*, 114.

109. Ibid.; Foner, *History of the Labor Movement*, vol. 2, 82–83.

110. Rayback, *History of American Labor*, 168.

111. Powderly, "Address," 1887, 1499–500.

112. Ibid., 1502, 1505.

113. Ibid., 1499, 1500.

114. Ibid., 1501.

115. Ibid.

116. Ibid., 1505.

117. Ibid., 1499.

118. Madison, *American Labor Leaders*, 44. See also Leon Fink, *Workingmen's Democracy: The Knights of Labor and American Politics* (Urbana: University of Illinois Press, 1985).

119. Powderly, "Address," 1880, 169.

120. Charles J. Stewart, "The Internal Rhetoric of the Knights of Labor," *Communication Studies* 42 (1991): 72–76.

121. Powderly, "Address," 1886, 42.

122. Ibid.

123. *Journal of United Labor* (10 September 1887): 2.

124. Powderly, "Address," 1886, 42.

125. *Journal of United Labor* (10 September 1887): 2.

126. Powderly, "Report," 1888, 16.

127. Ibid.

128. *Journal of the Knights of Labor* (3 July 1890): 1.

129. Ibid.

130. Ibid.

131. *Journal of the Knights of Labor* (12 February 1891): 1.

132. Ibid.

133. *Journal of the Knights of Labor* (9 June 1892): 2.

134. Ibid.

135. *Journal of the Knights of Labor* (29 April 1893): 1.

136. Powderly, "Annual Address," 1893, 2.

137. Ibid., 5.

138. Ibid., 6.

139. *Journal of the Knights of Labor* (12 February 1891): 2.

140. Powderly, "Annual Address," 1893, 2.

141. Samuel Gompers, "Address to the Machinists Convention," *American Federationist* (July 1901): 251.

142. "Report of the General Executive Board," *Proceedings* (November 1894): 71.

143. J. R. Sovereign, "Annual Address of the General Master Workman," *Proceedings* (November 1895): 1–2.

144. Rayback, *History of American Labor*, 181.

145. Fink, *Workingmen's Democracy*, 221.

146. Ibid., 230.

147. Ibid., xiii.

148. Ibid.

Fair Rhetoric

James Gilbert

10

> Most human beings operate like historians: they only recognize the nature of their experience in retrospect.
>
> —Eric Hobsbawm

For more than a hundred years, the World's Columbian Exposition, held at Chicago in 1893, has articulated memorable turn-of-the-century visions of American culture. First to tourists and visitors, then to a nation of newspaper and book readers, and finally to historians and their audiences, the Chicago World's Fair has been a useful and pliable symbol for the shape of early modern American society and culture. As the most important positive event in Chicago's history of that period, a time when the city was racked by a stupendous fire and momentous strikes and riots, the Fair represented a fantasy realization and a utopian reconstruction of the contemporary elements of modern industrial society and culture. It was an exposition of the possible meanings of an age. Because it was an enormous, varied, and culturally diverse event, it lent itself easily to different and, almost always, contested meanings. There never was—then or now—a single Fair, describable in the singular. Instead, there are many Fairs, many experiences of it, and a host of shaded meanings created and argued over by its various interpreters. This essay explores some of the ways that the Fair operated as a rhetorical subject, and how this rhetorical subject was, and still is, presented to various audiences for different purposes.

Planning the Fair

From the beginning, the World's Columbian Exposition had several distinct and even conflicting purposes, with advocates of these intentions who eagerly pushed a particular meaning in the press or other public arena. Over time, the sway of these ideas and purposes has shifted in relative importance. What mattered when the Fair opened in the spring of 1893 was not necessarily as significant by the fall closing. In several crucial areas, such as photography, for example, key personnel changed, and with the selection of a new official photographer came a flow of different "approved" images of the fairgrounds, its buildings, and exhibits. Consequently, over the summer the aesthetic presentation of the Fair shifted decisively. This visual history is especially noteworthy because of severe regulations limiting the private use of cameras on the grounds. Financial considerations also altered the public, cultural presentations sponsored at the Fair. When classical music concerts failed to attract sufficient audiences, the Fair management reversed itself and promoted different sorts of popular music events, designed to please an audience that preferred more accessible styles and orchestrations. Even prior to the opening of the Fair, significant changes in supervisory leadership of the Midway amusement section muted one sort of message and emphasized another. It should also be said that no experience of the event could be entirely unmediated. No matter what an audience witnessed at an exhibit or during a performance, whatever seemed to be happening was, in fact, subject to a cascade of competing interpretations. These, in turn, could and probably were shaped and reshaped in retrospect, as fairgoers read and heard about what they themselves had seen and experienced. Even their anticipations were carefully shaped by guidebooks, advertising, and an endless parade of journalism suggesting what to expect in Chicago and on the exhibit grounds.

The occasion (if not the purpose) of the Chicago Exposition was the celebration of Columbus and his claim to the discovery of the New World. How insignificant this was as a pretext, however, is suggested by the venue itself—Chicago—which was territory never inhabited by the Spanish (although they had vague claims to it at one point). Chicago, the great inland city, was anything but representative of the Spanish Empire, which was based on intensive extraction of gold and other raw materials. Nor would the city's founders claim any heritage backward to the Catholic culture that, beginning with Columbus, the Spanish imposed upon Native Americans. In fact, the affiliation with Columbus, other than his representing the first of a wave of European explorers and settlers, was most probably with the notion of empire itself, modernized, of course, and translated into a different idiom. There was, if nothing else, a sort of metaphoric unity between Chicago and the first European empire founded 400 years earlier. Chicago presented itself at the pinnacle of an economic, political, and commercial nexus, attached by tentacles of railway lines that connected and subordinated satellite cities and whole geographic areas to its commercial grasp. As the president of the Fair Corporation, Harlow Higginbotham, wrote, "The marvelous growth of Chicago from a frontier camp to the active city of more than a million souls, with a corresponding advance in commercial, industrial, and intellectual activities, can best typify the giant young nation whose discovery the projected Fair is to commemorate."[1] But Chicago was only one small portion of a larger American empire that was poised to acquire its first colonies and open spheres of interest five years later when it toppled the tottering remnants of Spanish power in Asia and the Caribbean. The purpose, then, of the Fair was to demonstrate the superiority of American society, its up-and-coming preeminence in a world heretofore dominated by Old World powers such as France, England, and Spain. The message it sought to convey was deeply patriotic in the most expansive sense of that term, being a celebration of the reconstitution of the nation (only twenty-eight years after the end of the Civil War), the military conquest of the West, the geographic completion of the nation—all in anticipation of new international adventures. In a way, this meaning reverberated through the dramatic enunciation of the "frontier thesis" by historian Frederick Jackson Turner during the Fair at a scholarly meeting in Chicago that summer.[2]

The choice of Chicago as host of the Fair was neither obvious nor inevitable. Severely contested by New York and by other Midwest cities like St. Louis, Chicago won the bid with political maneuvers and through financial guarantees. The very peculiarity of its success was incorporated into its narrative of self-promotion. In countless tracts, newspaper stories, guidebooks, and official statements, the Fair management played upon this anomaly. The Fair rose up on an uninhabited swamp inside a city just 60 years old, within a region that had belonged to the United States less than a century, inside a nation that was only 117 years old—if one starts counting with the Declaration of Independence. In this sense, Chicago perfectly represented the United States, particularly that aspect of its history that seemed to spring magically out of nothing. Chicago, the city less than one generation old, with one million inhabitants, the eighth largest city in the world, was surely also its greatest wonder.

James Wright Dickinson rendered this exuberant assessment in a poetic tribute published in 1892:

> O Mighty City! Earth's historic page
> Knows naught like thee. Alone, unrivaled, thou
> Hast sprung to life, like fabric of a dream;
> Like tale of magic from Arabian mind!
> E'en Desolation gives to thee new strength,
> And, from thy flames, like to the fabled bird,
> Hast thou arisen, thus renewing youth,
> E'en from thy ashes.[3]

Because Chicago could carry such dramatic nationalist metaphors on its impressive shoulders, once the selection was made, hesitations evaporated among most of its competitors. Gradually, in much of the nation's press Chicago's claim to speak for the nation found acceptance, and the act of going to the Fair was transformed into an act of patriotism. It is no accident, therefore, that the "Pledge of Allegiance (minus the contemporary reference to God) was developed for the Fair and practiced or witnessed by many of the tourists who attended its events.[4]

The nationalist mood of the Fair also inspired Chicago to express a gush of New World braggadocio. In 1889 Paris had assembled its splendid exhibit filled with anthropological wonders and industrial and consumer goods, and crowned by the Eiffel Tower, an ensemble that memorialized the culture and influence of that great empire. Chicago needed to do better, considering itself a competitor with the prior exhibition. What Paris could do, Chicago could surely surpass. At first this meant building a bigger and higher monument, sketched out in preliminary plans and often referred to as a new "Tower of Babel." The project, however, collapsed. But the competition with Paris received one gratuitous footnote in an exhibition on the Midway: a scale model of the Eiffel Tower, one-fiftieth its actual size. And the notion of "Babel" was applied time and again to the cultural juxtapositions in modern society and the new urban environment.

The Fair leadership looked elsewhere for symbolism and found it at least partially in the proposal of a gigantic amusement ride at the center of the Midway. When completed well after the opening of the Fair, this Ferris wheel carried plush-seated coaches high over the fairgrounds and the city. If the planners did not seem to recognize it, they had created a perfect metaphor for Chicago—a vertical railroad, revolving on a stationary axis that might have represented the city itself.[5]

Building the Fair: Architecture as Image

The Chicago businessmen who secured the federal license to construct the Columbian celebration resolved upon a number of statements they wanted to embed in the built environment, in the performative elements of the Fair, in publicity, in their own speeches, and through a careful censorship of the contents of exhibits. The attention they lavished on one section, the so-called White City because of the gleaming white surfaces and decor, and their seeming nonchalance toward the amusement center, Midway, were a reflection of an attempt to structure the meaning of the Fair and project that meaning to visitors of every sort. Even—or perhaps especially—the geography of the Fair exhibitions revealed an unmistakable purpose and hierarchy of values. Proximity to the "Court of Honor"—and what center of an imaginary city has ever conjured up a better name?—translated into a hierarchical scale of values. Architecture, art embellishments, and landscaping focused on a center that celebrated consumer products, manufacturing, art, education, and the liberal arts. All of the buildings in this central area (save one) were constructed of white-painted "staff," a compliant material of jute and plaster of Paris that could be shaped easily into neo-classical embellishment. Farther from the center stood less important buildings and areas—on one side, the dusty, raucous Midway, extending blocks away from the Court of Honor. To the north were the state exhibits and then those of other nations, close enough to be in the orbit of the commemoration of America contained in the central buildings, but still peripheral. To the south, less attractive economic endeavors like agriculture and mining were exhibited. But at the center, high art, consumer products, and manufacturing were intentionally grouped to project the values of the Fair managers and their desire to invest their own self-interest into a prediction of future American civilization.

The initial plan of the Fair, although modified over time, aimed to proclaim the majority of America alongside the grown-up world of European states. Further, businessmen like Marshall Field and Harlow Higginbotham; distinguished socialites like Bertha Honore Palmer, head of the Board of Lady Managers; and other officials believed that the Fair should also project a particular vision of Chicago. Built upon heavy industry like railroads, commodity shipments, and meatpacking, the city had a tough, raw reputation. The Fair leadership hoped to disguise this identity under a veneer of high culture. The much-vaunted White City was the result—a vision of what Chicago might and could look like, an integrated urban design based upon aesthetics and quiet, elite taste.

The buildings of the central court represented a remarkable architectural achievement. Built over enormous iron and steel frames, reminiscent of railway sheds, each building provided huge interior spaces for display. The resulting ensemble was a rhapsody of allusions to Greek and Roman culture, completely unreflective of the interior construction and immune to any suggestions of functionalism—this despite the displays of technological instruments and machinery inside. But the exteriors reflected the aspirations of the city's elite, who were attempting to persuade others, as well as convince themselves, that the crude capital accumulation and sprawling urban area of Chicago, constructed only in the last few decades, could be reshaped into a worthy and centralized cultural endeavor. Uncertain of their own originality, which was actually considerable in economics and merchandising, the planners copied what they believed were the prevailing standards of civilization.

Initially, the Fair planners hired John Root and Daniel Burnham to supervise the architectural ensemble. When Root died in 1891, the more conservative Burnham shouldered the responsibility alone. He demanded integration—that is, integrity of style—and coordination. Perspective and connection were key. Therefore buildings around the Court of Honor had to conform to a basic aesthetic; they had to function together to project the notion of a utopian center. The effect was nothing if not purposeful. Buildings, placement of walks and statues, canals, reflecting ponds, and plantings created multiple perspectives on the same fundamental theme—the ability of culture to transform crude power and wealth into moral and aesthetic energy. Inside the buildings, of course, were the jumbled styles of different displays and kiosks, quoting every conceivable architectural fashion and allusion. No product inside these buildings was offered for direct sale, but agents could take orders, and considerable business was transacted over the summer. That was the purpose of renting space inside these lavish temples to the functions of the modern economy. Thus the architecture not only was contrived to disguise the getting and spending inside, its purpose also was to recontextualize the mundane world of manufacturing, mining, and agriculture inside the elevating assumption that it all went together to produce the highest forms of civilization. What better way to make this impression than for Chicago to join the neo-classical building binge of late Victorian Europe?

Only one major architect, Louis Sullivan, had the prestige and courage to resist the seduction of this white, classical symbolism. His transportation building was oddly jarring—a transgression, in fact. Located akimbo to the Court of Honor, it employed Sullivan's particular and idiosyncratic version of the modern architect's dictum: "form should follow function." Actually, this meant the translation of function into an identifiable metaphor. So Sullivan graced his transportation building with a vast and ornate tunnel-like opening, the perfect allusion to the railways that converged upon and built Chicago. Yet nothing about the building celebrated the architectural structure that lay beneath the embellishment. Its difference from other buildings around the Court of Honor was a choice of poetry: Midwest vernacular American verse over against the Augustinian epic style. But it was all, still, illusion.

To integrate the high culture perspectives of the White City, the Fair managers hired Frederick Law Olmsted, designer of New York's Central Park and many other significant urban projects. Olmsted's trademark was also a manner of disguise. Olmsted believed in the restorative powers of nature, of walks, perspectives, and a restful eye fixed upon natural beauty. He wanted to shut the city out of its own center, to bring the soothing calm of natural beauty into a place that was accessible to the hurly-burly of the city. His project for the Fair was a wooded isle, located adjacent to the Court of Honor and surrounded by a lagoon that connected back to the central basin. Although he was deeply disappointed when the Fair management insisted upon placing a Japanese garden and temple in the center way of his walks and strolls, his effect upon the ensemble was significant. What is more, it helped articulate the central purposes of Burnham and his colleagues. Now, they believed, the name Chicago would perform as a cultural magnet, drawing wealthy visitors from the United States and the rest of the world to the Fair and to the city. There would be far less incentive, henceforth, for Americans to resort to London or Paris. Chicago would suffice.

Novelist Theodore Dreiser perfectly captured this spirit and pretense in his description of the Fair as "a garden of the gods." "One is reminded," he wrote, "of what the ancient Athenian capital must have been like. How its temples and public buildings, its statuary and its public ways must have adorned the ancient hills of Helos. One can understand, looking at the group of buildings, so gracefully sweeping away on every hand, why the Grecians were proud and how it came that men could meditate the sublime philosophies that characterized that mythic age."[6]

Presenting the Fair: The Rhetoric of Guidebooks

The purpose of the World's Columbian Exposition, from the perspective of the Chicago businessmen who commanded it into existence, was to alter the contemporary meaning of the city. No longer to be thought of as the black city of industrial strife, coal dust, traffic, with the sights and smells of its manufacturing and meatpacking industries intruding everywhere, Chicago would emerge in the vision of the nation and the eyes of its own citizens (who certainly knew better) as a great White City of high culture and elevated purpose. In this project the World's Fair planners received extraordinary support from the authors of guidebooks, travel writers, and journalists—all of whom had a vested interest in embellishing the story. Aiming their works at an audience that was wealthy enough to buy travel guides, or better, interested in making the journey to Chicago over the summer, these authors distributed the vision of the Fair that the Fair administration intended. At the same time, there were some interesting exceptions to this rhetorical presentation that emphasized a secondary view that grew in popularity over the summer.

Most of these works about travel to the Fair have very little in them that would surprise the modern reader, although there are certain omissions that might give pause. Indeed, the contemporary guidebook has much in common with these earlier pioneer versions. Their purpose is now and was then to encourage travel and provide the itinerary for a visit: what to see and, by implication, what to avoid. In Chicago during the 1890s, this meant making a complex triage of historical associations and geographic sections of the city. Chicago had much in its immediate past that required forgetting. There was the Chicago Fire of 1871, the railroad strikes of 1877, the Haymarket affair of 1886—all within striking distance of historical and personal memory, and an indelible part of the contemporary reputation of the city. Furthermore, of major American cities, Chicago had the greatest number of immigrants, with huge populations of Germans, Irish, and Scandinavians; a thriving foreign-language press; and a roiling population of Americans drawn into the city from the farms. In fact, the Fair had depicted this situation in two rather abstract ways: by its extraordinary attention to exhibiting ethnicity on the Midway and with a curious, plaintive painting in the exhibit of fine arts, deemed the favorite work of visitors. This latter was the nostalgic genre work of the American artist Thomas Hovenden called *Breaking Home Ties*. This sentimental painting depicts a young man preparing to depart home, presumably to join millions of other American youngsters on their trek to the city.

The strategies of the most important Chicago guidebooks followed a similar format. Some of the earlier guides, published for businessmen, tended toward advertising business opportunities. Others, such as the "gaslight" guides, presented a depiction of the most lurid pleasures the city could conjure up. But the 1890s guides were aimed at middle-class fairgoers. Their purpose was to present the most favorable and positive impression of the city and Fair possible and still convince the tourist to continue to rely upon the guide. This meant riding the edge of a contradiction. Guidebooks needed to reassure tourists at the same time as they warned against the arbitrary and aimless visit.

Much of the included material was simply useful: train schedules, hotel prices, and so on. Advisory itineraries structured the way visitors looked at the city, suggesting walks, describing buildings and parks, and ranking monuments and vistas according to importance. This ranking was generally based upon accepted wisdom and reputation, something that was highly favorable to city elites. Thus the Palmer House Hotel, Marshall Field's Department Store, and various other such commercial sites received special attention. Travel guides either failed to mention other parts of the city or warned patrons to avoid them. The city's huge immigrant sections warranted little discussion. The Chicago of guidebook culture was a small, circumscribed universe of high culture, swell hotels, and shopping, all resting upon a veiled world of heavy, sweated labor that made it possible.

For example, Flinn's popular guide, *Chicago: The Marvelous City of the West*, discouraged visiting working-class areas. "It was quite the 'fad' in fashionable circles not long since to 'go slumming' and the city detectives were frequently requested to conduct a party of young ladies and gentlemen through the various quarters of the city. It is no longer a 'fad' although the practice has by no means died out." If ever, this should be done only during the day. In a thirty-one-day self-guided tour of Chicago and the Fair, there was not a single excursion into any of the city's huge immigrant residential districts.[7]

Yet the rest of the city was present in the constant reference to the notion of Babel. A variety of books, like Charles Power's, *Heart of Chicago* and Robert Musket's, *Chicago, Yesterday and Today*, described the multicultural vision the voyager could enjoy from the comfort of downtown, standing on a street corner, watching the Chicago world pass by. This was a safer vantage point than venturing into the neighborhoods themselves. Exoticism and ethnic diversity were thus stereotyped and deracinated, rendering them safe and tame. Representatives from Babel could be observed at the heart of Chicago's Loop, and the visitor need travel no farther from this comfortable vantage point. Any serious encounter with the hundreds of thousands of immigrants who made up the huge population increase so boasted of by city boosters would be either accidental or limited. Just as it was on the fairgrounds, the urban Babel was separated from the commercial and cultural focus.[8]

Most guidebooks to the Fair situated their visit inside a tour of Chicago. They centered the experience within the remarkable urban conglomeration that had sprung up on the shores of Lake Michigan, and they frequently made cross-references between the two sites. Many saw the Fair itself as a metaphor for Chicago. With its gleaming Court of Honor and polyglot Midway, the Fair, with only a little imagination, could symbolize Chicago's Loop, with its emerging park system, opera and concert facilities, theater section, department stores, and attendant skyscrapers. Guidebooks asserted this notion of a city within a city with considerable self-congratulation and a tone of celebration. Bancroft's *Book of the Fair* was typical in its hyperbole. Chicago was "a city noted mainly as the incarnation of the eager, restless spirit of a commercial age, a city which, destroyed in a night, sprang almost as suddenly into yet more forceful life." Compared to the Exposition, this history made it "more of a wonder than the fairy-land of her creation."[9]

The *Official Directory* of the Fair was just as effusive in its praise of Chicago and certain of the metaphoric link between the Exposition and the city's brief, heroic history. The Fair crowned the work of a citizenry that in a few years transformed "prairies, marshes and huts into the Garden City—a city now universally recognized as one of the greatest in the world, and which had arisen from dire disaster of the most destructive conflagration ever known . . . to [become] the second city of the United States."[10] Or, as Carroll Ryan wrote in *Chicago the Magnificent*, the city had a truly magical, if short, history. It just shrugged off the fire in 1871, as if a variant of urban renewal: "but while the conflagration was raging and men were fighting the flames in one part of the city, gangs of laborers were set to work clearing the foundations over which the fire had swept, and new and better buildings went up almost as rapidly as the former had been burned down."[11]

What fascinates about this exaggerated gloss of tragedy is how much it appears as a matter of fact in guidebook after guidebook. Even nationalist overtones attached themselves to this self-presentation. After all, the United States itself was only a bit over a century old and used to presenting itself to other societies as remarkable and new. All such images became the potential repertoire for picturing the city and the Exposition. The usable past of the United States and Chicago really only meant a succession of statements about the future, predictions of triumph over adversity, and promises of greater progress. The very brashness of the language, the willful boasting, was itself the principal rhetorical frame of the Exposition.

If the countless and widely circulated guidebook literature structured the experience of the Fair for visitors, urging them to understand their experience in terms of the miraculous rebirth of Chicago and the promise of a new century of America's predominance in the world, it also sought to convey another, equally important impression. Just as the planners of the Fair careful devised a hierarchy of cultural values, dividing the grounds in two, between the White City and Midway, and then structuring once more the internal order within each segment, the guidebooks replicated these divisions. In some cases, the books failed to mention the Midway at all, presenting only the lustrous architectural and commercial wonders of the White City. Almost all the books offered a similar itinerary for visitors, starting at the Court of Honor and then working outward, reaffirming the scale of values inherent in the built environment. Even the displays of products followed an order that privileged the most refined—in this case, manufacturing—and thrust out to the periphery the traditional, less glamorous, and technologically less advanced activities like mining and agriculture. This structure was an intentional statement about the meaning of modern civilization, and the guidebooks did not miss it. Modern societies, in this dramatic presentation, produced the most refined machine-made products. Civilization diminished insofar as advanced production was absent.

If the guides were thorough (and they could vary enormously from an exhaustive catalog of buildings and displays to a short rushed visit to the high points), they might extend this message to an invidious comparison to the rest of the world, picturing Chicago as the future greatest city on earth. There were a number of large and complex exhibits built by European and other nations such as Japan. Sometimes these appeared to merit a visit and sometimes not. Thus *Conkey's Complete Guide* contained two sorts of lists. The first was an alphabetical list of major exhibits. This was followed by a hierarchical description, beginning in the White City, moving through the American state exhibits, to the foreign collections, and finally out onto the Midway.[12] Rand McNally's guide to the Fair, on the other hand, provided special attention to the Midway, explaining a number of attractions there, although organizing a visit in the order it believed would interest visitors most, emphasizing the Middle Eastern exhibits, the Ferris wheel, and then some of the more anthropologically inclined exhibits such as Dahomey and Zululand.[13] Flinn's *Official Guide to Midway Plaisance* preserved much the same order and listed entrance prices and accurate physical descriptions and measurements of the exhibits.[14]

That the guidebooks should impose this itinerary on a visit to the Midway was probably based upon an accurate prediction or recognition (some books were published after the Fair opened) of what might be popular in the amusement section. While these books did not tamper with the Fair administration's construction of hierarchy in the White City, or question that portion's superiority over the Midway, most tended to place their own order on presenting the scores of concessions.

This was certainly not the original intended purpose of the visit to the Midway. In the initial planning stages for the Fair, the administration had hoped to present an extensive anthropological exhibit to reflect the levels of modern civilization and the role that ethnicity and race played in this order. To this end, Burnham hired F. W. Putnam, a scientist from Harvard, to head the anthropological exhibit. Putnam devised a plan for a "Street of All Nations," so organized that it would begin with the lowest forms of civilization and rise in proximity to the White City and to European and American civilization: a stroll, as it were, through human evolution. This notion was probably not controversial to most Americans or even foreign visitors at the time, but Putnam hoped to explain the scientific justification for his arrangement. Before the opening of the Fair, however, Putnam was replaced by the entrepreneur and impresario Sol Bloom, who specifically rejected Putnam's lessons. Instead, he promoted entertainment and moneymaking—something the Fair administration also desired. And so the Midway actually conflated two sorts of order. Ranging from far to near the White City, one could follow the vague outlines of Putnam's original racial order, beginning with Dahomey from Africa and ending with the German Village. But, in fact, Bloom disrupted the prescribed flow from far to near and instead tried to draw visitors to the center, where, incidentally, his own exhibit, the Algerian Village, was located. Around this central area he placed all the "oriental" exhibits, plus the giant Ferris wheel, and these proved to be the most popular destinations of fairgoers.[15]

There was still another way that the administration hoped to structure the experience of the fairgoer and the impression gained worldwide about the Exposition. Burnham and his administration jealously guarded freelance and amateur photography within the fairgrounds, hiring C. D. Arnold as the official photographer. Arnold's stately, luminous, and monumental perspectives perfectly fit the grandiose aspirations of the Chicago boosters who initiated and directed the Fair. Although Arnold was finally replaced as official photographer toward the end of the summer, when many of the high culture aspirations of the administration had to be tempered with the aim to turning a profit, thousands of examples of his photographs circulated privately or appeared in guidebooks or later memory books of the Fair.

So heavy-handed was the administration in trying to control the visual memory of the Fair that it tried to inhibit private photography. The late nineteenth century was the beginning of the age of popular photography. Cheap Kodak cameras suddenly appeared everywhere, together with the "Kodak Fiend"—often pictured as an obtrusive woman, armed with a camera. To control photography and protect its monopoly, the administration severely limited the use of cameras by charging a $2 daily fee for use of handheld cameras (admission was only $.50). While this was less than prohibitive, it certainly cut down on the number of individualized shots and increased the sales of authorized postcards, photographs, and other scenes provided by the Fair management. Since these offerings tended to concentrate on views of the White City, the photographic record that made its way into private hands underscored the intended vision—even if the visitor had spent most of his or her time on the Midway.

Visiting the Fair

Despite the extensive visual and design ploys imposed upon fairgoers by guidebooks, the location of exhibits, the photography monopoly, sympathetic newspaper stories, and so on, the patron nevertheless had significant control over the portions of the Fair she or he visited. Fortunately, it is possible to estimate, with at least limited accuracy, the track of these visits to see if they in any way fulfilled the expectations of the management. Were the lessons of culture and civilization received as intended, or were they muted by unanticipated behavior? There are indications that millions of visitors ignored some of the proudest displays of the Chicago city fathers and avoided their cultural lessons. For example, the classical music concerts (much of it Wagnerian) offered by Maestro Theodore Thomas and the Chicago Symphony players had to be ended. Attendance at these concerts fell toward the end of the season, and Thomas quit.

Of course, a great many visitors spent time in the White City because everything conspired to send them there. Other exhibits, like those of Germany and Japan, evoked considerable notice in the newspapers. Another popular venue was the state exhibits, whose visiting books recorded the names and addresses of thousands of visitors—a great many of them hailing from the state. For the historian, however, the Midway offers the greatest accuracy in measuring visits because almost every exhibit charged admission, and those admissions were all reported to the Fair management.

Historians have generally accepted the notion that twenty-seven million people visited the World's Columbian Exposition, based upon the total number of turnstile figures. But this is hugely inaccurate. Many of the admissions were free (about six million). These included employees and guests, many of whom might not have attended the exhibits. Other groups included in the six million were children. Moreover, there is no way to know how many of these entries were by repeat visitors. It is probably more likely that about half the total were actually different visitors, making the estimate closer to twelve or thirteen million. While this is still an enormous number and a huge percentage of the American population for such an event, it lessens the number of personal experiences with the Fair. On the other hand, this increases the importance of journalistic and historical presentations of the Fair in establishing its meaning as the event was translated for the rest of the nation.

On the Midway, where individual behavior may be most accurately measured, it is clear that most visitors avoided the progression of civilization initially constructed by Putnam. Instead, they were drawn, as Sol Bloom hoped they would be, to the exoticism of the Oriental section focused toward the center. The areas with the least attraction were, like Dahomey Village, those with the most serious anthropological purpose. Dahomey collected only $113,152.50 in gross receipts. Assuming that one admission was $.25 (the standard charge for concessions), then there were approximately 400,000 visits, or about 3 percent of the total visitors to the Fair. The Moorish Palace had at least four times as many entries, and the German Village may have had as much as 2,500,000 visits. We cannot know how many of these were repeat encounters, but that does not change the relative popularity of each place. Taken together, admissions to the Oriental center of the Midway accounted for about one-eighth of the total revenues of all the concessions of the Midway. If the proceeds from the Ferris wheel, located at the same spot, are added to this total, it appears that about 20 percent of total concession revenues came from this area. Even if restaurant and other special features of some of these exhibits are subtracted from their totals, it is clear that this area accounted for much of the revenue associated with the anthropological exhibits.[16]

One of the striking conclusions that must be drawn from these gross concession figures is how few exhibits the average visitor actually entered on the Midway. The average expenditure per visitor was probably somewhere around $1.40. This sum included the cost for entrance to the Fair ($.50), food, souvenirs, cigars, special wheelchairs, guidebooks, and entrance to exhibits on the Midway. At most, then, fairgoers probably visited no more than one or two of the anthropological exhibits. Many visitors probably saw none at all. Yet it is still possible to speak of the Midway as a "Street of All Nations," because so much of the exhibition poured onto the street itself in the form of parades and miniperformances designed to draw patrons inside. Most visitors probably received their impression of Midway anthropology as a jumble of images: exotic costumes of players, advertisements, exteriors of buildings, and glances down into the interior courtyards of areas from the perspective of the Ferris wheel. This might not have been what Putnam or the planners of the Fair wanted or anticipated, but it probably represents typical Fair behavior, something that Sol Bloom, with his entertainment experience, both anticipated and encouraged. In fact, the Midway remained a confusing and exciting jumble of exhibits and kiosks, attracting a huge range of visitors who enjoyed animal shows, a glimpse at the "typical" workingman's home, inspection of the military encampment, rides, a visit to the American Indian Village, a swim in the natatorium, a consideration of the scale model of the Eiffel Tower, and a visit to ethnic restaurants, the Wisconsin Creamery, the Irish Blarney Castle, and so on.

Did visitors to the Fair, then, miss what was left of Putnam's point about the hierarchy of races? Did the display of their own tastes and inclinations to explore the exotic blind them to the racist implications of the anthropology? These are very difficult questions to answer, but I think the answer to both is no. Indeed, seeing became unnecessary and perhaps would have been unpleasant—as most of the guidebooks emphasized. And, while it had practically disappeared from the

Midway, Putnam's arrangement was frequently described in guidebooks, as if the hierarchical order were still readily visible—which, in fact, it was not. So it was possible for the average fairgoer to wander through the White City; ride the Ferris wheel; visit the Middle East, German, or Irish exhibits; eat in an ethnic restaurant; never see Dahomey; and yet come away with the impression of having experienced a hierarchy of civilizations and races.

Some guidebook descriptions of the Fair were very explicit about race. For example, Flinn's *Official Guide to Midway Plaisance* describes Dahomey Village this way: "Those who have visited the Javanese Village [scarcely more than saw Dahomey] will observe at once that there are very striking degrees of barbarism. The habits of these people are repulsive; they eat like animals and have all the characteristics of the very lowest order of the human family. Nearly all the women are battle-scarred; most of them are captives."[17] Such words no doubt discouraged visitors from entering the exhibit.

And whether or not, as the Rand McNally *Guide* proclaimed, the Tunisian and Algerian exhibits depicted life as it actually was lived in North Africa, the Street in Cairo was a complex mixture of anthropology and amusement, some things historical, some contemporary, and some salacious, such as the famous "danse du ventre" that appeared briefly.[18] The point is that whatever the pleasure-seeking patrons spent their meager funds on, the Midway experience—regardless of whether they actually saw it—was depicted for them in guidebooks and newspaper stories in terms of a "Street of All Nations."

The polyglot world exhibited in parades and displays along the "Street of All Nations" took on a special meaning because of the surroundings of the Fair and the beneficence of American culture, transforming diversity, confusion, and Babel into a vision of a peaceable kingdom. As Ben Truman wrote of the opening ceremony in his *History of the World's Fair*: "In the great procession, which was set in motion, were Teutons and Slavs and Frenchmen, and their hearts and feet beat time to the same music—that of 'the Star Spangled Banner.' Orangemen walked in that procession for the first time in their history of three hundred years, the Irish Celts walked with them in common cause. hereditary foes were brothers, and for once the descendants of warring European clans marched under the same flag."[19]

Interpreting the Fair: The Fair as Cultural Symbol

The fundamentally different possibilities of interpretation resulting from the evolution of the Fair as an enterprise and its implicit, conflicting messages and purposes made its impact as much an issue for debate in 1893 as it is today. Almost from the beginning, the event was indistinguishable from the rich overlay of symbolism and interpretation that surrounded the buildings, the events held in them, and the exhibits. Almost everyone associated with the Exposition—from the initial stages of planning through the fire that destroyed its remnants in 1894—believed that the Fair represented something grand and symbolic. It was constructed to speak a particular language of elite culture and then, emphasizing the vernacular, modified to make money through the sale of popular entertainments. Chicago's political, cultural, and business elite and the U.S. Congress that chose the site conceived of the project in large and grandiloquent terms. The fact that it opened in the midst of a terrible depression, and closed within a few months of the violent strike at the Pullman Railway works just south of the fairgrounds, opened such symbolic meanings to ironic interpretation: by 1894 the arrogance of Chicago became a metaphor for the tragic misunderstandings operating in American industrial relations. If the White City represented the height of industrial civilization, a catalogue raisonnee' of its accomplishments, then the destruction of the Fairgrounds and the strike at Pullman revealed its shabby and exploitive underpinnings.

Almost immediately, the Chicago World's Fair entered literature as a symbol summing up the civilization of late-nineteenth-century America. This occurred in two very different sorts of works. The first of these were by the great American writers Henry Adams and William Dean Howells, both of whom rendered Chicago and the Fair as a vision of the future, a symbol of the profoundest directions of modern society. Both men pointedly avoided the Midway in their assessments. In his famous *Education of Henry Adams*, Adams wrote that the Fair (and its advanced electrical technology) represented "the first expression of American thought as a unity." Adams made a reference to Babel in his work, not the cacophony of peoples and civilization, but rather "the loose and ill-joined . . . ill-defined and unrelated thought and half-thoughts" of the Exposition.[20]

William Dean Howells certainly visited the Midway and recognized its power, diversity, and confusion. Indeed, on first sight the whole ensemble of the Fair filled him with "rapture and despair." When he later collected his thoughts, they appeared in his fascinating utopian novel, *A Traveler from Altruria*, published in 1894. The planned White City, as opposed to the disorderly and aggressive capitalism seen on the Midway, was a ideal that Howells now adopted. Indeed, the author saw much of what Burnham intended him to see. Chicago was, despite all else, a foretaste of a new form of society.[21]

One of the most widely read contemporary accounts of the Fair was the chatty popular fiction called *The Adventures of Uncle Jeremiah and Family at the Great Fair*, published in 1893 by Laird and Lee, a company that also specialized in guidebooks, photo books, and other publications associated with the Exposition. *Uncle Jeremiah*, which, according to the publisher, sold 250,000 copies within the first few months of its appearance, was an adventure tale of a trip to the Fair by a rural family. The story involves false confidence, disguises, love, and distress about the disorder of the city. The Exposition itself also represents all of these possibilities. In the end, all of the difficulties are resolved, and the author leaves off talking about pickpockets and confusing city countenances to make his larger point: "If the Exposition has awakened the sentiments of patriotism and reverence in the minds of all of its visitors, it has broadened their views concerning mankind, and made more charitable their hearts toward the rest of the world."[22] For the author, the Midway becomes the centerpiece of the Fair and the urban experience of the late nineteenth century its referent.

These three works only begin to suggest some of the variety of literary comment that the Fair evoked from the beginning. The Exposition might either represent the possibilities of modern life, or its perils, or both. It was either very American, or very exotic, or both. And Chicago was the ambiguous harbinger of the future, the site upon which the fate of America might be predicted, for better or worse.

In their efforts to find a rhetoric that could contain, articulate, and focus the intended meanings of the Fair and its glorious urban situation, these authors, echoing the words of the city fathers, journalists, guidebook authors, and other observers, assembled an impressive list of descriptive terms that were at once religious, patriotic, modern, diverse, progressive, miraculous, and classical. If these might have suggested very different appraisals, the terminology was unified in one ultimate sense: its extravagance and exaggeration.

It is remarkable how the symbolic terms of the Fair, apparent from the beginning, have been passed on to modern historians almost intact—its various meanings still contending, its evaluation still open to conflicting interpretations. This modern writing is particularly noteworthy for its high quality, for its ingenuity, and finally, for the way it illustrates the inability of anyone to fix meaning onto the surface of an event as elusive and multifaceted as the Fair. Its meanings were never stable, from the beginning, and in fact evolved over time during the planning, building, and exposition stages. Diverse segments of the Fair always had distinct, sometimes competing, purposes. Different public presentations of the Fair stressed different camera angles of vision. And individuals constantly disrupted or revised the intended itineraries of its creators. At the same time, there can be no doubt that certain aspects of the Fair reverberated throughout American culture and reappeared in subsequent fairs, such as the one held in St. Louis in 1904, and in the urban planning movement known as the city beautiful movement. St. Louis, too, had magnificent white exposition buildings, plus a large midway section. A great many cities, influenced by the work of Daniel Burnham, rebuilt their centers in the heroic architectural style of the Chicago Fair, gathering together cultural and commercial institutions to create a unified aesthetic, economic, and cultural downtown. Architect Louis Sullivan (and those critics who followed his lead) denounced the pastiche of neo-classical architecture as a betrayal of the possibilities of modernism. He was right, of course, but modernist functionalism has also contributed its share of ungraceful buildings to American cities.

So the argument over the Fair has continued and, in its contemporary guise, even extended the language and symbolism of the Exposition into our own time. Besides the excellent, early depictions by such authors as Reid Badger and David Burg, and important work by historians Donald Miller and Neil Harris, among others, the Fair has continued to inspire moral contretemps among critics.[23] Two excellent works evaluate the Fair as a symbol for the transformation of modern American culture and society at the end of the century. Alan Trachtenberg's seminal *Incorporation of America* depicts the Fair as a crucial moment, summarizing into a visual landscape the gathering force, energy, and power of a burgeoning capitalist nation.[24] Robert Rydell's path-breaking work, *All the World's a Fair: Visions of Empire at American International Expositions, 1876–1916*, suggests that the Fair should be understood mostly in terms of the Midway.[25] Unlike so many previous historians and commentators who either agreed with Burnham or fought over his meaning, Rydell concentrated on the Midway, restoring the balance in the elements that had always been present in the event and the experience of its visitors.

Rydell contextualizes the Exposition in a fashion quite different from previous historians, placing it within the development of a modern European and American imperial vision. Taking Putnam at his word about the progression of the human races toward the ideal standard of white America, Rydell justly emphasizes the heavy, racially charged baggage of the Fair, suggesting that it provided a sort of handy guide to contemporary racial attitudes and imperial aspirations boiling up in American society. Rydell articulates implications of the Exposition that may not have been entirely explicit or even understood at the time, but which undoubtedly flowed into America's imperial ventures in the Philippines and Latin America during the next few years.

My own book, *Perfect Cities: Chicago's Utopias of 1893*, takes a somewhat different tack, stressing the contest of cultural forms within the Fair. Part of an extended dialogue about the meaning of modern urban culture, the Fair was, in this interpretation, the pinnacle of struggle between popular and elite visions of the city. While neither ever really triumphed, the contest itself became an axis along which attempts to solve urban problems in the twentieth century were located.[26]

There is not, nor can there ever be, a resolution to this contest of interpretation. The Fair was layered with different meanings and messages, a huge variety of existing interpretations, and the experiences and memories of millions of visitors, and all these contribute to the construction of the Fair as a remembered event. Historians are only separating and pulling at these threads of interpretation; they can never weave a complete or definitive tapestry of meaning. In doing their work, they are continuing the discussion that began as soon as the first architects and draftsmen set pen to paper in the early 1890s. They have continued to find various and contending meanings in an event that embodied the social, economic, ethnic, and racial contradictions of its era, plus its contradictory conceptions of culture. All of these observers, historians included, have, after all, only seen what was present in the first place: an environment, an event, a performance that spoke with diverse rhetorical devices, metaphors, and voices.

Notes

1. Harlow Higginbotham, *Report of the President to the Board of Directors of the World's Columbian Exposition* (Chicago: Rand McNally, 1898), 9.

2. Turner marked the U.S. Census Office's 1890 declaration that the frontier was closed in his essay. The frontier, he argued, had shaped American democracy, and, he warned, its shaping influence might well disappear also.

3. J. F. Martin, *Martin's World's Fair Album, Atlas and Family Souvenir* (Chicago: C. Ropp and Sons, 1892).

4. Robert Rydell, *All the World's a Fair: Visions of Empire at American International Expositions, 1876–1916* (Chicago: University of Chicago Press, 1982).

5. Rydell, *All the World's a Fair.*

6. Theodore Dreiser, "Last Day at the Fair," *Republic,* 23 July 1893, 6.

7. John J. Flinn, *Chicago: The Marvelous City of the West: A History, an Encyclopedia, and a Guide,* 2nd ed. (Chicago: Standard Guide, 1892), 579.

8. One measure of the huge immigrant population in Chicago is a profile of construction workers at the Fair. Almost twice as many foreign-born as native-born workers labored on the grounds. Of these, the largest percentages were Germans, Scandinavians, and Irish. These were the same populations that swelled city slums and immigrant ghettos. See Flinn, *Chicago.*

9. Hubert H. Bancroft, *The Book of the Fair* (Chicago: Bancroft, 1895), vol. 2, 972.

10. Moses P. Handy, *The Official Directory of the World Columbian Exposition* (Chicago: W. B. Conkey, 1893), 43.

11. Carroll Ryan, *Chicago the Magnificent: The Empire City of the West: A Souvenir of the World's Fair: Its Phenomenal Rise, Its Marvelous Status, Its Future Greatness* (New York: J. P. Williams, 1893), 21.

12. *Conkey's Complete Guide to the World's Columbian Exposition* (Chicago: W. B. Conkey, 1893), 21–22.

13. Rand McNally and Company, *Handy Guide to Chicago and World's Columbian Exposition* (Chicago: Rand McNally, 1893), 206.

14. John J. Flinn, *Official Guide to Midway Plaisance* (Chicago: Columbian Guide, 1893), 17–30.

15. This is based upon a calculation of the proceeds of all the Midway concessions. Those at the center did far and away the best business, with the exception of the Irish and German villages. See Higginbotham, *Report of the President,* appendix E.

16. Prices are from *Chicago Daily Columbian* (1893). For admission figures, see Higginbotham, *Report of the President,* appendix E, 482–91. Some exhibits charged multiple fees, so that the total admissions may be slightly lower.

17. Flinn, *Official Guide to Midway Plaisance,* 30.

18. Rand McNally, *Handy Guide,* 206.

19. Ben C. Truman, *History of the World's Fair, Being a Complete and Authentic Description of the Columbian Exposition from Its Inception* (Philadelphia: H. W. Kelly, 1893), 88.

20. Henry Adams, *The Education of Henry Adams* (Boston: Houghton, Mifflin, 1974), 340.

21. William Dean Howells, *A Traveller from Altruria* (New York: Harper and Brothers, 1894).

22. Quondam, *The Adventures of Uncle Jeremiah and Family at the Great Fair* (Chicago: Laird and Lee, 1893), 228.

23. David Burg, *Chicago's White City of 1893* (Lexington: University of Kentucky Press, 1976); Reid Badger, *The Great American Fair: The World's Columbian Exposition and American Culture* (Chicago: Nelson Hall, 1979). See also Neil Harris, *Grand Illusions: Chicago's World's Fair of 1893* (Chicago: Chicago Historical Society, 1993); and Donald L. Miller, *City of the Century: The Epic of Chicago and the Making of America* (New York: Simon and Schuster, 1996).

24. Alan Trachtenberg, *The Incorporation of America: Culture and Society in the Gilded Age* (New York: Hill and Wang, 2007).

25. Rydell, *All the World's a Fair.*

26. James Gilbert, *Perfect Cities: Chicago's Utopias of 1893* (Chicago: University of Chicago Press, 1991).

Anarchist Women and the Feminine Ideal: Sex, Class, and Style in the Rhetoric of Voltairine de Cleyre, Emma Goldman, and Lucy Parsons

Linda Diane Horwitz, Donna Marie Kowal,
and Catherine Helen Palczewski

11

Voltairine de Cleyre, Emma Goldman, and Lucy Parsons struggled amid the shifting sociopolitical climate of the late nineteenth and early twentieth centuries as part of a collective of labor, free thought, and anarchist agitators. Although anarchism is, broadly speaking, a political philosophy that regards individual autonomy as the fundamental basis for society, different strands of anarchist thought embraced differing conceptualizations of the role of the individual in society. These include individualist, communist, and syndicalist anarchism,[1] which are represented by the views of de Cleyre,[2] Goldman,[3] and Parsons, respectively. While their distinctive anarchist philosophies often meant they were critical of each other's ideas, these women sometimes worked together for the greater cause of anarchism and, on occasion, shared platforms.

Voltairine de Cleyre was best known for her advocacy of tolerance within the anarchist community. According to her biographer, Paul Avrich, she advocated "cooperation among all who sought the removal of authority, regardless of their economic preferences."[4] She also was a poet, a repeat eulogist at Haymarket memorials,[5] and a prolific writer of essays and speeches, as even a cursory review of her *Selected Works* demonstrates.[6] Along with her general work on anarchism, de Cleyre is recognized as developing one of the first complete analyses of sexuality from what is now understood as a feminist perspective.[7] Historian Margaret Marsh describes de Cleyre's rhetoric as "the most complete articulation of the anarchist-feminist position to appear in the nineteenth century."[8]

Emma Goldman, the most prominent of the three, became famous because of her agitative speeches, which led to her arrest and deportation to Russia in 1919. Goldman is also perhaps the most remembered of the three women rhetors examined in this essay because she was "rediscovered in the 1960s by a generation of feminists who celebrated her defiance of traditional womanly behavior."[9] In addition to delivering speeches on anarchism, birth control, sexuality, marriage, atheism, conscription, and numerous other subjects across the United States and abroad, she published the monthly journal *Mother Earth*, an influential forum for the expression of radical ideas, and her own bound collection of lectures and writings, *Anarchism and Other Essays*.[10] Her notoriety as "Red Emma" enabled her to promote anarchism widely to both working- and middle-class audiences and to position herself a spokesperson for freedom of speech and thought. Goldman clearly is an "influential figure in U.S. intellectual and social history."[11]

Lucy Parsons is best remembered as the widow of Albert Parsons, a labor activist and one of the Haymarket martyrs.[12] However, Lucy was more than simply his widow, even though she repeatedly evoked that persona. Active in the labor and anarchist movements for seventy years, she was one of the initial founders of the Industrial Workers of the World (IWW). Despite the fact that she was "black, a woman, and working class—three reasons people are often excluded from history," she "was a recognized leader of the predominantly white male working class movement in Chicago long before" Haymarket.[13]

The complex relationships among de Cleyre, Goldman, and Parsons involved a sense of camaraderie as well as a clash of interests. All their paths crossed. Parsons and de Cleyre attended some of the same rallies and meetings.[14] De Cleyre delivered a speech in defense of Goldman on the occasion of one of her arrests.[15] Although Goldman looked upon de Cleyre primarily as a survivor of "physical disability,"[16] she also regarded her as "the great forerunner of the revolution that is to come to America."[17] Although de Cleyre differed with Goldman on philosophy, she wrote, "*the spirit which animates Emma Goldman is the only one which will emancipate the slave from his slavery, the tyrant from his tyranny—the spirit which is willing to dare and suffer.*"[18] Finally, de Cleyre, Goldman, and Parsons all recognized the trial and hanging of the Haymarket martyrs as a defining moment of the labor movement. Even though Parsons actively participated in the events leading up and responding to the trial, sentencing, executions, and pardons, de Cleyre and Goldman rarely acknowledged any of her contributions. In return, Parsons criticized Goldman's egotism.

Taking these three women as representative of feminist anarchism in all its complexity produces a more complete understanding of women's diverse rhetorical styles. As has been noted by Karlyn Kohrs Campbell in her germinal work on women's rhetoric, *Man Cannot Speak for Her*, gender expectations enabled and constrained the rhetorical options of the women advocating suffrage, leading them to develop a "feminine style."[19] Campbell writes that their "style emerged out of their experiences as women and was adapted to the attitudes and experiences of female audiences."[20] However, as recent work on intersectionality suggests, women do not have experiences purely as women, but instead as individuals of a particular race, class, nationality, and sexuality.[21] Thus, when studying the rhetoric of early women anarchists, one must remember that their styles, often distinct not only from the suffrage rhetors contemporary to them but also from each other, emerged out of their experiences as working-class women, as immigrant women, and, in Parsons's case, as a racially ambiguous woman. Further, their styles were adapted to the attitudes and experiences of their working-class audiences.

If anarchism in its diversity can be represented by a sample, these three provide an excellent one. Each espoused a different ideological form of anarchism. In terms of class and ethnicity, their diversity also is clear: de Cleyre came from the lower working class, Goldman was a Russian Jewish immigrant, and Parsons was, possibly, a woman of color. Each woman's approach to the roles of wife and mother represents a different perspective on the fulfillment of social expectations. Parsons and Goldman married,[22] while de Cleyre rejected all permanent dependent relationships. Parsons and de Cleyre both gave birth, but de Cleyre left the child with its father and paternal grandmother.[23] In addition, their overlapping periods of activism allow for a clearer comparison of their speeches. Finally, these three were the most prominent women anarchists of their time.[24]

As historian Margaret Marsh notes, these women were anarchist-feminists who "possess a significance that extends beyond anarchism" because their lives provide insight into how "a group of women responded to the social, sexual, and economic upheavals of the late nineteenth and early twentieth centuries."[25] These three were not women who happened to be anarchists, or anarchists who happened to be women. Instead, their anarchism and their sex/gender were closely intertwined and mutually influential. As Marsh explains, anarchism offered many women "a way out of the gender trap," in part because it undergirded the "extreme lengths to which they carried their repudiation of traditional views about the nature of womanhood."[26] Marsha Hewitt echoes the perceived emancipatory potential of anarchist-feminism in her argument that the fusion of anarchism and feminism draws attention to "the political nature of sex," and, in so doing, "forces us to re-think the nature of revolution as *process*, as transformative praxis of thought, feeling and collective social activity."[27] Indeed, for de Cleyre, Goldman, and Parsons, anarchist-feminism was not merely a philosophical standpoint but a state of mind and a way of acting in the world that placed responsibility on women as well as men to achieve self-determination.

To comprehend the distinctive stylistic and substantive features of de Cleyre's, Goldman's, and Parsons's rhetoric, one must consider how each adopted a rhetorical persona that fit her identity as a woman from the working class. De Cleyre's persona matched her ideological commitment to absolute liberty, including in the area of sexuality. Goldman's persona implicated her liminal citizenship status as a Russian Jewish immigrant. Finally, Parsons's persona bracketed her uncertain racial status by constant reference to her marital status. These women did not believe that "but for their sex" they could have been doctors, lawyers, senators, or captains of business. They knew that because of their sex, class, race, and ethnicity, they faced lives of struggle and, often, poverty. Yet they spoke—repeatedly, loudly, anywhere an audience would gather, even when they had to break down doors and face imprisonment to do so. Voltairine de Cleyre, Emma Goldman, and Lucy Parsons were anarchists and agitators, rhetors worthy of note.

To initiate our analysis of the rhetoric of these three anarchist women, we consider the historical period from which they emerged and to which they responded, followed by a closer look at the individual life of each rhetor. We then provide the theoretical groundwork for our argument regarding the role of identity in rhetorical invention and engage in a critical analysis of de Cleyre, Goldman, and Parsons to illustrate the need for recognizing the ways women speakers rhetorically negotiated and enacted their complex identity positions. Finally, we close with a discussion of the diversity of women's rhetorical styles and its implications for the study of women's public address.

Anarchist Feminism in Time

The oppression of women in the United States during the late nineteenth and early twentieth centuries stemmed from and was maintained through legal, economic, social, political, and religious discourses and practices. The lack of the right to vote limited women's ability to influence policies that affected them; in many states women could not manage their property, control their earnings, or enter into business contracts. Eastern states were especially slow to make changes

ANARCHIST WOMEN AND FEMININE IDEAL: SEX, CLASS, AND STYLE IN THE RHETORIC OF VOLTAIRINE DE CLEYRE, EMMA GOLDMAN, AND LUCY PARSONS

311

in women's legal status, possibly because religious conceptions of women's inferiority prevailed there.[28]

In addition to restrictions on women's participation in the public sphere, social norms circumscribed women's ideal activities in and to the private sphere. Expectations of domestic life and religious mores relegated American women to the sphere of the home, where they were expected to practice the virtues of cooperation, piety, and submissiveness.[29] However, only economically privileged women had the luxury of the time and energy to pursue these ideals. Less economically privileged women were compelled to work outside the home to survive. In other words, because of their economic status, many women could not fulfill the social expectations of "true womanhood."[30] They worked in mills, factories, and various manufacturing jobs. As a result, femininity within the working class had been undergoing redefinition since the 1800s, when women who worked outside the home had to redefine the boundaries of public and private to do so.[31] Only at the end of the nineteenth century, when the clerical field opened, did new possibilities emerge for middle-class women in the workforce.[32]

Because of their limited legal status, immigrants, African Americans, women, and children were the least protected members of the workforce.[33] For working-class, minority, and immigrant women, all of whom were more likely to be employed than middle-class women, poverty rather than the denial of voting rights was the most significant form of oppression.[34] With industry unregulated, social and political influence was concentrated in the hands of wealthy business owners who took advantage of the cheap labor acquired through the exploitation of these groups. For example, working conditions for women in the U.S. textile industry parallel the typical contemporary "sweat shop" with a ten- to twelve-hour workday and wages amounting to about half of men's.[35] Living conditions for the working class were wretched, with widespread overcrowding and often abject poverty. To some extent, the exploitation of the rising immigrant population during the early 1900s was a response to their impressive numbers, crowded living spaces, and perceived vulnerability to big bosses. Finally, the public as a whole questioned the societal value and constitutional rights of racial and ethnic minorities.[36]

In response to the harsh conditions of factory work and working-class living, labor reform became important to women's liberation struggles, with many women joining unions and engaging in strikes. As detailed later, de Cleyre, Goldman, and Parsons each identified with the struggles of the working class. Working-class women like them were more likely to participate in radical movements than middle-class women because, as Glenna Matthews argues, "unruly" and "disorderly" working-class women were "less bound by decorous norms of appropriate female behavior."[37] In other words, their working-class position created possibilities for rhetorical activities that were notably different from middle- and upper-class women, who were more likely to participate in reform efforts like the woman suffrage movement.[38] However, de Cleyre, Goldman, and Parsons faced rhetorical constraints different from suffragists not only because of their respective class, ethnic, and racial identities but also because of society's rejection of their radical viewpoints.

Several events resulted in the public's fear of anarchists and labor agitators in the United States. The bombing of Chicago's Haymarket Square during a labor demonstration on 4 May 1886 raised public fears. Although the culprit was never identified, eight anarchists were convicted, seven of whom were immigrants. Four of the men were executed by hanging, including Parsons's husband, Albert.[39] The injustice of the arrests and convictions of the anarchists served as a wake-up call to radicals but concomitantly heightened the public's fear of them.

A second important event was the assassination of President William McKinley in 1901 by Leon Czolgosz, who identified himself as an anarchist inspired by Goldman, although he had no prior involvement with the anarchist movement or with

Goldman.[40] According to Robert K. Murray, a number of violent incidents, such as bombings, were blamed on anarchists, even though many of these accusations were unfounded and generated by media hype.[41] International events such as the Bolshevik Revolution of 1917 and 1919 that influenced parts of Europe, and the domestic establishment of two Communist parties in the United States, further exacerbated fear of radicals.[42] The Espionage Act of 1917 and the Sedition Act of 1918 repressed antigovernment speech, especially against the war. The Department of Justice embarked on a campaign to rid the country of radicals, particularly those who were foreign born. Official as well as unofficial harassment, intimidation, and arrest of dissenters were commonplace in 1919 and 1920. In this political climate, anarchist women who advocated the abolition of all institutions of power and who violated norms of "true womanhood" by speaking openly about sex were certainly looked upon with intense suspicion, not just curiosity.

Clearly, the arrival of the twentieth century was a critical time as women negotiated, in response to changing possibilities for participation in the workforce and in the polity, what it was to be a "public woman." Likewise, the era was a time when immigrants, racial and ethnic minorities, and the poor organized and spoke out against worker exploitation, even in the face of state-sanctioned repression of dissenting speech. The anarchist lifestyles charted by de Cleyre, Goldman, and Parsons emerged from and reacted to this unsettled sociopolitical climate.

The Lives of Three Anarchist-Feminists

VOLTAIRINE DE CLEYRE

Voltairine de Cleyre was born on 17 November 1866 in Leslie, Michigan, the daughter of Hector De Claire, a tailor, and Harriet Elizabeth Billings, a seamstress. Throughout her life, she worked as a teacher and anarchist lecturer and writer. Despite being raised in poverty, de Cleyre received formal schooling in a Catholic convent until the age of seventeen. Her experience in the convent influenced her turn to free thought and anarchism. In her speech "The Making of an Anarchist," she noted that "there are white scars on my soul yet" as a result of the convent life.[43]

In 1886 de Cleyre moved to Grand Rapids, Michigan, where she began her association with the free thought movement, a group that challenged the power of religious authority over human reason on matters of religious belief. While in Grand Rapids, she published her first essays and stories under the pseudonym Fanny Fern in the *Progressive Age*, a small free thought weekly.[44] She soon became its editor, a position she filled until she moved to Philadelphia in 1889. During her time in Philadelphia, from 1889 to 1910, de Cleyre increased her activism with the anarchist movement, began teaching English to Jewish immigrants (1891), and met Emma Goldman (1893). Also during this time, de Cleyre made her first suicide attempt after a particularly vicious fight with one of her lovers.

With Philadelphia as her home base, de Cleyre traveled to Britain and France in 1897, where she met Peter Kropotkin, Louise Michel, and Max Nettlau, among others. In 1903 she journeyed to Norway and Britain. This travel and work took their toll on both her mental and physical health. After extended stays in the hospital during 1904, she made a second suicide attempt in 1905. Emma Goldman's founding of *Mother Earth* in 1906 raised de Cleyre's spirit. She became a frequent contributor and met Alexander Berkman, with whom she had been corresponding since 1893.

Although originally driven to the free thought movement by her convent experience, she eventually embraced anarchism, motivated by four interlocking factors: the injustice of the Haymarket trial, her recognition of the plight of workers, her resistance to state interference in private affairs, and her rejection of women's traditional roles. De Cleyre referred to the Haymarket trial as "the specific occasion which ripened tendencies to definition."[45]

However, the Haymarket injustice alone did not transform de Cleyre into an anarchist. In "Why I Am an Anarchist," first delivered in 1897, de Cleyre described her conversion as growing from

> disgust with the subordinated cramped circle prescribed for women in daily life. . . . A sense of burning disgust that a mere legal form should be considered as the sanction for all manner of bestialities. . . . That in spite of all the hardship and torture of existence men and women should go on obeying the old Isra-elitish command; "Increase and multiply," merely because they have society's permission to do so, without regard to the slaveries to be inflicted upon the unfortunate creatures of their passions.[46]

De Cleyre functioned as "the leading apostle of tolerance within the anarchist movement, pleading for cooperation among all who sought the removal of authority, regardless of their economic preferences."[47] Her anarchism was without adjectives, rooted in the individual potential of each human being. This philosophy was best laid out in "Anarchism and American Traditions," which she delivered throughout 1909 and 1910.

De Cleyre's primary lesson of social protest is clear in her call to action: "The first act of our life was to kick against an unjust decree of our parents, and we have unflinchingly stood for the kicking principle ever since. Now, if the word kicking is in bad repute with you, substitute non-submission, insubordination, rebellion, revolution, whatever name you please which expresses non-acquiescence to injustice."[48] De Cleyre's anarchism led her to spend her life "making rebels wherever we can. By ourselves *living our beliefs*. . . . We are revolutionists. And we shall use propaganda by speech, deed, and most of all, life—*being* what we teach."[49] She lived among and taught immigrant laborers in Philadelphia and Chicago, lectured for anarchism and free thought, and never became dependent, emotionally or financially, on another person. Although her teaching fees were low, she never lived with any of her male companions, including James B. Elliot, Dyer D. Lum, T. Hamilton Garside, and Samuel Gordon.

In a particularly telling test of her convictions, she refused to press charges against a would-be assassin. While waiting for a streetcar on 19 December 1902, she was shot by a former student named Herman Helcher. She did not take legal action, arguing that the legal system would treat her attacker, whom she believed to be mentally ill, inappropriately. Instead, she initiated a fund-raising campaign to defray his legal expenses. Finally, when she bore a child (named Vermorel Elliot by de Cleyre, who later changed his name to Harry de Cleyre), she refused to care for him and instead left him in the care of his father, James B. Elliot, and his paternal grandmother.

Chronic sinus infections, which progressed to her middle ear and brain, coupled with psychological depression and the assassin's bullets that were never removed from her body, always made work, writing, and lecturing difficult and, sometimes, impossible. Yet despite her physical and financial constraints, de Cleyre was an active lecturer. Her speeches demonstrate a keen understanding of the range of oppressions faced by U.S. industrial workers and women.

Given the obstacles she faced, de Cleyre's extraordinary impact on her contemporaries was astounding. George Brown, the most popular anarchist orator in Philadelphia, wrote: "To me, she was the most intellectual woman I ever met. . . . She spent her tortured life in the service of an obscure cause. Had she done the same work in some popular cause, she would have been famous and the world would have acclaimed her . . . the greatest woman America ever produced."[50] Emma Goldman proclaimed her "one of America's great anarchists."[51] In 1910, after lecturing in New York, Ohio, and Michigan, de Cleyre resettled in Chicago, where she died two years later, on 20 June 1912. She is buried at Waldheim Cemetery in Chicago.

EMMA GOLDMAN

Emma Goldman was born in Kuana, Lithuania, in 1869, one of three daughters and two sons in a poor Jewish family. In many ways, argues historian Naomi Shepherd, Goldman's upbringing represented the negative side of the Russian Jewish tradition, particularly the dominion of the father over the family, the pressure to succumb to an arranged marriage, and the compulsion to bear children. The social contract for women under rabbinical law required women to enact the virtues of devotion to the home and husband, self-sacrifice, and sexual morality.[52] In her autobiography, *Living My Life*, Goldman describes the marriage of her parents as a loveless arrangement in accordance with Orthodox tradition, with her father dominating the household. She depicts her childhood as a nightmare because of her physically and verbally abusive father.[53]

Goldman's upbringing under a Russian Jewish cultural tradition influenced her public advocacy, including the emphasis she placed on intellectual pursuit. As Shepherd notes, although development of the intellect was a masculine gender role, Jewish women radicals identified with intellectual pursuit as a means of rejecting the subservient qualities of their mothers.[54] Goldman's respect for intellectual activity is clear in her contempt for middle-class "intellectual proletarians" who suffered from the repression of ideas in a capitalist economic system, in contrast to her compassion for manual laborers who were degraded by their class.[55] Goldman's commitment to reason and rational discourse is apparent in her tendency to use evidence from literary writers and modern philosophers to support her arguments; for her, anarchism was a political philosophy that "urges man to think, to investigate, to analyze every proposition."[56]

Goldman immigrated to the United States in 1886 at the age of seventeen in an attempt to flee what she saw as a restrictive and tragic life. Before she discovered anarchism soon after her arrival in Rochester, New York, the young Goldman married fellow Russian immigrant Jacob Kersner in accordance with Jewish custom. The marriage was a short-lived, unsatisfying experience, largely because of her husband's impotence.[57] Later, as an anarchist, Goldman denounced the institution of marriage as an "economic arrangement" that condemned women to "life-long dependency, to parasitism, to complete uselessness, individual as well as social."[58] However, in 1926, seven years after her deportation, Goldman married for a second time, to secure the protection of British citizenship. With her marriage, Goldman, "masquerading under the name Colton," could travel to Toronto, Canada, to be closer to her American comrades.[59]

Although Goldman's firsthand experience with the exploitation of immigrant workers served as a point of departure for her political activism, she, like de Cleyre and Parsons, attributed the awakening of her political consciousness to Haymarket. She viewed the "heroic deaths" of the anarchist men, seven of whom were also immigrants, as martyrs for "a great ideal."[60] The speeches of Johann Most, a prominent anarchist and editor of a German anarchist paper, about the Haymarket men, moved Goldman deeply. Impressed by Goldman's vivid personality, Most offered to train her as a public speaker. In response, Goldman moved to the Lower East Side of New York City in 1889 and entered the social circle of the anarchist and labor movement members as well as bohemian literary types. She delivered her early speeches in Yiddish, Russian, and German primarily to immigrant workers in New York City.[61]

During her first year in New York City, Goldman met anarchist comrade Alexander Berkman, with whom she had a long, tumultuous love affair before settling into a lifelong friendship.[62] In 1892, in the aftermath of the Homestead Steel Strike, Goldman participated in a failed effort to assassinate Henry Clay Frick by securing money and a gun for Berkman's use. Although Berkman was convicted and imprisoned for the assassination attempt, Goldman was neither arrested nor asked to serve as a witness in his trial. According to Marsh, Goldman's participation in the conspiracy to assassinate Frick was not clear until almost forty years later when she revealed it in her autobiography.[63] In 1901 Goldman was arrested and placed on trial for inspiring Leon Czolgosz in the assassination of President McKinley simply because he referred to her in his trial confession, even though she had no connection to him. She was later released from prison for lack of supporting evidence.[64] Goldman was arrested and imprisoned on several other occasions, including in 1893 for inciting to riot, in 1915–16 for lecturing and distributing information about birth control, and in 1917 for advocating against conscription.[65]

Despite repeated jail stints, from 1897 to 1899 Goldman crossed the United States on lecture tours. For over a decade beginning in 1906, she also published and wrote for her anarchist journal, *Mother Earth*. She used her public speeches and essays as a platform to encourage resistance against all forms of legal, moral, social, and economic oppression, especially those that contributed to inequality between the sexes. Combining anarchism and feminism, Goldman treated women's liberation as inseparable from the larger cause of human liberation. She considered the primary connection between women's liberation and human liberation to lie in the centrality of sexual freedom in the emancipation of human thought and action. She argued in "Marriage and Love" (1917) that sexual freedom entails not simply the practice of free love, free motherhood, and the dissolution of the institution of marriage, but also the enactment of a fundamental individual liberty, freedom of thought and expression. "The institution of marriage makes a parasite of woman, an absolute dependent," said Goldman, because "[i]t incapacitates her for life's struggle, annihilates her social consciousness, paralyzes her imagination, and then imposes its gracious protection, which in reality is a snare, a travesty on human character."[66]

Another formative influence on Goldman was her experience as an immigrant in the United States. Goldman encountered a new set of oppressive conditions working in the garment district of Rochester, New York, as a female immigrant laborer.[67] Living and working conditions were especially deplorable for immigrants like Goldman; these issues were recurring topics she addressed in her speeches and writings. She advocated solidarity among all workers and the use of "direct action, open defiance of, and resistance to, all laws and restrictions" as the means of achieving liberation.[68]

At times, Goldman used her speaking abilities and notoriety to support other groups that advocated freedom of thought and expression. She was influential in establishing the National Civil Liberties Bureau, which later became the American Civil Liberties Union.[69] From 1909 to 1912, she participated in a series of public debates in San Diego, California, regarding freedom of speech when authorities attempted to prevent IWW members from holding open public meetings. In response, Goldman was physically beaten, tarred, and feathered by IWW opponents.[70] Her public advocacy was frequently met with opposition from the mainstream public. The press typically depicted her as a public nuisance and danger to society.[71]

Goldman's immigrant status was a factor in her record of arrests and ultimately led to her deportation in 1919 under the Sedition Act amid the political climate of the Red Scare, the hysteria that targeted radicals whose beliefs and activities allegedly threatened the security of the United States. According to Robert K. Murray, official inquiries regarding Goldman's deportation began as early as 1907.[72] In 1917 she and Alexander Berkman formed the No-Conscription League and spoke out in opposition to the draft. Both were arrested and deported to Russia.

Goldman's deportation in 1919 did not put an end to her activist career. Disappointed by the outcome of the Bolshevik Revolution in Russia because it replaced one tyranny with another, she remained politically active in Europe and Canada for many years. Returning to the United States for a lecture tour in 1934, she delivered speeches reflecting on her life as an anarchist. Her final, most noteworthy achievement was serving as a spokesperson for the anarchist revolution in Spain from 1936 to 1939.[73]

Goldman died from a stroke in 1940 at the age of seventy in Toronto, Canada. Her body was transported to the United States, where she was buried along with de Cleyre and the Haymarket martyrs in Chicago's Waldheim Cemetery.

LUCY PARSONS

Lucy Parsons was probably born in 1853 in north-central Texas, although the exact date and her precise parentage remain unknown. Her ancestry was arguably part African American, although she consistently claimed to be American Indian and Spanish, probably so that she and her white husband, Albert Parsons, would escape miscegenation laws.[74] Adding to this confusion is the fact that Lucy Parsons used a range of different birth names on documents, only eventually settling on Gonzales.

After meeting Albert Parsons in the 1870s, the two lived as man and wife, although whether an "official" marriage ever took place is uncertain. Miscegenation laws may have prevented their marriage in Texas; no documents exist to verify that a marriage eventually took place once they moved to Chicago in 1873. From 1877 to 1882, they lived in a poor working-class German neighborhood, where Lucy was exposed to unemployment, deplorable working conditions, and protesting workers. Working as a printer, Albert joined a union. After hearing a lecturer from the Social Democratic Party of North America, he joined the party and became one of its spokespersons. Thus Lucy Parsons began her activism as a socialist rather than an anarchist when she and her husband became increasingly involved in union activities.

Eventually, as a result of his activism, Albert lost his job, and Lucy supported the family by working as a seamstress. By early 1879 Albert was editing the *Socialist*; Lucy, pregnant with their first child, was writing for the *Socialist* and speaking for the Working Women's Union. When the Knights of Labor first opened their doors to women in 1881, Lucy Parsons and Mary Harris "Mother" Jones were among the first to join. They were also the only two female founding members of the IWW in 1905.[75]

Lucy Parsons's anarchism emerged at the same time that anarchism first appeared in the United States, with the arrival of Johann Most in 1883 and the International Working People's Association's drafting of the Pittsburgh Manifesto on 14 October 1883.[76] As an anarchist, she gave speeches across the nation and Europe and edited newspapers, including *Freedom* and the *Liberator*. She also contributed articles to other publications throughout the states. In 1884 the International Working People's Association published the newspaper the *Alarm*. Albert Parsons was the editor, and the first issue's front page carried Lucy Parsons's article "To the Tramps," which ended with her famous line *"Learn the use of explosives!"* By 1885 Lucy Parsons was active in organizing seamstresses to demand an eight-hour workday.

Strikes and protests intensified in 1886, culminating on 4 May when an unknown assailant threw a bomb in Haymarket Square. Although Lucy and Albert were walking away from the crowd when the bomb was thrown and the police responded with gunfire, Albert was arrested with seven other men, who became known in anarchist circles as the "Haymarket martyrs," and convicted of inciting violence.

Lucy was an active speaker for the worker's movement before the Haymarket riot; her new exigence for speaking was Albert's incarceration and imposed silence. She believed that the system had imprisoned her husband and his comrades to stop the anarchist movement. Her duty, both to her husband and to the movement, was to maintain the anarchist agitation. Accordingly, Lucy resumed where her husband left off. Her goal was to motivate individuals to dedicate themselves to the anarchist cause. Speaking as the "Haymarket widow," she attained a new status and visibility in the movement.

During her sixty years as an activist, Parsons spoke, and was denied the right to speak, throughout the United States and England. Whenever her speeches were deemed newsworthy, the press reported her powerful words, her gender, and her race and/or ethnicity, but not always in that order. A typical newspaper report on Parsons was printed on 21 November 1887:

> Mrs. Parsons is a well-built young woman, apparently thirty-five years old. Her face is broad, [her] forehead low and head concealed beneath a wealth of fluffy, silken black hair. Her complexion is of a dull copperish color, and her skin is smooth and soft. She looks more like a low-country Mexican woman than a Negress, although in some respects she resembles the latter, her eyes being big, her lips full and thick and her speech soft and low, with now and then a touch of the Negro patois. Her knowledge of English is excellent, while she also talks Spanish. She is an Anarchist of the most rabid kind and declares that all political government is necessarily despotic.[77]

Although Parsons's rhetoric covered a range of subjects, her belief in the principles outlined in the Pittsburgh Manifesto never wavered.[78] The manifesto ended with six succinct goals:

> First—Destruction of the existing class rule, by all means—i.e. by energetic, relentless, revolutionary and international action.
> Second—Establishment of free society based upon co-operative organization of production.
> Third—Free exchange of equivalent products by and between the productive organizations without commerce and profit-mongery.
> Fourth—Organization of education on a secular, scientific and equal bases for both sexes.
> Fifth—Equal rights for all without distinction to sex or race.
> Sixth—Regulation of all public affairs by free contracts between autonomous (independent) Communes and associations, resting on a federalistic basis.[79]

Parsons's belief in these principles remained constant even as she helped found the IWW and while she worked with the Communists in the late 1930s and early 1940s. They guided her work as she edited anarchist newspapers such as *Freedom* and the *Liberator*, contributed articles to newspapers throughout the States, and delivered speeches across the nation and Europe.

She also commented on a number of specific issues, responding to the "woman question" in articles appearing in the journals *Freedom* (1892), *Firebrand* (1895),[80] and *Free Society* (1896). However, her most powerful speeches were those about the Haymarket martyrs, delivered as part of a tour that took place while Albert and the rest of the Haymarket martyrs were awaiting execution. Ultimately, Parsons worked with a variety of activist groups and "did not consider herself a representative of any organization, but the representative of the most oppressed of humanity, child laborers and prostitutes."[81] Along with de Cleyre and Goldman, Lucy Parsons is buried at Waldheim Cemetery in Chicago.

Performances of Anarchist Womanhood

Thus far, we have described the social and political contexts in which de Cleyre, Goldman, and Parsons emerged as anarchist activists and how these contexts influenced their distinct life histories. We are constantly cognizant that gender is not something determined by sex, but instead, as Judith Butler notes, is "performatively produced and compelled by the regulatory practices of gender coherence."[82] De Cleyre, Goldman, and Parsons performed differing conceptions of womanhood, all of which are gendered, but not necessarily in the same way. Thus they individually and collectively offer a way to identify where "gaps and fissures" emerge in the social inscriptions of gender.[83] If gender is understood as "the activity of managing situated conduct in light of normative conceptions of attitudes and activities appropriate for one's sex category,"[84] each woman's activities managed normative sex expectations in distinct ways. Basically, the three women share a sex, and were sex categorized in the same way, but their genders were distinct from each other and from privileged women. Voltairine de Cleyre saw herself as a poet and philosopher who could engage in lyrical elegance as well as in "cold, calculating" reason. Emma Goldman saw herself as an agitator whose primary goal was to awaken the masses to the necessity for anarchism. Lucy Parsons used her role as a widow to fellow anarchist and husband Albert Parsons as a point of departure for her activism. Each used stylistic elements uniquely her own, elements that were consistent with each woman's own conception of anarchism.

Despite their distinct personae, however, some commonalities exist. In particular, all three women grounded their appeals on the common experiences of the working class, rather than the common experiences of women. Each was willing to appeal to and act as an authority. For de Cleyre and Goldman, authority is expressed through their abstract and analytical approach to anarchism; absent are any references to their personal struggles or experiences. However, although de Cleyre's authoritative tone is guided by cool intellect, Goldman displays emotional arousal in her intense agitational speeches. The tone of Parsons's rhetoric is both authoritative and personal; she speaks directly, using self references extensively. This use of authority also led to deductive or direct refutation structures and quite confrontative speeches. The audience members were addressed not as social peers, but as political colleagues in the struggle, colleagues who would participate by engaging in collective action; in the collectivity, listeners could find power.

Anarchist women faced rhetorical constraints and opportunities as women, but they also confronted constraints and opportunities as anarchists. Thus they did not evolve a rhetorical style that could be considered conventionally feminine. These anarchist women used some elements of feminine style, but their rhetoric cannot be explained completely or accurately by the dimensions of the feminine style. Substantively, anarchist women acknowledged, as did suffrage advocates, that women were constrained by the lack of a ballot. However, anarchist women also recognized that the ballot would do little to alleviate the social, economic, and political ills women faced since it had done so little to help men. They sought other ways to exert political power. Stylistically, they had to develop strategies to gain audiences' attention not because they were women, but because they were anarchists and agitators. Their freedom to speak was restricted less by informal social constraints and far more by the formal legal restraints imposed by the Comstock Act, the Sedition Act, and other similar laws.

ANARCHIST WOMEN AND FEMININE IDEAL: SEX, CLASS, AND STYLE IN THE RHETORIC OF VOLTAIRINE DE CLEYRE, EMMA GOLDMAN, AND LUCY PARSONS

319

As the growing body of literature on intersectionality demonstrates, the very way women are women is influenced by a woman's race, class, education level, and nationality. Simply put, scholars argue that identity is multiplicative rather than additive.[85] One way to understand identity is as adding one element on top of another: woman + white + heterosexual + second-generation citizen. However, intersectionality theory suggests that identity makes more sense if one thinks of each identity element as inextricably linked with another: woman × white × heterosexual × second-generation citizen. All facets of identity are integral, interlocking parts of a whole. What it means to be black or white is influenced by being a woman, is influenced by one's class, is influenced by one's sexuality, and so forth. As Joan Wallach Scott explains, "Gender becomes so implicated in concepts of class that there is no way to analyze one without the other. One cannot analyze politics separately from gender, sexuality, the family. These are not compartments of life but discursively related systems; language makes possible the study of their interrelationships."[86] In other words, one cannot understand what it means to be a woman unless one understands what it means to be a woman of a class, of a race, of a religion, of an ethnicity, of a physical ability, of a sexual orientation. Although developed primarily to explain the intersections of Black women's identity, the concept can be used to explain any person's identity.

Our analysis demonstrates that these women clearly violated one model of femininity, but in so doing, created alternative models that were grounded in their political philosophies and in their class, sex, nationality, and race status. Theirs was not a feminine-anarchist style in which anarchism was moderated with a feminine style. Instead, it was an anarcho-feminist style in which their being feminine was reconstituted through their anarchism. Their rhetoric deserves attention because it can demonstrate how gender and its performances affect and are affected by the class, race, and sexuality of the speaker and of her or his audience.

Writing about how one can historicize discourse and experience, Kathleen Canning notes that subjects with agency can emerge within a "contested and fractured discursive domain" where agency can be viewed as a "site of mediation."[87] Class, throughout the nineteenth century, had been fracturing and contesting the discursive domain of gender; gender itself had become a fractured and contested domain.[88] Much as Canning claims that "female activists mobilized and recast their embodied experiences within the discursive fields of Weimar body politics,"[89] we argue de Cleyre, Goldman, and Parsons mobilized and recast their embodied experiences within the discursive fields of anarchist and working-class body politics. De Cleyre offered an interpretation of womanhood that was not dependent on motherhood, wifehood, or economic dependence; her model was overtly sexual. Goldman offered an interpretation of womanhood that recognized both biological and social forces. So, for example, she embraced motherhood (although a medical condition prohibited her bearing children) while rejecting compulsory motherhood.[90] Parsons's interpretation linked woman to her status as wife regardless of race, but also saw space for expanded activity in the economic and public realms.

All three women, through their unique interpretations, also subverted gender constraints, especially as gender was constrained through race, class, ethnicity, and sexuality. De Cleyre challenged gender expectations by using a logical, direct refutational style in much of her rhetoric. She also challenged gender norms by attacking marriage, motherhood, and prudishness concerning sexuality. Goldman's aggressive agitational style, ethnicity, and public sexuality challenged conventional conceptions of what a public woman was to be. Parsons subverted gender roles by appealing to them as she overtly played the role of the widow of a white man, challenging racist assumptions about miscegenation. Through the repeated evocations of her widowhood, she both highlighted her arguably illegal marriage and enabled herself to speak as a widow.

Finally, despite their individual expansion of gender roles, all three women internalized traditional roles. De Cleyre had a series of relationships with men, many which moved perilously close to the dependency she despised. Goldman constantly sought an ideal relationship. In playing the dutiful widow, Parsons enacted one role traditionally ascribed to women, although one sometimes not open to a woman of color.

Recognizing how individuals interpret, subvert, and internalize gender enables us to recognize Judith Butler's contributions concerning the inscription of gender while also allowing us to talk about the ways in which these women acted as agents, transforming themselves and the world around them. De Cleyre, Goldman, and Parsons negotiated the same constraints faced by privileged women, but they were aware that they not only were constrained by gender but also by race, class, ethnicity, and sexuality. They had to negotiate between who society dictated they were and what they wanted society to be. Their ideals enabled the inherent contesting and fracturing of gender, contesting and fracturing intensified by their status as working-class women and, in Parsons's case, as a woman of color.

This need to negotiate also explains the contradictions often found in all three women as they responded to the contradictory circumstances of a society in flux. As poor women, they had to work, yet feminine ideals said they should be domestic. As agitators, they had to act publicly, even as feminine ideals dictated they should be submissive. As anarchists, they critiqued established religion, even as feminine ideals said they should be pious. And they were sexual creatures in ways society condemned: de Cleyre refused to marry, Goldman spoke openly about her numerous lovers, and, at least in the eyes of some, Parsons engaged in miscegenation. Yet societal norms of femininity mandated that they should be pure.[91]

The need to negotiate between what was, what society expected, and what they thought the world should be explains the apparent contradictions produced by these women. Each woman at one time or another made contradictory statements or acted in a way that contradicted her statements. While one might condemn de Cleyre, Goldman, and Parsons for hypocrisy, we would rather speak of their need to negotiate an inherently contradictory world. Instead of condemning de Cleyre for engaging in a series of self-destructive relationships while she argued for women's nondependence, one should be attentive to the clash of individual ideals and social expectations in the midst of which she lived her life. Instead of condemning Goldman for rejecting compulsory motherhood as a benchmark for achieving womanhood when she also claimed all women possess the "mother instinct,"[92] one should be attentive to how this dance between positions enabled her to respect motherhood while critiquing its compulsory or institutionalized dimensions. Instead of condemning Parsons for playing the role of widow and for relegating women to the role of wife and mother when she was an independent agitator in her own right, one should be attentive to the unique demands her race placed upon her as a public rhetor. In what follows, we explore how de Cleyre, Goldman, and Parsons rhetorically negotiated and enacted their differing conceptions of womanhood.

VOLTAIRINE DE CLEYRE: A POET-PHILOSOPHER'S "ARTICULATE STORM"

From 1887 until her death on 20 June 1912, Voltairine de Cleyre lectured and wrote for and about the anarchist and free thought movements. Not as prominent as Emma Goldman, de Cleyre was nonetheless a powerful force. Although de Cleyre primarily was known for her writings, her biographer argues that it was as a speaker she "first made her mark in the radical movement, though she was not of the flamboyant, histrionic school of orators who overwhelm their audiences with tirades of venom or irony and capture them by main force."[93] In clear contrast to Emma Goldman, de Cleyre considered herself more of a lecturer than an orator. As their friend Carl Nold described their speaking styles, de Cleyre attracted her listeners with a violin, while Goldman used a base drum.[94] De Cleyre perceived her own style as "cold, calculated" in contrast to Goldman's "tongue of fire." That description may refer more to delivery style than content, however, because this comparison is preceded by three pages of fiery rhetoric in which she described the rich as "blood drinkers, tearers of human flesh, gnawers of human bones."[95]

Stylistically, de Cleyre combined the lyricism developed in her poetry with her exceptional reasoning and argumentation skills.[96] Having a deep appreciation of the power of language, she often decried those who took it for granted. She urged people to train themselves "to feel and hear the music of language . . . out of which come great organ tones, and trumpet calls, and thin flute notes, sweeping and wailing, an articulate storm—a conjuring key whereby all the passions of the dead, the millions of the dead, have given to the living the power to call their ghosts out of the grave and make them walk."[97]

This love of language led to a public performance style for de Cleyre that gave the impression of a professor or philosopher speaking. Avrich quotes Sadakichi Hartmann, who attended de Cleyre's lecture on Mary Wollstonecraft delivered at the Manhattan Liberal Club in 1894: "The even delivery, the subdued enthusiasm of her voice, the abundance of information, thought and argument, and the logical sequence of the same made a deep impression on me."[98] As Margaret Marsh notes in her study of anarchist women, "De Cleyre possessed one of the best minds among the American anarchists, and her essays, particularly in the early twentieth century, were sophisticated and subtle."[99]

Others also recognized her reasoning skills and the emotional reserve characteristic of her delivery. Joseph Kutera wrote of de Cleyre that it was "her logical, analytical mind that helped her to win an argument."[100] The *Detroit News-Tribune* described her: "Her appearance denotes refinement and culture, and in her lectures and public appearances there is nothing blatant or vulgar."[101] Yet only a month earlier her speeches were described as "sung in wild, weird verse, gospel of revenge and blood."[102] An article by S. E. Parker published in *Freedom* offers a way to reconcile de Cleyre's argumentative skill with her intense literary style: "At times her words seem to develop a white heat, and the reader is swept along by the force of her arguments."[103] She marshaled this articulate storm of "white heat" to advance her arguments for liberty in a rhetorical style marked by an intellectual aggressiveness that manifested itself in her use of direct refutation of named opponents, her systematic reasoning, and her use of dissociation. These stylistic elements were used to confront the main substance of her speeches: the capitalist system's oppression of women and workers.

Direct Refutation. De Cleyre was more than willing to directly identify points of disagreement, even with allies. For example, she articulated her own position, and distinguished herself from Goldman, in her December 1893 speech, "In Defense of Emma Goldman":

> Miss Goldman is a Communist; I am an Individualist. She wishes to destroy the right of property; I wish to assert it. I make my war upon privilege and authority, whereby the right of property, the true right in that which is proper to the individual, is annihilated. She believes that co-operation would entirely supplant competition; I hold that competition in one form or another will always exist, and that it is highly desirable it should.[104]

In typical fashion, de Cleyre was willing to detail points of disagreement as she systematically laid out her own position.

This precision of refutation led her to speak from carefully prepared texts. Given the literary and argumentative precision with which she constructed her speeches, de Cleyre eschewed extemporaneous speaking,[105] although she was willing to use that style on occasion.[106] Especially as restrictions on anarchist speakers became the norm, she turned to the delivery of transcribed speeches to protect herself from police harassment. The beginning of "On Liberty," delivered on 30 June 1909 as part of the Cooper Union Protest Meeting, explains her reliance on written texts and also typifies her argument style:

> I am in the habit of writing out what I have to say in advance: the reasons are several, but the principal one governing me in the present instance is, that I am speaking not only to the people here, but before a censorship so ignorant that it can neither understand nor correctly report what it does not understand; and in the event of my being called to account for what I did not say, I wish to be able to show in writing precisely what I did say. And in the event of my being pulled off the platform by the police before I have opened my mouth (as has happened to me before now), I may be able to say, "Here is what I would have said."[107]

De Cleyre explicitly stated her reasons and was willing to confront those with whom she disagreed. In fact, she always was willing to challenge the police. In her 1895 speech to the Ladies' Liberal League, in which she detailed the diverse topics and speakers heard by the league, she commented: "We will do our best to make these important issues interesting and instructive to the detectives and police of Philadelphia, and we sincerely hope that they may eventually be able to learn something." In her celebration of the Ladies' Liberal League, she also explicitly addressed the arguments presented by other lecturers to the group, such as Prof. E. D. Cope and Ralph Raleigh, dismissing them as men who only pretended to be a "friend of woman."[108]

De Cleyre's intellectually direct, precise style was honed to a cutting edge by her rapier wit. In one telling incident, after outlining her arguments against marriage, she declared: "Now my opponents know where to find me."[109] Further marking her as a distinctive anarchist-feminist voice, the maximization of freedom for women was found in de Cleyre's advocacy of economic independence for women coupled with a rejection of any "permanent dependent relationship" between men and women, her refusal to accept motherhood as definitive of womanhood, and her advocacy of sexual freedom.[110]

The most explicit example of de Cleyre's use of direct refutation is "They Who Marry Do Ill." She delivered this lecture on 28 April 1907 in response to Dr. Henrietta P. Westbrook's "They Who Marry Do Well." De Cleyre's use of direct refutation began with a definition of terms. The speech clearly articulated distinctions between what is commonly understood as marriage and what is necessarily a part of it. She uncoupled love from economic dependence, sexuality from procreation, and procreation from womanhood. Ultimately, she sought to prove that marriage, defined as "the permanent relation of a man and a woman, sexual and economical, whereby the present home and family life is maintained . . . is detrimental to the growth of individual character."[111]

Her use of direct refutation and dissociation combined to form clear attacks on those who would disagree. In one telling example, in "Sex Slavery," she addressed her opponents' argument that if women were so oppressed by marriage, "Why don't the wives leave?" Her response is one that leaves little question about de Cleyre's intellectually aggressive style:

> Why don't you run, when your feet are chained together? Why don't you cry out when a gag is on your lips? Why don't you raise your hands above your

head when they are pinned fast to your sides? . . . If there is one thing more than another in this whole accursed tissue of false society, which makes me angry, it is the asinine stupidity which with the true phlegm of impenetrable dullness says, "Why don't the women leave!" Will you tell me where they will go and what they shall do?[112]

De Cleyre did not mince words. In her 1896 speech "The Case of Woman vs. Orthodoxy," she engaged in a line-by-line analysis and humorous refutation of the thirty-first chapter of Proverbs, where King Lemuel asks and answers, "Who can find a virtuous woman?" Quoting each sentence of the passage, she then inserted her parenthetical interpretation.[113]

Although consistently cast as a movement philosopher, de Cleyre was not unerringly serious. Her letters to friends and family expose a person who was always quick to amuse and be amused. For example, in a letter to her mother dated 22 January 1893, she discussed a speech she had heard by an "old doctor" who believed Jesus Christ had no father and that 999 out of 1,000 species in the animal and vegetable kingdom reproduced nonsexually. She explained:

> I had made fun of them till everybody had a wide grin on his face. I said I had never heard the speaker's theory before, but since I had heard him soberly make the preceding statements I was inclined to believe him a case of virginal reproduction. It took half a minute for the grin to develop into a roar, and I don't think the old doctor will ever get over it. It was darned mean, but he shouldn't have been so stupid.[114]

These flashes of wit, often a very nonfeminine wit as it attacked others instead of engaging in self-deprecation, are sprinkled throughout her addresses and are just another form of direct refutation, ridiculing her opponents' positions to dissuade the audience from listening to them.

De Cleyre's ability to extract the core of her opponents' arguments and then distill them to their silliest was a recurring basis for her humor. When comparing men and women's skills in "The Gates of Freedom," she exclaimed, "Inferiority! Yes I am willing to admit that in certain things we are inferior to men. Also in certain things, men are inferior to crocodiles."[115]

Systematic Reasoning. Relying on a detailed reading of history and economics to justify her anarchism, de Cleyre rarely interjected her own personal experiences or anecdotes, even though she lived in grinding poverty.[116] De Cleyre's arguments often were supported by evidence from authority. Addressing her audience as political peers, she encouraged them to act from their own convictions, informed by the writings of great thinkers and the material realities of the prevailing economic conditions. Her goal was to make the condition of the workers visible to all and to mobilize the workers to defend themselves. As she offered a philosophical soul to the movement, her discourse often dealt with abstract principles, not personal experience. Perhaps this focus led historian Margaret Marsh to write that de Cleyre's discourse is "the most complete articulation of the anarchist-feminist position to appear in the nineteenth century."[117]

Even in "Why I Am an Anarchist," a speech delivered during her 1897 tour of England and Scotland as well as in Hammond, Indiana, de Cleyre eschewed injecting her personal experiences. Instead, the speech took the audience through the philosophical reasons and poetic sentiments that led her to anarchism. She systematically dispatched other proposed solutions to human misery and inequality, ultimately concluding that anarchism, and its attendant individual freedoms, is the lone solution.

She explained that she was motivated to search for a better world by the pressures of reason and emotion, focusing on "the question of bread": "The problem is not how to find a way to relieve temporary distress, not to make people dependent upon the kindness of others, but to allow every one to be able to stand on his own feet."[118] This focus led her to analyze the American Revolution and its resulting Constitution as a failure: "the political victory of America had been a barren thing." Given that the Constitution was "an irony in the face of facts," she concluded, "to be free one must have liberty of access to the sources and means of production." She then systematically dismissed socialism because the "individual would still be under the necessity of getting somebody's permission to go to work," land reform because "it did not offer any chance to the man who could actually bid nothing for the land . . . [and] because the theory of economic rent itself seemed to me full of holes," and the abolition of gold and silver and banking on the basis of security because it did not help the person who had nothing. Having rejected all alternatives, de Cleyre offered her own conclusion:

> That the way to get freedom to use the land is by no tampering and indirection, but plainly by the going out and settling thereon, and using it. . . .
>
> [T]hat as to the question of exchange and money . . . that the best thing ordinary workingmen or women could do was to organize their industry so as to get rid of money altogether. . . .
>
> [That e]very machine of any complexity is the accumulation of the inventive genius of the ages; no one man conceived it; no one man can make it; no one man therefore has a right to the exclusive possession of the social inheritance from the dead; that which requires social genius to conceive and social action to operate, should be free of access to all those desiring to use it. . . .
>
> [T]hat the assumptions as to women's inferiority were all humbug; that given freedom of opportunity, women were just as responsive as men, just as capable of making their own way, producing as much for the social good as men.[119]

Having systematically covered all areas of state regulation, she concluded: "the State had nothing left to do here; for it has never attempted to do more than solve the material difficulties, in a miserable, brutal way; and these economic independence would solve for itself." For her, the argument was logical: "[Anarchism] comes as the logical conclusion of three hundred years of revolt against external temporal and spiritual authority."[120] Given the broad principles that govern humanity, she concluded in "Why I Am an Anarchist" that anarchism was the only way to achieve full human potential.

Another example of de Cleyre's deductive and philosophically systematic approach is contained in "In Defense of Emma Goldman." There she argued:

> But the experience of this age has proven that metaphysical quantities do not exist apart from materials, and hence humanity can not be made equal by declarations on paper. Unless the material conditions for equality exist, it is worse than mockery to pronounce men equal . . . freedom, either of thought, speech, or action, is equally a mockery.[121]

Here de Cleyre did not speak of her own struggle to fill material needs, her low wages, and her dismal living conditions. Instead, she spoke to broad generalities. And in a move typical of her style, she added a twist of humor:

> I once read that one million angels could dance at the same time on the point of a needle; possibly one million angels might be able to get a decent night's

lodging by virtue of their constitutional rights; one single tramp couldn't. And whenever the tongues of the non-possessing class threaten the possessors, whenever the disinherited menace the privileged, that moment you will find that the Constitution isn't made for you.[122]

A similar approach was employed in her debate speech, "They Who Marry Do Ill." There she began with a definition of marriage as a "permanent dependent relationship."[123] Since all dependent relationships are bad, she concluded those who marry do ill. In those speeches not philosophically or deductively structured, a poetic or lyrical approach was her alternative, as evident in her Haymarket memorials.[124]

Dissociation. The strategy of dissociation was most evident in her speech "Sex Slavery," delivered in 1890 in defense of Moses Harman, who had been jailed on obscenity charges. She distinguished the prevailing legal understanding of adultery and rape from her interpretation of the terms: "for that is adultery where woman submits herself sexually to man, without desire on her part, for the sake of 'keeping him virtuous,' 'keeping him at home.' . . . And that is rape, where a man forces himself sexually upon a woman whether he is licensed by the marriage law to do it or not." In the same speech, she also explored the distinctions between legal and logical definitions of illegitimacy and obscenity.[125]

Yet even as she systematically addressed opponents' arguments by parsing the reality of the situation from the legal ideals, de Cleyre also employed strong emotional appeals. She argued vehemently: "But there is no refuge upon earth for the enslaved sex. Right where we are, there we must dig our trenches, and win or die," and

> that is the vilest of all tyranny where a man compels the woman he says he loves, to endure the agony of bearing children that she does not want, and for whom . . . they cannot properly provide. It is worse than any other human oppression; it is fairly *God*-like! To the sexual tyrant there is no parallel upon earth; one must go to the skies to find a fiend who thrusts life upon his children only to starve and curse and outcast and damn them![126]

Her cold and calculating style led her to declare: "The question of souls is old—we demand our bodies, now."[127]

"Why I Am an Anarchist" particularly typified de Cleyre's rhetoric because its logical appeals and lyrical language combined her philosophy and poetry. It also addressed the range of concerns present throughout her career as a speaker: anarchist philosophy, the plight of the worker, and the condition of women. In "Why I Am an Anarchist," with her focus on the individualistic and philosophic underpinnings of anarchism, de Cleyre presented eternal and abstract reasons for her beliefs. Even when explaining "why I am an Anarchist," she strove to keep her personal experiences out of her speeches. She insisted that adding details of her life might not be best "because in giving the reasons why I am an Anarchist, I may perhaps infuse too much of my own personality into the subject, giving reasons sufficient unto myself, but which cool reflection might convince me were not particularly striking as reasons why other people should be Anarchists." Although the speech proceeded to describe the various thought processes that brought de Cleyre to anarchism, the description is presented not as personal experience, but as the result of clear reasoning inspired by the principle of liberty: "I must do something with my brain. I cannot be content to regard the world as a mere jumble of happenings. . . . Neither can I be contented to take anybody's dictum on the subject; the thinking machine will not be quiet." In addition to "mental activity," "the possession of a very large proportion of sentiment" (sentiment being the "filtered and tested results of past efforts on the part of the intellect to compass the adaptation of the individual to its surroundings") led her to anarchism.[128] These two things compelled her to engage in "a study into history," which revealed that "the causes of discontent have chiefly been economic."[129] Even when she moved away from her more intellectual analyses of anarchism—for example, in her Haymarket memorial speeches—the personal does not appear.[130] Instead, her eulogies were attempts to create a secular afterlife for the Haymarket martyrs.

Overall, de Cleyre's emphasis on systematic reasoning, her use of direct refutation premised on dissociative moves, and her reliance on appeals to abstract values situated within material realities typify her style. However, although she may have arrived at clear conclusions about the benefits of anarchism and liberty, she would not dictate the actions of her audiences. Instead, she encouraged them to act based on their own reasons, informed by her arguments. Audience members were to follow her thinking, and then decide for themselves the appropriate response. For example, in "In Defense of Emma Goldman" she defended Goldman's right to urge expropriation, but did not urge it herself: "I would not say, 'take bread,' but take counsel with yourselves how to get the power to take bread." She explained her reasoning for this different counsel, closely linking it to her own support of individual rights: "I, as an anarchist, have no right to advise another to do anything involving a risk to himself."[131] Similarly, in "Why I Am an Anarchist" her goal is not to have the audience members inject themselves into her argument, especially because many members of her audience may not have been of the working class, but to allow them to follow her pattern of reasoning and commit themselves to action. Although she would not prescribe the manner of action, she did demand some form of action. Her speech was directive, absolute, and conclusive: the audience must act.

Direct action, whether it be on the part of workers or women, was a constant in de Cleyre's addresses. For example, in "The Gates of Freedom," she exhorted:

> Mind you, I never expect men to *give* us liberty. No, Women, we are not *worth* it, until we *take* it. How shall we take it? By the ballot? A fillip for your paper rag! The ballot hasn't made men free, and it won't make us free. . . . By *ourselves living our beliefs*. "Propaganda by the deed" is the favorite expression of the revolutionist. We are revolutionists. And we shall use propaganda by speech, deed, and most of all, life—*being* what we teach.[132]

Despite the power of this call, de Cleyre was not certain women would follow. Although she was more than willing to exclaim, "I say right here, candidly, that *as a class* I have nothing to hope from men," she also admitted discouragement because of the "apathy, the passivity, the can't-help-it-ness, or the religious slavishness of my own sex."[133]

De Cleyre's goal clearly was empowerment, but not merely the empowerment of women. Instead, she sought to instigate general resistance in all members of her audience. For example, she concluded her speech "The Past and Future of the Ladies' Liberal League" by celebrating what she called the "kicking principle," an active use of "non-submission, insubordination, rebellion, revolt, revolution" and "non-acquiescence to injustice."[134] De Cleyre sought audience action, whether it be protest at the injustice of the Haymarket hangings or the injustice done to workers and women.

De Cleyre's attention to women, and in particular women's sexuality, may be the most significant substantive element of her rhetoric. Unlike her contemporaries, de Cleyre attempted to negotiate both the pleasures and dangers attendant to sexuality and to combine her anarchism and feminism. Thus one cannot understand de Cleyre's rhetoric simply by attending to her biological sex; instead, her sexuality

ANARCHIST WOMEN AND
FEMININE IDEAL: SEX, CLASS,
AND STYLE IN THE RHETORIC OF
VOLTAIRINE DE CLEYRE, EMMA
GOLDMAN, AND LUCY PARSONS

327

and class must be recognized as well. When she spoke about the sexual needs of women, her persona was informed by her own sexual practices. For de Cleyre, the solution to women's economic servitude was not sexual servitude, as represented by permanent relationships. Instead, it was economic independence and hence sexual freedom.

When detailing the achievements of women reformers of this era, Matthews argues that the "most important cultural achievement for women of the late nineteenth century [was] the new freedom to talk publicly and openly about sexuality."[135] This freedom was one in which de Cleyre participated completely. De Cleyre was not bound by any attachment to the roles of wife, sweetheart, or mother. She refused to marry, and although she bore a child, she did not accept the role of mother. Accordingly, de Cleyre used a much broader ideology to critique sexual norms. Marsh dates the beginning of de Cleyre's active exploration of the woman question from 1891, a year after the birth of her son, arguing that "motherhood forced her to confront the consequences of her stance" regarding demands for freedom from the hindrances of feminine constraints.[136]

Sexual freedom was central in de Cleyre's thinking. For her, "the sex question" meant not only the question of what public role women should play but also what private role. In 1895 she argued that the sex question was "more intensely important to us than any other, because of the interdict which generally rests upon it, because of its immediate bearing upon daily life, because of the stupendous mystery of it and the awful consequences of ignorance of it."[137] Ultimately, she believed a free society required free women because "[y]ou can have no free, or just, or equal society, nor anything approaching it, so long as womanhood is bought, sold, housed, fed, and protected, as a chattel."[138] Her answer to the sex question is one that rings true today: she demanded women's autonomy over their bodies. She urged women to fight for their independence, writing in 1891:

> We have declared war—a few of us—and we accept no such treaty; we will be satisfied with nothing less than that maternity shall be put beyond the necessity of price–dependence. This means that we intend to be industrially independent; that we consider ourselves perfectly able to compete with men in a *free* field, and when our battle is won, as won it will be some day though none of us will live to see it, the body of women will be her own, and husbands must meet their wives on the proud footing of equality.[139]

This "proud footing of equality" was not one bound by the role of motherhood. De Cleyre rejected the idea that motherhood was necessary for womanhood. She argued that the twin traps of purity and motherhood go hand in hand to oppress women and deny the fulfillment of their "physical and mental appetites," appetites such as "the desire for sexual association, not for reproduction; the artistic desires; the desire to know . . . the desire to do."[140] Distinguishing herself from both prevailing and radical feminist thought of the time, de Cleyre denied that motherhood was inherent in women's identity, arguing "the development of individuality does no longer *necessarily* imply numerous children, nor indeed, *necessarily* any children at all."[141]

EMMA GOLDMAN: "TONGUE OF FIRE" AGITATOR

Labeled by the press as the "Queen of Anarchists" and "the Most Dangerous Woman in the World,"[142] Emma Goldman's position as a leader of the early anarchist movement is undeniable. The press regularly covered the speeches, arrests, and trials of Goldman and her comrade, Alexander Berkman, who, according to Marsh, "personified anarchism to Americans."[143] Previous scholarship about Goldman provides biographical and historical accounts of her life and highlights the distinctive features of her rhetoric.[144] Several writers have identified the importance of her ideas to feminist studies.[145] Despite her prominence as an anarchist, assessments of Goldman's rhetorical skill and contribution to feminism are mixed. For example, Martha Solomon notes that although Goldman's speeches and writings were probably persuasive to some select audiences, such as bohemian and intellectual types, ultimately they were too dogmatic, failed to communicate commonality with her listeners, failed to offer solutions to the societal ills she identified, and were tainted by biased and weak evidence.[146] While recognizing the significance of Goldman in the history of ideas about women, Bonnie Haaland questions the value of Goldman's ideas to feminism by characterizing her stance on sexuality as "biologically-determined and instinct-driven" and therefore essentializing womanhood along conventional lines.[147] This essay expands upon previous assessments by taking into consideration the influence of Goldman's immigrant and class status on the substance and style of her rhetoric.[148]

Goldman, Anarchism, and Women's Oppression. As noted earlier, Goldman's position on anarchism represents a communist approach to achieving individual autonomy. Unlike de Cleyre, Goldman rejected all property relations. As she explained in "What I Believe":

> "Property" means dominion over things and the denial to others of the use of those things. . . . It is the private dominion over things that condemns millions of people to mere nonentities, living corpses without originality or power of initiative, human machines of flesh and blood, who pile up mountains of wealth for others and pay for it with a gray, dull and wretched existence for themselves. . . . Anarchism is the only political philosophy that can and will do away with this humiliating and degrading situation.[149]

Goldman argued that autonomy could not be achieved without the elimination of private ownership of property, which she believed was responsible for creating the uneven distribution of power in society, including inequality between the sexes.

Goldman's rhetoric envisioned a society devoid of all systemic injustice, where individuals think and act freely and creatively, and are accountable for their own lives. She emphasized the autonomy of both women and men, through the elimination of relations of domination between the sexes, as the foundation for equitable human relations. Accordingly, the social relationship between women and men was a recurring theme in her speeches and writings. In "The Tragedy of Woman Emancipation,"[150] "Marriage and Love,"[151] and "The Traffic in Women,"[152] for example, Goldman critiqued societal institutions of suffrage, marriage, and prostitution, respectively. She argued that reform efforts aimed at gaining the right to vote were a waste of women's energy, which could better be applied to achieving the goals of anarchism. She proclaimed that marriage should be abolished as a form of social and economic slavery comparable to prostitution, and that the degrading conditions of prostitution, like marriage, would cease to exist with the abolition of capitalism.

Among anarchist women, Goldman was also notable as an advocate for birth control. Her lectures on birth control included technical information on how to use contraceptives.[153] Goldman believed that access to birth control for women was necessary to practice sexual freedom and realize her vision of open and equal human relationships. According to historian Linda Gordon, Goldman probably introduced the idea of birth control to Margaret Sanger, who is widely recognized as a pioneer in promoting family planning.[154] Unfortunately, only fragments of Goldman's writings on birth control and the practice of free love still exist.[155]

For Goldman, the centrality of sexual freedom in the emancipation of human thought and action was the basis for combining women's liberation with the larger cause of human liberation. As she indicated in her essay "Marriage and Love,"[156] sexual freedom refers not simply to the practice of free love and the dissolution of the institution of marriage, but to the unleashing of a creative energy and the enactment of a fundamental liberty, freedom of expression. When Goldman advocated sexual freedom, she recognized heterosexuality, homosexuality, and self-love as normal expressions of intimacy. Her inclusive position on sexuality is not well represented in her published works, but can be found in unpublished manuscripts.[157] For example, in a fragmented manuscript titled "Sexuality Instinct and Creativity," she wrote, "The concept of 'falling in love' may apply to self, to members of one's own or the opposite sex."[158]

Despite her emphasis on sexual freedom, Goldman's advocacy addressed a diversity of subjects that she directed sometimes at women and sometimes at a broad audience of all humans. Goldman's prominence, says Marsh, was the result of "her wide-ranging propaganda efforts that reached well beyond the confines of the anarchist movement."[159] For example, in "Minorities and Majorities,"[160] she argued that mass thought and action were the enemy of individual freedom, and in "The Individual, Society and the State,"[161] she provided a philosophical explanation of the relationship between the individual and collective. Subjects in various other speeches and essays included the conditions of workers, the atrocities of war and conscription, the role of intellectuals in the anarchist struggle, the philosophical bases of atheism, and analyses of European drama and literature.

The Reasoning Agitator. Regardless of her subject, Goldman's rhetorical style was a performance of a self-assigned role: agitator. Her powerful "tongue of fire" delivery style encompassed both the verbal and the nonverbal.[162] Her delivery is perhaps best described as burlesque or caricature-like in that she used her voice, facial expressions, and body in exaggerated ways, which often were captured in drawings of her that appeared in newspapers. Commenting on Goldman's remarkable ability to command and inspire an angry, frustrated audience of primarily unemployed people in New York City's Union Square in 1893, biographer Richard Drinnon writes: "As often happened at such times of crisis, she spoke almost in tongues, prophet-like, seemingly possessed by a truly incandescent indignation and sympathy; on these occasions she was so inspired—so filled with extra-human energy—that she drew her audience part of the way up to her own heights of feeling and consciousness."[163] The content of her rhetoric along with her larger-than-life platform style earned her such titles as "apostle of discord and dynamite," "nuisance to society," and "bitch of an anarchist."[164] As demonstrated in the following paragraphs, her speeches and writings were often sarcastic, chiding her audience/readers for lacking an anarchist consciousness. Acutely aware that her agitative style was offensive to some, she commented in an essay critiquing the woman suffrage movement, "Yes, I may be considered an enemy of woman; but if I can help her see the light, I shall not complain."[165]

Goldman's rhetorical style was characterized by a sarcastic tone; appeals to general truths, expert testimony, and logic; argument by analogy and metaphor; deductive structure; negotiating philosophical dichotomies; and inciting audience action. A representative example of Goldman's rhetorical style is "Anarchism: What It Really Stands For," published in her 1917 collection, *Anarchism and Other Essays*.[166] She also disseminated this essay in pamphlet form and probably delivered it as a lecture. After years on the public platform, however, Goldman came to prefer the written over the spoken word because "[t]he relation between the writer and the reader is more intimate."[167] In all probability, Goldman perceived writing to be a solution to the audience adaptation problems inherent in agitative speaking.[168]

Thus in 1906 she founded the journal *Mother Earth* to provide a written forum for anarchist philosophy and activism.

In "Anarchism: What It Really Stands For," Goldman provides a definition of and justification for anarchism. The essay opens with a poem in praise of anarchism by John Henry Mackay, and then proceeds to explain the implications of anarchism for property, religion, and government. Within this discussion, she identifies and refutes objections to anarchism, including concerns about maintaining public safety and social order. Her conclusion attempts to identify a practical method of "direct action" for achieving anarchism. This essay illustrates both the style and substance of Goldman's rhetoric, especially her agitative tone and appeals to authoritative sources and logic.

Probably the first feature one notices about Goldman's rhetorical style is its tone. Her sarcastic, authoritative, and impersonal tone is revealed early in the essay when she supplies a definition of anarchism:

> Anarchism urges man to think, to investigate, to analyze every proposition; but that the brain capacity of the average reader be not taxed too much, I also shall begin with a definition, and then elaborate on the latter.
>
> ANARCHISM:—The philosophy of a new social order based on liberty unrestricted by man-made law; the theory that all forms of government rest on violence, and are therefore wrong and harmful, as well as unnecessary.[169]

Her words convey a sense of confidence and certainty that anarchism is the logical solution to the world's ills. "In fact," explains Goldman, "there is hardly a modern thinker who does not agree that government, organized authority, or the State is necessary *only* to maintain or protect property and monopoly."[170] According to Goldman, these features of capitalism are the principal causes of human oppression, which only anarchism can relieve. By associating herself with "modern thinker[s]," Goldman writes from a position of mastery of her subject. Her distinct air of superiority is clear in her attitude toward her audience, whom she impels, by inference, to become enlightened modern thinkers. She writes, "[E]ven a flock of sheep would resist the chicanery of the State if it were not for the corruptive, tyrannical, and oppressive methods it employs to serve its purposes."[171]

Goldman typically utilized appeals to general truths, expert testimony, and logic to support her demands for agitation, rather than refer to personal examples or personalized anecdotes. In "Anarchism," she quoted the philosopher and poet Ralph Waldo Emerson to support her argument that all forms of government are inherently oppressive: "'All government in essence,' says Emerson, is 'tyranny.' It matters not whether it is government by divine or majority rule. In every instance its aim is the absolute subordination of the individual."[172] She also cited Oscar Wilde, George Bernard Shaw, Peter Kropotkin, Henry David Thoreau, and others. Of course, these radical poets, playwrights, and philosophers lent credibility to her claims only if the audience perceived them to be authorities. Goldman's most avid followers, typically young bohemians and intellectuals interested in anarchism as artistic self-expression, found such expert testimony persuasive.[173]

Goldman's reliance on "modern thinkers" demonstrated her attempt to expand the anarchist struggle to involve the activism of both intellectuals and laborers. This included encouraging the working-class masses to appreciate and incorporate the ideas of intellectuals in their activism. The goal of her agitation and activism is most clearly demonstrated by another essay, "Intellectual Proletarians," where she attempts to bridge "all those who work for their living, whether with hand or brain."[174] Goldman's tendency to refer to expert sources also suggests that she read widely and was influenced by the European intellectuals of her time. Her references to these authorities and her application of anarchist philosophy to various subjects encouraged fervent commitment to an ideal, a commitment premised on the ideas of intellectuals. However, such premises were probably only persuasive to those already sympathetic with the anarchist cause.

Another notable feature of Goldman's argumentation is her tendency to use analogies and metaphors. In making a comparison between the authoritarian institutions of government and religion, she wrote in "Anarchism," "The State is the altar of political freedom and, like the religious altar, it is maintained for the purpose of human sacrifice."[175] Goldman used such comparisons to demonstrate the pervasiveness of oppression. She likewise argued in "Woman Suffrage" that just as women's uncompromising support of religion resulted in their own oppression by religion, women's support of the right to vote also resulted in oppression by the very institution of politics to which they sought access. Goldman also repeatedly employed metaphors of slavery in "Anarchism." She used "enslaved," "captive," "oppressed," and similar terms to describe the physical and mental conditions of humans under capitalism.[176] Likewise, in her case for abolishing marriage in "Marriage and Love," Goldman defended free love by claiming that it transcends an arrangement made by the church and state; unlike marriage, she argued, free love cannot be "chained," "fettered," or "subdued."[177]

Goldman's reasoning was not always completely clear. For example, although an advocate for free love and sexual freedom and an ardent opponent of traditional roles for women, Goldman did not escape some of the sexual stereotypes of her day. She insisted that voluntary motherhood was "the highest fulfillment of woman's nature," clearly suggesting that childless women were somehow not fully complete.[178] She criticized motherhood as a social institution but named her journal *Mother Earth*. Thus, even as she advocated a radical philosophy of women's autonomy, she remained partially fixed within the confines of traditional gender roles. Such contradictions in argument appear within single works and within groups of works produced in a given period and therefore cannot be explained adequately as the alteration of arguments across time or in response to different audiences.[179]

Interpreting the Contradictions. The contradictions within Goldman's argumentation should not be immediately labeled as indicators of logical flaws. Although they are best understood through a more comprehensive analysis of a multitude of her works, a brief example is found in "Anarchism" in her treatment of the subject of political organizing. Political organizing posed a problem for anarchists because they rejected all forms of organized authority. Goldman herself recognized the confining aspects of organized liberation movements when she declared in "The Tragedy of Woman's Emancipation," "Now, woman is confronted with the necessity of emancipating herself from emancipation, if she really desires to be free."[180] Goldman's philosophy held that society should be organized entirely on the basis of the "free grouping of individuals." In "Anarchism," she explained why she could not propose an organized plan for anarchism: "[Anarchism is] a living force in the affairs of life, constantly creating new conditions. The methods of Anarchism therefore do not comprise an iron-clad program to be carried out under all circumstances. Methods must grow out of the economic needs of each place and clime, and of the intellectual and temperamental requirements of the individual."[181] Goldman urged her audiences to invent their own anarchism that would enable them to realize freedom of thought and expression. In order to achieve an anarchist society, however, organized political action was a pragmatic necessity. Thus Goldman also recommended organized activism in the form of "solidaric general protest" and "direct action" as the "logical, consistent method of Anarchism."[182]

From a neoclassical perspective, the "contradiction" between advocating radical autonomy and promoting organized action may be seen as faulty logic. However, neoclassical understandings of rhetoric that emphasize rules of decorum and logic are not necessarily appropriate for evaluating radical rhetoric that seeks to evade established rules. Indeed, rhetors like de Cleyre, Goldman, and Parsons who advocate radical change in a society that resists change necessarily find themselves in a difficult position. According to historian James Joll, the contradiction between advocating an antiauthority stance and the necessity for organized political action served as a great obstacle to advancing the anarchist cause.[183] In this light, contradictions in Goldman's argumentation are a negotiation of a philosophical dichotomy: the anarchist ideal of rejecting all organized authority and the pragmatics of working toward achieving that ideal. Likewise, Goldman's praise and criticism of the role of motherhood was a negotiation of "old" and "new" conceptions of womanhood, a negotiation that responded to the constraints of the historical moment.

As an anarchist agitator, not surprisingly Goldman defied norms of both decorum and logic. Goldman's anarchist philosophy itself urged audience action based on autonomous decisions removed from the influence of institutionalized thought and behavior. Similar to de Cleyre, Goldman attempted to instill a sense of autonomy in her audience, both women and men. Rather than instruct her audience of a specific solution or action, she encouraged them to reject authority and to act as free-thinking individuals. In "Anarchism," she explained that one must engage in "open defiance of, and resistance to, all laws and restrictions, economic, social, and moral. But defiance and resistance are illegal. Therein lies the salvation of man. Everything illegal necessitates integrity, self-reliance and courage." She further described anarchism as "the great liberator of man from the phantoms that have held him captive" and identified "the spirit of rebellion" as the means to carry it out.[184]

Goldman's invitation to her audience to join the anarchist cause was appropriately open and nondirective in that she ultimately defined anarchism as a revolutionary state of consciousness and being, rather than a matter of policy implementation. To become anarchists, Goldman's audience had to enact the traits of bravery and individual accountability in their everyday lives. A similar message was echoed in "Woman Suffrage," where she described the liberated woman: "Her development, her freedom, her independence, must come from and through herself."[185]

As noted earlier, however, Goldman's attitude toward her audience was at times quite condescending. For example, in "Woman Suffrage," she described suffragists as "lifeless and spineless ladies" and the suffrage movement as a "parlor affair, absolutely detached from the economic needs of the people."[186] Casting herself as superior and violating other expectations of traditional femininity garnered Goldman notoriety and a public hearing for the anarchist cause wherever she traveled. However, her condescending attitude probably also prevented her from being taken seriously by some audience members, especially those outside the anarchist movement, and thus limited the possibility for audience empowerment. Goldman's dominating presence, although certain to attract public attention, made her appear as a spectacle, removing her from the reality of everyday struggle even as she spoke on behalf of the plight of the working class. Yet she seemed to thrive in the starring dramatic role in which she cast herself. On the occasion of a rally to release Berkman from prison in 1917 (she was out on bail), authorities threatened that if Goldman spoke, the venue would be closed down. She rose to the speaking platform with a handkerchief stuffed in her mouth and "brought down the house."[187]

The various features of Goldman's agitative rhetorical style are a product of her identity. Just as de Cleyre spoke from the position of her sexuality and Parsons from her position as a married woman of color, Goldman spoke from her position as a female Russian Jewish immigrant. As an immigrant, her citizenship status was always subject to government scrutiny. Upon being deported to Russia, Goldman was truly "nowhere at home."[188] The combination of Goldman's ethnicity, gender, and class shaped her anarchist-feminist political philosophy and her rhetorical style. For example, although Goldman clearly rejected the religious

ANARCHIST WOMEN AND FEMININE IDEAL: SEX, CLASS, AND STYLE IN THE RHETORIC OF VOLTAIRINE DE CLEYRE, EMMA GOLDMAN, AND LUCY PARSONS

333

and moral codes of the Jewish tradition, she also was empowered by the emphasis it placed on the intellectual development of individuals as well as participation in political activism.[189]

Goldman's identification with Jewish culture is apparent in both public and private statements. In a 1908 lecture, for example, Goldman acknowledged the role of Jews in the revolution: "Because the Jews have never fought, it has been assumed that they would never rebel against existing conditions. Liberty cannot be obtained without struggle, and the Jews have become conscious of this truth. Their revolutionary spirit is growing powerful."[190] Moreover, Goldman identified herself culturally as Jewish. In a letter written in 1925, she commented: "I am too Jewish to become mystical or to ever accept anything but clear thinking."[191] These words reveal Goldman's identification with her Jewish background even as she sought to break away from it.

At times Goldman identified herself specifically as a Jewish woman. In an address delivered at a literary luncheon in London in 1933, she reflected back on her life: "Between the age of eight and twelve I dreamed of becoming a Judith. I longed to avenge the sufferings of my people, the Jews."[192] Her reference to the heroine Judith, who used her seductive charms and fearless courage to save the Israelites, is especially revealing. Shepherd notes that nineteenth-century Russian rabbis were troubled by Judith and other heroines because of these women's licentiousness.[193] However, Goldman, an advocate of women's sexual freedom, could fittingly identify with her. Goldman herself earned a reputation for torrid relationships with men.[194] Yet public scrutiny of Goldman's relationships did not hinder her political activism for, like de Cleyre and Parsons, she did not subscribe to the norms of female behavior expected of middle-class white women. Her unruly behavior and irreverence of social and moral codes enabled her to carry on her agitation despite public criticism. As Matthews notes, "Goldman lived her life as she chose and paid little heed to such considerations. Thus, her life and career constitute a benchmark in establishing the possibilities for public women by divorcing women's sexual conduct from public influence."[195]

LUCY PARSONS: THE HAYMARKET WIDOW

Lucy Parson's rhetoric, especially the interaction between her politics and her sex, is best understood through analysis of her constructed identity as the "Haymarket widow." Prior to the Haymarket riot Parsons was a local activist who led women's strikes and marches. Her activism extended beyond the bounds of Chicago when she began an extensive speaking tour immediately following the sentencing of those held responsible for the riot, including her husband, Albert. This tour made her so well known that the city of Chicago banned her from publicly speaking within the city limits.

During this tour, Parsons's public image evolved from a local anarchist speaking to other interested anarchists to the "Haymarket widow" addressing the nation. More important, her rhetorical persona as a Haymarket widow enabled her to circumvent her substantial dual disadvantages as an anarchist and as a woman of color. During the nineteenth century, widows enjoyed an unusual status. Approximately "10 percent of the adult females population were widows; half of the women who married became widows at some point in their lives."[196] Widowhood symbolized loss and hardship, but in some cases widowhood opened opportunities. Unlike other women, widows were sometimes forced to leave the domestic sphere for the good of the family.[197] With their husbands' deaths, many women became responsible for their own and their families' financial well-being.[198] As a result, many women became successful in running their husbands' farms or stores and created their own income.[199] Although widows were able to cross some traditional sex boundaries to provide for their families, they also were expected to reveal themselves as widows publicly through their dress, demeanor, and discourse. A widow was permitted to mourn publicly as she revered her husband's memory and could cross into the public sphere as long as she marked herself as a grieving spouse.[200]

The Haymarket Widow. Lucy Parsons's assumption of the role of the widow of a Haymarket martyr was deliberately strategic. Together, Albert and Lucy decided that he would accept the death sentence rather than appeal for clemency. The Illinois governor commuted the sentence to life imprisonment for two of Albert's comrades after they begged for clemency, but the Parsons hoped that his death would inspire action regarding the plight of working-class Americans.

By choosing to accept his sentence, Albert provided the opportunity for his death to be construed as martyrdom. In many ways, martyrdom is a rhetorical construct. To achieve the status of martyrdom, "the martyr must be confronted with a simple and immediate choice: conform or die (often unpleasantly). Both elements of the decision, deliberate refusal and positive acceptance of the consequence, must be in the form of a public and legal charade."[201] By declining to appeal for clemency, Albert hoped to frame his death as martyrdom. Lucy could then use her role as his widow to enhance her public advocacy for anarchism. Even before his execution, Lucy began her intense speaking tour to urge the anarchist case. Immediately after the sentencing, Lucy took Albert's hand, declaring: "My husband, I give you to the cause of liberty. I now go forth to take your place. I will herald abroad to the American people the foul murder ordered here today at behest of monopoly. I, too, expect to mount the scaffold. I am ready."[202] By speaking on behalf of her husband as well as herself, she was to become a more powerful voice for the movement than either of them had been on his or her own.

Even before Albert's execution on 11 November 1887, Lucy claimed the role of widow. Beginning her speaking tour on 9 October 1886, she declared:

> The world must hear from me now. The voice of my husband has been silenced, for the present at any rate, and perhaps forever in this world, but his life will speak in eloquent terms in the cause of suffering humanity until emancipation of wage-slavery comes. We are weak, tired, oppressed, but not discouraged nor disheartened. It is a day of struggle. Our cause is worth fighting for and worth dying for.[203]

Although her legal status as a widow was unclear, especially in the face of miscegenation laws, she consistently referred to herself as Mrs. Parsons. But her references to her widowhood did not entirely eclipse concerns about her racial identity. Reports from the tour often spoke of her appearance, explaining that she had an "African birth."[204] Some speculated that she was of "African descent . . . but claimed that her ancestors were Mexican,"[205] or that she had "evidence of Indian blood in her veins."[206] While some reports made wild guesses at her ancestry, others merely described her visual appearance as "copperish." She was also described as a "medium sized woman of good figure, of dark, brown-like complexion, high cheek bones with hair inclined to be kinky"[207] and as a "swarthy half mulatto half Indian face."[208] These varied reports of her racial background led the *New York Times* to note that one audience was "scattered here and there were a few sober-looking business men, who had evidently come to see what she looked like."[209] To combat the media's tendency to feature her ethnicity and gender, she was billed as "Mrs. Parsons! Wife of the Condemned Anarchist."[210] Accordingly, some audience members came to hear a "widow" of a possible martyr, although they might have had less interest in hearing a woman of color advocating radical social change.

The Widow as an Anarchist. During her tour, Lucy Parsons generally gave a standard prepared speech, which scholars have titled "I Am an Anarchist." The goal of this speech was to diminish the listeners' tendency to reject anarchism out of misunderstanding its tenets. By focusing on what anarchism advocated and differentiating it from mere anarchy, Parsons hoped to leave the audience with the thought: "If that is Anarchism then by ___ I'm an Anarchist."[211] Although no transcripts of this speech are available, newspaper accounts reported enough of her words for historians to reproduce what are considered to be accurate speech texts.[212]

This speech is an excellent example of how Parsons used the rhetorical strategy of transforming inartistic proofs into artistic rhetorical arguments. In this speech, Parsons transformed her appearance and her anarchism into rhetorical arguments. She utilized a strategy by which her speech responded directly to the preconceived notions of her audience and attempted to offer a new, stronger interpretation of her presence. In effect, Parsons acknowledged the inartistic proofs, the prespeech evidence of her reputation and her appearance, and strategically chose to transform them into enhanced ethos. She did this by using the inartistic proof of her race, sex, and ideological affiliation as premises in arguments instead of conclusions. By adding new premises and either drawing a conclusion or leaving the audience to complete the argument enthymematically, she drew on her reputation and appearance to build her case rather than to dissuade audiences from attending to her.

Parsons saw three points of her personal identity that worked inartistically against her ethos: her reputation as an anarchist, her sex, and her race.[213] Parsons responded to her sex and her anarchist status differently than she did her racial appearance. Addressing the culturally constructed labels "anarchist" and "female," she provided alternative meanings for each. She sought to alter her audience's preconceived assumptions through discursive reinterpretation.

During Parsons's lifetime, "anarchist" was a pejorative label. According to Carolyn Ashbaugh, in the late nineteenth century "the word 'anarchist' [came] to stand for almost any radical."[214] This negative connotation dates back until at least 1539. However, not until 1840 did the first person identify himself as an anarchist.[215] In 1886 most Americans had never met an anarchist; however, they had seen them portrayed in popular culture. The stereotype of the anarchist was of "poor, ugly, unwashed, animal-like, mentally deranged and dangerously violent foreigners."[216] One scholar describes the public image of the anarchist as being reduced to a hand holding a bomb.[217] While this image captured the views of some anarchists, it grossly oversimplified the ideology. Lucy Parsons did, in fact, encourage the use of explosives and other weapons, but her husband did not publicly advocate violence. Despite their differing views, both labeled themselves anarchists. That label, after 300 years of stereotyping, worked to the disadvantage of those involved in the Haymarket riot.

Lucy Parsons realized that understandings of anarchism could and did vary. She accepted the label, knowing that her audience perceived the term negatively. As she explained, "Webster gives the term [Anarchism] two definitions—chaos and the state of being without political rule. We cling to the latter definition. Our enemies hold that we believe only in the former."[218] Parsons recognized that her audience identified anarchism with chaos; she sought to depict anarchism as opposition to state control rather than support for anarchy.

In "I Am an Anarchist," Parsons attempted to redefine the term "anarchism" to mean a patriotic American. She began this stock speech with the statement: "I am an anarchist. I suppose you came here, the most of you, to see what a real, live anarchist looked like. I suppose some of you expected to see me with a bomb in one hand and a flaming torch in the other, but are disappointed in seeing neither."[219] By publicly and directly acknowledging her audience's preconceptions as she spoke in an orderly public forum, she enacted a different perspective on anarchism. Without explosive or inflammatory agitation, she explained that anarchy was a natural result of a failed democracy. The existence of anarchists, according to Parsons, was inevitable when the governmental system disappointed its constituents so horrifically. One example she gave was the erection of the Statute of Liberty (which occurred during her tour) in the face of the "victims of the rank injustice that permeates the system of government, and of political economy."[220]

After recasting anarchists as peaceful victims, she used the Haymarket riot as evidence that her audience might confront the same mistreatment. More than once she depicted the Haymarket meeting, prior to the riot, as a "peaceable meeting." She invoked authority, saying, "the mayor of Chicago, was there. He said it was a quiet meeting." She described the confrontation as being between the police and the entire assembly: "[the officer in command] ordered the police to charge those peaceable anarchists." By doing so, she characterized all of the attendees as peaceful. She then portrayed the police as the perpetrators of violence, calling them "murderous" and stating that "the police arrive[d] on the scene, with murder in their eyes, determined to break up that meeting." Additionally, she contended that the reaction of the bomber was understandable: "[H]ad I seen the liberties of my countrymen trodden under foot, I would have flung the bomb myself. I would have violated no law, but would have upheld the constitution."[221] By implication, her audience, listening to her explanations, risked being labeled as troublemakers if police decided to break up the meeting.

After suggesting that her audience was vulnerable to the same treatment as the so-called anarchists of Haymarket, Parsons explained that true patriots should choose to be anarchists. She did this by inverting the roles of the police and the anarchists. She argued that while the anarchists were considered criminals, they were the true patriots and that the police, charged with protecting America, violated the Constitution. Citing the Constitution, Parsons noted the rights of free speech, free press, and free assembly as the "crimes" of the anarchists. She explained that those assembled at Haymarket Square had the right to "repel the unlawful invasion of those rights."[222] Thus she argued that throwing the bomb at the police was a lawful action protected by the Constitution. Parsons contrasted the anarchists' "patriotic" defense of the Constitution with the police's demand for dispersal. She condemned the police as treasonous: "The meeting was held. It was peaceable. When [Captain John] Bonfield [of the Chicago police force] ordered the police to charge those peaceable anarchists, he hauled down the American flag and should have been shot on the spot." She then predicted the future for all Americans if the injustice of the Haymarket trial was not rectified:

> If this verdict is carried out it will be the death knell of America's liberty. You and your children will be slaves. You will have liberty if you can pay for it. If this verdict is carried out, place the flag of our country at half mast and write on every fold "shame." Let our flag be trailed in the dust. Let the children of workingmen place laurels to the brow of these modern heroes, for they committed no crime.[223]

Declaring "[l]iberty has been named anarchy,"[224] she insisted that the anarchists' cause is the cause of liberty and that anarchists were patriotic Americans rather than criminals.

On 25 October 1886 in Orange, New Jersey, Parsons, deviating from her prepared speech, delivered a speech now known as "The Red Flag." Although "The Red Flag" was an extemporaneous speech roughly patterned on "I Am an Anarchist," the texts varied significantly. "The Red Flag" speech situation was atypical for the tour because she had to fight for access to the speaking hall before being allowed to speak. Because an authority (the owner of the hall) attempted to prevent Parsons

ANARCHIST WOMEN AND FEMININE IDEAL: SEX, CLASS, AND STYLE IN THE RHETORIC OF VOLTAIRINE DE CLEYRE, EMMA GOLDMAN, AND LUCY PARSONS

337

from speaking, the speech situation was actually similar to the police interruption of the Haymarket meeting. Thus the facts of that evening enabled Parsons to alter her stock address.

Upon learning that the door to the hall was locked, Parsons turned to the crowd and shouted, "What do you call yourselves, men? Standing down there on the sidewalk when the weakest of you could have easily broken the door down." When no man came forward to break down the door, Parsons did so herself. Once inside the door, she called to the men: "Be free men. . . . Are you afraid to stay in a hall where one woman dares to stay?"[225] The statement invited the men inside, while taunting them, suggesting that if they did not come in, they were less than men since a mere woman was willing to remain.

While she did attempt to transform the meaning of the term *anarchist* during "The Red Flag" speech, Parsons did not claim this label for herself or the Haymarket martyrs. Instead of beginning her address with "I am an anarchist," she referred to herself as a "revolutionist" who was "sneered at as an Anarchist." She referred to her husband and his comrades as "the so-called Anarchists in Chicago."[226]

Parsons acknowledged the awkwardness of the speaking situation in both her introduction and her conclusion. In the introduction, Parsons explained: "I can't speak to you as I would like to. You know when you have to break open a hall you upset your nervous system and you can't get off your address as you would like to."[227] The situation put her on the defensive. In her conclusion, she tacitly admitted that her speech was not as successful as she would have liked it to be. She asked her audience: "What do you think of Anarchists now? If I could have made my regular address that takes two and a half hours, when you went away you would say as I've heard many men say: 'If that is Anarchism then by ___ I'm an Anarchist.'"[228] Clearly, Parsons realized that to transform the meaning of the term "anarchist" successfully, she needed to identify herself with the label.

Like the term "anarchist," "female" was a label Parsons assumed when she spoke publicly. Being a woman in 1886 was an obstacle to addressing large groups of primarily male workers. Parsons dealt with this problem by highlighting her roles as a wife and mother. From this perspective, she offered two acceptable reasons for her appearance on the public platform. First, she was speaking on behalf of her silenced husband, since he was unable to speak for himself. Second, she was making a personal plea for her condemned husband, evoking the ideal of "Labor's True Woman," who used her "moral authority in the home to justify [her] activism in the world."[229]

Just as Parsons responded differently in the two speeches to the obstacle of her reputation, she also articulated her status as a wife and mother differently in both speeches. Interestingly, in "I Am an Anarchist," where she identified herself as an anarchist, Parsons never referred directly to her sex or even to her role as a wife. Instead, the allusions to her sex and status were subtle and covert. For example, when discussing the scene of the Haymarket bombing, she referred to herself in the third person, saying that "he [Albert Parsons] took his wife . . . and his two children along."[230] While she does not say "I am the wife of Albert Parsons and the mother of his children," she was billed as "Mrs. Parsons"[231] and probably introduced that way. In contrast, in "The Red Flag" speech, she twice referred to Albert as "my husband."[232] Both references to Albert related to the fact that he was sentenced to die. Accordingly, her words compelled her audience to see in her obvious womanhood not only a courageous and loyal wife but also one on the brink of widowhood.

Parsons's third obstacle to her public speaking was her race. Unlike her approach to her anarchist and female labels, Parsons did not acknowledge her racial background when she spoke. Instead, she dealt with her audience's prejudice by keeping silent on her own background but critiquing race-based discrimination. She also discursively used her racial identity to enhance her arguments. In both instances, she sought to transform her appearance, an inartistic proof, into ethos, an artistic proof.

The reasons Parsons maintained silence regarding her racial identity are understandable. She assumed her audience was prejudiced against racial minorities. Miscegenation laws prevented her from acknowledging her racial background as the wife of a white man. Moreover, while she could have focused on the positive aspects of her sex, being a wife and mother, she found no such positive corollaries in her racial identity. In fact, explicit recognition of her race might deny her the ability to claim the role of widow, since societal norms did not always confer that status on women of color.

Furthermore, Parsons made improvements for the working class a priority over racial issues because she believed that racial discrimination was a by-product of class stratification. Although she was a strong believer in racial equality (the Pittsburgh Manifesto's fifth point called for "equal rights for all without distinction to sex or race"[233]), she also believed that African Americans were not oppressed because their skin was black but because they were poor. Parsons wrote in the *Alarm*: "Are there any so stupid as to believe these outrages [lynchings] have been, are being and will be heaped upon the Negro because he is black? Not at all. It is because he is *poor*. It is because he is dependent. Because he is poorer as a class than his white wage-slave brother of the North."[234] Parsons maintained that the way to equality for everyone was through anarchism because economic and political tyranny was the foundation for all discrimination.

Her personal silence combined with her critique of race-based discrimination implicitly argued that the racial identity of a speaker was unimportant. Even though she was not able to acknowledge her racial identity, she was able to transform the meaning of her racial appearance. By positioning the meaning of her racial identity as neutral, she sought to overcome an obstacle that could have prevented her from reaching her audience.

Parsons responded to the obstacles of her reputation as an anarchist, her sex, and her race by constructing herself as the "Haymarket widow." This persona signified that the Haymarket defendants were martyrs rather than criminals, personified her sex in terms of her wifely roles, and minimized her racial appearance. Seeking to discursively transform the three inartistic proofs (anarchist reputation, sex, and racial identity) into the artistic proof of ethos, she traveled the country lecturing on the perils of the working class and the injustice suffered by the Haymarket martyrs. Her name became synonymous with the Haymarket riot, although she had left the square before the bombing occurred, she did not speak at the Haymarket meeting, and she did not stand trial in connection with the riot. The success of her tour assured her status as a permanent fixture in the labor movement and the embodiment of the Haymarket riot.

Parsons's strategic construction of her ethos as the "Haymarket widow" had both personal and rhetorical consequences. On the personal side, consistently linking herself to her husband minimized her role as an independent agitator. Instead of being known as an independent leader of the labor movement, she was merely seen as the "wife" of someone else. Posters advertising her speaking engagements most often billed her as "Mrs. Parsons" or as the "Wife of Albert Parsons." Newspaper accounts referred to her in the same way and, after Albert's execution, as the "Haymarket widow" or as "Albert Parsons's widow." Lucy Parsons continued to fight against unjust employers and the plight of political prisoners fifty-seven years after the Haymarket riot.[235] Although remarried, she continued to call herself "Mrs. Parsons" and to be known as the "Haymarket widow." Unfortunately, scholars identifying significant historic women ignore her, seeing her as merely the "wife" of a more historically important man. The editors of Radcliffe's *Notable American Women* explained her exclusion from their publication: "she was

ANARCHIST WOMEN AND FEMININE IDEAL: SEX, CLASS, AND STYLE IN THE RHETORIC OF VOLTAIRINE DE CLEYRE, EMMA GOLDMAN, AND LUCY PARSONS

339

'largely propelled by her husband's fate' and was 'a pathetic figure, living in the past and crying injustice.'"[236] Similarly, Margaret S. Marsh's only statement about Parsons in her *Anarchist Women: 1870–1920* was that "Lizzie May Holmes and Lucy Parsons tended to take secondary roles, the former as assistant, the latter as wife. Perhaps because they were trying to attract working-class men, they preferred not to draw attention to themselves as women lest they court ridicule instead of respect."[237] Except for Angela Davis's short discussion of Parsons in *Women, Race and Class*, in a section on Communist women, the academic community has totally ignored her.[238]

The rhetorical consequence of her construction of the "Haymarket widow" was her improbable success as a public speaker. The "Haymarket widow" ethos empowered Parsons's arguments by layering three types of testimonials on top of every argument: convert testimony, expert testimony, and borrowed testimony. First, her rhetoric implicitly claimed to be convert testimony. Convert testimony denotes a speaker's retelling of a personal narrative, which functions rhetorically as a model for the audience.[239] In her role as "the martyr's widow," Parsons continually offered the story of her personal tragedy combined with her "sudden" activism as a model to her audience. She implied that they should actively work to change the plight of working people as a result of sharing her experience without having to endure tragedy firsthand.

Second, her depictions were also expert testimony. While many people spoke on labor issues, Parsons's expertise was known and revered. Parsons had been with the movement even before it became known as anarchism. Moreover, she was present at the Haymarket meeting preceding the bombing. She also witnessed the corruption of the subsequent trial. Thus, when she used the Haymarket experience as a touchstone for her speech, she produced a more effective argument than those who were merely sympathizers without firsthand expertise. While others had to give secondhand reports of the Haymarket crisis, Parson's personal memories functioned as anamnesis.[240]

Third, Parsons's self-presentation as the "Haymarket widow" also worked as borrowed testimony. By positioning herself as a stand-in for her husband, she successfully engaged in *eidolopoeia*, the act of speaking as the living embodiment of a dead person.[241] Even before he was executed, she engaged in *eidolopoeia* because she had successfully constructed his identity as a rhetorical "martyr." Using *eidolopoeia* resulted in her words coming from him as well as from her. The audience perceived that the couple was speaking in unison via Lucy's physical presence. This method of expanding her ethos to include his ethos was an unusually effective form of borrowed testimony.

As the "Haymarket widow," Parsons enacted her argument that anarchism in America was necessary, since the rights guaranteed under the Constitution were not distributed fairly among the classes. Parsons became a symbol of the anarchist movement. As the "Haymarket widow," Parsons proved that laborers were not afforded freedom to express their ideas and challenge the government. She was forced to speak on behalf of her husband, who because of his writing and speaking was incarcerated and was to be executed as an accessory to a bombing when he neither threw the bomb, advocated violence, nor was present during the riot. Parsons's use of enactment, coupled with convert, expert, and borrowed testimony, allowed her argumentative freedom and rhetorical power within the confines of the persona of the "Haymarket widow."

Identifying Anarcho-Feminine Styles

De Cleyre, Goldman, and Parsons performed differing conceptions of womanhood, all of which are gendered, but not necessarily in the same way. Thus they individually and collectively offer a way to identify where "gaps and fissures" emerge in the social inscriptions of gender. If gender is understood as "the activity of managing situated conduct in light of normative conceptions of attitudes and activities appropriate for one's sex category," each woman's activities managed normative sex expectations in distinct ways.[242] Basically, the three women share a sex, and were sex categorized in the same way, but their genders were distinct—from each other and from privileged women. De Cleyre saw herself as a poet and philosopher who could engage in lyrical elegance as well as in "cold, calculating" reason. Goldman saw herself as an agitator whose primary goal was to awaken the masses to the necessity for anarchism. Parsons rhetorically deployed her role as the widow of anarchist Albert Parsons as a point of departure for her activism. Each used stylistic elements uniquely her own, elements that were consistent with each woman's conception of anarchism and each of which challenged prevailing norms of femininity.

Despite their distinct personae, however, some commonalities exist. In particular, all three women based their appeals on the common experiences of the working class rather than the common experiences of women. Because of this, each was willing to appeal to, and act as, an authority. For de Cleyre and Goldman, authority was expressed through their abstract and analytical approach to anarchism absent any references to their personal struggles or experiences. However, although de Cleyre's authoritative tone was guided by cool intellect, Goldman displayed emotional arousal in the form of agitation. The tone of Parsons's authoritative, personal rhetoric was clear in her direct speaking style and her use of personal pronouns. This use of authority also led to noninductive structures and nonparticipatory speeches. The audience members were addressed not as social peers but as political colleagues in the struggle, colleagues who would participate by engaging in collective action; in joint action, they would find their power.

Although these three rhetors spoke directly to their audiences, their manner distinguished itself from the suffrage reformers' approach. De Cleyre, Goldman, and Parsons believed in the worth of the individual, but they also recognized that the power of the individual could only be found in collective action. Although each recognized how her own experiences shaped her beliefs, that was not the primary basis of their appeals. Appeals were made to "the people" not solely on the basis of personal experience.

Rational argumentation and reasoning were the primary means by which they supported their positions, yet these three anarchist women varied in the kind of evidence they supplied to support their claims. De Cleyre relied on systematic analysis of her subjects. Goldman provided expert testimony, metaphors, and analogies. Parsons presented herself as an authoritative source.

De Cleyre, Goldman, and Parsons structured their arguments deductively, beginning with broad principles and moving to specific applications. As with their use of evidence, however, variations occurred among these women. De Cleyre used deductive argument to develop a coherent philosophy of anarchy; Goldman employed it to negotiate diverse arguments concerning social roles; and Parsons used it to refute alternative solutions to the plight of the worker.

Despite their expert personae and use of nonparticipatory forms, all three women still saw a role for the audience, if not to participate in the speech then to participate in the anarchist movement. Since many of the speeches sought participation in the movement, addressing an audience as peers was not always possible. Listeners either needed to be motivated to act or were resistant to the movement with misperceptions that needed correcting. However, such an approach created

ANARCHIST WOMEN AND FEMININE IDEAL: SEX, CLASS, AND STYLE IN THE RHETORIC OF VOLTAIRINE DE CLEYRE, EMMA GOLDMAN, AND LUCY PARSONS

341

tensions with anarchism's celebration of individual autonomy. Because autonomy is a principal message of anarchist philosophy, empowerment of one's audience as individuals and as a collective entity is, not surprisingly, a significant feature of the rhetoric of these women. In this case, social conditions and political ideals created apparent contradictions in the women's discourse. Although they had to direct their audiences to act and educate them about the plight of the worker, they also had to create independent thinkers who would be willing to reject prevailing social norms on their own. The women negotiated these tensions in distinctive ways.

The stylistic elements detailed thus far combine to create a clear persona for each woman: de Cleyre was the philosopher-poet; Goldman the agitator; and Parsons the widow. Each persona represented a unique way to be gendered, defying feminine expectations in one way or another. Such performances also demonstrate that analyzing gender only through the lens of sex role expectations creates an incomplete understanding of the construct. Gender is more than the fulfilling of one's sex role. It affects and is affected by race, class, ethnicity, and sexuality. Ignoring these other elements would obscure important distinctions in these women's rhetorics. The same act may mean very different things for different women. For example, all three of the women anarchists used a slavery metaphor to discuss the plight of women and the working person. De Cleyre used the metaphor of "sex slavery" to define marriage.[243] Recall that Goldman, too, used metaphors of slavery to describe human oppression. The use of this slavery metaphor by all three women is easy to understand. At the turn of the century, slavery was a very effective and graphic image. However, it worked differently coming from Goldman and de Cleyre than coming from Parsons. As a person of color born in 1853, Parsons probably may have been born into slavery or have been the child of former slaves.[244] From a rhetorical perspective, however, whether she was ever actually a slave is unimportant because her appearance inevitably denoted close ties to people of color. Coming from a white peer, the argument is a simple condemnation of capitalism. Slaves are workers without rights or incomes; after emancipation, all workers should have rights and incomes. The same metaphor spoken by a person of color to a white audience, however, is no longer based on a common heritage but on two different racial experiences. A level of irony emerges as the similarity between a "wage slave" and an actual slave is disrupted by the numerous differences. The movement between the analogy and the irony gives the statement its power. Parsons made clear the difference between "wage slaves" and actual slaves by referring to actual slaves in her speeches. For example, in the speech "The Red Flag," Parsons declared, "[t]here is no slave so nice he won't dare assert his rights some time."[245]

Although de Cleyre, Goldman, and Parsons each faced identity constraints that influenced their arguments and personae, they all shared one thing that clearly distinguished their rhetoric from a rhetoric bound by the dictates of nineteenth-century femininity: they were anarchists. Because suffrage advocates were seeking inclusion through the vote, they had to adapt to the public norms. Although the effects of suffrage advocacy were, indeed, radical, advocates' means of presentation were not; their style employed the traditionally feminine.[246] However, the anarchist and labor movement represented a counterpublic sphere filled with alternative personae and operating with its own discursive norms that allowed women to be nondomestic—as workers, thinkers, agitators, and leaders. One alternative persona, identified by Matthews, is that of "disorderly women" in contrast to "Labor's True Woman." Although "Labor's True Woman," like the women who employed "feminine style," used "their moral authority in the home to justify their activism in the world," disorderly women, as working-class women, were "less bound by decorous norms of appropriate female behavior than middle class women."[247] Parsons may have approximated one of "Labor's True Women" as she embraced her widow role;

however, de Cleyre, Goldman, and Parsons were all disorderly women through their discursive enactment of anarchism.

In her analysis of nineteenth-century women's access to the public, Mary Ryan argues that women's "empowerment necessitated the construction of a separate identity and the assertion of self-interest."[248] The distinctiveness of disorderly women's rhetorical style presents a challenge because the history of women in public challenges us to listen carefully and respectfully for the voices of those who have long been banished from the formal public sphere and polite public discourse. Those most remote from public authorities and governmental institutions and least versed in their language sometimes resort to shrill tones, civil disobedience, and even violent acts in order to make themselves heard.[249]

Anarchists present this challenge, not only to expectations concerning public address but to expectations of femininity as well. Critics of public address must be attuned to the distinctive challenges faced by those who were most disenfranchised: the poor, the working class, persons of color, immigrants, the openly sexual, anarchists. What may be shrill, unfeminine, uncouth, or unusual may be the only option some of these speakers had. When we measure eloquence, we must not measure it against some supposedly neutral and abstract standard of aesthetics, but against a standard that can see and account for what was in the world of the speakers analyzed. Instead of searching for the timeless speech, perhaps we should attend to the speech most situated in time.

When Campbell wrote *Man Cannot Speak for Her*, she did so to "call into question what has become the canon of public address in the United States."[250] Campbell recognized that when measured against standards developed out of male discourse, women rhetors were often judged as failures. In response, she conceived the concept of feminine style to enable critics to see the innovative ways in which some women responded to their rhetorical challenges. However, if critics assess all women according to the elements of feminine style, then all anarchist women rhetors would be judged as failures, just as prevailing standards of public address long declared the suffragists failures. Even if we develop a set of criteria for anarcho-feminist rhetors, inevitably one or two of the three women studied here would fail. For this reason, we offer the idea that just as the rhetoric of women's liberation is an oxymoron,[251] the rhetoric of anarchist women is anarchic; there are no conventions of style, and there is an assumption of rule breaking. Given the privileging of individualism in anarchist thought, that these women differ is predictable. In particular, the absence of qualities associated with feminine style is understandable. Thus our use of the term "anarcho-feminine style" is not intended to indicate a set of rules or rhetorical conventions for these three women; rather, we use it simply as a way of drawing attention to the anarchic quality of their feminist discourse.

We also want to draw attention to the distinctively gendered personae of de Cleyre, Goldman, and Parsons. Campbell argues that many women "strategically adopted what might be called a feminine style to cope with the conflicting demands of the podium. That style emerged out of their experiences as women and was adapted to the attitudes and experiences of *female audiences*."[252] Although feminine style may have been one way to create gaps and fissures within socially inscribed gender norms, it was not the only way. Anarchist women had a distinct range of options because they were not bound by the expectations of a mainstream female audience, by working within the system, or by the confines of "true womanhood." When a speaker attempted to appeal to an audience broader than privileged women, the range of options expanded.

Unlike their more privileged counterparts, anarchist women were not bound by the conflicting demands of the podium engendered by the concept of "true womanhood": being pure, pious, domestic, and submissive. Parsons as a woman of color, de Cleyre as a woman of the lower working class, and Goldman as a Jewish

ANARCHIST WOMEN AND FEMININE IDEAL: SEX, CLASS, AND STYLE IN THE RHETORIC OF VOLTAIRINE DE CLEYRE, EMMA GOLDMAN, AND LUCY PARSONS

343

immigrant and worker were a priori denied the virtues of "true womanhood" because they had to leave the domestic sphere in order to earn wages. Their purity was suspect because they were associated with a movement linked to free love. As agitators, they clearly were not submissive, and atheistic anarchism was an affront to piety. Anarchist women did not violate "true womanhood" when they spoke; instead, their very being violated the qualities with which it was associated. Moreover, they were anarchists, part of a movement that aroused irrational fears in the public.[253]

Although all three women rejected "true womanhood," they still had to confront its demands because some in their audiences judged them by its norms, and social norms hold the power to inscribe particular gender performances. Both suffragists and anarchists had to confront the social expectations of femininity. However, the resources available—that is, the gaps and fissures within which to work—and the nongendered problems encountered by suffragists and anarchists differed. The suffragist and anarchist/labor movements operated as distinct, albeit perhaps sometimes overlapping, counterpublic spheres, "understood as critical oppositional forces within the society."[254] Given the long struggle of working women to redefine the public and private spheres, more expansive gaps and fissures in social inscriptions of gender existed for anarchist women. Consequently, a larger space for argument existed within the anarchist/labor movement. Nancy Fraser argues, ultimately, the existence of counterpublics expands the space for argument by challenging assumptions: "Still, insofar as these counterpublics emerge in response to exclusions within dominant publics, they help expand discursive space. In principle, assumptions that were previously exempt from contestation will now have to be publicly argued out." Fraser defines subaltern counterpublics as "parallel discursive arenas where members of subordinated social groups invent and circulate counterdiscourse to formulate oppositional interpretations of their identities, interests, and needs."[255] Because labor activists and anarchists were challenging some of the base assumptions of the social order, the challenging styles of de Cleyre, Parsons, and Goldman were more acceptable. This counterpublic relieved working women of many of the gender expectations faced by middle-class women. Clearly, diverse performances of gender may exist within a particular time, and the scope of rhetorical agency is influenced by the public in which one performs. Put differently, spheres of discourse create both obstacles and possibilities for rhetorical enactment, contingent upon the nature of a particular sphere.

Although we are not questioning the accuracy and value of Campbell's analysis of some early women's rhetoric, we do question the turn toward feminine style as the norm against which all women's rhetoric is judged and with which all women's speech is analyzed. Campbell herself eschews this essentializing practice. In many ways, scholars' reliance on feminine style is another example of how sex can be reinscribed and reiterated in the process of description.[256] As Butler warns, the process of "marking off will have some normative force and, indeed, some violence, for it can construct only through erasing; it can bound a thing only through enforcing a certain criterion, a principle of selectivity."[257] In other words, critics need to remember that feminine style is but one style among many styles and one version of the feminine among many. Otherwise, they simply reinscribe that which they are attempting to resist.

Anarchist women faced constraints as women, but those constraints and obstacles became areas of nongendered possibility—areas of possible systemic change, areas of possible rhetorical strategy—and did not evolve into a rhetorical style that could be considered conventionally feminine. Substantively, just as the suffrage advocates recognized that women were constrained by the lack of a ballot, so, too, did the anarchist women. However, anarchist women believed that the ballot would do little to alleviate the social, economic, and political ills women faced since it had done so little to help men. They instead sought other political and rhetorical approaches. Stylistically, they had to develop strategies to attract audiences not because they were women, but because they were anarchists and agitators. Their freedom to speak was restricted less by informal social constraints and more by the formal legal restraints imposed by the Comstock Act, the Sedition Act, and other similar laws.

Thus we offer this chapter as a beginning step in the development of a range of gendered styles available to women, a project called for by Celeste Condit in her contribution to the National Communication Association's "At the Helm" series. She argues: "Instead of trying to describe how men and women speak differently, we can begin to explore the range of gendered options available to people. Instead of merely repeating the apt insight that women's gender limits their speaking, and then rotely applying that insight to endless case studies, we can begin to explore the ways in which successful women . . . have constructed genderings that allowed them to speak effectively for their audiences."[258] Given the race, class, sexuality, and ethnicity of these women and their audiences, their constraints were different, and so were the ways they responded to them. Just as they would not be confined by the social constraints of what they saw as an unjust society, they should not be constrained by the theoretical demands of feminine style. Women can be philosopher-poets, agitators, and widows, as well as women.

Notes

1. L. Susan Brown, *The Politics of Individualism* (Montreal: Black Rose Books, 1993), 106.
2. Paul Avrich argues that de Cleyre eventually moved away from the focus on individualist anarchism; however, her thinking always maintained a strong focus on the individual and never moved toward the communist anarchism as Goldman once claimed. Instead, she preached tolerance among the many strands of anarchism. Paul Avrich, *An American Anarchist: The Life of Voltairine de Cleyre* (Princeton, N.J.: Princeton University Press, 1978), 147–55.
3. L. Susan Brown classifies Goldman's ideas as communist anarchist because Goldman emphasized the elimination of property relations as a necessary condition for achieving individual autonomy (*Politics of Individualism*, 115).
4. Avrich, *American Anarchist*, 153.
5. For a collection of extant Haymarket eulogies, see Voltairine de Cleyre, *The First Mayday: The Haymarket Speeches, 1895–1910*, ed. and intro. Paul Avrich (Minneapolis: Cienfuegos Press, Libertarian Book Club and Soil of Liberty, 1980).
6. Voltairine de Cleyre, *Selected Works of Voltairine de Cleyre*, ed. Alexander Berkman (New York: Mother Earth, 1914). De Cleyre's works also have been reprinted in Sharon Presley and Crispin Sartwell (eds.), *Exquisite Rebel: The Essays of Voltairine de Cleyre – Anarchist, Feminist, Genius* (Albany: SUNY Press, 2005) and A.J. Brigati (ed.), *The Voltairine de Cleyre Reader* (Oakland: AK Press, 2004).
7. Catherine Helen Palczewski, "Voltairine de Cleyre: Sexual Pleasure and Sexual Slavery in the 19th Century," *National Women's Studies Association Journal* 7 (Fall 1995): 54–68.
8. Margaret Marsh, *Anarchist Women, 1870–1920* (Philadelphia: Temple University Press, 1981), 132.
9. Ibid., 123.
10. Emma Goldman, *Anarchism and Other Essays* (1917; New York: Dover, 1969).
11. Martha Solomon, "Emma Goldman," in *Women Public Speakers in the United States, 1800–1925*, ed. Karlyn Kohrs Campbell (Westport, Conn.: Greenwood Press, 1993), 195.
12. The Haymarket martyrs were eight anarchists who were tried for and convicted of conspiring to detonate a bomb at a 4 May 1886 demonstration in Chicago's Haymarket Square. Seven police officers and four others were killed. More than 100 people were wounded. Even though no evidence was ever produced that the eight men had created, had placed, or even had prior knowledge of the bomb, all eight were found guilty of inciting the violence. Four were hanged (including

ANARCHIST WOMEN AND FEMININE IDEAL: SEX, CLASS, AND STYLE IN THE RHETORIC OF VOLTAIRINE DE CLEYRE, EMMA GOLDMAN, AND LUCY PARSONS

345

Albert Parsons), one allegedly committed suicide, and the remaining three were pardoned in 1893.

13. Carolyn Ashbaugh, *Lucy Parsons: American Revolutionary* (Chicago: Charles H. Kerr, 1976), 6. Parsons was a woman of color whose "true" racial identity was the subject of much speculation during her lifetime and remains unknown. Government records describe her husband as Caucasian. Her two children's birth certificates list them as "negro" or "nigger," while their death certificates maintain they were "white." See Ashbaugh, *Lucy Parsons*, 274.

14. Avrich, *American Anarchist*, 152.

15. Voltairine de Cleyre, "In Defense of Emma Goldman and the Right of Expropriation," in de Cleyre, *Selected Works*, 205–19. The speech was actually delivered on 16 December 1893.

16. Emma Goldman, "Voltairine de Cleyre Funeral Oration," 1914, 1, Joseph A. Labadie Collection, University of Michigan, Ann Arbor.

17. Emma Goldman, "America and the Russian Revolution," summary of lecture transcribed by E. J. Bamberger in "[Report to] Department of Justice," 18 January 1918, in *The Emma Goldman Papers*, ed. Candace Falk and Ronald J. Zboray, reel no. 48 (Alexandria, Va.: Chadwyck-Healey, 1991).

18. De Cleyre, "In Defense," 217.

19. Karlyn Kohrs Campbell, *Man Cannot Speak for Her*, vol. 1 (New York: Praeger, 1989). Campbell explains that "feminine style" was developed in order to push at sexist boundaries by using feminine gender expectations, thus developing a rhetoric that is "personal in tone"; relies "heavily on personal experience, anecdotes, and other examples"; is structured inductively; "invite[s] audience participation"; addresses the audience as peers; and has as its goal empowerment (*Man Cannot Speak for Her*, vol. 1, 10–12).

20. Ibid., 12.

21. Critical race feminists Adrien Wing and Kimberlé Crenshaw have articulated the theory of intersectionality, the notion that identity is multiplicative rather than additive. See Adrien Katherine Wing, ed., *Critical Race Feminism: A Reader* (New York: New York University Press, 1997); and Kimberlé Williams Crenshaw, "Mapping the Margins: Intersectionality, Identity Politics, and Violence Against Women of Color," http://www.hsph.harvard.edu/ grhf/WoC/feminisms/crenshaw. html, accessed 25 October 2000.

22. Goldman had a brief marriage to Jacob Kershner in 1887, not long after she immigrated to the United States and prior to her career as an anarchist activist. She married again in 1926 to a Canadian citizen; she used her acquired Canadian citizenship to reenter the United States years after her deportation in 1919.

23. Avrich, *American Anarchist*, 72.

24. Our focus on de Cleyre, Goldman, and Parsons is not meant to imply that they were the only anarchist women. In fact, many others were active at the time, including Margaret Anderson, Helena Born, Marie Ganz, Florence Finch Kelly, Molly Steimer, Kate Austin, and Lizzie Swank-Holmes. See Marsh, *Anarchist Women*, 176.

25. Ibid.

26. Ibid.

27. Marsha Hewitt, "Emma Goldman: The Case for Anarcho-Feminism," in *The Anarchist Papers*, ed. Dimitrios I. Roussopoulos (Montreal: Black Rose Books, 1986), 169–70.

28. Eleanor Flexner, *Century of Struggle* (Cambridge, Mass.: Harvard University Press, 1966), 62, 229.

29. Sara Evans, *Born for Liberty: A History of Women in America* (New York: Free Press, 1989), 68–69.

30. Barbara Welter, *Dimity Convictions: The American Woman in the Nineteenth Century* (Athens: Ohio University Press, 1976). Although Welter dates the "Cult of True Womanhood" as lasting from 1800 to 1860, she notes that its influence persisted even as the concept transformed itself into the "New Woman." See Welter, *Dimity Convictions*, 41.

31. Glenna Matthews, *The Rise of Public Woman: Woman's Power and Woman's Place in the United States, 1630–1970* (New York: Oxford University Press, 1992), see esp. chapters 5–8.

32. Flexner, *Century of Struggle*, 230–31.

33. Dorothy Schneider and Carl Schneider, *American Women in the Progressive Era, 1900–1920* (New York: Facts on File, 1993), 51.

34. Philip S. Foner, *Women and the American Labor Movement* (New York: Free Press, 1979), 85, 259.

35. Flexner, *Century of Struggle*, 247.

36. Richard Hofstadter, *The Age of Reform: From Bryan to F.D.R.* (New York: Knopf, 1977), 175–76.

37. Matthews, *Public Woman*, 197.

38. We do not mean to imply that the U.S. suffrage movement was class exclusive. Working-class women did play a role in the suffrage movement. See Ellen Carol Dubois, "Working Women, Class

Relations, and Suffrage Militance: Harriot Stanton Blatch and the New York Women's Suffrage Movement, 1894–1909," in *One Woman, One Vote*, ed. Marjorie Spruill Wheeler (Troutdale, Ore.: NewSage Press, 1995). However, the movement was predominantly middle and upper class, and this did have an effect on its rhetorical character. See Donna M. Kowal, "One Cause, Two Paths: Militant vs. Adjustive Strategies in the British and American Women's Suffrage Movements," *Communication Quarterly* 48 (Summer 2000): 240–56.

39. Marsh, *Anarchist Women*, 6–7.
40. Richard Drinnon, *Rebel in Paradise* (New York: Bantam Books, 1961), 68–77.
41. Robert K. Murray, *Red Scare: A Study in National Hysteria 1919–1920* (Minneapolis: University of Minnesota Press, 1955), 193.
42. Ibid., 7–16.
43. De Cleyre, *Selected Works*, 156.
44. De Cleyre borrowed this pseudonym from Sarah Payson Willis Parton, the first woman newspaper columnist in the U.S., the most highly paid newspaper reporter of her day, the first woman to praise *Leaves of Grass* in print, and the author of the best-selling *Ruth Hall*. See Joyce W. Warren, *Fanny Fern: An Independent Woman* (Rutgers University Press, 1994.)
45. De Cleyre, *Selected Works*, 156.
46. Voltairine de Cleyre, "Why I Am an Anarchist," *Mother Earth* 3 (March 1908): 20–21.
47. Avrich, *American Anarchist*, 153.
48. Voltairine de Cleyre, "The Past and Future of the Ladies' Liberal League," *Rebel* (20 October 1895): 18.
49. Voltairine de Cleyre, "The Gates of Freedom," *Lucifer* (29 May 1891): n.p.
50. Qtd. in Avrich, *American Anarchist*, 101.
51. Alix Kates Shulman, ed., *Red Emma Speaks: An Emma Goldman Reader* (New York: Schocken Books, 1983), 391.
52. Naomi Shepherd, *A Price Below Rubies: Jewish Women as Rebels and Radicals* (Cambridge, Mass.: Harvard University Press, 1993), 43–53, 278–79.
53. Emma Goldman, *Living My Life* (1931; New York: Dover, 1970), 59–60, 447.
54. Shepherd, *A Price Below Rubies*, 66.
55. Emma Goldman, "Intellectual Proletarians," in Shulman, *Red Emma Speaks*, 222–31.
56. Emma Goldman, "Anarchism: What It Really Stands For," in Goldman, *Anarchism and Other Essays*, 50.
57. Goldman, *Living My Life*, 21–23.
58. Emma Goldman, "Marriage and Love," in Shulman, *Red Emma Speaks*, 228. Also available in Emma Goldman, *Anarchism and Other Essays*, 3rd ed. (New York: Mother Earth, 1917; reprint, New York: Dover, 1969). For ease of reference, the version referred to throughout this essay will be the one published in Shulman, *Red Emma Speaks*, 227-39.
59. Goldman, *Living My Life*, 987.
60. Ibid., 8–10, 43.
61. Alix Kates Shulman, "Biographical Introduction," in Shulman, *Red Emma Speaks*, 23.
62. For a discussion on Goldman's relationships with men, see Candace Falk, *Love, Anarchy and Emma Goldman* (New Brunswick, N.J.: Rutgers University Press, 1990).
63. Marsh, *Anarchist Women*, 109.
64. Drinnon, *Rebel*, 68–77.
65. Marian J. Morton, *Emma Goldman and the American Left* (New York: Twayne, 1992), 156–57.
66. Shulman, *Red Emma Speaks*, 210–11.
67. Hippolyte Havel, "Emma Goldman: Biographic Sketch," in Goldman, *Anarchism and Other Essays*, 15–16.
68. Goldman, "Anarchism: What It Really Stands For," in Goldman, *Anarchism and Other Essays*, 65.
69. Marsh, *Anarchist Women*, 111.
70. Morton, *Emma Goldman*, 54.
71. For example, "Rebuff for Anarchists," *Portland Oregonian*, 19 May 1908; and Ben Boswell, "Old Red," review of *Living My Life*, by Emma Goldman, *Time*, 9 November 1931, 69.
72. Murray, *Red Scare*, 207.
73. For an account of Goldman's life after her deportation, see Alice Wexler, *Emma Goldman in Exile* (Boston: Beacon Press, 1989).
74. Ashbaugh, *Lucy Parsons*, 13–14.
75. Ibid., 30, 33–34, 217. Her husband, Albert Parsons, was the editor of the *Socialist*. For more information on the Working Women's Union and the introduction of women into the Knights of

ANARCHIST WOMEN AND FEMININE IDEAL: SEX, CLASS, AND STYLE IN THE RHETORIC OF VOLTAIRINE DE CLEYRE, EMMA GOLDMAN, AND LUCY PARSONS

347

Labor, see Emily Barrows, "Trade Union Organization among Women in Chicago" (Ph.D. diss., University of Chicago, 1927), 42.

76. Ashbaugh, *Lucy Parsons*, 44. Albert Parsons, Johann Most, and August Spies were on the drafting committee. Although Parsons did not write the manifesto, she embraced its theory of anarchism.

77. "The Female Anarchist," *Pittsburgh Leader*, 21 November 1886, clipping in Lucy Parsons's scrapbook, Albert Parsons Collection, State Historical Society of Wisconsin (SHSW), Madison.

78. Twenty years after its issue, while editing the *Liberator*, Parsons reprinted the entire manifesto in many of the issues.

79. "Declaration of Principles Adopted by the Anarchists' Congress Held in Pittsburgh, PA," *Liberator* 1, no. 22 (28 January 1906): 3.

80. Lucy Parsons, "Cause of Sex Slavery," *Firebrand* (27 January 1895), n.p.

81. Ashbaugh, *Lucy Parsons*, 217.

82. Judith Butler, *Gender Trouble: Feminism and the Subversion of Identity* (New York: Routledge, 1990), 24.

83. As sex is reiterated through performance or enactment, and in the process naturalized and thus made normal and inevitable, the reiteration also creates "gaps and fissures" or instabilities, "as that which escapes or exceeds the norms, as that which cannot be wholly defined or fixed by the repetitive labor of that norm" (Butler, *Gender Trouble*, 10). However, in Butler's work, the creation of fissures appears to be done across time, because the reiteration is a "temporal process," and not as the result of intentional acts by agents, as she makes explicit when she notes that "the agency denoted by the performativity of 'sex' will be directly counter to any notion of a voluntarist subject who exists quite apart from the regulatory norms which she/he opposes" (*Gender Trouble*, 15).

84. Candace West and Don H. Zimmerman, "Doing Gender," *Gender and Society* 1 (June 1987): 127.

85. Adrien Katherine Wing, "Brief Reflections," in Wing, *Critical Race Feminism*, 30

86. Joan Wallach Scott, *Gender and the Politics of History* (New York: Columbia University Press, 1988), 60.

87. Kathleen Canning, "Feminist History after the Linguistic Turn: Historicizing Discourse and Experience," *Signs* 19 (Winter 1994): 396.

88. For an excellent analysis of the influence of class on conceptions of woman's role and her emergence into the public sphere, see Matthews, *Public Woman*.

89. Canning, "Feminist History," 396.

90. For an expanded discussion, see Donna M. Kowal, "The Public Advocacy of Emma Goldman: An Anarcho-Feminist Stance on Human Rights" (Ph.D. diss., University of Pittsburgh, 1996).

91. For an exploration of the concept of "true womanhood" as pure, pious, domestic, and submissive, see Welter, *Dimity Convictions*, 21.

92. Emma Goldman, "The Tragedy of Women's Emancipation," in Shulman, *Red Emma Speaks*, 158–67.

93. Avrich, *American Anarchist*, 41.

94. Ibid., 88.

95. De Cleyre, "In Defense," 213, 214.

96. For examples of her poetry, see de Cleyre, *Selected Works*. For her explanation of the distinctions between poetry and prose, and of poetry's and literature's role in reform movements, see Voltairine de Cleyre, "The Poetry of Reform," unpublished manuscript, n.d., Joseph Ishill Collection, Houghton Library, bMS Am 1614 (250), Harvard University, Boston. For an analysis of the interactions between de Cleyre's essays, poetry, and speeches, see Eugenia C. DeLamotte, *Gates of Freedom: Voltairine de Cleyre and the Revolution of the Mind* (Ann Arbor: The University of Michigan Press, 2004).

97. Voltairine de Cleyre, "Literature the Mirror of Man," in de Cleyre, *Selected Works*, 379.

98. Ibid., 42.

99. Marsh, *Anarchist Women*, 104.

100. Joseph Kutera, "Voltairine de Cleyre: A Character Sketch," *Why?* 1 (August 1913): n.p.

101. *Detroit News-Tribune*, 25 January 1903, Joseph A. Labadie Collection, University of Michigan, Ann Arbor.

102. *Detroit News-Tribune*, December 1902, Joseph A. Labadie Collection, University of Michigan, Ann Arbor.

103. S. E. Parker, "Voltairine de Cleyre," *Freedom* (August 1914): 58, Joseph A. Labadie Collection, University of Michigan, Ann Arbor.

104. De Cleyre, "In Defense," 217.

105. Emma Goldman, *Voltairine de Cleyre* (Berkeley Heights, N.J.: Oriole Press, 1932), 15; Avrich, *American Anarchist*, 41–42.

106. Voltairine de Cleyre to Joseph Labadie, 11 May 1908, Joseph A. Labadie Collection, University of Michigan, Ann Arbor.

107. Voltairine de Cleyre, "On Liberty," *Mother Earth* 4 (July 1909): 151. A similar introduction was contained in "Our Police Censorship," a speech delivered on 8 October 1909 in Philadelphia at a public meeting in support of Emma Goldman (*Mother Earth* 4 [July 1909]: 297–301).

108. De Cleyre, "The Past," 32, 43.

109. Voltairine de Cleyre, "They Who Marry Do Ill," *Mother Earth* 2 (January 1908): 502.

110. De Cleyre, "They Who Marry," 502–6. See also Catherine Helen Palczewski, "Voltairine de Cleyre: Sexual Pleasure and Sexual Slavery in the 19th Century," *National Women's Studies Association Journal* 7 (Fall 1995): 54–68.

111. De Cleyre, "They Who Marry," 502.

112. Voltairine de Cleyre, "Sex Slavery," in de Cleyre, *Selected Works*, 351.

113. Voltairine de Cleyre, "The Case of Woman vs. Orthodoxy," *Boston Investigator*, 19 September 1986, 2.

114. Voltairine de Cleyre to her mother, Harriet Elizabeth de Claire, 22 January 1893, de Cleyre Papers, File 1, Joseph A. Labadie Collection, University of Michigan Library, Ann Arbor.

115. Voltairine de Cleyre, "The Gates of Freedom," *Lucifer* (15 May 1891): n.p.

116. The only example in which her own conversion to anarchism figured prominently is the essay "The Making of an Anarchist" (in de Cleyre, *Selected Works*, 154–63). Marsh notes this essay is "not typical" of de Cleyre because it is "deliberately personalized" (*Anarchist Women*, 138).

117. Marsh, *Anarchist Women*, 132.

118. De Cleyre, "Why I Am an Anarchist," 21.

119. Ibid., 22, 23, 25, 27–30.

120. Ibid., 30, 31

121. De Cleyre, "In Defense," 210.

122. Ibid.

123. De Cleyre, "They Who Marry," 502.

124. De Cleyre, *First Mayday*. See also Catherine Helen Palczewski, "Voltairine de Cleyre: Feminist Anarchist," in Campbell, *Women Public Speakers*, 143–55.

125. De Cleyre, "Sex Slavery," 342–58.

126. Ibid., 345, 352.

127. Ibid., 350.

128. De Cleyre, "Why I Am an Anarchist," 16, 17–18. In particular, her sentiments led to a "disgust with the subordinated cramped circle prescribed for women in daily life, whether in the field of material production, or in domestic arrangement, or in educational work; . . . an anger at the institutions set up by men, ostensibly to preserve female purity, really working out to make her a baby, an irresponsible doll of a creature not to be trusted outside her 'doll's house.' A sense of burning disgust that a mere legal form should be considered as the sanction for all manner of bestialities; that a woman should have no right to escape from the coarseness of a husband, or conversely, without calling down the attention, the scandal, the scorn of society" (de Cleyre, "Why I Am an Anarchist," 20).

129. Ibid., 21.

130. See de Cleyre, *First Mayday*.

131. De Cleyre, "In Defense," 216–17.

132. De Cleyre, "Gates of Freedom," *Lucifer* (29 May 1891): n.p.

133. Voltairine de Cleyre, "The Gates of Freedom," *Lucifer* (17 April 1891): n.p.

134. De Cleyre, "Ladies' Liberal League," 18.

135. Matthews, *Public Woman*, 178.

136. Marsh, *Anarchist Women*, 131–32.

137. De Cleyre, "Past," 43.

138. Voltairine de Cleyre, "The Gates of Freedom," *Lucifer* (24 April 1891): n.p.

139. Voltairine de Cleyre, "The Gates of Freedom," *Lucifer* (8 May 1891).

140. De Cleyre, "They Who Marry," 507.

141. Ibid., 506.

142. Alix Kates Shulman, *To the Barricades: The Anarchist Life of Emma Goldman* (New York: Thomas Y. Crowell, 1971), 3.

143. Marsh, *Anarchist Women*, 14–15.

144. Drinnon, *Rebel*; Falk, *Emma Goldman*; Morton, *Emma Goldman*; Shulman, *To the Barricades*; Martha Solomon, *Emma Goldman* (Boston: Twayne, 1987); Alice Wexler, *Emma Goldman: An Intimate Life* (New York: Pantheon Books, 1984); Elizabeth Berry, "Rhetoric for the Cause: The Analysis and Criticism of the Persuasive Discourse of Emma Goldman, Anarchist Agitator 1906–1919" (Ph.D. diss., University of California at Los Angeles, 1969); Kowal, "The Public Advocacy of Emma Goldman"; Andrea L. Rich and Arthur L. Smith, *Rhetoric of Revolution* (Durham, N.C.: Moore, n.d.); Vito Silvestri, "Emma Goldman: Enduring Voice of Anarchism," *Today's Speech* 17, no. 3 (1969): 20–25; Martha Solomon, "Ideology as Rhetorical Constraint: The Anarchist Agitation of 'Red Emma' Goldman," *Quarterly Journal of Speech* 74 (1988): 184–200; Solomon, "Emma Goldman."

145. Bonnie Haaland, *Emma Goldman: Sexuality and the Impurity of the State* (Montreal: Black Rose Books, 1993); Kowal, "The Public Advocacy of Emma Goldman"; Marsh, *Anarchist Women*; Solomon, "Emma Goldman."

146. Solomon, *Emma Goldman*, 131–48. This criticism of Goldman's rhetoric is echoed by Berry, "Rhetoric for the Cause"; and Rich and Smith, *Rhetoric of Revolution*.

147. Haaland, *Emma Goldman*, 183.

148. The analysis of Goldman's rhetoric presented here is partially based on Kowal, "Public Advocacy of Emma Goldman."

149. Emma Goldman, "What I Believe," in Shulman, *Red Emma Speaks*, 49–50.

150. Goldman, "Tragedy of Women's Emancipation," 158–67.

151. Goldman, "Marriage and Love," 204–13.

152. Goldman, "The Traffic in Women," in Shulman, *Red Emma Speaks*, 175–89.

153. Marsh, *Anarchist Women*, 93.

154. Linda Gordon, *Woman's Body, Woman's Right: A Social History of Birth Control in America* (New York: Grossman, 1976), 216–18.

155. Emma Goldman, [Sexual Instinct and Creativity] fragment and [Sexuality, Motherhood and Birth Control] fragment, in Falk and Zboray, *Emma Goldman Papers*.

156. Goldman, "Marriage and Love," 204–13.

157. Goldman's unpublished essays available only in fragment form suggest that she embraced both heterosexual and homosexual love. Haaland's argument that Goldman essentialized sexuality is based on a reading of her published speeches and writings only. For further discussion, see Kowal, "Public Advocacy of Emma Goldman," 113–20.

158. Goldman, [Sexual Instinct and Creativity] fragment.

159. Marsh, *Anarchist Women*, 123.

160. Emma Goldman, "Minorities and Majorities," in Shulman, *Red Emma Speaks*, 78–86.

161. Emma Goldman, "Individual Society and the State," in Shulman, *Red Emma Speaks*, 109–23.

162. De Cleyre, "In Defense," 214.

163. Drinnon, *Rebel*, 56.

164. "Rebuff for Anarchists," *Portland Oregonian*, 19 May 1908; Boswell, "Old Red," 69.

165. Emma Goldman, "Woman Suffrage," in Shulman, *Red Emma Speaks*, 202.

166. Originally appearing in Goldman, *Anarchism and Other Essays*. The version referred to was published in Shulman, *Red Emma Speaks*, 61–77.

167. Emma Goldman, "Preface," in *Anarchism and Other Essays*, 3rd ed. (1917; New York: Dover, 1969), 42.

168. Solomon, "Emma Goldman," 199.

169. Goldman, "Anarchism," 63.

170. Ibid., 69–70.

171. Ibid., 69.

172. Ibid., 68.

173. Marsh, *Anarchist Women*, 105–6.

174. Goldman, "Intellectual Proletarians," 222.

175. Goldman, "Anarchism," 69.

176. Ibid., 65, 68, 69.

177. Goldman, "Marriage and Love," 211.

178. Ibid.

179. For an extended analysis, see Kowal, "Public Advocacy of Emma Goldman."

180. Goldman, "Tragedy of Woman's Emancipation," 215.

181. Goldman, "Anarchism," 73, 74.

182. Ibid., 76–77.

183. James Joll, *The Anarchists*, 2nd ed. (Cambridge, Mass.: Harvard University Press, 1980), 167.

184. Goldman, "Anarchism," 65, 75–76.

185. Goldman, "Woman Suffrage," 202.

186. Ibid., 198, 199.

187. Shulman, "Biographical Introduction," 39–40.

188. Richard Drinnon and Anna Marie Drinnon, *Nowhere at Home: Letters from Exile of Emma Goldman and Alexander Berkman* (New York: Schocken Books, 1975).

189. Kowal, "Public Advocacy of Emma Goldman," 64–80; Shepherd, *Price Below Rubies*, 5–9.

190. Summaries and excerpt from lecture in William E. Carr "[Report to] United States Commissioner of Immigration," 19 April 1908, in Falk and Zboray, *Emma Goldman Papers*.

191. Emma Goldman to Minna Lowison, 12 May 1925, Labadie Goldman, Joseph A. Labadie Collection, University of Michigan, Ann Arbor.

192. Speech at Foyle's 29th Literary Luncheon, Grosvenor House, London, 1 March 1933, in Falk and Zboray, *Emma Goldman Papers*.

193. Shepard, *Price Below Rubies*, 31.

194. See Falk, *Emma Goldman*.

195. Matthews, *Public Woman*, 10.

196. Lisa Wilson, *Life after Death: Widows in Pennsylvania 1750–1850* (Philadelphia: Temple University Press, 1992), 1.

197. Wilson, *Life after Death*, 5.

198. Not until 1939, when Congress amended the 1935 Social Security Act to include them, did the U.S. government take responsibility for impoverished widows. See Arlene Scadron and Jerome H. Skolnick, eds., *Family in Transition*, 3rd ed. (Boston: Little Brown, 1980), xi.

199. Wilson, *Life after Death*, 101. As a widow of a "Haymarket martyr," Parsons was supported by the Pioneer Aid and Support Association; "the widows received $8 a week plus $2 each for the first two children and $1 for a third" (Ashbaugh, *Lucy Parsons*, 155). She also sold political pamphlets on the street and had a tailor shop.

200. Wilson, 11, 13.

201. Smith, *Rhetoric of Revolution*, 11.

202. Ashbaugh, *Lucy Parsons*, 104.

203. Qtd. in Ashbaugh, *Lucy Parsons*, 104.

204. "The Female Anarchist: Mrs. Parsons Talking at a Crowded Meeting at Claredon Hall," *New York Times*, 18 October 1886.

205. "Mrs. Parsons, the Wife of One of the Chicago Condemned Anarchists Stirs an Audience to a High Pitch of Enthusiasm," *Paterson (New Jersey) Morning Call*, 8 November 1886, clipping in Lucy Parsons's scrapbook, Albert Parsons Collection, SHSW.

206. "Mrs. Parsons Delivers an Anarchistic Address at Turner Hall Last Night," *St. Joseph (Missouri) Gazette*, 31 December 1886, clipping in Lucy Parsons's scrapbook, Albert Parsons Collection, SHSW.

207. "A Female Anarchist," *Baltimore American*, 20 November 1886, clipping in Lucy Parsons's scrapbook, Albert Parsons Collection, SHSW.

208. "Loud-Mouthed Treason: Mrs. Parsons Denounces the Law at Tobnener's Hall," *Kansas City Enquirer*, 20 December 1886, clipping in Lucy Parsons's scrapbook, Albert Parsons Collection, SHSW.

209. "Socialists and Anarchists: They Listen to one of Mrs. Parsons's Familiar Speeches," *New York Times*, 5 November 1886, clipping in Lucy Parsons's scrapbook, Albert Parsons Collection, SHSW.

210. Ashbaugh, *Lucy Parsons*, 149.

211. Lucy E. Parsons, "The Red Flag" assembled from partial transcriptions published in the *New York Globe*, *New York Herald*, and *Morning Journal*, 25 October 1886, by Robert J. Branham, unpublished, line 95.

212. The "I Am an Anarchist" and "The Red Flag" texts were constructed by piecing together newspaper accounts taken from Parsons's own scrapbook. The texts of the famous Lincoln-Douglas debates were pieced together in similar ways by Abraham Lincoln. See Paul M. Angle, *The Complete Lincoln-Douglas Debates of 1858* (1958; reprint, Chicago: University of Chicago Press, 1991), xlv. The most detailed text came from a speech given on 20 December 1886 at Kumps Hall in Kansas City.

213. Ashbaugh wrote of Parsons that "the burden of her sex, race, class and political beliefs made it imperative to 'act like a lady' to overcome the many prejudices which could lead to eviction and other forms of discrimination" (*Lucy Parsons*, 46).

214. Ibid., 43.

215. Franklin Rosemont, "A Bomb-Toting, Long-Haired, Wild-Eyed Fiend: The Image of the Anarchist in Popular Culture," in *The Haymarket Scrapbook*, ed. Dave Roediger and Franklin Rosemont (Chicago: Charles H. Kerr, 1986), 203. The first self-identified anarchist was Pierre-Joseph Proudhon, who seems to have originally adopted the label largely out of his predilection for paradox and scandal.

216. Rosemont, "Wild-Eyed Fiend," 203.

217. Ibid.

218. Lucy E. Parsons, "I Am an Anarchist," in *Lift Every Voice: African-American Oratory from 1787 to the Present*, ed. Philip S. Foner and Robert J. Branham (Tuscaloosa: University of Alabama Press, 1998), lines 6–8.

219. Ibid., lines 1–4.

220. Ibid., lines 16–17.

221. Ibid., lines 39, 40–41, 43, 44–46, 49–50, 109.

222. Ibid., line 38.

223. Ibid., lines 108–10, 131–36.

224. Parsons, "I Am an Anarchist," line 131.

225. "Lucy Broke Down the Door," *Orange (New Jersey) Journal*, 25 October 1886, in Lucy Parsons's scrapbook, Albert Parsons Collection, SHSW.

226. Parsons, "Red Flag," lines 12–13, 28, 33.

227. Ibid., lines 3–5.

228. Ibid., lines 92–95.

229. Matthews, *Public Woman*, 198.

230. Parsons, "I Am an Anarchist," lines 56–57.

231. Ashbaugh, *Lucy Parsons*, 149.

232. Parsons, "The Red Flag," lines 18, 45.

233. "Declaration of Principles," 3.

234. Lucy E. Parsons, "The Negro. Let Him Leave Politics to the Politician and Prayers to the Preacher," *Alarm* (Chicago), 3 April 1886, reprinted in Ashbaugh, *Lucy Parsons*, 64.

235. "On her last May Day—1941—Lucy Parsons rode as guest of honor on the Farm Equipment Workers float in the May Day Parade" (Ashbaugh, *Lucy Parsons*, 262).

236. Ibid., 6.

237. Marsh, *Anarchist Women*, 110.

238. Angela Y. Davis, *Women, Race and Class* (New York: Random House, 1981), 152–55. The only authority cited by Davis is Ashbaugh, *Lucy Parsons*.

239. Robert J. Branham, "The Role of the Convert in Eclipse of Reason and The Silent Scream," *Quarterly Journal of Speech* 77 (November 1991): 410.

240. Richard A. Lanham, *A Handlist of Rhetorical Terms* (Berkeley: University of California Press, 1991), 11.

241. Lanham, *Handlist*, 61–62.

242. West and Zimmerman, "Doing Gender," 127.

243. De Cleyre, "Sex Slavery."

244. Parsons's life before Chicago is sketchy at best.

245. Parsons, "Red Flag."

246. Campbell, *Man Cannot Speak for Her*, 12–13.

247. Matthews, *Public Woman*, 197–98.

248. Mary Ryan, "Gender and Public Access: Women's Politics in Nineteenth-Century America," in *Habermas and the Public Sphere*, ed. Craig Calhoun (Cambridge, Mass.: MIT Press, 1992), 284.

249. Ryan, "Gender and Public Access," 285–86.

250. Campbell, *Man Cannot Speak for Her*, 9.

251. Karlyn Kohrs Campbell, "The Rhetoric of Women's Liberation: An Oxymoron," *Quarterly Journal of Speech* 59 (February 1973): 74–86.

252. Campbell, *Man Cannot Speak for Her*, 12, emphasis added.

253. Avrich, *American Anarchist*, xiii.

254. Rita Felski, *Beyond Feminist Aesthetics* (Cambridge, Mass.: Harvard University Press, 1989), 166.

255. Nancy Fraser, "Rethinking the Public Sphere," in Calhoun, *Habermas and the Public Sphere*, 123, 124.

256. Although the attention devoted to analyzing the rhetoric of women who advocated suffrage was not meant to de-center other women, that focus, and the theory growing out of it, has had the unfortunate and unintended effect of shadowing the rhetorics of other women activists of the nineteenth century. Even though feminine style was developed specifically in response to the unique problems faced by early women suffrage advocates, other scholars have used feminine style as a method through which to analyze the speech of nonsuffrage and contemporary women. For example, Bonnie J. Dow and Mari Boor Tonn extend Campbell's concept of feminine style in two ways. First, they broaden the sphere of feminine style by arguing that it has application to discourses outside of the feminist movement, particularly mainstream politics, implying that feminine style need not serve feminist interests. Second, they argue that the effect of feminine style is not only strategic insofar as it serves to empower a female audience, but also philosophical in that it provides a political orientation to the world that values practical wisdom and judgment, emotional connections between people, and ultimately a nurturing relationship between a speaker and her audience. See Bonnie J. Dow and Mari Boor Tonn, "'Feminine Style' and Political Judgment in the Rhetoric of Ann Richards," *Quarterly Journal of Speech* 79 (1988): 286–302. Jane Blankenship and Deborah C. Robson share Dow and Tonn's vision of extending the construct of feminine style. See Jane Blankenship and Deborah C. Robson, "A 'Feminine Style' in Women's Political Discourse: An Exploratory Essay," *Communication Quarterly* 43 (1995): 353–66. They advocate the utility of feminine style for analyzing rhetoric across gender boundaries, including public policy discourse by women as well as some men, while recognizing that "[not] all women, monolithically, speak alike; rather, the intersections of gender, race, class, etc., mean that a multiplicity of voices help constitute variations within feminine style" (353). Indeed, the practice of using a single method in analyzing women's discourse, despite its complex diversity, is a problem.

   Unfortunately, the practice of using feminine style to analyze women's rhetoric over the years since its conception by Campbell suggests that it may represent *all* women's style and that it is the normative point of departure and even the measuring stick for the critical analysis of women's rhetoric, connections we wish to challenge. The crux of the problem lies not so much in the conceptualization of feminine style, or necessarily in individual critical essays, but in the singularity shown by its pattern of usage over time. Feminine style has become the terminisitic screen through which women's rhetoric is read. See Anne F. Mattina, "'Rights as Well as Duties': The Rhetoric of Leonora O'Reilly," *Communication Quarterly* 42 (Spring 1994): 196–205; Mari Boor Tonn, "Militant Motherhood: Labor's Mary Harris 'Mother' Jones," *Quarterly Journal of Speech* 82 (February 1996): 1–21; and Sara Hayden, "Re-Claiming Bodies of Knowledge: An Exploration of the Relationship between Feminist Theorizing and Feminine Style in the Rhetoric of the Boston Women's Health Book Collective," *Western Journal of Communication* 61 (Spring 1997): 127–63. In fact, recent critics of feminine style note that the concept and its extensions present problems in that they tend to overly constrain women's discourse within a framework that privileges a particular style of femininity. See M. Lane Bruner, "Producing Identities: Gender Problematization and Feminist Argumentation," *Argumentation and Advocacy* 32 (Spring 1996): 185–98.

257. Judith Butler, *Bodies That Matter: On the Discursive Limits of Sex* (New York: Routledge, 1993), 11.

258. Celeste M. Condit, "Gender Diversity: A Theory of Communication for the Postmodern Era," in *Communication: Views from the Helm for the 21st Century*, ed. Judith S. Trent (Boston: Allyn and Bacon, 1998), 183.

ANARCHIST WOMEN AND
FEMININE IDEAL: SEX, CLASS,
AND STYLE IN THE RHETORIC OF
VOLTAIRINE DE CLEYRE, EMMA
GOLDMAN, AND LUCY PARSONS

353

Passing the Torch of Women's Rights: Elizabeth Cady Stanton, Anna Howard Shaw, and Carrie Chapman Catt

Susan Schultz Huxman

12

Collectively, they spent seventy years of ceaseless campaigning on behalf of woman's rights in every state of the Union, in nineteen countries, in front of every imaginable audience, from presidents to pioneers, royalty to ruffians, learned to lay folks, supporters to skeptics. They were vaunted and vilified by the nation's press, clergy, politicians, and other reformers of their era. Though they rarely collaborated, each in her own way was considered an impressive speaker, an enactment of the evolved woman, and an indefatigable leader in securing the passage of the Nineteenth Amendment.

In an endurance test that not one of them imagined at the outset, Stanton, Shaw, and Catt "passed the torch" of woman's rights to each other in a marathon relay of Olympic proportions through the movement's three phases: inception (1848), tumult (1865–1915), and culmination (1920). Through crafty rhetorical maneuvering along the route, each emphasized distinct, but complementary, rhetorics that allowed for a woman's rights victory first only dimly perceived at Seneca Falls, New York.

Despite their connections, critics have never conceptualized these three leaders as a veritable relay team in the race for woman suffrage victory. This essay invites scholars to reappraise the way we study social movements and pay isolated tribute to woman's rights figures. Elsewhere, I have argued for the value of comparative critique in assessing the combined efforts of three pioneering reformers for woman's rights—Mary Wollstonecraft, Margaret Fuller, and Angelina Grimké—powerful rhetoricians who never met and whose circumstances were worlds apart, but whose rhetorics converged to form the nascent rhetorical vision of Seneca Falls.[1] Like that study, this one is undergirded by a distinct perspective. In my view, persuasion is often a slow, arduous process that places enormous burdens on the resources and momentum of movements. Since each movement must compete with other reform efforts, critics should consider how a movement relates, effectively or not, to particular historical forces during its own persistent evolution. As situations change and a movement evolves, its chances for success may be enhanced by the talents and contributions of diverse yet complementary leaders.

Rather than examining these three prominent leaders individually, this work attempts to preserve the "complex tapestry" of the early woman's rights movement by conducting a close inspection of the rhetorical choices of these three feminists.[2] I have selected what are arguably their most recognized and most important speeches for analysis: Stanton's "The Solitude of Self" (1892), Shaw's "The Fundamental Principle of a Republic" (1915), and Catt's "The Crisis" (1916).[3]

A Rationale for Comparative Critique of Stanton, Shaw, and Catt

Movements are rarely led by a single individual from start to finish. As Charles Conrad has argued, critics must preserve the "mosaic" of leaders' intersecting rhetoric in order to capture a collectivity's true nature.[4] Charles Stewart, Craig Allen Smith, and Robert Denton contend that as a movement matures, it needs new leadership, "a less impassioned and strident rhetoric as it enters the maintenance stage."[5] Similarly, Herbert W. Simons distinguishes between "militant" and "moderate" leaders, both of whom are necessary to movements in winning the support of antithetical, but important, power bases.[6] Furthermore, Stewart and his colleagues argue that movements need at least three types of leaders: prophets (visionaries who can express the ideology of the movement and set its moral tone), charismatic figures (persons who can generate enthusiasm and build membership), and pragmatists (organizational experts who can bring efficiency, common sense, and diplomacy to the cause).[7] These distinctive leadership types are necessary in order to appeal to a large cross section of potential converts and to align with three broad movement stages first enunciated by Leland Griffin as inception, crisis, and culmination.[8] Although such diverse leadership can produce discordance and splintering in movements, Ernest Bormann and Thomas Endres have separately suggested that the contribution of key "master plots"—namely, righteous, social, and pragmatic visions—could converge to create a "rhetorical vision" that appeals to a broad constituency.[9] Simply put, successful movements may draw on the distinctive rhetorical strengths of different leaders to craft a vibrant, multifaceted argument for their cause across time.

These contributions in movement scholarship suggest the usefulness of a focus on Stanton, Shaw, and Catt based on three factors: their prominence and longevity as distinctive leaders of the movement's key stages; their enactment of an evolving new model of womanhood stemming in part from the painful experiences in their formative years; and their rhetorical excellence as evidenced in the production of a classic speech.

Prominence and Distinctiveness as Rhetorical Leaders

Stanton, Shaw, and Catt represent the inception, crisis, and culmination stages of the woman's rights movement, a span of seventy-two years. Stanton was the most recognized leader in the inception phase, from her orchestrating the Seneca Falls convention in 1848 to her leading of the charge for including woman's enfranchisement of the Fourteenth and Fifteenth amendments in 1868. In passing the torch to

Shaw in the tortuously long crisis stage, 1870–1910, Stanton did not drop out of the race; she merely took a less prominent role. Likewise, Catt did not just appear at the end, but was being groomed alongside Shaw during the "doldrums" for her central role in the final, victorious stage between 1910 and 1920. All three were committed to a lifetime of suffrage activity and earned legendary reputations.

Of the three, Stanton was the best known and most persistent advocate of woman's rights in the nineteenth century, with a career that began at age twenty-five and did not abate until the age of eighty-seven. Even during her lifetime, she was called "the foremost American woman intellectual of her generation." Newspapers called her "America's Grand Old Woman" at the time of her death. She was the champion of a host of causes, including abolitionism, temperance, and labor reforms, but most notably she was a crusading figure for woman's rights broadly conceived. Her repertoire of woman's rights causes included suffrage, legal reform, coeducation, equal wages, birth control, property rights for wives, child custody rights for mothers, reform of divorce laws, dress reform, girls' sports and hygiene, and child care. She was a founder of the American Equal Rights Association, the National Women's Loyal League, and the National Woman Suffrage Association, and served as president of the merged National American Woman Suffrage Association (NAWSA). She was the first woman to run for the U.S. Congress.

Moreover, her speaking and writing output was prodigious. From 1869 to 1881, Stanton lectured for the New York Lyceum Bureau, often traveling to thirty cities in six weeks and speaking once daily. Her fees of $3,000 per year gave her enough income to provide higher education for her children. Her oratory was described as "the fire of genius" delivered in a "soothing alto voice" of "unshakable conviction" with a "logical incisiveness" that left audiences "spellbound," somewhat "intimidated," and even filled with "awe." Her journalistic career began early with the writing of a regular column for the *Lily*. She became editor of the *Revolution* (1868–70), assisted in editing the three volumes of *The History of Woman Suffrage* (1881, 1886), and wrote the controversial *The Woman's Bible* (1895, 1898).[10]

Anna Howard Shaw was also a legendary leader in her longevity and devotion to the cause. Shaw began speaking for temperance and suffrage in 1886 at the age of thirty-nine. Her work attracted the attention of Frances Willard, who asked her to serve the Woman's Christian Temperance Union (WCTU) as national lecturer. That spawned the beginning of a speaking career unparalleled in woman's rights advocacy. In 1887 the American Woman Suffrage Association hired Shaw as its national lecturer, and in 1890 NAWSA appointed her its national lecturer. In these posts, she made speeches on behalf of woman's rights, especially the right of suffrage, in every state of the Union. In 1915 she made 204 speeches in New York alone, and, as Wil Linkugel has tabulated, by the end of her career she had spoken more than 10,000 times. Newspapers called her "brilliant," "Queen of the Platform," and "the foremost orator of her generation." The *Boston Globe* even proclaimed that "her talent as an orator is unsurpassed [for] either sex," and an Oregon newspaper gushed that she was the "foremost woman speaker in the world." Catt herself said of Shaw: "She stood unchallenged throughout her career as the greatest orator among women the world has ever known."[11]

In 1892 she was named vice president of NAWSA and in 1904 named its president, a post she held for eleven years. During that time, NAWSA grew from a membership of about 13,000 to over two million in 1917. Karlyn Kohrs Campbell has concluded that "Shaw won more people for equal suffrage than any other advocate." In her final years, she became chairwoman of the Woman's Committee of the Council of National Defense, a post that won her the Distinguished Service Medal in 1919, the first living American woman to be so honored. She literally "died of overwork" on 2 July 1919 after a particularly grueling speaking tour in Indiana.[12]

Like her predecessors, Carrie Chapman Catt earned a reputation as an indefatigable leader of woman suffrage. Her career stretched from the 1880s to 1947, during which time she canvassed the globe on behalf of woman suffrage and the international peace movement. Best known as the leader who more than any other helped the Nineteenth Amendment become ratified in 1920, Catt first earned her leadership stripes in the Iowa Woman Suffrage Association and in the successful struggle for suffrage in the state of Colorado in 1893. After this victory, she was labeled "the new General" of the movement. She served ably as president of NAWSA from 1900 to 1904 and then again from 1915 to 1916, during which time she announced "the Winning Plan," a "tactical masterpiece."[13]

Like Shaw and Stanton, Catt maintained an exhausting speaking schedule. Robert Booth Fowler estimates that by 1900, she had traveled 13,000 miles and visited twenty states. By 1920 she had covered over 100,000 miles and spoken about 7,000 times. David Birdsell notes that her stage presence was described by the press as "perfect," her voice "splendid," her logic "unanswerable." As one reporter demurred: "There isn't much left to talk about when she gets through." On her fiftieth birthday, the front page of the *New York Times* declared her "one of the best-known women in the United States."[14]

The long-term commitment that each woman gave for the cause was one dimension that contributed to their success as leaders. Another was that each comfortably assumed one of the three central leadership roles that helped the cause move forward. Stanton became the movement's prophetic voice, a true intellectual and visionary who articulated ideology in uncompromising and righteous terms. Shaw assumed the movement's charismatic voice, enunciating a socially acceptable message in an effort to swell the ranks. Catt exemplified the movement's pragmatic voice, bringing an organizational efficiency and shrewd sense of diplomacy to secure the movement's aim.

Campbell has described Stanton as the movement's "pre-eminent thinker and publicist," "chief theorist," and "philosopher"; Beth Waggenspack labels her the movement's "agitator" and "philosopher"; Lois Banner describes her as the movement's "radical conscience" and "polemicist," who was "far more comfortable with confrontation rather than indirect political methods."[15] All of these assessments neatly support the idea that Stanton was the preeminent prophetic voice of the movement.

While Stanton articulated the philosophy of the movement, Shaw's job was to give that ideology mass appeal. "Shaw's contribution to the suffrage movement," according to Linkugel, "was not as a visionary"; rather, her role was to plough and sow rather than to plan the garden (Stanton's role) or reap the harvest (Catt's role).[16] Newspapers often reported that "greater entertainment is seldom enjoyed" than listening to Shaw, and "there [was] none . . . who [could] hold an audience with such pleasurable attention." Simply put, Shaw had a keen sense for how to entertain her audiences by inducing them to laugh at their fears by telling good stories and by engaging in playful repartee all in the name of a serious subject, woman suffrage. The movement could not have found a more effective charismatic.

Unlike Shaw, Catt "rarely spoke to entertain," according to Birdsell. Rather, critics have described her as "a rational pragmatist," "a great organizer," and "a practical politician." Shaw herself said of Catt: "She had the details of the plan of organization perfectly arranged. By her clearness and perfect understanding of methods, and by her tact in explaining and smoothing over difficult points, Mrs. Catt has greatly endeared herself to the suffrage world the world over." Catt assessed the importance of a movement's pragmatic leader in no uncertain terms: "Agitation for a cause is excellent; education is better; but organization is the only assurance of final triumph of any cause in a self-governing nation."[17]

As the movement's "radical conscience," Stanton found herself increasingly removed from the growing conservatism of the rank and file. From 1870 to 1880, she dropped out of the convention scene, objecting to its singular focus on suffrage and its accommodationist stance toward the politicians of both parties. Meanwhile, her incessant railing against organized religion so embarrassed many suffragists that in 1896 NAWSA officially rebuffed her. Stanton's view of Catt was cool. She did not consider her radical enough and did not approve of her single-minded concentration on suffrage.

Catt's view of Stanton was no more admiring. The first face-to-face visit between Stanton and Catt came in 1896 when Susan B. Anthony brought Catt to Stanton's home to explain why NAWSA had officially disavowed any connection to her book, *The Woman's Bible*. The meeting did not go well. Catt came away with the impression that Stanton was a selfish woman who had always gotten her own way and could not accept defeat or compromise. Later, Catt wrote that Stanton was "often out of control" and "irrational" and that "being a reformer could be counterproductive to the cause because reformers usually disdain politics and did badly when they tried to play the game."

Relations between Shaw and Catt were also tense, especially at the turn of the century. Both vied for the presidency of NAWSA, and losing to Catt hurt Shaw enormously. When Shaw did secure the presidency four years later, she gained many detractors. At sixty-eight, she was open to attack of a lack of energy, focus, and discipline. Catt joined the chorus of disenchantment. Shaw's main antagonists, however, were Alice Paul and Abigail Scott Duniway, the latter threatening to "have [Shaw] arrested if she tried to cross the border into Oregon." Toward the end of Shaw's tenure as NAWSA president, Catt averred with some condescension: "What is really needed is a truly great leader, and I, for one, feel that our movement never had one."[18]

Disputes of this sort between movement leaders are not unusual, especially between leaders who fulfill the vital roles of the cause. The righteous, social, and pragmatic voices of a movement are often "at war with one another." And yet, paradoxically, as Endres has observed, all three can coexist and complement one another within a given rhetorical community, and, in fact, are sometimes necessary to form a "tripartite public relations campaign."[19] These women's long record as rhetorical leaders stemmed, in part, from their ability to ground demands for woman's rights in their own personal experiences.

Enactment

With a slightly different label, enactment has already been suggested as a criterion for a comparative critique of suffrage rhetors.[20] A key determinant that united strong leaders such as Stanton, Shaw, and Catt in the woman suffrage battle was that each depicted her commitment to woman's rights as emerging from real-life experiences. Each woman felt a gradual tension between her own personhood and the socially constructed role of womanhood. For each, early life-shaping experiences with gender discrimination fueled a zealous commitment to woman's rights.

Stanton's memories of personal inequity are perhaps the sharpest. In 1819, upon the birth of her sister, Catherine, she heard many visitors remark regrettably that it was a pity the child was a girl. Then, at the age of eleven, her only brother, Eleazer, died. When she sought to comfort her father, Stanton remembered him saying: "Oh, my daughter, would that you were a boy!" As a teen and a member of the Presbyterian Girls' Club, Stanton saved pennies by baking and sewing to pay for the education of a man attending seminary. After his graduation, the club further assisted him by buying a new black suit and silk hat for him. But when the girls heard him preach his first sermon, he chose for his text 1 Timothy 2:21, "But I suffer not a woman to teach, nor to usurp authority of the man, but to be in silence." Stanton recalled leaving the church with her girlfriends in silent shock.[21]

In addition to these oft-cited episodes, her father's law practice revealed the many injustices endured by women seeking legal recourse. She heard the anguished stories of women who sought help in child-custody, property rights, and domestic violence cases, but were denied assistance from her father because women did not have legal rights in these areas. So offended was she by this condition that she sought to remedy the situation by cutting the unjust laws from her father's books.[22]

But more than anything else, Stanton traced her discontent to her utter isolation and increased domestic duties in Seneca Falls. Married for seven years to a reformer who was often traveling, and raising three of her eventual seven children in a desolate social environment, she wrote to Anthony: "How rebellious it makes me feel when I see Henry going about where and how he pleases. . . . He can walk at will through the whole world or shut himself up alone. As I contrast his freedom with my bondage, I feel that because of the false position of women I have been compelled to hold all my noblest aspirations in abeyance in order to be a wife, a mother, a nurse, a cook, and a household drudge."[23]

Shaw's personal discontent at woman's lot in life also began as a young girl. Shaw's father moved his entire family to the undeveloped northern forests of Michigan to establish a new colony when Anna was just twelve. Then, much to her puzzlement, he returned back East, leaving Anna and a younger brother to help their mother survive as best they could in the wilderness. This early lesson in self-reliance strengthened her resolve to pursue her dreams later in life, but also made her aware of the societal strictures of woman's lot in life.

When she entered Boston University Theological School at age twenty-seven, Shaw experienced the sting of discrimination in especially damaging ways. As the only female student in a class of forty-two, Shaw was neglected at every turn. Males were given free room and board; she was forced to rent a small attic room with no heat or running water and eat where she could find food. Though she persevered and finally accepted a call to be a pastor of a small Methodist church on Cape Cod, her troubles persisted. She had several altercations with townsfolk who frowned at the idea of a female minister. In part out of disillusionment, she embarked on a new career as a medical doctor in 1885.[24]

One of Catt's earliest lessons on the restricted role of women came during the presidential elections of 1872. Only thirteen, but enamored with politics, Carrie asked her mother why she was not changing her clothes to go vote with her father and the hired hands. When everyone laughed at this notion and her mother explained matter-of-factly that she was not allowed to vote, Carrie was speechless.

When Catt entered Iowa State Agricultural College in 1887, she was one of only six women in the school. While at Ames, she discovered several gender inequities, two of which she had a hand in changing. Through her efforts, physical education, which then was part of military training, was opened to women, and women were permitted to deliver speeches in the Literary Society.

Still, by her own admission, the nadir for Catt occurred in San Francisco in 1886, which she described as the worst year of her life. After the premature death of her first husband, Leo Chapman, she had moved to San Francisco to secure work in journalism. There she discovered that eking out a living as a single working female was virtually impossible. After a frightening evening when a male coworker attempted to assault her sexually, Catt realized for the first time what enormous pressures working women were under and became determined to do something for their protection.[25]

For each of these women, the "personal became the political." Each channeled her frustrations with discrimination into the same positive, energizing cause. From these early hurtful lessons in life, Stanton, Shaw, and Catt vowed to dedicate their lives to woman's rights. And true to form, each became a marathon reformer for the cause.

In their analysis of Anna Howard Shaw, Linkugel and Solomon examine the ways in which these suffrage rhetors specifically enacted their case. Recognizing that in order for woman's rights advocates to become effective as rhetorical leaders, Shaw had to model how women could retain their femininity, yet assert their worthiness as feminists. Calling it "the new woman," these scholars aver that the greater American public needed to witness suffrage leaders, like Shaw, pursuing new roles without sacrificing their womanly virtues; to see suffrage speakers demonstrate "the best of the old and the promise of the new." Few suffragists pulled this off with as much aplomb as Stanton, Shaw, and Catt. Each had an uncanny ability to enact "the new woman" in distinct, but compatible, ways.

Stanton was a radical feminist, but she was also, as Griffith has assessed, "a gracious, good-humored, charming mother of seven" who could shrewdly exploit her maternal identification to legitimize her revolutionary vocation. Waggenspack concurs, noting that Stanton's "ability to run a large household smoothly, successfully raise seven children without much help from her abolitionist husband, and her pride in housekeeping skills added to the matronly image of motherhood she wanted to foster." Banner maintains that journalists typically saw Stanton as a symbol of "benevolent maternity"; she was often compared to Martha Washington or Queen Victoria. One noted author of the time adroitly observed: "Stately Mrs. Stanton has secured much immunity by a comfortable look of motherliness and a sly benignancy in her smiling eyes, even though her arguments have been bayonet thrusts and her words gun shots." Stanton used her maternal experiences to discount the accepted "scientific truths" about women. She told audiences such things as her "experiment" while pregnant with her fifth child. During this time, she decided to challenge the belief that childbirth was an example of a woman's weak physiology and limited mental capacity. She exercised regularly, wrote prodigiously, and walked three miles the night before the child's birth. She had only her housekeeper present when the baby was delivered, and she resumed her normal routine immediately. Thus, rather cleverly, Stanton became the most radical spokesperson for woman's rights while still fulfilling the most traditional expectations of women.[26]

Because Shaw never married, the antisuffragists labeled her a "spinster suffragist," but her appearance, credentials, and subject matter undercut their depiction of a "lonely, barren, anti-woman activist." Linkugel and Solomon suggest that of all the leading suffragists' messages, Shaw's was the most conservative and least vulnerable to charges of upsetting the relations between the sexes.[27] She affirmed the importance of the home and the role of wife and mother; her affection and concern for children were well known. As a social worker in Boston for three years, she dealt principally with underprivileged children, an honorable and thoroughly feminine task. Further, she was never seen in public except in conservative clothing. She always wore black or her ministerial robes and insisted on being introduced as "the Reverend" Anna Howard Shaw. Like Stanton, Shaw found a delicate balance among her feminist arguments, keen intellect, professional credentials, logical brilliance, strong voice, verbal assault on opponents, and sheer physical endurance with a matronly appearance, a socially acceptable reform agenda, and humor.

Catt carved a middle road between Stanton and Shaw in enacting feminine and feminist ideals. Although she married twice, she never had children; while she treasured the marriage contract, she had a most unusual wifely role in each of her marriages. She became Leo Chapman's business partner as editor of the *Mason City (Iowa) Republican*. When he died suddenly from typhoid and she married George Catt, she insisted as part of the prenuptial that she have free one-third of every year to promote woman suffrage. While she couched her demands for suffrage in righteous terms, she was never a member of any church. Although her speeches were infused with "masculine qualities," such as battle metaphors, statistics, and scientific appeals, her ability to fraternize so easily with male politicians through backdoor diplomacy won her more male support from political quarters than any other suffragist. She was the only suffragist to have an enduring friendship with a sitting president, Woodrow Wilson. While most suffragists risked the "unpatriotic reformer" label in not supporting woman's role in the Great War, Catt was, according to Susan Zeiger, "the first prominent woman reformer to endorse American involvement," believing that wartime service was the necessary price for women's citizenship.[28] As NAWSA president, she demonstrated an amazing ability to diffuse conflict among members, let others take credit for movement gains, and play facilitator rather than authority. In all, Catt won over male politicians and female suffragists with a feminist message couched in practical, politically sellable ways.

Rhetorical Excellence

The campaign for woman's rights triumphed in part because Stanton, Shaw, and Catt were marathon advocates. Each of these women was a distinctive voice, an enactment of disenfranchisement, and, last but not least, an exceptional public speaker. Each delivered at least one "masterpiece" that inventively crystallized the vision of the movement and her role in it, received national accolades or demands for encore performances, and catapulted the speech and the rhetor into enduring prominence. Stanton's "The Solitude of Self," Shaw's "The Fundamental Principle of a Republic," and Catt's "The Crisis" are such classic speeches.

Stanton delivered "The Solitude of Self" three times over a three-day period, first to the House Committee on the Judiciary on 18 January 1892, then before the NAWSA convention on 20 January 20, and finally to the Senate committee on woman suffrage later that day. It evoked strong reactions from all three audiences. The speech was reprinted in the *Woman's Journal* and the *Congressional Record*. Susan B. Anthony stated it was "the strongest and most unanswerable argument and appeal made by the pen or tongue for the full freedom and franchise of women" and later "the speech of Mrs. Stanton's life." Shaw called it "an English classic," and Frederick Douglass said: "After her—silence." Karlyn Kohrs Campbell has summarized its enduring qualities by noting: "Today it has the power to speak to us, precisely because it transcends its time and place to talk of what it is to be human and of how our common humanity is the basis of all rights."[29] Though Stanton's leadership prowess was most recognized in the early phase of the movement, I chose this speech over others because it captured the understanding of woman's rights that she first enunciated in 1848, but in a more strikingly eloquent way to a much larger public more inclined to listen to a fresh, humanist appeal to self-sovereignty.

"The Fundamental Principle of a Republic" was Shaw's "all-occasion" signature speech. She gave it countless times to crowds everywhere. Campbell has noted that it quickly became known as "a masterpiece" and "a paradigmatic example of her skills and her strategies."[30] And yet given her predilection for extemporaneous speaking, she never gave it the same way twice. But the stock issues, anecdotes, and evidence of this speech are woven into many of her other addresses from 1888 to 1919. Linkugel explains that this speech best showed "Shaw's deadliest tactic" of exposing inconsistencies of the opposition in clever, even hilarious, ways.[31] The timing of this address was crucial in offsetting the growth of the antisuffragists and keeping the suffrage movement from stagnation, even decay.

"The Crisis" was Catt's strategic adaptation to a crisis that the movement faced in 1916. NAWSA was aimless and lurching from one defeat to another when Catt called an emergency convention in Atlantic City in September. The ranks divided over how best to secure woman's enfranchisement—whether to work exclusively for a federal amendment, concentrate on state legislatures, or continue working on both plans. Catt's address insisted that the federal amendment must be the movement's aim. The first unveiling of her "Winning Plan," the address was crafted expertly to raise the members' morale. It was, as Birdsell assesses it, a most "inspirational speech," a "major address that received much public attention" and conveyed brilliantly "her sense of urgency, opportunity, and mission." Remarkably, as Jacqueline Van Voris has concluded, the delegates were so impressed with her address that they hastily agreed with her plan, and when she asked for $1 million for the year's work, more than $800,000 was pledged immediately.[32]

Situational Constraints

If one knows nothing of the milieu in which Stanton, Shaw, and Catt were cast, the preceding analysis might suggest that through sheer fortitude, intellect, conviction, and rhetorical brilliance, these three women could run the race for woman's rights successfully. History, of course, tells us otherwise. From 1848 to 1920, the movement faced a plethora of roadblocks that stunted its growth, diminished its influence, derailed its focus, and, at times, nearly brought it to a complete standstill. As its torchbearers, these three leaders found themselves on an obstacle course, not a track. Some situational factors persisted, while others emerged only later in the movement's history. The persistent and evolving challenges remind us that movements are not discrete social phenomena; that their rhetorics co-opt other reform rhetorics; and that persuasion is an arduous process that burdens the resources and slows the momentum of any movement.

Persistent Obstacles

Resistance to change is part of human nature. Stanton, Shaw, and Catt understood that advocating changes in woman's position, however small, would invite suspicion, ridicule, and hostility. In her autobiography, Stanton observed philosophically: "The history of the world shows that the vast majority, in every generation, passively accept the conditions into which they are born, while those who demanded large liberties are ever a small, ostracized minority, whose claims are ridiculed or ignored."[33] After three decades of work for suffrage, Shaw conceded: "I have not yet won the great and vital fight of my life, to which I have given myself, heart and soul—the campaign for suffrage [and] when the ultimate triumph comes . . . I may not be in this world to rejoice over it."[34] Catt cut to the heart of the great resistance to their collective work: "The struggle for the vote was not what it appeared on the surface. Rather, it was an effort to bring men to feel less superior and women to feel less inferior."[35] All three were aware on some level of what Stanton had long noted: "the success of a movement depends much less on the force of its arguments, or upon the ability of its advocates, than the predisposition of society to receive it."[36]

Nonetheless, one can ask why this cause, especially woman suffrage, met with such fierce resistance. Why was woman suffrage fought longer and harder in the United States than in twenty-six other countries? Why did getting the word "male" out of the Constitution, as Catt calculated, "cost the women of the country 52 years of pauseless campaign"?[37] And why after the Nineteenth Amendment finally became law, passed by both houses of Congress, endorsed by the president, and duly ratified, did ten states still refuse to acknowledge that their female citizens could cast a ballot? Although the answers to these questions are complex, two stand out. First, the movement's demands were on a collision course with an intractable, long-standing view of male privilege and supremacy. Second, and equally important, the movement did not have a unified, consistent ideology. Because it was not tied to material interests or narrowly defined spiritual creeds, it often lacked focus and suffered division and distraction from within its ranks.

Summing up the daunting challenge suffragists faced in daring to defy the established order, Aileen Kraditor writes: "The movement of women to secure the vote was a conscious assault on ideas and institutions long accepted by most Americans." Americans were tied to the "sentimental vision of Home and Mother, equal in sanctity to God and the Constitution," and to dispute this eternal truth was to challenge theology, biology and sociology.[38] The ideals of chivalry, "true womanhood," and separate spheres undergirded cultural attitudes. In essence, the cultural attitude could be expressed axiomatically: women and men are constituted equally but differ in their destined relations in life as wife and mother, husband and provider. They represent different "spheres" of life, the woman's private, the man's public. These different but complementary spheres were necessary to preserve social, moral, and biological harmony. The respective genetic traits of man (assertive, logical, active, strong) and woman (reticent, emotional, sedentary, weak) are endowed by the Creator, made manifest by nature, and enforced by governing bodies.

Thus to many the campaign for woman suffrage was more than about going to the polls once a year; it was a threat to woman's physical and mental health. Women were incapable of undertaking the various intellectual and civic duties connected with voting; their physical constitutions were too delicate to withstand the turbulence of political life; their entrance into political life jeopardized the future good of humanity as it drew them away from their primary duties as mothers.

Advocacy for woman suffrage forced a battle over the definition of "woman's rights." From the standpoint of the established national consciousness, "sacrifice" (martyrdom) was the higher calling of woman, not her individual "rights" (selfish wants). As one leading eugenicist of the time put it: "The sacrifice of self . . . is the crown of woman's destiny. The eternal law of womanhood is suffering for the sake of the race."[39] And for that women could bask in the chivalric attention of men. As the Reverend James Todd explained in 1867: "It is her 'right' to be treated with the utmost love, respect, honor, and consideration in her sphere."[40] This position carried the imprimatur of many clergy; it was impervious to logic. When Stanton, Shaw, and Catt drew upon their considerable analytical and refutational skills to question this "truth," they confronted comments such as the one Catt fielded after a lengthy, incisively crafted suffrage speech: "We've been so used to keepin' our women down, 'twould seem queer not to";[41] or the comment made by a Senate Judiciary Committee member to Shaw after her vigorous appeal to that body: "There is no man living who can answer the argument of those women, but I'd rather see my wife dead in her coffin than voting, and I'd die myself before I'd vote to submit that amendment!"[42] Reactions like these prompted the ever-ebullient Shaw to remark: "Men are so sentimental. We used to believe that women were the sentimental sex, but they cannot hold a tallow candle compared with the arc light of the men."[43]

The other persistent problem women faced in fulfilling movement goals had to do with the very nature of their cause. Theirs was a broad, sometimes poorly defined cause (self-determination) without an official creed, specific material grievance, or political affiliation; its leaders were disenfranchised citizens. Kraditor's opening lines in *Ideas of the Woman Suffrage Movement* address part of this problem succinctly: "The woman suffrage movement had no official ideology. Its members and leaders held every conceivable view of current events and represented every philosophical position."[44] Stanton, for instance, viewed woman suffrage as just one of many goals of the movement; Shaw and Catt saw it as the centerpiece. Stanton derided organized religion as the central obstacle to the cause; Shaw used her position as a minister to advance the cause; while Catt, who was never affiliated with any church, claimed religion was a nonissue. The rank and file were even diverse demographically, composed of Republicans, Democrats, socialists, and anarchists; the religious and the irreligious; blacks and whites; laborers and elites; northerners, southerners, and westerners; native born and foreign born; single, married, and divorced; pacifists and militants. Shaw, for one, believed that this potpourri of personalities and ideas made the cause less threatening to society at large as she devoted great length to the issue in "A Fundamental Principle of the Republic."[45]

Joseph Gusfield has theorized that such movements, what he calls "status movements," are weakened in comparison to other movements precisely because they have no church, political, or associational unit that can explicitly defend their interests. Further, he explains, because such movements are looser collections of adherents formed out of sentiments rather than concrete objectified interests, the organization is less able to speak for its constituency.[46]

The woman's rights movement was weakened specifically from its multiple-ideological status in several ways. First, its leaders were committed to many causes simultaneously. Since woman's rights were grounded in human rights, Stanton, Shaw, and Catt found sympathy with and lent their leadership abilities generously to other movements working for the improvement of the human race. Before the Civil War, Stanton was a well-recognized abolitionist leader and founder of a temperance chapter. Shaw was the official lecturer for the WCTU. Catt was a founder and president of the International Woman's Peace Movement. Without leaders committing solely to woman's rights, the movement could easily drift. Anthony's admonishment of Shaw for dividing her loyalties between temperance and suffrage could have applied equally to Stanton and Catt: "You can't win two causes at once. You're merely scattering your energies. Begin at the beginning. Win suffrage for women, and the rest will follow."[47]

Second, the movement was weakened because its leaders were voteless citizens who, in remaining nonpartisan, gave politicians little incentive to listen to their demands. Refusing to play partisan politics gave the movement a veneer of respectability, but it came at a tremendous price. In not pinning their hopes to any one platform, they accentuated their disenfranchised status. This political act of remaining noncommittal was directly responsible for the movement's last and most bitter split.

Third, in crusading for different features of the cause, its leaders made the movement especially susceptible to disagreements and splits that slowed its momentum. In 1870 the movement split over differing reactions to the Fourteenth and Fifteenth amendments giving African American males the right to vote. The "conservative" American Woman Suffrage Association focused exclusively on suffrage through state ratification methods and encouraged male membership; the "radical" National Woman Suffrage Association retained the broad-based agenda of woman's rights, campaigning for suffrage through a federal amendment, and closed their doors to male members. Each published its own newspaper, conducted its own conventions, and vied for the same limited pool of movement members. Not until 1890 did the two factions unite.

The movement almost split again six years later over Stanton's publishing of *The Woman's Bible*, with a minority applauding Stanton's brilliance and brazenness and the majority denouncing her heresy and ineptitude. In fact, the movement split again, first in 1907 when Harriot Stanton Blatch, daughter of Elizabeth Cady Stanton, broke away from NAWSA to form the more radical Women's Political Union, and then more seriously in 1914, when disgruntlement over the nonpartisan position of the movement emerged. A "rebel" group, led by Alice Paul, founded the

PASSING THE TORCH OF WOMEN'S RIGHTS: ELIZABETH CADY STANTON, ANNA HOWARD SHAW, AND CARRIE CHAPMAN CATT

Congressional Union for Woman Suffrage, later the Woman's Party, as a semimilitant group that picketed "the party in power" (the Democrats) and openly solicited Republican support. These suffragists, Kraditor records, were upset because NAWSA merely asked men to give women the vote, and as long as women remained in the position of supplicants, men could continue to play political football with the demand of suffrage.[48]

All movements experience some dissension among their leaders and among the rank and file over the movement's aims and methods. Those movements without narrowly defined interests and restricted membership, however, are more prone to internal strife and have a more difficult time in mobilizing their resources to speak on behalf of the rank and file and to counter the competing persuaders of the established order.

Early Obstacles

Suffrage leaders had to be prepared for more than the intractable and persistent setbacks. Events of the day bore directly on the progress of the cause. When Stanton included woman suffrage as one element (number nine) in the "Declaration of Sentiments" (1848), its inclusion, no matter how innocuously placed, was nonetheless audacious. Male suffrage was still a relatively new concept in the United States. Not until 1828 did the advocates of male suffrage begin to win their battle. Until this time, most states had property qualifications for voting. In fact, not until 1850, two years after Seneca Falls, did North Carolina and Virginia finally relinquish the property rights stipulation and allow even nonlandowners to vote.

The cause of woman suffrage also suffered a major blow when the nation's press decided early on to wage an assault on its fledgling efforts. The three newspapers in the nation with the widest circulation during the antebellum period were published in New York City. The *New York Herald*, under the editorship of James Bennett, and the *New York Daily Times*, under the editorship of Henry Raymond, were openly hostile to the cause from its inception, calling the women who spoke on its behalf "unsexed" and "insane." Even Horace Greely's *New York Daily Tribune*, while supporting woman's rights early on, cooled on the cause during and after the Civil War.[49] Since most women were homebound and isolated from one another, they often did not see or hear the movement's leaders firsthand. They were often at the mercy of newspapers to form their initial impressions. Thus the movement's ability to attract a sizable following was thwarted from the start. Not until it generated enough resources to counter with newspapers of its own could it even begin to rebound and compete with such coverage.

Yet clearly the dominant obstacles to suffrage in its early stages were the Civil War and Reconstruction. "The dread artillery of war," Stanton resignedly admitted, "drowned alike the voices of commerce, politics, religion, and reform."[50] For fifteen years (1860–75) all reform efforts lost their glamour. Arthur Schlesinger has argued that "the moral letdown precipitated by this all-consuming war militated against social progress and naturally set back woman's rights."[51]

Despite the prospect that the nation might self-destruct, Stanton tried to put a positive spin on the Civil War's impact on the movement: "The war is music to my ears. It is a simultaneous chorus for freedom." By supporting the Union cause, Stanton firmly believed that women would earn the gratitude of abolitionists and Republicans and be rewarded with suffrage. She never anticipated an alternate outcome.[52] With her formation of the Woman's Loyal League, Stanton enlisted movement members to propagate the virtues of the Union cause, especially abolitionism, arguing that "there never can be a true peace in this Republic until the civil and political rights of all citizens of African descent and all women are practically established."[53] After the war's end, Stanton and others who had held their advocacy in abeyance to work on behalf of slaves were shocked, disillusioned, and embittered when Republican Party leaders informed them that "this is the Negro's hour" and that women must wait for their rights. After the war, five more years were consumed in writing the word "male" into the U.S. Constitution for the first time.

The ugly aftermath of the war, dubbed "Reconstruction," produced seething animosities and enduring controversies as Americans attempted to reunite their shattered national ethos. After Lincoln's assassination, the ascendant vice president, Andrew Johnson, was immediately slapped with impeachment proceedings. And though he was supported narrowly by a solitary vote not to impeach, the event cast a shadow on the presidency itself and seized the national interest for years.

The real harm that the war produced for the suffrage cause, however, was a generalized masculinization of the entire culture.[54] Catt expressed this change in nativist ways, observing that "the war had done two things to the immediate detriment of suffrage. . . . It had swept into their graves thousands of idealistic American men and it had opened the doors of America to thousands of unidealistic immigrant men."[55] Suzanne Marilley has noted that in their ratification debates over the Fourteenth and Fifteenth amendments, northern politicians unfurled a new objection to suffrage: military service was now a necessary qualification for voting. W. E. B. DuBois claimed that only the fine record of slaves' military achievements in the war made black enfranchisement possible. Charles Sumner and Horace Greeley echoed these sentiments, declaring that "the cause of human rights and of the Union needed the ballots as well as the muskets of colored men" and openly challenging Stanton by asking her "why women should have the ballot if they could not defend it with a bullet?"[56]

As the northern press gloated over the demise of the Confederacy, it concluded that southern men were no longer really men. Lee Whites keenly questioned: "To what extent had the loss of their public and political position reduced them so far that in addition to being unable to 'protect' their women they had been reduced to a position that was actually like that of their women?"[57] This kind of threat to their own self-worth and the entire chivalric way of life explains, in part, the fierce opposition to woman suffrage that arose in the South and produced such vile comments by southern politicians as: "We are not afraid to maul a black man over the head if he dares to vote, but we can't treat women, even black women, that way. No, we'll allow no woman suffrage. It may be right, but we won't have it."[58] Catt was not exaggerating when she said the turbulent years from 1870 to 1910 cost the women of this country "forty years during which they watched, prayed and worked without ceasing for the woman's hour that never came."[59]

Late Obstacles

While Stanton was consumed with trying to keep the torch for suffrage flickering during the early hazards, she was assisted by the emergent leadership of Shaw and Catt to confront later obstacles. Among those were an antisuffrage ascendancy fueled by the liquor interests, and distractions such as economic upheaval and international disputes. Upon her death, Stanton left it to Shaw and Catt to keep the suffrage hopes alive during World War I.

After the founding of the WCTU in 1874, the liquor interests responded to woman suffrage with a vengeance. Catt estimated that the liquor funds spent in political campaigns to defeat woman suffrage referenda, strong-arm politicians sympathetic to woman suffrage, and fill the coffers of candidates and parties resistant to the woman vote ranged upward to $10 million a year. With "amazed despair," she recollected, female advocates recognized that the liquor interests were "an invisible, devious and monstrous force against which suffrage was contending."[60]

Even with efforts such as Shaw's resignation as WCTU national lecturer in an effort to dissociate temperance from the woman question, woman suffrage remained linked to temperance. Shaw recalled that in the campaign for woman suffrage in Kansas, prospects for a victory looked exceedingly good until "the liquor dealers cast their united weight against suffrage by threatening to deny their votes to any candidate or political party favoring our Cause."[61] That ugly campaign became the precedent for countless others in the West.

The woman suffrage cause could not begin to compete with the monied interests of "demon rum." Perhaps what galled Catt and Shaw the most was the lavish amounts of money spent by liquor interests to prop up noted female antisuffragists in an attempt to pit woman against woman in what would be perceived as a silly, squabbling female dispute of little significance. Beginning in the late 1870s, a barrage of slick brochures and highly publicized speaking events by antisuffragists began to drown out the suffrage message. Everywhere one looked woman suffrage was being associated with divorce, promiscuity, looseness, and the neglect of children. Woman's rights figures were being portrayed as "noisy," "turbulent," "notoriety-seeking," "ambitious," "egotistical," and "strong-minded." Their real objective, according to antisuffragists, was to revolt against wifehood and motherhood as well as to urge anarchy of sex and reform against nature. As Stanton's agenda became more radical with age, she became a favorite target in the literature. Paraded as the "Stanton Stigma," antisuffragists associated her and the entire cause with an antifamily, prolabor, and an antichurch stance.[62] Catt noted that

> the women antis really aroused suffrage tempers in legislative hearings. Legislative committees divided the time equally between suffragists and antisuffragists and thus the appearance was given of a conflict between two groups of women, each presenting equal claims, before men who had the authority to act as judges. . . . When an anti with an ingratiating smile said, "Gentlemen, we trust you to take care of us and the government," almost any legislative committee could be counted on to beam with self-satisfaction in response.[63]

This precipitous rise in the power of the "antis" prompted Shaw to adopt what became her rhetorical signature, a solid logical yet entertaining refutation of the antisuffragists' case.

Countering the cacophony of shrill voices against the cause was one notable obstacle; trying to get the woman suffrage message heard through the turbulent events that cluttered the 1890s was another. The agrarian protests that grew out of the Populist revolt came to a fever pitch during this decade and overshadowed much suffrage maneuvering in the critical territories. The "Panic of 1893" began the most severe depression the nation had yet experienced, with 8,000 businesses failed, 156 railroads bankrupt, 500 banks closed, and 20 percent of the labor force out of a job. Between 1898 and 1902, the Spanish-American War and the conflict in the Philippines prompted the nation for the first time to look outward, feature international affairs over domestic, and envision its imperialistic prospects. Further, these battles reaffirmed "the ballot and the bullet" connection first touted after the Civil War. Black soldiers served admirably in these wars; one-quarter of the troops in the invasion of Cuba were black soldiers who worked alongside Teddy Roosevelt's "Rough Riders." Their patriotism did not go unnoticed by politicians or the press.[64]

Despite the fact that the American Woman Suffrage Association and the National Woman Suffrage Association united during the 1890s and appointed Stanton its president, Shaw its national lecturer, and Catt a chief organizer in the western states, little progress followed. Membership stagnated, and only three western states narrowly passed limited woman suffrage referenda. "The doldrums," as many scholars have pegged it, tested the character and commitment of its leaders. Stanton's death in 1902 seemed to foreshadow yet another slump in the movement's history.

After a brief surge of suffrage activity in the early part of the twentieth century, spurred on by the new era of progressivism, the movement faced another devastating setback: World War I, described by many historians as "the most savage conflict in history."[65] Even in the distracting years at the close of the nineteenth century the movement continued to receive some limited press coverage. But as Van Voris notes, by 1917 war news filled all the columns, and the suffragist cause was relegated to the category of nonnews. Suffragists were forced to use their limited financial resources on a few paid advertisements.[66]

More seriously, the war confronted suffragists with an ideological crucible. Both Catt and Shaw had spent decades as pacifists, arguing that the woman's vote would promote peace and work to end the brutality of armed conflict. Now in the throes of cataclysmic war, such rhetoric was unpatriotic, even seditious. As president of NAWSA and the International Women's Suffrage Alliance, Catt's position was scrutinized carefully. After much deliberation, Catt thought it politically astute to keep a low profile on peace during this time, especially if she wanted to preserve the friendship that she had cultivated with Woodrow Wilson and the momentum she had achieved on the Hill for her "Winning Plan" introduced just a year earlier. For this pragmatic decision, however, she was roundly criticized by both her friends abroad in the International Women's Suffrage Alliance and from certain religious blocks within the rank and file, like the Quakers. Shaw, who was freer to express her own opinions more stridently, having resigned the presidency of NAWSA just two years earlier, lent her voice in support of intervention and became chairwoman of the Woman's Committee of the Council of National Defense, a position for which she won the Distinguished Service Medal in 1919.

Expediency, patriotism, and patience in this case appeared to pay off. Unlike the aftermath of the Civil War, with its protracted debate over woman suffrage, the end of World War I brought a speedy House vote on the Nineteenth Amendment in early January 1918. Even in his own mind, Wilson's slogan that this was the war "to make the world safe for democracy" rang hollow without the enfranchisement of half of America's citizens. Enough representatives of both parties agreed. Though the Senate vote was more work, Shaw lived just long enough to see woman suffrage enacted into law in 1919, and Catt entered a voting booth to cast her ballot in the presidential election in 1920.

Passing the Torch of Woman's Rights

While the persistent early and late obstacles to woman suffrage were debilitating, movement leaders did not fail to seize a singular, but glimmering, opportunity provided by their historical milieu. Seeping into the national consciousness to challenge the well-established cultural ideal was an attractive discourse composed of various reform efforts all grounded in natural rights philosophy. In the 1840s (the "reform era") and again at the turn of the century (the "progressive era"), Americans were most susceptible to this rival, liberating philosophy. Stanton, Shaw, and Catt co-opted much of its appeal in legitimizing woman's rights.

Reform movements flourished in the early and latter stages of the nineteenth century, beckoning "do-gooders" to work simultaneously on any number of issues. Temperance, abolitionism, prison and mental asylum conditions, peace, labor and farm protections, and woman's rights rested on several presuppositions: that individuals could reach their full potential with protectionist legislation in a nation governed by democratic principles; that improved progress of humankind was inevitable; and that Americans were duty bound to express this impulse toward perfectionism. Above all, however, each reform movement touted the belief articulated in the Declaration of Independence that humans were created equal. As Schlesinger has noted, each reformer asked rhetorically, if all persons are created equal, why are women denied the right to vote, blacks held in bondage, farmers exploited, children abused, the sick and destitute held in deplorable conditions?[67]

The natural rights philosophy upon which all reforms were based evolved slowly, but was already gaining converts in the early stages of the nineteenth century as an established truth, not a debatable proposition. William Graham Sumner, a distinguished reformer of the era, carefully explained the radical ramifications of this new established truth. The medieval notion of rights was that they were grants or charters from the head of the state. Without action by civil authority, no human being had such rights. "Natural rights," as opposed to "chartered rights," meant that the fundamental presumption must be changed and that every human being must be regarded as free and independent, until some necessity had been established for restraint. Whatever rights the state might give to some should be given to all.[68]

Suffragists like Stanton, Shaw, and Catt based their demand for equality with men on the same ground as that of the nation's founders who fought for their independence from England. If all men were created equal and had the inalienable right to consent to the laws by which they were governed, women were created equal to men and had the same inalienable right to political liberty. Each of these three leaders in her "classic speech" stressed the ways in which men and women were similar. Men's and women's common humanity was the core of their plea.[69]

Existentialism, Methodism, and Social Darwinism

While Stanton, Shaw, and Catt associated themselves closely with other established movements besides woman's rights (abolitionism, temperance, and peace, respectively), their efforts at juggling dual causes in order to show that their real crusade was with human rights came with high political costs. Stanton's early connection with abolitionism alienated Southern women; Shaw's administrative post with temperance launched an antisuffrage ascendancy fueled by the liquor interests; Catt's avowed pacifism riled jingoistic politicians in both parties. All these movements had policy implications that made them controversial.

By contrast, when Stanton, Shaw, and Catt associated themselves rhetorically with three broad philosophic ideas (existentialism, Methodism, and social Darwinism, respectively), their efforts were more subtle and less subject to political polarization. Stanton's advocacy of self-determination, Shaw's sermonizing on the equality of men and women in the eyes of God, and Catt's pronouncements of the evolutionary progress of male/female relations held enthymematic power. Each was a promising new explanation of the value of a human rights philosophy, and co-opting the language of these ideas resonated with a larger, discerning public.[70]

If Stanton could be said to have possessed a motto, two phrases that she used with some regularity in her correspondence with others summarized it: "Self-development is a higher duty than self-sacrifice"; and "I place man above all governments, all institutions."[71] Throughout her career, Stanton emphasized the rights and responsibilities of individuals more than those of society or the state; self-sovereignty was the highest good. Long before Sartre, Camus, or De Beauvoir gave existentialism its recognition as a philosophical school, Stanton borrowed the themes of its earliest practitioners: Kierkegaard, Nietzsche, and Dostoyevsky. Her later works, in particular, show a strong affinity for the ideas embedded in these thinkers, including Kierkegaard's notion that the highest good for the individual is to find his or her own unique vocation without the aid of universal, objective standards; Nietzsche's disbelief in an orderly universe; and Dostoyevsky's view that human beings do not have a fixed nature but make choices that create their own nature.[72]

Events in the twilight of Stanton's suffrage career, no doubt, motivated her more inward, existentialist focus on woman's rights. She became increasingly disenchanted with what she perceived to be the movement's myopia—its all-consuming concentration on woman suffrage. The broader philosophic themes of individual autonomy seemed to have been swallowed up by this specific policy issue. She dropped out of the politicized convention scenes, arguing that "it is not in conventions that our best work begins. The radical reform must start in our homes, in our nurseries, in ourselves."[73] When her book *The Woman's Bible* was denounced by her own organization, she felt especially alienated and had cause to question the basic rationality of human beings, the inevitability of human perfection, and the final success of social reforms. Her response was to retreat and recapture the first principles of woman's genuine disaffection with the status quo.

"The Solitude of Self" resounds with the ideas of existentialist thought. From her startling opening remark ("The point I wish plainly to bring before you on this occasion is the individuality of each human soul") to her various illustrations of the aloneness of life ("the isolation of every human soul" and the "immeasurable solitude of self"), Stanton declares that woman must be "arbiter of her own destiny." Her familiarity with the work of Dostoyevsky is echoed in the story she tells of the fate of a Russian nihilist during his imprisonment in Siberia—an impassioned account of how liberal thought mitigated against his interminable solitude. Poignant stories like these punctuate the address and underscore her plea for giving women "all the opportunities for the full development of her faculties." Ultimately, they lead her to pronounce the irreducible "fact of human existence": "The strongest reason for giving woman all the opportunities . . . is the solitude and personal responsibility of her own individual life." In short, the speech is an eloquent manifesto of woman's rights couched in the tragic, but noble, themes of existentialism.

Shaw's Methodism subtly permeates her rhetoric. The height of Shaw's speaking career coincided with the phenomenal rise of Methodism in the United States. From 3 percent of all church members in 1776 to 34 percent in 1850, Methodists could boast by the 1880s that they were "far and away the largest religious body in the nation and the most extensive national institution other than the federal government."[74] The election of Methodist William McKinley to the presidency in 1896 further secured for John Wesley's heirs the centrality of Methodism in American life. Theologians Nathan Hatch and Russell Ritchey have argued that Methodism was so powerful in nineteenth-century America because it transcended class barriers and empowered common people to make religion their own. Methodists proclaimed a message of individual freedom, autonomy, responsibility, and achievement; they did not discourage preaching by anyone who felt the call. Thus it is no coincidence that women made up a substantial majority of Methodists in the United States and that Methodists were the first mainstream religious denomination to ordain women in the ministry. As a practical denomination, the faith presented itself as an alternative way of life to the hierarchical society of the Anglican gentry—a way of life that combined personal conversion and holiness with a radical, egalitarian social critique delivered in the republican language of U.S. civil religion.[75]

Shaw was drawn to Methodism while in high school when an itinerant Methodist minister from her district took a special interest in her rhetorical abilities.

PASSING THE TORCH OF WOMEN'S RIGHTS: ELIZABETH CADY STANTON, ANNA HOWARD SHAW, AND CARRIE CHAPMAN CATT

371

As Shaw noted, "Dr. Peck was ambitious to be the first presiding elder to have a woman ordained for the Methodist ministry."[76] Although Shaw quit the ministry to work full time for suffrage, she never quit the Methodist faith that propelled her into prominence. She continued to wear her ministerial gown and use the title of "Reverend."

Shaw's appeal to Methodism is embedded in "The Fundamental Principle of a Republic," although no direct references to the faith or its founder are mentioned. Her broad, opening appeal is to Protestantism: "Puritans left the old world to come to this country, led by the Divine ideal which is the sublimest and supremest ideal in religious freedom which men have ever known, the theory that a man has a right to worship God according to the dictates of his own conscience, without the intervention of any other man or any other group of men." She then articulates a specific Methodist belief in the equality of the sexes in the eyes of God: "And God said in the beginning: 'It is not good for man to stand alone' [Genesis 2:18]. That is why we are here tonight, and that is all woman's suffrage means; just to repeat again and again that first declaration of the Divine, 'It is not good for man to stand alone.'" She concludes with a more radical critique of government couched in patriotic language:

> Democracy . . . is more than a form of government; it is a great spiritual force emanating from the heart of the Infinite, transforming human character until some day, some day in the distant future, man by the power of the spirit of democracy, will be able to look back into the face of the Infinite and answer, as man cannot answer today, "One is our Father, even God, and all we people are the children of one family." And when democracy has taken possession of human lives no man will ask for himself any thing which he is not willing to grant to his neighbor, whether that neighbor be a man or a woman.

Shaw's peroration cements this patriotic-religious connection: "Men and women must go through this world together . . . it is God's way and it is the fundamental principle of a Republican form of government."

Similarly, Catt's devotion to the theories of human evolution approached religious fervor. She wrote: "I have spent my life in a sincere endeavor to help God's law of Evolution evolve."[77] The English philosopher Herbert Spencer was enormously popular in the 1870s and 1880s. The two great themes that dominated his philosophy were utilitarianism (liberty and happiness are the goals of man) and evolution (the natural law of "survival of the fittest" allowed societies to develop from simple to complex; from primitive to perfection). Although the scientist Charles Darwin appropriated many of Spencer's ideas, transforming evolutionary theory to reflect the laws of "natural selection," the notion of "social Darwinism" continued to reflect Spencer's view that individuals must have absolute freedom to struggle, to compete, and to gratify their instinct for self-interest.[78]

This idea, attractive to many suffragists of the time, captured the imagination of Catt in secondary school. By the time she was in college she had read all the works by Spencer and Darwin and penned her own optimistic message based on their ideas: "Human evolution is an invitation to people to speed the steady march of the human race to greater glory."[79]

"The Crisis" is Catt's invitation to the rank and file to spread the "steady march" of woman's enfranchisement: "Suffragists will accept the change [that the war hath wrought] as the inevitable outcome of an unprecedented world's cataclysm . . . and will trust in God to adjust the altered circumstances to the eternal evolution of human society. They will remember that in the long run, all things work together for good, for progress and for human weal." She issues a clarion call to a more perfect society and the inevitability of final victory: "The war will be followed by a mighty, oncoming wave of democracy. We will boldly lead in the inevitable march of democracy, our own American specialty. Sisters, let me repeat, the Woman's Hour has struck!"

Maximizing the benefits of co-opting these emergent ideas of human rights to support woman's rights required rhetorical savvy. Strategically, Stanton made no overt connection to Dostoyevsky, Nietzsche, or Kierkegaard; Shaw omitted any acknowledgment of John Wesley or the Methodist faith; Catt did not invoke the authority of a Spencer or Darwin. Co-optation efforts by their very design can obscure the demands of one cause for the other and constrain the ways in which a cause can be advanced.[80]

Yet the transparency of their co-optation efforts reaped a critical rhetorical advantage in piecing together a compelling message of woman's rights. Each rhetor exploited the logical persuasiveness of analogous reasoning. Co-opting the known to support the unknown reduces a rhetor's obligation to construct a full-blown rationale for a cause on its own grounds and eases the task of creating a new consciousness. Stanton, Shaw, and Catt cemented the historical connectedness of woman's rights to the emergent progressive ideas of existentialism, Methodism, and social Darwinism.

Patterns of Rhetorical Emphasis

As Stanton, Shaw, and Catt wove the ideas of their respective influences into their discourse of woman's rights, some well-defined patterns of rhetorical emphasis emerged. Stanton's co-optation of existential thought yielded an emphasis on *why* woman's rights were necessary. Her contribution to the meaning of woman's rights appealed to a universal audience. Shaw's co-optation of Methodism yielded a preoccupation with *who* must carry out the woman's rights agenda. Her piece of the message appealed to the general public. Catt's co-optation of social Darwinism yielded a fascination with *how* the movement could score a suffrage victory. Her addition to the message appealed to rank-and-file suffragists.

"The Solitude of Self" is a drumbeatlike repetition of Stanton's answer to the question: Why are woman's rights necessary? Her view that the facts of human existence embrace the demands of woman's rights is designed to strike a humanistic chord in all people. It is a timeless, enduring truth. Some of the many indisputable "facts" of human existence that Stanton weaves throughout the speech include: "the individuality of each human soul"; "the isolation of every human soul"; the necessity of "self-dependence, self-protection, and self-support"; "the birthright of self-sovereignty"; and "the responsibilities of life rest equally on man and woman." These facts form axiomatic principles that support woman's rights broadly conceived. In light of these facts, woman must be "arbiter of her own destiny"; the "incidental relations of life" [mother, wife, daughter] must not subordinate her rights and duties as an individual, as a citizen, and as a woman"; woman must be given "all the opportunities for the full development of her faculties" in order to "mitigate the solitude that at times must come to everyone."

In situating woman's rights in terms of the ultimate ground of existence, Stanton employs many water metaphors suggesting elemental sustenance and purity of woman's life. She is placed on a "solitary island"; each soul is "launched on the sea of life"; woman cannot be sheltered from "the fierce storms of life," "the terrible storms," or "the tidal wave [that] wrecks havoc on the shore." She must face the "darkness," "the cold night," "the silent stars," "the shadows" and "swim upstream," sometimes "drift[ing] with the current" before ultimately facing "death" alone. The existential facts of our humanness become all the more frightening when placed in the context of brutal scenic conditions, allowing Stanton to present her most eloquent plea for woman's rights:

> No matter how much women prefer to lean, to be protected and supported, nor how much men desire to have them to do so, they must make the voyage of life alone, and for safety in an emergency, they must know something of the laws of navigation. To guide our own craft, we must be captain, pilot, engineer; with chart and compass to stand at the wheel; to watch the winds and waves, and know when to take in the sail, and to read the signs in the firmament over all. It matters not whether the solitary voyager is man or woman; nature having endowed them equally, leaves them to their own skill and judgment in the hour of danger, and, if not equal to the occasion, alike they perish.

Stanton leaves us with the knowledge that "humans cannot change what Nature has bestowed," and thus "in the supreme moments of danger, alone woman must ever meet the horrors of the situation."

The preoccupation with why the cause is right allows Stanton to transcend the narrow policy debates over suffrage by associating woman's rights with the cosmic principle of solitude and self-sovereignty. That mystical emphasis, while downplaying the role of NAWSA in politicking for the vote, also strategically refutes the chivalric attitudes and protectionist legislation that underlie the prevailing view of separate spheres that deterred woman's advancement.

Shaw's "The Fundamental Principle of a Republic" is sensitive to the question: Who should be engaged in the battle for woman's rights? Careful not to cast the cause narrowly, or let inertia win the day, Shaw answers that the cause needs the help of everyone to succeed. She enacts the importance of individuals becoming actors. Self-references appear throughout the speech. "I" and "me" crop up no less that 117 times, compared with Stanton's two self-references. The ultimate aim of the speech is to unify the diversity of human agents.

The principal agents (suffragists) are referred to as "we," "the women of this country," and "I," but only occasionally as "suffragists." The coagents are "American men," whom Shaw coddles with comments such as "the average American man is a fairly good sort of a fellow" and "admirable people as far as they go." Shaw invests the American man with carrying out the noble ideals of a republic first enunciated by the nation's founders. With sweeping words of gratitude, Shaw acknowledges Puritans for being "sincere, honest and earnest men" of "profound conviction." She commends the good work of "the excellent ancestors of yours." She extols the virtues of "a great Democrat, Thomas Jefferson," and the work of both Republicans and Democrats for fostering "the evolution of a republic." Yet all the while Shaw reminds her audience with cutting humor that their efforts stopped short of a republic ideal. Even the antisuffragists are treated with respect: they are misguided, not vicious; quaint, not threatening. They are referred to as impersonal detractors, such as "those who oppose us," or "our opponents," or "they"; but just as frequently Shaw acknowledges them as friendly antagonists. They are "our good Anti friends," "the dear old Antis," and specifically "a young married woman from New Jersey" who "left her husband and home for three months to tell the women that their place was at home." In Shaw's discourse, human actors do not live so much in discord as with the possibility of harmonious coexistence.

Human agents are magnified in Shaw's discourse by associating them with all kinds of glorious and dubious acts. Shaw notes her own "speaking," "traveling," and "working" on behalf of suffrage. Other suffragists "are asking" for the vote and "merely asking" that "a republic that professes to be a republic, become a republic." The men of the country can "solve the problem" by "casting a ballot" to enfranchise their helpmeets. Puritans "practiced persecution," "drove," "burned," and "ducked" outsiders. The nation's founders "wrote" the Declaration of Independence and the Constitution; they "rubbed out" the word "taxpayer" and "wrote in the word white." Antisuffragists are "forever crying, the goblins will catch you if you don't watch out." They are preoccupied with "gathering more statistics than any other person I ever saw," and they "will tell you" that "suffragists are all sorts of creatures."

The featuring of those who should carry out the woman's rights agenda secures for Shaw's audience a belief in their own rational abilities to correct wrongs, to unify Americans as citizens of a true republic, and ultimately to take responsibility eagerly in casting aside the old protectionist views. The central action for all the characters in Shaw's discourse who speak for or against suffrage is dialogue. In reenacting witty exchanges with both men and women of her audience, Shaw achieves an intimacy with them that might be expected at a religious gathering where one is encouraged to take personal responsibility for one's own salvation.

Catt's pragmatism is the energizing feature of "The Crisis." In that vein, she meets the question of how woman suffrage will be achieved head on. In bolstering the commitment of the rank and file, Catt overcomes the perceived stagnation of the movement to focus on the multitude of ways in which women are propelling the cause upward and onward. Agents (women of the rank and file) become empowered agencies (a functional, unstoppable force when working as a unit). The speech has a decidedly up-tempo "forward march" pace to it that features the critical dimensions of the means necessary to bring about final victory.

Catt transforms individual suffragists into a potent, indestructible force, "a great Niagara" in ushering in the woman's vote. First, she establishes that the world war helped the world over to see women as functional "war assets," as "women [capable of] holding together the civilization for which men are fighting." Using the most utilitarian of metaphors, Catt proclaims that a realization has set in that "the woman 'doormat' in every land has unconsciously become a 'doorjamb.' . . . She will wonder how she ever could have been content lying across the threshold now that she discovers the upright jamb gives so much broader view of things. . . . The 'jamb' will never descend into a 'doormat' again."

Emboldened by the power of their collective might and muscle in the war, Catt argues that women must now channel their energies in "the inevitable march" for suffrage activity. They must now proceed as "suffrage master-masons," as the "builders of the suffrage roof." With exuberance, Catt intones, "shall we, like the builders of old, chant, 'Ho! all hands, all hands, heave to!' and while we chant, grasp the overhanging roof and with a long, pull, a strong pull and a pull together, fix it in place forevermore?" If so, she commands, "prepare for the forward march."

In accordance with a utilitarian philosophy, Catt emphasizes how the movement must proceed if it hopes to succeed. Suffragists are the conduit to no greater purpose than victory. Purpose is cast in a narrowly defined pragmatic way: passage of the Nineteenth Amendment is the end goal. In fact, the word "victory" is repeated fourteen times in the speech and is only exchanged for a rousing and repeated slogan, "The Woman's Hour has struck," an allusion to the victory of the Fourteenth and Fifteenth amendments when it was the "Negroes' Hour." In all, Catt's pragmatism energizes the appeal of a belief in human evolution and undercuts the passivity that impedes progress. In a fitting Darwinian summary, Catt announces: "As the most adamantine rock gives way under the constant dripping of water, so the opposition to woman suffrage in our own country has slowly disintegrated before the increasing strength of our movement."

Philosopher, Apologist, Mobilizer

To complete an examination of the complex tapestry that composed the rhetoric of woman's rights requires an inspection of the way in which Stanton's, Shaw's, and Catt's personae worked together in their classic speeches. Each woman comfortably assumed one of the distinctive roles of social movements (prophecy, charisma, pragmatism) to articulate a message most appealing to their primary audience. The way in which each rhetor co-opted an existing cause (existentialism, Methodism, and social Darwinism) to support her own philosophy of woman's rights created ideological tensions at a surface level, but ultimately allowed for a culminating transcendent rhetorical message to emerge.

As the movement's philosopher/agitator, Stanton's "Solitude of Self" is typified by penetrating, poignant, and disarming passages intended for a "universal audience," an audience of persons that transcend time and circumstance. Even though the speech was repeated to three specific audiences on diverse occasions (to two groups of legislators and to woman's rights supporters), in the typical style of philosophic discourse it remains virtually devoid of any references that an actual audience exists.

That pattern of poignant introspection (existential philosophizing on the fundamental purpose of life) followed by a jarring observation (agitation for a "righteous" cause) is commonplace in the speech. For instance, Stanton depicts the feeling of alienation with haunting repetition:

> When death sunders our nearest ties, alone we sit in the shadow of our affliction. Alike amid the greatest triumphs and darkest tragedies of life, we walk alone. On the divine heights of human attainment, eulogized and worshipped as a hero or saint, we stand alone. In ignorance, poverty and vice, as a pauper or criminal, alone we starve or steal; alone we suffer the sneers and rebuffs of our fellows; alone we are hunted and hounded through dark courts and alleys, in by-ways and highways; alone we stand in the judgment seat; alone in the prison cell we lament our crimes and misfortunes; alone we expiate them on the gallows.

Then Stanton disarms her auditor with cutting remarks: "Seeing then that life must ever be a march and a battle, that each soldier must be equipped for his own protection, it is the height of cruelty to rob the individual of a single natural rights. To throw obstacles in the way of a complete education is like putting out the eyes; to deny the rights of property, like cutting off the hands."

Elsewhere, she captures the terror of impending tragedy: "When suddenly roused at midnight with the startling cry of 'Fire! Fire!' to find the house over their heads in flames, do women wait for men to point the way to safety? And are the men, equally bewildered, and half suffocated with smoke, in a position to do more than try to save themselves?" Then she caustically asks: "[I]s it not the height of presumption in man to propose to represent her at the ballot box and the throne of grace, to do her voting in the State, her praying in the church and to assume the position of High Priest at the family altar?" But perhaps her most memorable lines as philosopher/agitator occur at the end. Poetic introspection ("Our inner being which we call ourselves, no eye or touch of man or angel has ever pierced. It is more hidden than the caves of the gnome; the sacred adytum of the oracle; the hidden chamber of Eleusinian mystery, for to it only Omniscience is permitted to enter") gives way to rueful shaming ("Such is individual life. Who, I ask you, can take, dare take on himself the rights, the duties, the responsibilities of another human soul?").

As the movement's apologist/entertainer, Shaw's "The Fundamental Principle of a Republic" is filled with humor, charm, and self-effacement altogether fitting for her audience composed of the general public, principally curiosity seekers, who have joined together in the town square to enjoy yet another speaker on the lyceum circuit. The pattern of witty repartee followed by self-effacement goes a long way toward fulfilling the needed leadership trait of charisma and enunciating an accompanying nonthreatening social message. Humor permeates the speech. Upon noting that antisuffragists claim that women would not use the vote, even if given it, Shaw retorts: "If we would not use it, then I really cannot see the harm of giving it to us, we would not hurt anybody with it and what an easy way for you men to get rid of us. No more suffrage meetings, never any nagging you again, no one could blame you for anything that went wrong with the town, if it did not run right, all you would have to say is, you have the power, why don't you go ahead and clean it up." This passage is followed by the humorous refutation of another antisuffrage argument: that the woman's vote is useless because wives will vote like their husbands. Shaw jabs: "[E]ven if we have no husbands, that would not affect the result because we would vote just as our husbands would vote if we had one." To the argument that women would have to sit on juries if given the right to vote, Shaw gets downright silly: "I have seen some juries that ought to be sat on, and I have seen some women that would be glad to sit on anything." And so it goes, one-liner after one-liner effectively diffusing the charges against suffrage, with Shaw playing the apologist/entertainer role to perfection.

Fueling this entertaining romp against the antisuffragist charges is Shaw's humble demeanor. In addition to repairing the damage done to the cause itself, Shaw's task is to purify the image of the agents, like herself, advocating the cause. No strident, elitist feminist delivers this message. On the contrary, more along the lines of a humble country preacher extolling an idealistic cause, Shaw makes her audience like her. She tells her audience intimate testimonials of growing up: "When I was a girl, years ago, I lived in the back woods"; and "Thirty-five years ago I lived in the slums of Boston." She tells them she has little sophistication: "I ask what that [feminism] is and no one is able to tell me. I would give anything to know what a feminist is." And elsewhere, "A clergyman asked me the other day, 'by the way, what church does your official board belong to?' I said I don't know. . . . Really it never occurred to me, but I will hunt them up and see." She tells them she is not ambitious: "[T]hey tell us that if women were permitted to vote that they would take office. . . . I don't think women have much chance, especially with our present hobbles." This humor/self-effacement pattern produces a winning apologia that features a likable agent who acts admirably on behalf of a socially desirable, even religiously inspired, cause.

Catt's "The Crisis" is a much-needed wake-up call to an audience of suffrage members committed to the cause but still languishing in the movement's "doldrums." As the movement's organizer/mobilizer, Catt infuses her speech with rhythmic pacing and evolutionary zeal. Her confidence in collectivities to secure their aim is at first simply announced matter-of-factly: "The object of the life of an organized movement is to secure its aim. Necessarily, it must obey the law of evolution and pass through the stages of agitation and education and finally through the stage of realization." Then her confidence in the success of the cause and in the political system that will embrace it is boldly pronounced:

Let us then take measure of our strength. Our cause has won the endorsement of all political parties. Every candidate for the presidency is a suffragist. It has won the endorsement of most churches; it has won the hearty approval of all great organizations of women. It has won the support of all reform movements; it has won the progressives of every variety. The majority of the press in most States is with us. Great men in every political party, church and movement are with us. The names of the greatest men and women of art, science, literature and philosophy, reform religion and politics are on our lists.

PASSING THE TORCH OF WOMEN'S RIGHTS: ELIZABETH CADY STANTON, ANNA HOWARD SHAW, AND CARRIE CHAPMAN CATT

Catt's supreme confidence sets the stage for a lengthy inspirational peroration designed to reenergize and recommit the rank and file to become the vital agencies to secure the movement's pragmatic aim: suffrage victory. In addition to repeating the word "victory" fourteen times in the speech, Catt fashions a rousing slogan: "The Woman's Hour has struck," which she repeats five times in the closing appeal. With dramatic flair, Catt proclaims:

> Awake, arise, my sisters, let your hearts be filled with joy,—the time of victory is here. Onward March. . . . Let us sound a bugle call here and now to the women of the Nation: "The Woman's Hour has struck." Let the bugle sound from the suffrage headquarters of every State at the inauguration of a State campaign. Let the call go forth again and again and yet again. Let it be repeated in every article written, in every speech made, in every conversation held. Let the bugle blow again and yet again. The political emancipation of our sex calls you, women of America, arise! . . . [T]he final battle is on.

Stanton's haunting speech was designed to disrupt an audience; Shaw's humorous speech was designed to cajole an audience; Catt's hopeful speech was designed to energize an audience. When taken together, these three speeches produced, paradoxically enough, both discordance and harmony.

Tensions between the speeches are obvious, echoing the competitiveness between leadership functions. The prophetic voice of Stanton envisioned woman's rights as encompassing "the complete emancipation from all forms of bondage, of custom, dependence, [and] superstition." Her plea was that liberal learning be open to all persons. The social and pragmatic voices of Shaw and Catt, on the other hand, envisioned woman's rights as a narrowly defined goal: woman suffrage. While Shaw and Catt based their entire plea on the need for "the vote," Stanton only mentioned "the ballot box" one time in her entire speech.

This difference in objectives led to other points of friction. Catt's speech especially espouses political efforts. She quoted noted male politicians throughout the address in order to grant legitimacy to the cause. Shaw had faith in the political system as well, though she poked fun at its shortsightedness. Stanton's address, however, is decidedly antipolitical. The speech is devoid of any reference to the power of political bodies to effect positive change; in fact, her whole existential premise sharply limited what political action can do to alter the human condition.

In the end, the way in which each co-opted the ideas of other causes (existentialism, Methodism, social Darwinism) contributed to the surfacing of these tensions. Stanton elevated the power of individual freedom in changing woman's subjugated position; Catt elevated the power of collectivities to improve woman's condition. And yet this notable difference produced an ironic similarity: both became camouflaged rhetors; their personalities in the movement were eclipsed by the philosophical views they espoused. Stanton referred to herself only twice; Catt offered only a few more self-references. Shaw's emphasis, on the other hand, elevated her presence. She became an omnipresent rhetor; her role in the movement took center stage, as an apologist's should. The stark difference between the speeches is most profoundly felt by comparing Stanton's and Shaw's closing remarks. Stanton soberly avers: "And so it ever must be in the conflicting scenes of life, in the long weary march, each one walks alone." Shaw optimistically concludes, "Men and women must go through this world together from the cradle to the grave, it is God's way and it is the fundamental principle of a Republican form of government."

Despite the incongruencies that these three speeches generated, their congruencies are more consequential. Their distinctive prophetic, charismatic, and pragmatic voices worked in harmony to combat their shared nemeses: an array of rhetorical obstacles that thwarted the cause. Each found a way to persuasively subvert "the old theory of the divine right of sex," as Shaw called it.[81]

Shaw good-humoredly showed the irrelevance of chivalry today: "I know that they say that men protect us now and when we ask them what they are protecting us from, the only answer they can give us is from themselves. . . . Now this old-time idea of protection was all right when the world needed this protection, but today the protection in civilization comes from within and not from without." More condemnatory, Stanton said: "The talk of sheltering woman from the fierce storms of life is the sheerest mockery [for] whatever the theories may be of woman's dependence on man, in the supreme moments of her life, he cannot bear her burdens." With supreme confidence and devastating clarity that comes from a grand historical perspective, Catt simply declared the end of the outworn view:

> From the beginning of things, there have been Antis. The Antis drove Moses out of Egypt; they crucified Christ . . . they have persecuted Jews in all parts of the world; they poisoned Socrates, the great philosopher; they cruelly persecuted Copernicus and Galileo, the first great scientists . . . they egged Abbie Kelley and Lucy Stone and mobbed Susan B. Anthony. Yet, in proportion to the enlightenment of their respective ages, these Antis were persons of intelligence and honest purpose. They were merely deaf to the call of Progress and were enraged because the world insisted upon moving on. . . . Give to them a prayer of forgiveness for they know not what they do; and prepare for the forward march.

With the old views deposed of whether through good humor, scolding, or bold pronouncement, a new perspective on woman's rights could emerge. Stanton, Shaw, and Catt used their collective voice to give that message clarity, mass appeal, and urgency. Stanton, the philosopher, reminded her audience that women are individuals first, and hence their rights are entailed by the human condition. To clarify this basic truth, she used the term "self-sovereignty" four times in her address, an expression that reinforced the speech's humanistic appeal. Shaw, the apologist, recalled that consent of its governed is the unifying principle of a republic. To give that truth mass appeal, she used the term "republic" an amazing thirty-six times. Thus, through a patriotic appeal, Shaw gave her listeners another glimpse of the rightness of the cause. Catt, the mobilizer, demonstrated that woman suffrage was the inevitable next stage of evolutionary progress. To give that truth urgency of implementation, she used the phrase "the Woman's Hour" seven times. Thus, through a progressive appeal, Catt gave her audience the final dimension of the new message.

When these three themes converge, they form a transcendent message of woman's rights that is compelling for an entire social order: woman's rights are grounded in natural rights. All three rhetorics supported this feminist philosophy; all three rhetors in their own way helped perfect it.

Conclusion

This analysis began by identifying the advantages of comparative critique in appraising the artistry and effectiveness of the rhetoric of the early woman's rights movement. Three considerations—longevity and distinctive leadership, enactment of the cause, and rhetorical excellence—were advanced to validate Elizabeth Cady Stanton, Anna Howard Shaw, and Carrie Chapman Catt as a veritable relay team in the race for woman's rights. In retracing the "laps" each ran, the essential task of retelling the lives of feminist foremothers was framed in a new light. Rather than concentrate on the rhetorical brilliance of these movement leaders singularly considered, this analysis supported the view so aptly expressed by Virginia Woolf that "masterpieces are not single and solitary births; they are the outcome of many years of thinking in common."[82] By comparing the rhetorical efforts of Stanton, Shaw, and Catt, this analysis sought to preserve the complex rhetorical mosaic of the movement's identity and to better articulate the dynamic of its feminist core.[83]

The comparative critique supported the idea that movements need leaders who can enunciate its philosophy (prophecy), give it mass appeal (charisma), and ensure victory (pragmatism). In metaphoric terms, critics have suggested that leaders must be like accomplished gardeners. It takes someone to plan the garden, another to plough and sow, and yet another to reap the harvest.[84] Or, consistent with the theme emphasized here, movements need relay teams to pace them through its three central stages: inception, crisis, and consummation. Stanton, Shaw, and Catt fulfilled these three critical functions well. Even though these roles are often in conflict, they were needed to mount a multifaceted public relations campaign in the securing of an enlightened view of woman's rights.

This essay has exposed individual rhetorical choices with an eye toward seeing how they formed a collective rhetorical body that relied upon conventional patterns of usage.[85] Campbell has noted that "in seeking to effect change, great works by women exploit existing symbolic resources." Stanton's existentialism, Shaw's Methodism, and Catt's social Darwinism were examined to show the extent to which feminism could be filtered through the most popular philosophies of the nineteenth century. These co-optation efforts demonstrated that "the principle of rhetorical invention is subversion"; that rhetors must "[use] the master's tools to undermine . . . the master's house." Similarly, all three enacted the view that "persona has been a singular rhetorical resource for women."[86] Stanton's role as philosopher, Shaw's role as apologist, and Catt's role as mobilizer were discussed to show how each woman captured a crucial audience necessary to the advancement of the cause; namely, a universal audience, a skeptical public, and converts already in the ranks. Each assumed a familiar and authoritative role for her audiences, then "strategically reconstructed [her role] to gain access to and legitimate [her] use of the argumentative resources ordinarily limited to males."[87] Stanton's existential appeal to universal human experience gave her "Solitude of Self" speech a haunting quality that disrupted auditors. Shaw's idealism gave her "Fundamental Principle of a Republic" a patriotic quality that cajoled auditors. Catt's pragmatism gave her "Crisis" speech a hopeful quality that energized auditors. Each woman appropriated conventional resources and used them ingeniously to contribute to a unified feminist message.

The discussion of situational constraints, named "persistent," "early," and "late" obstacles, reconstructed a historical terrain so full of pitfalls for woman's rights advocates of the nineteenth century that the rhetorical maneuverings of Stanton, Shaw, and Catt seem all the more spectacular. The recurring metaphor that these rhetors "passed the torch" of woman's rights to each other in a "marathon relay of Olympic proportions" does not seem overblown when viewed against a seventy-two-year backdrop of obstacles, including inertia, internal divisiveness, legal obstacles, negative press, Civil War, Reconstruction, antisuffragist ascendancy, monied opposition, other protest movements clamoring for attention, economic depressions, and the Great War. Further, the historical grounding of the movement supported the assumptions that persuasion is an arduous process that burdens the resources and slows the momentum of a movement's aim, and that movements are not discrete social phenomena and must compete with other reform efforts for the attention of an easily distracted public.

Stanton, Shaw, and Catt faithfully carried the torch of woman's rights through the movement's long, tumultuous course toward suffrage victory. But as Catt said upon ratification of the Nineteenth Amendment: "Nothing stops here." Her statement was prescient. Leaders like Betty Friedan, Gloria Steinem, and Bella Abzug would be waiting in turn to advance the cause and to perfect its message.

Notes

An earlier, condensed version of this essay appeared as "Perfecting the Rhetorical Visions of Woman's Rights: Elizabeth Cady Stanton, Anna Howard Shaw, and Carrie Chapman Catt," *Women's Studies in Communication* 23, no. 2 (Fall 2000): 307–36.

1. Susan Schultz Huxman, "Mary Wollstonecraft, Margaret Fuller, and Angelina Grimké: Symbolic Convergence and a Nascent Rhetorical Vision," *Communication Quarterly* 44, no. 1 (Winter 1996): 16–28.

2. Charles Conrad, qtd. in Martha Solomon, "Autobiographies as Rhetorical Narratives: Elizabeth Cady Stanton and Anna Howard Shaw as 'New Women,'" *Communication Studies* 42, no. 4 (Winter 1991): 355.

3. The published versions of "The Solitude of Self," "The Fundamental Principle of a Republic," and "The Crisis" are compiled in Karlyn Kohrs Campbell, *Man Cannot Speak for Her*, vol. 2 (New York: Praeger, 1989), 371–84, 433–60, 483–502. For an alternate, considerably longer, version of Catt's speech, see Terry Desch Croy, "The Crisis: A Complete Critical Edition of Carrie Chapman Catt's 1916 Presidential Address to the National American Woman Suffrage Association," *Rhetoric Society Quarterly* 28, no. 3 (Spring 1998): 49–73. Croy argues that "The Crisis" speech actually contained "The Winning Plan"; they were not separate speeches, as other sources have suggested. The 400-line addition in Croy's version does not alter the subsequent analysis of the speech offered here.

4. Charles Conrad, "The Transformation of the 'Old Feminist' Movement," *Quarterly Journal of Speech* 67 (1981): 288.

5. Charles J. Stewart, Craig Allen Smith, and Robert E. Denton Jr., *Persuasion and Social Movement*, 2nd ed. (Prospect Heights, Ill: Waveland Press, 1989), 43.

6. Herbert W. Simons, "Requirements, Problems, and Strategies: A Theory of Persuasion for Social Movements," *Quarterly Journal of Speech* 56 (February 1970): 1–11.

7. Stewart, Smith, and Denton, *Persuasion*, 39.

8. Leland M. Griffin, "The Rhetoric of Historical Movements," *Quarterly Journal of Speech* 38 (April 1951): 184–88.

9. Ernest Bormann, "Symbolic Convergence Theory: A Communication Formulation," *Journal of Communication* 35, no. 4 (Autumn 1985): 128–38; Thomas G. Endres, "Co-Existing Master Analogues in Symbolic Convergence Theory: The Knights of Columbus Quincentennial Campaign," *Communication Studies* 45 (Fall–Winter 1994): 295.

10. Elisabeth Griffith, *In Her Own Right: The Life of Elizabeth Cady Stanton* (New York: Oxford University Press, 1984), preface; Lois Banner, *Elizabeth Cady Stanton: A Radical for Woman's Rights* (Boston: Little, Brown, 1980), 69; Beth Waggenspack, *The Search for Self-Sovereignty: The Oratory of Elizabeth Cady Stanton* (Westport, Conn.: Greenwood Press, 1989) 69; Jeanne Stevenson-Mossner, "Elizabeth Cady Stanton, Reformer to Revolutionary," *Journal of the American Academy of Religion* 62, no. 3 (Fall 1994): 677; Campbell, *Man Cannot Speak for Her*, vol. 1; Karlyn Kohrs Campbell, *Women Public Speakers in the United States, 1800–1925* (Westport, Conn.: Greenwood Press, 1993).

11. Wil A. Linkugel and Martha Solomon, *Anna Howard Shaw: Suffrage Orator and Social Reformer* (Westport, Conn.: Greenwood Press, 1991), 3, 8, 9, 11, 97, 98.

12. Ibid.; Campbell, *Man Cannot Speak for Her*, vol. 1, 159.

13. Campbell, *Man Cannot Speak for Her*, vol. 1, 165.

14. David S. Birdsell, "Carrie Lane Chapman Catt: Leadership for Woman Suffrage and Peace," in Campbell, *Women Public Speakers*, 321; Campbell, *Man Cannot Speak for Her*, vol. 1, 165; Robert Booth Fowler, *Carrie Catt: Feminist Politician* (Boston: Northeastern University Press, 1986), 17, 115; Jacqueline Van Voris, *Carrie Chapman Catt: A Public Life* (New York: Feminist Press, 1987), preface.

15. Campbell, *Man Cannot Speak for Her*, vol. 1, 143, 144; Waggenspack, *Search for Self—Sovereignty*, 89; Banner, *Elizabeth Cady Stanton*, 45, 70, 101, 119.

16. Wil A. Linkugel, "Anna Howard Shaw: A Case Study in Rhetorical Enactment," in Campbell, *Women Public Speakers*, 409–20; Linkugel and Solomon, *Anna Howard Shaw*, 97, 109, 197, 417.

17. Birdsell, "Carrie Lane Chapman Catt," 321; Fowler, *Carrie Catt*, 17, 40, 127, 131; Van Voris, *Carrie Chapman Catt*, 60, 199.

18. Fowler, *Carrie Catt*, 22, 26, 43, 45, 107, 121, 222; Linkugel and Solomon, *Anna Howard Shaw*, 98; Banner, *Elizabeth Cady Stanton*, 45, 69, 70, 101, 155, 164–65; Griffith, *In Her Own Right*, 138, 165.

19. Endres, "Co-Existing Master Analogues," 295.

20. Solomon, "Autobiographies," 354–70.

21. Waggenspack, *Search for Self—Sovereignty*, 8–9; Jeanne Stevenson-Moessner, "Elizabeth Cady Stanton, Reformer to Revolutionary," 673.

22. Solomon, "Autobiographies," 359.

23. Banner, *Elizabeth Cady Stanton*, 29, 31.

24. Linkugel and Solomon, *Anna Howard Shaw*, 5, 11.

25. Van Voris, *Carrie Chapman Catt*, 6, 8.

26. Griffith, *In Her Own Right*, 163; Waggenspack, *Search for Self-Sovereignty*, 4; Banner, *Elizabeth Cady Stanton*, 51, 122, 123.

27. Linkugel and Solomon, *Anna Howard Shaw*, 109.

28. Susan Zeiger, "Finding a Cure for War: Women's Politics and the Peace Movement in the 1920's," *Journal of Social History* 24, no. 1 (Fall 1990): 75.

29. Campbell, *Man Cannot Speak for Her*, vol. 1, 135, 140, 141, 142; Waggenspack, *Search for Self-Sovereignty*, 82; Griffith, *In Her Own Right*, 203–4.

30. Campbell, *Man Cannot Speak for Her*, 1: 159.

31. Linkugel, "Anna Howard Shaw," 415.

32. Birdsell, "Carrie Lane Chapman Catt," 327; Van Voris, *Carrie Chapman Catt*, 132–33.

33. Elizabeth Cady Stanton, *Eighty Years and More: Reminiscences 1815-1897* (New York: Schocken Books, 1971), 317.

34. Anna Howard Shaw, *The Story of a Pioneer* (New York: Harper, 1915), 121.

35. Carrie Chapman Catt and Nettie Rogers Shuler, *Woman Suffrage and Politics* (New York: Charles Scribner's Sons, 1926), 73.

36. Stanton made this statement in 1888 before the U.S. Senate Committee on Woman Suffrage. See Campbell, *Women Public Speakers*, 85.

37. Catt, qtd. in Campbell, *Man Cannot Speak for Her*, vol. 1, 157.

38. Aileen Kraditor, *The Ideas of the Woman Suffrage Movement: 1890–1920* (New York: Columbia University Press, 1965), 14.

39. Lorna Duffin, "Prisoners of Progress: Women and Evolution," in *The Nineteenth-Century Woman: Her Cultural and Physical World*, ed. Sara Delamont and Lorna Duffin (New York: Barnes and Noble, 1978), 78.

40. Rev. John Todd, *Woman's Rights* (Boston: Lee and Shepard, 1867), 13–14.

41. Incident as related in "The Crisis" speech, 1916.

42. Linkugel, "Anna Howard Shaw," 418.

43. Shaw, "Fundamental Principles," 1915.

44. Kraditor, *Woman Suffrage Movement*, vii.

45. One section of Shaw's speech that tackles this issue at length is quoted here only in part: "A clergyman asked me the other day, 'By the way, what church does your official board belong to?' I said I don't know. He said, 'Don't you know what religion your official board believes?' I said, 'Really it never occurred to me, but I will hunt them up and see, they are not elected to my board because they believe in any particular church. We had no concern either as to what we believe as religionists or as to what we believe as women in regard to theories of government, except that one fundamental theory in the right of democracy. We do not believe in this fad or the other. . . . That is all there is to it.'"

46. Joseph Gusfield, *Symbolic Crusade: Status Politics and the American Temperance Movement*, 2nd ed. (Chicago: University of Illinois Press, 1986), 21.

47. Shaw, *Story of a Pioneer*, 182.

48. Kraditor, *Woman Suffrage Movement*, 231.

49. Sylvia D. Hoffert, "New York City's Penny Press and the Issue of Woman's Rights, 1848-1860," *Journalism Quarterly* 70, no. 3 (Autumn 1993): 657.

50. Stanton, *Eighty Years*, 234.

51. Schlessinger, qtd. in Joseph Gusfield, *Protest, Reform, and Revolt: A Reader in Social Movements* (New York: John Wiley, 1970), 129.

52. Griffith, *In Her Own Right*, 108.

53. Stanton, *Eighty Years*, 236.

54. LeeAnn Whites, *The Civil War as a Crisis in Gender* (Athens: University of Georgia Press, 1995), 135.

55. Catt and Shuler, *Woman Suffrage and Politics*, 160.

56. Suzanne M. Marilley, "Frances Willard and the Feminism of Fear," *Feminist Studies*, 19, no. 1 (Spring 1993): 135.

57. Whites, *Crisis in Gender*, 135.

58. Catt and Shuler, *Woman Suffrage and Politics*, 89.

59. Ibid., 108.

60. Ibid., 141.

61. Shaw, *Story of a Pioneer*, 252.

62. Richard N. Current, T. Harry Williams, Frank Freidel, and Alan Brinkley, eds., *American History: Since 1855*, vol. 2, 7th ed. (New York: Knopf, 1987), 615; Griffith, *In Her Own Right*, xv.

63. Catt and Shuler, *Woman Suffrage and Politics*, 272.

64. Current et al., *American History*, 587.

65. Ibid., 649.

66. Van Voris, *Carrie Chapman Catt*, 137, 143.

67. Schlesinger, qtd. in Gusfield, *Protest, Reform, and Revolt*, 128.

68. William Graham Sumner, *Social Darwinism: Selected Essays* (Englewood Cliffs, N.J.: Prentice-Hall, 1963), 65–66.

69. Kraditor, *Woman Suffrage Movement*, 74.

70. Americans of the educated class were familiar with the writings of these thinkers. Kierkegaard was required reading at most universities, even in all-women's schools. Dostoyevsky's *Notes from the Underground* (1864) received much press in the United States. John Wesley found his most sympathetic audience in America, and Herbert Spencer was considered "the supreme ideologue of the Victorian period." See Duffin, "Prisoners of Progress," 59.

71. See Waggenspack, *Search for Self-Sovereignty*, preface; Banner, *Elizabeth Cady Stanton*, 75.

72. See Alasdair MacIntyre, "Existentialism," in *The Encyclopedia of Philosophy*, vol. 3, ed. Paul Edwards (New York: MacMillan), 147, 149; Solomon, "Autobiographies," 597; Alice Leuchtag, "Elizabeth Cady Stanton: Freethinker and Radical Revisionist," *Humanist* 56, no. 5 (September/October 1996): 29; http://www.connect.net/ron/exist.html.

73. Stanton, qtd. in Banner, *Elizabeth Cady Stanton*, 75.

74. Nathan Hatch, "The Puzzle of American Methodism," *Church History* 63 (June 1994): 143.

75. Ibid.; Russell Richey, *Early American Methodism* (Bloomington: Indiana University Press, 1991), xvii; Earl Kent Brown, *Women of Mr. Wesley's Methodism* (New York: Edwin Mellen, 1983), xi.

76. Shaw, *Story of a Pioneer*, 58.

77. Fowler, *Carrie Catt*, 59.

78. Current et al., *American History*, 507.

79. Fowler, *Carrie Catt*, 9.

80. If the parallels between woman's rights and existentialism, Methodism, and social Darwinism were pushed too far, the strategy might have lost rhetorical force. In its purist sense, existentialism is antithetical to the impulse of rhetoric to change the human condition and stresses the limitations of social reform. In many quarters by the turn of the century, Methodists elected to ignore Wesley's plea for female equality and had reverted to limiting woman's authority in the church, many denominations even banning the ordination of women. Social Darwinism was also used by opponents of woman suffrage to argue that "what was decided among the prehistoric Protozoa cannot be annulled by Act of Parliament . . . the moral sphere, not the political sphere, is woman's province and vital to the future of human evolution." See Duffin, "Prisoners of Progress," 63.

81. All three rhetors effectively staged a counterassault to the chivalric views on women. Stanton, however, ignored the other obstacles that plagued the movement. Shaw concentrated on combating the "late obstacle" of suffrage ascendancy and took aim at the "ballot and the bullet" argument, a manifestation of the masculinization of culture that permeated the post–Civil War culture. Catt, however, attempted to refute most of the obstacles—persistent, early, and late—that plagued the movement.

82. Woolf, qtd. in Karlyn Kohrs Campbell, "Inventing Women: From Amaterasu to Virginia Woolf," *Women's Studies in Communication* 21, no. 2 (1998): 123.

83. Adrienne Rich aptly describes the harm in approaching the work of feminist leaders singularly: "Each feminist work has tended to be received as if it emerged from nowhere; as if each one of us had lived, thought, and worked without any historical past or contextual present. This is one of the ways in which women's work and thinking has been made to seem sporadic, errant, and orphaned from any tradition of its own." See Adrienne Rich, *On Lies, Secrets and Silence* (London: Virago, 1980), 11.

84. See Linkugel and Solomon, *Anna Howard Shaw*, 197.

85. Thus, while this essay is especially indebted to the many separate probative analyses of Stanton, Shaw, and Catt, it is more closely aligned methodologically with a few studies engaged in movement or rhetor comparisons. See Huxman, "Mary Wollstonecraft"; Solomon, "Autobiographies"; Cynthia Griffin Wolff, "Emily Dickinson, Elizabeth Cady Stanton and the Task of Discovering a Usable Past," *Massachusetts Review* 30 (1989): 629–44; and Nicholas McGuinn, "George Eliot and Mary Wollstonecraft," in Delamont and Duffin, *Nineteenth-Century Woman*, 188–205.

86. Campbell, "Inventing Women," 119.

87. Ibid.

BIBLIOGRAPHY

Ackerman, Jessie. "Noble Women." *Presbyterian Messenger*, 6 April 1894. Temperance and Prohibition Papers (Microfilm Edition), Woman's Christian Temperance Union National Headquarters Historical Files, Ohio Historical Society and Michigan Historical Collections , WCTU series, roll 42, frame 377.

Adams, Henry. *The Education of Henry Adams*. Boston: Houghton, Mifflin, 1974.

Anderson, James D. *The Education of Blacks in the South, 1860–1935*. Chapel Hill: University of North Carolina Press, 1988.

Anderson, Judith, ed. *Out-Spoken Women: Speeches by American Women Reformers, 1635–1935*. Dubuque, Iowa: Kendall/Hunt, 1983.

Anderson, Walter Truett. "Four Different Ways to Be Absolutely Right." In *The Truth about the Truth*, ed. Walter Truett Anderson, 110–16. New York: G. P. Putnam's Sons, 1995.

———. "Introduction: What's Going on Here?" In *The Truth about the Truth*, ed. Walter Truett Anderson, 1–17. New York: G. P. Putnam's Sons, 1995.

Andrews, James, and David Zarefsky, eds. *American Voices: Significant Speeches in American History, 1640–1945*. New York: Longman, 1989.

Andrews, John, and W. D. P. Bliss. *History of Women in Trade Unions*. Vol. 10 of *Report on the Condition of Women and Child Wage-Earners in the United States*. Washington, D.C.: Government Printing Office, 1911. Reprinted in Rosalyn Baxandall, Linda Gordon, and Susan Reverby, eds., *America's Working Women: A Documentary History–1600 to the Present*, 63–66. New York: Vintage Books, 1976.

Angle, Paul M., ed. *The Complete Lincoln-Douglas Debates of 1858*. 1958. Reprint, Chicago: University of Chicago Press, 1991.

Aptheker, Bettina. "Woman Suffrage and the Crusade against Lynching, 1890–1920." In *Woman's Legacy: Essays on Race, Sex, and Class in American History*, ed. Bettina Aptheker. Amherst: University of Massachusetts Press, 1982.

Argersinger, Peter H. "Ideology and Behavior: Legislative Politics and Western Populism." *Agricultural History* 58 (January 1984): 43–69.

———. "The Most Picturesque Drama: The Kansas Senatorial Election of 1891." *Kansas Historical Quarterly* 38 (1972): 43–64.

———. "Pentecostal Politics in Kansas: Religion, the Farmers' Alliance, and the Gospel of Populism." *Kansas Quarterly* 1 (1969): 24–35.

———. *Populism and Politics: William Alfred Peffer and the People's Party.* Lexington: University of Kentucky Press, 1974.

———. "Road to a Republican Waterloo: The Farmers' Alliance and the Election of 1890 in Kansas." *Kansas Historical Quarterly* 33 (1967): 443–69.

Arnesen, Eric. "American Workers and the Labor Movement in the Late Nineteenth Century." In *The Gilded Age: Essays on the Origins of Modern America*, ed. Charles W. Calhoun, 39–62. Wilmington, Del.: Scholarly Resources, 1996.

Ashbaugh, Carolyn. *Lucy Parsons: American Revolutionary.* Chicago: Charles H. Kerr, 1976.

Atkinson, Linda. *Mother Jones: The Most Dangerous Woman in America.* New York: Crown, 1978.

"The Atlanta Exposition." *New York Times*, 19 September 1895.

Avrich, Paul. *An American Anarchist: The Life of Voltairine de Cleyre.* Princeton, N.J.: Princeton University Press, 1978.

Badger, Reid. *The Great American Fair: The World's Columbian Exposition and American Culture.* Chicago: Nelson Hall, 1979.

Bagehot, Walter. *Physics and Politics.* Westport, Conn.: Greenwood Press, 1973.

Balthrop, V. William. "Culture, Myth, and Ideology as Public Argument: An Interpretation of the Ascent and Demise of 'Southern Culture.'" *Communication Monographs* 51 (1984): 339–52.

Bancroft, Hubert H. *The Book of the Fair.* 2 vols. Chicago: Bancroft, 1895.

Banner, Lois. *Elizabeth Cady Stanton: A Radical for Woman's Rights.* Ed. Oscar Handlin. Boston: Little, Brown, 1980.

Bare, Mrs. J. C. "A Call for Continued Action." *Jeffersonian* (Lawrence), 10 November 1892, 1.

Barnes, Djuna. *Interviews.* Ed. Alyce James Barry. Washington, D.C.: Sun and Moon Press, 1985.

Barr, Elizabeth N. "The Populist Uprising." In *A Standard History of Kansas and Kansans*, ed. William E. Connelley, 1115–95. Chicago: Lewis, 1918.

Barrows, Emily. "Trade Union Organization among Women in Chicago." Ph.D. diss., University of Chicago, 1927.

Barthes, Roland. *Mythologies.* Trans. Annette Lavers. New York: Hill and Wang, 1957.

Basche, Françoise. "Introductory Essay." In *The Diary of a Shirtwaist Striker*, by Theresa S. Malkiel. Ithaca, N.Y.: ILR Press, Cornell University, 1990.

Baxandall, Rosalyn. *Words on Fire: The Life and Writings of Elizabeth Gurley Flynn.* New Brunswick, N.J.: Rutgers University Press, 1987.

Baxandall, Rosalyn, Linda Gordon, and Susan Reverby, eds. *America's Working Women: A Documentary History–1600 to the Present.* New York: Vintage Books, 1976.

Beals, Carleton. *The Great Revolt and Its Leaders: The History of Popular American Uprisings in the 1890's.* New York: Abelard-Schuman, 1968.

Bennett, Lerone, Jr. *Before the Mayflower: A History of Black America.* New York: Penguin, 1962.

Benoit, William L. "Sears Repair of Its Auto Service Image: Image Restoration Discourse in the Corporate Sector." *Communication Studies* 46 (1995): 89–105.

Berlin, Ira, Marc Favreau, and Steven F. Miller, eds. *Remembering Slavery: African Americans Talk about Their Personal Experiences of Slavery and Freedom.* New York: New Press, 1998.

Berry, Elizabeth. "Rhetoric for the Cause: The Analysis and Criticism of the Persuasive Discourse of Emma Goldman, Anarchist Agitator 1906–1919." Ph.D. diss., University of California at Los Angeles, 1969.

Bicha, Karel D. "Jerry Simpson: Populist without Principle." *Journal of American History* 54 (1967): 291–306.

Biesecker, Barbara. "Coming to Terms with Recent Attempts to Write Women into the History of Rhetoric." *Philosophy and Rhetoric* 25 (1992): 140–61.

Birdsell, David S. "Carrie Lane Chapman Catt: Leadership for Woman Suffrage and Peace." In *Women Public Speakers in the United States, 1800–1925*, ed. Karlyn Kohrs Campbell, 321–38. Westport, Conn.: Greenwood Press, 1993.

Bjork, Daniel. *The Victorian Flight: Russell Conwell and the Crisis of American Individualism.* Washington, D.C.: University Press of America, 1978.

Black, Edwin. *Rhetorical Criticism: A Study in Method.* New York: Macmillan, 1965.

Blankenship, Jane, and Deborah C. Robson. "A 'Feminine Style' in Women's Political Discourse: An Exploratory Essay." *Communication Quarterly* 43 (1995): 353–66.

Blocker, Jack. *American Temperance Movements: Cycles of Reform*. Boston: Twayne, 1989.

Boa, Xialon. "Chinese Mothers in New York City's New Sweatshops." In *The Politics of Motherhood: Activist Voices from Left to Right*, ed. Alexis Jetter, Annelise Orleck, and Diana Taylor, 127–40. Hanover, N.H.: University of New England Press, 1997.

Bocock, Kemper. "The Southern Social Problem." *Social Economist* 4, no. 1 (1893): 22–28.

Bordin, Ruth. *Frances Willard*. Chapel Hill: University of North Carolina Press, 1986.

Bormann, Ernest. "Symbolic Convergence Theory: A Communication Formulation." *Journal of Communication* 35 (Autumn 1985): 128–38.

Boston Post. Woman's Christian Temperance Union National Headquarters Historical Files, Ohio Historical Society and Michigan Historical Collections Microfilms.

Boswell, Ben. "Old Red." *Time*, 9 November 1931, 69.

Boydston, Jeanne, Mary Kelley, and Anne Margolis. *The Limits of Sisterhood: The Beecher Sisters on Women's Rights and Woman's Sphere*. Chapel Hill: University of North Carolina Press, 1988.

Brands, H. W. *The Reckless Decade: America in the 1890s*. New York: St. Martin's Press, 1995.

Branham, Robert J. "The Role of the Convert in *Eclipse of Reason* and the *Silent Scream*." *Quarterly Journal of Speech* 77 (1991): 407–26.

Briffault, Robert. *The Mothers*. Abbrev. ed. Ed. G. R. Taylor. New York: MacMillan, 1959.

Brinkley, Alan, Richard N. Current, Frank Freidel, and T. Harry Williams. *American History: Since 1855*. Vol. 2. 7th ed. New York: Knopf, 1987.

Brinson, Susan L., and William L. Benoit. "Dow Corning's Image Repair Strategies in the Breast Implant Crisis." *Communication Quarterly* 44 (1996): 29–41.

Broadhead, Michael J. *Persevering Populist: The Life of Frank Doster*. Reno: University of Nevada Press, 1969.

Brown, Earl Kent. *Women of Mr. Wesley's Methodism*. New York: Edwin Mellen, 1983.

Brown, L. Susan. *The Politics of Individualism*. Montreal: Black Rose Books, 1993.

Bruner, Jerome. "The Ontogenesis of Speech Acts." *Journal of Child Language* 2 (1975): 1–19.

Bruner, M. Lane. "Producing Identities: Gender Problematization and Feminist Argumentation." *Argumentation and Advocacy* 32 (Spring 1996): 185–98.

Bryan, William Jennings. "America's Mission." In *William Jennings Bryan: Orator of Small-Town America*, ed. Donald Springen, 141–48. New York: Greenwood Press, 1991.

———. "'Cross of Gold' Speech July 9, 1896, at the Democratic National Convention, Chicago." Ed. Donald Springen. Tennessee Tech University. http://www.tntech.edu/history/ crosgold.html.

———. "Democracy's Deeds and Duties." In *William Jennings Bryan: Orator of Small-Town America*, ed. Donald Springen, 149–71. New York: Greenwood Press, 1991.

———. "Imperialism." In *Imperialism*, ed. Jim Zwick. 1995. http://www.boondocksnet.com/ailtexts/ bryanimp.html.

———. "The Prince of Peace." In *The Prince of Peace*, 3–63. London: Funk and Wagnalls, 1915.

———. "The Value of an Ideal." In *Speeches of William Jennings Bryan*. 2 vols. New York: Funk and Wagnalls, 1909.

Bryan, William Jennings, and Mary Baird Bryan. *The Memoirs of William Jennings Bryan*. Chicago: John C. Winston, 1925.

Burg, David. *Chicago's White City of 1893*. Lexington: University of Kentucky Press, 1976.

Burke, Kenneth. *Attitudes toward History*. 3rd ed. Berkeley: University of California Press, 1984.

———. *Counterstatement*. 2nd ed. Berkeley: University of California Press, 1968.

———. *A Grammar of Motives*. Berkeley: University of California Press, 1962.

———. "Ideology and Myth." *Accent* 7 (1947): 195–205.

———. *Permanence and Change*. Berkeley: University of California Press, 1984.

———. *Philosophy of Literary Form*. Berkeley: University of California Press, 1973.

———. *The Rhetoric of Motives*. Berkeley: University of California Press, 1969.

Burkholder, Thomas R. "Kansas Populism, Woman Suffrage, and the Agrarian Myth: A Case Study in the Limits of Mythic Transcendence." *Communication Studies* 40 (1989): 292–307.

———. "Mythic Conflict: A Critical Analysis of Kansas Populist Speechmaking, 1890–1894." Ph.D. diss., University of Kansas, 1988.

Burkholder, Thomas R., and Karlyn Kohrs Campbell. *Critiques of Contemporary Rhetoric*. 2nd ed. Belmont, Calif.: Wadsworth, 1997.

Burr, Agnes Rush. *Gleams of Grace*. Philadelphia: J. B. Lippincott, 1887.

———. *Russell H. Conwell: The Work and The Man*. Philadelphia: John C. Winston, 1905.

———. *Russell H. Conwell and His Work*. Philadelphia: John C. Winston, 1926.

Butler, Judith. *Bodies That Matter: On the Discursive Limits of Sex*. New York: Routledge, 1993.

———. *Gender Trouble: Feminism and the Subversion of Identity*. New York: Routledge, 1990.

Butler, Sherry Devereaux. "The Apologia, 1971 Genre." *Southern Speech Communication Journal* 37 (1972): 281–89.

Cain, Richard H. "Civil Rights Bill." In *Negro Orators and Their Orations*, ed. Carter G. Woodson, 328–38. New York: Russell and Russell, 1925.

Calais (Maine) Times, 23 June 1891. Woman's Christian Temperance Union National Headquarters Historical Files, Ohio Historical Society and Michigan Historical Collections Microfilms.

Calhoun, Charles W. "Introduction." In *The Gilded Age: Essays on the Origins of Modern America*, ed. Charles W. Calhoun, xi–xix. Wilmington, Del.: Scholarly Resources, 1996.

———. "The Political Culture: Public Life and the Conduct of Politics." In *The Gilded Age: Essay on the Origins of Modern America*, ed. Charles W. Calhoun, 185–214. Wilmington, Del.: Scholarly Resources, 1996.

Cameron, Ardis. *Radicals of the Worst Sort: Laboring Women in Lawrence, Massachusetts, 1860–1912*. Urbana: University of Illinois Press, 1955.

Camp, Helen C. *Iron in Her Soul: Elizabeth Gurley Flynn and the American Left*. Pullman: Washington State University Press, 1995.

Campbell, Karlyn Kohrs. "Femininity and Feminism: To Be or Not to Be a Woman." *Communication Quarterly* 31 (1983): 101–8.

———. *Man Cannot Speak for Her*. 2 vols. New York: Praeger, 1989.

———. "Mary Church Terrell." In *Women Public Speakers in the United States, 1925–1993: A Bio-Critical Source Book*, ed. Karlyn Kohrs Campbell, 108–19. Westport, Conn.: Greenwood Press, 1994.

———. "The Rhetoric of Mythical America Revisited." In *Critiques of Contemporary Rhetoric*, 2nd ed., ed. Karlyn Kohrs Campbell and Thomas R. Burkholder, 202–12. Belmont, Calif.: Wadsworth, 1997.

———. "The Rhetoric of Women's Liberation: An Oxymoron." *Quarterly Journal of Speech* 59 (1973): 74–86.

———, ed. *Women Public Speakers in the United States, 1800–1925*. Westport, Conn.: Greenwood Press, 1993.

Campbell, Karlyn Kohrs, and Celeste M. Condit. "Inventing Women: From Amaterasu to Virginia Woolf." *Women's Studies in Communication* 21, no. 2 (1998): 111–26.

Canning, Kathleen. "Feminist History after the Linguistic Turn: Historicizing Discourse and Experience." *Signs* 19 (Winter 1994): 368–404.

Carlson, Cheree. "Narrative as the Philosopher's Stone: How Russell H. Conwell Changed Lead into Diamonds." *Western Journal of Speech Communication* 53 (1989): 342–55.

Carnegie, Andrew. "Wealth." *North American Review* 148 (1889): 653–64.

Cashman, Sean Dennis. *America in the Gilded Age: From the Death of Lincoln to the Rise of Theodore Roosevelt*. 3rd ed. New York: New York University Press, 1988.

Catt, Carrie Chapman. "The Crisis." In *Man Cannot Speak for Her*, vol. 2, ed. Karlyn Kohrs Campbell, 483–502. New York: Praeger, 1989.

———. "Letter to Mary Church Terrell." 19 January 1939. Mary Church Terrell Papers, Library of Congress.

Catt, Carrie Chapman, and Nettie Rogers Shuler. *Woman Suffrage and Politics*. New York: Charles Scribner's Sons, 1926.

Caudill, Edward. *Darwinian Myths: The Legends and Misuses of a Theory*. Knoxville: University of Tennessee Press, 1977.

Cherny, Robert W. *A Righteous Cause: The Life of William Jennings Bryan*. Ed. Oscar Handlin. Boston: Little, Brown, 1985.

Chicago Evening Journal. 22 March 1871. Woman's Christian Temperance Union National Headquarters Historical Files, Ohio Historical Society and Michigan Historical Collections Microfilms.

"Chicago's Peace Jubilee." *New York Times*, 17 October 1898.

Chodorow, Nancy. *The Reproduction of Mothering: Psychoanalysis and the Sociology of Gender*. Berkeley: University of California Press, 1978.

Christian Advocate. 5 March 1896. Woman's Christian Temperance Union National Headquarters Historical Files, Ohio Historical Society and Michigan Historical Collections Microfilms.

Christian Century (30 October 1940): 1346.

Clanton, O. Gene. "Intolerant Populist? The Disaffection of Mary Elizabeth Lease." *Kansas Historical Quarterly* 34 (1968): 189–200.

———. *Kansas Populism: Ideas and Men*. Lawrence: University Press of Kansas, 1969.

Clements, Kendrick A. *William Jennings Bryan: Missionary Isolationist*. Knoxville: University of Tennessee Press, 1982.

Clinton, Katherine B. "What Did You Say, Mrs. Lease?" *Kansas Quarterly* 1 (1969): 52–59.

Coletta, Paolo E. *William Jennings Bryan: Political Evangelist, 1860–1908.* 3 vols. Lincoln: University of Nebraska Press, 1964.

Collins, Patricia Hill. *Black Feminist Criticism: Knowledge, Consciousness and the Politics of Empowerment.* New York: Routledge, 1991.

Condit, Celeste M. "Gender Diversity: A Theory of Communication for the Postmodern Era." In *Communication: Views from the Helm for the 21st Century*, ed. Judith S. Trent, 177–83. Boston: Allyn and Bacon, 1998.

Conkey's Complete Guide to the World's Columbian Exposition. Chicago: W. B. Conkey, 1893.

Conrad, Charles. "The Transformation of the 'Old Feminist' Movement." *Quarterly Journal of Speech* 67 (1981): 284–97.

"Constitution of the General Assembly of the ********." *Records* (1–4 January 1878): 29.

Conwell, Russell H. "Above the Snake Line." *Christian Century* (29 October 1925): 1335–38.

———. "Acres of Diamonds." *Executive Speeches* 10, no. 6 (1996): 31–36.

———. "Acres of Diamonds." In *Three Centuries of American Discourse: An Anthology and a Review*, ed. Ronald F. Reid, 573–86. Prospect Heights, Ill.: Waveland Press, 1988.

———. *The Angel's Lily.* Philadelphia: Judson Press, 1920.

———. "Fifty Years on the Lecture Platform." In *Russell H. Conwell: Acres of Diamonds and His Life and Achievements*, ed. Robert Shackleton, 171–81. New York: Harper and Brothers, 1915.

———. *Gleams of Grace.* Philadelphia: J. B. Lippincott, 1887.

———. *How a Soldier May Succeed after the War.* New York: Harper and Brothers, 1918.

———. *Observation: Every Man His Own University.* New York: Harper and Brothers, 1917.

———. *The Romantic Rise of a Great American.* New York: Harper and Brothers, 1924.

———. *Sermons for the Great Days of the Year.* New York: George H. Doran, 1922.

———. *Unused Powers.* New York: Fleming H. Revell, 1922.

———. *What You Can Do with Your Will Power.* New York: Harper and Brothers, 1917.

———. *Why Lincoln Laughed.* New York: Harper and Brothers, 1922.

———. *Woman and the Law.* Boston: B. B. Russell, 1876.

Cooper, Anna Julia. *A Voice from the South.* Aldine, 1892. Reprint, New York: Oxford University Press, 1988.

Cope, E. D. "Two Perils of the Indo-European." *Open Court* 3, no. 126 (1890): 2052–54.

Cott, Nancy F. "What's in a Name? The Limits of 'Social Feminism'; or, Expanding the Vocabulary of Women's History." *Journal of American History* 76 (1989): 809–29.

Creelman, James. "The Atlanta Exposition." *New York World*, 19 September 1895. In *The Booker T. Washington Papers*, vol. 4, ed. Louis R. Harlan, Stuart B. Kaufman, and Raymond W. Smock, 12–14. Urbana: University of Illinois Press, 1974.

———. "South's New Epoch." *New York World*, 19 September 1895. In *The Booker T. Washington Papers*, vol. 4, ed. Louis R. Harlan, Stuart B. Kaufman, and Raymond W. Smock, 15–17. Urbana: University of Illinois Press, 1974.

Crenshaw, Kimberlé Williams. "Mapping the Margins: Intersectionality, Identity Politics, and Violence against Women of Color." http://www.hsph.harvard.edu/grhf/WoC/ feminisms/crenshaw.html.

Crosby, W. C. "Acres of Diamonds." *American Mercury* 14 (1928): 104.

Croy, Terry Desch. "The Crisis: A Complete Critical Edition of Carrie Chapman Catt's 1916 Presidential Address to the National American Woman Suffrage Association." *Rhetoric Society Quarterly* 28 (Spring 1998): 49–73.

Crummell, Alexander. *Africa and America: Addresses and Discourses.* Springfield, Mass., 1891.

Crunden, Robert. *A Brief History of American Culture.* New York: Paragon House, 1994.

Cumnock, Robert M., ed. *Choice Readings for Public and Private Entertaining.* rev. ed. Chicago: A. C. McClurg, 1898.

———. Letter to Anna Gordon, 2 April 1898. Temperance and Prohibition Papers (Microfilm Edition), Woman's Christian Temperance Union National Headquarters Historical Files, Ohio Historical Society and Michigan Historical Collections, WCTU series, roll 27, frame 53.

Curti, Merle. *The Growth of American Thought.* New York: Harper and Brothers, 1951.

Curtis, Wardon Allen. "The Ultimate Solution of the Negro Problem." *American Journal of Politics* 3, no. 4 (1893): 352–58.

Chillicothe Daily News, 24 October 1890.

Daniels, Roger. "The Immigrant Experience in the Gilded Age." In *The Gilded Age: Essays on the Origins of Modern America*, ed. Charles W. Calhoun, 63–90. Wilmington, Del.: Scholarly Resources, 1996.

Davenport, Henry, Joseph R. Gay, and I. Garland Penn. *The College of Life; or, Practical Self-Educator: A Manual of Self-Improvement of the Colored Race*. Chicago: Chicago Publication and Lithograph, 1895.

Davis, Angela Y. *Women, Race and Class*. New York: Random House, 1981.

Davis, Kenneth S. *Kansas: A History*. New York: W. W. Norton, 1984.

DeBois, Carol. *Woman Suffrage Women's Rights*. New York: New York University Press, 1998.

Debs, Eugene V. "To the Rescue of Mother Jones!" *Appeal to Reason* (3 May 1913): 1.

"Declaration of Principles Adopted by the Anarchists' Congress Held in Pittsburgh, PA." *Liberator* 1, no. 22 (1906): 3.

de Cleyre, Voltairine. "The Case of Woman vs. Orthodoxy." *Boston Investigator*, 19 September 1986, 2.

———. "In Defense of Emma Goldman and the Right of Expropriation." In *Selected Works of Voltairine de Cleyre*, ed. Alexander Berkman, 205–19. New York: Mother Earth, 1914.

———. *The First Mayday: The Haymarket Speeches, 1895–1910*. Ed. and intro. by Paul Avrich. Minneapolis: Cienfuegos Press, Libertarian Book Club and Soil of Liberty, 1980.

———. "The Gates of Freedom." *Lucifer* (17 April 1891): n.p.

———. "The Gates of Freedom." *Lucifer* (24 April 1891): n.p.

———. "The Gates of Freedom." *Lucifer* (15 May 1891): n.p.

———. "The Gates of Freedom." *Lucifer* (29 May 1891): n.p.

———. Letter to Harriet Elizabeth de Claire. 22 January 1893. Voltairine de Cleyre Papers, Joseph A. Labadie Collection, University of Michigan, Ann Arbor.

———. Letter to Joseph Labadie. 11 May 1908. Voltairine de Cleyre Papers, Joseph A. Labadie Collection, University of Michigan, Ann Arbor.

———. "Literature the Mirror of Man." In *Selected Works of Voltairine de Cleyre*, ed. Alexander Berkman, 359–80. New York: Mother Earth, 1914.

———. "The Making of an Anarchist." In *Selected Works of Voltairine de Cleyre*, ed. Alexander Berkman, 154–63. New York: Mother Earth, 1914.

———. "On Liberty." *Mother Earth* 4 (July 1909): 151–55.

———. "Our Police Censorship." *Mother Earth* 4 (July 1909): 297–301.

———. "The Past and Future of the Ladies' Liberal League." *Rebel* (20 October 1895): 18.

———. "The Past and Future of the Ladies' Liberal League." *Rebel* (20 November 1895): 31–32.

———. "The Past and Future of the Ladies' Liberal League." *Rebel* (January 1896): 43–44.

———. "The Poetry of Reform." Unpublished manuscript, n.d. Joseph Ishill Collection, Houghton Library, Harvard University, Cambridge, Mass.

———. *Selected Works of Voltairine de Cleyre*, ed. Alexander Berkman. New York: Mother Earth, 1914.

———. "Sex Slavery." In *Selected Works of Voltairine de Cleyre*, ed. Alexander Berkman, 342–58. New York: Mother Earth, 1914.

———. "They Who Marry Do Ill." *Mother Earth* 2 (January 1908): 500–511.

———. "Why I Am an Anarchist." *Mother Earth* 3 (March 1908): 16–31.

Decosta-Willis, Miriam. *The Memphis Diary of Ida B. Wells*. Boston: Beacon Press, 1995.

Degler, Carl N. *In Search of Human Nature: The Decline and Revival of Darwinism in American Social Thought*. New York: Oxford University Press, 1991.

The Democrat. 12 February 1882. Woman's Christian Temperance Union National Headquarters Historical Files, Ohio Historical Society and Michigan Historical Collections Microfilms.

Dennis, Michael. "The Skillful Use of Higher Education to Protect White Supremacy." *Journal of Blacks in Higher Education* 32 (Summer 2001): 115–23.

Detroit News-Tribune. December 1902. Joseph A. Labadie Collection, University of Michigan, Ann Arbor.

Detroit News-Tribune. 25 January 1903. Joseph A. Labadie Collection, University of Michigan, Ann Arbor.

Diggs, Annie L. *The Story of Jerry Simpson*. Wichita, Kans.: Jane Simpson, 1908.

Douglass, Frederick. "Self-Made Men." In *The Frederick Douglass Papers*, vol. 5, ed. John W. Blassingame et al., 545–75. New Haven, Conn.: Yale University Press, 1992.

———. "Speech at Rochester." In *Negro Orators and Their Orations*, ed. Carter G. Woodson, 197–223. New York: Russell and Russell, 1925.

———. "A Speech before the National Unitarian Association." In *The Booker T. Washington Papers*, vol. 3, ed. Louis R. Harlan, Stuart B. Kaufman, and Raymond W. Smock, 477–78. Urbana: University of Illinois Press, 1974.

Dow, Bonnie. "Frances E. Willard: Reinventor of 'True Womanhood.'" In *Women Public Speakers in the United States, 1800–1925*, ed. Karlyn Kohrs Campbell, 476–90. Westport, Conn.: Greenwood Press, 1993.

———. "The 'Womanhood' Rationale in the Woman Suffrage Rhetoric of Frances E. Willard." *Southern Communication Journal* 56 (1991): 298–307.

Dow, Bonnie J., and Mari Boor Tonn. "'Feminine Style' and Political Judgment in the Rhetoric of Ann Richards." *Quarterly Journal of Speech* 79 (1988): 286–302.

Dreiser, Theodore. "Last Day at the Fair." *Republic* (23 July 1893): 6.

Drinnon, Richard. *Rebel in Paradise*. New York: Bantam Books, 1961.

Drinnon, Richard, and Anna Marie Drinnon, eds. *Nowhere at Home: Letters from Exile of Emma Goldman and Alexander Berkman*. New York: Schocken Books, 1975.

Dubois, Ellen Carol. *Feminism and Suffrage: The Emergence of an Independent Women's Movement in America 1848–1869*. Ithaca, N.Y.: Cornell University Press, 1978.

———. "Working Women, Class Relations, and Suffrage Militance: Harriot Stanton Blatch and the New York Women's Suffrage Movement, 1894–1909." In *One Woman, One Vote*, ed. Marjorie Spruill Wheeler, 221–44. Troutdale, Ore.: NewSage Press, 1995.

DuBois, W. E. B. "The Conservation of Races." In *W. E. B. DuBois Speaks: Speeches and Addresses 1890–1919*, ed. Philip S. Foner, 73–85. New York: Pathfinder, 1970.

———. "The Economic Future of the Negro." *Publications of the American Economic Association* 7 (1906): 219–42.

———. "Is Race Separation Practicable?" *American Journal of Sociology* 13 (1908): 834–38.

———. Letter to Booker T. Washington. 24 September 1895. In *The Booker T. Washington Papers*, vol. 4, ed. Louis R. Harlan, Stuart B. Kaufman, and Raymond W. Smock, 26. Urbana: University of Illinois Press, 1974.

———. "The Niagara Movement." *Voice of the Negro* (September 1905): 619–22.

———. "Of Alexander Crummell." In *The Souls of Black Folk: Essays and Sketches*, 170–79. Chicago: A. C. McClurg, 1903. Reprint, New York: Alfred A. Knopf, 1993.

———. "On Mr. Booker T. Washington and Others." In *The Souls of Black Folk: Essays and Sketches*. Reprinted in Ronald F. Reid, ed., *American Rhetorical Discourse*, 2nd ed., 569–77. Prospect Heights, Ill.: Waveland Press, 1998.

———. *The Souls of Black Folk: Essays and Sketches*. Chicago: A. C. McClurg, 1903. Reprint, New York: Alfred A. Knopf, 1993.

———. "The Talented Tenth." In *DuBois on Education*, ed. Eugene F. Provenzo Jr., 75–92. Walnut Creek, Calif.: AltaMira Press, 2002.

———. "The Training of Negroes for Social Power." *Colored American Magazine* (May 1904): 333–39.

Duffin, Lorna. "Prisoners of Progress: Women and Evolution." In *The Nineteenth-Century Woman: Her Cultural and Physical World*, ed. Sara Delamont and Lorna Duffin, 57–91. New York: Barnes and Noble, 1978.

Dunn, Frederick. "The Educational Philosophies of Washington, DuBois, and Houston: Laying the Foundations for Afrocentrism and Multiculturalism." *Journal of Negro Education* 62, no. 1 (1993): 24–34.

Earhart, Mary. *Frances Willard*. Chicago: University of Chicago Press, 1944.

Ecroyd, Donald H. "The Agrarian Protest." In *America in Controversy: History of American Public Address*, ed. Dewitte Holland, 171–84. Dubuque, Iowa: William C. Brown, 1973.

———. "The Populist Spellbinders." In *The Rhetoric of Protest and Reform, 1878–1898*, ed. Paul H. Boase, 132–52. Athens: Ohio University Press, 1980.

"Editorial: The Outlook." *AME Review* 6 (April 1890): 503–4.

Edwards, Ishmell Hendrex. "History of Rust College 1866–1967." Ph.D. diss., University of Mississippi, 1994.

Edwards, Paul Denyce, ed. *The Encyclopedia of Philosophy*. Vol. 4. New York: MacMillan, 1967.

Eisinger, Chester E. "The Freehold Concept in Eighteenth Century American Letters." *William and Mary Quarterly* 3rd ser. 4 (1947): 42–59.

———. "The Influence of Natural Rights and Physiocratic Doctrines on American Agrarian Thought during the Revolutionary Period." *Agricultural History* 21 (1947): 12–23.

Ekrich, Arthur A., Jr. *Progressivism in America: A Study of the Era from Theodore Roosevelt to Woodrow Wilson*. New York: New Viewpoints, 1974.

Eliade, Mircea. *Myth and Reality*. Trans. Willard R. Trask. New York: Harper and Row, 1963.

Elkins, Stanley, and Eric McKitrick. *The Founding Fathers: Young Men of the Revolution*. Vol. 1 of *Myth and the American Experience*, ed. Nicholas Cords and Patrick Gerster. New York: Glencoe Press, 1973.

Elliott, R. B. "The Civil Rights Bill." In *Negro Orators and Their Orations*, ed. Carter G. Woodson, 309–28. New York: Russell and Russell, 1925.

Endres, Thomas G. "Co-Existing Master Analogues in Symbolic Convergence Theory: The Knights of Columbus Quincentennial Campaign." *Communication Studies* 45 (Fall–Winter 1994): 294–308.

Epstein, Barbara. *The Politics of Domesticity*. Middletown, Conn.: Wesleyan University Press, 1981.

Erlich, Howard S. "Populist Rhetoric Reassessed: A Paradox." *Quarterly Journal of Speech* 63 (1977): 140–51.

Evans, Sara. *Born for Liberty: A History of Women in America*. New York: Free Press, 1989.

Evanston Index. 16 July 1881. Woman's Christian Temperance Union National Headquarters Historical Files, Ohio Historical Society and Michigan Historical Collections Microfilms.

Evening Gazette (Galena). n.d. Woman's Christian Temperance Union National Headquarters Historical Files, Ohio Historical Society and Michigan Historical Collections Microfilms.

Falk, Candace. *Love, Anarchy and Emma Goldman*. New Brunswick, N.J.: Rutgers University Press, 1990.

Farmer, Hallie. "The Economic Background of Frontier Populism." *Mississippi Valley Historical Review* 10 (1924): 406–27.

Fehlandt, August. *Century of Drink Reform in the U.S.* Cincinnati: Dennings and Graham, 1904.

Felski, Rita. *Beyond Feminist Aesthetics: Feminist Literature and Social Change*. Cambridge, Mass.: Harvard University Press, 1989.

"A Female Anarchist." *Baltimore American*, 20 November 1886, n.p. Lucy Parsons's Scrapbook, Albert Parsons Collection, State Historical Society of Wisconsin, Madison.

"The Female Anarchist." *Pittsburgh Leader*, 21 November 1886, n.p. Lucy Parsons's Scrapbook, Albert Parsons Collection, State Historical Society of Wisconsin, Madison.

"The Female Anarchist: Mrs. Parsons Talking at a Crowded Meeting at Claredon Hall." *New York Times*, 18 October 1886.

"Female Suffrage." *Ladies Repository* 27 (1867): 504–6.

Ferkiss, Victor C. "Populist Influences on American Fascism." *Western Political Quarterly* 10 (June 1957): 350–73.

Fetherling, Dale. *Mother Jones, the Miners' Angel: A Portrait*. Carbondale: Southern Illinois University Press, 1974.

Filippelli, Ronald L. *Labor in the USA: A History*. New York: Alfred A. Knopf, 1984.

Fink, Leon. *Workingmen's Democracy: The Knights of Labor and American Politics*. Urbana: University of Illinois Press, 1985.

Fishel, Leslie H., Jr. "The African-American Experience." In *The Gilded Age: Essay on the Origins of Modern America*, ed. Charles W. Calhoun, 137–62. Wilmington, Del.: Scholarly Resources, 1996.

Fisher, Walter R. *Human Communication as Narration: Toward a Philosophy of Reason, Value, and Action*. Columbia: University of South Carolina Press, 1987.

Fiske, John. *The Destiny of Man: Viewed in Light of His Origin*. Boston: Houghton, Mifflin, 1892.

Fitzhugh, George. "What's to Be Done with the Negroes?" *DeBow's Review* (1866): 577–81.

Flexner, Eleanor. *Century of Struggle*. Cambridge, Mass.: Harvard University Press, 1966.

Flexner, Eleanor, and Ellen Fitzpatrick. *Century of Struggle: The Woman's Rights Movement in the United States*. Cambridge, Mass.: Belknap Press of Harvard University Press, 1996.

Flinn, John J. *Chicago: The Marvelous City of the West: A History, an Encyclopedia*. 2nd ed. Chicago: Standard Guide, 1892.

———. *Official Guide to Midway Plaisance*. Chicago: Columbian Guide, 1893.

Flynn, Elizabeth Gurley. "Early Notes." Holograph, 1907 or 1908. Elizabeth Gurley Flynn Papers, Tamiment Library, New York University.

———. "Evaluation of Labor Leaders." Holograph, n.d. Elizabeth Gurley Flynn Papers, Tamiment Library, New York University.

———. *I Speak My Own Piece: Autobiography of "The Rebel Girl."* Rev. ed. New York: International Press, 1973.

———. "Jungle Law." Holograph, 1908. Elizabeth Gurley Flynn Papers, Tamiment Library, New York University.

———. "On Arrests and Indictments." 6 August 1948. Elizabeth Gurley Flynn Papers, Tamiment Library, New York University.

———. "Opposition to the Confirmation of Tom Clark as Associate Justice of the Supreme Court." 10 August 1949. Elizabeth Gurley Flynn Papers, Tamiment Library, New York University.

———. "The Political Significance of Defense Work." 1950. Elizabeth Gurley Flynn Papers, Tamiment Library, New York University.

———. "Problems Organizing Women." Holograph, 1916. Elizabeth Gurley Flynn Papers, Tamiment Library, New York University.

———. "Public Speaking Notes." Holograph, n.d. Elizabeth Gurley Flynn Papers, Tamiment Library, New York University.

———. "Radio Address." 1947. Elizabeth Gurley Flynn Papers, Tamiment Library, New York University.

———. *Sabotage: The Conscious Withdrawal of the Workers' Industrial Efficiency*. Cleveland: I.W.W. Publishing Bureau, 1917. Wayne State University Industrial Workers of the World Collection, Archives of Labor and Urban Affairs.

———. "Small Families—a Proletarian Necessity." Holograph, 1915. Elizabeth Gurley Flynn Papers, Tamiment Library, New York University.

———. "Speech by Elizabeth Gurley Flynn." *Political Affairs*, n.d. Elizabeth Gurley Flynn Papers, Tamiment Library, New York University.

———. "Statement at the Smith Act Trial." In *We Shall Be Heard: Women Speakers in America*, ed. Patricia Scileppi Kennedy and Gloria Hartmann O'Shields, 239–43. Dubuque, Iowa: Kendall/Hunt, 1983.

———. "Summation in the Smith Act Trial." 6 January 1953. Elizabeth Gurley Flynn Papers, Tamiment Library, New York University.

———. "The Truth about the Paterson Strike." 31 January 1914. Elizabeth Gurley Flynn Papers, Tamiment Library, New York University.

———. "Woman." Holograph. 1909. Elizabeth Gurley Flynn Papers, Tamiment Library, New York University.

Foner, Philip S., ed. *Mother Jones Speaks: Collected Speeches and Writings*. New York: Monad Press, 1983.

———. *Women and the American Labor Movement*. New York: Free Press, 1979.

Fowler, Robert Booth. *Carrie Catt: Feminist Politician*. Boston: Northeastern University Press, 1986.

Franklin, John Hope, and Alfred A. Moss Jr. *From Slavery to Freedom*. 7th ed. New York: McGraw-Hill, 1994.

Fraser, Nancy. "Rethinking the Public Sphere." In *Habermas and the Public Sphere*, ed. Craig Calhoun, 109–42. Cambridge, Mass.: MIT Press, 1992.

Frederickson, Mary. "'I Know Which Side I'm On': Southern Women in the Labor Movement in the Twentieth Century." In *Women, Work, and Protest: A Century of U.S. Women's Labor History*, ed. Ruth Milkman, 156–80. Boston: Routledge and Kegan Paul, 1985.

French, Bryant Morey. *Mark Twain and the Gilded Age: The Book That Named an Era*. Dallas: Southern Methodist University Press, 1965.

Friedman, Milton. "The Crime of 1873." *Journal of Political Economy* 98 (1990): 1159–94.

Frye, Northrop. *Anatomy of Criticism: Four Essays*. Princeton, N.J.: Princeton University Press, 1957.

———. *The Critical Path: An Essay on the Social Context of Literary Criticism*. Bloomington: Indiana University Press, 1973.

———. "Literature and Myth." In *Relations of Literary Study*, ed. James Thorpe, 27–41. New York: Modern Language Association of America, 1967.

Galton, Francis. "Hereditary Talent and Character." *Macmillan's Magazine* 12 (1865): n.p. In *The Bell Curve Debate*, ed. Russell Jacoby and Naomi Glauberman, 393–409. New York: Random House, 1995.

Gehring, Mary Louise. "Russell H. Conwell: American Orator." *Southern Speech Communication Journal* 20 (1954): 117–24.

Giddings, Paula. *When and Where I Enter: The Impact of Black Women on Race and Sex in America*. New York: Bantam, 1984.

Gifford, Carolyn DeSwarte. "Frances E. Willard." In *Women Building Chicago, 1790–1990: A Biographical Dictionary*, ed. Rima Lunin Schultz and Adele Hast, 968–74. Bloomington: Indiana University Press, 2001.

———. "'The Woman's Cause Is Man's'? Frances Willard and the Social Gospel." In *Gender and the Social Gospel*, ed. Wendy Deichmann Edwards and Carolyn DeSwarte Gifford, 21–34. Urbana: University of Illinois Press, 2003.

———. *Writing Out My Heart: Selections from the Journal of Frances E. Willard, 1855–1896*. Urbana: University of Illinois Press, 1995.

Gifford, Carolyn De Swarte and Amy Slagell. *"Let Something Good Be Said": Speeches and Writings of Frances E. Willard*. Urbana: University of Illinois Press, 2007.

Gilbert, James. *Perfect Cities: Chicago's Utopias of 1893*. Chicago: University of Chicago Press, 1991.

Gilligan, Carol. *In a Different Voice: Psychological Theory and Women's Development*. Cambridge, Mass.: Harvard University Press, 1982.

Glad, Paul W., ed. *McKinley, Bryan, and the People*. Philadelphia: J. B. Lippincott, 1964.

Gold, Ellen Reid. "Political Apologia: The Ritual of Self-Defense." *Communication Monographs* 45 (1978): 306–16.

Goldman, Emma. "America and the Russian Revolution." Summary of lecture transcribed by E. J. Bamberger in "[Report to] Department of Justice." 18 January 1918. In *The Emma Goldman Papers*, ed. Candace Falk and Ronald J. Zboray, reel no. 48. Alexandria, Va.: Chadwyck-Healey, 1991.

———. "Anarchism: What It Really Stands For." In *Anarchism and Other Essays*, 47–67. New York: Mother Earth, 1917. Reprint, New York: Dover, 1969.

———. "Anarchism: What It Really Stands For." In *Red Emma Speaks*, ed. Alix Kates Shulman, 61–77. New York: Schocken Books, 1983.

———. *Anarchism and Other Essays*. New York: Mother Earth, 1917. Reprint, New York: Dover, 1969.

———. "An Anarchist Looks at Life." Speech at Foyle's 29th Literary Luncheon. 1 March 1933. In *The Emma Goldman Papers*, ed. Candace Falk and Ronald J. Zboray, reel no. 52. Alexandria, Va.: Chadwyck-Healy, 1991.

———. "The Individual, Society, and the State." In *Red Emma Speaks*, ed. Alix Kates Shulman, 109–23. New York: Schocken Books, 1983.

———. "Intellectual Proletarians." In *Red Emma Speaks*, ed. Alix Kates Shulman, 222–31. New York: Schocken Books, 1983. Reprint, Atlantic Heights, N.J.: Humanities Press, 1996.

———. Letter to Minna Lowensohn. 12 May 1925. Labadie Goldman, Joseph A. Labadie Collection, University of Michigan, Ann Arbor.

———. *Living My Life*. New York: Alfred Knopf, 1931. Reprint, New York: Dover, 1970.

———. "Marriage and Love." In *Red Emma Speaks*, ed. Alix Kates Shulman, 204–13. New York: Schocken Books, 1983.

———. "Minorities and Majorities." In *Red Emma Speaks*, ed. Alix Kates Shulman, 78–86. New York: Schocken Books, 1983.

———. "[Report to] United States Commissioner of Immigration." Summaries and excerpt from lecture transcribed by William E. Carr in *The Emma Goldman Papers*, ed. Candace Falk and Ronald J. Zboray, reel no. 47. Alexandria, Va.: Chadwyck-Healey, 1991.

———. "[Sexual Instinct and Creativity] Fragment." In *The Emma Goldman Papers*, ed. Candace Falk and Ronald J. Zboray, reel no. 54. Alexandria, Va.: Chadwyck-Healy, 1991.

———. "[Sexuality, Motherhood and Birth Control] Fragment." 1935. In *The Emma Goldman Papers*, ed. Candace Falk and Ronald J. Zboray, reel no. 54. Alexandria, Va.: Chadwyck-Healy, 1991.

———. "The Traffic in Women." In *Red Emma Speaks*, ed. Alix Kates Shulman, 175–89. New York: Schocken Books, 1983.

———. "The Tragedy of Women's Emancipation." In *Red Emma Speaks*, ed. Alix Kates Shulman, 158–67. New York: Schocken Books, 1983.

———. *Voltairine de Cleyre*. Berkeley Heights, N.J.: Oriole Press, 1932.

———. "Voltairine de Cleyre Funeral Oration." 1914. Joseph A. Labadie Collection, University of Michigan, Ann Arbor.

———. "What I Believe." In *Red Emma Speaks*, ed. Alix Kates Shulman, 48–60. New York: Schocken Books, 1983. Reprint, Atlantic Heights, N.J.: Humanities Press, 1996.

———. "Woman Suffrage." In *Red Emma Speaks*, ed. Alix Kates Shulman, 190–203. New York: Schocken Books, 1983.

Gompers, Samuel. "Address to the Machinists Convention." *American Federationist* (July 1901): 251.

———. *Journal of the Knights of Labor* (3 July 1890): 1.

Goodwyn, Lawrence. *Democratic Promise: The Populist Moment in America*. New York: Oxford University Press, 1976.

Gordon, Anna. *The Beautiful Life of Frances E. Willard*. Chicago: Woman's Temperance Publishing Association, 1898.

Gordon, Linda. *Woman's Body, Woman's Right: A Social History of Birth Control in America*. New York: Grossman, 1976.

Gould, Stephen J. "William Jennings Bryan's Last Campaign." *Natural History* 96 (1987): 16–26.

Graham, Sara Hunter. *Woman Suffrage and the New Democracy*. New Haven, Conn.: Yale University Press, 1996.

Griffin, Leland M. "The Rhetoric of Historical Movements." *Quarterly Journal of Speech* 38 (1952): 184–88.

Griffith, Elisabeth. *In Her Own Right: The Life of Elizabeth Cady Stanton*. New York: Oxford University Press, 1984.

Grimes, Alan P. *The Puritan Ethic and Woman Suffrage*. New York: Oxford University Press, 1967.

Griswold, A. Whitney. "The Agrarian Democracy of Thomas Jefferson." *American Political Science Review* 40 (1946): 657–81.

Gunderson, Robert. "The Calamity Howlers." *Quarterly Journal of Speech* 26 (1940): 401–11.

Gusfield, Joseph R. "Functional Areas of Leadership in Social Movements." *Sociological Quarterly* 7 (1966): 137–56.

———. *Protest, Reform, and Revolt: A Reader in Social Movements.* New York: John Wiley, 1970.

———. *Symbolic Crusade: Status Politics and the American Temperance Movement.* 2nd ed. Chicago: University of Illinois Press, 1986.

Haaland, Bonnie. *Emma Goldman: Sexuality and the Impurity of the State.* Montreal: Black Rose Books, 1993.

Hackney, Sheldon. *Populism: The Critical Issues.* Boston: Little, Brown, 1971.

Hamilton, William Baskerville. *Holly Springs, Mississippi, to the Year 1878.* Holly Springs, Miss.: Marshall County Historical Society, 1984.

Hammell, George M., ed. *The Passing of the Saloon.* Cincinnati: F. L. Rowe, 1908.

Hammers, J. L. "Our Demands." *Anthony Weekly Bulletin*, 8 April 1892, 8.

Hance, Kenneth G., H. O. Hendrickson, and Edwin W. Schoenberger. "The Later National Period, 1860–1930." In *A History and Criticism of American Public Address*, vol. 1, ed. William Norwood Brigance, 111–52. New York: Russell and Russell, 1960.

Handlin, Oscar. "Reconsidering the Populists." *Agricultural History* 39 (April 1965): 68–74.

Handy, Moses P. *The Official Directory of the World Columbian Exposition.* Chicago: W. B. Conkey, 1893.

Handy, Robert T., ed. *The Social Gospel in America.* New York: Oxford University Press, 1966.

Harrell, Jackson, B. L. Ware, and Wil A. Linkugel. "Failure of Apology in American Politics: Nixon on Watergate." *Speech Monographs* 42 (1975): 245–61.

Harris, Neil. *Grand Illusions: Chicago's World's Fair of 1893.* Chicago: Chicago Historical Society, 1993.

Hatch, Nathan. "The Puzzle of American Methodism." *Church History* 63 (June 1994): 175–89.

Hawkins, Mike. *Social Darwinism in European and American Thought, 1860–1945.* Cambridge: Cambridge University Press, 1997.

Hayden, Sara. "Re-Claiming Bodies of Knowledge: An Exploration of the Relationship Between Feminist Theorizing and Feminine Style in the Rhetoric of the Boston Women's Health Book Collective." *Western Journal of Communication* 61 (Spring 1997): 127–63.

Haynes, Frederick Emory. "The New Sectionalism." *Quarterly Journal of Economics* 10 (1896): 269–95.

Hearit, Keith Michael. "'Mistakes Were Made': Organizations, Apologia, and Crises of Self Legitimacy." *Communication Studies* 46 (1995): 1–17.

Heath, Robert L. "Alexander Crummell and the Strategy of Challenge by Adaptation." *Central States Speech Journal* 26 (1975): 178–87.

Herrick, Genevieve Forbes, and John Origen Herrick. *The Life of William Jennings Bryan.* Chicago: Grover C. Buxton, 1925.

Hewitt, Marsha. "Emma Goldman: The Case for Anarcho-Feminism." In *The Anarchist Papers*, ed. Dimitrios I. Roussopoulos, 169–75. Montreal: Black Rose Books, 1986.

Hicks, John D. "The Farmer Protests: Populism." In *The American Story: The Age of Exploration to the Age of the Atom*, ed. Earl Schenck Miers, 219–24. New York: Charmel Press, 1956.

———. *The Populist Revolt.* Minneapolis: University of Minnesota Press, 1931.

Higginbotham, Harlow. *Report of the President to the Board of Directors of the World's Columbian Exposition.* Chicago: Rand McNally, 1898.

"Hoarse." *New Yorker*, 26 October 1946, 23.

Hochschild, Arlie, and Anne Machung. *The Second Shift: Working Parents and the Revolution at Home.* New York: Viking, 1989.

Hoffert, Sylvia D. "New York City's Penny Press and the Issue of Woman's Rights, 1848–1860." *Journalism Quarterly* 70 (Autumn 1993): 656–65.

Hofstadter, Richard. *The Age of Reform: From Bryan to F.D.R.* New York: Alfred A. Knopf, 1955. Reprint, New York: Alfred A. Knopf, 1977.

———. "The Democrat as Revivalist." In *William Jennings Bryan and the Campaign of 1896*, ed. George F. Whicher, 89–102. Boston: D. C. Heath, 1953.

———. *Social Darwinism in American Thought.* Boston: Beacon Press, 1955.

———. *Social Darwinism in American Thought.* Rev. ed. New York: George Braziller, 1959.

Holland, Frederick May. "Shall Colored Citizens Be Banished?" *Open Court* 3, no. 128 (1890): 2079–81.

Hostetler, Michael J. "William Jennings Bryan as Demosthenes: The Scopes Trial and the Undelivered Oration, 'On Evolution.'" *Western Journal of Communication* 62 (1998): 18–25.

Howells, William Dean. *Traveler from Altruria.* New York: Harper and Brothers, 1894.

Hurtado, Aida. "Relating to Privilege: Seduction and Rejection in the Subordination of White Women and Women of Color." *Signs* 14 (1989): 833–55.

Hutton, Mary M. Boone. "Ida B. Wells Barnett (1862–1931), Agitator for African-American Rights." In *Women Public Speakers in the United States, 1800–1925: A Bio-Critical Sourcebook*, ed. Karlyn Kohrs Campbell, 462–75. Westport, Conn.: Greenwood Press, 1993.

Huxman, Susan Schultz. "Mary Wollstonecraft, Margaret Fuller, and Angelina Grimke: Symbolic Convergence and a Nascent Rhetorical Vision." *Communication Quarterly* 44 (Winter 1996): 16–28.

———. "Perfecting the Rhetorical Visions of Woman's Rights: Elizabeth Cady Stanton, Anna Howard Shaw, and Carrie Chapman Catt." *Women's Studies in Communication* 23, no. 2 (2000): 307–36.

Huxman, Susan Schultz, and Denise Beatty Bruce. "Toward a Dynamic Generic Framework of Apologia: A Case Study of Dow Chemical, Vietnam, and the Napalm Controversy." *Communication Studies* 46 (1995): 57–72.

Japp, Phyllis M. "'A Spoonful of Sugar Makes the Medicine Go Down': Dr. Conwell's 'Feel Good' Cultural Tonic." *Speaker and Gavel* 27 (1990): 2–10.

Jetter, Alexis, Annelise Orleck, and Diana Taylor, eds. *The Politics of Motherhood: Activist Voices from Left to Right*. Hanover, N.H.: University Press of New England, 1997.

Joll, James. *The Anarchists*. 2nd ed. Cambridge, Mass.: Harvard University Press, 1980.

Jones, Beverly W. "Mary Church Terrell and the National Association of Colored Women, 1896 to 1901." In *Church and Community among Black Southerners 1865–1900*, 350–63. New York: Garden, 1994.

Jones, Mary Harris. *The Autobiography of Mother Jones*. Ed. Mary Field Parton. 3rd ed. Chicago: Charles Kerr, 1980.

Josephson, Matthew. *The Robber Barons*. New York: Harcourt, Brace, 1934.

Kammen, Michael. *People of Paradox*. Ithaca, N.Y.: Cornell University Press, 1990.

Kennedy, Patricia, and Gloria O'Shields, eds. *We Shall Be Heard*. Dubuque, Iowa: Kendall/Hunt, 1983.

Kessler-Harris, Alice. "Problems of Coalition-Building: Women and Trade Unions in the 1920s." In *Women, Work, and Protest: A Century of U.S. Women's Labor History*, ed. Ruth Milkman, 110–38. Boston: Routledge and Kegan Paul, 1985.

Kimble, James. "Frances Willard as Protector of the Home." In *Lives of Their Own: Rhetorical Dimensions of Autobiographies of Women Activists*, ed. Martha Watson, 47–62. Columbia: University of South Carolina Press, 1999.

Kincaid, James. *Tennyson's Major Poems*. New Haven, Conn.: Yale University Press, 1975.

Kingston, Ian Randle. *From Chattel Slaves to Wage Slaves: The Dynamics of Labour Bargaining in the Americas*. Bloomington: Indiana University Press, 1995.

Kowal, Donna M. "One Cause, Two Paths: Militant vs. Adjustive Strategies in the British and American Women's Suffrage Movements." *Communication Quarterly* 48 (Summer 2000): 240–56.

———. "The Public Advocacy of Emma Goldman: An Anarcho-Feminist Stance on Human Rights." Ph.D. diss., University of Pittsburgh, 1996.

Kowal, Donna M., Andrea L. Rich, and Arthur L. Smith. *Rhetoric of Revolution*. Durham, N.C.: Moore, n.d.

Kraditor, Aileen. *The Ideas of the Woman Suffrage Movement: 1890–1920*. New York: Columbia University Press, 1965. Reprint, New York: Norton, 1981.

Kruse, Noreen Wales. "Apologia in Team Sport." *Quarterly Journal of Speech* 67 (1981): 270–83.

Kutera, Joseph. "Voltairine de Cleyre: A Character Sketch." *Why?* 1 (August 1913): n.p.

Kvale, Steinar. "Themes of Postmodernity." In *The Truth about the Truth*, ed. Walter Truett Anderson, 165–80. New York: G. P. Putnam's Sons, 1995.

Lamont, Corliss. *The Trial of Elizabeth Gurley Flynn by the American Civil Liberties Union*. New York: Horizon, 1968.

Langer, Susanne Katherina Knauth. *Philosophy in a New Key: A Study in the Symbolism of Reason, Rite and Art*. Cambridge, Mass.: Harvard University Press, 1957.

Lanham, Richard A. *A Handlist of Rhetorical Terms*. Berkeley: University of California Press, 1991.

Lantz, Herman R., and J. S. McCrary. *People of Coal Town*. New York: Columbia University Press, 1958.

Lease, Mary Elizabeth. "Address at Cooper Union." *Kansas Agitator* (Garnett), 8 March 1894, 1, 6.

———. "Speech before the Labor Congress." *Abilene (Texas) Monitor*, 7 September 1893, 8.

Leavenworth (Kansas) Daily Press. 16 May 1880. Woman's Christian Temperance Union National Headquarters Historical Files, Ohio Historical Society and Michigan Historical Collections Microfilm.

Lee, Howard B. *Bloodletting in Appalachia*. Morgantown: West Virginia University Library, 1969.

Leeman, Richard. *"Do Everything" Reform: The Oratory of Frances E. Willard*. New York: Greenwood Press, 1992.

Lerner, Gerda, ed. *Black Women in White America: A Documentary History*. New York: Vintage Books, 1972.

———. *The Creation of Patriarchy*. New York: Oxford University Press, 1986.

Leuchtag, Alice. "Elizabeth Cady Stanton: Freethinker and Radical Revisionist." *Humanist* 56 (September/October 1996): 29–32.

Lewelling, Lorenzo D. "Speech at Huron Place, Kansas City, July 26, 1894." Kansas State Historical Society, Topeka.

Life. 18 February 1893. Woman's Christian Temperance Union National Headquarters Historical Files, Ohio Historical Society and Michigan Historical Collections Microfilms.

Linkugel, Wil A. "Anna Howard Shaw: A Case Study in Rhetorical Enactment." In *Women Public Speakers in the United States 1800–1925*, ed. Karlyn Kohrs Campbell, 409–20. Westport, Conn.: Greenwood Press, 1993.

Linkugel, Wil A., and Martha Solomon. *Anna Howard Shaw: Suffrage Orator and Social Reformer*. Westport, Conn.: Greenwood Press, 1991.

Lipscomb, Drema R. "Anna Julia Cooper." In *African-American Orators: A BioCritical Sourcebook*, ed. Richard W. Leeman, 41–50. Westport, Conn.: Greenwood Press, 1996.

Logan, Rayford. *The Negro in American Life and Thought: The Nadir, 1877–1901*. New York: Dial, 1954.

Long, Priscilla. *Mother Jones, Woman Organizer*. Cambridge, Mass.: Red Sun Press, 1976.

"Loud-Mouthed Treason: Mrs. Parsons Denounces the Law at Tobnener's Hall." *Kansas City Enquirer*, 20 December 1886. Lucy Parsons's Scrapbook, Albert Parsons Collection, State Historical Society of Wisconsin, Madison.

Lucas, Stephen E. "Booker T. Washington." In *African-American Orators: A BioCritical Sourcebook*, ed. Richard W. Leeman, 341–57. Westport, Conn.: Greenwood Press, 1996.

"Lucy Broke Down the Door." *Orange (New Jersey) Journal*, 25 October 1886, morning ed. Albert Parsons Collection, State Historical Society of Wisconsin, Madison.

L.W.B. "Is He a New Negro?" *Chicago Inter Ocean*, 2 October 1895, 7. In *The Booker T. Washington Papers*, vol. 5, ed. Louis R. Harlan, Raymond W. Smock, and Barbara S. Kraft. Urbana: University of Illinois Press, 1976.

Lyotard, Jean-François. *The Postmodern Condition: A Report on Knowledge*. Trans. Geoff Bennington and Brian Massumi. Minneapolis: University of Minnesota Press, 1993.

MacIntyre, Alasdair. "Existentialism." In *The Encyclopedia of Philosophy*, vol. 3, ed. Paul Denyce Edwards, 147–54. New York: MacMillan, 1967.

Madison, Charles A. *American Labor Leaders: Personalities and Forces in the Labor Movement*. New York: Frederick Unger, 1960.

Marilley, Suzanne M. "Frances Willard and the Feminism of Fear." *Feminist Studies* 19 (1993): 123–46.

Marot, Helen. "A Woman's Strike—An Appreciation of the Shirtwaist Makers of New York." *Proceedings of the Academy of Political Science of the City of New York* 1 (October 1910): n.p. Reprinted excerpts in Rosalyn Baxandall, Linda Gordon, and Susan Reverby, eds., *America's Working Women: A Documentary History–1600 to the Present*, 187–94. New York: Vintage Books, 1976.

Marsh, Margaret. *Anarchist Women, 1870–1920*. Philadelphia: Temple University Press, 1981.

Martin, J. F. *Martin's World's Fair Album, Atlas and Family Souvenir*. Chicago: C. Ropp and Sons, 1892.

Matthews, Glenna. *The Rise of Public Woman: Woman's Power and Woman's Place in the United States, 1630–1970*. New York: Oxford University Press, 1992.

Mattina, Anne F. "'Rights as Well as Duties': The Rhetoric of Leonora O'Reilly." *Communication Quarterly* 42 (Spring 1994): 196–205.

Mattingly, Carol. *Well-Tempered Women*. Carbondale: Southern Illinois University Press, 1998.

McGuinn, Nicholas. "George Eliot and Mary Wollstonecraft." In *The Nineteenth-Century Woman: Her Cultural and Physical World*, ed. Sara Delamont and Lorna Duffin, 188–205. New York: Barnes and Noble, 1978.

McMurry, Linda O. *To Keep the Waters Troubled: The Life of Ida B. Wells*. New York: Oxford University Press, 1998.

McVey, Frank L. "The Populist Movement." In *Selected Readings in Rural Economics*, ed. Thomas Nixon Carver, 666–98. Boston: Ginn, 1916.

Meier, August. *Negro Thought in America, 1880–1915*. Ann Arbor: University of Michigan Press, 1963.

Mellen, Bertha. "Calamity Howlers." *Kansas Agitator* (Garnett), 15 September 1892, 8.

Meridian (Mississippi) News. 17 April 1889.

Metzler, Milton. *Bread and Roses: The Struggle of American Labor 1865–1915*. New York: Knopf, 1967.

Miller, Diane Helene. "From One Voice a Chorus: Elizabeth Cady Stanton's 1860 Address to the New York State Legislature." *Women's Studies in Communication* 22 (Fall 1999): 152–89.

Miller, Donald L. *City of the Century: The Epic of Chicago and the Making of America*. New York: Simon and Schuster, 1996.

Miller, Peggy. "Teasing as Language Socialization and Verbal Play in a White Working-Class Community." In *Language Socialization Across Cultures*, ed. Bambi B. Schieffelin and Elinor Ochs, 199–212. New York: Cambridge University Press, 1986.

Miller, Raymond Curtis. "The Background of Populism in Kansas." *Mississippi Valley Historical Review* 11 (1925): 469–89.

Monmouth (New Jersey) Democrat. 10 February 1887. Woman's Christian Temperance Union National Headquarters Historical Files, Ohio Historical Society and Michigan Historical Collections Microfilms.

Mooney, Fred. *Struggles in the Coal Fields: The Autobiography of Fred Mooney*. Morgantown: West Virginia University Library, 1967.

Morgan, H. Wayne. "Populism and the Decline of Agriculture." In *The Gilded Age*, rev. ed., ed. H. Wayne Morgan, 149–70. Syracuse, N.Y.: Syracuse University Press, 1970.

Morison, Samuel Eliot, Henry Steele Commager, and William E. Leuchtenburg. *A Concise History of the American Republic*. 2nd ed. New York: Oxford University Press, 1983.

Morris, Lloyd. *From Postscript to Yesterday*. New York: Random House, 1947, Elizabeth Gurley Flynn Papers, Tamiment Library, New York University, n.p.

Morton, Marian J. *Emma Goldman and the American Left*. New York: Twayne, 1992.

Mossell, Gertrude B. *The Work of the Afro American Woman*. 1894. Reprint, New York: Oxford University Press, 1988.

"Mother Jones, Mild Mannered, Talks Sociology." *New York Times*, 1 June 1913.

"Mother Jones at Jop[l]in." *Workers' Chronicle* (Pittsburg, Kans.), 17 September 1915.

"Mother Jones Fiery." *Toledo (Ohio) Bee*, 24 March 1903.

"Mrs. Parsons, the Wife of One of the Chicago Condemned Anarchists Stirs an Audience to a High Pitch of Enthusiasm." *Paterson (New Jersey) Morning Call*, 8 November 1886. Lucy Parsons's Scrapbook, Albert Parsons Collection, State Historical Society of Wisconsin, Madison.

"Mrs. Parsons Delivers an Anarchistic Address at Turner Hall Last Night." *St. Joseph (Missouri) Gazette*, 31 December 1886. Lucy Parsons's Scrapbook, Albert Parsons Collection, State Historical Society of Wisconsin, Madison.

Murray, Robert K. *Red Scare: A Study in National Hysteria 1919–1920*. Minneapolis: University of Minnesota Press, 1955.

Muscatine (Iowa) Daily Journal. 2 May 1890.

Nimmo, Dan, and James E. Combs. *Subliminal Politics: Myths and Mythmakers in America*. Englewood Cliffs, N.J.: Prentice-Hall, 1980.

Nordloh, David J. *William Jennings Bryan*. Boston: G. K. Hall, 1981.

Nugent, Walter T. K. "How the Populists Lost in 1894." *Kansas Historical Quarterly* 31 (1965): 245–55.

———. "Some Parameters of Populism." *Agricultural History* 40 (1966): 255–70.

———. *The Tolerant Populists: Kansas Populism and Nativism*. Chicago: University of Chicago Press, 1963.

Oberschall, Anthony. *Social Conflict and Social Movements*. Englewood Cliffs, N.J.: Prentice-Hall, 1973.

Ochs, Elinor. "From Feelings to Grammar: A Samoan Case Study." In *Language Socialization Across Cultures*, ed. Bambi B. Schieffelin and Elinor Ochs, 1–13. New York: Cambridge University Press, 1986.

O'Hara, Maureen, and Walter Truett Anderson. "Psychotherapy's Own Identity Crisis." In *The Truth about the Truth*, ed. Walter Truett Anderson, 170–81. New York: G. P. Putnam's Sons, 1995.

Oldfield, John R. *Civilization and Black Progress: Selected Writings of Alexander Crummell on the South*. Charlottesville: University of Virginia Press, 1995.

Oliver, Robert T. *History of Public Speaking in America*. Boston: Allyn and Bacon, 1965.

Olmstead, Audrey Perryman. "Agitator on the Left: The Speechmaking of Elizabeth Gurley Flynn, 1904–1964." Ph.D. diss., Indiana University, 1971.

O'Neill, William. *Everyone Was Brave: A History of Feminism in America*. Chicago: Quadrangle Books, 1969.

Our Brother in Red. 19 March 1896. Woman's Christian Temperance Union National Headquarters Historical Files, Ohio Historical Society and Michigan Historical Collections Microfilms.

Page, Thomas Nelson. "The Lynching of Negroes—Its Cause and Its Prevention." *North American Review* 178, no. 1 (1904): 33–48.

———. "The Negro: The Southerner's Problem: Slavery and the Old Relation Between Southern Whites and Blacks." *McClure's* 22, no. 5 (1904): 548–45.

———. "Second Paper: Some of Its Difficulties and Fallacies." *McClure's* 22, no. 6 (1904): 619-26.

———. "Third Paper: Its Present Condition and Aspect, as Shown by Statistics." *McClure's* 23, no. 1 (1904): 96–102.

Palczewski, Catherine Helen. "Voltairine de Cleyre: Feminist Anarchist." In *Women Public Speakers in the United States, 1800–1925: A Bio-Critical Sourcebook*, ed. Karlyn Kohrs Campbell, 143–55. Westport, Conn.: Greenwood Press, 1993.

———. "Voltairine de Cleyre: Sexual Pleasure and Sexual Slavery in the 19th Century." *National Women's Studies Association Journal* 7 (Fall 1995): 54–68.

Parker, S. E. "Voltairine de Cleyre." *Freedom* (August 1914): 58. Joseph A. Labadie Collection, University of Michigan, Ann Arbor.

Parsons, Lucy. "Cause of Sex Slavery." *Firebrand* (27 January 1895): n.p.

———. "I Am an Anarchist." In *Lift Every Voice: African-American Oratory from 1787 to the Present*, ed. Philip S. Foner and Robert J. Branham, 655–60. Tuscaloosa: University of Alabama Press, 1998.

———. "The Negro. Let Him Leave Politics to the Politician and Prayers to the Preacher." *Alarm* (Chicago), 3 April 1886. Reprinted in Carolyn Ashbaugh, *Lucy Parsons: American Revolutionary*, 64–66. Chicago: Charles H. Kerr, 1976.

———. "The Red Flag." *New York Globe*, 25 October 1886.

———. "The Red Flag." *New York Herald*, 25 October 1886.

———. "The Red Flag." *Morning Journal*, 25 October 1886.

Patemen, Carole. *The Sexual Contract*. Palo Alto, Calif.: Stanford University Press, 1988.

Peffer, William A. "Speech to the Cincinnati Convention." *Alliance Monitor* (Abilene), 5 June 1891.

———. "Speech to the Cincinnati Convention." *American Nonconformist and Kansas Industrial Liberator* (Winfield, Kans.), 28 May 1891, 1, 4, 5.

———. "Speech to the Cincinnati Convention." *Central Advocate* (Marion), 12 June 1891, 1.

Perelman, Chaim. *The Realm of Rhetoric*. Notre Dame, Ind.: University of Notre Dame Press, 1982.

Perkins, Sally J. "The Myth of the Matriarchy: Annulling Patriarchy through the Regeneration of Time." *Communication Studies* 42 (1991): 371–83.

Pettey, Sarah Dudley. "What Role Is the Educated Negro Woman to Play in the Uplifting of Her Race?" In *Twentieth Century Negro Literature*, ed. D. W. Culp, 182–85. 1902. Reprint, New York: Arno Press, 1969.

Phillips, Myron G. "William Jennings Bryan." In *A History and Criticism of American Public Address*, vol. 2, ed. William Norwood Brigance, 891–918. 1943. Reprint, New York: Russell and Russell, 1971.

Pollack, Norman. "Fear of Man: Populism, Authoritarianism, and the Historian." *Agricultural History* 39 (April 1965): 59–67.

Porter, Glenn. "Industrialization and the Rise of Big Business." In *The Gilded Age: Essays on the Origins of Modern America*, ed. Charles W. Calhoun, 1–18. Wilmington, Del.: Scholarly Resources, 1996.

Powderly, Terence. "Address of the General Master Workman." *Proceedings of the General Assembly of the Knights of Labor* (6 October 1886): 38–43.

———. "Address of the General Master Workman." *Proceedings of the General Assembly of the Knights of Labor* (October 1887): 1477–540.

———. "Address of the General Master Workman." *Proceedings of the General Assembly of the Knights of Labor* (November 1893): 1–40.

———. "Address of the Grand Master Workman." *Proceedings of the General Assembly of the Knights of Labor* (7 September 1880): 169–76.

———. "Address of the Grand Master Workman." *Proceedings of the General Assembly of the Knights of Labor* (6 September 1881): 271–74.

———. "Address of the Grand Master Workman." *Proceedings of the General Assembly of the Knights of Labor* (16 September 1882): 274–86.

———. "Address of the Grand Master Workman." *Proceedings of the General Assembly of the Knights of Labor* (5 September 1883): 400–11.

———. *Journal of the Knights of Labor* (3 July 1890): 1.

———. *Journal of the Knights of Labor* (17 July 1890): 1.

———. *Journal of the Knights of Labor* (18 September 1890): 1.

———. *Journal of the Knights of Labor* (23 October 1890): 1.

———. *Journal of the Knights of Labor* (15 January 1891): 2.

———. *Journal of the Knights of Labor* (9 June 1892): 2.

———. *Journal of the Knights of Labor* (30 March 1893): 1.

———. *Journal of the Knights of Labor* (29 April 1893): 1.

———. *Journal of United Labor* (15 May 1880): 12.

———. *Journal of United Labor* (June 1882): 241.

———. *Journal of United Labor* (26 March 1887): 2330.

———. *Journal of United Labor* (10 September 1887): 2.

———. *Journal of United Labor* (31 December 1887): 2.

———. *Journal of United Labor* (24 March 1888): 2.

———. *Journal of United Labor* (21 April 1888): 2.

———. *Journal of United Labor* (26 May 1888): 1

———. *Journal of United Labor* (2 August 1888): 2.

———. *Journal of United Labor* (27 December 1888): 1.

———. *Journal of United Labor* (14 March 1889): 1.

———. *Journal of United Labor* (12 February 1891): 2.

———. *The Path I Trod.* New York: Columbia University Press, 1940.

———. "Report of the General Master Workman." *Proceedings of the General Assembly of the Knights of Labor* (5 October 1885): 6–26.

———. "Report of the General Master Workman." *Proceedings of the General Assembly of the Knights of Labor* (10 November 1888): 3–20.

———. "Report of the General Master Workman." *Proceedings of the General Assembly of the Knights of Labor* (November 1889): 1–9.

———. "Report of the General Master Workman." *Proceedings of the General Assembly of the Knights of Labor* (November 1890): 1–15.

———. *Thirty Years of Life and Labor, 1859–1889.* Philadelphia, 1890.

"Preamble." *Records of a Convention of the *********.* (1 January 1878): 28–32.

Press, Donald E. "Kansas Conflict: Populist versus Railroader in the 1890's." *Kansas Historical Quarterly* 43 (1977): 319–33.

Price, Joseph Charles. *New York Age,* 11 October 1890, 3.

Provenzo, Eugene F., Jr. *DuBois on Education.* Walnut Creek, Calif.: AltaMira Press, 2002.

Quondam. *The Adventures of Uncle Jeremiah and Family at the Great Fair.* Chicago: Laird and Lee, 1893.

Rand McNally and Company. *Handy Guide to Chicago and World's Columbian Exposition.* Chicago: Rand McNally, 1893.

Rapier, James T. "Civil Rights Bill." In *Negro Orators and Their Orations,* ed. Carter G. Woodson, 338–56. New York: Russell and Russell, 1925.

Ray, Angela. *The Lyceum and Public Culture in the Nineteenth-Century United States.* East Lansing: Michigan State University Press, 2005.

Rayback, Joseph G. *A History of American Labor.* New York: Macmillan, 1959.

"Rebuff for Anarchists." *Portland Oregonian,* 19 May 1908.

Reid, Ronald F. *Three Centuries of American Discourse: An Anthology and a Review.* Prospect Heights, Ill.: Waveland Press, 1988.

"Report of the General Executive Board." *Proceedings of the General Assembly of the Knights of Labor* (November 1894): 70–73.

Reynolds, Samuel. "Equal Suffrage." *Jeffersonian* (Lawrence, Kans.), 9 August 1894, 4.

Rich, Adrienne. *On Lies, Secrets and Silence.* London: Virago, 1980.

Rich, Andrea L., and Arthur L. Smith. *Rhetoric of Revolution.* Durham, N.C.: Moore, n.d.

Richey, Russell. *Early American Methodism.* Bloomington: Indiana University Press, 1991.

Rickard, Louise E. "The Impact of Populism on Electoral Patterns in Kansas, 1880–1900: A Quantitative Analysis." Ph.D. diss., University of Kansas, 1974.

Robinson, James Oliver. *American Myth, American Reality.* New York: Hill and Wang, 1980.

Rosemont, Franklin. "A Bomb-Toting, Long-Haired, Wild-Eyed Fiend: The Image of the Anarchist in Popular Culture." In *The Haymarket Scrapbook,* ed. Dave Roediger and Franklin Rosemont, 203–12. Chicago: Charles H. Kerr, 1986.

Rowland, Robert C. "On Mythic Criticism." *Communication Studies* 41 (1990): 101–16.

———. "The Value of the Rational World and Narrative Paradigms." *Central States Speech Journal* 39 (1988): 204–17.

Royster, Jacqueline Jones. "Introduction: Equity and Justice for All." In *Southern Horrors and Other Writings: The Anti-Lynching Campaign of Ida B. Wells, 1892–1900,* by Ida B. Wells, ed. Jacqueline Jones Royster. Boston: Bedford/St. Martin's, 1997.

Ruddick, Sara. *Maternal Thinking: Towards a Politics of Peace.* New York: Ballantine Books, 1989.

Ruffin, George L. "A Look Forward." *AME Review* 2 (July 1885): 29–33.

Rushing, Janice Hocker. "*E.T.* as Rhetorical Transcendence." *Quarterly Journal of Speech* 71 (1985): 185–203.

———. "Mythic Evolution of 'The New Frontier' in Mass Mediated Rhetoric." *Critical Studies in Mass Communication* 3 (1986): 265–96.

———. "The Rhetoric of the American Western Myth." *Communication Monographs* 50 (1983): 14–32.

Rust College. "About Rust." http://www.rustcollege.edu.

Ryan, Carroll. *Chicago the Magnificent: The Empire City of the West: A Souvenir of the World's Fair: Its Phenomenal Rise, Its Marvelous Status, Its Future Greatness.* New York: J. P. Williams, 1893.

Ryan, Mary. "Gender and Public Access: Women's Politics in Nineteenth-Century America." In *Habermas and the Public Sphere*, ed. Craig Calhoun, 259–88. Cambridge, Mass.: MIT Press, 1992.

Rydell, Robert W. *All the World's a Fair: Visions of Empire at American International Expositions, 1876–1916.* Chicago: University of Chicago Press, 1982.

Saint Peter Minnesota Tribune. 24 November 1886. Woman's Christian Temperance Union National Headquarters Historical Files, Ohio Historical Society and Michigan Historical Collections Microfilms.

Saloutos, Theodore. "The Professors and the Populists." *Agricultural History* 40 (1966): 235–54.

Scadron Arlene, and Jerome H. Skolnick, eds. *Family in Transition.* 3rd ed. Boston: Little, Brown, 1980.

Schaef, Ann Wilson. *Women's Reality: An Emerging Female System in a White Male Society.* San Francisco: Harper and Row, 1981.

Schecter, Patricia A. *Ida B. Wells-Barnett and American Reform, 1880–1930.* Chapel Hill: University of North Carolina Press, 2001.

Schneider, Dorothy, and Carl J. Schneider. *American Women in the Progressive Era, 1900–1920.* New York: Facts on File, 1993.

Scott, Joan Wallach. *Gender and the Politics of History.* New York: Columbia University Press, 1988.

Scott, Robert L., and Donald K. Smith. "The Rhetoric of Confrontation." *Quarterly Journal of Speech* 55 (1969): 1–8.

Scruggs, Lawson. *Women of Distinction: Remarkable in Works and Invincible in Character.* Raleigh, N.C.: Author, 1893.

Shackleton, Robert, ed. *Russell H. Conwell: Acres of Diamonds and His Life and Achievements.* New York: Harper and Brothers, 1915.

Shafer, Elizabeth. "St. Frances and the Crusaders." *American History Illustrated* 11 (1976): 24–33.

Shaw, Anna Howard. "The Fundamental Principle of a Republic." In *Man Cannot Speak for Her*, vol. 2, ed. Karlyn Kohrs Campbell, 433–60. New York: Praeger, 1989.

———. *The Story of a Pioneer.* New York: Harper, 1915.

Shepherd, Naomi. *A Price Below Rubies: Jewish Women as Rebels and Radicals.* Cambridge, Mass.: Harvard University Press, 1993.

Shulman, Alix Kates. "Biographical Introduction." In *Red Emma Speaks*, ed. Alix Kates Shulman, 20–47. New York: Schocken Books, 1983.

———, ed. *Red Emma Speaks.* New York: Schocken Books, 1983. Reprint, Atlantic Heights, N.J.: Humanities Press, 1996.

———. *To the Barricades: The Anarchist Life of Emma Goldman.* New York: Thomas Y. Crowell, 1971.

Silvestri, Vito. "Emma Goldman: Enduring Voice of Anarchism." *Today's Speech* 17, no. 3 (1969): 20–25.

Simons, Herbert W. "Requirements, Problems, and Strategies: A Theory of Persuasion for Social Movements." *Quarterly Journal of Speech* 56 (1970): 1–11.

Simpson, Jerry. "Speech Delivered at Wichita, September 15, 1891." *Kansas Commoner* (Wichita), 24 September 1891.

Slagell, Amy Rose. "A Good Woman Speaking Well: The Oratory of Frances E. Willard." Ph.D. diss., University of Wisconsin, 1992.

———. "The Rhetorical Structure of Frances E. Willard's Campaign for Woman Suffrage, 1876–1896." *Rhetoric and Public Affairs* 4 (2001): 1–23.

Smith, Albert Hatcher. *The Life of Russell H. Conwell.* Boston: Silver, Burdett, 1899.

Smith, Henry Nash. *Virgin Land: The American West as Symbol and Myth.* New York: Vintage Books, 1957.

Smith, Wilda M. "A Half Century of Struggle: Gaining Woman Suffrage in Kansas." *Kansas History* 4 (1981): 74–95.

"Socialists and Anarchists: They Listen to One of Mrs. Parsons's Familiar Speeches." *New York Times*, 5 November 1886. Albert Parsons Collection, State Historical Society of Wisconsin, Madison.

Solomon, Martha. "Autobiographies as Rhetorical Narratives: Elizabeth Cady Stanton and Anna Howard Shaw as 'New Women.'" *Communication Studies* 42 (Winter 1991): 354–70.

———. *Emma Goldman.* Boston: Twayne, 1987.

———. "Emma Goldman." In *Women Public Speakers in the United States, 1800–1925*, ed. Karlyn Kohrs Campbell, 195–205. Westport, Conn.: Greenwood Press, 1993.

———. "Ideology as Rhetorical Constraint: The Anarchist Agitation of 'Red Emma' Goldman." *Quarterly Journal of Speech* 74 (1988): 184–200.

———. "The 'Positive Woman's' Journey: A Mythic Analysis of the Rhetoric of Stop ERA." *Quarterly Journal of Speech* 65 (1979): 262–74.

Sovereign, J. R. "Annual Address of the General Master Workman." *Proceedings of the General Assembly of the Knights of Labor* (November 1895): 1–5.

Sprague, Rosetta Douglass. "What Role Is the Educated Negro Woman to Play in the Uplifting of Her Race?" In *Twentieth Century Negro Literature*, ed. D. W. Culp, 167–71. 1902. Reprint, New York: Arno Press, 1969.

Springen, Donald. *William Jennings Bryan: Orator of Small-Town America*. New York: Greenwood Press, 1991.

Stanton, Elizabeth Cady. *Eighty Years and More: Reminiscences 1815–1897*. New York: Schocken Books, 1971.

———. "The Solitude of Self." In *Man Cannot Speak for Her*, vol. 2, ed. Karlyn Kohrs Campbell, 371–84. New York: Praeger, 1989.

Steel, Edward M. *The Correspondence of Mother Jones*. Pittsburgh: University of Pittsburgh Press, 1985.

———, ed. *The Speeches and Writings of Mother Jones*. Pittsburgh: University of Pittsburgh Press, 1988.

Stepto, Robert B. *From Behind the Veil: A Study of Afro-American Narrative*. Urbana: University of Illinois Press, 1979.

Stetson, George R. "The Developmental Status of the American Negro." *Public Opinion* (21 February 1895): 171–72.

Stevenson-Mossner, Jeanne. "Elizabeth Cady Stanton, Reformer to Revolutionary." *Journal of the American Academy of Religion* 62 (Fall 1994): 673–97.

Stewart, Charles J. "The Internal Rhetoric of the Knights of Labor." *Communication Studies* 42 (1991): 67–82.

———. "Labor Agitation in America: 1865–1915." In *America in Controversy: History of American Public Address*, ed. DeWitte Holland, 153–69. Dubuque, Iowa: William C. Brown, 1973.

Stewart, Charles J., Craig Allen Smith, and Robert E. Denton, Jr. *Persuasion and Social Movements*. 4th ed. Prospect Heights, Ill.: Waveland Press, 2001.

Still, William. Letter to Booker T. Washington. 19 September 1895. In *The Booker T. Washington Papers*, vol. 4, ed. Louis R. Harlan, Stuart B. Kaufman, and Raymond W. Smock, 18–19. Urbana: University of Illinois Press, 1974.

Stokes, John W. *The Man Who Lived Two Lives*. New York: Vantage Press, 1973.

Stone, Elizabeth. *Black Sheep and Kissing Cousins: How Our Family Stories Shape Us*. New York: Times Books, 1978.

Sumner, William Graham. "The Forgotten Man." In *Social Darwinism: Selected Essays of William Graham Sumner*, 110–35. Englewood Cliffs, N.J.: Prentice-Hall, 1963.

———. *Social Darwinism: Selected Essays of William Graham Sumner*. Englewood Cliffs, N.J.: Prentice-Hall, 1963.

———. *What Social Classes Owe to Each Other*. New York: Harper and Brothers, 1883.

Tannen, Deborah. *Talking Voices*. New York: Cambridge University Press, 1989.

Temperance and Prohibition Papers. Woman's Christian Temperance Union National Headquarters Historical Files, Ohio Historical Society and Michigan Historical Collections Microfilms.

"Temple University Gets $5 Million Gift." *New York Times*, 31 March 1985.

Terrell, Mary Church. *A Colored Woman in a White World*. 1940; Reprint, New York: Arno Press, 1980.

———. "The Duty of the National Association of Colored Women to the Race." *AME Church Review* (January 1900): 340–54. Reprinted in Beverly Washington Jones, ed., *Quest for Equality: The Life and Writings of Mary Eliza Church Terrell, 1863–1954*, 139–50. Brooklyn, N.Y.: Carlson, 1990.

———. "The Effects of Disenfranchisement Upon the Colored Women of the South." 13 typed pages, Library of Congress, ms. 16976, reel 23, container 32, 385–97. Qtd. in *Man Cannot Speak for Her: A Critical Study of Early Feminist Rhetoric*, vol. 1, by Karlyn Kohrs Campbell. New York: Praeger, 1989.

———. "First Presidential Address to the National Association of Colored Women." In *Quest for Equality: The Life and Writings of Mary Eliza Church Terrell, 1863–1954*, ed. Beverly Washington Jones, 133–38. Brooklyn, N.Y.: Carlson, 1990.

———. "Graduates and Former Students of Washington Colored High School." *Voice of the Negro* (June 1904): 221–27. In *Quest for Equality: The Life and Writings of Mary Eliza Church Terrell, 1863–1954*, ed. Beverly Washington Jones, 159–66. Brooklyn, N.Y.: Carlson, 1990.

———. "The History of the Club Women's Movement." *Aframerican Woman's Journal* (Summer-Fall 1940): 34–38. In *Quest for Equality: The Life and Writings of Mary Eliza Church Terrell, 1863–1954*, ed. Beverly Washington Jones, 315–26. Brooklyn, N.Y.: Carlson, 1990.

———. "The Justice of Woman Suffrage." *Crisis* 4 (September 1912): 243–45. In *Quest for Equality: The Life and Writings of Mary Eliza Church Terrell, 1863–1954*, ed. Beverly Washington Jones, 307–10. Brooklyn, N.Y.: Carlson, 1990.

———. "Lynching from a Negro's Point of View." *North American Review* (June 1904). In *Quest for Equality: The Life and Writings of Mary Eliza Church Terrell, 1863–1954*, ed. Beverly Washington Jones, 167–82. Brooklyn, N.Y.: Carlson, 1990.

———. "N.A.C.W. Department Announcement." *Woman's Era* (1896): 3–4. In *Quest for Equality: The Life and Writings of Mary Eliza Church Terrell, 1863–1954*, ed. Beverly Washington Jones, 131–32. Brooklyn, N.Y.: Carlson, 1990.

———. "Needed: Women Lawyers." In *Quest for Equality: The Life and Writings of Mary Eliza Church Terrell, 1863–1954*, ed. Beverly Washington Jones, 327–30. Brooklyn, N.Y.: Carlson, 1990.

———. "Peonage in the United States: The Convict Lease System and the Chain Gangs." *Nineteenth Century* (August 1907): 306–22. In *Quest for Equality: The Life and Writings of Mary Eliza Church Terrell, 1863–1954*, ed. Beverly Washington Jones, 255–73. Brooklyn, N.Y.: Carlson, 1990.

———. "A Plea for the White South by a Coloured Woman." *Nineteenth Century and After* (July 1906): 70–84.

———. "The Progress of Colored Women." *Voice of the Negro* (1904): 291–93.

———. "Service Which Should Be Rendered the South." *Voice of the Negro* (February 1905): 182–86. In *Quest for Equality: The Life and Writings of Mary Eliza Church Terrell, 1863–1954*, ed. Beverly Washington Jones, 205–12. Brooklyn, N.Y.: Carlson, 1990.

———. "What It Means to Be Colored in the Capital of the United States." *Independent* (24 January 1907): 181–86. In *Quest for Equality: The Life and Writings of Mary Eliza Church Terrell, 1863–1954*, ed. Beverly Washington Jones, 283–92. Brooklyn, N.Y.: Carlson, 1990.

———. "What Role Is the Educated Negro Woman to Play in the Uplifting of Her Race?" In *Twentieth Century Negro Literature*, ed. D. W. Culp, 172–77. 1902. Reprint, New York: Arno Press, 1969.

Thames, Richard H. "A Flawed Stone Fitting Its Nineteenth Century Setting: A Burkeian Analysis of Russell Conwell's 'Acres of Diamonds.'" *Speaker and Gavel* 27 (1990): 11–19.

Tipple, John. "Big Businessmen and a New Economy." In *The Gilded Age*, rev. ed., ed. H. Wayne Morgan, 13–30. Syracuse, N.Y.: Syracuse University Press, 1970.

Todd, Rev. John. *Woman's Rights*. Boston: Lee and Shepard, 1867.

Tonn, Mari Boor. "Elizabeth Gurley Flynn's *Sabotage*: 'Scene' as Both Controlling and Catalyzing 'Acts.'" *Southern Speech Communication Journal* 1 (1995): 59–75.

———. "Mary Harris 'Mother' Jones (1830?–1930), 'Mother' and Messiah to Industrial Labor." In *Women Public Speakers in the United States, 1800–1925: A Bio-Critical Sourcebook*, ed. Karlyn Kohrs Campbell, 229–41. Westport, Conn.: Greenwood Press, 1993.

———. "Militant Motherhood: Labor's Mary Harris 'Mother' Jones." *Quarterly Journal of Speech* 82 (1996): 1–21.

Tonn, Mari Boor, and Mark S. Kuhn. "Co-constructed Oratory: Speaker-Audience Interaction in the Labor Union Rhetoric of Mary Harris 'Mother' Jones." *Text and Performance Quarterly* 13 (1993): 1–18.

———. "Elizabeth Gurley Flynn (1890–1964), Advocate Who Merged Feminism and Radical Labor Organizing." In *Women Public Speakers in the United States, 1925–1993: A Bio-Critical Sourcebook*, ed. Karlyn Kohrs Campbell, 221–37. Westport, Conn.: Greenwood Press, 1994.

Townes, Emilie. "Ida B. Wells-Barnett: An Afro-American Prophet." *Christian Century* 106 (1989): 285–86.

Trachtenberg, Alan. *The Incorporation of America: Culture and Society in the Gilded Age*. New York: Hill and Wang, 2007.

Truman, Ben C., et al. *History of the World's Fair, Being a Complete and Authentic Description of the Columbian Exposition from its Inception*. Philadelphia: H. W. Kelly, 1893.

Turner, Henry McNeal. "The Democratic Return to Power: Its Effect." *AME Review* 1 (January 1885): 246–48.

———. "I Claim the Rights of a Man." In *The Voice of Black America: Major Speeches by Negroes in the United States 1797–1971*, ed. Philip S. Foner, 357–66. New York: Simon and Schuster, 1972.

———. *The Negro in All Ages*. Savannah, Ga.: D. G. Patton, 1873.

———. "Will It Be Possible for the Negro to Attain, in This Country, Unto the American Type of Civilization?" In *Twentieth Century Negro Literature*, ed. D. W. Culp, 42–45. 1902. Reprint, New York: Arno Press, 1969.

Turner, James. "Understanding the Populists." *Journal of American History* 67 (1980): 354–73.

U.S. Congress. House, Subcommittee of the Committee on Mines and Mining. *Conditions in the Coal Mines of Colorado*. 63rd Cong., 2nd sess., H. Res. 387. Washington, D.C.: Government Printing Office, 1914.

University of Missouri–Kansas City School of Law. "Trial of Joseph Shipp et al. 1907." lynchingsstate. html.

Van Voris, Jacqueline. *Carrie Chapman Catt: A Public Life*. New York: Feminist Press, 1987.

Vartabedian, Robert A. "Nixon's Vietnam Rhetoric: A Case Study of Apologia as Generic Paradox." *Southern Speech Communication Journal* 50 (1985): 366–81.

Vonnegut, Kristen. "Listening for Women's Voices." *Communication Education* 41 (1992): 26–39.

Waggenspack, Beth. *The Search for Self-Sovereignty: The Oratory of Elizabeth Cady Stanton*. Westport, Conn.: Greenwood Press, 1989.

Wake, C. Staniland. "The Race Question." *Open Court* 4, no. 148 (1890): 2353–55.

Wakeman, T. B. "Planetary Statesmanship and the Negro." *Open Court* 4, no. 154 (1890): 2433–35.

Walsh, James F., Jr. "An Approach to Dyadic Communication in Historical Social Movements: Dyadic Communication in Maoist Insurgent Mobilization." *Communication Monographs* 53 (1983): 1–15.

———. "Paying Attention to Channels: Differential Images of Recruitment for Students for a Democratic Society, 1960–1965." *Communication Studies* 44 (1993): 71–86.

Ware, B. L., and Wil Linkugel. "They Spoke in Defense of Themselves: On the Generic Criticism of Apologia." *Quarterly Journal of Speech* 59 (1973): 273–83.

Ware, Norman J. *Labor Movement in the United States, 1860–1895: A Study in Democracy*. Gloucester, Mass.: P. Smith, 1959.

Washington, Booker T. "An Abraham Lincoln Memorial Address in Philadelphia." In *The Booker T. Washington Papers*, vol. 5, ed. Louis R. Harlan, Raymond W. Smock, and Barbara S. Kraft, 32–38. Urbana: University of Illinois Press, 1976.

———. "An Account of a Speech in Washington, D.C., 7 April 1894." In *The Booker T. Washington Papers*, vol. 3, ed. Louis R. Harlan, Stuart B. Kaufman, and Raymond W. Smock, 397–402. Urbana: University of Illinois Press, 1974.

———. "An Address at a Mass Meeting in Washington, D.C." In *The Booker T. Washington Papers*, vol. 3, ed. Louis R. Harlan, Stuart B. Kaufman, and Raymond W. Smock, 184–94. Urbana: University of Illinois Press, 1974.

———. "An Address at the Harvard Alumni Dinner." In *The Booker T. Washington Papers*, vol. 4, ed. Louis R. Harlan, Stuart B. Kaufman, and Raymond W. Smock, 183–85. Urbana: University of Illinois Press, 1974.

———. "An Address at the National Peace Jubilee." In *The Booker T. Washington Papers*, vol. 4, ed. Louis R. Harlan, Stuart B. Kaufman, and Raymond W. Smock, 490–93. Urbana: University of Illinois Press, 1974.

———. "Address before the National Education Association." In *The Booker T. Washington Papers*, vol. 4, ed. Louis R. Harlan, Stuart B. Kaufman, and Raymond W. Smock, 188–99. Urbana: University of Illinois Press, 1974.

———. *The Booker T. Washington Papers*. Ed. Louis R. Harlan. Urbana: University of Illinois Press, 1972.

———. "Cotton States Exposition Address." In *American Rhetorical Discourse*, 2nd ed., ed. Ronald F. Reid, 564–67. Prospect Heights, Ill.: Waveland Press, 1998.

———. "National Unitarian Association." In *The Booker T. Washington Papers*, vol. 3, ed. Louis R. Harlan, Stuart B. Kaufman, and Raymond W. Smock, 476–79. Urbana: University of Illinois Press, 1974.

———, ed. *The Negro Problem: A Series of Articles by Representative American Negroes of Today*. New York: James Pott, 1903.

———. "A Speech before the New York Congregational Club." In *The Booker T. Washington Papers*, vol. 3, ed. Louis R. Harlan, Stuart B. Kaufman, and Raymond W. Smock, 25–32. Urbana: University of Illinois Press, 1974.

———. "A Speech Delivered before the Women's New England Club." In *The Booker T. Washington Papers*, vol. 3, ed. Louis R. Harlan, Stuart B. Kaufman, and Raymond W. Smock, 279–88. Urbana: University of Illinois Press, 1974.

—. "The Standard Printed Version of the Atlanta Exposition Address." In *The Booker T. Washington Papers*, vol. 3, ed. Louis R. Harlan, Stuart B. Kaufman, and Raymond W. Smock, 583–87. Urbana: University of Illinois Press, 1974.

Washington, Mary Helen. "Introduction." In *A Voice from the South*, by Anna Julia Cooper, xxvii–liv. New York: Oxford University Press, 1988.

Webber, Josie. "Woman Suffrage and Prohibition." *Kansas Agitator* (Garnett), 1 March 1894.

Weekly Censor. 13 January and 5 May 1887. WCTU Series, Microfilm.

Wells, Ida B. *Crusade for Justice: The Autobiography of Ida B. Wells*. Ed. Alfreda M. Duster. Chicago: University of Chicago Press, 1970.

—. *Southern Horrors and Other Writings: The Anti-Lynching Campaign of Ida B. Wells, 1892–1900*, ed. Jacqueline Jones Royster. Boston: Bedford/St. Martin's, 1997.

—. "Lynch Law in All Its Phases." In *With Pen and Voice: A Critical Anthology of Nineteenth-Century African-American Women*, ed. Shirley Wilson Logan, 80–105. Carbondale: Southern Illinois University Press, 1995.

—. "The Reason Why The Colored American Is Not in the World's Columbian Exposition." In *Selected Works of Ida B. Wells-Barnett*, ed. and comp. Trudier Harris, 46-137. New York: Oxford University Press, 1991.

—. *A Red Record*. 1895. Reprint, New York: Arno Press, 1969.

—. "A Red Record Made Public." In *Selected Works of Ida B. Wells-Barnett*, ed. and comp. Trudier Harris, 140–52. New York: Oxford University Press, 1991.

—. *Southern Horrors: Lynch Law in All Its Phases*. 1892. Reprint, New York: Arno Press, 1969; New Orleans: Ayer Press, 1990.

—. "Southern Horrors: The Lynch Law in All Its Phases." In *Selected Works of Ida B. Wells-Barnett*, ed. and comp. Trudier Harris, 16–45. New York: Oxford University Press, 1991.

Welter, Barbara. "The Cult of True Womanhood: 1820–1860." *American Quarterly* 18, no. 2 (1966): 151–74.

—. *Dimity Convictions: The American Woman in the Nineteenth Century*. Athens: Ohio University Press, 1976.

Werstein, Irving. *Labor's Defiant Lady: The Story of Mother Jones*. New York: Thomas Y. Crowell, 1969.

West, Candace, and Don H. Zimmerman. "Doing Gender." *Gender and Society* 1 (June 1987): 125–51.

Wexler, Alice. *Emma Goldman: An Intimate Life*. New York: Pantheon Books, 1984.

—. *Emma Goldman in Exile*. Boston: Beacon Press, 1989.

Whites, LeeAnn. *The Civil War as a Crisis in Gender*. Athens: University of Georgia Press, 1995.

Whitman, Mrs. T. J. "Importance of Correct Education." *Topeka (Kansas) Advocate*, 6 August 1890.

Wiebe, Robert H. *The Search for Order: 1877–1920*. New York: Hill and Wang, 1967.

Willard, Frances. "Address at the Colorado State WCTU Convention." *Denver Daily News*, 10 August 1883. Woman's Christian Temperance Union Series. Microfilm. Reprinted in Amy Rose Slagell, "A Good Woman Speaking Well: The Oratory of Frances E. Willard," 335–40. Ph.D. diss., University of Wisconsin, 1992.

—. "Address before the House Judiciary Committee." Woman's Christian Temperance Union Series. Microfilm. Reprinted in Amy Rose Slagell, "A Good Woman Speaking Well: The Oratory of Frances E. Willard," 235. Ph.D. diss., University of Wisconsin, 1992.

—. *Address before the Second Biennial Convention of the World's Woman's Christian Temperance Union, and the Twentieth Annual Convention of the National Woman's Christian Temperance Union*. Chicago: Woman's Temperance Publishing Association, 1893.

—. "Address before the Senate Committee on Woman Suffrage." In *Miscellaneous Documents of the Senate of the United States*. 50th Cong., 1st sess. Doc. 114, 19–21. Washington, D.C.: Government Printing Office, 1888. Reprinted in Amy Rose Slagell, "A Good Woman Speaking Well: The Oratory of Frances E. Willard," 445–50. Ph.D. diss., University of Wisconsin, 1992.

—. "Address before the World's WCTU." In *Address by Frances E. Willard President of the World's Woman's Christian Temperance Union at its Third Biennial Convention*, 1–95. London: White Ribbon, 1895.

—. "Address to President Garfield." In *Woman and Temperance*, 265–71. Hartford, Conn.: Park Publishing, 1883. Reprint, Chicago: Woman's Temperance Publishing Association, 1897.

—. "Address to the Committee on Resolutions of the Republican National Convention." *Patriot* (26 June 1884): 344. Reprinted in Amy Rose Slagell, "A Good Woman Speaking Well: The Oratory of Frances E. Willard," 341–45. Ph.D. diss., University of Wisconsin, 1992.

—. "Address to the Michigan State WCTU." Woman's Christian Temperance Union National Headquarters Historical Files, Ohio Historical Society and Michigan Historical Collections Microfilms.

Reprinted in Amy Rose Slagell, "A Good Woman Speaking Well: The Oratory of Frances E. Willard," 373–84. Ph.D. diss., University of Wisconsin, 1992.

———. "The Coming Brotherhood." *Arena* 6 (August 1892): 317–24.

———. "The Dawn of Woman's Day." *Our Day* 2 (November 1888): 345–60. Reprinted in Amy Rose Slagell, "A Good Woman Speaking Well: The Oratory of Frances E. Willard," 466–83. Ph.D. diss., University of Wisconsin, 1992.

———. *Do Everything: A Handbook for the World's White Ribboners.* Chicago: Woman's Temperance Publishing Association, 1895.

———. *Eleventh Presidential Address before the National WCTU, November 14, 1890, Atlanta, Georgia.* Chicago: Woman's Temperance Publishing Association, 1890.

———. "Eulogy to John Finch." In Amy Rose Slagell, "A Good Woman Speaking Well: The Oratory of Frances E. Willard," 430–31. Ph.D. diss., University of Wisconsin, 1992.

———. "Everybody's War." In Amy Rose Slagell, "A Good Woman Speaking Well: The Oratory of Frances E. Willard," 160–74. Ph.D. diss., University of Wisconsin, 1992.

———. *Glimpses of Fifty Years: The Autobiography of an American Woman.* Chicago: Woman's Christian Temperance Publishing Association, 1889.

———. *A Great Mother.* Chicago: Woman's Christian Temperance Publishing Association, 1894.

———. *Hints and Helps in Our Temperance Work.* New York: National Temperance Society and Publication House, 1875.

———. "Home Protection." In *The Home Protection Manual.* Broadway, N.Y.: Independent Office, 1879. Reprinted in Amy Rose Slagell, "A Good Woman Speaking Well: The Oratory of Frances E. Willard," 249–67. Ph.D. diss., University of Wisconsin, 1992.

———. "Home Protection Address." Woman's Christian Temperance Union National Headquarters Historical Files, Ohio Historical Society and Michigan Historical Collections Microfilms. Reprinted in Amy Rose Slagell, "A Good Woman Speaking Well: The Oratory of Frances E. Willard," 184–97. Ph.D. diss., University of Wisconsin, 1992.

———. *How to Win: A Book for Girls.* New York: Funk and Wagnalls, 1886.

———. Interview. *Great Thoughts* (February 1893). Woman's Christian Temperance Union National Headquarters Historical Files, Ohio Historical Society and Michigan Historical Collections Microfilms.

———. "Man in the Home." *Chautauquan* (February 1887): 279–81.

———. "The New Chivalry." In Amy Rose Slagell, "A Good Woman Speaking Well: The Oratory of Frances E. Willard," 128–41. Ph.D. diss., University of Wisconsin, 1992.

———. "A New Departure for Woman's Higher Education." In *Papers and Letters Presented at the First Woman's Congress of the Association for the Advancement of Women,* 94–99. New York: Mrs. Wim. Ballard, 1874. Reprinted in Amy Rose Slagell, "A Good Woman Speaking Well: The Oratory of Frances E. Willard," 147–59. Ph.D. diss., University of Wisconsin, 1992.

———. *Nineteen Beautiful Years.* New York: Harper and Brothers, 1864.

———. "On the Embellishment of a Country Home." In *Transactions of the Illinois State Agricultural Society,* ed. S. Francis, 466–71. Springfield, Ill.: Baihache and Baker, 1859.

———. "Personal Liberty." In Amy Rose Slagell, "A Good Woman Speaking Well: The Oratory of Frances E. Willard," 315–29. Ph.D. diss., University of Wisconsin, 1992.

———. "Presidential Address." In *Minutes of the National Woman's Christian Temperance Union,* 64–82. Brooklyn, N.Y.: Union Argus Steam Printing, 1881.

———. "Presidential Address." In *Minutes of the National Woman's Christian Temperance Union,* 47–67. Cleveland: Home Publishing, 1883.

———. "Presidential Address." In *Minutes of the National Woman's Christian Temperance Union,* 50–74. Chicago: Woman's Temperance Publication Association, 1884.

———. "Presidential Address." In *Minutes of the National Woman's Christian Temperance Union,* 62–93. Brooklyn, N.Y.: Martin and Niper, 1885.

———. "Presidential Address." In *Minutes of the National Woman's Christian Temperance Union,* 70–90. Chicago: Woman's Temperance Publishing Association, 1886.

———. "Presidential Address." In *Minutes of the National WCTU 14th Annual Meeting* [1887 Convention], 71–95. Chicago: Woman's Temperance Publishing Association, 1888.

———. "Presidential Address." In *Minutes of the National Woman's Christian Temperance Union,* 1–64. Chicago: Woman's Temperance Publishing Association, 1888.

———. "Presidential Address." In *Minutes of the National Woman's Christian Temperance Union,* 92–163. Chicago: Woman's Temperance Publishing Association, 1889.

———. "Presidential Address." In *Minutes of the National Woman's Christian Temperance Union*, 84–226. Chicago: Woman's Temperance Publishing Association, 1891.

———. "Presidential Address." In *Minutes of the National Woman's Christian Temperance Union*, 53–148. Chicago: Woman's Temperance Publishing Association, 1893.

———. "Presidential Address." In *Minutes of the National Woman's Christian Temperance Union*, 81–189. Chicago: Woman's Temperance Publishing Association, 1894.

———. *Report of the International Council of Women*. Washington, D.C.: Rufus Darby, 1888. Reprinted in Amy Rose Slagell, "A Good Woman Speaking Well: The Oratory of Frances E. Willard," 437–44. Ph.D. diss., University of Wisconsin, 1992.

———. *Should Women Vote?* Chicago: Ruby Gilbert, n.d.

———. "Social Purity: The Latest and Greatest Crusade." *Voice Extra* (June 1886). Woman's Christian Temperance Union National Headquarters Historical Files, Ohio Historical Society and Michigan Historical Collections Microfilms. Reprinted in Amy Rose Slagell, "A Good Woman Speaking Well: The Oratory of Frances E. Willard," 353–72. Ph.D. diss., University of Wisconsin, 1992.

———. "Speech at Queen's Hall, London." *Citizen and Home Guard* (23 July 1894). Woman's Christian Temperance Union National Headquarters Historical Files, Ohio Historical Society and Michigan Historical Collections Microfilms. Reprinted as "The Average Woman" in Amy Rose Slagell, "A Good Woman Speaking Well: The Oratory of Frances E. Willard," 619–25. Ph.D. diss., University of Wisconsin, 1992.

———. *Temperance and the Labor Question*. Chicago: Ruby Gilbert, n.d.

———. *A Wheel within a Wheel: How I Learned to Ride the Bicycle*. New York: F. H. Berell, 1895.

———. "White Cross in Education." In *National Education Association Journal of Proceedings and Addresses*, 159–78. Topeka: Clifford Baker, Kansas Publishing House, 1898. Reprinted in Amy Rose Slagell, "A Good Woman Speaking Well: The Oratory of Frances E. Willard," 502–28. Ph.D. diss., University of Wisconsin, 1992.

———. "White Life for Two." *Chautauqua Assembly Herald*, 3 August 1891. Woman's Christian Temperance Union National Headquarters Historical Files, Ohio Historical Society and Michigan Historical Collections Microfilms. Reprinted in Amy Rose Slagell, "A Good Woman Speaking Well: The Oratory of Frances E. Willard," 575–88. Ph.D. diss., University of Wisconsin, 1992.

———. "Woman and Philanthropy." *Christian Union* 35, no. 25 (9 May 1887): n.p. Reprinted in Amy Rose Slagell, "A Good Woman Speaking Well: The Oratory of Frances E. Willard," 395–406. Ph.D. diss., University of Wisconsin, 1992.

———. *Woman and Temperance*. Hartford, Conn.: Park, 1883. Reprint, Chicago: Woman's Temperance Publishing Association, 1897.

———. "The Woman's Cause Is Man's." *Arena* 5 (1892): 717–24.

———. "Women and Organization." In *Transactions of the National Council of Women of the United States*, 23–57. Philadelphia: J. B. Lippencott, 1891. Reprinted in Amy Rose Slagell, "A Good Woman Speaking Well: The Oratory of Frances E. Willard," 529–74. Ph.D. diss., University of Wisconsin, 1992.

———. "Women in Journalism." *Chautauquan* (July 1886): 576–79.

Willard, Frances, Helen Winslow, and Sallie White, eds. *Occupations for Women*. New York: Success, 1897.

Wilson, Charles Morrow. *The Commoner: William Jennings Bryan*. Garden City, N.Y.: Doubleday, 1970.

Wilson, Gerald L. "A Strategy of Explanation: Richard M. Nixon's August 8, 1974, Resignation Address." *Communication Quarterly* 24 (1976): 14–20.

Wilson, Kirt H. *The Reconstruction Desegregation Debate: The Politics of Equality and the Rhetoric of Place, 1870–1875*. East Lansing: Michigan State University Press, 2002.

Wilson, Lisa. *Life After Death: Widows in Pennsylvania 1750–1850*. Philadelphia: Temple University Press, 1992.

Wing, Adrien Katherine. "Brief Reflections toward a Multiplicative Theory and Praxis of Being." In *Critical Race Feminism: A Reader*, ed. Adrien Katherine Wing, 27–34. New York: New York University Press, 1997.

———, ed. *Critical Race Feminism: A Reader*. New York: New York University Press, 1997.

Wittenmyer, Annie. *History of the Women's Temperance Crusade*. Philadelphia: Office of the Christian Woman, 1878.

Wolff, Cynthia Griffin. "Emily Dickinson, Elizabeth Cady Stanton and the Task of Discovering a Usable Past." *Massachusetts Review* 30 (1989): 629–44.

Wood, Andrew F. "Managing the Lady Managers: The Shaping of Heterotopian Spaces in the 1893 Chicago Exposition's Woman's Building." *Southern Communication Journal* 69, no. 4 (2004): 289–302.

Woodward, C. Vann. "The Populist Heritage and the Intellectual." *American Scholar* 29 (1959–60): 55–72.

———. *The Strange Career of Jim Crow.* New York: Oxford University Press, 1957.

Zeiger, Susan. "Finding a Cure for War: Women's Politics and the Peace Movement in the 1920's." *Journal of Social History* 24 (Fall 1990): 69–86.

ABOUT THE AUTHORS

THOMAS R. BURKHOLDER is an associate professor and the chair in the Department of Communication Studies at the University of Nevada at Las Vegas. His research interests are in presidential rhetoric and American public address. With Karlyn Kohrs Campbell, he is coauthor of *Critiques of Contemporary Rhetoric*.

A. CHEREE CARLSON is a professor in the Hugh Downs School of Human Communication at Arizona State University. A former editor of the *Western Communication Journal*, she has published extensively in the areas of Burkean criticism, women's discourse, and social change. She is the author of *The Crimes of Womanhood: Defining Femininity in a Court of Law*.

JAMES GILBERT is a Distinguished University Professor in the Department of History at the University of Maryland at College Park. He has authored eight monographs. His most recent works are *Explorations of American Culture* and *Redeeming Culture: American Religion in an Age of Science*. His *Perfect Cities: Chicago's Utopias of 1893* was chosen by the *New York Times* as one of its Notable Books of 1991. His *A Cycle of Outrage: America's Reaction to the Juvenile Delinquent in the 1950s* was the Oxford University Press entry for the Pulitzer Prize. The holder of several fellowships, including an NEH and Fulbrights to Australia and Sweden, he has also been a Fellow of the Woodrow Wilson Center, the Rutgers University Center for Historical Analysis, and the Rockefeller Center at Bellagio, Italy. He is founder of the Center for Historical Studies at the University of Maryland.

LINDA DIANE HORWITZ, Ph.D., Northwestern University, is assistant professor of Communication at Lake Forest College. She teaches courses in rhetorical theory, rhetorical criticism, feminist argumentation, and pop culture criticism. Her research interests are in rhetorical theory and criticism, with special emphasis in the rhetoric of African American women.

SUSAN SCHULTZ HUXMAN is director of the Elliott School of Communication at Wichita State University. Having won numerous awards and recognition for her teaching, she has published nearly two dozen scholarly articles and book chapters in the field of rhetorical criticism and is coauthor with Karlyn Kohrs Campbell of *The Rhetorical Act: Thinking, Speaking, and Writing Critically*.

DONNA MARIE KOWAL is an associate professor in the Department of Communication at the College at Brockport, State University of New York. Her research focuses on the rhetoric of social movements and representations of gender, race, ethnicity, class, and cultural identities in public discourse. She is a recipient of the Eastern Communication Association's Caroline Drummond Ecroyd Award and the New York State Chancellor's Award for Excellence in Teaching.

RICHARD W. LEEMAN is a professor in the Department of Communication at the University of North Carolina at Charlotte, where he has been on the faculty since 1989. He has authored, coauthored, or edited five books: *The Rhetoric of Terrorism and Counterterrorism; "Do-Everything" Reform: The Oratory of Frances E. Willard; African-American Orators: A Bio-Critical Sourcebook;* (with Bill Hill) *The Art and Practice of Argumentation and Debate;* and (with Bernard K. Duffy) *American Voices : An Encyclopedia of Contemporary Orators*.

SHIRLEY WILSON LOGAN is an associate professor in the Department of English at the University of Maryland, College Park, where she has directed the Professional Writing Program. She has also served as Chair of the Conference on College Composition and Communication and the Alliance of Rhetoric Societies. In addition to several journal articles, she is the author of *"We Are Coming": The Persuasive Discourse of Nineteenth-Century Black Women* and editor of *With Pen and Voice: A Critical Anthology of Nineteenth-Century African-American Women*.

CATHERINE HELEN PALCZEWSKI is a professor in the Department of Communication Studies at the University of Northern Iowa. Her research interests include rhetorical theory and criticism, feminist theory and criticism, political communication, social movements, and argumentation theory. Within these areas, she focuses on the rhetorical constructions and implications of speaking from the margin. She also directs the university's intercollegiate policy debate program. A UNI Summer Research Fellowship supported her work on the chapter in this volume.

SALLY PERKINS currently teaches part-time at Butler University and Indiana University–Purdue University in Indianapolis. Her research focuses on feminist rhetoric, early women's rights rhetoric, and instructional communication. She recently coauthored a rhetorical criticism textbook and has been awarded an Outstanding Teaching Award at California State University, Sacramento, where she taught full-time for twelve years.

AMY R. SLAGELL is an associate professor in the English Department at Iowa State University, where she heads the speech program. Her research interests are American public address and women's discourse. She is co-editor of *"Let Something Good Be Said": Speeches and Writings of Frances E. Willard* (Urbana: University of Illinois Press, 2007).

CHARLES J. STEWART is a professor in the Department of Communication at Purdue University. His research interests include persuasion and the rhetoric of social protest. He is coauthor of the popular text *Persuasion and Social Movements*.

MARI BOOR TONN is an associate professor at the University of Maryland, College Park, where she specializes in feminist and rhetorical criticism, with a special emphasis in women labor movement leaders and feminist rhetoric. She received the Karl Wallace Memorial Award for excellence in rhetorical scholarship from the National Communication Association in 1997 and the Past President's Award for excellence in scholarship and service from the Eastern Communication Association in 2000. Among other places, she has published in the *Quarterly Journal of Speech* and *Rhetoric and Public Affairs*.

MARTHA S. WATSON is dean of the Greenspun College of Urban Affairs and Sanford Berman Professor in the Department of Communication Studies at the University of Nevada, Las Vegas. A former editor of the *Quarterly Journal of Speech* and the *Southern States Communication Journal*, she has also served as president of the National Communication Association. She has published extensively in American public address with an emphasis on social change and women's discourse.

INDEX

abolitionism, 6–8, 20, 23, 31, 256; woman's
    rights and, xviii, 180–81, 357, 365–67, 369–70

Abzug, Bella, 381

accommodationists: African-American, 2–5
    17, 20–21, 27–28, 32n. 8, 200–201; woman
    suffragist, 359

Ackerman, Jessie, 163

action: Conwell and transforming scene through,
    78–82; de Cleyre and call to, 327; Goldman
    and call to, 330–33; Terrell and call to, 205–7;
    Wells and clear paths of, 48, 54–56, 58–59

Adam and Eve, 24, 176

Adams, Henry, **Works**: *Education of Henry Adams*,
    304

Adams, John, 134

adaptation strategy, 28

ad hominem attacks, 229

*Adventures of Uncle Jeremiah and Family at the Great
    Fair, The*, 304

advertising, 294–95, 339

Aesop's Fables, 111

a fortiori argument, 53, 214

Africa, 3, 11, 13–15, 26

African Americans: abolitionists and, 6–7;
    assimilationists, accomodationists,
    integrationists, and separationists, defined,
    2–4; Conwell on opportunity and, 76;

declining rights of, xvi–xviii, xxvi, 1–2, 37–40;
education of, xvii; "equal chance" theme and,
5–6; gender and, and Wells, xxiii–xxiv, 43,
50; gender and class and, and Parsons, 310,
317, 320–21, 335, 338–39, 342–43; gender
and class and, and Terrell, 195–221; labor
movement and, 55, 237, 238, 312; lyceums
and, 43; lynching and, xviii, xxiii–xxiv, 37–63,
195, 207–12; migrations of, from South, xvii–
xviii; military service and, 6, 21, 368; press
and, 55, 58; reform rhetoric and, xxiii–xxiv,
1–35; social Darwinism and, xix, 3–5, 9–11,
13–14, 16–32; strategies for advancement of,
Du Bois and Washington, vs. Terrell, 200–203;
voting rights of, xvi–xvii, 1–2, 8, 27–28, 30,
37–41, 52, 216, 233, 365, 367–68; woman
suffrage and, xiv, xviii–xix, 216, 365, 367–68;
women's clubs and, 203–7; World Columbian
Exposition and, 46. *See also* race(s); racial
discrimination (racism, prejudice); *specific
individuals*

African Methodist Episcopal (AME) Church, 23

Afro-American League, 3

agitator persona, xxv, 51, 224–25, 228–30, 311,
    319–21, 328–34, 341–42, 344–45, 376,
    379–80

agrarian myth: conspiracy of evil and, 97–98,

109–12; Conwell's "comic frame" and, 66–69; cultural defense and, 99–100, 104; defined, 89–92; gospel of wealth vs., 92–94, 98, 118–19; Conwell's "comic frame" and, 66–69; limits of, 96, 116–19; Populists and, 88–92, 98, 100–19; yeoman farmer as central to, 105–9

agriculture and farmers: African Americans and, xvii–xviii, 2; Bryan and, 140–41, 148, 151; freehold concept and protection of, 90–91, 112; industrialization and, x–xiii, xvii, 69, 94–98, 298; laborers linked to, 102–4, 106–8, 118, 238; social Darwinism and, xxii; World's Columbian Exposition and, 296–98, 300. *See also* Populism; sharecroppers; yeoman farmer archetype

Alabama, xvii, 39, 207

Alarm (newspaper), 317, 339

Alaska *Labor News*, 224

Albert, Prince Consort, 177

Alcott, Louisa May, 42

Alexander the Great, 177, 181

Alger, Horatio, myth, 69

Algerian Village, 301, 303

All the World's a Fair (Rydell), 305

Alpha Suffrage Club, 47

Altgeld, John Peter, 140

amalgamationists, xiii, 2–3, 13, 32n. 7

AME Review, 3

American Anarchist, An (Avrich), 345n. 2

American Civil Liberties Union (ACLU), 226, 229, 231, 234, 236, 250n. 73, 316

"American Dream," 69

American Equal Rights Association, 357

American Federation of Labor (AFL), xiii, xvi, xxv, 261, 265, 277–84, 286–87

American Federation of Labor-Congress of Industrial Organizations (AFL-CIO), 277, 288

American foundation or heritage myth, xxiv, 106, 128, 130, 133–37, 139–40, 142, 145–53; realist vs. patriotic version, 155–56

American Indian Village, 302

American Journal of Politics, 29

American Missionary Magazine, 217

American Negro Academy, 8

American Railway Union, 287

American Revolution, 21, 112, 130, 134, 145–46, 171, 325

American Woman Suffrage Association (AWSA), x, 357, 365, 368

analogy: Bryan and, 131, 135, 139, 156; Goldman and, 330, 332, 341; religious, and Flynn, 244; social Darwinism and, xx; women's rights and, 172–75, 180–81, 373

Anarchism and Other Essays (Goldman), 310, 330

"Anarchism: What It Really Stands For" (Goldman), 330–33

anarchists, xxv, 92, 106, 261, 365; feminist, 309–53; Knights of Labor and, 273, 275–77,

283–85

Anarchist Women: 1870–1920 (Marsh), 340

Anderson, Margaret, 346n. 24

Anderson, Walter Truett, 137, 156

Anglo-Saxons, xiii–xiv, 28, 144, 146

antebellum era, 6, 8, 10, 23

Anthony, Susan B., xix, 162, 168, 359–60, 362, 365, 379

anthropology, 300, 302–3

Anti-Caste (magazine), 56

Anti-Lynching Association, 46

antilynching campaign, xviii, 37–63, 196, 198, 207, 218n. 15

Anti-Lynching Society of England, 204

anti-Semitism, 108

antisuffragists, xiv, xix, xxviiin. 90, 362, 367–68, 370, 374–75, 377, 379–80

antithesis, 102, 149, 154

antitrust legislation, 124, 150–51

aphorism, 19, 174

apologists, 255, 289n. 32; African Americans and, 196, 199; lynching and, 49–50, 52, 54, 207–12; Powderly as, xxv, 283–86; woman suffrage and, 376–80

Appeal to Reason (newspaper), 229

Aptheker, Bettina, 57

arbitration, 256, 259–61, 286

archetypes, 69

architecture, x, 296–97, 305

Argersinger, Peter H., 95–96, 113

argumentation: Bryan and, 126, 139–40; de Cleyre and, 322; Wells and, on lynching, 52–54, 57

Arkansas, xvii, 39

Arkansas Race Riot, The (Wells), 48

Armour, Philip, xv

Armstrong, Samuel C., 17

Arnesen, Eric, xv–xvi, xviii, xx

Arnold, C. D., 301

Arnold, Matthew, 197

art, 296

Arthur, Chester A., xvii

Arthur, T. S., 164

Aryan race, 4–5

Ashbaugh, Carolyn, 336, 352nn

Asiatic "races," xiii

assimilationists, xiii, 2–3, 13, 32n. 7

Astor, John Jacob, 74

atheism, 310

Atilla, 177

Atlanta Constitution, 20, 22, 211

Atlantic Monthly, 201

atonement, 135–36

audience: anarchist women and, 310, 319, 327, 330, 333, 341–42, 345; Bryan and myth and, 100, 124–25, 140; Conwell and desires of, 71, 76; Jones and, 242–43; narratives as transforming devices for, 82–83; Terrell and white, 199, 208, 211, 213–15, 217; Wells and,

international peace movement, 358, 365

International Socialist News, 224

International Socialist Review, 229

International Union of Machinists and Blacksmiths of the United States of America, 257–58, 272

International Woman's Peace Movement, 365

International Women's Suffrage Alliance, 369

International Workingmen's Association, 278–79

International Working People's Association, 317

intersectionality, 195–96, 310, 320, 346n. 21

Iowa prohibition, 165

Iowa State Agricultural College, 360

Iowa Woman Suffrage Association, 358

Irish immigrants, xiii, 9, 229–30, 298, 306n. 8

Irish Rebellion, 230, 250n. 63

Irish Village, 302–3, 306n. 15

Iron in Her Soul (Camp), 248nn

Italian immigrants, xiii, xiv

Jacks, James W., 204–6

Jacksonian tradition, 103

Jacquard, Mrs., 75

Japan, 238, 297, 300–301

Jefferson, Thomas, 90–91, 94, 103–4, 109, 134, 147, 154, 263, 374

Jetter, Alexis, 247

Jews, xii, xiv, 108, 130, 155, 227–28, 313, 315, 334, 343–44, 379

Jim Crow laws, xix, 2, 38–42, 195, 203, 213, 238

Johnson, Andrew, 367

Joll, James, 333

Jones, Beverly Washington, 219n. 26, 220n. 53

Jones, Jim, 155

Jones, Mary Harris "Mother," xxiv, 225–26, 228–48, 248nn, 250nn, 317; **Speeches:** Central Federated Union, 1904, 233; Central Labor Council, 1902, 233–34; Children's March, 239; congressional testimony, 226, 244; Colorado, 1903, 237, 239; Cooper Union, 1915, 234–35; Joplin, Missouri, 1915, 243; Pittsburg, Kansas, 1914, 242; Pittsburg, Kansas, 1915, 246; Seattle, 1914, 230; UMWA conventions, 235–39, 241; West Virginia, 1912, 235–36, 238, 242; **Works:** *Autobiography of Mother Jones, The*, 226, 230, 249n. 17

Journal of the Knights of Labor, 262, 266, 272–73, 279–80, 284, 286

Journal of United Labor, 262, 266–70, 275, 284, 286

Kammen, Michael, 68, 69

Kansas: African Americans and, xviii, 6; boom and bust in, xii, 95–97; elections of 1890–92 and, 113; elections of 1894 and, 113–14, 116–17; woman suffrage and 113–15, 118; Populist movement in, xxiv, 87–122

Kansas Farmer (newspaper), 113

Kansas People's Party manifesto, 88

Kelley, Abbie, 379

Kelley, Florence, 224

Kelley, Mary, 190n. 30

Kelly, Florence Finch, 346n. 24

Kersnner, Jacob, 315, 346n. 22

Kessler-Harris, Alice, 226

"kicking principle," 314, 327

Kierkegaard, Søren, 371, 373, 383n. 70

Kimble, James, 170, 172, 190n. 17

Kincaid, James, 180

King, Martin Luther, Jr., 171

Kipling, Rudyard, 243–44

Knights of Labor, xvi, xvii, xxv, 180, 228, 255–91; external assaults and, 267–83; founded, 256; internal dissension and, 263–67; Parsons and, 317; women and, 347–48n. 75

Knights of the White Camellia, 40

Kosher butcher shops looting, 228

Kowal, Donna Marie, xxv, 309–53

Kraditor, Aileen, 364, 366

Kropotkin, Peter, 313, 331

Ku Klux Klan, 1, 39–41, 52

Ku Klux Klan Act (1871), 38

Kutera, Joseph, 322

Labor, Department of, 287

laborers, xi–x; African Americans as, 15, 207; Bryan and, 140–41, 148, 151; cheap, unskilled, 255, 256, 286, 312; Populists and, 98, 100, 102–4, 106–8, 114, 116–18; women and, in home, 182–83; World's Columbian Exposition and, 298–99, 306. *See also* working class

labor movement, x, xiii, xv–xvi; AFL and trade vs. industrial unions and, xvi, 277–82; African Americans and, xviii, 2, 15; anarchist women and, 309–10, 317; Knights of Labor and, 255–91; Willard and, 182, 188; women organizers as radicals in, xxiv–xxv, 223–53; women's rights movement and, 160, 231–32, 312, 357, 365, 368–69. *See also* Haymarket bombing; *specific boycotts, strikes, and organizations*

"Labor's True Woman" ideal, 338, 342

"labor theory" of value, 100, 107

Ladies Liberal League, 323

Ladies Pictorial, 46

Ladies Repository, 168

Laird and Lee company, 304

laissez-faire ideology, xxi, xxii, 5, 7, 13, 15–16, 32, 33n. 18, 35n. 94

land: natural right to own, 90–91, 93–94, 100, 102; reform, 288, 325; speculation, 95

Langer, Susanne, 127

Latin America, 305

Latino workers, 237

Lawrence, Massachusetts, textile strikes, xiii, 224, 227–28, 241–42, 245, 248n. 11

"laws of nature," xxiii, 8–9

Rauschenbusch, Walter, 158n. 37

Rayback, Joseph, 260, 261, 275, 287

Raymond, Henry, 366

Reading Railroad, 271

Realm of Rhetoric, The (Perleman), 49

Reason Why the Colored American Is Not in the World's Columbian Exposition, The (Wells, Douglass, Penn, and Barnett), 46, 48, 51

Reconstruction, xvi, xvii, 1–6, 10, 23, 31–32, 203, 209; Supreme Court and, 38–39; woman suffrage and, 366–67, 380

Reconstruction Act (1867), 2

Red Record, A (Wells), 47–48, 51, 53–55, 58, 61n. 87

Red Scare, 316

Reese, Maggie, 53

reform movement, x, xiii–xiv, xxvi; African Americans and, xviii–xix, 1–35; Bryan and, 152; home as model for, xxiv, 159–94; labor and, 255, 258–59, 262, 286–87, 312, 329; Populists and, 87, 98; social Darwinism and, xxi–xxiii; woman suffrage and, 369–70

refutation: Bryan and, 139, 142, 144–45, 155; de Cleyre and, 319–20, 322–24, 327; Populists and, 104; Terrell and, 208–11; Wells and, xxiv, 48, 52–54, 57

religion (clergy); African Americans and, 19, 38; anti-immigrant sentiment and, xiv; Bryan and, 126, 129–31, 135–37; de Cleyre and, 313, 321; Goldman and, 321, 331–34; Knights of Labor and, 260, 262, 282–84; labor unions and, xiii; Populists and, 112; Shaw and, 365, 371–72; social Darwinism and, 4; Stanton and, 359–60, 365; Terrell and, 214; women's rights and, 312, 364–65, 369; World's Columbian Exposition and, 304; yeoman farmer and, 90. *See also* Bible; Christ myth; *specific denominations*

repetition, 58, 217, 243, 372–73, 375–76, 378–79

"representative anecdote," 67–68

Republican Party, 160, 260; African American and, xvii, xviii, 6; Bryan attacks on, 144, 147, 149; business and, xiv, xv; Populists and, 87–88, 97–98, 107–10, 113–14, 115–17; Wells and, 40–41; Willard and, 161; woman suffrage and, 114, 365–67, 374

Revolution (journal), 357

Reynolds, Samuel, 101; **Speeches**: Douglas County Farmer's Alliance, 116

rhetoric: accommodationist, 3–4; action, call to, 48, 54–56, 58–59, 205–7, 327, 330–33; action, transforming scene through, 78–82; African-American reform, 1–36; aggregation, 49; ambivalent, 8–17; anarcho-feminine style, 309–54; analogy, xx, 131, 135–36, 139, 156, 172–76, 180–81, 330, 332, 341, 244, 373; anecdote, "representative," 67–68; antisuffrage, xxviiin. 90; antithesis, 102, 149, 154; aphorism, 19, 174; apologetic or defensive, xxv, 49–50, 52, 54, 207–12, 196, 199, 255, 262–88, 289n. 32, 376–80; assimilationist, 2–3; boasting, 299; borrowed testimony, 340; canon, 177; central motif, home as, xxiv, 159–88; characterization, 140–46, 151; classical images, 105; clear, plain facts, 48, 51–52; cliché, xxii; "comic frame," 65–68, 74–76, 80–83; confrontational, 22–28, 59, 88, 99–100; constraints and challenges, and women rhetors, 48, 58–59, 312; conversational tone, 175; convert testimony, 340; co-optation, 17–22, 28–32, 35n. 80, 165, 363, 369–70, 373, 376, 378, 380; cultural defense, 99–100, 123; "cunning identification," 73; deceptive frame, 83; deductive reasoning, 144, 229, 319, 325–26, 330, 341; de facto reasoning, 4, 31–32; definition, and redefinition, 69–70, 73–74; definition, argument from, 4, 7, 24, 127–30, 135–36, 140, 149, 152, 155, 323, 326, 331, 336; deliberative political, 123; denotive statements, 153–54; dialectical terms, 70; dialogue, 375; dialogue, "constructed," 243; dichotomies, 330, 333; diction, 211, 215; differentiation, 277–79, 284; distancing and disassociating, 271, 274, 276–78, 281–82, 284, 323, 326–28; dramatic images, 127–28, 134–35, 140, 145; education in elocution, 41–42, 46, 175; effective public advocacy, 59; *eidolopoeia*, 340; emphasis patterns, 373–75; empowerment, 327, 333, 340, 342; enactment, 243, 359–62, 379; enthymemes, 100, 214, 336, 370; ethos, 50, 54, 208, 211, 228, 336–40; evaluative statements, 153–54; evidence, 48, 50, 54, 57–59, 155, 324, 341, 362; examples, xxiv, 48, 53–54, 58–59, 82–83, 213–15; expert testimony, 330, 331–32, 340–41; "feminine style," xxv, 243, 310–11, 319, 341, 343–45, 346n. 19, 353n. 256; "fidelity" of narrative, 148, 154–55; "frame," 81–83; historical allusions, xxvi, 105; historically transcendent principles, 135; humor, 106–7, 130, 132, 229, 323–26, 376–77; hyperbole, 299; identification strategies, 199, 208, 211, 214–15, 242–43; identity, challenges of, 48, 58–59, 111, 311, 320, 333–34, 336–39, 342–45; ideology, 100, 103–4, 127, 131, 187, 336, 364–65; importance of, in Gilded Era, xxiii; inartistic proofs transformed into artistic, 336–39; "incompatibility" strategy, 126; inductive reasoning, 243; integrationist, 3–4; interrogative statements, 153; irony, 213, 236; leadership styles and "master plots," 356–59, 359; "let the Negro alone," 6–8, 13, 17, 31–32; logic, 206–7, 123–24, 126, 137, 139, 155, 320, 322, 330–33, 364; lyricism, 322, 341; manipulation of act, agency, and scene, 69–82; martyrdom construct, 335;

Wilson, Charles Morrow, 124, 129, 157n. 32

Wilson, Kirt, 39

Wilson, Woodrow, 124, 127, 149–50, 233, 362, 369

Wing, Adrien, 346n. 21

"Winning Plan," 358, 363, 369, 381n. 3

Wollstonecraft, Mary, 322, 355

Woman and Temperance (Willard), 169

womanhood: anarchist-feminist interpretation of, 320, 329, 333, 341; new model of, and Stanton, Shaw and Catt, 356, 359–62; Willard and new understanding of, 178. *See also* "true womanhood"

"womanliness," 162–63, 165, 168

Woman of the Future, A (pamphlet), 224

"woman question," 318, 328

Woman's Bible, The (Stanton), 357, 359, 365, 371

Woman's Building, x

"Woman's Cause" (Willard), 194n. 155

Woman's Christian Temperance Union (WCTU), xxiv, 159–60, 164–72, 174, 176–79, 181, 185, 191n. 54, 357, 365, 367–68

woman's clubs, 198, 203–7

Woman's Committee of the Council of National Defense, 357, 369

Woman's Congress of the Association for the Advancement of Women, 172–73

Woman's Crusade of 1873–74, 165–67, 169, 191n. 46

Woman's Era, 205

Woman's International Council, 168

Woman's Journal, 362

Woman's Party (*formerly* Congressional Union for Woman Suffrage), 366

woman's/women's rights movement, x, xviii–xix, xxiv–xxvi, xxviiin. 89, 6: passing torch of, Stanton, Shaw and Catt and, 355–84; Willard and, 160–62, 166–70, 177. *See also* feminism; labor movement, women organizers; woman suffrage; temperance movement; *and specific advocates*

Woman Suffrage and the New Democracy (Graham), xxviiin. 90

woman suffrage movement, x, xiv, xxiii, xxv–xxvi; African American women and, 47, 198, 216; anarchist feminists and, 311–12, 319, 329, 333, 341, 344–45; Bryan and, 124, 127, 137, 150; Conwell and, 76, 82; early obstacles in, 366–67; existentialism, Methodism, and social Darwinism and, 370–73, 383n. 80; female labor activists and, 227, 231–34; "feminine

style" and, 353n. 256; late obstacles, 367–69; Native American men's rights and, 12; "new woman" and, 359–62; passing of torch of, and Stanton, Shaw, and Catt, 355–81; Populists and, 87, 113–19; Powderly and, 256; Willard and, home protection and, 160, 162, 164, 166, 168, 170, 184, 187; working-class women and, 312, 346–47n. 38

"Woman versus the Indian" (Cooper), 12

Women and Economics (Gilman), 224

Women of Distinction (Scruggs), 60nn

Women, Race and Class (Davis), 340, 352n. 238

women's clubs, 22, 45, 47, 56, 215–16

Women's Era Club, 56, 204

Women's Loyal Union, 56

Women's Political Union, 365

Women Under Socialism (Bebel), 224

Wood, Andrew, x

Woodhull, Victoria, 190n. 33

Woodward, C. Vann, 87

Woolf, Virginia, 380

Words on Fire (Baxandall), 248n. 13

Workers Defense Union, 234

working class, xiii, 139, 148, 224, 232, 234, 238, 240–41, 245–46, 252, 298–99, 310–12, 317, 319–21, 327, 331, 333, 339–40, 342–43, 346–47n. 38. *See also* laborers; labor movement

working conditions, xv–xvi, xxii, 227, 256, 260, 286–87

Working Women's Union, 317, 347–48n. 75

World's Columbian Exposition (Chicago, 1893), x, xxv–xxvi, 46, 293–307; **Guidebooks**, 294, 297–303; *Official Directory,* 299; *Official Guide to Midway Plaisance,* 300, 303

World's Woman's Christian Temperance Union, 160

World War I, xviii, xx, 76, 124, 150, 225, 229, 233, 236, 238, 249n. 36, 313, 362, 367, 369, 375, 380

World War II, 227, 238

Wright, Martha Coffin, 193n. 132

Yale University, 67

Yankee in Rome, The (Twain), 111

yeoman farmer archetype, 69, 89–91, 93–100, 102–11, 114, 117–18

Youmans, Letitia, 164

Zeiger, Susan, 362

Zululand exhibit, 300